The JOURNAL of SOUTHERN HISTORY

VOLUME XLI

February–November 1975

Published Quarterly by the Southern Historical Association

CONTENTS OF VOLUME XLI

ARTICLES:

The Historian as Teacher: Professional Challenge and Opportunity. Gilbert C. Fite 3

Black Violence and White Response: Louisiana, 1862. William F. Messner 19

A Man but Not a Brother: Abraham Lincoln and Racial Equality. George M. Fredrickson 39

The Fortieth Annual Meeting. Richard Maxwell Brown 59

The Antebellum Southern Herdsman: A Reinterpretation. Forrest McDonald and Grady McWhiney 147

Black Militancy in Readjuster Virginia, 1879–1883. James T. Moore 167

The Demise of the Colored Farmers' Alliance. William F. Holmes 187

Southern History in Periodicals, 1974: A Selected Bibliography .. 201

Annual Report of the Secretary-Treasurer. Bennett H. Wall ... 233

Charles Colcock Jones and the Southern Evangelical Crusade to Form a Biracial Community. Donald G. Mathews 299

Black Ironworkers and the Slave Insurrection Panic of 1856. Charles B. Dew 321

The Commercial-Civic Elite and City Planning in Atlanta, Memphis, and New Orleans in the 1920s. Blaine A. Brownell .. 339

The Black Family in Transition: Louisiana, 1860–1865. C. Peter Ripley 369

Protestantism and Afro-Americans in the Old South: Another Look. Kenneth K. Bailey 451

Using the Testimony of Ex-Slaves: Approaches and Problems. John W. Blassingame 473

Southern Mountain Republicans and the Negro, 1865–1900. Gordon B. McKinney 493

NOTES AND DOCUMENTS:

Andrew Johnson and Reconstruction: A British View. Edited by Eric Foner 381

Northern Institutions in Southern Financial History: A Note on Insurance Investments. B. Michael Pritchett 391

Jefferson Davis Ponders His Future, 1829. Edited by Lynda J. Lasswell 517

A Note on Evidence: The Personal History of Madison Hemings. Dumas Malone and Steven H. Hochman 523

BOOK REVIEWS 89, 240, 397, 529

BOOK NOTES 283, 436, 583

HISTORICAL NEWS AND NOTICES 135, 291, 438, 589

INDEX 601

THE JOURNAL OF SOUTHERN HISTORY

FEBRUARY 1975
Vol. XLI, No. 1

ublished Quarterly by the Southern Historical Association

The Journal of Southern History

Published Quarterly by

THE SOUTHERN HISTORICAL ASSOCIATION

New Orleans, Louisiana

Printed by WILLIAM BYRD PRESS,
RICHMOND, VIRGINIA

The present constitution of the Southern Historical Association is printed in the February 1974 issue of the *Journal of Southern History*, Volume XL, Number 1.

Contributions and correspondence relating to articles, book reviews, and any other editorial matters should be sent to the Managing Editor, *Journal of Southern History*, Rice University, Houston, Texas 77001.

The subscription rate is $10.00 a year for a regular membership, $12.00 for family membership, $5.00 for enrolled student, and $3.00 for retired members. Upon payment of $200.00 any person may become a life member of the Southern Historical Association. Single numbers of the *Journal* are available at $3.00 plus postage. Changes of address must be made six weeks in advance of the publication of an issue in order for the change to be effective with that issue. A charge of $2.50 will be made for forwarding copies returned because of incorrect addresses.

Subscriptions, membership applications, and orders for current issues of the *Journal* should be sent to Bennett H. Wall, Secretary-Treasurer, History Department, Tulane University, New Orleans, Louisiana 70118. *Notice of nonreceipt of an issue must be sent to the Secretary-Treasurer within sixty days following publication of the issue.* Inquiries concerning noncurrent back issues of the *Journal* should be directed to Johnson Reprint Corporation, 111 Fifth Avenue, New York, New York 10003.

The Southern Historical Association disclaims responsibility for statements made by contributors.

Second-class postage paid at New Orleans, Louisiana, and at additional mailing offices.

The Journal of
SOUTHERN HISTORY

VOLUME XLI FEBRUARY 1975 NUMBER 1

Contents

The Historian as Teacher: Professional Challenge and Opportunity
By Gilbert C. Fite 3

Black Violence and White Response: Louisiana, 1862
By William F. Messner 19

A Man but Not a Brother: Abraham Lincoln and Racial Equality
By George M. Fredrickson 39

The Fortieth Annual Meeting *By Richard Maxwell Brown* 59

Book Reviews 89

Historical News and Notices 135

Book Reviews

McWhiney, *Southerners and Other Americans,* by Paul M. Gaston 89
Olson, *Anglo-American Politics,* by Vernon O. Stumpf 90
Nash, *Red, White, and Black,* by Donald J. Berthrong 91
Rainbolt, *From Prescription to Persuasion,* by C. Robert Haywood 93
Giraud, *A History of French Louisiana,* Vol. I, by Jack D. L. Holmes 94
Berkeley and Berkeley, *Dr. John Mitchell,* by George W. Knepper 94
Onuf, ed., *Maryland and the Empire,* by Robert J. Chaffin 96
Conkin, *Self-Evident Truths,* by Merrill D. Peterson 97
Hawke, *Paine,* by Malcolm Lester 98
Morris, *Free Men All,* by Anne C. Loveland 99
Bloom, ed., *The American Territorial System,* by Robert H. Jones 100
Bell, *Party and Faction in American Politics,* by William Bruce Wheeler 101
Chase, *Emergence of the Presidential Nominating Convention,* by Joseph H. Harrison, Jr. 103
McDonald, *The Presidency of George Washington,* by Richard E. Ellis 104
Bowman, *The Struggle for Neutrality,* by Dale M. Royalty 105
Baker, *John Marshall,* by James W. Ely, Jr. 106
Brodie, *Thomas Jefferson,* by Holman Hamilton 107
Malone, *Jefferson the President, 1805–1809,* by Morton Borden 109
Starobin, ed., *Blacks in Bondage,* by Charles B. Dew 110
Mooney, *William H. Crawford,* by Herbert J. Doherty, Jr. 112
Württemberg, *Travels in North America,* by John E. Stealey, III 113
Huston, *Deaf Smith,* by Joseph Milton Nance 115
Jones, *The American Problem in British Diplomacy,* by James A. Casada 115
Horton, *Samuel Bell Maxey,* by Jack B. Scroggs 116
Evitts, *A Matter of Allegiances,* by David E. Meerse 118
Quarles, *Allies for Freedom,* by Robert R. Davis, Jr. 119
Barney, *The Secessionist Impulse,* by Robert E. May 120
Davis, *Arming the Union,* by Bowling C. Yates 121
Cullen, *The Peninsula Campaign,* by Peter Maslowski 122
Vaughn, *Schools for All,* by William C. Harris 123
Harlan *et al.*, eds., *The Booker T. Washington Papers,* Vol. 3, by Emma Lou Thornbrough 125
Weiss, *The National Urban League,* by Roger W. Lotchin 126
Burts, *Richard Irvine Manning,* by James T. Moore 127
Barbeau and Henri, *The Unknown Soldiers,* by Robert V. Haynes 128
Hobson, *Serpent in Eden,* by Walter W. Isle 129
Barnard, *Dixiecrats and Democrats,* by Hugh Davis Graham 131
Yarnell, *Democrats and Progressives,* by E. Berkeley Tompkins 132
Foner, *Blacks and the Military,* by Carl R. Osthaus 133

The Historian as Teacher: Professional Challenge and Opportunity

By GILBERT C. FITE

THE MOST ENJOYABLE TASK WHICH THE PRESIDENT OF THIS ASSOCIATION has is preparing and delivering a presidential address. That is, after he decides what to say. First let me confess that after about thirty years of teaching and research, I have no great historical theory to expound. Moreover, having been away from my research for three years, I cannot bring you anything new or exciting from some original and unused sources. Perhaps I should have attempted to entertain you. But that would be out of character for me and certainly out of character with the times. There is little that is humorous in our profession today. Indeed, we have regrettably left what now seems to have been the golden age of our profession when students crowded our classes and jobs were plentiful for historians. In contrast, we have descended into what some consider the dark age of declining enrollments, professional unemployment, and a growing rejection of history by many students who seem to agree with Henry Ford that history is "bunk."

After thinking a great deal about what most needs to be said in our profession today, I decided to talk about teaching—specifically, the teaching of history. There has probably been more talk about improved teaching and less done about it than almost anything else in higher education. Nevertheless, I want to place the spotlight on something I am afraid we have taken for granted—superior performance in the classroom. As strange as it may seem, this is an aspect of our profession which has been largely ignored. During the last fifteen years historians have dealt with about everything from free love to vegetarianism, while the real problems of our profession languished for attention and solution. I dare say that if we had spent as much time and effort improving our teaching, redesigning our courses, and promoting the intellectual and

MR. FITE is president of Eastern Illinois University. This paper was delivered as the presidential address at the annual meeting of the Southern Historical Association at Dallas, Texas, on November 7, 1974.

THE JOURNAL OF SOUTHERN HISTORY
Vol. XLI, No. 1, February 1975

cultural values of history as we have chasing after every passing social issue, we might have kept our students, maintained our academic position, and greatly reduced what is commonly referred to as the crisis in history. I might add that there is no crisis in history; the crisis is among historians. History and history teaching is what we make it.

A survey of the *Reader's Guide to Periodical Literature* over the last quarter century quickly emphasizes that not much serious study has been done on the teaching of history at the college and university level. Scores of books and articles have been written about history, but very little about teaching the subject in post-secondary schools. Moreover, the leaders of our profession have given little or no attention to this important matter. A study of the addresses of presidents of the major historical associations shows that our professional leadership has conspicuously neglected the question. In 1956 Dexter Perkins did talk about teaching in his presidential address before the American Historical Association. This is part of what he said:

> We have tended . . . to exalt the written over the spoken word in the practice of our profession. Both carry their special messages, but for most of us the possibility of reaching large audiences through what we write is not great. Our best chance of making impact on others will come through the influence we can exert in the classroom, through the enthusiasms we kindle, through the interests we arouse, through the wisdom that history teaches and that we can strive to disseminate. Here, as I see it, for all but the greatest and most imaginative scholar, is our greatest chance of usefulness, our largest hope.[1]

But Perkins's advice was all but ignored, and we can generally look in vain for serious discussion of history teaching beyond the high school.

This is a rather strange phenomenon. The great majority of professional historians have been, and still are, hired to teach. Classroom instruction is our first and foremost responsibility to the institution which employs us. Every September we walk into our classes, meet a group of students, and begin the teaching process. At the end of the month we receive a paycheck in return for those

[1] Dexter Perkins, "We Shall Gladly Teach," *American Historical Review*, LXII (January 1957), 291–309 (quotation on page 293). Elmer Ellis also dealt with some problems relating to superior teaching in his presidential address before the Mississippi Valley Historical Association in 1951. "The Profession of Historian," *Mississippi Valley Historical Review*, XXXVIII (June 1951), 3–20.

teaching duties. In most colleges and universities historians are also expected to pursue scholarly work, do some research, as well as perform certain types of university and public service. But teaching students is our main responsibility and the reason we are employed and get paid. Teaching is what students, parents, private donors, and taxpayers expect us to do, and to do well. Since this is our foremost responsibility, we might assume that a great deal of attention would have been given by individual historians and history departments to the question of increasing classroom effectiveness. It might have been expected even that some serious research would have been done on the subject of improved teaching. But, alas, that has not been the case.

This is not to say that we historians have shown no interest in the quality of history teaching or that we are bad teachers. Indeed, I believe just the opposite is true. There are many distinctive and outstanding teachers of history, and many of them have given a great deal of time and effort to improved classroom instruction. Unfortunately, most of those efforts have been confined to history teaching at the secondary level. The American Historical Association has had a Committee on Teaching for many years. Several of us here have served on that committee. Through the Committee on Teaching the American Historical Association sponsored conferences, seminars, and workshops for high school history teachers. Moreover, the United States Office of Education funded hundreds of institutes in the 1960s which were designed to improve history teaching in the secondary schools. Many of us also participated in those institutes.

For some unknown reason most professional historians who have helped with the various programs to improve teaching in the secondary schools seldom or ever raised the question of the kind and quality of teaching in their own classrooms or departments. It seemed to be assumed that performance in college classrooms was good, if not superior, and therefore there was no use to waste time or antagonize colleagues by raising the issue of teaching effectiveness. It is entirely possible that discussion of teaching in history departments has been avoided because it smacked somehow of teacher training and professional education, which were, and still are, anathema to most historians. In any event, one of the great givens in our profession has been that college history teaching was excellent and needed little or no improvement. At least, this assumption has been held by the professors if not by the students.

Thus, for a generation we went along confident and content. In the postwar years enrollments in history courses expanded rapidly, we added faculty at an amazing rate, and as a profession we throve and waxed prosperous. Seldom did we stop to ask ourselves what kind of a job we were doing in the classroom, what our goals were, or indeed whether we had any achievable goals as teachers. What difference did it make? Our classes were full and overflowing. It was easy to conclude that we were good teachers. We must be; look how we draw students.

What we failed to realize was that we had captive audiences. Certain institutional requirements assured us students in both the survey and advanced courses. In some states legislation required one or more courses in American history, adding thousands of students to the pool of enrollees. The combination of increasing college and university enrollments along with various institutional and state requirements placed history in a favorable position. Then about 1970 or 1971 conditions suddenly changed. Total enrollments in the senior colleges began to level off or even decline. Many institutions loosened general requirements, and history was no longer mandatory in some programs. To make matters worse, history found itself competing with sociology, psychology, and other social sciences which claimed to be more relevant and meaningful in helping students to understand modern society.

The result of these and other factors has been a sharp decline in the number of students taking history courses. My survey of history departments in the spring of 1974 revealed that nearly 75 percent of them were experiencing a decline in enrollment.[2] Even more distressing was the fact that history enrollments have dropped proportionately further than overall institutional registrations. As a result, in some institutions the position of the history faculty became not only difficult but precarious. Not only were there no openings for newly trained scholars, but some currently employed people were dismissed. A near panic situation existed on a few campuses.

[2] On March 15, 1974, questionnaires dealing with enrollment trends and problems surrounding teaching were sent to seventy-six history departments. I received sixty-one replies. I promised all participants that I would keep their comments confidential.

These conditions suddenly produced a new concern in the profession about teaching. The burst of interest in the quality of instruction during the last two years might be compared to a deathbed conversion. As the fires of professional hell began to light up, individual historians, departments, and even some of our major associations finally admitted that salvation might be found in better teaching and more appropriate courses.

At its meeting on November 30, 1973, the Executive Board of the Organization of American Historians devoted considerable attention to problems surrounding the teaching of history. While the board emphasized the status of history rather than instructional methods, it was clear that a new concern had developed in regard to history teaching at the college level. At about the same time the editor of the *Newsletter* of the American Historical Association conceded that the association had "devoted comparatively little effort directly to improving the state of historical studies in the classroom." The review board recommended the establishment of a teaching division which would "invest the teaching function with a status and recognition equal to that previously reserved for research."[3] If further evidence is needed to demonstrate a new seriousness about teaching, one need only point to the sessions scheduled at the American Historical Association meeting in December 1973 and at the meeting of the Organization of American Historians in April 1974, which dealt with history teaching in colleges and universities. In January 1974 the issue of the American Historical Association's *Newsletter* announced that many members wanted "more news on teaching methods." The editor promised to publish "a continuing list of new approaches to teaching undergraduate history."[4]

Now that we have at last begun to give some attention to the teaching function, we must be careful to ask the right questions. One of the dangers is that we will become engulfed in a study of methods and techniques and fail to analyze the more important problems of goals and objectives. If we concentrate too much attention on method, we will be little if any better off than we are now. Our first task is to decide why we are teaching history. The "how"

[3] AHA *Newsletter,* XI (November 1973), 24–26 (quotation on pages 24–25).
[4] *Ibid.,* XII (January 1974), 1.

or the method should only be determined after we have established our objectives. This seems almost too elementary and simplistic to mention, but simple things are sometimes the most profound. The basic and fundamental question is to determine what we want to do in our classrooms and why. Once we determine the ends, then we can adopt the proper means. Let us be careful not to get the ends and the means confused.

In April 1974 I mailed seventy-six questionnaires to historians who I believed could properly evaluate what was going on in their departments in regard to the matter of improved teaching. The answers to the specific questions and the textual comments which accompanied the returns, as well as conclusions drawn from my own thirty years of experience, have convinced me that history teaching can be greatly improved by (1) creating an atmosphere where teaching is considered of first importance in fact as well as in word; (2) by demonstrating more enthusiasm for the subject; (3) by carefully delineating our goals and objectives for both our total curriculum and the individual courses; and (4) by developing courses for the students rather than for members of the faculty.

First, let us look at the matter of establishing an atmosphere, as well as actual conditions, where teaching receives the highest priority among departmental activities. This cannot be done simply by proclaiming it. Teaching must be kept uppermost in the entire range of decisions extending from recruitment to financial rewards. In regard to employment, no clear answer developed from my questionnaire on what factor was most important in hiring new personnel. Most departments, however, indicated that both teaching and research were important. But there is considerable evidence that relatively little attention has been given in the interview process to the candidate's ability to teach effectively. I have seen candidates, as I know you have, subjected to a barrage of questions about what they had written or planned to write, but hardly a query about his or her view of teaching. It seems to have been assumed that the person could and would teach effectively. In many cases this turned out to be true, but it happened more by accident than by design.

Once a historian is employed, proper reward should be given to the best teachers. This, of course, involves judgments and evaluation of teaching. Evaluation is something that not only historians but other academicians have tried to avoid at all costs. We have all heard it said that teaching varies so much that effectiveness cannot be properly judged. One respondent to my questionnaire wrote: "Instruction is too personal, too subjective and too closely associated with schools of education to get much attention." Another said: "Concepts of good teaching [are] too varied for meaningful discussion." I am sure there are people in this audience who believe that. I think it is hogwash. The best teachers are known on every campus. So are the worst. It is not that we do not know who the best teachers are; we have too often been afraid to identify and properly reward them. But if we want to give teaching its proper place, we must identify it and reward it adequately. This does not mean rewarding someone who simply claims greater effectiveness in the classroom because he or she is not doing research. Self-claim to good teaching is often a cop-out and an excuse for not doing any research or scholarly work. But, regardless of the pitfalls, we must get more serious about the evaluation process.

For some reason there is a basic reluctance to consider improved teaching seriously at the departmental level. While some departments have explored the problem in a systematic way, both through a committee structure and by the department as a whole, I received report after report testifying to the lack of serious departmental discussions of the teaching function. A senior professor at a leading southern university said his department was "apathetic" to the matter. Another historian said in answer to the question, whether his department ever devoted a full meeting to improved classroom instruction, "not only no, but Hell no." From a leading Big Ten department came the reply that there had been "lots of talk" in the department, but no sensible conclusions had been reached or any action taken. Another respondent said that "the feeling is that teaching is not improved by discussions in departmental meetings."

Why, over the years, has there been such a negative reaction among faculty members to any type of teaching evaluation? The opposite attitude persists in the area of research. Research, like teaching, is a very personal and individual activity, but when we publish our work, it is always scrutinized and judged by others in the field. We all know professors who impatiently look forward to a review of their latest book in a professional journal, but who would lock the classroom door if they thought a colleague might drop in. But attitudes are changing. The chairman of a department in a Big Ten university wrote: "We are now in the process of working on means of measuring teaching effectiveness whereby all instruction in the department will be evaluated, from teaching assistants to full professors." But, he added, I think only half facetiously, "should we ever perfect such a technique, get general acceptance of various instruments, and otherwise solve the evaluation of teaching at all levels, I suspect we will apply for either a patent or a copyright, or both!"

My survey indicates that individuals in most history departments are somehow trying to upgrade the position of teaching and are discussing, at least informally, how history instruction might be improved. They see the problem and are thinking seriously about it but have not quite come to grips with the issue. There is ferment, but at this point that is about all. However, I would add that this ferment may lead to good results. If anything worthwhile is accomplished, we will do it at the individual and departmental level. The best professional committee from any of our major associations is not going to change Professor Dullard at X University. If we think someone off campus will solve our problems, we are only deluding ourselves. While, as I said, to proclaim good teaching will not achieve it, to admit and declare a need for better instruction is the first step toward improvement. We need to make our intentions clear in this regard and then develop the means to achieve the best results.

Besides elevating the role of teaching in our departments, we need to do some other things. We should do research on teaching effectiveness. We need to develop instruments which will evaluate better what we are trying to do. This should include peer, student, administration, and even outside evaluation. Moreover, we need to consider the other side of teaching, namely learning. There is a vast body of literature on the theories of learning. Better acquaintance with such information would, I believe, be highly useful to us as history teachers.

Secondly, I am convinced that many college and university

professors have lost their enthusiasm for teaching. One respondent to my questionnaire referred to this condition as "a certain dullness and indifference" in the classroom. He added that, "It seems to me that the quality which should be most assiduously cultivated is that of enthusiasm." Lack of enthusiasm is nothing new. Carl Lotus Becker wrote that average students and ordinary class sessions bored him. In 1929 he said, "Everything as dull here as usual. . . . Handing out the same old stuff . . . and mystifying ten seminarians with the old jokes and paradoxes."[5] Students also now and in the past report a seeming lack of enthusiastic commitment to our discipline. Observation over many years confirms that students often take professors rather than courses. Course choices are often made on the basis of what one student tells another. In discussing a particular course in 1926 Carl Becker wrote: "It will be as good as the man is."[6] Indeed, it is the professor who counts. At one prominent midwestern university the professor of ancient history won the outstanding teacher award based on student input. It has been commonly said that ancient history is so irrelevant to modern students that they avoid it in droves. This evidently depends upon who is teaching it.

In the undergraduate curriculum it is the survey courses in Western civilization and American history that are in the most serious trouble. In other words, our survey courses are in general decline. This has resulted from, among other things, the dropping of requirements. A member of one of the nation's most distinguished departments wrote, "Our enrollment in the American survey and in the large upper division courses all dropped greatly when the college . . . abolished course requirements in American history . . . ." Besides the abolition of requirements, we have been thrown into the competitive jungle with other disciplines which are vying for the students who traditionally took history courses.

To meet the competition and recover our former position among students we will have to teach better and increase the attractiveness of our courses. To be enthusiastic about what we are doing is the first step in this direction. One student told me that her professor

[5] Quoted in Michael Kammen, ed., "*What Is the Good of History?*" *Selected Letters of Carl L. Becker, 1900–1945* (Ithaca and London, 1973), xx.

[6] *Ibid.*, 111.

announced in the first class session, "I hate this course, and I wish I did not have to teach it." While I am certain that such attitudes are the exception rather than the rule, anything resembling a lack of faith and commitment to what we are doing can only lead to further deterioration of our enrollments.

Challenges to effective teaching are undoubtedly greater than ever before. This is partly because mass education at the college level has brought people to our classes who have little or no commitment to the intellectual efforts required in higher education. Yet we do not want to overemphasize this point, because we have always had students in our courses who were indifferent, if not actually hostile. Nevertheless, it is probably more difficult to develop student interest in history today than in years past. Students have higher expectations, there is great emphasis on presentism, and teaching performance must compete with programs delivered on television by media experts. These and other factors have increased and complicated the problems of teaching history. But if students are more indifferent to the values of history, if they are resisting the subject and the courses more vigorously than in the past, our job as teachers is obviously more difficult and challenging. In that case, greater effort and imagination must be used in our classrooms. It means that we must adopt every technique, develop every approach, and examine every method which will attract students to history courses. But more important than anything else is our responsibility to show how history is meaningful and relevant to the lives of people. We cannot just assume that students will see this. We must carefully explain the value of history to our students and not leave this important matter to chance.

I believe the most significant improvement in history instruction will come only after we have carefully determined our goals and objectives. In other words, we must be clear in our own minds why we are teaching a particular course. Historians have advanced numerous reasons to justify the inclusion of history in the curriculum. We argue that people must know the past if they are to understand the present. We insist that a knowledge of history contributes to intelligent citizenship so necessary in a democracy. We say that the study of history helps people learn how to think, to reason, and to draw intelligent conclusions from specific evidence.

Some insist that history is simply interesting and adds joy and pleasure to life. Others argue that history should improve students' abilities in the area of decision making and in dealing with unexpected results which happen so often in our society. One historian has said that, "The most important professional goal of teaching history is to encourage people's sense of change over time . . . ."[7] These are only a few of the familiar reasons given for studying history.

While many professional historians would agree on at least some common objectives, it is not necessary that we teach with the same goals in mind. That would be tragic in a democracy. We do not want to define our purposes as the Chinese historian Chou Yi-liang did in a paper delivered in 1963. That year I attended an international history conference at Lahore, Pakistan. In his paper Professor Yi-liang said that the purpose of history was to "educate people in patriotism and internationalism." "Research," he continued, "must include analytical study guided by correct theories and leading to certain views and conclusions."[8] We do not want to be governed by any "correct theories" laid down by the state or by anyone else. However, as individual teachers it is highly important, yes, absolutely essential, that we have clear and obtainable objectives and that our students have a fairly good idea of what these are. Unless we do establish goals for a course about all we will do is cover a certain amount of material. I believe that large numbers of students have been turned off from history simply because teachers have had the unstated but implied goal of covering a certain period or topic without ever making it clear why it is important or worthwhile to do so.

In the first place, we need to ask ourselves the fundamental question of whether as teaching scholars we are trying to train professional historians or attempting to increase the general level of historical understanding in our society. The answer to that question is clear. We should be teaching, I believe, for greater public in-

[7] Committee on History in the Classroom, *Newsletter*, No. 5 (September 1973), 4. This mimeographed newsletter is issued by a rank-and-file group of some three hundred members of the American Historical Association. The secretary is Professor John A. Scott of the School of Law, Rutgers University, Newark, N.J.

[8] Chou Yi-liang, "The Teaching of History in New China's Universities" (mimeograph copy in author's possession).

telligence. Most of our students will never take up history as a profession. While we do have the responsibility of training professional historians, that is not the primary task for most of us. Nevertheless, we too often teach as though all of our students were going to become master's or doctoral candidates, or at least history majors.

Since World War II many historians have concentrated on teaching upper-division or graduate students. They have been concerned about preparing more historians for professional jobs in teaching or elsewhere. The emphasis has been to increase the number of majors and specialists. We judged individuals and departments by the number of students majoring in history and those going on to graduate school. We forgot that most of our students would become businessmen, salesmen, housewives, plant managers, lawyers, civil servants, etc., and that only a very small percentage of the individuals who attended our classes would ever earn a graduate degree or make a living as a professional historian. I think that most of us would agree that history is the premier intellectual and cultural subject. But have we designed our courses to meet the intellectual and cultural needs of the majority of our students, who may never take more than one, two, or three history courses in a college career, or have we proclaimed the values of history and then largely ignored the masses of our students who need it most?

This brings me back to the survey courses. As I stated, my study shows that the old standby surveys in Western civilization and American history are in deepest trouble. As a result, there have been intense campaigns to get requirements restored in order to rebuild enrollments in those courses. This sudden love affair with required courses strikes me as both somewhat hypocritical and as a frantic reaching for the professional life raft. If we honestly believed that the survey courses were so valuable for students, how was it that many professors taught them as a chore rather than as a challenge. The truth is that we have given only meager attention to the nonmajors forced into our classes by requirements. We have all too often moved through those classes as quickly and with as little effort as possible so that we could get on with our advanced courses filled mainly with majors. It seems clear to me that we did not really care a great deal about the masses of students who were required to take history, or who took it by choice, and that we made very little effort to design courses which would meet the needs of the student who would not study history professionally. We often refer to the surveys as service courses. They were and are considered second class. With few exceptions, these courses have been the ugly ducklings of most departments. Little energy and less imagination has been devoted to discovering ways to make survey courses into something that will be meaningful and useful to the nonmajor student who has to take them.

How often have we even raised the question about the needs of nonmajors who fill our survey courses? Have we asked ourselves what we are trying to accomplish in those courses? Have we any definite goals? Do we really think the courses are beneficial to students, and, if so, how? If we do have clear objectives in our own minds, have we made these clear to the students?

Many historians have devoted a great deal of time and energy trying to show how history has a vocational function. We have tried to answer the question of students, "What can I do with a history major?" Departments have published lists of professions and employment opportunities open to those with training in history, and we have argued that a history major can prepare one for satisfying and useful employment. To some degree, this is true. But, again, I think we have been trying to answer the wrong question. One need only look at the employment statistics to know that there are relatively few positions for professional historians, not only at this time, but ever. Why did we not admit the obvious and concentrate our efforts on teaching history as part of a broad liberal education which will serve as a tool for the businessman, the politician, the civil servant, and everyone else. When the student comes to us asking what he can do with history, I believe our answer should be that, except for a few, it offers little in the area of employment, but that it has tremendous value in this complex and dangerous world in which we live; that it will be beneficial regardless of the career a student may follow. To be sure, there are a limited number of professions where historians are absolutely essential and a high level of training is necessary. But if we are going to place our hope in finding enough professional jobs for our majors in history, we are only deluding ourselves and our students. If our major function is to help students evaluate their society and the world more intelligently, we must show students how important history is in every aspect of our society in a clear and simple way. We need to be direct, precise, and insistent on the values of history and teach with the goal of achieving that result.

There is much to be discouraged about in our profession today. But to me the most discouraging thing is the evident lack of influence which we have had on the millions of students who have gone through our courses. Have our students, as a result of studying history, been more perceptive than other people? Do they understand the complexity of life and society better than those who never had a history course? Daniel Patrick Moynihan said when he left his position as White House adviser on urban affairs, "One of the greatest weaknesses of Americans is the habit of reducing the most complex issues to the most simplistic moralisms."[9] Have our courses reduced this dangerous habit? If we are going to have any real impact on individuals or society, we must do something besides just cover the material. It is absolutely essential that we decide what we hope to achieve and then select the historical material and methods to accomplish that purpose. Other than providing jobs for some historians, it will do no good to have ever so many students in our classes unless those individuals are somehow changed. If we have no effect on the student's thought processes as a result of his or her having had our courses, what good have we accomplished?

I believe that we have been careless in the development of objectives. More than this, we have generally avoided developing any kinds of tests to determine whether courses in history achieve what we are trying to do. For example, does the course in Western civilization give students a better perspective of the world in which they live? I do not know. I do know that not many of us have tried to find out.

Finally, I want to talk briefly about our curriculum. I maintain that we have designed too many of our courses and too much of the curriculum to meet the desires of particular faculty members rather than the needs of the students. How many times have departments given serious consideration to the history courses which would be

[9] Quoted in Association of Collegiate Schools of Business, *Bulletin*, IX (January 1973), 6.

most valuable and useful to students in this complex world? Not often, I fear. The question generally is, what does the instructor want to teach? If the new professor is a specialist in Patagonian culture, immediately there is a rush to get a new course approved on Patagonia. This may be a slight exaggeration, but not much. Seldom is the question asked whether the students need such a course or whether it fits departmental objectives. All of us have seen departments bring in a new professor and add several new courses in his specialty. In two or three years that professor leaves and is replaced by one who wants to teach something else. So we add more courses, again with little thought of what is best for the students.

I do not believe that the students should determine the curriculum. I think that professional historians know better than anyone else what should be offered. What I object to is our failure to give serious attention to the curriculum and our willingness to juggle courses for individual faculty convenience rather than developing courses most needed by and useful to the students. Furthermore, we seldom ask how particular courses fit into what we as individuals and departments are trying to do.

Again, I come back to goals. It probably makes little if any difference what courses we offer so long as we expect no definite results. If we are just covering the material with the vague hope that there will be some worthwhile fallout among our students, one course may be as good as another. The problem here is that we have too often, perhaps unwittingly, assumed that the interests of the students and the faculty are the same. This can be true, but probably it is not regularly the case. For example, it would be easy for me to rationalize that my department should permit me to offer a course in twentieth-century farm movements. Indeed, there is not a professor here who cannot make a strong case for his or her specialty. But our self-interest does not necessarily coincide with the interests and needs of students. The curriculum in our departments should be developed to meet the general and specialized needs of students, and the faculty should fulfill those needs by offering the courses which will meet the established goals.

There are many problems connected with the things I have been talking about, and the implications are many. Perhaps, we have not had better teaching because it is very tedious and hard work. That is, it is tiring and boring, as Carl Becker said, until students begin to respond. Then it is the most glorious of all professions. I believe that we can have more glorious moments in our teaching if we address ourselves to the problems which I have raised. If we become convinced that teaching is genuinely important, if we demonstrate the enthusiasm in the classroom that we sometimes show in our research and writing, if we decide what we are trying to accomplish and make this clear to the students, and finally, if we give up some of our professional selfishness and help develop a curriculum which will meet the needs of students as we see them, then I think we as teachers will have fewer boring experiences and more glorious ones.

Black Violence and White Response: Louisiana, 1862

By William F. Messner

A curious duality marked antebellum thought regarding the black slave: the black image was a mixture of Sambo and Nat Turner, fawning simpleton and flaming revolutionary. White Americans explained this apparent anomaly in terms of the acculturation process which the plantation regimen imposed upon all slaves. By nature blacks were savage brutes, but through contact with the higher civilization of the white South the African had been domesticated. As long as the discipline of the white man was secure, the slave would remain a Sambo; but remove the authority of the master, and blacks would revert to type as bloodthirsty savages.[1] Although this pattern of thought was not peculiar to the South, in that region its influence was particularly pervasive, for the southerner's belief in the black man's violent potential tended to reinforce the widely held opinion that a profitable production of staples could only be accomplished through the maintenance of a stable labor force. Slavery, therefore, had the complementary functions of ensuring white control over a potentially subversive minority population and of maximizing profits by the stabilization of labor.

The outbreak of civil war in 1861 sparked among whites a fear of imminent black violence, and in southern war zones the exodus of slaves from plantations accompanied by sporadic acts of servile violence only sharpened in the white mind the image of the manic Afro-American. In Louisiana especially the racial stability secured by the slave system shattered beneath the weight of the Federal assault on New Orleans in the spring of 1862, and the resulting

[1] See George M. Fredrickson, *The Black Image in the White Mind: The Debate on Afro-American Character and Destiny, 1817–1914* (New York and other cities, 1971) for a discussion of racial imagery in nineteenth-century America.

Mr. Messner is a member of the faculty of Keystone Junior College, La Plume, Pennsylvania, and wishes to acknowledge a faculty research grant which facilitated preparation of this article.

turmoil convinced both native whites and Federal military officials of the necessity for establishing mechanisms to check the black threat to law and order. While most southerners favored a reinstitution of the slavery regime, Federal military officials during 1862 devised a series of contraband programs which stabilized the racial situation by placing blacks under white control and which also aided the Union war effort. Prompted initially by the white fear of black violence, these programs served as precursors for future Federal efforts among the freedmen of the Southwest during the Civil War and Reconstruction.[2]

As soon as Federal warships appeared at the mouth of the Mississippi River early in 1862 plantation owners along the coast of Louisiana and Mississippi began to take precautions against the feared uprising of their slaves. Whites increased security measures, issued fewer passes for travel, and resorted more often to the whip. So fearful were planters of black violence that they refused to allow their slaves to congregate in large numbers even for such vital functions as repairing crevasses in the levee.[3] White fears were seemingly justified as blacks began to escape from their owners and to make their way by rowboat to the Federal staging area on Ship Island.[4] Other slaves bided their time until the Union assault on New Orleans was completed in May 1862. Believing the Union army had come to free them, slaves in the immediate vicinity of the city fled from their plantations and flocked into Union camps surrounding New Orleans. At Camp Parapet, just north of the city, 450 black refugees resided less than a month after the arrival of Union troops, and their number swelled to over a thousand by the end of the summer.[5]

[2] Extended discussions of contraband programs in Louisiana can be found in Louis S. Gerteis, "From Contraband to Freedman: Federal Policy Toward Southern Blacks, 1861–1865" (unpublished Ph.D. dissertation, University of Wisconsin, 1969); J. Thomas May, "Continuity and Change in the Labor Program of the Union Army and the Freedmen's Bureau," *Civil War History,* XVII (September 1971), 245–54; and William F. Messner, "The Federal Army and Blacks in the Gulf Department, 1862–1865" (unpublished Ph.D. dissertation, University of Wisconsin, 1972). For a general treatment of black behavior during the war see Bell I. Wiley, *Southern Negroes, 1861–1865* (New Haven and London, 1938).

[3] George H. Hepworth, *The Whip, Hoe, and Sword; or, The Gulf-Department in '63* (Boston, 1864), 151; Eliza McHatton-Ripley, *From Flag to Flag: A Woman's Adventures and Experiences in the South During the War, in Mexico, and in Cuba* (New York, 1889), 20–21.

[4] Neal Dow, *The Reminiscences of Neal Dow* (Portland, Maine, 1898), 668–69.

[5] Harrison Soule to his parents, May 8, 15, 1862, Harrison Soule Papers (Michigan Historical Collections, University of Michigan, Ann Arbor, Mich.); Frank D. Harding to his father, May 3, 1862, Eddy Harding Correspondence (State Historical Society of Wisconsin,

Federal military officials were perplexed by the black exodus. "What shall I do with my niggers?" asked the hard-pressed commander at Fort Macomb.[6] "I am placed in an awkward dilemma," complained the commander at Fort Saint Philip; "I have no authority to feed them [the slaves] . . . or send them away. I cannot have them in the fort, and know not what to do."[7] A New Hampshire officer noted in his diary that the blacks were "coming into camp by the hundred and are a costly curse. They should be kept out or set at work, or freed or colonized or sunk or something."[8] The sentiments of an enlisted man were expressed in a letter from a private in the Fourth Wisconsin Volunteers. "Potatoes are knee high, & beans to the top of the poles," he wrote from Baton Rouge. "It is a nice country if it were not for the negroes."[9]

Accompanying the exodus of blacks from plantations were incidents of black violence which solidified in the white mind the image of the barbaric black man freed from the restraints of white discipline. During the summer reports abounded concerning black unrest in the parishes of southern Louisiana. ". . . there is an uneasy feeling among the slaves," reported a correspondent of the New York *Times* in late July; "they are undoubtedly becoming insubordinate, and I cannot think that another sixty days can pass away without some sort of demonstration."[10] Three weeks later the same reporter wrote that the slaves in two nearby parishes were in a state of "semi-insurrection."[11] The correspondent of the New York *Herald* concurred in these conclusions. "There is no doubt that the negroes, for more than fifty miles up the river, are in a state of insubordination," he reported from New Orleans. "The country is given to pillage and desolation . . . . The slaves refuse obedience and cannot be compelled to labor."[12] On a Plaquemines Parish estate the owner recorded the following disturb-

---

Madison, Wis.); John W. De Forest, *A Volunteer's Adventures: A Union Captain's Record of the Civil War,* edited by James H. Croushore (New Haven and London, 1946), 17, 39–40; Dow, *Reminiscences,* 673–74.

[6] O. W. Lull to Benjamin Butler, May 11, 1862, Benjamin F. Butler Papers (Manuscript Division, Library of Congress, Washington, D. C.).

[7] New York *Times,* June 23, 1862.

[8] John M. Stanyan, *A History of the Eighth Regiment of New Hampshire Volunteers* (Concord, N. H., 1892), 105–107.

[9] De Have Norton to his parents, June 9, 1862, De Have Norton Correspondence (State Historical Society of Wisconsin).

[10] New York *Times,* August 1, 1862.

[11] *Ibid.,* August 26, 1862.

[12] New York *Herald,* September 9, 1862.

ing scene: "We have a terrible state of affairs here negroes refusing to work and women all in their houses. The negroes have erected a gallows in the quarters and give as an excuse for it that they are told they must drive their master . . . off the plantation . . . and that then they will be free."[13] On a neighboring plantation the slaves had already driven off the overseer and taken over the estate for their own use, and on another place blacks killed an overseer who had beaten slaves for refusing to work.[14] Frustrated in their own attempts at quelling the racial turmoil, slaveowners turned to the Union army as the only means for restoring order in the parishes.[15]

The tide of racial turmoil extended even into New Orleans. On the outskirts of the city violent confrontations often occurred between police and black refugees attempting to enter Union lines. Disgusted with such militant actions, the New Orleans *Daily Picayune* declared in July 1862 that the slaves had "become impudent, disobedient and reckless. This morning fifteen, armed with clubs and cane knives, came up from a plantation below the city."[16] Two weeks later a New Orleans citizen noted in his diary that "late last night & early this morning there was a speck of servile war in the lower part of the city." Forty slaves had overpowered the police and were only routed when Federal troops arrived on the scene.[17] Once inside the city the behavior of blacks improved very little. Police reports for the Third District of New Orleans reflect the racial instability which gripped the city. Arrests of slaves accused of impudent and violent behavior were daily occurrences during the summer, and a constant stream of fugitive bondsmen flowed in and out of the city's jails.[18] Especially disturbing to whites was the frequency with which police arrested slaves for insulting and even assaulting their owners. One such incident

[13] Quoted in J. Carlyle Sitterson, *Sugar Country: The Cane Sugar Industry in the South, 1753–1950* ([Lexington, Ky.], 1953), 209–10.

[14] *Ibid.*; New Orleans *Daily Picayune*, October 11, 1862.

[15] Throughout the summer of 1862 military headquarters in New Orleans received a constant stream of requests from planters for aid in controlling their slaves. New York *Times*, August 26, 1862; W. Mitthoff to Benjamin Butler, May 29, 1862, Benjamin F. Butler, *Private and Official Correspondence of Gen. Benjamin F. Butler During the Period of the Civil War* (5 vols., Norwood, Mass., 1917), I, 525–27; Polycarpe Fortier to Butler, June 4, 1862, *ibid.*, 553–54.

[16] New Orleans *Daily Picayune*, July 22, August 14, 1862.

[17] MS diary of "A Louisiana Rebel," entry for August 4, 1862 (New-York Historical Society, New York City).

[18] Day and Night Police Reports, Third District, New Orleans Police Department (New Orleans Public Library, New Orleans, La.).

was recorded by the *Picayune:* "A savage old nigger named Ben, forgetting all past benefits conferred upon him, was brought into court for insulting his mistress. Among other disloyal expressions the old rascal said that he wanted to get arrested, for then he could become a soldier, fight his mistress, and do what he pleased. He was sent to prison for three months."[19] Disturbances such as this confirmed the *Picayune*'s opinion that "Recent events have made many of the negroes in this city and neighborhood almost unmanageable."[20]

The Union commander charged with the responsibility for restoring order to the Gulf Department was Major General Benjamin Franklin Butler.[21] At first glance Butler appears to have been an unlikely choice for the command of the Union expedition against New Orleans. A professional politician, he had no military experience prior to 1861 save for the command of a brigade of Massachusetts militia. As a lifelong Democrat, the general had supported the Buchanan administration throughout its tumultuous term of office, and in 1860 he had campaigned for the election of John Cabell Breckinridge, the one Democratic candidate whom Butler believed had a chance of defeating Abraham Lincoln for the Presidency. But with the secession of South Carolina the Massachusetts politician decided to divest himself of the robes of Hunker Democracy and took up the cause of the national government. In attempting to rid himself of the stigma of his Democratic past, Butler informed Massachusetts governor John Albion Andrew well before the outbreak of hostilities that he was ready to serve with the militia in case of an emergency. Eager to gain Democratic support for the Union war effort, Governor Andrew was only too glad to appoint the willing Butler commanding general of the state militia in the field. Only a month after Fort Sumter, Butler evoked the public's notice when, in response to severe criticism from the radical wing of the Massachusetts Republican party for having returned slaves to their master, he labeled three fugitive slaves who came into his lines at Fort Monroe, Virginia, contraband of war and refused to return them to

[19] New Orleans *Daily Picayune,* August 22, 1862.

[20] *Ibid.*, July 22, 1862.

[21] Although the boundaries of the Gulf Department shifted during the war with the fortunes of the Union army, for the purposes of this study the Gulf Department is defined to include those parishes in southern Louisiana which President Lincoln excluded from the operation of the Emancipation Proclamation. These parishes are St. Bernard, Plaquemines, Jefferson, St. John, St. Charles, St. James, Ascension, Assumption, Terrebonne, Lafourche, St. Mary, St. Martin, and Orleans.

their owners. Butler justified his politic maneuver on the basis of military necessity. The slaves had previously been aiding the Confederate war effort, and Butler's actions simply shifted their energies to support the cause of the Union.[22]

Despite having earned the reputation of a foe of slavery during his command at Fort Monroe, Butler was initially disinclined to tamper with the peculiar institution in southern Louisiana. His goal in the Gulf Department was to restore Louisiana to the Union by assuaging the fears of the planting and propertied interests who were "well-disposed toward the Union, only fearing lest their negroes should not be let alone . . . ."[23] Confiscation of slaves would have been, in Butler's opinion, an "injustice to the bona fide loyal creditor, whose interest the Government will doubtless consider."[24] Contributing to his determination to ensure that slaves remained under the control of their masters was his dread of the blacks' potential for violence. Deeply disturbed by the racial instability he met in New Orleans, Butler outlined his thoughts on slavery in a letter to Secretary of the Treasury Salmon Portland Chase: "Be sure that I shall treat the negro with as much tenderness as possible but I assure you it is quite impossible to free him here and now without a San Domingo. A single whistle from me would cause every white mans throat to be cut in this city. Accumulated hate has been piled up here between master and servant, until it is fearful. . . . There is no doubt that an insurrection is only prevented by our *Bayonets.*"[25]

Convinced of the necessity for maintaining civil order, Butler attempted to reassure the native white population that the Union army would not tolerate further racial unrest. During the first week of the Federal occupation he publicly declared that "All rights of property, of whatever kind, will be held inviolate, subject only to the laws of the United States." The object of the military in Louisiana was "to restore order out of chaos . . ." and "to have every species of disorder quelled." He also promised that all persons aiding this cause would not be disturbed in either their persons or property.[26] Determined to fulfill these promises, Butler

[22] Butler's contraband policy at Fort Monroe is discussed in Gerteis, "From Contraband to Freedman," 14–31.

[23] Butler to Edwin Stanton, June 29, 1862, Butler, *Private and Official Correspondence*, II, 13–16 (quotation on page 14).

[24] Butler to Stanton, May 25, 1862, Butler Papers.

[25] Butler to Chase, July 10, 1862, Salmon Portland Chase Papers (Historical Society of Pennsylvania, Philadelphia, Pa.).

[26] Proclamation, May 1, 1862, Butler, *Private and Official Correspondence*, I, 433–36.

directed his troops to confiscate only those slaves whose owners had committed an overtly treasonable act. All other black refugees who could not be employed by the army were to be excluded from Union lines.[27]

Butler delegated primary responsibility for implementing his slave-exclusion policy in New Orleans to the city police, for War Department orders prohibited military authorities from returning slaves to their owners. Throughout the summer of 1862 police officers gathered and imprisoned fugitive slaves from the streets of New Orleans and delivered them to their owners on demand.[28] Outside the confines of the city, however, the task of restraining blacks from leaving their owners belonged by default to the Federal army. Contrary to both national law and military orders, the army not only excluded slaves from its lines during the summer but also returned slaves to their owners and disciplined recalcitrant black workers.[29] Even the navy became involved in maintaining civil order. During the unsuccessful naval assault on Vicksburg in June blacks succeeded in boarding Union vessels despite the efforts of ship commanders to exclude them. Naval regulations required that these slaves be hired as laborers on the flotilla, but many were returned to owners who claimed loyalty to the Union.[30]

Although most officers in the Gulf Department agreed with Butler's contention regarding the slaves' potential for violence, not all concurred in his methods for controlling blacks. The most notable critic of the commander's contraband policy was Brigadier

[27] General Order No. 32, May 27, 1862; Special Order No. 45, May 27, 1862; General Order No. 44, June 21, 1862, *The War of the Rebellion: A Compilation of the Official Records of the Union and Confederate Armies* (70 vols. in 128, Washington, 1880–1901), Ser. I, Vol. XV, 445–46, 492; cited hereinafter as *O.R.*

[28] New York *Tribune*, August 13, 1862; New Orleans *Daily Picayune*, June 4, August 2, 1862; Police Reports, Third District, New Orleans Police Department. During the summer over one hundred slaves were arrested as "runaways" in the Third District of New Orleans alone. In addition, city police jailed slaves for "safekeeping" on the request of their owners. Military authorities also permitted city jailers to whip insubordinate slaves and city newspapers to print notices of fugitive slaves. New York *Tribune*, August 5, 1862; New Orleans *Daily Picayune*, June 6, October 1, 1862; J. P. M. to Butler, July 18, 1862, Butler, *Private and Official Correspondence*, II, 84–86.

[29] New Orleans *Daily Picayune*, May 13, 24, 29, 1862; New York *Times*, August 18, 1862; New York *National Anti-Slavery Standard*, August 30, 1862; R. Smith to Butler, May 21, 1862, Butler Papers; Harrison Soule to his parents, May 8, 1862, Soule Papers.

[30] New York *Times*, August 6, 14, 1862; New York *Tribune*, August 2, 1862; New York *National Anti-Slavery Standard*, August 16, September 27, 1862; David D. Porter to Thomas T. Craven, June 24, 1862, *Official Records of the Union and Confederate Navies in the War of the Rebellion* (30 vols., Washington, 1894–1922), Ser. I, Vol. XVIII, 571–72; Selim E. Woodworth to Porter, July 1, 1862, *ibid.*, 664–66.

General John Wolcott Phelps, a regular army officer who first articulated much of the thinking which would later shape Federal efforts among the freedmen of the Southwest. An outspoken proponent of the primacy of the Anglo-Saxon race and the efficacy of free labor, Phelps believed that the presence of the black slave thwarted the extension of northern laborers and institutions throughout the South. He hoped the war would result in the abolition of slavery and the exportation of the slaves, but he believed special measures had to be taken during the war to care for blacks who, left to shift for themselves, would either initiate a race war or align with the rebels in response to native white promises of protection. In order to stabilize and control the black population Phelps proposed the organization of blacks into military units and the establishment of a rigorous educational program for all slaves. At the end of hostilities he hoped to utilize his black troops as the vanguard of a black exodus to Africa for exploiting the "underdeveloped riches" of the Dark Continent.[31]

Immediately upon his arrival in the Gulf Department Phelps began implementing his antislavery beliefs despite General Butler's policy of buttressing the slave system. During the first weeks of Federal occupation slaveowners besieged the commander with complaints that their chattels were being given refuge at Camp Parapet, the headquarters of General Phelps. Butler attempted to cajole and then to scold his balky subordinate into submission, but all his efforts proved unavailing. Phelps believed that if the army continued to support slavery, "the danger of a violent revolution, over which we can have no control, must become more imminent every day," and therefore he continued to accept fugitive slaves into his camp and subsequently began a system of rudimentary black education and military training.[32]

Phelps's utilization of black troops placed him on a direct collision course with his commander. By writing department headquarters in late July and requesting provisions for his new troops, he precipitated the final confrontation with General Butler. As justification for the enlistment of slaves, Phelps argued that his

[31] Phelps's ideas must be pieced together from his correspondence, essays, and diaries, John Wolcott Phelps Papers (New York Public Library, New York City). His first recorded public statement on slavery was made in December 1861 shortly after his arrival at Ship Island. James Parton, *General Butler in New Orleans* (New York, 1864), 198–200.

[32] Phelps to R. S. Davis, June 16, 1862, *O.R.*, Ser. I, Vol. XV, 486–90 (quotation on page 487). For a complete discussion of the Phelps-Butler controversy see Messner, "The Federal Army and Blacks in the Gulf Department," 30–38.

program was "the best way of preventing the African from becoming instrumental in a general state of anarchy."[33] Butler reacted heatedly to this latest provocation. He wrote to his wife that Phelps was "mad as a March Hare on the 'nigger question.' "[34] Not even deigning to consider Phelps's proposal, Butler directed his subordinate to employ his "contrabands" in cutting down the trees around his camp. Regarding Butler's orders as an affront and unwilling to perform the functions of a "slave-driver," Phelps tendered his resignation.[35] By the end of the summer he had left the Gulf Department and the army, but his ideas lingered on. Through his efforts Phelps popularized the notion that programs could be established for transforming blacks into a positive element in the war effort and for eliminating the slaves' disruptive potential.[36] Even before his departure from the Gulf Department, Phelps's beliefs were beginning to replace the more conservative practices of General Butler.

The necessity for a basic alteration in the army's confiscation program was impressed upon Butler by a combination of local and national developments. Within the Gulf Department, despite the best efforts of the military, blacks continued to manifest their discontent with the institution of slavery, and black insubordination remained as the leitmotif of labor relations on sugar plantations. In Butler's opinion, the continuing racial instability threatened to make his department a "Sodom & Gomorrah," with the slaves acting as the "fire and brimstone" of God. At his wits' end concerning the unruly blacks, the commander exclaimed to his wife, "we shall have a negro insurrection here I fancy. If something is not done soon, God help us all. The negroes are getting saucy and troublesome, and who blames them?"[37]

At this juncture in the late summer of 1862, although Butler

[33] Phelps to R. S. Davis, July 30, 1862, *O.R.*, Ser. I, Vol. XV, 534–35.

[34] Butler to his wife, August 5, 1862, Butler *Private and Official Correspondence*, II, 154.

[35] R. S. Davis to Phelps, July 31, 1862, Parton, *General Butler*, 506; Phelps to Davis, July 31, 1862, *O.R.*, Ser. I, Vol. XV, 535; Phelps to Lorenzo Thomas, August 2, 1862, Butler, *Private and Official Correspondence*, II, 146–47.

[36] To the end of his stay in the Gulf Department Phelps continued to stress the need for constructing new mechanisms for controlling the slaves. In August he informed Butler that Louisiana society was "on the verge of dissolution, and it is the true policy of the Government to seize upon the chief elements of disorder and anarchy, and employ them in favor of law and order." According to Phelps the black man threatened "to be a fearful element of ruin and disaster, and the best way to prevent it is to arm and organize him on the side of the Government." Phelps to Butler, August [6], 1862, Butler, *Private and Official Correspondence*, II, 155–57 (quotations on page 157).

[37] Butler to his wife, July 28, 25, 1862, *ibid.*, 115, 117, 109.

was still convinced of the necessity of maintaining control over the black population, he was no longer certain that this goal could be accomplished through the medium of slavery. Rather, over the last three months of the year Butler instituted programs which simultaneously signaled the demise of slavery in southern Louisiana and the reinstitution of white control over blacks. The final impetus for this change came from the national level. Administration spokesmen, such as Secretary of War Edwin McMasters Stanton and Secretary of the Treasury Salmon Chase, informed Butler during the late summer of a shift in national sentiment toward the abolition of slavery. They suggested that he place himself at the head of this movement by acting decisively against the peculiar institution in the Gulf Department.[38] Their opinion was confirmed by the passage of the Second Confiscation Act on July 17, which freed all slaves of rebel masters as soon as they came within Union lines.[39] Butler's politically astute wife analyzed the growth of antislavery sentiment for her husband in early August. She wrote: "Emancipation, and arming the negroes is held in check for a little . . . [as] soon as there is a plausible hope of success it will be brought forward again. . . . Phelps' policy prevails instead of yours. The abolitionists will have this a war to free the slaves at once if possible, nothing else is thought of. The Administration will assent to it just as fast and as far as the country will sustain it."[40] Ever responsive to shifts in the political winds, this information, coupled with the army's inability to control blacks as slaves, prodded Butler into a more radical direction regarding slavery.

The first action by General Butler which marked a movement away from his former policy of buttressing the institution of slavery was the enlistment of blacks into the Union army. Although he had been initially disinclined to utilize black soldiers, by the end of the summer Butler was faced with a dire need for more soldiers to bolster his increasingly diffused command. His

[38] Chase to Butler, July 31, 1862, Chase Papers; Stanton to Butler, August 7, 1862, *O.R.*, Ser. I, Vol. XV, 543.

[39] Butler was informed of the passage of the Second Confiscation Act in early August by Secretary Stanton. Stanton to Butler, August 7, 1862, *O.R.*, Ser. I, Vol. XV, 543. See James M. McPherson, *The Struggle For Equality: Abolitionists and the Negro in the Civil War and Reconstruction* (Princeton, 1964), 106–18, for a discussion of the growth of antislavery sentiment in the North during the summer of 1862.

[40] Mrs. Butler to her husband, August 8, 1862, Butler, *Private and Official Correspondence*, II, 164. See also Mrs. Butler's letter of September 28, 1862, to her husband regarding the political gains which could be made by arming the slaves. *Ibid.*, 335–36.

need for additional troops, combined with his awareness of favorable administration sentiment and the necessity to discipline blacks, convinced him to "call on Africa to intervene . . ." in the war effort. On August 14 he informed Secretary of War Stanton that he was enlisting into the Union service a brigade of free black men raised the year before by the Confederates.[41] Butler's action was a reflection of his political astuteness. The Rebel regiment, entitled the Native Guards, was composed of New Orleans freemen and had originally been organized in May 1861 by Louisiana governor Thomas Overton Moore. Because of the Confederate origin of his new soldiers and their free status, Butler believed he had insulated himself from criticism. "I have kept clear of the vexed question of arming the slaves," he explained to Henry Wager Halleck, general-in-chief of the Union army. "I am fortified by precedents of a half century's standing, acted upon by the Confederate authorities within six months, and I believe I have done nothing of which the most fastidious member of Jefferson Davis' household political can rightfully complain . . . ."[42]

Butler's black military organization was an immediate success. Within two weeks after its founding over eighteen hundred black men had enlisted in the Native Guards, and by the end of the year Butler had formed three infantry regiments and two batteries of heavy artillery from his black recruits.[43] The reason for Butler's phenomenal success in locating recruits for his new organization was explained by a Native Guards officer: "Any negro who could swear that he was free, if physically good, was accepted . . . ."[44] Utilizing this tactic, the army was able to recruit slaves as well as free blacks for the Native Guards. Indeed, by the end of 1862 the overwhelming majority of enlisted men in the black organization were former slaves. For Butler to have followed any other practice would have been foolish, since the army desperately needed troops and fugitive slaves needed the discipline which only the military could provide. George S. Denison, customs collector for the port of New Orleans and Butler's political colleague, recognized

[41] Butler to Stanton, August 14, 1862, *O.R.*, Ser. I, Vol. XV, 549.

[42] Butler to Halleck, August 27, 1862, *ibid.*, 555–56. A discussion of the Rebel origins of the Native Guards can be found in Mary F. Berry, "Negro Troops in Blue and Gray: The Louisiana Native Guards, 1861–1863," *Louisiana History*, VIII (Spring 1967), 167–70.

[43] Berry, "Negro Troops," 174–76; New York *Times*, September 29, 1862.

[44] Joseph T. Wilson, *The Black Phalanx; A History of the Negro Soldiers of the United States in the Wars of 1775–1812, 1861–'65* (Hartford, 1888), 195, see also George Denison to Salmon Chase, September 24, 1862, Salmon P. Chase Correspondence (Manuscript Division, Library of Congress).

this rationale for arming slaves: "One individual can control 50,000 disciplined men," he wrote Secretary Chase, "but cannot control a mob of fifty."[45] Blacks were not only utilized as enlisted men by Butler but were also given commissions in the Native Guards. Sixty-six black men, most of them "free men of color," received commissions as captains and lieutenants during 1862. The military's desire for racial stability also played a role in the decision to utilize free blacks as officers. Butler believed that the enthusiasm and intelligence of the freemen made them prime officer material and that their presence as Native Guards officers would have a stabilizing effect on the enlisted men. Racial hostility could be avoided if the slaves were treated fairly by being armed and given officers of their own color. Any other policy, according to Butler, would not only be unfair to the black man but would also be "an injustice which is pregnant with dangerous consequences."[46]

Butler's emphasis upon controlling the dangerous proclivities of Afro-Americans and inculcating them with the essentials of military discipline was reflected by the use which the army made of its black auxiliaries. Very rarely were black troops in the Gulf Department permitted to assume combat roles. Rather, military efficiency and discipline, combined with the supposed immunity of blacks to climatic diseases, dictated that the Native Guards be placed in the role of a fatigue and garrison force. The army's utilization of the first three Native Guard regiments during 1862 was indicative of this pattern of thought. The first regiment spent two weeks repairing railroad track and bridges and then devoted the rest of the year to foraging. The second regiment guarded the railroad at Opelousas for the whole of 1862 and then traveled to desolate Ship Island, where it spent the next three years on prison guard duty. In late November the third regiment saw its first military duty clearing the sugar-cane fields in the Teche district for the next year's crop. After many weeks of this arduous labor the regiment closed out the year foraging the surrounding countryside.[47] The vaunted servility of the black man when placed firmly under white control made the Native Guards perfectly suited for these labor details, and Butler's utilization of black troops during

[45] Denison to Chase, October 8, 1862, Chase Correspondence.

[46] Berry, "Negro Troops," 174–76; Wilson, *Black Phalanx*, 169–70.

[47] Butler to Godfrey Weitzel, October 30, 1862, *O.R.*, Ser. I, Vol. XV, 587–88; Berry, "Negro Troops," 176–79; *Senate Reports*, 37 Cong., 3 Sess., No. 108: *Report of the Joint Committee on the Conduct of the War* (Serial 1154, Washington, 1863), Pt. 3, pp. 358–59.

1862 established a pattern which would be uniformly followed in the Gulf Department for the remainder of the war.[48]

The second phase of General Butler's program for stabilizing the black population of the Gulf Department was the establishment of a wage-labor system on the sugar plantations of southern Louisiana. Sugar was the mainstay of Louisiana's economy, and the commander realized that the revitalization of this most important industry was an integral part of the reconstruction process in his department. But before any progress could be made in the restoration of the industry, sugar producers first had to acquire a reliable labor force. In the past slaves had assumed this role, but during the summer of 1862 blacks manifested an increasing reluctance to continue laboring as chattels. The situation was doubly irritating to planters because the sugar crop then reaching maturity was even more promising than it had been in record-setting 1861. Butler was aware of the planters' plight, if only because he was the unwelcome recipient of many slaves who had formerly composed the work force of the sugar plantations. On September 1 he reported to the War Department that his commissary was issuing twice as many rations to black refugees as it was to the troops of his command. "They are now coming in by the hundreds nay thousands almost daily," he lamented to General Halleck. "Many of the plantations are deserted along the 'coast'. . . . Crops of sugar cane are left standing to waste which would make millions of dollars worth of sugar."[49]

Prohibited by the Second Confiscation Act from excluding slaves any longer from his lines, Butler turned to wage labor as a means for placing blacks back on plantations, where they could aid in the development of the Gulf Department's agricultural resources. Secretary of the Treasury Chase had been urging the general throughout the summer to institute a wage-labor program, and Butler had received similar advice from Edward Lillie Pierce, who had established a comparable program in the Sea Islands of South Carolina.[50] In addition, many planters had become con-

[48] Even during the one major battle in which blacks assumed a combat role in the Gulf Department, the Battle of Port Hudson, the most important contribution of the Native Guards to the Union effort was the completion of extensive labor details. Messner, "The Federal Army and Blacks in the Gulf Department," 301–36; Dudley T. Cornish, *The Sable Arm: Negro Troops in the Union Army, 1861–1865* (New York, 1956), 142–44.

[49] Butler to Halleck, September 1, 1862, Butler Papers; New York *Times* December 21, 1862.

[50] Chase to Butler, July 31, 1862, Butler, *Private and Official Correspondence,* II, 131–35; Pierce to Butler, August 20, 1862, Butler Papers; see also annual report of Secretary of War Stanton, December 1, 1862, *O.R.*, Ser. III, Vol. II, 910–12, for a similar opinion concerning the institution of wage labor in the South.

vinced that wage labor was the only means by which blacks could be induced to work once again on sugar plantations. According to a New York *Times* correspondent, the planters of southern Louisiana were convinced that "so utterly disorganized have the slaves become, that the institution, under its old order, is forever destroyed and worthless, no matter what Mr. LINCOLN or anyone else may say on the subject."[51] While this sentiment was by no means universal among sugar planters, there were many businessmen in the Gulf Department willing to utilize black wage labor if they could be reasonably assured of making a profit from sugar production.

By December the military in conjunction with sugar planters had developed the framework of a wage-labor program to be utilized on Gulf Department sugar plantations. The army's standard wage-labor contract provided a ten-dollar monthly wage for all black workers, with three dollars to be deducted for clothing. Employers also were required to provide their laborers with food and medicine as well as protection for the immediate relatives of workers incapacitated by sickness or old age. In return, the military required all blacks to return to plantations and to labor ten hours a day, twenty-six days a month. Butler forbade "cruel or corporal punishment" but promised to punish refusal to work or insubordination by "imprisonment in darkness on bread and water." The army guaranteed to provide each planter with an adequate supply of laborers as well as guards and patrols to "preserve order and prevent crime."[52] General supervision of the labor contract was placed in the hands of a three-man Sequestration Commission. This body was to supply laborers to planters and also to work for the government any plantations which had been abandoned by their owners. Because of the need for laborers and the army's desire to establish white control over black workers, the commissioners required that all black refugees return to plantations under the stipulations of Butler's wage contract. The commission placed its workers under military guard and delivered them on request to planters and private businessmen leasing abandoned plantations from the army.[53]

Despite the seemingly liberal compensation called for in

[51] New York *Times*, November 3, 1862.

[52] Parton, *General Butler*, 523–24; G. Strong to G. Weitzel, November 2, 1862, *O.R.*, Ser. I, Vol. XV, 162–63.

[53] General Order No. 91, November 9, 1862, *ibid.*, 592–94.

Butler's wage contract, few workers profited from the wage-labor program. Anxious to rid themselves of their black burden, many military commanders simply delivered blacks to planters with little or no regard for the wages promised to the laborers. Concurrently, many refugees, equally anxious to escape the drab and often unhealthy environs of the contraband camp, signed on with planters despite the meager recompense offered to them.[54] Even in those situations where workers were promised full wages, many employers simply turned off their employees after the harvest without paying them. On the Star Plantation, leased by Charles Weed from the army in the fall of 1862, the workers were still waiting for their first wages in July 1863.[55] The 330 workers on the David Pugh Plantation, hired at ten dollars a month, harvested a crop for their employer valued at $36,000, for which they received shoes and rations totaling $1,500. Sixty percent of the workers received no pay at all.[56] Cases such as these were by no means unique. In January 1863 General William Helmsby Emory reported to department headquarters that "it appears that those who have been working for their own profit the abandoned plantations have in many cases turned off the hands without payment, food or clothing." As a result, blacks in a "wretched and destitute condition" were once again flocking into military posts and contraband camps.[57]

Although the army gave only perfunctory attention to the payment of workers, great care was taken to ensure the subordination of black laborers to white employers. General Butler had promised planters that the military would "preserve order" on sugar plantations by providing guards and patrols to "prevent abuse on one side and insubordination on the other." These military guards generally construed their role to be that of overseers for the plantation owner, and employers found it an easy matter to enlist the sympathy, and police powers, of Union soldiers on their behalf.

[54] F. S. Nickerson to William Hoffman, December 23, 1862, Records of United States Continental Army Commands, 1821–1920, Department of the Gulf, Box 5, Record Group 393 (National Archives, Washington, D. C.); cited hereinafter as RG 393, NA.

[55] Report of the Star Plantation, July 22, 1863, Records of Civil War Special Agencies of the Treasury Department, Third Special Agency of the Treasury Department, Vol. 71, Record Group 366 (National Archives).

[56] Benjamin Smith to Nathaniel Banks, March 7, 1863, Department of the Gulf, Box 3, RG 393, NA.

[57] Emory to William Hoffman, January 27, 1863, *ibid.*; see also John Clark to Richard B. Irwin, January 30, 1863, *ibid.; Second Annual Report of the New England Freedmen's Aid Society (Educational Commission)* (Boston, 1864), 46.

Numerous incidents of plantation guards aiding planters in cheating workers were referred to Superintendent of Contrabands George H. Hanks, who reported to his commander that he had "no doubt of their truth . . . and that many other cases of like injustices will be brought to light."[58] The military's emphasis on black subordination did not end with the termination of General Butler's command in the Gulf Department at the end of 1862. Although his successor, General Nathaniel Prentiss Banks, eliminated some of the grosser inequities from the wage-labor program, the military continued to stress, in Banks's words, the need to "induce" blacks to return to plantations and the necessity of requiring them to "work diligently and maintain respectful deportment to their employers, and perfect subordination to their duties."[59] Under Banks the anomaly of a system of compulsory free labor reached its zenith in the Gulf Department, for only through such a program was the military confident that the "necessity of toil" could be impressed upon the black man.[60]

By the end of 1862 most Federal officials and northern observers considered General Butler's wage-labor program an unqualified success. True, only one-third of the plantations within Federal lines had been worked and the harvest was only a fraction of the record total of the year before, but these debits were offset by the experiment's clear evidence that staples could be grown at a profit by free black labor. On plantations where the experiment was tried, "sugar was manufactured more rapidly than during any previous season," reported a correspondent for the *Times*, ". . . the same number of negroes, with the same machinery, producing a hogshead and a half more of sugar each day than under the old system."[61] The wage-labor program successfully refuted the theories by which southerners had justified slavery. "The labour necessary to the Working of Sugar Plantations can be done without the Aid of the Slave Drivers Whip," John Wilson Shaffer, Butler's chief quartermaster, reported to President Abraham Lincoln "Free labour on Sugar Plantations. Thank God, [it] is no longer an Experiment, it has been tried and found to be the better

[58] Hanks to Banks, March 5, 1863; B. F. Smith to Banks, March 7, 1863, Department of the Gulf, Box 3, RG 393, NA; De Forest, *A Volunteer's Adventures,* 76; Edwin B. Lufkin, *History of the Thirteenth Maine Regiment* . . . (Bridgeton, Maine, 1898), 42–43.

[59] *De Bow's Review,* Ser. II, Vol. III (January 1867), 100–101.

[60] General Order No. 23, February 3, 1864, *O.R.*, Ser. I, Vol. XXXIV, Pt. II, 227–31. See Messner, "The Federal Army and Blacks in the Gulf Department," 106–200, for a description of Banks's free-labor program.

[61] New York *Times,* January 16, 1863.

System."[62] The magnitude of the program's success was not lost on its founder. In late November Butler reported to the President that his program had proven that "Black labor can be as well governed, used, and made as profitable in a state of freedom as in slavery . . . ." Despite the opposition of some planters who refused to give up the use of the lash, Butler predicted the program would show enough profit to finance the department's relief measures for at least a half year. Although he believed that gradual emancipation was the most effective means for controlling blacks and restructuring the social institutions of the South, he thought it "quite feasible" for free blacks to be put to work immediately "with profit and safety to the white," but he asserted that it could "be best done when under military supervision."[63]

Two weeks after reporting the success of his wage-labor program to the President, Butler was relieved of his command and replaced by General Nathaniel Banks, another Massachusetts political general. But the removal of Butler did not imply administration disapproval of his contraband programs.[64] Rather, the military utilized Butler's attempts at controlling blacks as the basis of its efforts among blacks in the Gulf Department during the remainder of the war and even into the period of Reconstruction. Specifically, the commander's emphasis upon "military supervision" was at the core of his successor's publicized efforts among the freedmen. Under Banks's leadership Gulf Department officials between 1863 and 1865 established an extensive series of contraband programs, including the institution of black wage labor throughout all of southern Louisiana, further black military enlistment, educational programs for the freedmen, and various relief measures for unemployed blacks. In all these programs the army stressed the necessity for maintaining firm control of its black wards. Soon after Banks's arrival in the Gulf Department the

[62] Shaffer to Lincoln, December (?), 1862, Robert Todd Lincoln Collection, Abraham Lincoln Papers (Manuscript Division, Library of Congress); see also George Denison to Chase, November 14, 1862, Chase Correspondence.

[63] Butler to Lincoln, November 28, 1862, Butler, *Private and Official Correspondence*, II, 447–50; quotations on page 450.

[64] Butler was removed from the command of the Gulf Department for political reasons. His controversial activities in Louisiana had alienated a good portion of the New Orleans diplomatic community, and his Democratic background and volatile behavior were considered detrimental to the delicate process of restoring Louisiana to the Union. Charles Sumner to Butler, January 8, 1863, *O.R.*, Ser. I, Vol. LIII, 546. Banks, on the other hand, was a moderate Republican politician who had shown a genius for placing himself in the mainstream of national political movements. Fred H. Harrington, *Fighting Politician; Major General N. P. Banks* (Philadelphia and London, 1948).

military developed the technique of the police dragnet, which it used with great success throughout the remainder of the war as a means of eliminating black vagrants from the towns and cities of southern Louisiana. Banks eliminated the black officer corps of the Native Guards because of white dissatisfaction with this administrative innovation. Compulsion became the watchword under the new commander in the army's efforts to recruit blacks for military and plantation labor. Even the efforts of the military to provide for black education and relief were utilized by Banks as a means of controlling the anarchic tendencies of the freedmen and of shaping them into productive farm workers.[65]

By the end of the war freedmen in the Gulf Department were the objects of a wide variety of contraband programs and were probably more secure physically than in any other area of the South. But the freedmen's security was purchased at a price. Under both Butler and Banks the fear of black violence played a role in shaping the army's contraband programs. Both commands considered strict white control to be essential in structuring freedmen's activities. Gulf Department officials considered independent thoughts and actions on the part of blacks as threatening to the reconstruction process, and the military's contraband programs therefore de-emphasized and even discouraged the growth of black economic and political autonomy.[66] The goal of Federal officials relative to the freedmen was the development of an efficient and stable plantation labor force, and within this framework there was little room for the uncurbed, and potentially subversive, gropings of black individuals.

A final result of the army's institution of contraband programs was a reshaping of the black image in the white mind. Just as the outbreak of war had given emphasis to the image of the black man as manic revolutionary, so had the reimposition of order by the Union military signaled a reversion to the Sambo image of the Afro-American. In explaining the success of blacks as wage laborers and soldiers, military officials in the Gulf Department never tired of emphasizing the innate docility of the black man. In the summer of 1863 General Banks appointed two former abolitionists to assess the progress made in the implementation of

[65] Messner, "The Federal Army and Blacks in the Gulf Department," Chaps. III–VII.

[66] Although Banks gave lip service to the ideal of black proprietorship of farm land, during his administration the military made neither land nor credit available to aspiring black farmers. Rather, under both Butler and Banks the army placed sole emphasis upon compelling blacks to work on plantations as field laborers under white direction and control. *Ibid.*, 242–57.

a wage-labor program in southern Louisiana.[67] The conclusion reached by these inspectors was that on those plantations where the army's experiment had been faithfully carried out the black workers were "docile, industrious, & quiet."[68] A year later Banks's superintendent of Negro labor reported that the blacks were "more willing to work, and more patient than any set of human beings I ever saw. . . . The negroes willingly accept the condition of labor for their own maintenance . . . ."[69] A similar line of thinking characterized white explanations of the freedmen's success as soldiers. A Massachusetts soldier characterized the suitability of the black man for the army in the following terms: "Their docility, their habits of unquestioning obedience, pre-eminently fit them for soldiers. To a negro an order means obedience in spirit as well as letter."[70] In the estimation of General Daniel Ullmann, a commander of black troops in the Gulf Department, the freedman's outstanding qualification as a soldier was his "habit of subordination."[71] According to General Butler black soldiers were "more exact, inasmuch as they are more obedient."[72]

Even before the conclusion of the war, then, the black image in the white mind had come full circle, and blacks who in 1861 had been feared for their violent potential were now praised for their docile behavior. This development is of more than passing interest, for the reimposition of white control over blacks significantly diminished the need felt by whites for instituting new programs for southern freedmen. Just as fear had been the catalyst for many of the military's contraband programs, so had the abatement of the white man's violent racial fantasies marked the end of the army's innovation in the field of freedmen's affairs. By 1865 the Union army had successfully reestablished racial order by putting

[67] Banks's inspectors were George Hughes Hepworth and Edwin Wheelock, both of whom were Unitarian ministers from Massachusetts and active members of the antislavery movement.

[68] Wheelock and Hepworth to Banks, April 9, 10, June 15, 28, 1863, Nathaniel P. Banks Papers (Manuscript Division, Library of Congress).

[69] George Hanks to James McKaye, March 28, 1864, quoted in J. McKaye, *The Mastership and Its Fruits: The Emancipated Slave Face to Face with His Old Master* (New York, 1864), 17.

[70] Quoted in Henry T. Johns, *Life with the Forty-ninth Massachusetts Volunteers* (Washington, 1890), 166–70; quotation on page 167.

[71] Ullmann to Henry Wilson, December 4, 1863, *O.R.*, Ser. III, Vol. III, 1126–28; quotation on page 1126.

[72] Testimony of Benjamin Butler before the American Freedmen's Inquiry Commission, General Correspondence and Related Records, Records of the Adjutant General's Office, Record Group 94, National Archives Microfilm Series M-256, roll 200, frames 79–84. See Fredrickson, *The Black Image In the White Mind,* 168–71, for a discussion of the relationship between black Union soldiers and the Sambo image.

young black males under military discipline and by placing the remainder of the Gulf Department's black population back on plantations as wage laborers under white control. These programs, first inaugurated under General Butler, checked the black threat to law and order and transformed the slave population into a positive element in the Union war effort. Having thus stabilized the racial situation in Louisiana, federal authorities during the period of Reconstruction felt little compulsion to move beyond the wartime experiences of the army in expanding upon the meaning of freedom for the former slave.

A Man but Not a Brother: Abraham Lincoln and Racial Equality

By George M. Fredrickson

"In all my interviews with Mr. Lincoln," Frederick Douglass recalled in the 1880s, "I was impressed with his entire freedom from popular prejudice against the colored race."[1] But in an oration delivered in 1876 at the unveiling of a monument to Lincoln, Douglass felt obliged to remind his black audience that "Abraham Lincoln was not, in the fullest sense of the word, either our man or our model. In his interests, in his associations, in his habits of thought, and in his prejudices, he was a white man. He was preeminently the white man's President, entirely devoted to the welfare of white men. He was ready and willing at any time during the first years of his administration to deny, postpone, and sacrifice the rights of humanity in the colored people to promote the welfare of the white people of this country."[2]

Although these statements may seem contradictory, they provide a good point of departure for a reconsideration of Lincoln's racial attitudes. Taken together, they suggest that the Civil War President was neither a common Negrophobe nor a principled champion of racial equality. Any such refusal to put Lincoln in a ready-made category would of course undercut the recent popular debate on his racial views and policies, a heated discussion which has generated sharply conflicting moral judgments. Marshaling the evidence that supports its case, one side portrays Lincoln as a hero of the egalitarian tradition, while the other dismisses him as a typical white racist.[3] Spokesmen for both positions

[1] Allen T. Rice, ed., *Reminiscences of Abraham Lincoln by Distinguished Men of His Time* (New York, 1888), 193.

[2] Douglass, "Oration Delivered on the Occasion of the Unveiling of the Freedman's Monument in Memory of Abraham Lincoln, Washington, D. C., April 14, 1876," in Benjamin Quarles, ed., *Frederick Douglass* (Englewood Cliffs, N. J., 1968), 74.

[3] For the opposing views see Lerone Bennett, Jr., "Was Abe Lincoln a White Supremacist?" *Ebony*, XXIII (February 1968), 35–38, 40, 42; and Herbert Mitgang, "Was

Mr. Fredrickson is professor of history at Northwestern University. Earlier versions of this essay were presented as papers to the Columbia University Seminar in American Civilization and to a session of the Southern Historical Association annual meeting in November 1972.

The Journal of Southern History
Vol. XLI, No. 1, February 1975

are apparently in search of a usable Lincoln, whose humanity or bigotry—as the case may be—can serve as an object lesson for those concerned with the current state of race relations. Participants in the debate are in danger of losing sight of the fact that Lincoln's racial beliefs derived from a situation and climate of opinion different in many respects from our own. Obviously, the viewpoint of the man often sanctified as "the Great Emancipator" is bound to be relevant to any historically based perspective on black-white relations in the United States. But to understand what Lincoln means today, one must determine more precisely what his attitudes were and where they came from. As Douglass's comments suggest, this is not as simple a matter as some have made out, and its resolution demands that one resist the temptation to seek direct support for contemporary ideological positions.

A basic problem confronting any student of Lincoln's thought and attitudes is how to distinguish the deeply held convictions of the man from the evasion and equivocation of the politician responding to public opinion. This essay is based on the assumption that a careful reading of Lincoln's public and private utterances over a long period of time can provide an insight into his actual beliefs, provided one always takes into account the conditioning effect of the political context in which he operated. As a professional politician Lincoln had to make his compromises and adjustments, and he was always careful to work within the limits allowable by public opinion at a given time. But these limits were not always clearly defined, and even when they were, options might exist inside the prevailing consensus. The position Lincoln was to take on the race question in the 1850s was not totally predetermined by political calculation. If his key utterances of that period are located in the larger context of a pattern of belief that manifested itself throughout his career, one finds a complex process at work, involving the conscientious effort to adapt a certain set of personal principles and preferences to the circumstances of the time. These principles and preferences can perhaps be traced back to Lincoln's early decision to affiliate with the party of Henry Clay rather than that of Andrew Jackson.

In one of the debates with Stephen A. Douglas in 1858 Lincoln described Clay as "my beau ideal of a statesman, the man for

---

Lincoln Just a Honkie?" *New York Times Magazine*, February 11, 1968, pp. 34–35, 100–107. Better balanced discussions of Lincoln's racial ideas and policies can be found in Benjamin Quarles, *Lincoln and the Negro* (New York, 1962); and Arvarh E. Strickland, "The Illinois Background of Lincoln's Attitude Toward Slavery and the Negro," Illinois State Historical Society, *Journal*, LVI (Autumn 1963), 474–94.

whom I fought all of my humble life."[4] It is more than probable that Lincoln was initially attracted to the embryonic Whig or anti-Jacksonian party in the 1830s by his admiration for Clay and his sincere adherence to the Kentuckian's principles and programs. In identifying himself as a Clay supporter at the outset of his political career in 1832, Lincoln was by no means taking the easy and opportunistic course for a young Illinois politician on the make. The lines between Clay and Jackson were already drawn, and it is clear that the Jacksonians were the majority in Illinois and even, at that time, in Lincoln's own Sangamon County.[5] What Clay meant to Lincoln did not become fully apparent until the 1850s when the latter delivered his moving eulogy and then went on to assume self-consciously the mantle of Clay as a moderate opponent of slavery. But from the beginning of his career the Clay influence and example powerfully affected Lincoln and shaped his thinking.

What is relevant here, of course, is not the full scope of Clay's nationalist philosophy as it affected Lincoln but rather the enduring influence of Clay's perspective on slavery and race. Time and again in the 1850s Lincoln would have recourse to Clay in the debate over the extension of slavery in the territories. He quoted Clay, paraphrased him, and at times virtually plagiarized from him, not merely for the practical political purpose of winning recalcitrant Whigs to the Republican cause but because he indeed thought of himself as taking up where Clay had left off. If the Clayite foundations of Lincoln's free-soil Republicanism have not been fully apparent to historians, it is because they have fixed their attention on Clay as the Great Compromiser and have tended to lose sight of Clay's significance as a racial moderate and proponent of gradual emancipation. Clay, it must be admitted, was not entirely consistent in these matters. As a practical politician with presidential ambitions who represented a border slave state in Congress, he was subject to pressures that forced him at times to compromise his principles and muffle his antislavery sentiments. Clay began his political career in 1799 as an outspoken advocate of gradual emancipation in Kentucky, but by the end of the 1830s he was responding to the antiabolitionist hysteria infecting all the slaveholding states by taking positions that brought him for a time perilously close to the southern proslavery camp. Yet Clay never retracted his early pronouncements that slavery

[4] Roy P. Basler *et al.*, eds., *The Collected Works of Abraham Lincoln* (8 vols. and index, New Brunswick, N. J., 1953–1955), III, 29; cited hereinafter as Basler, ed., *Collected Works*.

[5] Albert J. Beveridge, *Abraham Lincoln, 1809–1858* (2 vols., Boston and New York, 1928), I, 115.

was an evil—"a universally acknowledged curse"—or repudiated his hope that the institution would eventually disappear.[6] In 1849, after giving up his presidential ambitions, he once again took up the cause of gradual emancipation in Kentucky and wrote a public letter to Richard Pindell on behalf of this unsuccessful movement, demonstrating anew his strong personal preference for a society based on free labor.[7]

Clay differed from the South's outspoken defenders of slavery not only in his underlying attitude toward "the peculiar institution" but also in his characteristic estimate of the black character. In 1829 Clay affirmed that blacks are "rational beings, like ourselves, capable of feeling, of reflection, and of judging of what naturally belongs to them as a portion of the human race."[8] In the 1830s and 1840s, when an insurgent racism was denying the basic humanity of blacks, Clay held back from such judgments. In his Pindell letter of 1849 he openly attacked the argument for slavery based on inferiority of race. In a passage later quoted by Lincoln he wrote:

> An argument in support of reducing the African race to slavery is sometimes derived from their *alleged* intellectual inferiority to the white races; but, if this argument be founded on fact (as it *may* be, but which I shall not now examine), it would prove entirely too much. It would prove that any white nation which had made greater advances in civilization, knowledge and wisdom than another white nation, would have a right to reduce the latter to a state of bondage. Nay, further, if the principle of subjugation, founded upon intellectual superiority, be true, and be applicable to races and to nations, what is to prevent its being applied to individuals? And then the wisest man in the world would have a right to make slaves of all the rest of mankind![9]

These statements reveal that Clay was something less than a convinced proponent of racial equality. But set against the climate of Negrophobia in the mid-nineteenth century they seem relatively benign. Clay was arguing that blacks are human beings, who have, in rudimentary form at least, the same basic desires and capabilities as whites. In his attempted *reductio ad absurdum* of the proslavery racial argument he admitted the possibility that blacks are intellectually inferior to whites. But Clay's tentativeness

[6] On Clay's attitude towards slavery see Clement Eaton, *Henry Clay and the Art of American Politics* (Boston and Toronto, 1957), 118–36; and Calvin Colton, ed., *The Works of Henry Clay* (10 vols., New York and London, 1904), VI, 335.

[7] Clay to Pindell, February 17, 1849, Colton, ed., *Works of Henry Clay*, III, 346–52.

[8] *Ibid.*, I, 213.

[9] *Ibid.*, III, 347. Italics are mine.

on this question, his denial of its applicability to the slavery issue, and his willingness to equate black "inferiority" with the backwardness of some white nations stood in sharp contrast with currently fashionable assertions that black inferiority was exceptional and inherent.[10] Furthermore, as a lifelong proponent of African colonization Clay denied the fundamental racist argument that blacks were incapable of self-government. He defended colonization in his Pindell letter of 1849 by arguing that in Africa blacks could "enjoy the great blessings of liberty, and sivil [*sic*], political, and social equality . . . ."[11]

Clay's colonizationism, of course, had other implications. As one of the founders and leading spirits of the American Colonization Society, Clay maintained with others of his persuasion that gradual emancipation was impracticable unless accompanied by colonization. Deportation of freed blacks was deemed necessary because of the allegedly deep-seated and unconquerable prejudices of the whites, prejudices which would lead to race war if freed blacks were put in a position to demand political and social equality. At the root of this popular revulsion to blacks, Clay argued, was a horror at the prospect of intermarriage with human beings of a different color.[12] In defending colonization and opposing emancipation on the soil because of the power of white prejudice, Clay made two notable statements that were later paraphrased by Lincoln for his own purposes. In denouncing the abolitionist proposal for immediate emancipation in 1842 Clay asserted that "such are the feelings—prejudice, if you please (and what man, claiming to be a statesman, will overlook or disregard the deep-seated and unconquerable prejudices of the people?)—in the slave states, that no human law could enforce a union between the two races."[13] In 1849 in the Pindell letter he maintained that any plan for emancipation must be accompanied by colonization, because "the color, passions, and prejudices would forever prevent the two races from living together in a state of cordial union."[14]

These basic views of Clay were to be reaffirmed by Lincoln, who absorbed not only the doctrines but even some of the terminology of his precursor. In his fundamental attitudes toward slavery and

[10] See George M. Fredrickson, *The Black Image in the White Mind: The Debate on Afro-American Character and Destiny, 1817–1914,* (New York, 1971), 43–164, *passim.*

[11] Colton, ed., *Works of Henry Clay,* III, 352.

[12] See Fredrickson, *Black Image,* 1–42; and Colton, ed., *Works of Henry Clay,* I, 210–14, 219–20.

[13] Clay's reply to Mr. Mendenhall, Richmond, Indiana, October 1, 1842, Colton, ed., *Works of Henry Clay,* I, 220.

[14] *Ibid.,* III, 349.

race Lincoln remained, apparently to the end of his career, a Henry Clay–type Whig colonizationist. Or, more accurately perhaps, he was Henry Clay relieved of the burden of slaveholding and a slaveholding constituency, a difference in situation which permitted Lincoln a greater freedom in implementing Clay's basic philosophy than the Kentuckian himself had ever enjoyed.

The earliest hint of Lincoln's attitude toward slavery came in 1837 when he and one other member of the Illinois state legislature protested for the record against a previously approved resolution condemning abolitionism. They objected, not out of sympathy for the abolitionists, whom they conceded did more harm than good, but because the original resolution had not made it clear that slavery was an evil institution, "founded on both injustice and bad policy . . . ."[15] This early attempt to be antislavery in principle while steering clear of abolitionism foreshadowed Lincoln's position in the 1850s.

Four years later, in 1841, Lincoln described privately his direct impression of a coffle of south-bound slaves encountered on an Ohio riverboat. Contrary to his later recollection of the incident, he was struck at the time by the apparent happiness of the slaves rather than by their misery. It is significant, however, that he did not draw the obvious racist conclusion by generalizing about the peculiarities of the black temperament but instead made his perception the basis of a general observation about human nature. The slaves' contentment was "a fine example . . . for contemplating the effect of *condition* upon human happiness." It illustrated the supposedly universal truth that God "renders the worst of human conditions tolerable, while He permits the best, to be nothing better than tolerable."[16] Such philosophizing was hardly indicative of antislavery zeal, and it can easily be condemned as a manifestation of complacency, insensitivity, or lack of imagination. But it was nevertheless based on the assumption, increasingly rare in the 1840s, that blacks responded to conditions in a way that could be understood in terms of a common humanity and not as the result of peculiar racial characteristics.

Lincoln had no occasion before the 1850s to discuss explicitly the phenomenon of racial prejudice. But in his temperance address of 1842 and elsewhere he held to the conservative principle that firmly established public opinion on any question must be respected because it was providential and would therefore change only in God's good time.[17] Clearly, if opposition to black equality con-

[15] Basler, ed., *Collected Works,* I, 75.
[16] Lincoln to Mary Speed, September 27, 1841, *ibid.,* 260.
[17] *Ibid.,* 275.

stituted a strong and general conviction of the white community, Lincoln would be prepared to accept it as a fact of life, not readily altered even if morally wrong.

After the passage of the Kansas-Nebraska Act in 1854 Lincoln emerged as an important spokesman for free-soil principles. In his well-known speeches during the half-dozen years before his election to the Presidency he promulgated a racial philosophy that combined the principles adumbrated above: moral opposition to slavery, acceptance of the basic humanity of blacks, and a conservative position on the prospects for racial equality in the United States. To see these views in perspective, it is important to recognize that the years after 1854 not only saw an effort to extend and nationalize slavery but also provided the occasion for a torrent of racist propaganda. Extreme racism, based on the pseudoscientific concept of genetic inferiority, was employed by some proslavery apologists to demote blacks to the status of domestic animals, by Douglas and the advocates of popular sovereignty to demonstrate that democracy and the Declaration of Independence applied only to whites, and by some Republicans who saw the containment of slavery as the penning up of a radically inferior black population.[18] The fact that spokesmen for all positions in the debate over slavery extension made racist appeals would seem to suggest that differences in racial philosophy had little to do with the ideological origins of the Civil War.[19] A strong case can be made for this point of view. Certainly, there was a clash of sectional interests and on a deeper level, perhaps, an irrepressible conflict of societies with differing value systems. But the argument can be pressed too far. Inseparable from the conflict of interests and ideologies were differences in the degree, emphasis, and application of racism. There *were* Republicans who rivaled the Democrats and the southerners in their racism—many of them were in fact ex-Democrats who cut their political teeth in a party that had condoned race baiting since the time of Jackson. There were also Republicans, usually from a Liberty party, Free-Soil, or Conscience Whig background who came close to accepting the radical abolitionist premise of racial equality.[20] But at the center of the

[18] Fredrickson, *Black Image,* 43–164; Eugene H. Berwanger, *The Frontier Against Slavery: Western Anti-Negro Prejudice and the Slavery Extension Controversy* (Urbana, 1967), 123–37.

[19] See David M. Potter, *The South and the Sectional Conflict* (Baton Rouge, 1968), 113–18, for a discussion of how the emphasis of historians on the North-South racial consensus has led away from the kind of understanding of sectional differences required to explain the Civil War.

[20] On the spectrum of Republican racial attitudes see Eric Foner, *Free Soil, Free Labor, Free Men: The Ideology of the Republican Party Before the Civil War* (New York, 1970), 261–300.

party, representing its basic position in the 1850s, were ex-Whigs of mildly antislavery antecedents like Abraham Lincoln, the compromise candidate of 1860, who not only held a middle ground on questions of antislavery policy but also espoused a moderate racial philosophy in the tradition of Henry Clay. Men of this persuasion offered some resistance to extreme racism while at the same time carefully avoiding what they regarded as the dangerous racial utopianism of the abolitionists. They reflected, to some extent at least, the racial views of an earlier America—the conservative, quasi-environmentalism of the Founding Fathers and the early colonizationists. Their importance was that they gave the Republican party a racial emphasis compatible with a practical defense of white supremacy—and hence acceptable to public opinion—without going to the extreme of denying black humanity and thereby undermining the moral basis of opposition to slavery.

It is to Lincoln's speeches that one turns for the fullest exposition of this philosophy. That Lincoln was opposed to the extension of slavery on moral as well as economic and social grounds has been conclusively demonstrated by Don E. Fehrenbacher and should require no further elaboration.[21] But Lincoln's specifically racial pronouncements could stand reexamination. The question of innate biological differences between the races was avoided by Lincoln until the senatorial campaign of 1858. In his reply to Douglas at Ottawa he conceded that there was "a physical difference between the two [races], which in my judgment will probably forever forbid their living together upon the footing of perfect equality . . . ." This of course is the classic statement often used to demonstrate Lincoln's dyed-in-the-wool racism. But it should be noted that Lincoln made this concession in the course of refuting Douglas's argument that the Negro was not a man entitled to equality by the Declaration of Independence. Lincoln concluded this section of his speech by saying: "I agree with Judge Douglas he is not my equal in many respects—certainly not in color, perhaps not in moral or intellectual endowment. But in the right to eat the bread, without the leave of anybody else, which his own hand earns, *he is my equal and the equal of Judge Douglas, and the equal of every living man*."[22] Here Lincoln distinguished between an elemental human equality affirmed by the Declaration of Independence and denied by slavery and a full social and political equality that might legitimately be withheld on racial grounds. And what was the nature of these crucial racial differences? All that Lincoln was willing to affirm un-

[21] Fehrenbacher, *Prelude to Greatness: Lincoln in the 1850's* (Stanford, Calif., 1962).
[22] Basler, ed., *Collected Works*, III, 16; see also *ibid.*, II, 520.

equivocally was white superiority in color. He was, following the example of Henry Clay's Pindell letter of 1849, tentative on the question of intellectual and moral distinctions.

In the context of the time, when dogmatic statements of innate inferiority were heard on almost every hand, such tentativeness denoted a relatively open-minded or liberal position. Even some of the most radical Republicans were ready to concede the probability, if not the certainty, of innate white superiority of some sort.[23] But what can be made of Lincoln's unequivocal statement that blacks are inferior in color? It seems reasonable to assume that Lincoln sensed in the attitudes of white Americans, and probably in himself as well, a strong distaste for Negroid physical features and a powerful preference for white pigmentation as the human norm. If one were to follow the thinking of the sociologist Harry Hoetink, one might argue that Lincoln had laid bare a basic source of racial prejudice—the "somatic norm image" (or ideal of physical beauty) inevitably possessed and treasured by the dominant group in a racially "segmented society."[24] If pushed too far, such a mode of explanation can easily lead to a psychological determinism that obscures the importance of immediate social and economic factors. But if there is any truth at all in Winthrop D. Jordan's analysis of early American racial attitudes, it becomes difficult to deny that anti-Negro feelings and actions derive, to some extent at least, from a color complex deeply rooted in Western culture—a predisposition that can turn into virulent racial prejudice when associated with social fears and economic interests.[25] Like many comparatively benevolent or "liberal" whites throughout American history, Lincoln could reject the most blatant forms of racist ideology without escaping an underlying emotional commitment to whiteness and white supremacy. Lincoln differed from some others similarly disposed in that his political situation, and perhaps his fundamental honesty as well, impelled him to make his attitude explicit. In 1854, for example, he confessed that his "own feelings" would not allow him to contemplate the political and social equality of blacks.[26] Was Frederick Douglass therefore deceived in his belief that Lincoln was free from "popular prejudice against the colored race"? Douglass of

[23] Congressman Owen Lovejoy, the most radical of Illinois Republican leaders, conceded in 1860 that blacks were inferior but denied that racial inferiority constituted a justification of slavery. Cited in Fredrickson, *Black Image*, 51.

[24] Hoetinck, *The Two Variants in Caribbean Race Relations: A Contribution to the Sociology of Segmented Societies* (London, New York, and Toronto, 1967), *passim*.

[25] Jordan, *White over Black: American Attitudes Toward the Negro, 1550–1812* (Chapel Hill, 1968).

[26] Speech at Peoria, October 16, 1854, Basler, ed., *Collected Works*, II, 256.

course did not meet Lincoln until the summer of 1863 and by then the latter's feelings may have changed. But another possibility exists. Perhaps Lincoln's exceptionally egalitarian manner resulted from a depth of self-awareness that made it possible for him to control his prejudices precisely because he acknowledged their existence and recognized their irrational character.

Whatever the validity of such psychological speculations, it is clear that Lincoln confronted the phenomenon of racial prejudice in himself and others and applied his findings in a cautious and pragmatic fashion to questions of policy. In his Peoria speech of 1854 he justified his reluctance to recommend immediate emancipation to the people of the South by pointing to what he believed was the practical impossibility of elevating the freed blacks to a position of equality: "Free them, and make them politically and socially, our equals? My own feelings will not admit of this; and if mine would, we well know that those of the great mass of white people will not. Whether this feeling accords with justice and sound judgment, is not the sole question, if indeed, it is any part of it. A universal feeling, whether well or ill-founded, can not be safely disregarded."[27] Here Lincoln echoed Clay's conservative doctrine that a statesman must adjust himself to "the deep-seated and unconquerable prejudices of the people" and provided the real underpinning for his later contention that the races could never live together in "perfect equality," or, as Clay had put it, "in . . . cordial union."

Lincoln's well-known advocacy of colonization as the only solution to the race problem followed inevitably from his premise that insurmountable white prejudices made racial equality impossible in the United States. His first opportunity to comment publicly on the colonization idea was his 1852 eulogy to Henry Clay. After praising Clay for his lifelong devotion to the cause of black expatriation, Lincoln concluded: "If as the friends of colonization hope, the present and coming generations of our countrymen shall by any means, succeed in freeing our land from the dangerous presence of slavery; and, at the same time, in restoring a captive people to their long-lost father-land, with bright prospects for the future; and this too, so gradually, that neither *races nor individuals* shall have suffered by the change, it will indeed be a glorious consummation."[28] In the Peoria speech of 1854 Lincoln alluded to emancipation accompanied by colonization as the only practical way of getting rid of slavery, but conceded that the plan's "sudden execu-

[27] *Ibid.*

[28] *Ibid.*, 132.

tion is impossible."[29] In 1855 he addressed the Illinois Colonization Society; the surviving outline of his speech suggests that it consisted largely of a sympathetic account of the history of the colonization movement, a subject on which Lincoln was apparently well versed.[30]

In his 1857 Springfield speech Lincoln once again took up the subject of colonization: "The enterprise is a difficult one," he conceded; "but 'when there is a will there is a way;'. . . . Will springs from the two elements of moral sense and self-interest. Let us be brought to believe it is morally right, and, at the same time, favorable to, or, at least, not against, our interest, to transfer the African to his native clime, and we shall find a way to do it, however great the task may be." Lincoln went on to argue on this occasion that the Republican belief in the "manhood" of the Negro was more likely to create a "public sentiment" on behalf of colonization than the Democrat's effort to "crush all sympathy for him, and cultivate and excite hatred and disgust against him . . . ." Colonization would not succeed, Lincoln was arguing, unless accompanied by a humanitarian interest in the Negro and some respect for his capabilities. By apparently denying his humanity, Douglas and other supporters of popular sovereignty were laying the groundwork for "the indefinite outspreading of his bondage." Furthermore, he added, the Republican program of restricting slavery to its present domain had the long-range benefit of denying slaveholders a chance to sell their surplus bondsmen at high prices in new slave territories, thus encouraging them to begin the process of gradual emancipation by sending the excess to Liberia.[31] Here Lincoln laid bare the full thrust of his antislavery program by revealing the close connection in his thinking between the restriction of slavery and the promotion of colonization. Southern slaveholders, he implied, would never be induced to emancipate and colonize their slaves unless they were driven by necessity. It was partly to create such a necessity that Lincoln and other sincerely antislavery Republicans advocated restriction of slavery to its existing limits. In the last analysis, their hopes for both the end of slavery and expatriation of the black population depended on the creation of economic and population pressures in the South that would compel the acceptance of gradual emancipation and colonization. Perhaps the only basic fallacy in such a program was

[29] *Ibid.*, 255.
[30] *Ibid.*, 298–99.
[31] *Ibid.*, 409–10.

the assumption that the South would allow such a situation to develop without adopting desperate measures to prevent it.

Since colonization was such an important element in Lincoln's long-range scenario for ending slavery, it may seem surprising that he did not stress his hopes for black expatriation in the 1858 senatorial campaign against Douglas. In the great debates themselves he did no more than quote the section of his Peoria speech that alluded to the long-range hope for colonization.[32] Perhaps Lincoln kept his colonizationism under wraps because he was unsure of his political ground, uncertain whether an emphasis on black expatriation would add to or subtract from his vote total. Although often endorsed by notables and public figures, colonization had never been a genuinely popular movement, even in the North. It promised to get rid of an allegedly dangerous and undesirable free black population, but it was also likely to be a very complex and costly enterprise, requiring large appropriations by state and federal governments and necessitating a greater degree of centralized planning and direction than antebellum opinion was characteristically willing to tolerate. It may be surmised that many Negrophobes in Illinois would have been happy to get rid of the free blacks in the state and even to see slavery disappear gradually in the South but were reluctant to pay the price of even the most limited and partial colonization scheme. Lincoln also knew that his chances for victory depended not only on winning a share of the anti-Negro vote but also on holding within the Republican coalition the radical, quasi-abolitionist minority of northern Illinois. To some of these radicals colonization was anathema because it was a concession to "the caste spirit" and an affront to their egalitarian idealism. There is every reason to believe, however, that the long-range prospect of colonization was in the back of Lincoln's mind when he spoke of the "ultimate extinction" of slavery in the "House Divided" speech. In his reply to Douglas at Ottawa he elaborated on the House Divided statement, arguing that once the public mind was again secure in its former belief that slavery was "in the course of ultimate extinction. The crisis would be past and the institution might be let alone for a hundred years, if it should live so long, in the States where it exists, yet it would be going out of existence in the way best for both the black and the white races."[33] What he undoubtedly meant by the "best way" was a process of gradual, voluntary emancipation accompanied by the colonization of freedmen outside the United States.

[32] *Ibid.*, III, 14–15.
[33] *Ibid.*, 18.

In one little-noticed speech of the 1858 campaign Lincoln demonstrated how colonization was related to a liberal hope that all men everywhere would someday enjoy the blessings of self-government. According to the newspaper report of his speech at Carlinville, Lincoln contended that "Negroes have natural rights . . . as other men have, although they cannot enjoy them here, and even [Chief Justice] Taney once said that 'the Declaration of Independence was broad enough for all men.' But though it does not declare that all men are equal in their attainments or social position, yet no sane man will attempt to deny that the African *upon his own soil* has all the natural rights that instrument vouchsafes to all mankind." But those who would countenance the extension of slavery were apparently not sane men, because their view that the Negro was subhuman meant to Lincoln that "even upon his own soil he has no rights which white men are bound to respect."[34]

If the report of this speech was correct, Lincoln was saying in effect that every race had the right and capability of self-government but only on its "own soil." In one respect this was an antiracist position, because it conflicted with the concept of racial imperialism promulgated during this period not only by southern expansionists, who dreamed of a Caribbean slave empire, but also, as Harry V. Jaffa has demonstrated, by Stephen A. Douglas and the other northern Democratic proponents of an unrestrained Manifest Destiny under the banner of popular sovereignty for whites only.[35] The idea of whites moving into the tropics and denying the possibility of self-government to other races was apparently unacceptable to Lincoln. The promise of colonization was that it would transplant blacks to regions where they could rule themselves and develop their own democratic institutions free of white interference. This concept of a democratic world of distinct races enjoying perfect self-government on their "own soil" repudiated internationalist racism while affirming the inevitability of domestic racism. It implied "the ideal of racial homogeneity," the belief that equality in a given nation or climatic zone could exist only for the one racial group which had attained a dominant position because of its superior adaptability to the physical environment. It followed that a society guaranteeing equality for all its inhabitants would have to be racially homogeneous.[36] There can be little doubt that Lincoln accepted this basic doctrine. In the Peoria

[34] *Ibid.*, 79–80. Italics are mine.

[35] Harry V. Jaffa, *Crisis of the House Divided: An Interpretation of the Issues in the Lincoln-Douglas Debates* (Garden City, N. Y., 1959), 48–49, 65–69, 99–103.

[36] See Fredrickson, *Black Image*, 130–64.

speech of 1854 he conceded Douglas's dictum that "this government was made for the white people and not for the negroes."[37] At Ottawa in 1858 he acknowledged that when two distinct races inhabited the same territory "necessity" dictated that one be supreme. He then added, "I, as well as Judge Douglas, am in favor of the race to which I belong, having the superior position."[38] Lincoln, like some of the founders of the American Colonization Society, was a pragmatic white supremacist in his concept of domestic race relations but indulged a principled egalitarianism in his world outlook. Although this combination actually offered little benefit to American blacks, it did help give substance to the claim that Republicans adhered more closely to the democratic ideal than the proponents of slavery or popular sovereignty.

On the surface Lincoln's racial philosophy seems logically consistent. But deeper probing reveals an unresolved conflict at the root of his thought. The contradiction in Lincoln's racial ideology came, as Richard Hofstadter has suggested, from his somewhat arbitrary distinction between slavery and white supremacy.[39] Slavery, according to Lincoln, flagrantly contradicted the Declaration of Independence, but the denial to blacks of political and civil equality did not. To make this point Lincoln distinguished between the natural rights of life, liberty, and the pursuit of happiness, and the full privileges of citizenship, which the majority could grant or withhold from any minority as it saw fit.[40] Harry V. Jaffa, a leading student of Lincoln's thought, has argued in *The Crisis of the House Divided* that Lincoln was not only consistent but completely justified in taking such a position: "Lincoln did not believe he had a moral right to deprecate the opinion of his countrymen which denied political equality to Negroes. To have done so would have meant denying the right of white men to judge the conditions under which their government could best secure their rights. But the Declaration of Independence asserts that the people have an indefeasible right to judge of the security of their rights, and Lincoln could not deny the legitimacy of their judgment concerning the status to be accorded the Negro without denying that right."[41] Unfortunately, this argument tends to undermine the moral distinction that Jaffa is elsewhere so concerned with making between Lincoln's free-soilism and Douglas's popular sovereignty. If the white

[37] Basler, ed., *Collected Works,* II, 281.

[38] *Ibid.,* III, 16.

[39] Hofstadter, *The American Political Tradition and the Men Who Made It* (New York, 1948), 116–17.

[40] See Basler, ed., *Collected Works,* II, 265–66, 405–407, 499–501, 520.

[41] Jaffa, *Crisis of the House Divided,* 377.

majority believed that the defense of its rights required that blacks be denied social and political equality, what prevented it from going one step further and deciding, on the basis of popular sovereignty, that the protection of its liberty also required black enslavement? Only the abstract and legalistic distinction between natural rights and the privileges of citizenship. And, as critics of this distinction have often pointed out, no group can in fact exercise or protect its "natural rights" without having a voice in how it is governed.

On one occasion Lincoln himself made what amounted to an open admission that his distinction was a legalistic evasion of the spirit of democratic government. In the Peoria speech he attacked slavery by appealing to the Declaration of Independence and in particular to the concept of the "consent of the governed." Slavery, he contended, was a flagrant denial of the Declaration because it allowed one man "to govern another man, *without that other's consent*." Pushing the concept of government by consent to its logical outcome, Lincoln concluded with the following imperative. "Allow ALL the governed an equal voice in the government, and that, and that only is self government." Realizing perhaps that he had just obliterated any clear distinction between natural and political rights, he quickly added that he was not of course "contending for the establishment of political and social equality between the whites and blacks" or "combating the argument of NECESSITY, arising from the fact that the blacks are already amongst us . . . ."[42] Lincoln, in other words, conceded here that denial of black citizenship was inconsistent with his basic political doctrines and fell back on the argument from practical "necessity." Ultimately, then, an alleged racial necessity forced a violation of the principle of government by consent and consigned blacks to an inferior political and civil status. But the trouble with the pragmatic argument of racial necessity was that it could also be used as a justification for slavery itself and even for the extension of slavery. At the core of his thinking, then, Lincoln was trapped by what Gunnar Myrdal has called "the American dilemma," and for him it was truly insoluble. Blacks as men were entitled to equality, but whites were unalterably prejudiced against them and would never permit the actual attainment of equal rights. For Lincoln the Negro was—to alter the abolitionist battle cry—a man but not a brother.

Yet the very fact that Lincoln was caught in a moral and ideological dilemma sets him off from those racists who avoided the

[42] Basler, ed., *Collected Works,* II, 266.

dilemma completely by defining blacks as subhuman. When Douglas in effect denied the full humanity of the Negro and told cheering crowds that the Declaration of Independence applied to whites only, Lincoln objected in vigorous terms, condemning in principle a situation that he in fact found himself powerless to alter. In the 1858 campaign Douglas attempted to make race the main issue by accusing the Republicans of advocating a political and social equality and thereby promoting the "amalgamation" of the races. Lincoln responded defensively by denying the charge and then tried to turn the tables on proponents of popular sovereignty by arguing that since slavery was the chief cause of miscegenation in the United States, the restriction of its spread would in fact reduce the possibilities of race mixture.[43] In these attempts to neutralize the race issue as it affected the North while seeking to focus attention on the abstract inequity of slavery as an institution, Lincoln came close to arguing, in the manner of other leading midwestern Republicans, that his party, and not the Democrats, was "the white man's party."[44]

When he campaigned in Ohio in 1859, again at the heels of Douglas, who was stumping the state for the Democrats, Lincoln's strategy underwent a subtle change of emphasis which brought out more clearly the relatively benign side of his racial philosophy. He made much in his speeches of a recent statement of Douglas in which "the Little Giant" had maintained that he was for the Negro against the crocodile but for the white man against the Negro. Lincoln described this statement as part of a Democratic campaign to debauch the public mind on the slavery issue by demoting the Negro "from the rank of a man to that of a brute."[45] Douglas's statement, he told his Ohio audience, meant that "As the negro ought to treat the crocodile as a beast, so the white man ought to treat the negro as a beast."[46] Lincoln apparently believed that Douglas had gone too far in articulating a crude Negrophobia. What the latter was now saying was perhaps acceptable to the voters of southern Illinois but too extreme for those of Ohio and many other northern states. Lincoln correctly assumed that an explicit denial of Negro humanity was incompatible with moral opposition to the extension of slavery and therefore unacceptable to a growing northern free-soil majority. Despite the ambivalence of his own position, he emerged in the Ohio campaign as a functional op-

[43] *Ibid.*, III, 80, 84, 88–89.
[44] See Berwanger, *Frontier Against Slavery*, 133–34.
[45] Basler, ed., *Collected Works*, III, 423–24.
[46] *Ibid.*, 432; see also p. 444.

ponent of extreme racism. In his speech in Cincinnati he went so far as to deny that there was "a necessary conflict between the white man and the negro" and affirmed "that there is room enough for us all to be free . . . ."[47]

Lincoln, however, had not given up his belief that the only way blacks could become fully free was by emigrating from the United States. After his election to the Presidency and the outbreak of the War for the Union, Lincoln believed for a time that Providence had provided a golden opportunity for realizing his long-standing dream, inherited from Henry Clay, of ending slavery and solving the race problem by a carefully organized program of gradual emancipation and colonization. The story of Lincoln's hesitant progress toward emancipation and his determined but abortive effort to set in motion some kind of colonization program is so well known that it seems unnecessary to go over it again.[48] A more fruitful approach is to concentrate on the principal question that remains in dispute: Did Lincoln toward the end of the war change his basic views on racial equality in such a way as to affirm the possibility of a biracial democracy?[49]

The best point of departure is Lincoln's address of August 14, 1862, to a delegation of blacks whom he had invited to the White House. The purpose of the meeting was to arouse black interest in colonization, and Lincoln repeated his long-standing view that racial equality was impossible on American soil: "You and we are different races. We have between us a broader difference than exists between almost any other two races. . . . this physical difference is a great disadvantage to us both, as I think your race suffer very greatly, many of them by living among us, while ours suffer from your presence." When blacks ceased to be slaves, Lincoln continued, they were still "far removed from being placed on an equality with the white race. . . . The aspiration of men is to enjoy equality with the best when free, but on this broad continent, not a single man of your race is made the equal of a single man of ours." Whatever one

[47] *Ibid.*, 446.

[48] See for example the excellent accounts in Quarles, *Lincoln and the Negro* and in V. Jacque Voegeli, *Free but Not Equal: The Midwest and the Negro During the Civil War* (Chicago and London, 1967). For detailed discussions of specific colonization projects see Warren A. Beck, "Lincoln and Negro Colonization in Central America," *Abraham Lincoln Quarterly*, VI (September 1950), 162–83; and Paul J. Scheips, "Lincoln and the Chiriqui Colonization Project," *Journal of Negro History*, XXXVII (October 1952), 418–53.

[49] For an exchange on this question see Ludwell H. Johnson, "Lincoln and Equal Rights: The Authenticity of the Wadsworth Letter," *Journal of Southern History*, XXXII (February 1966), 83–87; Harold M. Hyman, "Lincoln and Equal Rights for Negroes: The Irrelevancy of the 'Wadsworth Letter,' " *Civil War History*, XII (September 1966), 258–66; and Johnson, "Lincoln and Equal Rights: A Reply," *ibid.*, XIII (March 1967), 66–73.

thought about this situation, he went on, it was an unalterable fact of life, and "It is better for us both, therefore, to be separated." Lincoln's argument, ostensibly at least, derived from a conservative fatalism about popular attitudes and not from personal Negrophobia; in accord with the traditional colonizationist philosophy it made white prejudice and not natural black incapacity the main barrier to equality. In calling for educated free blacks to lead the exodus, Lincoln invoked an ethnocentric kind of environmentalism. In his opinion, newly freed bondsmen, "whose intellects are clouded by Slavery . . . ," needed the direction of blacks "capable of thinking as white men," because they had not been "systematically oppressed."[50] The address to the Negro deputation stands as the classic statement of Lincoln's quasi-racism, because it simultaneously denied black equality as practical option for American society while affirming it as a theoretical possibility in another place and under other circumstances.

Turning directly now to the question of whether Lincoln gave up these doctrines in the last year and a half of the war, one confronts a fragmentary and confusing record. Faced with the practical failure of all his deportation schemes, Lincoln had by 1864 apparently "sloughed off that idea of colonization," or so his secretary John Hay reported.[51] Yet according to General Benjamin F. Butler, Lincoln conferred with him in early April 1865, shortly before the assassination, about the possibility of colonizing freed blacks and especially those who had borne arms for the Union. "But what shall we do with the negroes after they are free?" Lincoln reportedly asked Butler. "I can hardly believe that the South and North can live in peace, unless we can get rid of the negroes. Certainly they cannot if we don't get rid of the negroes whom we have armed and disciplined and who have fought with us . . . . I believe that it would be better to export them all to some fertile country with a good climate, which they could have to themselves." After appealing to Butler for logistical advice on black removal, Lincoln laid bare the root of his fears: "If these black soldiers of ours go back to the South I am afraid they will be but little better off with their masters than they were before, and yet they will be free men. I fear a race war, and it will be at least a guerilla war because we have taught these men how to fight."[52] Historians are naturally reluctant to take Ben Butler's word for anything, but some recent scholars have found

[50] Basler, ed., *Collected Works,* V, 371–73.

[51] Tyler Dennett, ed., *Lincoln and the Civil War in the Diaries and Letters of John Hay* (New York, 1939), 203.

[52] Butler, *Autobiography and Personal Reminiscences of Major-General Benj. F. Butler: Butler's Book* (Boston, 1892), 903.

good reason to accept his account of this conversation. Ludwell H. Johnson has pointed out that Butler had no conceivable motive for lying in this instance, and Herman Belz has found that the basic thrust of Lincoln's comments was "in accord with views . . . [he] expressed elsewhere concerning reconstruction."[53] If Butler's recollection is substantially correct, as it appears to be, then one can only conclude that Lincoln continued to his dying day to deny the possibility of racial harmony and equality in the United States and persisted in regarding colonization as the only real alternative to perpetual race conflict.

The thesis that Lincoln changed his views on the possibility of equal rights rests almost entirely upon two statements he made recommending a partial black suffrage for the reconstructed government of Louisiana. In a letter of March 1864 to the newly elected loyalist governor of that state, he proposed that the upcoming constitutional convention consider extending the suffrage to "very intelligent" blacks and "those who have fought gallantly in our ranks," adding cautiously that "this is only a suggestion, not to the public, but to you alone."[54] Lincoln may have been inspired to make this recommendation because of a visit he had received the previous day from two wealthy and cultivated representatives of the free mulatto population of New Orleans. The visitors presented a petition demanding the right to vote, signed by a thousand freeborn men of color, all of whom were substantial property owners.[55] Hence, the possibility exists that Lincoln saw the free blacks of Louisiana as a peculiar case with some claim to special consideration. The convention failed to enact a partial black suffrage, however, and Lincoln accepted its decision. In the last public speech before his assassination he made a final plea for congressional recognition of the Louisiana government. In answering the objection of Radical Republicans that "the elective franchise is not given to the colored man," he confessed that he himself would "prefer that it were now conferred on the very intelligent, and on those who serve our cause as soldiers." But he went on to point out that under the new constitution the legislature was empowered to confer the suffrage on blacks and that the best policy was to recognize the government in the hope that extension of the suffrage would come in good time.[56]

Before concluding that Lincoln had become a convinced and op-

[53] Johnson, "Lincoln and Equal Rights: A Reply," 68; Herman Belz, *Reconstructing the Union: Theory and Policy During the Civil War* (Ithaca, 1969), 282–83.

[54] Lincoln to Michael Hahn, March 13, 1864, Basler, ed., *Collected Works*, VII, 243.

[55] Quarles, *Lincoln and the Negro*, 227–28.

[56] Basler, ed., *Collected Works*, VIII, 403–404.

timistic advocate of political equality for blacks by April 1865, other possibilities have to be taken into account. One, already mentioned, is that Louisiana, with its unique caste of educated, freeborn mulattoes, was regarded by Lincoln as a special case and not as a source of precedent for the reconstruction of other states. Another is that Lincoln was recommending partial suffrage as a way of heading off an impending Radical demand for full political equality. A few months later President Andrew Johnson, whose opposition to racial equality was clear and unequivocal, would propose a limited black suffrage to the provisional governor of Mississippi with exactly this purpose in mind.[57] Furthermore, Lincoln at no point contemplated making even limited suffrage a condition for readmission to the Union. Black suffrage, if it came, would have to stem from the voluntary action of southern whites. Local white preferences, in other words, would be allowed to determine the extent of black political participation. Finally, Lincoln's particular concern with suffrage for blacks who had served in the Union army may take on a new connotation if the fears he expressed to Butler are given credence. It was the ex-soldiers whom Lincoln allegedly saw as the possible catalyst for race war, and it may be that he was subtly suggesting to white southerners that the best way to neutralize this potential source of trouble was to give black veterans the vote, thereby satisfying their personal demands for equality in the hope that this would make them contented and willing to forgo strenuous agitation on behalf of their voteless brothers.

All this is frankly speculative. But equally speculative and, on balance, less plausible is the theory that Lincoln did an about-face in the last year and a half of the war and ended up as a convinced believer in the possibility of full racial equality. Lincoln was a flexible man, but the deeply rooted attitudes and ideas of a lifetime do not change easily. Although no final answer can be given to the question of whether Lincoln changed his mind, the weight of evidence and logic seems to support the hypothesis that Lincoln died with the same basic views on black-white relations that he had held tenaciously throughout his public life.

[57] Eric L. McKitrick, *Andrew Johnson and Reconstruction* (Chicago, 1960), 166, 190.

The Fortieth Annual Meeting

By Richard Maxwell Brown

THE 1974 MEETING OF THE SOUTHERN HISTORICAL ASSOCIATION was held in Dallas, Texas, on Wednesday through Saturday, November 6–9. With convention headquarters in the Adolphus Hotel (supplemented by facilities in the adjacent Baker Hotel), over thirteen hundred registrants were greeted by a program of fifty-three regular and special sessions embodying 220 participants from 156 colleges, universities, and other organizations. The large attendance at the fortieth annual meeting was especially gratifying, since last year at this time the program chairman, members of the Program Committee, and officers of the Association worried that continued adverse effects of inflation and the so-called energy crisis might seriously diminish the turnout for the 1974 convention. Fortunately, the gloomy forebodings of last winter were belied by the reality of the very successful fortieth annual meeting. Perhaps the only disappointment was the cold, rainy weather that afflicted those who from time to time wandered away from the convention hotels to such nearby attractions as the Neiman-Marcus department store and Brennan's restaurant.

The business of the Association was smoothly transacted at the customary early Thursday afternoon meeting, whose substance will be reported in the next issue of this magazine. That evening a near capacity crowd of 450 assembled in the Grand Ballroom of the Adolphus to listen to Gilbert C. Fite, president of the Association, deliver a hard-hitting address on "The Historian as Teacher: Professional Challenge and Opportunity." Fite's provocative remarks are printed elsewhere in this issue of the *Journal*. Introducing Fite with grace and wit was his presidential predecessor, George B. Tindall of the University of North Carolina at Chapel

---

MR. BROWN is professor of history at the College of William and Mary. As program chairman he wishes to acknowledge the assistance of his extremely capable student secretary, Carol E. Radford, and the support of his department chairman, Ludwell H. Johnson, III, and the College of William and Mary. Other acknowledgments appear in the final paragraph of the report.

Hill. In addition there were four special sessions: three luncheon meetings and a Wednesday night general session (all reported below).

The program of forty-seven regular sessions, Thursday through Saturday, was strong and well balanced in regard not only to diversity of subject matter but to the age, standing, sex, race, region, and institutional affiliation of the participants. The core of the program comprised the twenty-seven sessions that dealt with southern history. The bulk of these sessions were concerned with the antebellum South, the Civil War and its aftermath, aspects of the New South, slavery, black history, and racism. Interwoven among those sessions was substantial treatment of the history of women in the South in addition to a panel session dealing generally with critical issues in women's history.

Dallas was an apt location for sustained attention to the great Southwestern subregion of the South, and eight sessions, keynoted by Frank E. Vandiver's address on "The Southwest: South or West?" reflected this concern. In regard to nonsouthern U. S. history a ground-breaking session on the methodology of diplomatic history tested the utility of paradigms and models. There were eleven carefully conceived, well-attended, and well-received sessions on British, European, and Latin American history ranging from Irish and Italian Jacobins to totalitarian diplomacy in the era of World War II. For the second year in a row there was a session on African history, and for the first time in several years there was an Asian history session. The program was rounded out by a session on history teaching in the secondary schools and a cluster of sessions on the burgeoning fields of historical societies, preservation, and administration.

Compelling personal and professional reasons caused certain individuals to withdraw from their original commitment to participate in the program, but they did so responsibly and with ample notice to the program chairman. It is a good showing that only one person (noted below) inconsiderately resigned from the program. The session summaries that follow reflect these changes in the program as originally printed. According to long-established precedent these summaries are based mainly upon the reports submitted by the session chairmen. Unless otherwise indicated all rooms mentioned were in the Adolphus Hotel.

The Dallas annual meeting got underway before a near capacity crowd in the Grand Ballroom at the Wednesday evening general session as Frank E. Vandiver, provost and professor of history at Rice University, essayed the difficult task of throwing new light on an old but ever significant subject, "The Southwest: South or West?" After a light, bantering exchange with the session chairman, Ben H. Procter of Texas Christian University, Vandiver got down to serious business and rose magnificently to the challenge of his topic. His wide-ranging, elegantly delivered address was studded with fresh insights on the role of evangelical religion among blacks and whites as the irreducible southern core of Texas life, on Texas's own "interior fall line"—the Balcones Fault, on Walter Prescott Webb's overemphasis of the physiographic frontier at the expense of the cultural frontier's clash between southerners and Hispanos as well as Indians versus whites, and on the replacement of the antebellum cotton kingdom by the cattle kingdom and, in intellectual terms, the displacement of the myth of the Old South by the myth of the cowboy and, ultimately, the myth of the oil wildcatter. Vandiver thus aptly keynoted an annual meeting that featured among its fifty-three regular and special sessions a number of symposia on Texas and the Southwest.

The Golden Age of Texas Scholarship was, in effect, a highly successful contribution to oral history. A fascinated audience of about eighty gathered Thursday morning in the Renaissance Room to listen to the single paper by William A. Owens, Columbia University, on "Webb, Dobie, Bedichek, and Boatright." Before Owens read his paper, the session chairman, Robert C. Cotner, University of Texas, Austin, introduced the widow of Walter Prescott Webb and also Llerena Friend, Barker Texas History Center. In a personalized and reminiscent paper Owens stressed the post–Civil War era, prosouthern background which they transcended toward the ends of their lives. The work of these men was shaped, too, by their common experience in an educationally impoverished but culturally rich Southwest. They were intellectual mavericks and to a considerable extent, despite the academic status of three (Webb, Dobie, Boatright), antiacademic, especially in their contempt for pedantry. Most important was their "community of effort" in regard to the production of thirty-nine books (plus articles and edited books) in which their relationship with each other (especially Webb, Dobie, and Bedichek) was "convivial, critical, and creative." By the end, in contrast to their early years, ideas no longer terrified them, and they had become serene, philosophical old masters. Two witty, evocative, and at times touchingly reminiscent comments were offered by protégés and former students of these notable men: Joe B. Frantz, University of Texas, Austin, and W. Eugene Hollon, University of Toledo. Frantz felt that Boatright, for all his importance as a scholarly folklorist, was somewhat out of place in this session and thus emphasized the three old-time Texas cronies, Webb, Dobie, and Bedichek, in his critique, as did Hollon. Mrs. Webb graciously acknowledged that she had learned some things about her late husband that she hadn't known and that, recognizing him to be a great man, she had been delighted to say yes when he asked her to marry him. Appropriate comments from the audience by Frank Wardlaw, Texas A&M University Press, and Walter Brown, University of Arkansas, concluded a remarkable session.

Sixty-five persons attended the session on *Southern Economic Development After the Civil War* in the Advertising Club Room on Thursday morning. Joel R. Williamson, University of North Carolina at Chapel Hill, presided over a two-paper meeting. The first paper, "Planter-Merchant Conflict in Reconstruction Alabama," was offered by Jonathan M. Wiener of the University of California, Irvine, who argued that the planter-slaveholder class effectively used the lien system in the postwar world to continue to seize the surplus product of labor and to transform itself into a planter-merchant class. At the same time, they practically displaced the nonlandowning merchants in the black belts, leaving them to exploit only the farmers of the white counties. Jay R. Mandle of Temple University presented the second paper, "The Plantation System as an Obstacle to Economic Development," in which he offered the thesis that abundant, cheap, and caste-fixed labor deprived planters of the necessary incentives to upgrade inputs into the productive process. The first commentator, Ronald L. Davis, California State University, Northridge, commented that Wiener had failed to compute the details of the operations of merchants or to identify in depth the planter-merchant class of which he spoke. Davis believed that Mandle had underestimated the mobility of labor in the postwar decades. Pete Daniel, University of Tennessee, Knoxville, asked that Wiener define the differences between planters and merchants and utilize additional manuscript collections. Daniel observed, too, that Mandle could have clarified his thesis by looking closely at individual farmers in the areas of the South utilized in his model and concluded by calling for a more humanistic approach to postwar economics in the South. From the floor came expressions advising caution concerning the membership and the persistence of the planter-merchant class and the assumption that those people were wholly exploitative.

The Thursday morning session on *Southern Reformers in the 1920s* drew about fifty people to the French Room, where Martha M. Bigelow, Michigan Department of State, served in the chair.

Byrle Kynerd, Mississippi Department of Archives and History, in his paper, "Some Glad Day: The W.C.T.U. in Mississippi in the 1920s," stressed the renewed activity of the W.C.T.U. in Mississippi in that decade. He pointed out that, although the primary purpose of the W.C.T.U. was to see that prohibition was enforced, the aims and activities of the members embraced a wide range of social reforms that should entitle them to a higher measure of respect as reformers than they are usually accorded. William F. Mugleston, Albany Junior College, in his paper on "The Crusades of a Georgia Editor: Julian Harris in the 1920s" presented the thesis that Harris, editor of the Columbus *Enquirer-Sun*, was a reformer in the mold of individuals like Grover Hall and that his contributions have been ignored. Harris was one of the earliest fighters against the Ku Klux Klan and was vitriolic in his editorials against the Klan and other evils. Mugleston declared that the effort of Harris to be his own man and thus to emerge from the shadow of his famous father, Joel Chandler Harris, may have made him overly pugnacious. A synthesis of the two papers was given in the comment by Hugh C. Bailey, Samford University, who placed them in relationship to general press and reform movements of the South and pointed out that, although Julian Harris was not liberal in certain areas and the W.C.T.U. helped give the South the reputation of being a "benighted region," both Harris and the W.C.T.U. showed that the progressive reform spirit was not dead in the South of the twenties. Bailey's principal point was the complexity of any particular reform movement.

John E. Selby, Institute of Early American History and Culture, was chairman of the session on *North American Slavery in a Revolutionary Age*, which had a Thursday morning attendance of about sixty-five. Gerald W. Mullin of California State University, Sacramento, read a paper on "Slavery in an Age of Revolution: British-American Plantation Societies, 1763–1807" in which he compared the different development of slavery in the British West Indies and on the North American mainland. Because of the large number of blacks in the West Indies the orientation of new slaves was handled by other blacks rather than by whites as in Virginia, and the newcomers retained their African culture much longer. Also, on islands on which all the land was not suitable for staple-crop production slaves were forced to produce their own food, resulting in extralegal but well-recognized property rights which might even be passed on by inheritance. The first commentator, Peter H. Wood, Harvard University, observed that rewards such as extralegal property rights might be even more effective than punishment in denying liberty and exploiting slaves. The second commentator, David Barry Gaspar of the University of Virginia, confirmed most of Mullins's findings from his own studies of eighteenth-century Antigua and noted that, in contradiction of recent studies by Richard Dunn and others which argue that the West Indies were unable to develop a stable society, this evidence indicated that the black societies on the islands were quite stable. Members of the audience joined the panel in a vigorous and stimulating discussion of comparative aspects of North American slavery in this Texas Room, Baker Hotel, session.

The session on *Paradigms and Models: What Utility for Diplomatic History?* convened Thursday morning in the Danish Room. Chaired by Samuel R. Williamson, Jr., North Carolina at Chapel Hill, the session was attended by seventy persons. Melvin Small, Wayne State University, read a paper (coauthored by J. David Singer, University of Michigan) on "The Application of Quantitative Techniques to Diplomatic History." In it the authors focused on the paucity of contact between quantitative international politics and diplomatic history, offered several explanations for this, and then detailed possible areas of fruitful collaboration between traditionalists and those who "count." The second paper on "Theories of Bureaucratic Politics" was presented by Ernest R. May, Harvard. Reviewing the images developed by Graham Allison, May suggested how they could alter one's evaluation of the behavior of the U. S. State Department for the years 1945–1947. He also noted that paradigms, if used judiciously, might help explain other puzzling outcomes in history such as the Stamp Act of 1765. In his comment Wayne S. Cole, University of Maryland, College Park, while applauding efforts for interdisciplinary cooperation, worried about the time needed to acquire quantitative skills and the amounts of data necessary for the successful use of models. The second commentator, Jamie W. Moore, The Citadel, who warned of the dangers of overselling quantification as a technique, underscored May's consistent use of models, and wondered whether business techniques offered another fruitful set of paradigms. From the audience, Enno E. Kraehe, University of Virginia, expressed skepticism about using bureaucratic models for early-nineteenth-century diplomatic history. Other comments centered upon the impact of quantitative methodology upon teaching and on the problems of interdisciplinary communication.

Monroe Billington of New Mexico State University presided over a session on *The Impact of Federal Policy on Blacks*. Thomas R.

Johnson of the U. S. Air Force addressed himself to "Reconstruction Politics in Washington: A Test Tube Experiment for the Radical-Negro Alliance," in which he pointed out that the nation's capital city had served as an early unsuccessful experiment for black suffrage, the failure of that experiment being a portent of failures to come in the various southern states. A. L. King of the University of Missouri–St. Louis read a paper entitled "The Nixon Administration and the Desegregation of Southern Public Schools," in which he held that the less than constructive policy of the Nixon administration in regard to school desegregation has increased the problems of race relations in the United States. Commentators J. Carleton Hayden of Howard University and Walter Fisher of Morgan State College agreed with the general themes of both papers, but each had specific criticisms. Hayden was concerned that Johnson did not make clear who Washington's black Reconstruction leaders were and whether they represented the black masses in the District of Columbia. Fisher noted that King's paper relied too heavily on sources critical of Nixon. Questions and comments from a Thursday morning audience of about thirty persons in the Civic Center I Room were relevant and perceptive.

About eighty persons attended the session on *Southern Women and Racism* held Thursday morning in the Civic Center III Room. With Emma Lou Thornbrough of Butler University presiding, Barry A. Crouch, Bowie State College, read a paper, "Freedom with Honor: Black Women in Texas, 1865–1870," which was replete with examples of responses of individual women to the transition from slavery to freedom. In her comment Lou Holloway of Tougaloo College said that the paper was valuable for the information extracted from hitherto unexplored source materials and would contribute to a future synthesis of research on black women in the first years of freedom. In a second paper, "White Southern Women as Racial Liberals: The Case of Lillian Smith," Morton P. Sosna of the National Endowment for the Humanities examined Smith's life and environment and how they contributed to her development as a writer who made a powerful moral indictment of racism and segregation. Commentator Letitia W. Brown of George Washington University questioned whether Smith was in fact a "type" of southern woman and raised questions about the special insights on race attributed to southern white women. Most of the audience discussion centered on Sosna's paper. Elliott Rudwick, Kent State University, pointed out that as a racial liberal Smith was more of a propagandist than an activist, and a question from A. Elizabeth Taylor, Texas Woman's University, elicited discussion on the relations between white women and black women in the fight against racism.

About fifty persons came to the session on *Mass Violence in Colombian History* held Thursday morning in the Florentine Room and chaired by J. León Helguera, Vanderbilt University. In his paper on "Disaffection Under the Radical Republic: The Colombian Civil War of 1876–1877," Miguel A. Bretos, Oberlin College, discussed the causes and course of this civil conflict, noting its significance as the last stand of Colombian Radical Liberalism. In his comment Charles W. Bergquist, Duke University, asserted the need for more detailed socioeconomic research in the period, a point strongly seconded by the chairman. The second paper, "Traditionalism and Violence in Rural Colombia: A Modern History of Tolima," by James D. Henderson, Grambling College, surveyed the department of Tolima as a sounding board for the stresses and strains of Colombian national politics from 1930 to 1965 and emphasized the high incidence of political and social violence there. In his comment Gabriel Marcella, U. S. Army War College, called for a comparative approach to explain political violence that would include a greater exploration of political ideology. Bergquist, in an extensive commentary on Henderson's paper, stressed the continuity of violence in Colombian history and the importance of integrating a regional approach with national and international economic trends as well as the dominant social and economic interests of the elites. Further discussion by members of the audience revolved around the relationship of violence and the professionalization of the military sector in Colombia's past.

Under the guidance of Steven T. Ross of the Naval War College the session on *Jacobins in Ireland and Italy* met in the Emerald Room with about forty persons present. W. Benjamin Kennedy, West Georgia College, speaking on "The Irish Jacobins," discussed the complexities of Irish Jacobinism. He noted that Irish radicals included both moderate Whig reformers and Catholic peasant nationalists. The inability of groups opposed to British rule to cooperate effectively partially explained the failure of the 1798 revolt. Leonard A. Macaluso, University of South Alabama, delivered a second paper on "The Italian Jacobins" in the 1796–1799 period. He noted that Italian Jacobins also included reformers and real revolutionaries. The French tended to support the moderate reformers, while the radicals turned to clandestine activities. Both groups failed to appeal to the peasantry and consequently lacked mass support. In a single comment Carl B. Cone of the University of Kentucky conceded that both papers contributed to the study of non-French revolutionary movements during the 1790s and declared that the relationship between French and non-French radicalism was indeed complex and worthy of further study.

The Thursday morning session on *Religion and Social Change in Africa* in the English Room, Baker Hotel, drew a slim audience. The meeting featured two papers on Zaire: "The Indigenous Missionary Movement in Zaire" by William M. Rideout, Florida State University, and "Christian Mission and Social Change in Zaire" by Ben C. Hobgood, Southern Methodist University. (Hobgood deserves special commendation for his contribution of a paper on a short two-months notice following the irresponsibly late withdrawal from the session of a previously announced participant.) Charles H. Long, University of North Carolina at Chapel Hill, was the commentator, while the chairman was David M. Foley, University of Georgia.

At the Phi Alpha Theta luncheon in the Rose Room on Thursday the title of the address of the featured speaker, Frank L. Klement, Marquette University, echoed the Watergate affair and similar seamy aspects of our own political scene while pursuing a resolutely historical topic as he delivered remarks on " 'Dirty Tricks' and Civil War Politics: Republican Political Propaganda and Postwar Politics." Donald B. Hoffman presided at this session.

An overflow audience of nearly 350 persons assembled Thursday afternoon in the Renaissance Room for the session, *The Psychosexual Origins of Racism Revisited,* chaired by Jimmie L. Franklin, Eastern Illinois University. In an incisive paper, "Sex, Racism, and Democracy: Alternatives to the Jordan Hypothesis," Robert M. McColley, University of Illinois at Urbana-Champaign noted that his criticism of Winthrop D. Jordan's *White over Black* (the real concern of this session) would "hardly diminish the stature of a remarkable book." Following a discussion of what he characterized as the "Jordan Hypothesis," McColley admitted that most of the ingredients included in Jordan's position "were beyond dispute" but that the way Jordan combined them in patterns of cause and effect called for close examination. Perhaps the most important criticism McColley offered was his rejection of the notion that the white man's perception of color differences between Africans and Europeans resulted from "repressed sexual instincts." He also readily dismissed the contention that slavery in seventeenth-century America represented an "unthinking decision." Viewing his own creation six years after publication in "*White over Black:* A Retrospective," Jordan, University of California, Berkeley, responded graciously to McColley's dignified critique and said that if he had it to do over again he would explore more fully the English cultural revolution on the eve of contact with Africans. Such a probe would go a long way toward explaining why the English (and the Dutch) developed "the most hostile, pervasive, and persistent racism toward Africans." Commentators for the two papers, Willie Lee Rose and August Meier of Johns Hopkins and Kent State universities, respectively, lauded the strengths of *White over Black*, but Meier, in a model version of a negative judgment, believed the papers at this session were weak. That few questions came from the audience testified, in the opinion of the chairman, to the inhibiting effects of a large crowd, the general strength of the papers, and the perceptive commentaries which followed. All in all, this was an outstanding session—the sort that keeps people coming to scholarly conventions.

Chairman Sheldon Hackney of Princeton University reported that an audience of fifty people, "evidently more interested in eschatology than sex," met in the Advertising Club Room on Thursday afternoon to consider *The Idea of Progress in the Old South*. Jack P. Maddex, Jr., University of Oregon, in his paper "Slavery and the Millennium: The Eschatology of Southern Calvinists, 1840–1870," traced the development of "postmillennial" perfectionist ideas of southern Presbyterian churchmen as those ideas were used to support the institution of slavery. Maddex mounted an impressive display of research results to substantiate his claim and to trace the nuances of the argument at the intersection of theology and social thought. Similarly, William H. Longton, University of Toledo, in a second paper on "Process and Development in Science and Society in the South, 1820–1860" delineated the stubborn persistence of Baconian and teleological scientific theories, as opposed to evolutionary, developmental, and chance-based theories which were increasingly popular outside the South and which were more in conformity with the accumulating evidence. Longton inferred from this lag in southern scientific thought that southern scientists needed to espouse systems of knowledge which would undergird the challenged southern social system based on slavery. Neal C. Gillespie, Georgia State University, in his comment (read in his necessary absence by George-Anne Willard, also of Georgia State University) raised a series of questions about Presbyterian thinking and mildly took to task both speakers for missing a great opportunity to take southern intellectual history seriously enough to write about ideas for their own sake and not in relation to the controversy over slavery. The second commentator, Klaus J. Hansen of Queen's University of Canada called for more sophisticated, more cosmopolitan, and more comparative intellectual history so as to distinguish in what ways southern thought differed within itself and what role ideas played in the South. Following the papers and comments an interested audience delved into the Sellers "guilt" hypothesis and into the function of intellectual history.

The session on *Political Parties in the South After World War I* focused on the Democratic domination of southern politics and the inability of the Republican party to counter Democratic hegemony. John C. Weaver of McMaster University, in his paper "Lawyers, Lodges, and Kinfolk: The Workings of a Southern Democratic Organization, 1920–1936," dealt with the political career of South Carolina Fourth District Congressman John J. McSwain, who took advantage of the limited and relatively homogeneous electorate to fashion a friends-and-neighbors personal organization that ensured the congressman an extended and largely unchallenged incumbency. In "The Republican Party in the South and the Harding Years: The Failure of Reform" Roger M. Olien, University of Texas, Permian Basin, reported on the Republican National Committee's unsuccessful efforts to formulate a strategy for revitalizing its moribund southern wing. In their comments both Charles M. Dollar, National Archives and Records Service, and Ralph A. Stone, Sangamon State University, questioned the extent to which generalizations could be validly drawn from the two studies, since Olien's paper focused on relatively narrow party questions and Weaver studied a congressional district probably atypical of the southern norm. Questions and comments from the audience were generally favorable. About twenty-five people attended this session held Thursday afternoon in the French Room under the chairmanship of Numan V. Bartley, University of Georgia.

Approximately thirty persons attended the session on *Black Politics and the Contemporary Urban South: Atlanta and Memphis* convened Thursday afternoon in the Texas Room of the Baker Hotel and chaired by Zane L. Miller, University of Cincinnati. In his paper entitled "Atlanta and Memphis: Black Political Awareness in the Urban South" Duncan R. Jamieson, University of Alabama, argued that black political awareness ran higher in Atlanta than in Memphis because of Atlanta's differing black and white socioeconomic structure. Warren E. Stickle of Purdue University spoke on "Atlanta and Memphis: Black Political Participation in the Urban South, a Quantitative Approach" and emphasized the role of Crump's machine as a political training ground for blacks. He contrasted the Memphis experience with Atlanta's tradition of black activism in voluntary civic organizations, institutions, and political clubs. Stickle contended that blacks in Memphis turned out to vote in about the same proportion as blacks in Atlanta despite the different structure of the two black communities. The commentator, Jessie T. Moore, Jr., University of Rochester, questioned the effectiveness for blacks of either coalition or independent politics, asserted that both black and white leaders in Atlanta pursued essentially conservative policies and suggested that high levels of black participation in politics may veil a fundamental alienation from the system and represent an attempt to take over the system to make it serve the real as well as symbolic interests of blacks. He concluded that race has been, is, and will continue to be a critical political issue in cities across the country.

The session on *British Political Parties and Party Loyalty in the Age of Gladstone and Disraeli* met Thursday afternoon in the Danish Room with Joseph O. Baylen, Georgia State University, presiding and approximately sixty persons in attendance. In the first paper, "The Liberal Party Leadership and the General Election of 1868," Thomas F. Gallagher, Xavier University of Louisiana, explained the "class harmony" facilitating the Liberal party victory in 1868 in terms of the party's need for middle-class and working-class support, the advocacy of the same policies by the party and the workingmen candidates, and the "remarkably modest demands" of the workingmen. In the second paper, on "The Farmers' Alliance and the General Election of 1880," Norman H. Pollock of Old Dominion University reviewed the *raison d'être* for the Farmers' Alliance and concluded that the Alliance failed to achieve its objectives because it was unable to dispel the farmers' fears of being identified with Irish and/or urban radicalism, because "its issues were largely irrelevant and some of its candidates unsuitable," and because local and sectarian factors militated against the success of the organization. In his commentary Sheldon Rothblatt, University of California, Berkeley, offered some perceptive remarks on the background, context, and perspective of the 1868–1880 era in British history, made suggestions on how Gallagher and Pollock might strengthen their research, and pointed out that Pollock had dealt with the county franchise, which has been largely ignored by historians. Rothblatt's remarks were followed by audience discussion and a meeting of the Southern Conference on British Studies.

One of America's most interesting but least studied cultural minorities was the subject of the session on *A Response to Mr. Longfellow: The Louisiana Acadians Revisited* held Thursday afternoon in the chilly Civic Center I Room under the guidance of Philip D. Uzee, Nicholls State University. Both papers—"The

Acadians: A Rebel Breed?" by Glenn R. Conrad of the Center for Louisiana Studies and "Nineteenth-Century Acadiana" by Vaughan Baker of the University of Southwestern Louisiana—were historical case studies of the myth-versus-reality dichotomy in regard to a subject that has been bedeviled with oversimplification. Conrad dwelled on the success of the Acadians in reconstructing and protecting the way of life they had developed in Acadia until twentieth-century developments began to puncture the walls of Cajun isolation. Baker discussed the contrast between Cajun residents along well-traveled waterways, who early on acculturated significantly to the Old South life-style of Louisiana, and the more isolated rural Cajuns, who preserved in much purer form the Nova Scotian heritage. A. Otis Hebert of the State Archives, Louisiana, opened his comment by stating that this session on the Acadians was the first in the history of the Association. Hebert commended both papers and devoted himself to a plea for wide-ranging further research to dispel prevailing contradictory and erroneous concepts about the Acadians. There was a lively and good-humored exchange of views among individuals in the audience of fifty and the panelists, who were all declared to be honorary Cajuns

About thirty-five persons attended the session on *New Perspectives in Mexican-American History* held on Thursday afternoon in the Civic Center III Room. A. Rolando Andrade, University of Oklahoma, concluded in his paper that Juan N. Cortinas was neither a Mexican-American bandit nor a Robin Hood but a Texan who sought private revenge against Anglo-Texans. In the second paper Joseph P. Sanchez, University of Arizona, discussed the use of anti-Mexican themes by Lone Star Republic writers to develop Texas nationalism. In the third paper Guillermo Lux, New Mexico Highlands University, sorted out the *raza* types to establish proper use of the term Chicano, showed *raza* group interaction, and illustrated Movimiento activities by other *raza* than Chicanos. Manuel A. Machado, Jr., University of Montana, commented on the three presentations. According to him, Andrade's paper suffered from methodological, syntactic, and organizational problems; Sanchez's paper placed too much emphasis on anti-Mexicanism in the formation of Texas nationalism; and Lux's paper was a confusing attempt to create a Chicano typology. The session was chaired by Manuel P. Servin, Arizona State University.

Distinguishing the Thursday afternoon, Emerald Room session on *Historical Preservation* was "An Appraisal of the Historical Preservation Movement," copiously illustrated by slides, presented by Ernest Allen Connally, National Park Service. Connally's richly detailed critique traced the history of the preservation movement since the early nineteenth century with careful attention to federally sponsored efforts that have increased greatly since 1935. The current threat of economically induced demolition of historic structures and the need for a vast increase in the financial resources of preservation as well as the philosophy of preservation were stressed, too, by Connally. James Morton Smith, State Historical Society of Wisconsin, and William S. Powell, University of North Carolina at Chapel Hill, were acute commentators at this session presided over by Samuel Proctor, University of Florida.

A near capacity crowd of over a hundred gathered Thursday afternoon in the Florentine Room to consider *Western Aspects of Totalitarian Diplomacy* under the chairmanship of Earl R. Beck, Florida State University. In his paper on "Hitler's 'International': The Activities of Nazi Party Groups Outside Germany, 1933–1945" Donald M. McKale, Georgia College, crisply demonstrated many points of similarity between the "Nazintern" (directed by the flamboyant Ernst Bohle) and the Comintern. "The Response of the Democracies to Japanese Totalitarian Aggression: 'Running with the Hare and Hunting with the Hounds'—France, the Powers, and the Far Eastern Crisis, 1937–1939" by John E. Dreifort, Wichita State University, was the medium for his emphasis on the ambivalent and indecisive aspects of French foreign policy during the years treated. Basically favorable commentaries by Jay W. Baird of Miami University (Ohio) and William Roger Louis of the University of Texas, Austin, were the prelude for a lively floor discussion which, among other points, questioned whether the relationship of "Race and Reich" had real meaning abroad.

The session on *Jesuit Wealth: An Economic Factor in Eighteenth-Century Spanish America* featured papers on "The Wealth of the Jesuits in Mexico, 1670–1767" by James D. Riley, Catholic University, who discussed the successes and failures of Jesuit agricultural projects, and on "The Jesuit Temporalities at the Disposal of the Reforming Bourbons, 1767–1814" by Charles J. Fleener, St. Louis University, who addressed himself to the administrative structures established to control the confiscated Jesuit properties. Both discussants, Ursula Ewald, University of Heidelberg, and Charles W. Polser, S. J., Arizona State Museum, emphasized the failure of both papers to place their subjects within a general economic framework or to deal adequately with either agricultural or bureaucratic innovation. Comment from the audience of fifty was confined largely to the accessibility and location of relevant manuscripts. This session met Thursday afternoon in the English Room of the Baker Hotel with John G. Clark, University of Kansas, in the chair.

The session on *Confederate Military Leadership* occurred Friday morning in the Renaissance Room with approximately eighty persons present and Charles P. Roland, University of Kentucky, serving as chairman. Grady McWhiney, Wayne State University, presented a paper on "Jefferson Davis and the Art of War," in which he argued that Davis as Confederate President was not heavily influenced by the military theories of Baron Henri Jomini as some historians have speculated but was the product of his experience in the Mexican War. William C. Davis, *Civil War Times Illustrated,* spoke on "Secretary of War John C. Breckinridge and Confederate Defeat" and contended that Breckinridge more than any other man in the position of secretary of war influenced Jefferson Davis in the conduct of affairs and that Breckinridge's advice helped to bring about the honorable surrender of Confederate armies instead of their piecemeal deterioration. Peter F. Walker, University of North Carolina at Chapel Hill, commented on McWhiney's paper, suggesting the need for a deeper psychological analysis of Davis in order to understand his military policies. Herman M. Hattaway of the University of Missouri–Kansas City, discussed both papers; he took issue with McWhiney on the ground that, despite the lack of explicit evidence of Jominian influence on Confederate generals and on Davis, perhaps there may well have been an "unconscious" Jominian influence on them. Hattaway agreed with William C. Davis's main theme but questioned his implication that Breckinridge had never been confident of Confederate success. A brief discussion followed the papers and commentaries.

Nearly one hundred persons gathered in the Advertising Club Room of the Adolphus for a significant Friday morning panel session on *Editing and Publishing the Papers of Black Americans: Problems and Prospects.* Arthur S. Link of Princeton University, editor of *The Papers of Woodrow Wilson,* presided. The panelists made informal presentations. Alton Hornsby, Jr., of Morehouse College, editor of the papers of John Hope, told about the discovery of a large quantity of exciting new papers relating to Hope and about his own plans for publication. Louis R. Harlan of the University of Maryland, College Park, editor of *The Booker T. Washington Papers,* commented on the vast scope of the Washington collection, the problems of selection, and the progress of his project. John W. Blassingame of Yale University, editor of the papers of Frederick Douglass, remarked on the way in which his documentary materials illustrate the life and career of perhaps the most distinguished black American of the nineteenth century. Edgar A. Toppin of Virginia State College, president of the Association for the Study of Afro-American Life and History and a member of the National Historical Publications Commission, reported on the interest and involvement of these two organizations in the publication of papers illustrating the lives of American Negroes. The panelists and the chairman agreed that historians are just now on the threshold of what might become one of the important undertakings in American historical scholarship. They also agreed that documentary materials exist in great abundance, that letterpress editions are much more useful than microfilm editions, and that money can probably be found for any worthy undertakings. There were no commentators, but discussion from the floor was vigorous and lively, extending for more than an hour. In summary, all agreed that there were new opportunities for work in the much-neglected field of the publication of documentary materials illustrating the lives and careers of a large number of black Americans.

Norman L. Crockett, University of Oklahoma, headed the timely session, *Historical Perspectives on the Energy Crisis,* that attracted about forty persons to a Friday morning meeting in the French Room. Bennett H. Wall, Tulane University, delivered a paper on "Henry L. Doherty and the Struggle for Oil Conservation in the 1920s." Doherty, founder of the Cities Service Company, warred with the Federal Oil Conservation Board, the American Petroleum Institute, and any other groups unwilling or reluctant to adopt oil-conservation techniques during the decade. A pioneer in the field, Doherty convinced other leaders in the petroleum industry to accept some modified form of conservation. In a second paper John A. DeNovo, University of Wisconsin, Madison, dealt with "Anglo-American Discord over Middle Eastern Oil During World War II," in the course of which he discussed mutual Anglo-American suspicion relating to Middle Eastern oil rights between December 1943 and the signing of the first Anglo-American Oil Agreement in August 1944. As two of several conclusions, DeNovo suggested that the discord over oil represented only one of several strains between the two countries and that both nations sensed the need to serve the general international interest but not at the expense of compromising their separate national interests. In commenting on both papers Gerald D. Nash, University of New Mexico, indicated that future historians were likely to concentrate research efforts on the values of leaders in the petroleum industry rather than its technology. Specifically, Nash suggested that Doherty was more a publicist than a thinker and certainly not alone in the fight for oil conservation during the twenties. American fear of British expansion in the Middle East, he argued, was perhaps well founded and in part the result of American fear of declining oil reserves in the Western Hemisphere. Audience participation revolved around current Third World attitudes toward natural resources, French reaction to the 1944 Anglo-American agreement, and British relations with the Arab states.

John Hebron Moore, Florida State University, guided a highly technical Friday morning session on *Manufacturing in the Old South* in the crowded Tally Ho Room of the Baker Hotel. Over thirty persons were on hand to hear a collaborative paper on "Profitability in Antebellum Southern Manufacturing" that was prepared by three economists,Fred Bateman and James D. Foust of Indiana University and Thomas J. Weiss, University of Kansas, and read by Weiss. In their analysis of the profitability of various southern industries, based mainly on manuscript schedules of the 1850 and 1860 censuses on manufacturing, Bateman, Foust, and Weiss determined that all industries brought in substantially better returns on invested capital than did plantation agriculture. They also observed that planters generally failed to take advantage of opportunities to invest their profits in manufacturing enterprises. In the first commentary historian Charles B. Dew of the University of Missouri–Columbia praised the effort that had gone into the analysis of the census data as well as the formula devised by the authors to measure profitability but questioned the reliability of the historical statistics inserted into their equation. Dew suspected that the authors of the paper underestimated the cost of slave wages while overestimating the amounts received from the sale of manufactured products, errors that would make industries appear more profitable than they were. The second commentator, economist Gavin Wright, University of Michigan, commented that the authors' formula did not take transportation costs into account. Speculating that transportation costs sometimes created local manufacturing monopolies, Wright doubted that profitability statistics calculated for industries on a statewide basis were really useful. He also doubted that planters actually had many chances to invest in manufacturing enterprises, for they were usually financed by the savings of the owners augmented by investments made by friends and acquaintances.

The session on *Southern Baptists in the 1920s* was held Friday morning in the Danish Room. Chaired by David Edwin Harrell, Jr., University of Alabama in Birmingham, the session was attended by about forty-five persons. In his paper on "Edgar Young Mullins and the Crisis of Moderate Southern Baptist Leadership" William E. Ellis, Eastern Kentucky University, pictured Mullins as a responsible denominational leader who tried to thwart radical Fundamentalists and yet retain a leadership role in his conservative church. Commentator Paul A. Carter, University of Arizona, pointed out that the Fundamentalist-modernist controversy was a national one and that Mullins's career indicated that the Southern Baptists may have reached a more reasonable compromise than did most northern churches. C. Allyn Russell, Boston University, read the second paper on "J. Frank Norris: Irascible Fundamentalist." Norris's role as a controversialist was emphasized in the paper; his extreme tactics probably slowed the growth of liberal thought in the Southern Baptist Church. In his comment Robert Moats Miller, University of North Carolina at Chapel Hill, observed that, while Norris was destructive and dangerous, he was not a charlatan. He pointed to the need for understanding the psychology of such corrosive religious leaders. Very few persons left before the session ended, and the audience obviously appreciated the efforts of the panel.

Arthur H. DeRosier, University of Mississippi, was chairman of a three-paper session on *Indians of the South and Southwest* that assembled Friday morning in the Civic Center I Room. Two papers dealt with the Cherokees, while the third was devoted to the Quapaw Indians. In "Poor Little Rich Indians: The Quapaw Story" W. David Baird of the University of Arkansas, Fayetteville, recounted the discovery of lead and zinc ore on the Quapaw reservation in northeast Oklahoma in the first three decades of the twentieth century and assessed the impact of the large royalty payments accruing to the tribe in terms of individual and governmental reaction. Baird concluded that the resultant federal supervision left the Quapaws rich in wealth but poor in personal freedom. The paper on "Black Slavery Among the Cherokees" by Rudi Halliburton, Jr., of Northeastern State College (Oklahoma) was preceded by the presentation of Diana G. Vari, Utah State University, on "Rather Red than Dead: The Worcester Case and the Origins of the Cherokee Removal Faction." In his paper Halliburton traced the historical evolution of the institution of black slavery, which by the time of the removal to the West had become a pervasive one among prominent Cherokee families. Cherokee acceptance of slavery was enhanced by the gradual loss of their hunting lands and the examples of surrounding white colonial plantations, with the result that by 1800 among the Cherokees some full-scale plantations based on slave labor were in existence and black codes were being formulated. The commentator for all three papers was Robert A. Trennert of Arizona State University.

The session on *August Bebel and German Socialism,* held on Friday morning in the Civic Center III Room and chaired by Konrad H. Jarausch, University of Missouri–Columbia, was attended by about sixty people. In her paper on "The Evolution of August Bebel's Social-Political Philosophy, 1864–1871" Sarah C. Neitzel of Pan American University argued that the leader of German socialism was prompted more by his resentment of Bismarck's conquest of Germany, by his friend Liebknecht, by Catholic journeymen's societies, and by his own natural sympathy for the oppressed than by *Das Kapital.* The topic of the paper by William H. Maehl, Auburn University, was "August Bebel's Role in the Development of a German Socialist Foreign Policy, 1878–1896," and in it Maehl traced the emergence of a less internationalist and antimilitarist attitude towards foreign policy to Bebel's gradual acceptance of defensive war against tsarist absolutism and stressed that his pro-English stand stemmed more from nationalism than from domestic anti-imperialism. In his comment on Neitzel's paper Vernon L. Lidtke of Johns Hopkins University questioned the importance of St. Ambrose as the inspiration for Bebel, explored the ambiguities of subjective versus objective Marxism, and suggested a psychological answer to Bebel's espousal of Marxist ideas. In his critique of Maehl's paper Lidtke raised the issue of what constituted a "Marxist" foreign policy in this period, rejected the definition of a "responsible" stance in terms of nationalism, and argued that Bebel's ideas were influenced by domestic motives.

Under the presiding direction of Mary E. Young, University of Rochester, around forty persons gathered Friday morning in the Emerald Room for the session on *Cultural Crisis in the 1890s: The Problem of Appalachia.* The lone paper on "The Invention of Appalachia as a Resolution of a Cultural Crisis, 1895–1925" was presented by Henry D. Shapiro of the University of Cincinnati. Shapiro argued that in the 1890s, as a result of Americans' uncertainty about their national identity, benevolent groups working with southern mountaineers first identified the population of Appalachia as deviants requiring help from social reformers and then came to redefine the area as a legitimate "region" with peculiar but positively deviant characteristics. In his critique Paul K. Conkin of the University of Wisconsin, Madison, charged that the definition of "Americans" in Shapiro's paper was neither sharply delimited nor firmly evidenced. Conkin maintained that intellectual historians cannot give evidence of a generalized opinion or state of mind even among the elite and that consequently they cannot validly describe what "Americans" of the 1890s believed. Questioners from the floor sought to establish the opinions of special classes of observers: students of the ballad, businessmen investing in the southern mountain region, and philanthropic organizations and their agents in the area. The discussion elicited evidence that stereotypes of the area did not take account of actual variations within it; the focus of the paper emphasized changing stereotypes rather than changing conditions. Shapiro claimed that he had in fact identified both individuals and classes of individuals to whom the views he analyzed might be attributed.

Two *Aspects of the Sacred and Profane in the Colonial Chesapeake Region* were treated in the Friday morning session of that title in the Florentine Room. One aspect was a contribution to the "new social history" of the colonial period, while the other was another study in the long-term consideration of the quality of colonial Episcopalian clerics. The first paper, "The Structure of Household Labor in Late-Seventeenth-Century Virginia: Surry County, a Case Study," was read by Kevin P. Kelly of the Institute of Early American History and Culture. Through a study of Surry's tithable tax lists Kelly argued that in the face of declining white immigration Surry planters, especially the small and moderate-sized ones who keyed their actions to booms in the tobacco market, turned to slave labor as an alternative as early as the 1670s. The pace of the shift accelerated until by the late 1680s black slaves dominated the household labor force. Thus, Kelly found that at the century's end, although the number of slaves owned by any one planter was small, slaveowners as a group had virtually turned away from white labor. In his comment Darrett B. Rutman, University of New Hampshire, questioned Kelly's use of tithe lists and urged him to adhere to a less narrow approach to his study. In "Sinners and Saints: The Character of the Eighteenth-Century Anglican Clergy in Maryland" by Gerald E. Hartdagen, Indiana University–Purdue University at Indianapolis, and David Curtis Skaggs, Bowling Green State University, the authors assessed post-1945 scholarship and advocated a more complex view of the Maryland clergy that would fully credit the estimable performance of the ministry. Discussant Alison Gilbert Olson, University of Maryland, College Park, scored the Hartdagen-Skaggs presentation for lack of clear focus in too loosely categorizing ministers as good and bad. Nearly forty attended this session headed by Hugh F. Rankin, Tulane University.

The Camellia Room, Baker Hotel, snugly accommodated the Friday morning audience of forty at the session on *Indian, Spaniard, and Anglo in the Southwest: The Preservation of a Legacy* under the chairmanship of Merrill J. Mattes, National Park Service (Denver). "The Private Citizen, the Professions, and Preservation" by Charles R. McGimsey III, University of Arkansas Museum, reviewed three major pieces of federal legislation, 1966–1974, that have greatly enhanced preservation efforts, while the second paper, "The Past Is Tomorrow," read by Michael Weber, Museum of New Mexico, in behalf of Spencer Wilson of the New Mexico Cultural Properties Review Committee, used slides to illustrate New Mexican compliance with the legislation. Commentator Donald E. Worcester, Texas Christian University, noted that our vision should not be limited to the physical remains since the cultural legacy is much greater and called for the purgation of traditional attitudes toward non-Anglos. Animated discussion from the floor concluded the session.

Sixty persons attended the Latin American History luncheon on Friday in the Century Club Room with William S. Coker, University of West Florida, presiding. The address by Severo Gómez, assistant commissioner, Texas Education Agency, on "Bilingualism and Bilingual Education in the Borderlands," in which the speaker described the bilingual education program that now assists nearly a million non-English-speaking Texas children in making the transition from home to school, touched off an active discussion period by a responsive audience. At the Friday European History Section luncheon in the Rose Room about eighty people heard Harold T. Parker, Duke University, voice extremely perceptive "Reflections on Thucydides: Coalition War in Modern European History." Parker discerned significant resemblances in the formation and behavior of coalitions, with difficulty of genesis and speedy postwar dissolution particularly marking such alliances. George V. Taylor, University of North Carolina at Chapel Hill, presided.

The more than one hundred persons who came to the session on *Recent Texas Writing: Larry McMurtry and the* Texas Observer *Group* were amply repaid for their interest by being present for a penetrating symposium on the significant yet relatively neglected cultural enterprise of contemporary Texas writing. Under the chairmanship of Lon Tinkle, Southern Methodist University, the Friday afternoon gathering was called to order in the Renaissance Room. Warren I. Susman, Rutgers University, read a paper on "The Fiction of Larry McMurtry" and delivered a perceptive interpretation of McMurtry as one whose writing (heightened by the film versions of his books) updates traditional southwestern myths of life, violence, and the like in terms of the contemporary national suburbanized culture. The result of all this, concluded Susman, is that McMurtry deals tellingly, if not conclusively, with national questions of culture from the base of Texas life and lore. Composed of equal parts of analysis and personal memoir was the acute paper of Lawrence C. Goodwyn, Duke University, on "The *Texas Observer:* The Personal Journalists." Goodwyn, a former *Observer* staff member, pictured writing for the *Observer* as an apprenticeship leading to a "loss of innocence" politically for a number of young Texans, who have gone on to achieve national audiences and acclaim. Goodwyn praised founding editor Ronnie Dugger for his "education" of his staff, for his development of what was, in effect, the "new journalism" long before the term was thought of, and for his unrelenting editorial crusade against Texas corruption. In an incisive comment on both papers Richard H. Pells, University of Texas, Austin, concluded that the chief function of both McMurtry and the *Texas Observer* has been, indeed, observation—observation of what has happened to the past and what is happening in the present; in the sense of observation both McMurtry and the *Observer* group have done much to shape the national consciousness of the present. Audience discussion featured a story by Frank Wardlaw, Texas A&M University Press, about Larry McMurtry's first manuscript and general agreement that Pells's summation of the papers and the significance of McMurtry and the *Observer* group were correct.

Approximately seventy people attended the session on *Sex and Race in the Twentieth-Century South* held Friday afternoon in the Advertising Club Room and chaired by Elliott Rudwick, Kent State University. In her paper on "Revolt Against Chivalry: Jessie Daniel Ames and the Women's Campaign Against Lynching" Jacquelyn Dowd Hall, University of North Carolina at Chapel Hill, examined the career of the Texas suffragist who used the political influence of white women to combat mob violence against blacks. Ames's attack against lawlessness was also an attack against the code of chivalry which imprisoned southern women in old sexual stereotypes. In the second paper, "Racial Revolt and Sexual Consciousness: Women in the Civil Rights Movement, 1960–1965," Sara M. Evans, University of North Carolina at Greensboro, noted that white women participants developed a heightened sense of strength and self-worth within the movement, which provided the basic thrust for their revolt against being treated only as sexual objects, houseworkers, and clerks. In his comment on both papers William H. Chafe, Duke University, contrasted Ames's more limited challenge to the norms of her culture with the radical commitment to change of the civil rights activists of the sixties. He suggested that Ames was a "loner," whose early sense of limited personal worth made her fear complete public rejection and contributed to her inability to challenge many prevailing values. On the other hand, the civil rights activists of the sixties not only had a high sense of personal worth but were deeply alienated from southern cultural norms. Compared to Ames, activists of the sixties also operated in a social milieu far more conducive to social change.

An entranced audience of nearly one hundred was present in the French Room Friday afternoon for a distinctive session on *Southern Music* headed by Ronald L. Davis, Southern Methodist University. In his paper on "Country Music and the South" Bill C. Malone, Tulane University, argued that country music has reflected the inner tensions of southern life—a traditionalistic, rural, family-centered society that at the same time has been conscious of change. He played a tape and sang examples. In his comment Charles R. Townsend, West Texas State University, asked Malone to be more specific in his definition of country music and recommended that the South's music be studied in comparison with that of the rest of the nation rather than as an isolated phenomenon. The second paper, "Southern Protest Music," presented by Joe Glazer, U. S. Information Agency, pointed out four categories of social, economic, and political protest songs. Glazer played the guitar and sang examples from each category: (1) Hard Times, (2) The Union Is Behind Us, (3) The Fighting Side of Me, and (4) Progressive Country. Townsend in his commentary urged Glazer to broaden his concept of protest music to include issues of a sociopsychological nature.

A capacity crowd of sixty persons attended the session on *Radical Republicans: North and South* held on Friday afternoon in the Tally Ho Room of the Baker Hotel and chaired by Allen W. Trelease, University of North Carolina, Greensboro. Glenn M. Linden, Southern Methodist University, in his paper "Politics or Principle?: Voting by Congressmen on the Thirteenth, Fourteenth, and Fifteenth Amendments," found that two-thirds of the congressmen were consistent in their voting on measures relating to the Negro in the years 1838–1869. Of the minority, most increased their support of the Negro in voting on the civil rights amendments, 1864–1869. Both commentators, William McKee Evans, California State

Polytechnic University, and William C. Harris, North Carolina State University, argued that many of the prewar antislavery measures were not necessarily regarded as pro-Negro by the congressmen voting on them; some members were motivated by anti-Negro sentiment, for instance, in opposing slavery expansion. Richard L. Hume, Washington State University, in his paper on "Carpetbaggers in the Black and Tan Constitutional Conventions of 1867–1869," gave a summary account of 158 northern-born delegates, using primarily the manuscript census of 1870 and the convention journals. Their constituencies typically contained many blacks and were comparatively urbanized; they were rather well-to-do economically; they led in the movements for Negro political and legal rights and public education; and most of them remained in the South. The commentators generally praised the papers while pointing to worthwhile areas of further research. Evans pointed out that carpetbaggers brought economic as well as political progress and settled in towns partly for purposes of community and protection.

Two case studies of North Carolina and Arkansas with long-range implications highlighted the session on *Federal Relief in the 1930s: Its Impact on Southern States,* called to order Friday afternoon in the Danish Room by J. Joseph Huthmacher, University of Delaware. Forty persons were present. Both papers, one titled "Federal Relief in Arkansas," by Stephen F. Strausberg of the University of Arkansas, Fayetteville, and the other, "The Impact of the New Deal on Welfare in North Carolina," by Thomas S. Morgan of Winthrop College, on the basis of exhaustive research in each case, emphasized the effect of the contention between "the State House crowd" and "the federal crowd" and the restraints of "local practices and mores" on provision of adequate assistance to the needy. Commentator Donald Holley of the University of Arkansas at Monticello praised the usefulness of such state and local studies in explicating New Deal failures, while Roger Daniels, State University of New York College at Fredonia, stressed the utility of the grass-roots perspective in exposing the negative impact of Depression-era programs on poor people.

A probing panel session on *Critical Issues in Women's History: O'Neill's* Everyone Was Brave *in Retrospect* was led Friday afternoon by A. Elizabeth Taylor, Texas Woman's University. There were four panelists: Jill K. Conway, University of Toronto; Allen F. Davis, Temple University; Nancy Schrom Dye, University of Kentucky; and William L. O'Neill, Rutgers University. Davis commended O'Neill's *Everyone Was Brave* for placing the feminist movement in its proper context in the broad sweep of American history. Dye, too, saluted O'Neill for putting the Nineteenth Amendment in correct perspective but criticized his classification of feminists as "social" or "radical" as being too narrow and thus inadequate. Conway, disagreeing, considered these classifications to be useful analytical devices and expressed agreement with O'Neill about the ideological poverty of the feminist movement. In response, O'Neill clarified his use of the terms "social" and "radical" and pointed out that his book had been published some years ago, asking that it be judged in that context and not in the light of more recent studies in women's history. The lively audience of about sixty that met in the Civic Center I Room raised the issues of the place of feminism in women's history, the influence of industrialization on the role of woman, the need for more studies of working-class women, and the problems of structuring courses on women's history.

In the Friday afternoon session on *Bluejackets and Ironclads: The Mid-Victorian Royal Navy* Colin F. Baxter, East Tennessee State University, read a paper on "The Great Debate over the Creation of the British Ironclad Navy, 1859–1866." His central point was that fear, induced by French naval building, slowly dragged Britain into iron ships, and the new ships moved England and the world toward the age of the dreadnought. Eugene L. Rasor of Emory and Henry College then presented his paper on "The Admiralty and the Lower Deck, 1859–1866." His findings suggest that improvement in the treatment of enlisted men in these years produced higher motivation among the sailors. Wilbur Devereux Jones, University of Georgia, commentator for the session, pointed out that the new-type sailors, who benefited from humane reforms, fought no better than their less coddled predecessors. Jones rated both papers as well conceived and well researched. The audience of over sixty persons in the Civic Center III Room asked questions and made comments relating to technological changes in the British navy and specific living conditions aboard a man-of-war. John K. Mahon, University of Florida, was chairman of the session.

The Mexican Borderlands session treated the years of Mexican sovereignty after 1821. The young Mexican nation inherited all the problems Spain had known in the late decades of its rule—distance, lack of population, bothersome Indians, and aggressive neighbors. In his paper "New Mexico in the Mexican Period" Gerald Theisen, University of Albuquerque, focused on the state of education. Attempts to establish a system of public education were less than successful; private schools filled the gap within the province, with the controversial Padre Martinez quite influential and the contributions of far-off Saint Louis University, at the other end of the Santa Fe Trail, far from negligible. Félix D. Almaráz, University of Texas, San Antonio, covered a number of "Aspects of Mexican Texas" in his presentation. The most significant was his emphasis on little-recognized instances of bilingual cooperation between Tejanos and Anglos in opposing the centralizing efforts of Santa Anna. He also noted many enlightened efforts of Mexico to develop Texas prior to the 1830s in regard to matters of Indian policy, population increase, and general economic development. Provocative comment was offered by Manuel P. Servín, Arizona State University, and Ralph H. Vigil, University of Nebraska–Lincoln. Fifty-odd interested folk attended this Friday afternoon session in the Emerald Room under the chairmanship of John Francis Bannon, St. Louis University.

About twenty persons attended the session on *The Anomalous Positions of Hong Kong and Taiwan,* held Friday afternoon in the Florentine Room. The panel was chaired by Richard Smith, Rice University. John R. Moore, University of Southwestern Louisiana, delivered a paper on "The U. S.–Taiwan Mutual Defense Treaty and the Future of Taiwan," emphasizing the numerous and vexing policy problems presented by Taiwan's anomalous position in international affairs. In his comments Walter E. Hugins, Jr., State University of New York, Binghamton, elaborated on the origins of the treaty and discussed the implications of its possible abrogation. The paper by David P. Aldstadt, Chinese University of Hong Kong, entitled "The Sino-British 'Unequal Treaties' and the Future of Hong Kong," traced Hong Kong's evolution into an entity "neither totally Chinese nor totally British" and outlined several future options for the crown colony. Raymond M. Lorantas, Drexel University, indicated in his comment that the people of Hong Kong had become a kind of special "minority," which might at some time be administered by the People's Republic of China as an "autonomous region." Similar suggestions for the resolution of Taiwan's anomalous situation were also discussed. The panelists generally agreed that Western policy remains an important factor in the present status of Hong Kong and Taiwan and that both now and in the foreseeable future pragmatic considerations will blunt the thrust of China's determined quest for complete national integration.

Career opportunities for young historians was the central issue of the panel session on *The Work of Historical Societies* under the chairmanship of Daniel J. Reed, National Archives and Records Service, Friday afternoon in the English Room of the Baker Hotel.

The substantial audience of forty-five heard panelists Wilcomb E. Washburn, Smithsonian Institution, Edward M. Riley, Colonial Williamsburg Foundation, and Russell W. Fridley, Minnesota Historical Society, discuss employment possibilities and trends in regard to "Museums," "Research Collections," and "Historic Sites and Preservation." A vibrant conversation among panelists and audience led to the agreement that there were notable opportunities in the fields discussed for aspiring historians at the B.A., M.A., and Ph.D. levels.

About fifty persons attended the session on *Teaching History in the Secondary Schools: The Controversy over the Inquiry Method* held Saturday morning in the Renaissance Room under the chairmanship of Glenn M. Linden of Southern Methodist University. In "A Mode of Inquiry, Value Clarification, and the Teaching of History: Are They Compatible?" Allan Kownslar of Trinity University discussed the way "Inquiry" could be used in the classroom and answered some of the major objections to this teaching method. The second effort, "The American Experience—An Inquiry Approach to the Teaching of Humanities: A Multimedia and Panel Presentation" by Sylvia Butler, Rosemary Thomas, Anne-Marie Hodges, and Bill Nelson of the W. T. White High School of Dallas (assisted musically by twenty of their students), illustrated the way "Inquiry" can be used in an interdisciplinary setting. The commentator, Floyd B. Pitts of the Dallas Independent School District, responded positively to these two endorsements of "Inquiry," while audience reaction focused on the problem of adequate financial and administrative support for this innovative method.

Revisionistic scholarship and avant garde methodology characterized the Saturday morning session on *The Southern Redeemers Reexamined* in the Advertising Club Room. Charles E. Wynes, University of Georgia, presided over the gathering of thirty. The initial paper by Catherine Silverman, New York State Division of Human Rights, on "Attitudes of the Redeemers Toward Social Change in Virginia and North Carolina" presented a strongly negative portrait of the Redeemers as failed "natural leaders." Discussant Joseph F. Steelman, East Carolina University, questioned her estimate in several respects and noted in race relations a similar failure by old abolitionists, leading Radicals, and others. A high point of the second paper by Carl V. Harris, University of California, Santa Barbara, on "The South in Congress, 1875–1896" was his use of statistical analysis to challenge C. Vann Woodward's claim that Redeemer congressmen generally supported the economic policies of northeastern interests; instead, Harris saw residual agriculturalist tendencies determining their voting record. Second commentator Raymond H. Pulley, Appalachian State University, asked whether quantification could really be enlightening on Redeemer congressional behavior and stressed Redeemer complexity in representing "many Souths."

A satisfactory audience was present Saturday morning in the French Room for the session on *Black Americans in the Nineteenth Century.* In her paper Nell Irvin Painter, University of Pennsylvania, explored "Millennial Aspects of the Exodus to Kansas of 1879," which, she held, primarily affected the Louisiana-Mississippi portion of that movement. Next, Carl R. Stockton, Talladega College, dealt with "Alexander Crummell and the Black Intelligentsia, 1872–1898" and concluded that the most lasting contribution of the influential black nationalist Crummell was the founding of the American Negro Academy, an attempt to counter long-standing antiblack racial stereotypes. Also appearing before the attentive gathering were the two commentators, Donnie E. Bellamy of Fort Valley State College and Gossie H. Hudson of Lincoln University (Missouri) and session chairman Walter B. Weare of the University of Wisconsin, Milwaukee.

Conflicting views and the active participation of the audience of thirty attended the analysis of *Dissent in the New South* under the careful chairmanship of Richard L. Watson, Jr., Duke University, on Saturday morning in the Danish Room. In "Walter B. Hill: Dissent in Southern Academe" G. Ray Mathis of Troy State University etched Hill, University of Georgia chancellor from 1899 to 1905, as a tactful critic of intolerance and southern society and a racist who was sympathetic to black people. William E. Nicholas of Birmingham-Southern College concentrated on serious abridgments of academic freedom and professorial civil liberties at Tulane and the universities of Texas and Virginia in his paper on "Academic Dissent in the South During World War I." The two discussants, Mollie C. (Davis) Abernathy of Queens College and Bruce L. Clayton of Allegheny College, thoughtfully commented on many issues of interpretation and historical context raised by the two papers, while, among salient contributions from the floor, Daniel W. Hollis, University of South Carolina, noted that the published histories of Tulane, Texas, and Virginia glossed over the episodes described in depth by Nicholas.

A good Saturday morning gathering of nearly forty attended the session on *The Diplomacy of Reaction: The Great Powers and the*

Greek Revolt, 1821–1822 held in the Civic Center I Room under the guidance of Arthur G. Haas, University of Tennessee, Knoxville. Irby C. Nichols, Jr., North Texas State University, contended that Austrian and British Russophobia led to a pro-Turk stand in the episode he probed under the title of "Hellas Scorned: The Ambassadorial Address to the Greeks." In the second paper, "Metternich, the Papacy, and the Greek Revolt," Alan J. Reinerman of Boston College investigated Metternich's efforts to keep Rome from supporting Greek rebels as fellow Christians. Both commentators, Douglas D. Hale, Jr., of Oklahoma State University and Enno E. Kraehe of the University of Virginia, praised the originality of research of the two papers while questioning certain interpretations in each of them.

Another spirited Saturday morning assemblage (numbering nearly forty) was present for the session dealing with *Colombia's Self-Image and Diplomacy During the First Century of Independence.* In "The Vicissitudes of Bolivarian Grandeur in New Granadan Diplomacy" by John W. Kitchens of Tuskegee Institute and "Picking up the Pieces: The Mil Dias, Panama, and the Diplomacy of Rafael Reyes" by Joseph L. Arbena of Clemson University the audience heard two strongly researched papers that scanned the issues of internal order and international standing (often in terms of tensions between isolationism and internationalism) in regard to two contrasting periods, 1842–1854 and 1904–1909, of Colombian history and diplomacy. Harold A. Bierck, Jr., University of North Carolina at Chapel Hill, presided over the commentaries by Ron L. Seckinger of the University of North Carolina at Chapel Hill and Helen V. Delpar of the University of Alabama and the audience discussion.

A dialogue combining a review of practical experience with speculative opinion marked the Saturday morning session on *University Training for Historical Administration* held in the Florentine Room. William T. Alderson, Jr., of the American Association for State and Local History presided over the group of thirty in the unavoidable absence of V. Jacque Voegeli. A successful enterprise was surveyed in "The Cooperstown Graduate Program: A Decade in Retrospect," a paper read by Lonn Taylor, Winedale Inn Museum of the University of Texas, in behalf of Peter C. Welsh, New York State Historical Association. "University Training for Historical Administration: Problems and Potential" by Barnes Riznik of Old Sturbridge Village and the comment by Edward P. Alexander, University of Delaware, discussed (with sometimes contrary opinions) such issues as internships, museum-site training, and employment prospects. A responsive audience discussion followed.

Serving with the program chairman in the arrangement of the sessions for the fortieth annual meeting were the following diligent, inspired members of the Committee on Program: Amos E. Simpson, University of Southwestern Louisiana, vice-chairman for non–U. S. history; William T. Alderson, Jr., American Association for State and Local History; William S. Coker, University of West Florida; Robert F. Durden, Duke University; Willard B. Gatewood, Jr., University of Arkansas, Fayetteville; Arrell M. Gibson, University of Oklahoma; Jane DeHart Mathews, University of North Carolina at Greensboro; Walter Rundell, Jr., University of Maryland, College Park; Arvarh E. Strickland, University of Missouri–Columbia; and Harold D. Woodman, Purdue University. All members of the Committee on Program, especially the chairman, are greatly indebted to President Fite for his generous advice and encouragement and to Secretary-Treasurer Bennett H. Wall, a tower of strength during the long two-year process of preparing the program. For the usual outstanding production of the annual meeting we may all thank Secretary-Treasurer Wall, his administrative assistant, Neva Wall, convention coordinator Don R. Byrnes, and the other members of the convention staff.

Book Reviews

Southerners and Other Americans. By Grady McWhiney. (New York: Basic Books, c. 1973. Pp. xiv, 206. $7.95.)

Professor McWhiney's first graduate-school seminar paper, a splendid analysis of "The Ghostly Legend of the Ku Klux Klan," is included in this collection of twelve essays, half of which have not previously been published. It is also one of the best, revealing a healthy skepticism toward received truths, a good eye for an interesting story, and an ability to get a lot out of relatively few sources. Polished and revised by McWhiney's first seminar instructor, the late Francis Simkins, it sensibly shows that blacks during Reconstruction were quite properly frightened more by guns and threats of violence than they were by the thought that Klansmen were ghosts of Confederate dead.

The iconoclastic spirit infusing McWhiney's first essay is happily present in most of his subsequent writings, at least in the dozen essays of this volume, which span more than two decades of scholarship. In one way or another several of them do battle with the belief that the Old South was a unique civilization. Sensitive to the forces in American culture that have bound and homogenized citizens of all regions, McWhiney informs several essays with this insight. For example, in his well-known essay on Alabama Whigs he argues against the notion that party division in the state followed class lines. In another piece, on the morals of antebellum West Pointers, he writes that, contrary to its claims, the academy did not turn out officers and gentlemen with morals different from those of other Americans.

These and most of the other essays—including a piece on the coming of the Civil War, an analysis of Jefferson Davis's selection of his generals, Grant's military education, and the reasons for the Confederate defeat—deal with mid-nineteenth-century history. A previously unpublished essay on the proscription of black rights in the thirty-five years after the Civil War is strangely uninformed by the debate brought on by C. Vann Woodward's *The Strange Career of Jim Crow.*

Two essays deal with twentieth-century topics. The best one, apparently another graduate-school paper, is a fine analysis of the socialist movement and the 1912 election in Louisiana. Published in this journal twenty years ago, it deftly traces the rise of "rustic radicalism" and intelligently explores the relationship between the labor movement and radical politics in Louisiana. Considerably less impressive is the more recent, and previously unpublished, piece entitled "Black History or Propaganda?" This essay, which already appears remarkably dated, is an angry reply to the black-studies movement of the late sixties. Abandoning the detachment and gentle touch of the earlier essays, McWhiney replaces skepticism with a sledgehammer that he uses to demolish an obscure teachers' handbook on black history. One suspects that this essay will be read in later years (as, indeed, many will read it now) as an example of the perturbation with which many white historians received the black-studies movement.

Apart from the suggestion in some of the essays that the South's presumed uniqueness needs to be questioned more rigorously because of the common culture and history Americans share, there is no unifying theme that ties the essays together. *Southerners and Other Americans* stands, then, as a collection of twelve pieces of uneven value. The best of them were previously published.

University of Virginia PAUL M. GASTON

Anglo-American Politics 1660–1775: The Relationship Between Parties in England and Colonial America. By Alison Gilbert Olson. (New York and Oxford: Oxford University Press, 1973. Pp. xvi, 192. $7.50.)

Professor Olson describes the diverse conditions of the first British empire out of which developed Anglo-American political parties. She argues that several conditions were important to the acceptance of parties as part of the political process of the empire. The conditions were the growth of legislative power relative to the executive, the multiplication of interest groups seeking political outlets in the colonial legislatures, the change in the nature of issues over which men divided, a corresponding change in attitudes towards dissent, and the changing idea of government in relation to the communities. Her interpretation differs from that of Caroline Robbins.

She recognizes that Namieristic studies are essential to a definitive analysis of colonial political parties, but she disclaims that her study is Namieristic or definitive. Rather, she sees her book as a suggestive essay that will encourage further studies in the history of early American politics and the American Revolution.

In the first fifteen years of the Restoration, according to her, provincial authorities were left free to suppress local opponents, while opposition leaders searched for legitimate means to operate within the imperial political framework. The Navigation Act of 1673, which required customs officials to be sent to the colonies, provided potential rivals to the governors around which their enemies could rally. Thus, Charles II contributed to the divisions within the colonies and the weakening of the governors. This was particularly true after the Exclusion Crisis, when the king depended on customs duties for revenue. Edward Randolph's suggestion that the crown ought increasingly to favor the moderates against the ruling classes in the colonies was accepted. In appointing enemies of the local governors to office, dissent was legitimized. Michael G. Hall disagrees with the view that royal policy built up loyal but weaker and less organized groups in each colony. He concludes that the Massachusetts moderate party actually disintegrated under the Dominion of New England.

After the Glorious Revolution, the author asserts, the colonial governors were able to create Court parties to support their policies except in North Carolina and Virginia. In doing this, the governors strengthened their associations with their British patrons. She should reconsider the excluding of North Carolina, because several governors there had Court parties. For example, Governor Tryon could not have quelled the Regulators without loyal support.

The author believes that the importance of the 1750s lies in the growing estrangement between English and American parties. The failure of the governors to develop long-run connections at Whitehall emphasized the futility of attempting to revive the workable transatlantic partisan connections that had flourished between 1689 and 1714. The crown's decisions in 1763 and afterwards are important as major turning points in colonial policy. The gulf between the Anglo-American parties was further widened by the Stamp Act of 1765, which revealed the power of popular pressure groups in the colonies. The weakness of English officials in the face of colonial mobs and the ignominious treatment of colonial agents forced American politicians to rethink their positions. Their conclusions eventually led them to the founding of our nation.

This well-written book is recommended reading for all Anglo-American historians and political scientists. Once this book is in a paperback edition, it should prove to be a useful teaching tool.

Campbell College VERNON O. STUMPF

Red, White, and Black: The Peoples of Early America. By Gary B. Nash. (Englewood Cliffs, N. J.: Prentice-Hall, c. 1974. Pp. xviii, 350. Paper, $5.95; cloth, $9.95.)

To make United States colonial history "more understandable to an ethnically, socially, and intellectually diverse undergraduate audience" (p. xvi), Professor Nash embarked upon readings in anthropological and ethnohistorical studies and African and Latin American history to widen his perspectives about the lives of Indian, African, and European peoples who inhabited colonial America. By focusing upon "social and cultural *process* and *change*," Professor Nash draws upon his readings to write a "history of the *peoples* of eastern North America," not another Eurocentric colonial American history (p. 4).

European colonists chose to acquire wealth by the production of goods and the acquisition of land, achieving their goals "at a terrible price in exploitation and human suffering, enslavement and alienation" (p. 319). White colonial leaders realized that a nonassimilationist policy permitted the appropriation of Indian lands and exploitation of African labor. If Indians were Christianized and educated, they would be rivals for agricultural land, and where blacks outnumbered whites, the implications of Christianity and learning were dangerous to the dominant whites. To prevent unified Indian resistance, white colonial leaders used the principle of dividing the Native Americans until tribal strength had been undermined. European colonists rationalized that Indians and Africans were so unlike themselves that absorption of those culturally different peoples into a common society was undesirable.

White Americans treated with disdain the African peoples upon whom they depended for labor, while Indians who were capable of warring upon and killing white settlers were reluctantly respected. Such behavior was due to the chattel condition of the blacks and the military strength of the Indians. Ironically, however, the African people who were "enslaved, degraded and despised survived and flourished demographically . . ." (p. 313), while Indians who maintained their autonomy saw their people gradually diminish in number. European admiration of the Indians' "hospitality, generosity, bravery and the spirit of mutual caring" (p. 318) did not save Indians from the devastating effects of epidemic diseases, alcohol, and war, which eroded their cultural and political independence.

Comparative history is used effectively by Professor Nash. He contrasts demographic and social change in colonial America to similar trends in other British, French, Spanish, and Portuguese possessions in the Western Hemisphere. Some scholars of Indian history still might wish that Professor Nash had compared Spanish Indian policy after 1609 toward the Pueblos, Apaches, and Navajos with the English and French experience with eastern Indian groups. Others might wish that the author had devoted more attention to the power and importance of the Indian tribes north of the Ohio River who were sought as allies by the Iroquois during and after the 1750s. The lack of intertribal unity north of the Ohio River cannot be explained solely by analysis of British and French Indian policies. Too many of the tribes of the Old Northwest in the eighteenth century remembered the Iroquois raiding parties which swept through the forests in the seventeenth century, driving other Indian tribes from their domains to defensive villages in the Fox and Wisconsin river valleys.

The question to which Professor Nash does not address himself is whether or not there were viable alternatives to the policies adopted by European political administrators toward Indian and black peoples. Scholars of recent Indian history conclude that the assimilationist policies of the United States government destroyed Indian culture. Correctly, Professor Nash states that the colonials rejected cultural absorption of the Indians. If, however, both nonassimilation and assimilation ruined Indian culture, what alternatives other than cultural, social, and political isolation remained for Indian tribes? For a scholar searching for new facts, this volume contains few. But historians and students looking for a book that differs from the traditional colonial histories will find it challenging.

Purdue University DONALD J. BERTHRONG

From Prescription to Persuasion: Manipulation of Eighteenth Century Virginia Economy. By John C. Rainbolt. (Port Washington, N. Y., and London: Kennikat Press, 1974. Pp. x, 218. $8.95.)

The thesis of this volume holds that the provincial leadership in seventeenth-century Virginia (inadvertently printed as eighteenth century on the title page) deliberately sought to mold the economic and social life of the colony, first to conform to the mercantilistic theories of the empire and later to devise a system of provincial mercantilism. In the expectation of gaining greater social stability, they advanced projects calling for diversification of the economy, promotion of towns, exploration of the West, and opposition to large proprietary grants. Although these were major concerns, the effort of the leadership "elite to transform the colony's economic and social condition between 1650 and the early eighteenth century was a critical factor in most major political decisions and disputes" (p. 7). The early leadership (1650–1676), operating from a weakened base, failed largely because of the "leadership techniques" of prescription in the form of burdensome taxes, tobacco controls, and trade regulations, which were resisted by fellow colonists and were insufficiently reinforced by the home government. The result was rebellion. The second period (1676–1710) saw a change in the style of leadership, involving greater participation and consent of the governed. Following Bacon's Rebellion "economic innovation was now offered as the route toward provincial autonomy rather than an expression of the integrated interests of crown and colony" (p. 100). The goals were scarcely altered, but the new rationale was a portent of significance in the coming break with the crown and in the principles embraced by the new frame of government.

Professor Rainbolt supports this thesis with closely marshaled and exhaustive detail. He makes a good case. But beyond the central theme there are other insights of considerable merit. The discussion of the underlying currents in Bacon's Rebellion, the motivations of various provincial leaders, governors, and units of the royal bureaucracy are particularly helpful. The weakest point comes in his projection of the effect of the shift in leadership style beyond the years covered by the main body of the study. At one point Rainbolt observes: "The town act which resulted from a combination of a weak governor and a depressed economy was . . . the last major effort at government-induced diversification until the closing years of the colonial period" (p. 157). In fact, the *Statutes at Large of Virginia*, the *Journals of the House of Burgesses*, the *Virginia Gazette*, and the personal correspondence of planters and politicians reflect numerous proposals for and some success with schemes for an expanded diversification of the economy.

Beyond this the scholarship is impeccable, and the book will be indispensable to any future examination of seventeenth-century colonial economic or political history. A review of political style in the colonial period, its origin and its effect, is a contribution of considerable importance which should serve as a distinguished model for other such studies. Unfortunately, they will not come from the pen of John C. Rainbolt, whose untimely death occurred in October 1973.

Washburn University C. ROBERT HAYWOOD

A History of French Louisiana. Volume I: *The Reign of Louis XIV, 1698–1715.* By Marcel Giraud. Translated by Joseph C. Lambert. (Baton Rouge: Louisiana State University Press, c. 1974. Pp. xvi, 398. $15.00.)

When the Presses Universitaires de France brought out the first volume of Marcel Giraud's history of French Louisiana in 1953 scholars throughout the world paid homage to the solid research of the brilliant professor. Here was a worthy modern historian who had drunk deeply from the fountains of such notables as LePage du Pratz, Villiers du Terrage, Delanglez, and Parkman.

Giraud notes the contributions of these pioneers, but he is more at home examining the original documents located in archives and libraries throughout the French-speaking world. He seems equally at home in Paris or Nantes, in Quebec or the "Newb" in Chicago. Where the intrepid missionaries, *coureurs de bois,* or French colonial administrators left their records, Giraud has tirelessly explored them. The result, as seen in the first of four volumes translated into English, is stupendous.

Joseph C. Lambert's translation is careful, and for scholars who are not at home in French he has rendered yeoman service. If the prose seems at times stilted, Lambert has little cause for concern; the original French is hardly a masterpiece of concise and literary history. And this is probably the major criticism of the book: its style is heavy.

Although Giraud "revised and corrected" the original French edition, as the publisher points out, the omission of such solid studies as Charles O'Neill's *Church and State in French Colonial Louisiana* (Yale University Press, 1966), weakens his aim for complete grasp of the subject.

Giraud's introductions from the French and English editions explain his self-imposed limitations (pp. xi–xii): "Only limited space will be given to such matters as relations with the English colonies, the strife with the Spanish crown, and the conflict between France and England over domination of the Mississippi Basin, thus reducing the need for documentation from foreign sources."

In examining events within France, Canada, and Louisiana itself Giraud has rendered a solid contribution, and scholars should look forward to the appearance of the following volumes in the monumental study of French Louisiana by one of the greatest scholars of our day.

University of Alabama, Birmingham JACK D. L. HOLMES

Dr. John Mitchell: The Man Who Made the Map of North America. By Edmund Berkeley and Dorothy Smith Berkeley. (Chapel Hill: University of North Carolina Press, c. 1974. Pp. xx, 283. $12.50.)

This handsome volume from the University of North Carolina Press rescues Dr. John Mitchell (1711–1768) from undeserved obscurity. Most professional historians know Mitchell only as the maker of the "Map of the British Colonies in North America . . ." (1755), which was used by peace commissioners in 1782 and 1783 to define the boundaries of the newly independent United States, and used subsequently to reconcile boundary disputes.

While the title indicates the source of John Mitchell's public recognition, for the most part this book deals with the limited but active world of early-eighteenth-century natural science, with its main focus resting on botany. That remarkable, largely unstructured network involving scientific societies, publications, botanical gardens, and collectors was sustained by an extensive correspondence among European, British, and American enthusiasts, among whom was Dr. John Mitchell.

Born in Virginia and trained as a doctor of physic at Edinburgh, Mitchell practiced as a physician in his native province until his health forced him to move to England. He devoted more of his life to natural science than to medicine. His familiarity with exotic species from his native America made him especially valued as a correspondent and as a source of specimens and seeds for his English friends. His special studies—on the opossum, Virginia pines, skin pigmentation, "yellow fever," and potash, among others—were much valued by his contemporaries, who elected him a fellow in the Royal Society of London. Through influential friends—Franklin, Bartram, and Colden in America; Collinson, the Earl of Bute, Catesby, the Duke of Argyll in Britain—Mitchell was in touch with the main scientific currents of his time.

The Berkeleys, whose previous works on John Clayton and Dr. Alexander Garden have made them authorities on eighteenth-century American botanists, have accomplished an impressive research effort in ferreting out Dr. Mitchell's story. Unfortunately, little is known of John Mitchell the man; only the sketchiest portrait emerges from the meager sources. It is a pity since these hints suggest an attractive person.

Perhaps the least successful portion of the book, ironically, deals with Mitchell the mapmaker. Not until page 175 will the reader find a discussion of Mitchell's cartographic efforts. These appear to have been motivated largely by a conviction that the French were encroaching upon legitimate British claims in the interior parts of North America. Why Mitchell should feel so keenly about the French claims is not explained convincingly, but it is known that Mitchell made his 1755 map at the urging of Lord Halifax and the Board of Trade in order to enhance the British position in negotiations with France. Since it is difficult for the reader to follow the detailed discussion of Mitchell's map without a copy to refer to, the Berkeleys should have identified place names more precisely and, in the process, they should have corrected some misinformation that now stands unchallenged in the narrative. Nevertheless, this is a worthy study. We are the richer for knowing Dr. John Mitchell, by profession a physician, by inclination a botanist and natural scientist, and almost by chance a mapmaker and shaper of nations.

University of Akron GEORGE W. KNEPPER

Maryland and the Empire, 1773: The Antilon–First Citizen Letters. Edited by Peter S. Onuf. (Baltimore and London: Johns Hopkins University Press, c. 1974. Pp. xii, 236. $10.00.)

Few debates reveal the ideological dimensions of the American Revolution better than the eight "Antilon–First Citizen" letters, which first appeared in the *Maryland Gazette* in 1773. This new edition is a welcome addition to the growing list of recently published pamphlet and newspaper literature of the Revolution.

Governor Robert Eden's 1770 fee proclamation sparked the debate between Daniel Dulany, "Antilon," and Charles Carroll, "First Citizen." As a result of a conflict between the Maryland house and council the inspection law had lapsed. Eden issued a proclamation which established the same fee schedule as called for in the old law. He did so, he said, to protect the people from exorbitant fees. Delegates replied that the governor had denied them the right to be taxed by their own representatives. Around these issues of prerogative and taxation, then, the debate centered.

Dulany supported Eden's actions. Already a polished pamphleteer, Dulany had opposed the Stamp Act. Now a defender of the government, he maintained that the governor had the constitutional right to issue such proclamations. Both the law and history supported his position, he argued. Carroll, later to achieve lasting fame as a signer of the Declaration of Independence, took the more popular view. As throughly educated as Dulany, Carroll showed the same breadth of knowledge. He believed that the proclamation created new fees and thus a form of taxation. In the absence of a law, he suggested that officials should bring suit for their fees and allow juries to decide the proper amount.

Dulany answered that in the past all three branches of government had individually set fees. Because taxes could be established only by representatives and since branches other than lower houses had fixed fees Dulany was convinced that such charges were not taxes. Carroll brushed aside Dulany's examples, arguing that his precedents were exceptions to basic principles.

The letters make ponderous reading. They have the dry character of legal briefs, which is not surprising since both authors were lawyers. How much impact the letters between two intellectual elites had upon Maryland is questionable. Few people probably read them; fewer still understood them.

Onuf does an admirable editorial job, and his long introduction helps to put the letters in their proper setting. If he had indicated the impact of the letters upon Maryland, it would have proved helpful. Nonetheless, the letters show the distinctive character of some arguments colonists used to support their points of view.

University of Wisconsin, Oshkosh ROBERT J. CHAFFIN

Self-Evident Truths: Being a Discourse on the Origins & Development of the First Principles of American Government—Popular Sovereignty, Natural Rights, and Balance & Separation of Powers. By Paul K. Conkin. (Bloomington and London: Indiana University Press, c. 1974. Pp. xii, 211. $7.95.)

Paul Conkin's latest book demonstrates once again that he is about the most versatile as well as the most clearheaded of American intellectual historians. In *Self-Evident Truths* he turns his attention to eighteenth-century political ideas, and while his book contains nothing startlingly new, it is distinguished by the exceptional clarity with which certain first principles of American government are elucidated and expounded. Conkin is a historian of ideas in the Lovejoy tradition. Great nuclear ideas like natural rights have an inner life of their own which carries their meaning over time, and thus their role in history is to be understood by philosophical analysis rather than by contextual analysis of forces and events that surround them. This formalistic approach is refreshing at a time when the critical political ideas of the Revolutionary era have been engulfed by ideology.

The "self-evident truths" Conkin studies are popular sovereignty, natural rights, and separation of powers. One might question whether the third conformed to the logic of self-evidence and also whether federalism should have been omitted from the first principles. Each nuclear idea is first examined in the light of its origin and development in Western thought, then in American Revolutionary discourse, and finally in its constitutional implementation. The biographies of the ideas are traced through the classic political theorists from Plato and Polybius through Locke, Montesquieu, and Vattel. This is a bit textbooky, and the course of political theories known to modern scholars is not the same as the history of these ideas known to the Founding Fathers. As Conkin recognizes, they never heard of Althusius, seldom read Hobbes, and may have been more influenced by *Cato's Letters* than by Locke's *Second Essay.* They got as much of their political doctrine from historians, moral philosophers, and polemicists as from the classic theorists. There is then, despite the rewards of the formalistic approach, a certain gap between what is in Conkin's mind and what was in the mind of the Founding Fathers. The analysis of the American development and institutionalization of the ideas is perceptive and refined. Ambiguities are noted, subtle distinctions are drawn, and the logical relationships among the ideas are carefully worked out. Conkin's brief but deft account of the evolution of separation of powers out of mixed-government doctrine and the ultimate American resolution in the new doctrine of checks and balances is a model of its kind. He seems to think, however, that mixed government was achieved in attenuated form in the first state constitutions, an assessment that goes along with his exaggerated estimate of John Adams's political theory. But it is not easy to find fault with any of Conkin's interpretations.

In a short epilogue Conkin reflects on the changes wrought by two centuries of history on the first principles of government. While there has been some erosion, even some displacement, he is impressed by the capacity of the principles to adapt to change and survive. Institutionally, he remarks, Americans are still very close to the world of the Founding Fathers, but they lack the fathers' concern with normative theory and first principles, to which he urges a return. But what has changed, of course, are not primarily the principles but the moral and intellectual foundations that supported them and made normative theory possible. One wishes that Conkin would now turn his fine philosophical mind to the grave and difficult problem of putting new moral and intellectual foundations under the old principles.

University of Virginia MERRILL D. PETERSON

Paine. By David Freeman Hawke. (New York and other cities: Harper and Row, c. 1974, Pp. x, 500. $15.00.)

David Freeman Hawke's biography of Thomas Paine is an appropriate bicentennial commemoration of Paine's arrival at Philadelphia from England in 1774. Hawke's biography, the most satisfactory yet published, is one of three Paine biographies appearing this year in the flood of writings marking the bicentennial years of the Age of Revolution. As the author of a valuable study of the Declaration of Independence, a sprightly biography of Benjamin Rush, and a highly regarded textbook on the history of colonial and Revolutionary America, Professor Hawke is eminently qualified to write of the life, times, and work of Thomas Paine.

Regrettably though, Hawke's biography falls somewhat short of being a definitive treatment, but perhaps there never can be such an account. The difficulty lies not with the biographer but with the personality of Paine and the nature of his writings. Hawke perceptively observes of Paine (p. 107) that "he was flawed and often so were his writings." Yet the Paine biographer is confronted with more than a flawed personality. The stage upon which the drama of Paine's life was played included three countries—England, the United States, and France—each of which during his lifetime was undergoing revolutionary change in thought, politics, and economics, change extremely difficult for the biographer to narrate and analyze. Moreover, the bits and pieces of Paine's saga have been collected and scrambled by previous biographers, some hostile and vindictive, some uncritically adulatory and sympathetic. Paine was dead for nearly a century before the life by Moncure Conway, the first substantial biography, was published in 1892. Joel Barlow in 1809, shortly after Paine's death, counseled that it was not the time to write his biography and observed that Paine's writings were the best life. Wise as this observation may have been, the reader must remember that Paine's writings, all polemical in nature, were often flawed by invective and the passion of the moment, as Hawke reminds us. The critic of a Paine biography must also recollect that many of Paine's papers have been destroyed or lost like his bones and that there is still no definitive edition of his extant writings.

Despite the difficulties besetting the biographer of Paine, Professor Hawke has written a successful biography. Although Crane Brinton's masterful essay in the *Dictionary of American Biography* should never be overlooked nor Harry Hayden Clark's useful introduction to *Thomas Paine: Representative Selections* (1944), the only scholarly book-length life of Paine prior to 1974 with which Hawke's can be compared is Alfred Owen Aldridge's *Man of Reason* (1959). Hawke's book is better written and livelier, and it gives a more comprehensive understanding of the times. While Hawke has an especially good account of Paine's confrontation with Edmund Burke, his treatment of Paine's role in the history of British radicalism should have been expanded. But all things considered, we are indebted to Hawke for a fair and judicious as well as sympathetic biography. It is indeed a timely book, for when we ponder the terrible abuse of government power threatening us today, Thomas Paine's lifelong rebellion against the unwarranted use of that power over the individual must always be instructive and inspiring.

Davidson College MALCOLM LESTER

Free Men All: The Personal Liberty Laws of the North, 1780–1861. By Thomas D. Morris. (Baltimore and London: Johns Hopkins University Press, c. 1974. Pp. xiv, 253. $12.50.)

Thomas Morris terms his book "a study of the ways people translated into law the presumption that all persons are born free and cannot be deprived of that freedom except by due process of law, even though they might be slaves" (p. x). Specifically, he is concerned with those statutes known collectively as the personal liberty laws, which utilized such legal processes as trial by jury and the writs of habeas corpus and replevin to deal with cases of fugitive slavery and to protect free blacks from kidnapping and enslavement. His study is confined to five representative states—Pennsylvania, New York, Massachusetts, Ohio, and Wisconsin—though an appendix provides a checklist of personal liberty laws passed in other states.

In tracing the development of personal liberty laws during the eight decades preceding the Civil War, Morris emphasizes the difficult constitutional questions faced by proponents of such legislation and the extent to which compromise and caution influenced the shaping of such laws, particularly in the early years. The commitment to the notion that all men are free until proven otherwise by due process was "bounded not only by ardent unionism but by the imperatives and uncertainties of federalism, by a continued recognition of the lawful holding of persons as property, and by a sometimes shortsighted appraisal of social reality" (p. 24). Even in the 1840s and 1850s personal liberty laws remained an essentially moderate approach to the slavery question. Both noncooperation and interposition were efforts to follow what Morris calls a "middle way between revolution and submission" (p. 159). They were part of the larger strategy of containment of slavery. Not until 1859 did a movement emerge calling upon the states to repudiate their obligation under the fugitive-slave clause of the Constitution. But moderates, joined by conservatives, were successful in defeating such an attempt to make the personal liberty laws an engine of radical abolitionism.

Morris makes no extravagant claims for the importance of his study in explaining the sectional crisis and Civil War. He concedes that the territorial question was of primary significance in precipitating the crisis and reinforces this view by demonstrating that many of the personal liberty laws were passed in response to issues raised by the territorial question. Nor does he exaggerate the extent of the northern commitment to freedom. The personal liberty laws, he observes, "are only one side of a complex set of legal systems—systems which reflected both idealism and meanness" (p. x). Having chosen to focus on the idealism, Morris provides us with a balanced, comprehensive, essentially factual account of one aspect of "a continuous, and richly varied, commitment to the idea of liberty under law" (p. 218).

Louisiana State University ANNE C. LOVELAND

The American Territorial System. Edited by John Porter Bloom. (Athens, Ohio: Ohio University Press, c. 1973. Pp. xvi, 248. $10.00.)

In November 1969 the National Archives and Records Service sponsored the first conference on the history of the territories. The papers then presented are reprinted here. The editor conceived the book "as an introduction to the subject [of territorial history] and an indication of its richness and its importance . . ." (p. xiii). The book also served as a tribute to the late Clarence E. Carter, veteran scholar and the editor of *The Territorial Papers of the United States.*

Divided into five major sections, each part included an editor's introduction, two short articles, a "Discussion of Sources" (often more valuable than the papers themselves), and, for several of the sections, the commentator's views and a summary of discussion that followed a particular session.

The first section, "The Northwest Ordinance," led off with Arthur Bestor, who traced the development of a consensus among national leaders concerned with the public domain that the territories "would receive . . . not only every privilege of republican self-government but also unqualified admission to the Union . . ." (p. 32) on the same basis in every respect as the original states. Robert F. Berkhofer, Jr., perceived the Northwest Ordinance as "the culmination of American thinking about the nature of a colonial system for a republican empire" (p. 45).

In the second section, "The Territories and the Congress," Jo Tice Bloom discussed the problems and politics of "Early [Territorial] Delegates in the House of Representatives," while Robert W. Johannsen took the reader to the Senate with Stephen A. Douglas. Johannsen argued convincingly for Douglas as a concerned advocate of all the territories and expansionism.

The third section dealt with the "Territorial Courts of the Far West," providing an interesting debate on this neglected subject between historian John D. W. Guice and lawyer William L. Knecht. In the fourth part, "The Territories: Land and Politics," Thomas G. Alexander examined the land survey system in the Rocky Mountain West after 1870, while Kenneth N. Owens explored western territorial politics. Owens observed the emergence of a one-party pattern in the territories as they moved toward statehood.

The last section, "The Territories in the Twentieth Century," opened with Robert W. Larson's paper on Theodore Roosevelt's protégé, Governor George Curry of New Mexico Territory; then Robert R. Robbins looked at "United States Territories in Mid-Century." This view of the Caribbean and Pacific territories and the international questions that involved the United Nations led directly to the final address by Harrison Loesch of the Interior Department, "The American Territories of Today and Tomorrow."

The papers themselves were of uneven quality, with this reviewer most impressed by those of Bestor, Johannsen, Owens, and Robbins. To be fair, however, all the papers suffered from the mandatory brevity imposed by their oral delivery at the conference. Yet they provided exactly what the editor of the volume hoped they would: an *introduction* to the subject. It is not a *comprehensive* view of the territorial system.

Graduate students and other scholars whose pathways take them into some phase of territorial history are beholden to Leonard Rapport, Charles E. South, Marion M. Johnson, and John P. Heard, who expertly discussed the available sources. This may be the most important contribution of the volume and as such will be most welcome on the research shelf.

University of Akron ROBERT H. JONES

Party and Faction in American Politics: The House of Representatives, 1789–1801. By Rudolph M. Bell. *Contributions in American History*, Number 32. (Westport, Conn., and London: Greenwood Press, c. 1973. Pp. xiv, 311. $13.95.)

Whatever its problems and pitfalls, the use of quantification by historians has affected historical scholarship in two beneficial ways: 1) statistical analyses have often confirmed what earlier scholars had hypothesized from less complete evidence, and 2) occasionally these newer studies have overturned traditional beliefs and stimulated scholars to see the past from different perspectives. In many respects this study by Rudolph Bell does both.

Bell has analyzed over five hundred roll-call votes cast in the House of Representatives from 1789 to 1801 to show how the rising two-party system gradually enveloped the more fluid, issue-oriented factions which characterized the House during its early years. Dividing the majority of roll calls into four general issue groups (the extent of federal authority, the West, economic policy, and foreign policy), he demonstrates how each general category brought forth temporary though relatively stable legislative factions bent on promoting rival policy alternatives. These issue-oriented factions were marked by their nonsectional compositions and their lack of cohesiveness from issue to issue. Thus men could (and did) join each other in one faction on one day while voting on one issue, yet found themselves in different camps the next day when a different issue was introduced.

Party discipline began to replace the looser factional system by the mid-1790s but, claims Bell, at a price. Instead of being primarily concerned with issues and policy formulation, the emerging political parties, Bell believes, were more interested in winning offices and therefore found it prudent to appeal to a more heterogeneous group than had earlier factions. Thus, states Bell, legislative innovation and serious responses to issues by elected representatives disappeared almost as soon as parties became predominant. It was the earlier factions and not the evolving but ideologically bereft parties which fleshed out the Constitution and established direction for the young republic.

Bell's analysis is certain to excite scholars and stimulate controversy. Some will feel that he is too hard on political parties, that their pursuit of power was and is for the expressed purpose of altering previous policy decisions, that they provide continuity while simultaneously giving opportunity for ideological conflict within parties if not always between them. Others will charge that Bell has been unfair to the Jeffersonians in that many of their differences with Federalism were too subtle for Bell's methodology to detect and also that Jeffersonian negativism was in itself a rather consistent policy which most Republicans sincerely believed was best for the infant nation. Concentration on the House of Representatives alone, still others will note, gives Bell too narrow a lens to study the essence of the evolving party system.

Though each comment has *some* validity, Bell's work should stand as a thought-provoking study which deserves scrutiny by students of American politics far beyond the Federalist era. Indeed, it is always refreshing to see scholarly precision and bold interpretations so nicely married in a stimulating volume.

University of Tennessee, Knoxville WILLIAM BRUCE WHEELER

Emergence of the Presidential Nominating Convention, 1789–1832. By James S. Chase. (Urbana, Chicago, and London: University of Illinois Press, c. 1973. Pp. xviii, 332. $8.95.)

Few parts of the American body politic, as it limps towards the last quarter of the twentieth century, are more frequently pronounced to be ailing, even moribund, than our party system. No aspect of that system has been less satisfactory of late than the national nominating convention; but it is hard to imagine the parties of the past functioning without it, and it is by no means clear that it can be dispensed with even now.

These facts add significance to the work of Professor Chase who here gives us the prenatal history of the nominating convention in some detail. He examines, of course, the evolution of the Republican congressional caucus from 1800 to the fatal year 1824, shows the development of several devices for party or factional nominations in the states, treats the party realignment in the administration of John Quincy Adams with considerable attention to the rise of anti-Masonry, and concludes with the successive nominating conventions, triumphantly unveiled, of 1831 and 1832.

He has done this clearly and well, has firmly avoided digression, and has successfully digested impressive quantities of manuscript, newspaper, and secondary material. This reviewer could have wished for a more detailed anatomization of "King Caucus," whom Professor Chase rather downgrades. He emphasizes that the original function of the caucus was the choice of vice-presidential running mates for the recognized party leader. He does not think that it could have imposed Crawford on the country, had it nominated him instead of Monroe in 1816; and he finds the caucus a joke in 1820. Under these circumstances its relative vitality four years later appears mildly surprising.

Professor Chase is highly informative about state legislative caucuses, "mixed caucuses" (with representation from districts where the party was without legislators), and the early conventions in New York and Pennsylvania. He shows that the idea of a national convention was launched, and abandoned, by Thomas Ritchie in the early 1820s. He is good on the administration of the second Adams and brings out the ironic fact that Andrew Jackson shared, though not incurably, Adams's principled dislike of political partisanship. The genesis of anti-Masonry is especially well done, and so is the treatment of the conventions which nominated William Wirt, Henry Clay, and Martin Van Buren.

On some matters of detail Professor Chase may, like all of us, be faulted. Clay, for example, did not share in the "common and intensive [*sic*] dislike of Crawford" attributed to the Georgian's opponents in 1824 (p. 43). It is doubtful if "distrust of central power and the glorification of the states' rights . . . served the interests [as distinguished from the prejudices] of most . . . [Virginians]" (p. 47). Contemporaries would not, I think, have ascribed a merely "moderate nationalism" to Calhoun in 1824 (p. 55); nor was George M. Dallas a senator at that time. John

McLean cannot be counted as a cabinet member under Adams (p. 75), since the postmaster general had not yet been accorded that status. And that hard-shelled Federalist James Kent would probably have boggled at being called a "disciple" (p. 223) of Henry Clay.

More serious is the bibliographical omission of the Adams papers, which would have strengthened one of the best parts of Professor Chase's volume. In any case, it is a work which belongs on the shelf with those of Noble Cunningham, Richard McCormick, and Robert Remini.

Auburn University JOSEPH H. HARRISON, JR.

The Presidency of George Washington. By Forrest McDonald. (Lawrence, Manhattan, and Wichita: University Press of Kansas, c. 1974. Pp. xiv, 210. $10.00.)

Like everything else Forrest McDonald has written, this book has real strengths and weaknesses. It is intelligent, knowledgeable, incisive, highly capable in its lucid handling of complicated financial and economic problems, and well written to the point of being entertaining. Yet it also suffers from the workings of an overly fertile imagination, a perverse desire to be clever and to shock rather than to be insightful or thoughtful, and an infuriating tendency to make wild generalizations, and sometimes even important ones, on the basis of no evidence or on research that cannot be checked out and verified.

This volume covers much the same ground that Joseph Charles did in *The Origins of the American Party System*, but there are important differences. Whereas Charles was hostile to Alexander Hamilton and denigrated George Washington, McDonald makes a hero out of the Treasury secretary, is biased against Jefferson and almost all other southern planters, and is somewhat more gentle with Washington, whom he views as "indispensable, but only for what he was, not for what he did" (p. 186). More important, in dealing with political developments during Washington's administrations McDonald not only describes national issues as does Charles, but he also attempts to show how these national issues did and did not relate to state politics. This is a significant and healthy departure from the tendency of students of the 1790s to disregard the fact that state politics continued to be very important even after the adoption of the Constitution and to ignore local issues and alignments. By trying to confront the elusive question of how state and national politics interacted during the 1790s McDonald has focused on an important but unexplored area of the political history of the early national period. While it is doubtful that many of McDonald's glib assertions will pass the test of close scrutiny, he has nonetheless raised a number of meaningful questions about how politics operated outside the national arena, particularly in regard to the role of the Democratic-Republican societies and popular sentiment on the Jay Treaty.

The book concludes with an interesting "Historiographical and

Bibliographical Note." In it McDonald observes that his *We the People: The Economic Origins of the Constitution* (1958) "was widely praised, in no small measure because many reviewers erroneously read it as an effort to restore the sainted Founding Fathers to the holy niches from which Beard had removed them." He then goes on to argue that his *E Pluribus Unum: The Formation of the American Republic, 1776–1790* (1965) was coolly received because in it he "attempted to show that the Founders were not only preoccupied with getting rich, but also drank intoxicants and not infrequently violated the Seventh Commandment" (p. 197). This comment reveals a great deal about McDonald's view of human nature, and it also raises the very relevant and ultimately damning historiographical question of why it was that those historians of the 1950s who believed in an "idealistic" interpretation of the Constitution so enthusiastically embraced *We the People.*

State University of New York, Buffalo RICHARD E. ELLIS

The Struggle for Neutrality: Franco-American Diplomacy During the Federalist Era. By Albert Hall Bowman. (Knoxville: University of Tennessee Press, c. 1974. Pp. xviii, 460. $13.50.)

Drawing on French and American sources, Professor Bowman traces the course of American policy toward France as well as French policy toward the United States from 1793 to 1800. His examination of French policy will interest American historians looking for a wider perspective on the development of United States foreign policy during the Federalist era.

Bowman's interpretation of Jay's Treaty, "the central event of the Federalist period" (p. viii), follows the French view of the treaty as a deliberate attempt by the Federalists in Washington's administration to undermine the Franco-American alliance, and thus he sees the Directory's harsh reaction to American policy as entirely justified. Most significant is his view that Talleyrand, far from supporting the Directory's belligerent policy following Jay's Treaty, was the leading advocate of accommodation. According to Bowman it was chiefly Talleyrand's efforts that paved the way for the settlement of Franco-American difficulties in the Convention of 1800, next to the Anglo-American treaty of 1783 "the most fortunate peace settlement ever negotiated by the United States" (pp. 434–35).

In contrast to his treatment of the French side of Franco-American relations, Bowman's evaluation of American policy leaves much to be desired. United States foreign policy is viewed almost entirely as a function of the controversy between Hamilton and Jefferson, their differing concepts of America's power to influence events in the eighteenth century, and their contrasting visions of America's future. Bowman's sympathies are so clearly with Jefferson that his objectivity in assessing American foreign policy is sometimes compromised. Jefferson, "designed by Nature to counterbalance Hamilton" (p. 25), adopted a policy that "flowed from a sympathetic understanding of America's direction which Hamilton did not share" (p. 38). Hamilton, on the other hand, was "Britain's effective agent" (p. 144), and his towering ambition might have led the United States to a "militaristic oligarchy" or even to a dictatorship under an American Bonaparte (p. 434). Students of the Federalist period will also be interested to learn that Hamilton's enemies "might have considered him foppish" (p. 18).

Bowman's reading of French policy toward the United States during the Federalist period will be of interest to diplomatic historians. However, his interpretation of American domestic politics and the origins of American foreign policy must be read with caution and not without a critical reading of the sources cited and consideration of the views of historians less sympathetic to Jefferson.

East Tennessee State University DALE M. ROYALTY

John Marshall: A Life in Law. By Leonard Baker. (New York: Macmillan Publishing Co.; London: Collier Macmillan, 1974. Pp. xvi, 846. $17.95.)

Anyone expecting a significant reexamination of John Marshall's place in American history will be disappointed by Baker's biography of the famous Chief Justice. Indeed, the lengthy descriptive passages and the ample attention given to Marshall's private life suggest that this volume was intended for a popular rather than a scholarly audience. Almost half the work is devoted to Marshall's career as soldier, lawyer, diplomat, and politician, including an extended treatment of the XYZ Affair. The final portion considers Marshall's years on the bench, with a thorough, if unoriginal, discussion of the landmark decisions rendered by the Chief Justice. Baker is very sympathetic to his subject and praises Marshall's struggle for judicial independence and federal supremacy.

Unfortunately, the book is marred by a number of analytical failures. Developing the questionable notion that judicial proceedings are a substitute for military combat, Baker exaggerates the importance of judicial review in American history. It is startling to read that "the development of judicial review is almost synonymous with the development of a civilized state" (p. 381), and that "there could be no modern United States without a Supreme Court empowered with judicial review . . ." (p. 767). In addition, Baker is confusing about the role of law in society. Although he recognizes "that the law develops, builds, and even changes . . ." (p. 554), the author often presents law as a system of fixed principles to which scrupulous adherence is mandated. Thus, in one paragraph he explains that "The relationship between the American people and their government was, as it must always be, an uncertain one," and then inconsistently refers to "the strict limits allowed by the Constitution" (p. 669).

Similarly, Baker has difficulty with the concept of democracy. He concludes that the "unifying theme" of Marshall's opinions is "man's need to democratically arrive at just laws and then to observe them" (p. 710). Yet democracy is never adequately defined—"a law which offers all men the opportunity to solve their problems in a fair and just manner . . ." (p. 228). While the author declares that "Judges are not expected to be representative or responsive to the people . . ." (p. 372), he makes no attempt to reconcile majority rule with judicial review, and his contention that Marshall was a democrat fails to convince this reviewer.

Moreover, the text is flawed by numerous overstatements and a good deal of dubious history. Granted that the *Marbury* opinion is a major state paper, it was hardly "one of mankind's greatest achievements" (p. 409). Judicial review was recognized in post-Revolutionary America, but it was certainly not "common" (p. 381). Jefferson's conduct concerning the Burr treason trial was not his finest hour, but this reviewer questions whether it "was government tyranny at its worst" (p. 302). The views of Spencer Roane and John Taylor did not make the Civil War "inevitable" (p. 609). Is "the purpose of the Supreme Court in American life" really "to determine what America needs, what its purpose requires it to have" (pp. 580–81)? Less serious but equally bothersome is the author's propensity to trite or meaningless phrases—"the law is what its words say it to be, and all men must obey the law . . ." (p. 172). He has a maddening tendency to cite "family tradition" as an authority for comments on Marshall's personal life.

Lastly, Baker's presentation of Marshall's views leaves much to be desired. He does not make it clear that Marshall personally affirmed the constitutionality of the Sedition Act of 1798, and he overstates Marshall's criticism of slavery. The author neglects the substantial intellectual legacy of Alexander Hamilton to Marshall's opinions. There are also a few factual errors.

In short, one wishes the author had exhausted the possibilities of his fascinating subject. Rather than a scholarly contribution, this work must be judged a popular biography.

Vanderbilt Law School JAMES W. ELY, JR.

Thomas Jefferson: An Intimate History. By Fawn M. Brodie. (New York: W. W. Norton and Co., c. 1974. Pp. 591. $12.50.)

This book has valuable assets. Stylistic felicities distinguish many pages. The drama of nation-founding events, frequently described by other authors, is produced anew with engaging freshness. Such contributions apply not alone to the American scene of Jefferson's day but almost equally to international, especially French, features. Yet, through them all Mrs. Brodie never leaves her man long enough for readers to forget her principal purpose, which is to develop her version of Thomas Jefferson's "intimate history."

From several standpoints of craftsmanship (one may even say art) the volume is a model for writers to study—with particular reference to stage settings, smooth transitions, concentration on a main theme, and often judicious applications of peripheral etching.

The "shocker" for numerous nonhistorians is the presentation of Sally Hemings, one of Jefferson's slaves, as his concubine for years and the mother of many Jefferson children. Scholars, of course, have long been acquainted with remarks about "Dusky Sally" made and repeated during Jefferson's lifetime. Dumas Malone, Merrill D. Peterson, and Winthrop D. Jordan are among modern authors who preceded Mrs. Brodie in discussing the purported relationship in book form. In the Brodie judgment the allegations are true. Her case rests, mainly but not exclusively, on two considerations. One is a statement made in 1873 by Madison Hemings, a son of Sally. The second is the point that Jefferson was where Sally was nine months before the birth of each child.

So far as the alleged liaison is concerned, Mrs. Brodie assuredly does not strengthen her case by some of her ventures into the psychohistorical. If Jefferson had a mulatto concubine during part of his mission to France (which I doubt), there is absolutely nothing to be learned from the appearance of the word "mulatto" eight times in twenty-five pages of a travel account penned by him. Jefferson simply was describing the soil and using a word suited to that purpose. It is most unconvincing to project the notion that this had anything to do with Sally. Here, we have an excellent example of Mrs. Brodie's strainings for the conjectural.

The book contains many errors of fact or of judgment involving a wide historical spectrum. These range from an unsupportable statement—which would be important if true—about Abraham Lincoln (p. 23) to giving Jefferson Davis a strange name, "Thomas Jefferson Davis" (p. 469). Mrs. Brodie confuses "Light Horse Harry" Lee with Richard Henry Lee (p. 125) and with "Black Horse Harry" Lee (p. 444). She calls Edward M. House the "president-maker" of Woodrow Wilson (p. 301). And so forth. Perhaps the worst error is the supposition that Jefferson's unproved Sally Hemings relationship affected his attitudes toward emancipation in general.

It is true that Mrs. Brodie's mistakes in some matters do not necessarily demonstrate limitations on other points. But those mistakes are of a piece with her failure to underscore every one of Madison Hemings's misstatements. He erred at least four times in ten lines in that part of his reminiscences reproduced near the bottom of p. 472. On the basis of this portion of his story, is it possible for anyone to know whether other segments were similarly inaccurate? Madison Hemings says Sally was "*enciente*" (one of the few words he or his amanuensis misspelled) when she returned to Virginia from France; the child, however, "lived but a short time" (p. 473). This does not accord with the Brodie impression about a Jefferson son named "Tom," whom Madison never mentions. In sum, the closest thing to hard evidence in the book is limited to circumstantial evidence—that Jefferson and Sally were in the same place when her children were conceived.

The volume's last chapter is entitled "The Monticello Tragedy." The biographical tragedy is that the author chose not to eliminate a large number of dubious inclusions and worse. (Among the better materials are the reminiscences of Israel Jefferson, another former Monticello slave, who also said in 1873 and in the same newspaper: "I can as conscientiously confirm his [Madison Hemings's paternity] statement as any other fact which I believe from circumstances but do not positively know" [p. 482].) Possessing literary talent of a high order, Mrs. Brodie harms her offering by deficiencies in discrimination. Her book is long on speculation and suggestion. But neither speculation nor suggestion nor circumstantial evidence clinches the case.

University of Kentucky HOLMAN HAMILTON

Jefferson the President: Second Term, 1805–1809. By Dumas Malone. *Jefferson and His Time,* Volume V. (Boston: Little, Brown and Co., 1974. Pp. xxxii, 704. $14.50.)

Vastly successful during his first presidential term, Thomas Jefferson's fortunes descended steadily during his second, reaching the nadir of his entire public career. In 1804 he could report to Philip Mazzei that "The spirit of republicanism is now in almost all its ancient vigor . . . ." Four years later Jefferson was less sure of the American future. His tone was subdued rather than confident, tired rather than exuberant, and he was glad to leave "the boisterous ocean of political passions" (p. 668) for the quiet pleasures of Monticello. The Burr conspiracy troubled Jefferson, and he committed errors of judgment, but it was foreign affairs which especially bedeviled the second administration, creating problems which the passage of time could not dissipate nor the best statesmanship resolve. The embargo, though supported by a majority of the nation, failed to make any impression abroad and roused Federalist expectations of being restored to office. "I felt the foundations of the government shaken under my feet by the New England townships," Jefferson later recalled (p. 613). In the closing months frustration led to impotence, and Jefferson refused to make executive decisions which both Albert Gallatin and James Madison pressed upon him. Even his influence in Congress had eroded. His final nomination, that of William Short as minister to Russia, was unanimously rejected by the Senate.

Naturally, this administration has been an easy mark for historical critics. Some reviewers have expected Dumas Malone to rebut them, point by point, as if he were a partisan attorney writing a legal brief for Jefferson. (Garry Wills, for example, in the *New York Review of Books,* May 16, 1974, says Malone trusts Jefferson "totally," likens him to James St. Clair defending Richard Nixon, and concludes that the defense is inadequate.) Actually, Malone observes a careful professional line between explaining and defending his subject. The text is liberally sprinkled with assessments which describe Jefferson's actions as "unfortunate," "unwise," "gullible," and "disingenuous." Where other scholars have made unsupported or questionable evaluations, and Malone disagrees, he takes exception. Thus, from time to time Malone, in passing, footnotes his areas of disagreement with Henry Adams, Albert Beveridge, A. T. Mahan, Walter McCaleb, Bradford Perkins, and Leonard Levy. Malone's understanding of Jefferson's character is acute, his sympathy apparent, but his book is not, nor is it meant to be, an unqualified appreciation of Jefferson. He writes not as a poet or journalist or lawyer, but as a historian, constantly measuring what Jefferson did against the practical alternatives of the moment. What emerges from this work of prodigious scholarship and attention to detail is a Jefferson who, being human, errs as well as accomplishes, and both errors and accomplishments are placed in the context of circumstances. "It seems to me not far from the truth," writes Malone, "to say that in the domestic field he was seeking to reconcile the irreconcilable, and in the foreign field to solve the insoluble" (p. xxi).

Seventeen years of retirement followed, a fruitful period when politics passed into the background, which Malone will cover in a sixth and final volume. One looks forward to the summing up when "the sage and builder and educational statesman could emerge" (p. 668).

University of California
Santa Barbara

MORTON BORDEN

Blacks in Bondage: Letters of American Slaves. Edited by Robert S. Starobin. (New York: New Viewpoints, 1974. Pp. xviii, 196. Paper, $3.95; cloth, $8.95.)

Anyone who has been following current debate over the nature of the American slave system should put this volume near the top of his reading list. *Blacks in Bondage* offers a remarkable collection of letters written by American blacks while they were enslaved or shortly after they had escaped from slavery. Almost all of these documents were culled from manuscript depositories by the late Robert S. Starobin and have not been published before. This book amply demonstrates, as did his earlier study of industrial slavery in the antebellum South, that Professor Starobin had a command of relevant primary materials that was probably unsurpassed among current scholars investigating the South's peculiar institution. There can be little doubt that he would have made additional significant contributions to the history of American slavery if his life had not ended in 1971.

Included in this collection are letters written by slaves in a surprisingly wide range of situations. As might be expected, there is more correspondence from house servants, drivers, and managers than from any other occupational groups, but letters from field hands, artisans, fugitive slaves, and blacks caught up in the domestic slave trade are also present. One section dealing with slave insurrection contains the confessions and trial testimony of a number of blacks who were convicted of complicity in Gabriel's rebellion in 1800, and a final chapter consists of letters from Liberian émigrés who had formerly belonged to John McDonogh of Louisiana. Professor Starobin cautions in his introduction that scholars must do a considerable amount of reading between the lines if they are to grasp the full meaning of most of these documents because the letters "are loaded with subtleties of meaning, irony, double entendres, and outright put-ons" (p. xiv). Care and sensitivity are needed even when using letters addressed to other blacks, since slaves were well aware that whites might intercept their communications. Despite these difficulties, Professor Starobin seems fully justified when he claims that these sources constitute "one of the best tools historians may find for an understanding of slavery from the black man's perspective" (p. xiv).

In many ways, the most striking thing about this collection is the prevalence of three major themes running through much of the correspondence: a tremendous concern and affection for the slave's own family; an intensely felt Christianity that emphasized personal salvation; and, from those former slaves in a position to write fully about the subject, a consuming desire for freedom and bitter resentment of the racism present in antebellum America. The first two themes are perhaps best illustrated in a poignant letter written in 1858 by a slave named Abream Scriven after he had been sold away from his family by the Reverend Charles Colcock Jones of Liberty County, Georgia. "Give my love to my father & mother and tell them good Bye for me," he wrote from Savannah to his wife Dinah, who had remained on one of Jones's plantations, "and if we Shall not meet in this world I hope to meet in heaven. My Dear wife for you and my Children my pen cannot Express the griffe I feel to be parted from you all" (p. 58). Black disillusionment with white America comes through most clearly in the letters from the Liberian settlers: " . . . I will never consent to leave this country for all the pleasures of America combined together to live," remarked a black man who had purchased his freedom from McDonogh, "for this is the only place a colored person can enjoy his liberty for there exists no prejudice of color in this country but every man is free and equal" (p. 181).

The one frustrating feature of this book is that the lives of the slaves mentioned in these scattered pieces of correspondence cannot be followed in more detail. If Professor Starobin had been able to consult Robert Manson Myers's *The Children of Pride,* published in 1972, he would have been able to supply additional information on some of the more fascinating individuals discussed in the letters, the slaves of the Reverend Charles C. Jones. Abream Scriven, for example, appears twice in *The Children of Pride,* first as he is grievously awaiting sale in Savannah in 1858 (p. 442) and then six years later when a member of the Jones family encounters him near Atlanta. "He had not heard of Dinah's death," the writer relates, "and said he had never married until pretty recently, for he had always hoped something would turn up and he would be able to go back to Liberty" (p. 1147). Even though we cannot learn as much as we would like about the black men, women, and children mentioned in

Professor Starobin's volume, these extraordinary documents still provide some rare and enormously valuable glimpses into the interior lives of a number of American slaves. *Blacks in Bondage* deserves the widest possible readership, and those who helped bring this book into print following Professor Starobin's death deserve the thanks of everyone interested in trying to understand what it meant to be black and to be a slave in the white man's South.

University of Missouri, Columbia CHARLES B. DEW

William H. Crawford, 1772–1834. By Chase C. Mooney. (Lexington: University Press of Kentucky, c. 1974. Pp. xii, 364. $15.00.)

In this book the late Professor Mooney took upon himself a difficult task. No sizable collection of Crawford papers exists, and not a single letter remains between Crawford and any member of his family. Mooney painstakingly searched scores of libraries, collections, and governmental depositories and has put together perhaps as thorough a story as can be told. It is not, however, biography in the fullest sense, but rather a history of the events through which Crawford moved.

The author treats four significant phases of the Crawford career: service in the United States Senate, foreign service as minister to France, membership in the cabinets of Madison and Monroe, and Georgia activities after the end of his national career. The third phase occupies eight of thirteen chapters and includes his unsuccessful attempt to attain the Presidency.

Crawford went to the Senate in 1807 and won the admiration of Albert Gallatin because of his broad constructionism in fighting for recharter of the Bank of the United States in 1811. The author asserts that this put him outside the fold of the "old Republicans." Hostile to much of Madison's foreign policy, he supported measures of the war party including war itself. He was mortified by Madison's disavowal of intervention in Florida in 1812, in which Crawford had been involved. Minor errors flaw the author's account of the Florida events.

From 1813 to 1815 Crawford served abroad as the United States minister to France, the only minister in Western Europe. The main purpose of his mission—to get reparations for damages to American shipping and more favorable commercial arrangements—was not accomplished. He did keep Secretary of State Monroe informed on political and military affairs and recommended sensible reorganization of the consular service. The qualities that served him well as a senator, however, appear not to have made him an effective diplomat.

From August 1815 to October 1816 he served as Madison's secretary of war, bringing innovations and starting programs others were to carry forward. He differed with Andrew Jackson about Indians, defending their just claims under existing treaties. His 1816 report on Indian affairs suggested Indian-white intermarriage as a solution to the Indian problem, a suggestion which overshadowed other items of genuine merit in the report and which haunted him the rest of his days.

In August 1816 he became secretary of the Treasury, holding that office until 1825. The three chapters on his work at the Treasury are most detailed and constitute a veritable administrative history. Again, he advocated a strong bank as an essential instrument of policy and worked most harmoniously with Langdon Cheves during his tenure at the bank. Both favored severe retrenchment to cope with the depression of 1819. Those members of Congress who supported the policy were identified as "radicals and partisans of Crawford" (p. 156). The name "radical" stuck to the Crawfordites, but Mooney recognizes that it cannot be ideologically defined.

President Monroe ran a collegial administration, but the harmony of his second-term cabinet was disrupted by policy disagreements sharpened by the presidential ambitions of Crawford, Calhoun, and Adams. As presidential front-runner—having declined caucus nomination in 1816 and been instrumental in preventing a caucus in 1820—Crawford was everyone's target. Attempts of opponents to alienate him from Monroe failed, but Crawford's influence waned after 1822. By this time the Van Buren faction was maneuvering to make Crawford the 1824 candidate through caucus nomination, while partisans of other candidates denounced that mode of selection. Crawford's prolonged illness, which began in September 1823, was the deathblow to his national ambitions.

The chapters dealing with one-party politics, the caucus, and the election of 1824 are disappointing. Though detailed, they are not alive; there is no excitement in them. The chapter on the Georgia years, 1825–1834, portrays Crawford as a state judge, engaging in the civic activities one might expect, ridiculing Calhoun and the nullifiers, and on the eve of his death seeking appointment from Jackson to the United States Supreme Court.

Professor Mooney was fully aware of the limitations upon the writing of a Crawford biography, and no good purpose is served by being overly critical of his pedestrian style. The book is thorough, reasonably detailed, and obviously the product of a considerable amount of hard scholarly work.

University of Florida HERBERT J. DOHERTY, JR.

Travels in North America, 1822–1824. By Paul Wilhelm, Duke of Württemberg. Translated by W. Robert Nitske and edited by Savoie Lottinville. (Norman: University of Oklahoma Press, c. 1973. Pp. xxxiv, 456. $20.00.)

By the time of his death in 1860 Friedrich Paul Wilhelm, Duke of Württemberg, had explored the American West more extensively than any other foreigner. Stimulated by the scientific education afforded by the Stuttgart gymnasium and inspired by the writings of Alexander

Freiherr von Humboldt, he initially traveled to the United States in 1822. Despite the vast knowledge of the Trans-Mississippi that he gathered in seven sojourns, including four major trips, the German and his explorations (with the present exception) have remained relatively obscure. Duke Paul Wilhelm, a thoroughly trained and internationally recognized natural scientist, consigned himself and his attainments to the oblivion of succeeding generations because he forsook reporting his data and compiling his travel journals. Instead, he concentrated upon additional exploration and upon the accumulation of probably the largest private European collection of American botanical, zoological, and ethnological objects.

The youthful duke's systematic journal of his first American experience traces his progress in the sixteen-month trip (October 1822–February 1824) from Hamburg to the hinterland of present South Dakota and his return to Havre-de-Grace. Upon reaching New Orleans, he followed von Humboldt's footsteps by sailing to Cuba for a brief visit before ascending the Mississippi by steamer. His intended destination was Pittsburgh, but the unavailability of steamboat transportation above the Falls of the Ohio confined his progress eastward to Louisville. He then proceeded to St. Louis, where he made arrangements with the Berthold, Chouteau, and Pratte fur company to travel to the upper Missouri by cordelle boat.

Most American historians will find Paul Wilhelm's account of limited use, but those interested in natural science, geography, Indians and ethnology, and western exploration will deem the methodical narrative quite important. In sometimes trying physical circumstances, the duke carried the manuals of previous naturalists, classified the flora and fauna with precision, and collected the diverse species along with minerals and Indian artifacts. Violating his intention of keeping the journal scientific, the author fortunately permitted his temperament to moderate the clinical narrative. His observations about people lack detailed and colorful portraiture; however, his friendly comments about Louisiana Creoles, Kentuckians, General William Clark, and the Chouteau family are revealing. While harboring skepticism about frontier marksmanship and disdaining American whiskey, his fellow countrymen at Harmony, Indiana, half-breeds, Irish, and squatters, Paul Wilhelm displayed great knowledge and understanding about the life and plight of the Indians that he encountered, particularly the Iowa, the Omaha, the Otos, the Pawnee, and tribes of the Sioux nation. The work's most striking aspect is the feeling it gives of the impact of the "cutting edge" of frontier settlement upon the natural environment. In this regard, no traveler was more observant or better qualified to comment than the duke.

The editor's comprehensive introduction and the brief, descriptive, and corrective annotations benefited from the collaboration of two Sooner natural scientists. Historians of western exploration and natural science can hope that the Duke of Württemberg's remaining journals surface and receive equally skillful editorial treatment.

Shepherd College JOHN E. STEALEY, III

Deaf Smith: Incredible Texas Spy. By Cleburne Huston. (Waco: Texian Press, 1973. Pp. xii, 141. $10.00.)

This is the first attempt at a book-length biography of Erastus (Deaf) Smith, the noted spy of the Texas Revolution, who "left no personal papers or correspondence, received no written military orders and made his reports verbally, direct to the commander-in-chief . . ." or other superior officer of the Texan forces (p. ix). All this attests to the fact that Smith's education was far more limited than author Cleburne Huston admits. The author by necessity has relied largely upon secondary materials rather than upon primary sources. Nevertheless, he has presented in this small volume a clearer, more complete, and more authentic picture of Deaf Smith's private life and public activities than has ever been offered before. At times the author speculates and assumes much in putting the story together. He is aware of conflicting statements and reports about Smith that make it impossible to state exactly what transpired. His assumptions and conclusions, however, appear to be reasonable, and his evaluation of Smith's military service in the Texas Revolution is sound.

Born in 1787 in Dutchess County, New York, Erastus Smith migrated in 1798 with his parents, brothers, and sisters to Mississippi. He made a trip to Texas in 1817 before coming to live permanently in the San Antonio area in 1821. From childhood his hearing was greatly impaired, causing him to avoid noisy company and creating the impression that he was a "loner." The Mexicans in Texas called him "el Sordo" (the Deaf One). He married the widow Guadalupe Ruiz Duran in 1822, became a citizen of Mexico, and received a land grant of one Spanish league across the Cibolo River from the present town of La Vernia, thus becoming the first Anglo-American landowner in what is now Guadalupe County.

Smith sought to remain neutral at the beginning of the Texas Revolution. He had been away from home when General Martin Perfecto de Cos occupied San Antonio, and when Smith attempted to enter the town to see his family, Cos sought to arrest him, believing no doubt that he had been too friendly toward the Anglo-Americans.

At this point Smith definitely went over to the Texan side, and his well-known talents as a scout were utilized effectively throughout the revolution. His invaluable services were greatly appreciated by Sam Houston, but his unauthorized clandestine attack upon the inhabitants of Laredo in the spring of 1837 was criticized by Houston, and Smith was forced to retire from the rangers. He then settled at Richmond, Texas, where he died on November 30, 1837, and was buried in the town.

Deaf Smith: Incredible Texas Spy is worthy of reading by anyone interested in the history of Texas, and especially by those interested in the revolutionary period.

Texas A&M University JOSEPH MILTON NANCE

The American Problem in British Diplomacy, 1841–1861. By Wilbur Devereux Jones. (Athens: University of Georgia Press, c. 1974. Pp. xii, 260. $13.50.)

This work offers a fresh perspective on mid-nineteenth-century Anglo-American relations, a field which has been examined exhaustively by American historians but generally neglected by students of British diplomacy. The reason for this apparent imbalance lies in foreign-policy formulation as conceived on opposite sides of the Atlantic—England loomed quite large in American eyes, whereas European affairs were of paramount concern in London. Accordingly, these contrasting viewpoints give rise to the rather unusual circumstance that Professor Jones's study, while written from a British vantage point and solidly grounded in British private and official papers, will probably prove of greatest interest to specialists in American history. Yet this fact should not be viewed as a criticism of the book; indeed, the author's novel approach provides important modifications of standard interpretations of such American diplomatic landmarks as the Webster-Ashburton Treaty, the Clayton-Bulwer Treaty, and the complex question of the Monroe Doctrine in its application to the Mosquito Protectorate controversy.

The closely related central themes pursued by Jones in analyzing the recurrent crises and variegated ministerial approaches of the two decades leading up to the Civil War are (1) an evaluation of Anglo-American relations in the context of internal politics, imperial concerns, and the current state of European affairs; and (2) a careful scrutiny of the tactics employed by successive British statesmen in seeking solutions to controversies with the United States. He brings impressive credentials to his task, in that he is the author of a number of earlier books on various aspects of the early Victorian era, and the present work leans heavily on his other studies. This is particularly true of *Lord Aberdeen and the Americas,* and it comes as no surprise that the incisive treatment of Aberdeen's essentially benevolent attitude on American problems is one of the high points of the book. Lord Palmerston's belligerency (tinctured by a strong undercurrent of caution resulting from his knowledge of America's growing strength), Lord Malmesbury's attempts to counteract what he construed as American bluffs, and Lord Granville's rather genial ineptitude are likewise covered in a sensible, urbane fashion.

All in all, this is a fine piece of diplomatic history, and Jones's smooth-flowing prose brings lucidity to even the most intricate and vexatious of diplomatic tangles. My one major criticism is the dearth of maps. Surely such a subject deserves more than a single, rather indifferent map (of the Mosquito Coast and Central America). Otherwise, the author's exhaustive researches in manuscript materials, his obvious if unobtrusive knowledge of the period, and his objective and telling comments on the interpretations of previous writers ensure this work of a prominent place in the literature on the subject.

Winthrop College JAMES A. CASADA

Samuel Bell Maxey: A Biography. By Louise Horton. (Austin and London: University of Texas Press, c. 1974. Pp. xii, 222. $10.00.)

In this biography of Samuel Bell Maxey the author has resurrected from relative obscurity an unusual post–Civil War politician, whose life was shaped by both his native state of Kentucky and the frontier state of Texas. Born in Kentucky, Maxey was educated at West Point, where he was associated with a stellar group of classmates destined to play conspicuous leadership roles in both the Union and Confederate armies. After service in the Mexican War he studied law, joined his father's law firm, and held minor political posts in Clinton County, Kentucky. After his marriage in 1853 the Maxey family moved to Texas, where he and his father established their own law firm.

Maxey's political fortunes improved in his new location in northeast Texas, and in 1861 he was elected to the state Senate. His political career was interrupted, however, when he obtained the approval of President Davis to raise a regiment of troops for the Confederacy. In 1874, as a part of the general defeat of Republicans in Texas, Maxey was elected to the United States Senate, a position which he held until 1887, when he was defeated by John H. Reagan. It is this period in Maxey's career to which the author devotes the greater part of her study.

Maxey served in the Senate while the lingering efforts of Congressional Reconstructionists were being abandoned by Republican leaders and destroyed by determined Democrats. In such an atmosphere the Texas senator became known for his moderation, although he consistently supported the southern position on issues of sectional division, particularly those of interest to his adopted state. As the author notes, by "reason and moderation" Maxey "gained friends among the northern Republicans as well as among the Democrats . . ." (p. 194). This position established the senator as a leader in amelioration of lingering sectional emotion in national politics.

The author used an impressive amount of manuscript documents in compiling the data for this biography, the most important of which were the papers of Maxey and of his associates. As a biography this work is essentially sound and readable, although the principal often gets lost in the maze of political machinations. The reader cannot but sympathize with this plain man of modest intellectual qualities who viewed service to his constituency as a matter of honor and obligation. His accomplishments, not widely known, even at the time, were achieved by dint of hard work and perseverance, and his comments on associates in politics demonstrate in succinct form the homely political shrewdness of a conservative Henry Clay Whig.

A few questionable historical interpretations do not appreciably detract from the value of the work, with its focus on the role of Maxey in state and national affairs. One could quarrel with the author's assertion that his work "extended well into the period of the Progressive Movement" (p. ix), since he was elected at the end of the Republican regime in Texas, served until 1887, and died in 1895, before there was any recognizable Progressive Movement. Further, from the evidence presented it is doubtful that Maxey occupies a historical niche quite so exalted as the author claims. Nevertheless, for historians of the postwar period Louise Horton has provided in a scholarly work additional insight into the efforts of southern moderates of Whig lineage to affect reconciliation of the sections.

North Texas State University JACK B. SCROGGS

A Matter of Allegiances: Maryland from 1850 to 1861. By William J. Evitts. *The Johns Hopkins University Studies in Historical and Political Science*, Series XCII, No. 1. (Baltimore and London: Johns Hopkins University Press, c. 1974. Pp. xii, 212. $11.00.)

Allegiance—defined as "loyalty, affiliation, endorsement, identification" (p. 3)—is the organizing theme used to explain the transformation of Maryland politics during the critical antebellum decade. The two major allegiances, Unionism and southernism, drawing Marylanders' loyalties at the decade's outset, were compatible. But by 1861 Marylanders had to choose between these two allegiances. The choice of Unionism resulted from a complex interaction of state and local factors with national trends. Basic to an understanding of these factors was the state's division into three geographic and economic regions: the diversified-farming, limited-slaveholding Eastern Shore; the tobacco-growing, slaveholding, "old society" south (p. 9); and agriculturally-diversified, industrializing western Maryland. Baltimore, a mushroom, immigrant city facing a host of urban problems because of architectural, social, and governmental difficulties resulting from chronic legislative underrepresentation, was the headquarters of the last section. In 1850 the Whigs controlled the first two sections and, narrowly thereby, the state; western Maryland and Baltimore were Democratic strongholds. The combination of national Whig debility, the local unpopularity of its 1852 presidential candidate Winfield Scott, and the identification of the Democracy with state constitutional reform overthrew the dominant party. But Democratic victory and Whig disappearance were too complete; internal Democratic squabbling and heightening tensions resulting from Baltimore's urban problems produced, first, independent prohibition-reform movements and, subsequently, Native Americanism. Although inheriting the Whig's Unionism, Native Americanism was not Whiggery; the Eastern Shore and south Maryland moved into Democratic ranks, while in Baltimore and the west nativism flourished. Nativism in power, however, was not nativism campaigning; the Know-Nothings abandoned their platform in favor of electoral chicanery to maintain themselves in power. Centering in Baltimore, their violence and vote fraud carried the state for Fillmore in 1856. Again the victory was too complete; city reform elements, determined to cleanse the political process, made significant progress in 1858 and 1859. Outside the city increasing Democratic strength and the increasing prosouthern identification of the Democracy indicated continuing southern allegiance. John Brown's raid, originating on Maryland soil, abruptly reinterjected national issues into the political arena and laid the groundwork for the 1860 presidential campaign. Once again local issues influenced the outcome of national political campaigns: offsetting the reemergence of old Whig-Unionists frightened by John Brown, the identification of the Constitutional Unionist party with the thoroughly discredited Baltimore Native Americans cost John Bell votes and gave the state to John C. Breckinridge by a paper-thin margin. Once these local factors were removed and Marylanders had to face the crisis of choosing the Union or the South, the state's basic, but fragile, Unionism reasserted itself. Even in the 1861 incidents that might have precipitated unthinking state secession, Lincoln's furtive February journey through Baltimore and the April mob violence against Massachusetts troops, Unionists maintained their control, ensuring Maryland's ultimate allegiance.

Well grounded in the available newspapers and manuscripts, this study buttresses its case by an unobtrusive use of statistical analysis. Maryland is indeed fortunate that this author joins Gerald Henig and Jean Baker to complete the long-needed reexamination of *the* critical border state.

State University of New York
Fredonia

DAVID E. MEERSE

Allies for Freedom: Blacks and John Brown. By Benjamin Quarles. (New York: Oxford University Press, 1974. Pp. xvi, 244. $7.95.)

In 1972 Benjamin Quarles edited *Blacks on John Brown*, a collection of personal letters, eulogies, sermons, and essays written by blacks on the subject of John Brown. It is not surprising, therefore, that Professor Quarles was motivated to write a monographic study concerning not only the attitudes of Afro-Americans, past and present, regarding the enigmatic Brown, but also a study which explores in depth the interaction of blacks, both free and slave, with Brown while he lived.

Historians who have come to appreciate the combination of painstaking methodology and lucid penmanship characteristic of Quarles's earlier books will not be disappointed with *Allies for Freedom*. The author has done a great deal of spadework and, more significant, has diligently attempted to separate historical fact from romanticized fiction, not an easy task considering the subject matter. Quarles points out, for example, that the stereotyped and oft-repeated image of Brown kissing a black baby en route to the gallows "was the invention of a newspaper reporter . . ." (p. 121). Not only were women and children officially barred from the execution site, but Brown himself was continually surrounded by guards during his trek from cell to noose, contrary to Whittier's "Brown of Osawatomie," Louis Ransom's "John Brown on His Way to Execution," and Thomas Hovenden's "The Last Moments of John Brown."

Unlike most writers on John Brown, whose accounts invariably end with his abortive Harpers Ferry foray and his subsequent execution, Quarles devotes a significant portion of this book to the historical aftermath of Harpers Ferry and to the canonization of Brown by American blacks. By actively seeking the friendship and camaraderie of Afro-Americans during his lifetime Brown was (and is) viewed as being a man devoid of race prejudice, consumed with the desire to destroy any and all institutions which perpetuated such prejudice. "Down to the black power revolution of the mid-1960's," Quarles concludes, "Brown continued to be a bright and morning star in the racial remembrance of Negro Americans" (p. 192).

Ohio Northern University ROBERT R. DAVIS, JR.

The Secessionist Impulse: Alabama and Mississippi in 1860. By William L. Barney. (Princeton, N. J.: Princeton University Press, c. 1974. Pp. xvi, 371. $14.50.)

In this book Professor Barney provides an intricate analysis of party leadership and voting behavior in Alabama and Mississippi during and after the presidential election of 1860 as a means to a more exact understanding of the secession movement. Utilizing a wide range of manuscript and secondary sources and carrying out exhaustive research in published and manuscript census returns as well as newspapers, Barney shows that the Breckinridge forces were led by young, ambitious lawyer-planters. Threatened by high slave prices and a growing scarcity of fertile land at the very time when they were achieving or aspiring to achieve planter status, these parvenus saw the Union as an obstacle to their ambitions. In reaction, they demanded such radical programs as slave expansion in the Caribbean and the reopening of the African slave trade, programs unobtainable within the Union, particularly after Lincoln's election. Barney also describes their conservative Bell and Douglas opponents, qualifying the traditional stereotype of Whiggery. Bell and Douglas leaders tended to be older, and Whig voting strength was derived from urban centers and rural regions past their agricultural prime, while Douglas drew support from nonslaveholders and the foreign-born. Party profiles provide Barney with a means of explaining why the Breckinridge forces won the 1860 Alabama and Mississippi elections and how they mobilized the people for secession.

The book's main asset is its quantitative approach to party leadership and voting behavior, which provides many insights into the dynamics of Mississippi and Alabama society in 1860. But a price is paid for his focus. Since Barney is primarily concerned with the thrust of local politics, events in Congress and at the state level become secondary and sometimes hidden, and key Alabama and Mississippi figures (other than the governors) at each of these levels have little importance. Thus, William Lowndes Yancey is accorded the most token mention, Henry S. Foote's colorful stump campaign for Douglas is unnoticed, and Jefferson Davis becomes virtually irrelevant because he is off in Washington and supposedly out of touch with local reality. An emphasis on group behavior may be a useful corrective to elite-centered history, but we still need the whole picture. Because Barney is looking at society at a point in time, his evidence led him away from the careers of men whose significance may have been their transformation over time. Jeremiah Clemens of Alabama was a leading cooperationist in 1860 but had been a prominent "ultra" in 1850. Innumerable southern politicians followed Clemens's path, many going the opposite direction, and some passing through a number of ideological contortions. Barney's very premise that party affiliation and political behavior related to specific socioeconomic traits should have made case studies of such men of particular relevance.

This study, however, is more informative than those of Denman and Rainwater on Alabama and Mississippi and contributes tremendously to our understanding of what was really going on in the South as a whole in 1860. Its significance transcends its group-behavior dimension. Barney's evidence of slaveholder control of all parties challenges Fletcher Green's view of an increasingly powerful yeomanry before the war, while it simultaneously reminds us of the complex nature of planter hegemony. Many studies have described the impotence of cooperationism, but Barney's is particularly discerning. He has delivered an effective blow for antirevisionism historiography. Like Steven Channing, Barney emphasizes a crisis of fear in 1860, but he contends that the crisis was artificially contrived by the Breckinridge forces. Although Barney oversimplifies southern expansionism, his insistence on the importance of land acquisition demonstrates that issue's vitality. The radicals, the dynamic core of the antebellum South, acted with forethought to defend their society and way of life.

Purdue University ROBERT E. MAY

Arming the Union: Small Arms in the Civil War. By Carl L. Davis. (Port Washington, N. Y., and London: Kennikat Press, 1973. Pp. xiv, 207. $12.50.)

Carl Davis has produced a useful, informative, and well-balanced book on a topic which has not previously had an overall treatment. The acquisition of weapons was a function of the Ordnance Department, which in 1860 was small, antiquated, and ill-prepared to undertake a major mission that had to be performed in haste. Appreciation and promotions went to combat units; and ordnance duties were not well understood, as the author explains, but the department performed in a creditable manner.

The limited supply of available arms and the tremendous demand made purchases abroad natural. To secure these arms and to deprive the Confederacy of them meant rivalry in the market, and many second-rate weapons were purchased in haste.

With the loss of the armory at Harpers Ferry, government production of small arms was a responsibility of the Springfield Armory in Massachusetts. Under Captain Alexander B. Dyer in 1864 this armory produced 300,000 arms each day at a low cost of $11.97 each. By the end of the war the armory was the largest in the world both in total production and in capacity. It "produced eight hundred two thousand rifled muskets and, by supplying gauges, patterns and advice, had aided private manufacturers in tooling for hundreds of thousands more" (p. 71).

Arms firms besieged the Ordnance Department for contracts, but once they had awards, the department had to fight to get production. Dr. Davis describes the problems with the laggards as well as the accomplishments of such reliable firms as the Sharps Rifle Company and the Spencer Repeating Rifle Company.

Both breech-loading and repeating weapons were purchased. The Sharps Rifle Company, most productive of the firms making breech-loaders, delivered 80,000 carbines and about 10,000 rifles, while the Spencer Repeating Rifle Company made 50,000 carbines and 12,000 rifles. The Spencer with the metallic cartridge and repeating firepower was the favored gun at the end of the war.

Both types of carbines were issued to cavalry units, since their men had to reload in the saddle. Horsemen soon learned that fighting dismounted with the new weapons, they could produce a devastating firepower. Davis asserts that "Firepower appeared on the Civil War battlefields as it had never been seen before. . . . During the Civil War, firepower came of age . . ." (p. 145).

The book includes footnotes and a useful bibliography, along with a number of well-chosen photographs. The work is broad in scope and replete with interesting detail. Despite the complexity of his subject, the author presents his material so as to inform without confusing, no small achievement.

Reinhardt College BOWLING C. YATES

The Peninsula Campaign, 1862: McClellan & Lee Struggle for Richmond. By Joseph P. Cullen. (Harrisburg, Pa.: Stackpole Books, c. 1973. Pp. 192. $8.95.)

Joseph P. Cullen, a public affairs officer for the National Park Service in Richmond, Virginia, attempts "to present new interpretations of already known facts . . ." (p. 182) concerning the generalship of Lee and McClellan during the Peninsula Campaign, with particular emphasis on McClellan's performance. The book is based on well-known and often-used sources, and as the author admits, his only effort to introduce new material concerns a peacemaking mission initiated by McClellan when he sent his aide-de-camp to confer with the Confederacy's General Howell Cobb. Unfortunately, the book is not footnoted, and Cullen mentions only that he took his account of the incident from Series I of the *Official Records.*

Cullen's appraisal of Lee is traditional. He readily admits that the southern general made mistakes, especially at Malvern Hill, but concludes that "The important thing was that Lee, despite the mistakes, had proved himself a competent and daring field commander who would learn from experience" (pp. 168–69). Some historians, notably Thomas L. Connelly, have recently questioned whether Lee learned much from his mistakes. In many respects Antietam and Gettysburg seem as futile and as wasteful of the South's precious manpower as Malvern Hill. Also, although Cullen criticizes McClellan for misunderstanding the importance of the western theater, he ignores the same fault in Lee.

The author treats McClellan harshly. He belittles the idea that actions taken by Lincoln and Stanton, such as the recall of McDowell's corps just as the campaign began, seriously affected McClellan's plans. He hints, on the basis of flimsy circumstantial evidence, that McClellan hoped to subvert the President's constitutional position as commander-in-chief. By building his army to 300,000 men, writes Cullen, McClellan believed "he would then be in a position to tell the president and the government what he intended to do and when, whether they liked it or not" (p. 172). Cullen also tries hard to deny McClellan any praise. For example, he writes that McClellan "cannot be given credit for any of the battles fought during the maneuver . . ." from the York to the James because "he wasn't even on the field" (p. 179). Yet there is evidence that McClellan *was* on the battlefield for varying lengths of time at Mechanicsville, Savage's Station, and Malvern Hill.

Few will deny that McClellan's handling of the Peninsula Campaign is subject to criticism, but Cullen has carried the criticism too far. Readers of this volume would be well advised to read Warren W. Hassler's biography of McClellan before drawing any conclusion about "The Young Napoleon's" conduct during the campaign.

Despite Cullen's strong anti-McClellan bias, his book provides interesting and oftentimes lively reading. However, it should appeal more to Civil War buffs than to specialists in the field.

University of Nebraska, Lincoln PETER MASLOWSKI

Schools for All: The Blacks & Public Education in the South, 1865–1877. By William Preston Vaughn. (Lexington: University Press of Kentucky, c. 1974. Pp. x, 181. $12.50.)

Despite the recent outpouring of books and articles on Negro history, the story of black education during Reconstruction has not received the attention that it deserves. Although the movement failed to realize the idealistic objectives of its northern founders, the crusade to provide elementary schooling for blacks in the Reconstruction South achieved impressive results. Largely due to the efforts of northern missionary and benevolent societies in cooperation with officials of the Freedmen's Bureau more than 25 percent of the former slave population could read and write by 1870. The percentage would increase during the early 1870s as Republican-sponsored public school systems were established throughout the South.

Professor Vaughn has attempted the first comprehensive account of the Reconstruction experiment in mass education for blacks. He only partly succeeds in his task. Solidly documented, despite the absence of any reference to the voluminous and revealing papers of the American Missionary Association at the Amistad Research Center, Dillard University (now available on microfilm), the book focuses on the pre-Republican movement to establish schools for blacks, the hammering out of the school article in the state constitutional conventions of 1868, the struggle in Louisiana and South Carolina over racial mixing in the public schools and the state universities, and the unsuccessful Radical attempt in Congress to prohibit segregation in southern classrooms. Of particular significance is Vaughn's detailed account of the black effort in the "Black and Tan" conventions and the early Republican legislatures to prevent the establishment of segregated schools. Supported only by a handful of white Radicals, black leaders demonstrated far more opposition to segregation than historians have realized. But only in Louisiana, where state superintendent of education Thomas W. Conway, a white Republican, led the movement for integration, did racial mixing become a reality in the postwar public schools. Even in this state integration was limited to New Orleans, where approximately one third of the schools were racially mixed. In 1873 the University of South Carolina after a long struggle became the only southern institution of higher education to open its doors to students of both races. By 1875 one-half of the student body of 166 was black. Despite the meager numbers involved and the violent opposition of conservatives, Vaughn concludes that integration worked well where it was tried.

Unfortunately, Vaughn's preoccupation with the issue of mixed schools has caused him to overlook other important aspects of the history of black education during Reconstruction. He attributes the shortcomings (or failure, as in the case of rural Louisiana) of the Republican school systems either to white hostility to Negro learning or to the fear of forced integration. As a result he ignores the serious economic plight of the postwar South, which created a shortage of tax revenues and undermined financial support for the infant school programs. In addition, Vaughn leaves unexplored the story of segregated black schools, which existed everywhere in the South except in the Cresent City and were an integral part of the educational experience of Reconstruction Negroes. Readers of this book will search in vain for discussions of administration, curricula, and the quality of instruction in these schools.

Although the book is not definitive, Vaughn has written an informative and lucid account of the postwar effort to provide blacks with an educational base in freedom.

North Carolina State University — William C. Harris

The Booker T. Washington Papers. Volume 3: *1889–95.* Edited by Louis R. Harlan and others. (Urbana, Chicago, and London: University of Illinois Press, c. 1974. Pp. xxx, 618. $17.50.)

Volume 2 of the Washington Papers spanned a period of almost thirty years (1860–1889). Volume 3 covers less than six years, from May 21 1889, to September 18, 1895—evidence of the increasing abundance of documents. The correspondence includes letters written by Washington and a substantial number of letters written to him. The editors also include numerous speeches, a few articles written by Washington, and significant contemporary newspaper and periodical articles. The bulk of the contents is from the Washington Papers in the Library of Congress. Some are from the Tuskegee Institute Archives. A few are from other manuscript collections. The contents are remarkably varied. They throw light on Washington and his career and also illuminate the condition of the black population in the South.

A considerable part of the volume deals with Washington's personal life and his role as principal of Tuskegee. Of particular interest are the letters from Margaret James Murray ("Maggie"), who was appointed lady principal of Tuskegee in 1890 and who became Washington's third wife in 1892. It is fitting that this volume is dedicated to her memory. The letters show her devotion to Washington and to his children by his previous marriages, although before her marriage she confessed: ". . . I can not feel toward Portia [Washington's daughter by his first marriage] as I should." She added: "I wonder Mr. Washington if it is a wise and Christian thing for me to love you feeling as I do [toward Portia]" (pp. 177–78)?

As lady principal Maggie encountered numerous problems relating to student discipline and relations among faculty and staff which she related to Washington in long letters during his absences from Tuskegee. One problem was "gentlemen teachers" who spent too much time talking to girl students. A woman teacher showed too much interest in a sixteen-year-old boy pupil. Other letters show dissatisfaction of students with treatment by some of the staff. Most problems ultimately came to Washington for settlement, and no detail about the school was too trivial for his attention.

There is correspondence with Samuel Chapman Armstrong and with white philanthropists who were interested in Tuskegee. These included a number of women, among them Caroline Phelps Stokes and Olivia Egleston Phelps Stokes, as well as such male donors as Collis P. Huntington. There are also numerous speeches by Washington, usually before northern audiences. They emphasize the need of southern blacks for industrial and moral education and foreshadow the accommodationist stance of the Atlanta address. There are some exceptions to the usual pattern, notably a speech to the Women's New England Club in 1890, in which Washington explicitly criticized Henry W. Grady and protested the denial of political rights to blacks.

Included also are numerous letters from blacks of varied background and status, which show the increasingly influential role which Washington was beginning to play among members of his own race. Some of the correspondence deals with his criticism of the black clergy and his opposition to Henry M. Turner's African emigration schemes. Events preceding Washington's appearance at the Cotton States and International Exposition are covered, and the volume ends with the Atlanta address.

The editorial work in the present volume, as in the first two, shows meticulous scholarship. In addition to identifying nearly all correspondents and persons mentioned, the editors have included succinct biographies of most of them, a feature which will make the volume especially valuable to scholars.

Butler University EMMA LOU THORNBROUGH

The National Urban League, 1910–1940. By Nancy J. Weiss. (New York: Oxford University Press, 1974. Pp. xiv, 402. $12.50.)

In a smooth-flowing, judicious, painstaking, and fair-minded narrative, Nancy J. Weiss carries the story of the National Urban League from 1910 to 1940. She relates the particular activities of the organization to reform, to the history of labor, to urbanization, to the First World War, to immigration, to the Depression, to the experience of the black masses and black protest groups, to the broader stream of American history, and to many other matters of relevance. Despite her disclaimers about the unevenness of her sources, the completeness of her analysis is striking.

Yet *The National Urban League* is not a comfortable book to read. It recounts the league's skillful, varied, and hopeful efforts to enhance the status of American blacks; but in many ways Professor Weiss's study is a deterministic one, bristling with "No Exit" signs. The program of the league was minimal, constrained by the middle-class values of its personnel, by the context of the times, and by the sources of its funds. Time and again the organization settled "for the best possible rather than the most desirable" (p. 308); and just as often Weiss is forced to conclude that this was about all the league could have achieved. It could conceivably have been more militant, but militancy was not in vogue in the twenties; and in the thirties radicalism did not work even for whites, much less for blacks. The black reformers might possibly have gained more from the unions, but these were the captives of a prejudiced membership and leadership. Perhaps they could have pushed harder with the politicians, but the latter were unconcerned with government solutions in the twenties and politically vulnerable to the attacks of a race-conscious South during the New Deal. The league might have taken a more forceful line in all that it did; but it wasn't easy to devise radical solutions on Rockefeller's money even if the leaders' bourgeois values had permitted the effort. One senses in the author a tension between her humanitarian impulse to point out a method by which the league could have found a quick and dramatic way to scale the walls of prejudice surrounding the black community and her scholarly imperative to be realistic. Probably, Professor Weiss was no more comfortable with her conclusions that the reader is; nevertheless, she is usually convincing.

Perhaps the only place where she fails to persuade is in her discussion of the pathology of black urban life in the twenties. In contrast to her meticulous coverage of the "Great Migration" of the war years, she unaccountably neglects the large migration of the 1920s. She explains the Great Migration in the usual way—as a matter of southern push (worsening economic and racial conditions) and northern pull (wartime industrial prosperity). The narrative makes it quite obvious that blacks derived solid benefits from their new city experience. In the 1920s, however, the pull of wartime prosperity did not endure; yet the large-scale migration of blacks continued. If the "Black Metropolises" were as pathological as the author contends, then it is difficult to understand why the migrants continued to crowd into them. A more thorough discussion of the continuing flight to the cities would have cleared up this seeming contradiction of growing urban pathology and continuing black willingness to volunteer for it. This is a flaw in the work, yet it must be balanced against many more strengths.

University of North Carolina
Chapel Hill
ROGER W. LOTCHIN

Richard Irvine Manning and the Progressive Movement in South Carolina. By Robert Milton Burts. (Columbia, S.C.: University of South Carolina Press, 1974. Pp. xii, 259. $9.95.)

In this study Professor Burts traces the career of Richard I. Manning, an outstanding progressive who served as South Carolina's governor from 1915 to 1918. In some respects Manning was an unlikely figure to lead a movement for social and economic change. Born into an aristocratic family which had produced five previous governors, he first came to prominence as a gentleman farmer during the turbulent post-Reconstruction years. He was elected to the state legislature during the agrarian upheaval of the 1890s, but he showed little sympathy for the democratic objectives of the Tillman movement. Instead, he devoted his energies to attacks on electoral corruption. In the early 1900s he gave evidence of an expanding social consciousness, however, and he emerged as a champion of public education and tax reform. Combating the influence of the demagogic Cole Blease, Manning captured the governor's mansion in 1914 and moved to energize the entire state government. He pressed for improvements in the public schools, colleges, prisons, and mental institutions. Prodded by Manning, moreover, the legislature revamped South Carolina's election machinery and enacted a more restrictive child labor law. The legislators also responded to gubernatorial pressure by establishing state commissions to equalize tax burdens, mediate labor disputes, and regulate insurance companies. Capping this list of achievements, Manning proved to be one of the nation's most effective wartime governors as well, collaborating fully with President Wilson in bond sales and other defense endeavors.

Avoiding unnecessary verbiage, Professor Burts describes the foregoing events in a clear-cut, factual manner. The book's value is further enhanced by its author's extensive research in primary sources, research which enables him to shed considerable light on some of the more obscure and intricate controversies of the day. Of particular interest are his accounts of Governor Manning's behind-the-scenes efforts to curb lynching, enforce the liquor-control laws, and suppress the antiwar and anti-Wilson activities of Cole Blease's followers. Such information adds significantly to our knowledge of the period.

On the negative side, by way of contrast, this biography suffers from a number of serious flaws. For one thing, it offers little insight into the governor's personal or business relationships. Instead, the focus is almost exclusively on politics, producing an essentially one-dimensional portrait with inevitable distortions. More significantly, perhaps, there are also unfortunate deficiencies in Burts's treatment of political affairs. He makes no real attempt, for example, to explain the influences which transformed Manning from a youthful "Bourbon" to a reformist Democrat in his mature years. Indeed, Manning's motives—his ideas and aspirations—are neglected throughout the book. Compounding this problem, moreover, the author demonstrates a similar narrowness in his approach to the rank-and-file progressive elements in the Palmetto State. He fails to analyze election returns or legislative roll-call votes, thus leaving the reader in almost total ignorance as to which groups and areas actually supported Manning's program. Finally, Burts's efforts to relate South Carolina's progressive upsurge to national or regional trends are also, for the most part, inadequate. In this connection it should be noted that his bibliography lists none of the numerous books on national or southern Progressivism which have appeared since he received his Ph.D. degree in 1957. Analysis of these studies would undoubtedly have improved the interpretive character of his work.

Virginia Commonwealth University JAMES T. MOORE

The Unknown Soldiers: Black American Troops in World War I. By Arthur E. Barbeau and Florette Henri. (Philadelphia: Temple University Press, c. 1974. Pp. xviii, 279. $10.00.)

This study of black participation in World War I by two young black scholars, one a professional historian and the other a free-lance writer, seeks to fill a long-standing void in Afro-American history. As soon as the United States entered the war white southerners, with some degree of success, tried to limit black military involvement to service roles, but the War Department, under intense pressure from Afro-Americans, eventually created two black combat units. The 92d Division was made up entirely of draftees, while the 93d Division, which never attained full strength, consisted mostly of National Guardsmen. Upon reaching France the four regiments of the incomplete 93d Division were assigned to the French sector, where they were used to relieve battle-weary French troops. Equipped with unfamiliar French weapons and rations, the men of this outfit performed surprisingly well under fire. In contrast, the record of the 92d Division was less praiseworthy, and at least one regiment, the 368th, was withdrawn from the front in disgrace.

As the authors clearly demonstrate, the shortcomings of black soldiers in combat resulted primarily from inadequate training, incompetent officers (mostly white), and obsolete equipment, but not, as their critics insisted, from inherent character weaknesses or lack of intelligence. Furthermore, white commanders had no confidence in black officers or enlisted men, and these attitudes often proved to be self-fulfilling prophecies. In addition to detailing the exploits of black soldiers—both combatants and noncombatants—in France, the authors also describe the discriminations endured by blacks at home and abroad as well as the naïve hopes of a large number of Afro-Americans that their active participation in the war effort would serve to ease racial tensions and improve postwar conditions. When neither of these happened, disillusionment set in, culminating in a brief period of unprecedented racial violence.

Although this study provides a good general synthesis, it is hardly definitive, and much work remains to be done. In fact, the book contains little that will be new to specialists in the field. Furthermore, it is not without a few minor errors. For instance, the Houston riot of 1917, involving the 24th Infantry, occurred on San Felipe Street not Filipo Street, and 118, not 156, men were court-martialed. Finally, the authors have an unfortunate habit of pleading their case rather than describing and interpreting the events as they unfold. Nevertheless, Barbeau and Henri have made a lasting contribution to Afro-American history.

University of Houston ROBERT V. HAYNES

Serpent in Eden: H. L. Mencken and the South. By Fred C. Hobson, Jr. Foreword by Gerald W. Johnson. (Chapel Hill: University of North Carolina Press, c. 1974. Pp. xvi, 242. $8.95.)

In 1920 H. L. Mencken fixed an image of southern culture in his essay "The Sahara of the Bozart." Southern reaction was immediate and extreme. While defenders of the South were outraged, a number of young writers and journalists scattered through the region believed they had found a voice.

Starting with this cultural event, Fred C. Hobson, Jr., examines all the ramifications of H. L. Mencken's relationship to the South and especially to the beginnings of the southern literary renaissance in the 1920s. Mr. Hobson makes excellent use of newly available Mencken correspondence to supplement Carl Bode's recent biography in this area of one of

Mencken's strongest special interests. His examination of Mencken's role as cultural critic and stimulant in the South also complements Douglas C. Stenerson's recent and more general study of this aspect of Mencken's character.

As Mr. Hobson works outward from that 1920 essay, he shows how Mencken himself tried to change the Sahara into fertile land, or, more correctly, how he worked to encourage those writers already active in the South whose work would prove him wrong. All the forces of Puritanism, romanticism, and provincialism which Mencken so violently attacked would eventually fall before writers like William Faulkner and Thomas Wolfe.

Mr. Hobson's particular emphasis, however, is on the few years in the twenties immediately preceding the major achievements of Faulkner and Wolfe. He shows Mencken actively supporting little magazines such as the *Double Dealer* in New Orleans and, especially, the *Reviewer* in Richmond, and encouraging editors and writers alike to work toward a new, realistic portrait of the South. Mencken's interests and efforts at reform also went beyond the little magazines and poetry societies to active social criticism, to the work of journalists and students of southern society who were willing to speak out. Mr. Hobson's discussion of Mencken's relations with Howard W. Odum, Gerald W. Johnson, and, later, W. J. Cash is a particularly valuable part of his study.

Given Mencken's penchant for realism and outspoken social criticism, his championing of James Branch Cabell as the finest of southern writers is puzzling. Mr. Hobson's intelligent discussion of the relationship gives us perhaps as clear an understanding as we can have of the similar attitudes toward the South and, finally, toward human nature that drew such different men together.

H. L. Mencken has faded from the center of literary interest almost as completely as James Branch Cabell. Perhaps a partial explanation for such a reversal can be seen in Mr. Hobson's discussion of Mencken's failure to recognize fully the talents of the Fugitives, of writers like Allen Tate and John Crowe Ransom, who were to be much closer to the center of modern literature than most of the writers Mencken directly championed. Similarly, Mencken's support of the *Reviewer* and writers like Julia Peterkin was part of a failure to value properly the less provincial and more important *Double Dealer*.

Mr. Hobson does follow through with a fine discussion of the Agrarians (most of them former Fugitives) and of Mencken's relationship to their ideas in the early thirties. He shows, finally, how southern literature went beyond Mencken, beyond his iconoclasm to a genuine renaissance, and how Mencken's own limitations kept him from recognizing the significance of *Look Homeward, Angel* and *The Sound and the Fury*.

Mr. Hobson has incorporated his scholarship into a clear, continuously interesting study of H. L. Mencken and of an important decade in the history of southern literature.

Rice University WALTER W. ISLE

Dixiecrats and Democrats: Alabama Politics, 1942–1950. By William D. Barnard. (University, Ala.: University of Alabama Press, c. 1974. Pp. viii, 200. $7.95.)

This able monograph focuses on the early political career of James E. Folsom. It begins in 1942 when he ran second to the conservative Chauncey Sparks in Alabama's Democratic primary for governor, peaks with his election as governor in 1946, and concludes in 1950 with the victories of the Folsom-backed Loyalists over the Dixiecrats in the fight for control of the Democratic State Executive Committee and over Loyalist Gordon Persons in the gubernatorial primary. A broader concern of the book is an analysis of the origins of Democratic factionalism in Alabama's history, of the state's economic and political geography, and of the interplay of race, class, and ideology. The political dynamics of the intense bifactionalism setting Alabama's New Dealish liberals against her Bourbon and Big Mule conservatives are highlighted by the gubernatorial contests of 1942 and 1946, the dueling between Folsom and the conservative-dominated legislature, the Senate elections of Lister Hill and John Sparkman, and the Dixiecrat revolt of 1948.

Barnard is clearly sympathetic to the New Deal tradition and also to Folsom's neopopulism, although he is not uncritical of Folsom's simplistic Jacksonian faith, and his assessment of the conservatives is fair-minded. Indeed, we gain more insight into the mind of the conservative former governor, Frank M. Dixon, than into the enigmatic Folsom, and this seems to be largely a function of Barnard's major internal sources of evidence, which were the papers of Dixon and Chauncey Sparks, and the disappointing Folsom papers. Barnard is sensitive to what Richard Hofstadter called "the process of deconversion from reform to reaction," as he traces the devolution of old southern progressives into Dixiecrats and of onetime ardent Rooseveltians like John Temple Graves into shrill opponents of reform. He makes an apt distinction between the "good government" progressives, who never seriously threatened the disfranchisement and malapportionment that had entrenched the conservatives and the much more rare and thoroughgoing reformers like "radical democrat" Folsom, who like Huey Long terrified the conservatives, but who lacked Huey's skill and persistence in mastering his political enemies. Barnard is also keenly attuned to the conservatives' legislative maneuverings that so frustrated the erratic Folsom and limited his first-term achievements to such minor and largely negative victories as unmasking the revived Ku Klux Klan and vetoing a loyalty oath.

With his Strawberry Pickers hillbilly band, his suds bucket for contributions, and his corn-shuck mop to clean the rascals out, Big Jim Folsom's traveling road show offers fascinating details of political campaigns and their stratagems, but Barnard disappointingly relegates the elections themselves to the appendix and to an occasional summary footnote (printed, annoyingly, at the back of the book). His seven county maps are good, but they are buried in the appendix rather than placed in the text, where they might have demanded more ecological analysis. In this sense V. O. Key's friends-and-neighbors maps and crude scatter plots in *Southern Politics* (1949) are in some ways more illuminating of bifactional patterns as revealed by aggregate data, and it is disappointing that Barnard fails to take advantage of this important mode of analysis. To the degree that an assertion of continuity in Alabama's bifactionalism is central to Barnard's concern, simple regression analysis would offer a revealing measure, for instance, of voter continuity in the alliance between the northern hill counties and the Wiregrass. Similarly, his brief allusions to disfranchisement and malapportionment are historically quite correct, but they could easily have been strengthened by a simple arithmetical analysis of aggregate data that are readily obtainable.

But this is to criticize Barnard for what he has not attempted to do; what he has attempted to accomplish he has brought off quite well, together with a good bibliographical essay and useful photographs and editorial cartoons. One senses in his brief epilogue an essential sadness at the direction of events in Alabama and the South, a trend symbolized by the resurgence and then the lingering demise of Folsom, "the little man's big friend," who retired to Cullman a broken man, his vast potential unachieved, his neopopulist dream of uniting the masses of the white and black poor yet another bitter tribute to the primacy of the politics of race over the politics of economic class in the enduring South.

University of Maryland HUGH DAVIS GRAHAM
Baltimore

Democrats and Progressives: The 1948 Presidential Election as a Test of Postwar Liberalism. By Allen Yarnell. (Berkeley, Los Angeles, and London: University of California Press, 1974. Pp. xiv, 155. $8.95.)

In this interesting and well-researched volume Professor Yarnell examines the impact of the Progressive party on the conduct and outcome of the 1948 presidential election. In doing so, he also attempts to evaluate "the conventional wisdom concerning third parties" (p. 111). The results of his analysis place him in opposition to both the traditional view of third parties in American politics and the position of such other noted commentators on this particular election, as Rexford Tugwell, David Shannon, and Richard Kirkendall.

Although history has treated the colorful and feisty President from Missouri kindly, in 1948 Harry Truman's reputation was at a low ebb; and he was engulfed by virulent criticism from people with diverse ideological tenets. Leading the attack from the left was the respected quondam secretary of agriculture and erstwhile Vice-President, Henry A. Wallace. Wallace was an enigmatic and outspoken man, whose naïve but strongly held and vociferously uttered critiques of Truman's foreign policy caused the President to relieve him of his post of secretary of commerce.

Wallace at first hoped to win control of the Democratic party in 1948 and prevent Truman from being renominated. When this proved impossible, he assumed the leadership of the Progressive party, a heterogeneous assembly of individuals bound together by their dislike of the Truman administration's aggressive position vis-à-vis the Soviet Union. However, as Professor Yarnell notes (p. 63), foreign policy was tactically "a poor issue on which to found a new party . . . ," and the electorate did not respond enthusiastically.

Skillfully aided by Clark Clifford, whose "importance in the Truman victory of 1948," Yarnell asserts, "cannot be exaggerated" (p. 28), the President was able to fend off adroitly Wallace's awkward attack. While giving the rhetorical illusion of a move to the left, Truman actually did not shift his established position on major issues. As a result Truman was able to hold together the most important elements of the New Deal coalition and retain the Presidency. The Progressive party not only failed to make an impressive showing in the election, gaining only 2.5 percent of the popular vote, but it also failed to have any significant ideological effect on the Democratic party. "It is," Yarnell concludes, "a hard and cold fact that the Wallace forces did not push the Democratic party into new positions. The fabled Truman shift did not occur" (p. 86).

Professor Yarnell has researched his subject assiduously and marshaled his evidence effectively. His analyses of the Democratic party and the ephemeral Progressive party in this important election are quite cogent. If the book has a major flaw, it is the author's virtually total neglect of the equally intriguing phenomenon of the revolt of the southern right wing of the Democratic party in 1948; but one may hope that Professor Yarnell will use the commendable analytical skill which he displays here to complete the story of this political *annus mirabilis* in a future volume.

National Historical Publications Commission — E. BERKELEY TOMPKINS

Blacks and the Military in American History: A New Perspective. By Jack D. Foner. (New York and Washington: Praeger Publishers, c. 1974. Pp. x, 278. $10.00.)

Foner's *Blacks and the Military in American History* surveys the black man's attempts to prove himself by fighting the nation's foes and the segregation and discrimination which have been the black soldier's lot. From the Revolution to the 1950s the worthy contributions of black heroes and heroines and black regiments have contrasted with the reluctance to accept blacks as soldiers and officers, the segregation of black troops, the tendency to limit their service and opportunities to the dirty tasks of army life, and the occasional gross miscarriages of military justice such as in the Brownsville affair in 1906 and the Houston mutiny and riot of 1917. World War II seems to have been a turning point for the black soldier, although Foner labels the improved conditions and new opportunities "inconsiderable." In the postwar period the pressure-group tactics of black leaders, President Truman's need to outbid Henry Wallace for the black vote in 1948, and, in Korea, the necessity of rebuilding depleted white regiments with black soldiers resulted in an end to segregation in the armed forces. As Vietnam approached blacks viewed the military favorably and believed it offered greater career opportunities than civilian life. But soon that changed. For the first time a significant number of black leaders opposed the participation of blacks in an American war effort, and blacks came to regard Vietnam as their own particular incubus—a war which destroyed black youth and consumed scant financial resources needed to achieve equality at home.

Blacks and the Military reveals how racism handicaps a society at war. Until Korea black manpower was not fully utilized. Black troops had appeared threatening, and their use and promotion challenged traditional racial stereotypes. But not to make use of black troops hurt America's war efforts and led to dissatisfaction among whites who were called into the service and to the front line. The end of segregation and the dawn of an official policy of equality eased this dilemma, but as Foner's summary of recent events makes clear, racial problems still infest the military. Racial tension and fighting, the problems of promotion and equitable assignment of blacks and whites, and the doubts of blacks about the impartiality of military justice have so disrupted the military that, according to Navy secretary John W. Warner in 1972, "Race relations have now been elevated to the same top priority as combat readiness" (p. 243).

Professor Foner's survey of blacks and the military is a competent work, although uneven in emphasis and readability. The first three brief chapters, which conclude with the end of the Civil War, lack the certainty and ease of the later chapters. The subtitle, "a new perspective," is somewhat misleading, for Foner's study, based largely on secondary sources, presents a generally familiar story. Although the book's value lies in its overall view, one wishes that Foner had offered new insights and more research on the high black casualty rates and the intimations that historically black soldiers were more than equal at the front in wartime (an occurrence which, if it has any validity, may apply only to Korea and Vietnam). The book has an annotated bibliography but no footnotes.

Oakland University CARL R. OSTHAUS

Historical News and Notices

THE ASSOCIATION

The forty-first annual meeting of the Southern Historical Association will be held November 12–15, 1975, at the Shoreham Hotel in Washington, D. C.

At the annual business meeting of the Association at Dallas on November 7, 1974, Richard N. Current of the University of North Carolina at Greensboro succeeded Gilbert C. Fite of Eastern Illinois University as president. Since there had been no additions to the nominations of the Nominating Committee published in the May issue of the *Journal*, it was announced that Frank E. Vandiver of Rice University had been elected vice-president, and James C. Bonner of Georgia College, Ernest M. Lander, Jr., of Clemson University, and Hans A. Schmitt of the University of Virginia had been elected to three-year terms on the Executive Council. No mail ballot was necessary.

The Executive Council at its meeting on November 6 approved the nominations of Noble E. Cunningham, Jr., of the University of Missouri at Columbia and Richard Lowitt of the University of Kentucky as members of the Board of Editors of the *Journal*. They succeed E. David Cronon of the University of Wisconsin at Madison and Holman Hamilton of the University of Kentucky. The Executive Council also approved establishment of the Francis Butler Simkins Prize in cooperation with Longwood College. Details are given below.

President-designate Frank E. Vandiver has appointed the following program committee to serve for the forty-second meeting of the Association, which will be held in Atlanta, Georgia, November 10–13, 1976: Edwin A. Miles, University of Houston, chairman; Jerah W. Johnson, University of New Orleans, vice-chairman for non–United States history sessions; Monroe L. Billington, New Mexico State University; Blaine A. Brownell, University of Alabama in Birmingham; Judith F. Gentry, University of Southwestern Louisiana; William C. Harris, North Carolina State University; J. Leon Helguera, Vanderbilt University; Merl E. Reed, Georgia State University; Norman K. Risjord, University of Wisconsin; Robert M. Weir, University of South Carolina; Edward L. Weldon, New York State Archives; and Lorraine A. Williams, Howard University.

The committee held its first meeting in Dallas on November 8, 1974, at which time it discussed preliminary plans for the 1976 program. Since the meeting will be held during the bicentennial year of American independence, it was agreed that some special attention would be given to the era of the American Revolution, though the committee will strive to arrange a balanced program within the guidelines laid down by the bylaws of the Association. At least one-half of the sessions will deal with southern history, broadly interpreted, but there will also be sessions dealing with other aspects of United States history, as well as the history of Europe, Latin America, and other areas. In addition, there will be sessions relating to the teaching of history, historical methodology, and the nonteaching fields of the historical profession.

The committee welcomes suggestions for papers, sessions involving two or more papers, and panels. A one- or two-page résumé summarizing the content, thesis, and significance of each proposed paper would greatly assist the committee in its evaluation of suggestions received. Each prospective participant not listed in the sixth edition of the *Directory of American Scholars*, Volume I, *History* (1974), should submit a brief curriculum vitae, giving information concerning educational background, research interests, and recent publications. The committee hopes to complete most of its plans for the program at this year's meeting of the Association, so the deadline for the acceptance of proposals will be November 1, 1975. To assure earlier consideration, however, prospective participants are urged to make their proposals as soon as possible. Suggestions should be sent to Edwin A. Miles, Department of History, University of Houston, Houston, Texas 77004.

NOTE: In the text of the review of *Coozan Dudley LeBlanc* by Floyd Martin Clay, published in the November 1974 issue of the *Journal* (XL, 674–75), the author is mistakenly referred to as Martin rather than Clay. The *Journal* regrets this error.

SYDNOR AWARD

The Charles Sackett Sydnor Award for a distinguished book in southern history for 1972 and 1973 was awarded to Thomas B. Alexander of the University of Missouri at Columbia and Richard E. Beringer of the University of North Dakota for *The Anatomy of the Confederate Congress: A Study of the Influences of Member Characteristics on Legislative Voting Behavior, 1861–1864*, published in 1972 by the Vanderbilt University Press. The award is made in even-numbered years and carries a stipend of $500. The members of the Sydnor Award Committee were Charles P. Roland of the University of Kentucky, chairman, Willard B. Gatewood, Jr., of the University of Arkansas at Fayetteville, and George C. Rogers, Jr., of the University of South Carolina.

GRADUATE STUDENT AWARD

The Graduate Student Award for the best article by a graduate student published in the *Journal of Southern History* in 1972 and 1973 was awarded to Warren A. Ellem for his article "Who Were the Mississippi Scalawags?" published in the May 1972 issue (XXXVIII, 217–40). The award is made in even-numbered years and carries a prize of $50. The members of the award committee were Carol K. Rothrock Bleser of

Colgate University, chairman, Hugh C. Bailey of Samford University, and A. V. Huff, Jr., of Furman University.

THE FRANCIS BUTLER SIMKINS PRIZE

The Southern Historical Association in cooperation with Longwood College has established the Francis Butler Simkins Prize to honor the late Francis Butler Simkins, eminent scholar, former president of the Southern Historical Association, and long-time professor of history at Longwood College. The prize will be awarded in odd-numbered years for a distinguished scholarly first book in the general field of southern history published in the preceding biennium. The formal presentation will be made at the annual meeting of the Southern Historical Association. The first award will be made at the 1977 annual meeting for a book published in 1975 or 1976. It will carry a stipend of $200 and include a certificate suitably inscribed and framed. The monetary value of the award may be increased from time to time. It will be funded by the Simkins Memorial Fund, which is administered by the Department of History at Longwood College, with the chairman or another member of the department designated by him acting as liaison with the Association.

The winner of the prize will be chosen by the Simkins Prize Committee, to consist of three members appointed by the president of the Association biennially, beginning in the fall of 1974. The chairman of the committee will maintain liaison with the Longwood Department of History. Members of the committee will assess the merits of eligible books and decide the winner by majority vote not later than six weeks before the prize is to be awarded. Publishers may nominate one or more books, sending copies directly to each of the members of the prize committee. Authors may also submit their own books in the same fashion. Such submissions *must be made by March 1 of the year of the award*. Entries must be a first book by the author or authors, be scholarly, be in the general field of southern history, and have been published in the specified biennium. Winners of the Sydnor Award may also be considered for this prize if their books conform to the above criteria.

EUROPEAN HISTORY SECTION

The European History Section of the Southern Historical Association at its annual business meeting in Dallas on November 8, 1974, elected the following officers: Enno E. Kraehe of the University of Virginia, chairman; Joel Colton of the humanities section of the Rockefeller Foundation, vice-chairman; Amos E. Simpson of the University of Southwestern Louisiana, secretary-treasurer; and Walter R. Craddock of the University of Southwestern Louisiana, managing editor of the *European History Newsletter*.

The European History Section's John L. Snell Memorial Prize for the best seminar research paper completed during the academic year

1973–1974 (including the summer of 1973) was awarded to Robert C. Thomas of the University of Maryland, a student of Louis M. Greenberg, for his essay "Orleanist Spoliation Claims Debates, 1834–1835." The award carried a stipend of $100. The selection committee included Irby C. Nichols of North Texas State University, chairman; Gerard E. Silberstein of the University of Kentucky; and Richard C. Marius of the University of Tennessee at Knoxville.

PERSONALS

Office of Air Force History: Stanley L. Falk named chief historian.

University of Alabama, Huntsville: Lee E. Williams, II, appointed instructor.

State College of Arkansas: Eugene J. Corcoran appointed assistant professor; Harry W. Readnour promoted to associate professor and William Mayes to assistant professor; John Buckner has retired.

Auburn University: Donathon Carnes Olliff promoted to assistant professor.

Bishop College: Edward Rice-Maximin promoted to assistant professor.

Carson-Newman College: Robert M. Burts named chairman of Social Sciences Division and James L. Baumgardner coordinator of History/Political Science Department.

Columbus College: Mark L. Berger promoted to associate professor.

Duke University: Barry Gough appointed visiting associate professor for fall semester and Dennis Conrad, Sara Evans, Jeffery A. Gunsburg, and John M. Lindley instructors.

East Tennessee State University: James L. Odom and Dale J. Schmitt promoted to associate professor.

East Texas State University: Margaret Patoski appointed assistant professor; Keith D.McFarland promoted to associate professor.

Elon College: Robert W. Delp named chairman.

Fairmont State College: Harold D. Peters named assistant to dean of academic affairs; Robert L. Daugherty appointed assistant professor; Carl Hunt promoted to assistant professor.

Florida State University: Jeanne V. Conner and Darrell Levi appointed assistant professors; Paul G. Halpern and Mary Elizabeth Thomas promoted to professor and Edward F. Keuchel, William O. Oldson, and Paul W. Strait to associate professor.

Franklin D. Roosevelt Library: William R. Emerson named director.

Georgetown University: Michael Hudson appointed lecturer.

Georgia College: Rosemary E. Begemann appointed assistant professor.

Georgia Southern College: Stephen Gurr promoted to associate professor.

Hendrix College: John A. Ziegler appointed associate professor and named chairman.

Jacksonville University: George E. Buker promoted to associate professor.

John Brown University: Richard L. Niswonger promoted to associate professor; William H. Burnside on leave.

Kent State University: Kenneth R. Calkins, John T. Hubbell, and James P. Louis promoted to associate professor.

Lincoln University (Missouri): Roland Johnson, Maynard Jordan, and Franklin Powell appointed to the staff; Dan D. Bradbury promoted to associate professor; Gary Kremer on leave.

Livingston University: James P. Pate named chairman; Fred W. Sakon promoted to associate professor.

University of Missouri, Columbia: Gerard H. Clarfield and Charles E. Timberlake on leave fall semester and N. Gerald Barrier and Richard Thomas Bienvenu spring semester; William Francis English has retired.

Nicholls State University: Thomas Becnel promoted to associate professor.

North Carolina Central University: G. W. Reid named chairman; Lydia Lindsey appointed instructor.

North Carolina Division of Archives and History: Robert Edwin Stipe named director and Larry E. Tise assistant director.

University of North Carolina, Charlotte: Paul D. Escott appointed assistant professor.

University of North Carolina, Wilmington: Alan D. Watson promoted to associate professor.

North Texas State University: Irby C. Nichols, Jr., on leave spring semester.

Oklahoma College of Liberal Arts: John Dexter Marble promoted to assistant professor; Irene E. Mitchell has retired.

Pembroke State University: Jeffrey A. Mirus appointed assistant professor.

Rockefeller Foundation: Joel Colton named director for humanities.

University of South Florida: George H. Mayer on leave.

Southern Methodist University: Luis Martin on leave for spring semester.

Spring Hill College: Howard W. Smith named acting chairman.

Stetson University: Gilbert L. Lycan has retired.

Tennessee State University: Johnny Louis Burchett appointed instructor.

Tennessee Wesleyan College: Thomas J. Baker, Jr., named chairman.

Texas A&M University: Roger A. Beaumont and Arnold P. Krammer appointed associate professors, Ralph J. Q. Adams assistant professor, and Keith A. Sutherland visiting assistant professor; Thomas Lloyd Miller has retired.

Texas Woman's University: Leonard C. Schlup appointed assistant professor and Martha Helen Swain instructor.

Union College: William S. Oxendine named head of the department; Erwin S. Bradley has retired.

Union University: Gay Semrav appointed instructor.

Vanderbilt University: William T. Alderson appointed adjunct professor for spring semester.

Virginia Commonwealth University: Leland C. Barrows appointed assistant professor; Sandra M. Hawley promoted to assistant professor.

Virginia Polytechnic Institute and State University: Michael C. Hurst appointed visiting professor for fall quarter and Harry D. Bralley assistant professor; Robert P. Grathwol, William E. Mackie, and J. Dean O'Donnell on leave.

Washington and Lee University: Robert B. Jeans, Jr., appointed assistant professor; Leon Franklin Sensabaugh has retired.

Washington University: David T. Konig on leave spring and fall semesters 1975.

Wayland College: Estelle Owens appointed assistant professor.

College of William and Mary: Jess H. Stone appointed assistant professor; Judith Ewell on leave.

Winston-Salem State University: James McLaughlin appointed instructor.

Xavier University: Sister Barbara Hughes named chairman; Thomas F. Gallagher appointed associate professor.

ANNOUNCEMENTS AND ACTIVITIES

The National Historical Publications Commission has approved many publication grants, six of which are for new projects including letterpress publication of the papers of William Livingston, Henry Bouquet, and Josiah Bartlett, and of a selective edition of papers relating to the American Revolution in the West Indies, and microfilm publication of the papers of Tench Coxe and William R. Shafter. Five additional grants were made to the Adams family and the Franklin, Hamilton, Jefferson, and Madison papers. Appropriations were also made for continuing letterpress publication of the papers of John C. Calhoun, Jefferson Davis, Ulysses S. Grant, James K. Polk, Jonathan Trumbull, Booker T. Washington, and for editing and publishing the papers of Henry Clay, Frederick Douglass, Samuel Gompers, Marquis de Lafayette, Benjamin Henry Latrobe, John Marshall, George Washington, Daniel Webster, and the First Congress. At its September 21, 1974, meeting, the Commission made its first subvention grants to seven university presses to offset publication deficits of eleven editorial series volumes. Eight new and continuing microfilm projects received Commission funds including the Emily Howland, Jane Addams, Rutherford B. Hayes, Richard Pettigrew, Ezra Stiles, and Samuel "Golden Rule" Jones papers, and the American Federation of Labor and Panton, Leslie, and Company records.

The Commission has also undertaken a revision of the *Guide to Archives and Manuscripts in the United States,* edited by Philip Hamer (1961). Anne Harris Henry will coordinate the revision, which will seek to produce a comprehensive survey of manuscript resources in institutional repositories of the United States.

The Commission will continue its program of fellowships in advanced editing of documentary sources for American history. As many as eight will be made in 1975–76, each bearing a stipend of $11,000. Information about the Commission's educational programs may be obtained from the Executive Director, National Historical Publications Commission, National Archives Building, Room 100, Washington, D. C. 20408.

The Mrs. Simon Baruch University Award for 1974 has been awarded to Professor Sarah Woolfolk Wiggins of the University of Alabama for her manuscript entitled "Scalawags in Alabama Politics, 1865–1881." The award was established by the United Daughters of the Confederacy in 1904.

The American Revolution Bicentennial Commission of Florida will hold its fourth annual symposium dealing with Florida's role in the American Revolution March 21–22, 1975, at Florida State University. The theme for the meeting will be "Eighteenth Century Florida and the Revolutionary South." Inquiries and reservations should be directed to Samuel Proctor, Chairman, Bicentennial Symposium, Division of Continuing Education, Hecht House, Florida State University, Tallahassee, Florida 32306.

The tenth annual Walter Prescott Webb Memorial Lectures will be delivered April 3, 1975, at the University of Texas at Arlington. Papers on Professor Webb and the influence of his ideas will be presented by Professors W. Eugene Hollon, W. Turrentine Jackson, Joe B. Frantz, and George Wolfskill. Further information may be obtained from the Webb Lecture Committee, Department of History, University of Texas, Arlington, Texas 76019.

"Black Local History and Genealogy: Problems and Prospects" will be the conference topic for the Southwest Research Center and Museum for the Study of Negro Life and Culture meeting at Bishop College, April 3–5, 1975. Those interested in further information should write Harry Robinson, Jr., Coordinator, Southwest Research Center and Museum for the Study of Negro Life and Culture, Bishop College, Box 866, Dallas, Texas 75241.

Northeastern Oklahoma State University will sponsor a symposium on the American Indian on May 1–2, 1975. The meeting will examine "The American Indian and American Ideals: 200 Years After Independence." Program and reservation information may be obtained from Billy Joe Davis, Director, Symposium of the American Indian, Division of Social Sciences, Northeastern Oklahoma State University, Tahlequah, Oklahoma 74464.

The United States Army Command and General Staff College has established a chair of military history for a visiting professor. The visiting professor for 1974–1975 is Harry L. Coles of Ohio State University. Two other qualified civilian historians are to be appointed annually to conduct courses in military history and to develop research for the Departments of Tactics and Strategy. Joseph R. Goldman will serve with the Department of Strategy and Lynn L. Sims with the Department of Tactics.

LIBRARIES AND ARCHIVES

The Library of Congress Manuscript Division has recently acquired the following material of interest to southern historians: a holograph by an unknown hand docketed "A Description of the City of Washington, Decr. 14. 1799"; additions to the papers of Secretary of War James McHenry (1753–1816); a nineteen-reel microfilm of the thirty-nine volumes constituting Foreign Office 47 (Liberia) in the British Public Record Office (1848–1905); the papers of Washington *Post* owner-publisher Eugene Meyer (1875–1959); and 24,000 items from the Leadership Conference on Civil Rights (1963–73).

New material in the National Archives and Records Service of interest in the field of southern history includes 48 cubic feet of records of the National Council on Indian Opportunity, 1968–74; tabulations prepared by the Bureau of the Census for the Office of Economic Opportunity from the 1970 census entitled "Poverty Neighborhoods in 105 Large Central Cities"; and 4,000 photographs from the Bureau of Mines of the Department of the Interior made by the Medical Survey Group of the Coal Mines Administration–Navy, 1946–47.

New National Archives publications include *Documents from America's Past,* General Information Leaflet No. 13.

Recent archives microfilm publications are M739, Letters Sent by the War Department Relating to Naval Matters, January 3, 1794–June 14, 1798; M927, Letters, Orders for Pay, Accounts, Receipts, and Other Supply Records Concerning Weapons and Military Stores, 1776–1801; M965, Case Files in Suits Involving Consuls and Vice Consuls and the Repeal of Patents of the United States District Court for the Southern District of New York, 1806–60; M977, Navy Department General Orders and Circulars, 1798–1862.

The Kansas City Archives Branch has arranged and described 120 cubic feet of records of the U. S. Coast Guard and its predecessor agencies from the mid-1840s to 1960 including material from the port of St. Louis.

The Dwight D. Eisenhower Library has declassified records of the President's Committee on Migratory Labor, 1938–66, and has made available Orval Faubus's transcript from the Columbia University Oral History Project.

The South Carolina Archives has accessioned the following state materials: records of the comptroller general and annual statements of county treasurers (1953–55); records of the state House of Representatives including bills defeated and vetoed (1971–72), budgets (1940–63), correspondence, congressional (1951–72), photographs of members (1900–58), and reports (1938–72); records of the Industrial Commission including accident register (1936–48) and docket case listing (1935–47); records of the Military Department, Office of the Adjutant General, including muster rolls and enlistment papers (1907–22), miscellaneous records (1886–1913), property account books (1911–22), and Spanish–American War veterans list (1898); records of the Department of Social Services including Civilian Conservation Corps recruiting plan for South Carolina (1938–42); records of the state treasurer, including appropriation ledgers (1938–64), general deposit ledgers (1958–64), revenue ledgers, general accounts (1940–58), revenue ledgers, special accounts (1945–58), and special deposit ledgers (1958–64).

Recent acquisitions of the East Carolina Manuscript Collection, East Carolina University, include the papers (1932–74) of Major General John Albert Lang, Jr., secretary of the North Carolina Department of Military and Veterans Affairs; missionary papers of Catherine Parham (1920–72, Congo), Jessie L. Wolcott (1939–50, China), and Venetia Cox (1939, China); tobacco records of the Greenville office of the Export Leaf Tobacco Company (1912–40), the eastern North Carolina offices of Imperial Tobacco Company, Ltd. (1902–66), and of the Growers Cooperative Warehouse, Inc., of Wilson, N. C. (1948–72); papers (1958–74) of attorney general and U. S. senator-elect Robert Morgan; papers (1925–69) of poetess Lucy Cherry Crisp with notes from an interview with George Washington Carver; and the Getsinger family papers (1847–1944) containing correspondence of the Mexican War.

The Maryland Historical Society has added the following material to its manuscript collections: the Shriver Family Papers from Union Mills, Maryland, MS. 2085; the copybook of Baltimore printer and publisher Fielding Lucas, Jr., c. 1800, MS. 2083; the Frank W. Buschman Collection, 1916–1923, MS. 2082; the Troop Family letters, 1815–1891, MS. 2060; the account book of Baltimore merchant Thomas Moale, 1790–1802, MS. 2087; and the Hamilton Downs Business Collection, including the receipts of this Williamsport merchant, 1852–1875, MS. 2048.

The Auburn University Archives has a number of collections of interest to southern and American historians, including Civil War materials, business records, and a variety of other materials. A brief description of the holdings may be obtained from Professor Allen W. Jones, Department of Archives, Auburn University, Auburn, Alabama 36830.

turn the page, please

THE SOUTHERN HISTORICAL ASSOCIATION

THE JOURNAL OF SOUTHERN HISTORY

MAY 1975
Vol. XLI, No. 2

Published Quarterly by the Southern Historical Association

The Journal of Southern History

Published Quarterly by

THE SOUTHERN HISTORICAL ASSOCIATION

New Orleans, Louisiana

Printed by WILLIAM BYRD PRESS,
RICHMOND, VIRGINIA

The present constitution of the Southern Historical Association is printed in the February 1974 issue of the *Journal of Southern History,* Volume XL, Number 1.

Contributions and correspondence relating to articles, book reviews, and any other editorial matters should be sent to the Managing Editor, *Journal of Southern History,* Rice University, Houston, Texas 77001.

The subscription rate is $10.00 a year for a regular membership, $12.00 for family membership, $5.00 for enrolled student, and $3.00 for retired members. Upon payment of $200.00 any person may become a life member of the Southern Historical Association. Single numbers of the *Journal* are available at $3.00 plus postage. Changes of address must be made six weeks in advance of the publication of an issue in order for the change to be effective with that issue. A charge of $2.50 will be made for forwarding copies returned because of incorrect addresses.

Subscriptions, membership applications, and orders for current issues of the *Journal* should be sent to Bennett H. Wall, Secretary-Treasurer, History Department, Tulane University, New Orleans, Louisiana 70118. *Notice of nonreceipt of an issue must be sent to the Secretary-Treasurer within sixty days following publication of the issue.* Inquiries concerning noncurrent back issues of the *Journal* should be directed to Johnson Reprint Corporation, 111 Fifth Avenue, New York, New York 10003.

Second-class postage paid at New Orleans, Louisiana, and at additional mailing offices.

The Journal of SOUTHERN HISTORY

VOLUME XLI MAY 1975 NUMBER 2

Contents

The Antebellum Southern Herdsman: A Reinterpretation
By Forrest McDonald and Grady McWhiney 147

Black Militancy in Readjuster Virginia, 1879–1883 *By James T. Moore* 167

The Demise of the Colored Farmers' Alliance
By William F. Holmes 187

Southern History in Periodicals, 1974: A Selected Bibliography 201

Annual Report of the Secretary-Treasurer
By Bennett H. Wall 233

Book Reviews 240

Book Notes 283

Historical News and Notices 291

Book Reviews

GENOVESE, *Roll, Jordan, Roll,* by Bertram Wyatt-Brown 240
FINSTER, ed., *The National Archives and Urban Research,* by Leonard P. Curry 242
COLEMAN, *Debtors and Creditors in America,* by Gerald Sorin 243
SHERIDAN, *Sugar and Slavery,* by Gerald W. Mullin 245
WOOD, *Black Majority,* by George C. Rogers, Jr. 246
PRICE, ed., *North Carolina Higher-Court Records,* by Nannie M. Tilley 248
CROWLEY, *This Sheba, Self,* by Phinizy Spalding 249
KETCHAM, *From Colony to Country,* by Joyce O. Appleby 250
CALDWELL, *Tennessee,* by Charles W. Crawford 251
AMMERMAN, *In the Common Cause,* by John A. Neuenschwander 252
O'DONNELL, *Southern Indians in the American Revolution,* by Henry T. Malone 253
BARTLETT, *The New Country,* by Walter Rundell, Jr. 255
BOYD and LESTER, eds., *The Papers of Thomas Jefferson,* Vol. 19, by Robert M. McColley 256
BRUCE, *And They All Sang Hallelujah,* by John B. Boles 258
LUMPKIN, *The Emancipation of Angelina Grimké,* by Jane H. Pease ... 259
SWISHER, *History of the Supreme Court of the United States,* Vol. V, by Phillip S. Paludan 260
BAUER, *The Mexican War,* by Seymour V. Connor 262
MORRISON, ed., *The Memoirs of Henry Heth,* by Frank L. Byrne 263
SWORD, *Shiloh,* by James L. Baumgardner 264
FISCHER, *The Segregation Struggle in Louisiana,* by Robert G. Sherer .. 265
SHOFNER, *Nor Is It Over Yet,* by Robert H. Jones 266
MOORE, ed., *The Juhl Letters to the* Charleston Courier, by W. Calvin Smith 267
MATHIS, ed., *College Life in the Reconstruction South,* by Howard W. Smith 268
MOORE, *Two Paths to the New South,* by William J. Cooper, Jr. 269
KOUSSER, *The Shaping of Southern Politics,* by William F. Holmes 270
WILSON, *Coming of Age,* by Thomas M. Deaton 272
GARSON, *The Democratic Party and the Politics of Sectionalism,* by Keith L. Bryant, Jr. 273
PARKER, *The Morrison Era,* by James L. McCorkle, Jr. 274
ROSENGARTEN, *All God's Dangers,* by Howard N. Rabinowitz 275
BAKER, *The Southern Baptist Convention and Its People,* by William A. Poe 277
ELOVITZ, *A Century of Jewish Life in Dixie,* by Arnold Shankman 278
ALVEY, *History of Mary Washington College,* by Lucille Griffith 279
EDWARDS, *Pioneer-at-Law,* by Charles C. Alexander 280
BAKER, *Catch the Vision,* by Ottis Clark Skipper 281

The Antebellum Southern Herdsman: A Reinterpretation

By Forrest McDonald and Grady McWhiney

In 1860 hogs and other southern livestock were worth half a billion dollars—more than twice the value of that year's cotton crop. Not all of the Old South's animals were sold each year, of course, but in 1850 the Patent Office (the statistics-gathering predecessor of the Department of Agriculture) reported that one relatively small area of the South—some two hundred miles square of piney woods in southern Mississippi, eastern Louisiana, and western Alabama—had "raised, . . . for 20 years past, one million head of cattle yearly" and sold them for "from $10 to $12 per head." Two-thirds of the nation's hogs were grown in the South. In 1860 ten southern states—Alabama, Texas, Georgia, Mississippi, Arkansas, Kentucky, North Carolina, Missouri, Tennessee, and Virginia—could boast of a hog population of more than a million; only four northern states—Illinois, Indiana, Ohio, and Pennsylvania—could claim so many. Nor were these southern animals merely valueless "razorbacks," so often described as bone and gristle. In 1860 the hogs and other livestock slaughtered in the South were worth some $106,555,000; this was $327,000 more than all the livestock slaughtered in the North.[1]

[1] *Agriculture of the United States in 1860 . . . Compiled from . . . the Eighth Census . . .* (Washington, 1864), 184–87; *Report of the Commissioner of Patents, for the Year 1850:* Part II, *Agriculture* (Washington, 1851), 260; cited hereinafter as *Patent Office Report, 1850.* The average price for middling upland cotton between 1856 and 1860 was 11.5 cents on the New York market and 6.7 cents on the Liverpool market. The weighted average price in 1860 on the New Orleans market was 11.1 cents per pound. M. B. Hammond, *The Cotton Industry: An Essay in American Economic History* (New York, 1897), Appendix I; Lewis C. Gray, *History of Agriculture in the Southern United States to 1860* (2 vols., Washington, 1933), II, 1027. For this study an average price of 10 cents per pound was used. It should be noted that cotton prices fluctuated "as much as 5 cents per pound—and more—throughout the season in every market . . . ." Harold D. Woodman, *King Cotton & His Retainers: Financing & Marketing the Cotton Crop of the South, 1800–1925* (Lexington, 1968), 19–20.

This essay presents a tentative and a preliminary statement of a thesis on this and related

Messrs. McDonald and McWhiney are professors of history at Wayne State University. Mr. McWhiney will be professor of history at the University of Alabama after June 1, 1975.

The Journal of Southern History
Vol. XLI, No. 2, May 1975

Despite their numbers and value, southern animals—as well as the people who raised them—have received far less attention than their importance in the economy warranted.[2] Hogs especially have been neglected. This neglect of livestock in works on the South seems to be the result of a strong historiographical tradition. Part of the problem is that historians, especially those who synthesize, usually write about what other historians have written about. This is necessary, of course, because no individual can become an expert on all topics and in all areas. So historians borrow from and build upon previous scholarship; they also follow trends, just as do other people. Textbook writers and other generalists have ignored the importance of animals in the South's history because specialists have ignored livestock. In 1965 a distinguished agricultural historian stated: "There are no works dealing with southern farm livestock except for rather sketchy and inadequate treatment of livestock production in the Tennessee-Kentucky region."[3]

Another reason why livestock and those who raised it have received little attention[4] may be that historians have been intimidated by one or both of two overwhelming historiographical in-

subjects on which we are currently doing research toward a book. We offer it now, complete with possible imperfections, on the ground that it will be several years before we publish the book and we would like to stimulate criticism and research in this immensely rich area right away. For critical comments and suggestions, we are grateful to Professors James C. Bonner, E. Merton Coulter, David Herbert Donald, Ari Hoogenboom, John Hebron Moore, Charles P. Roland, V. Jacque Voegeli, and Bennett H. Wall.

[2] Julian A. C. Chandler *et al.*, eds., *The South in the Building of the Nation* (13 vols., Richmond, 1909–1913), V, 242–57, allot a mere fifteen pages to the animal industry of the South and only a short paragraph (125 words) to hogs; Wendell H. Stephenson and E. Merton Coulter, eds., *A History of the South* (9 vols. to date, [Baton Rouge], 1947–   ), devote only thirty of the more than four thousand pages in these volumes to livestock. See also Francis B. Simkins and Charles P. Roland, *A History of the South* (4th ed., New York, 1972); William B. Hesseltine and David L. Smiley, *The South in American History* (2d ed., Englewood Cliffs, N. J., 1960); and Monroe L. Billington, *The American South: A Brief History* (New York, 1971). An exception to this pattern is Charles P. Roland's forthcoming volume on the recent South, which has much information on livestock and poultry production since World War II.

[3] James C. Bonner, "Plantation and Farm: The Agricultural South," in Arthur S. Link and Rembert W. Patrick, eds., *Writing Southern History: Essays in Historiography in Honor of Fletcher M. Green* ([Baton Rouge], 1965), 169.

[4] There are some exceptions. Gray, *History of Agriculture*, devotes many pages to livestock. So does Sam B. Hilliard, *Hog Meat and Hoecake: Food Supply in the Old South, 1840–1860* (Carbondale and Edwardsville, Ill., London, and Amsterdam, 1972). Other scholars who have not ignored the subject include John H. Moore, *Agriculture in Ante-Bellum Mississippi* (New York, 1958); James C. Bonner, *A History of Georgia Agriculture, 1732–1860* (Athens, 1964); Everett Dick, *The Dixie Frontier: A Social History of the Southern Frontier from the First Transmontane Beginnings to the Civil War* (New York, 1948); Clement Eaton, *A History of the Old South* (New York, 1949); Clement Eaton, *The Growth of Southern Civilization, 1790–1860* (New York, 1961); Paul W. Gates, *The Farmer's Age: Agriculture, 1815–1860* (New York, 1960); and, of course, Frank L. Owsley, *Plain Folk of the Old South* ([Baton Rouge], 1949). See also note 22.

fluences. No single individual has exerted more influence upon interpreting the history of the South, especially the antebellum South, than Ulrich Bonnell Phillips. In his two most important works—*American Negro Slavery* and *Life and Labor in the Old South*—Phillips insisted that plantations and slavery determined the nature of southern society. At the top were the agriculturists who owned much land and many Negroes and grew the great staple crops. Because his interests centered on the plantation, Phillips neglected those people who were not large slaveholders and landowners. He failed to mention hog raisers in *American Negro Slavery* though he noted that bacon was a staple in the slave diet and was, along with chicken, one of the plantation's "standard meats."[5] It is not that Phillips totally ignored southerners who raised and drove livestock to market. He was aware that such people existed, but he minimized their importance by giving them little space in his books. He spent less than a page on livestock drovers in *Life and Labor.*[6]

By allotting so little space to people like drovers, who were not a part of the plantation itself but without whom the plantation system could not have existed, Phillips distorted both the composition of antebellum southern society and the importance of certain occupations. He also perpetuated the misconception that almost every antebellum southerner was, or wanted to be, a grower of great staple crops. "Wanted: lands like those of the Bluegrass, in the climate of middle Georgia, on rivers flowing smoothly to the sea, under laws favorable to the holding of Negroes in bondage. Such a notice," Phillips contended, "might well have been signed by any of ten thousand men in the 'teens; and the 'twenties, 'thirties, 'forties and 'fifties brought no end to the demand."[7]

Phillips arranged his evidence to convince readers that the only worthwhile activity in the Old South was the growing of plants, *and that success, not occupation, determined a man's place in society.* What caused the differences in wealth between planters and farmers, he argued, was simply "the variance of talent, resolution, health and mere luck. The divergencies furthermore, were not sharply between rich and poor but of continuous gradation from millionaires to paupers; and the classes were by no means constant in personnel." Long before Frank Lawrence Owsley wrote a book

[5] Phillips, *American Negro Slavery: A Survey of the Supply, Employment and Control of Negro Labor as Determined by the Plantation Régime* (New York and London, 1918), 265, 276, 279, 297, 312 (quotation).

[6] Phillips, *Life and Labor in the Old South* (Boston, 1929), 144–45.

[7] *Ibid.*, 99.

about the "plain folk" Phillips had "discovered" them—only to obscure them by painting them in false colors. "These and their fellow millions," he wrote, "cannot be lumped as 'poor whites' and dismissed . . . ." They were yeoman farmers who grew plants; all of them aspired to possess land and slaves, many owned land, and some owned a few slaves. "Their standards of comfort and propriety, their manners and morals, varied with the vicinage, with health and wealth, with education and opportunity, and with individual proclivities and predilections," Phillips claimed,[8] but he saw all as a part of a competitive agricultural society and system in which everyone tried to better himself by acquiring land and slaves.

What Phillips completely missed in his analysis of antebellum society was the importance of the herdsmen. In some ways this is a curious oversight, since Phillips used certain references to herdsmen which suggest that their role was far more significant than his brief mention of them would indicate. For example, he quoted a Virginia mountaineer, who wrote in 1828: "I am not making any money at present, and cannot until I sell my corn to Hog-drovers, from which I never have failed to make every fall something like four or five hundred dollars." This letter alone suggests that hog driving was a sizable—and distinct—economic operation. Such a conclusion is confirmed by another letter quoted by Phillips from a settler near Chattanooga who complained in 1850 that a drought had reduced local crops by half: "I do not know what the poor hog drovers will do for corn this season if they drive as many as they did last. They must have drove some 80 thousand . . . last season, and it would take no inconsiderable part of the corn raised in our valley . . . to feed that number during their passage this season. The mules have commenced going already. For the last two weeks there has hardly been a day that a drove or two has not passed."[9]

Apart from Phillips, the man most responsible for distorting the southern herdsmen's role was Frederick Jackson Turner. If Phillips's vertical model of antebellum southern society minimized the importance of the herdsmen by placing them near the bottom of a chain of ambition, Turner's horizontal model of successive frontiers relegated the herdsmen to a transitory and impermanent existence. They were to him merely a stage in frontier development—"fur-trader, miner, cattle-raiser, and farmer." As Turner described this process, "each type of industry was on the march toward the West, impelled by an irresistible attraction. Each passed in successive waves across the continent. Stand at Cumber-

[8] *Ibid.*, 346, 340.

[9] *Ibid.*, 144–45.

land Gap and watch the procession of civilization, marching single file—the buffalo following the trail to the salt springs, the Indian, the fur-trader and hunter, the cattle-raiser, the pioneer farmer—and the frontier has passed by. Stand at South Pass in the Rockies a century later and see the same procession . . . ."[10]

This Turnerian emphasis upon the herdsman as a transitory figure always being pushed westward by farmers is evident in even the most careful studies of southern livestock raisers. Lewis Cecil Gray, who devoted considerable space to animal husbandry in his massive history of agriculture in the Old South, concluded: "Before the outbreak of the Civil War the advance of agriculture was driving the herding industry into the semiarid districts of western Texas."[11]

Turner's influence is also apparent in the best analysis of the antebellum southern livestock grazers ever written—the twenty-eight pages Frank L. Owsley allotted to herdsmen in his study of the Old South's plain folk.[12] Owsley made a valuable contribution to the understanding of the livestock industry by showing that "grazing was a major occupation in the South . . ." and that grazers were "a large and important element" in antebellum southern society.[13] But he also argued that herdsmen "were the typical pioneers." Some, essentially hunters and trappers who grazed animals only as a "secondary pursuit," constantly moved "from place to place in search of better pastures and more game"; others, "who were the main body of frontiersmen, occupied the zone of unsurveyed lands at a reasonably safe distance from the Indian border. They were the genuine herdsmen."[14] Owsley believed that, as a rule, herdsmen ultimately either became farmers or were driven out as grazing regions became more settled. "A cattleman usually began as a poor young man, and if he became wealthy he settled down in some well-selected spot, usually as a planter . . . ," he wrote. "Frequently, too, the smaller herdsmen settled as farmers on land which they had purchased . . . ." But "Many others . . . grazed their cattle and hunted from one frontier to another until at last there was no frontier left except the great pine barrens and the broken mountainous regions."[15]

[10] Turner, "The Significance of the Frontier in American History," in Turner, *The Frontier in American History* (New York, 1920), 12.

[11] Gray, *History of Agriculture,* II, 834.

[12] Owsley, *Plain Folk,* 23–50; see also Owsley, "The Pattern of Migration and Settlement on the Southern Frontier," *Journal of Southern History,* XI (May 1945), 147–76.

[13] Owsley, *Plain Folk,* 27, 24.

[14] *Ibid.,* 24–25.

[15] *Ibid.,* 33–34, 25.

Table 1

FARMS AND PRODUCTION IN SELECTED ALABAMA COUNTIES, 1860

Counties	Farms Under 50 Acres	Farms Over 500 Acres	Total Number of Farms	Total Number of Hogs	Total Value of Livestock	Average Number of Hogs Per Farm	Average Value of Livestock Per Farm	Average Value of Cotton Per Farm*
Black Belt:								
Dallas	116	193	711	55,145	$1,716,129	78	$2,414	$3,567
Greene	72	166	793	49,701	1,746,454	63	2,202	2,919
Lowndes	249	160	1,033	56,394	1,661,362	55	1,608	2,078
Marengo	187	166	778	58,457	1,699,142	75	2,184	3,210
Monroe	299	39	764	30,661	673,257	40	881	954
Montgomery	117	169	800	63,134	1,748,273	79	2,185	2,944
Perry	229	118	926	41,767	1,305,872	45	1,410	1,927
Black Belt Counties	1,269	1,011	5,805	355,259	$10,550,489	61	$1,818	$2,474
Pine Belt and Upland:								
Bibb	370	7	878	42,158	$608,458	48	$693	$878
Coffee	433	4	829	23,859	392,032	29	473	255
Coosa	841	24	1,631	35,810	909,070	22	557	343
Covington	312	5	517	20,527	324,362	40	627	156
Fayette	758	0	1,189	21,963	501,713	18	422	184
Lauderdale	456	71	996	24,101	845,171	24	849	444
Randolph	1,508	3	2,202	37,596	679,785	17	309	117
Washington	136	117	725	15,314	295,576	21	408	190
Pine Belt and Upland Counties	4,814	231	8,967	221,328	$4,556,167	25	$508	$250

SOURCE: Agriculture in the United States in 1860, pp. 2-5, 193. The counties are those selected by Owsley, Plain Folk, 157-62, 181-93.
* An average price of 10 cents per pound was used for cotton.

Owsley's explanation of why the herdsmen moved so often was the same as Turner's, though with a twist that explained how herdsmen could remain in the East while being pushed ever westward—namely, that they were driven to the "inner frontier." "It was agriculture . . . ," insisted Owsley, "that drove the herdsmen from frontier to frontier and finally into the pine barrens, hills, and mountains. After the Civil War this phenomenon was repeated when the farmers or nesters swarmed into the Great Plains and crowded the cattle ranchers farther into the more arid regions."[16]

Though Owsley believed that farmers drove out the herdsmen, he did not believe that slavery and the plantation system drove out the small farmers. Indeed, he argued that small and large plant growers managed to live together in harmony. But, astonishingly, he did not go on to observe that animal growers and plant growers could also coexist in large areas of the South. As a result, he ignored the probability that half or more of the people he listed as small farmers (Owsley estimated that 70 percent of the people of the lower South owned farms)[17] raised animals worth more than their crops and that many of the rest raised plants such as corn primarily to supply animals. (Table 1 illustrates the prevalence of

[16] *Ibid.*, 51.
[17] *Ibid.*, 9.

livestock culture in precisely those counties that Owsley used to illustrate the opposite.)

Livestock growers have suffered some misunderstanding in the works of Phillips and even the most conscientious Turnerians, such as Owsley, because all these historians shared a Jeffersonian bias; their ideal types—Phillips's planter and the Turnerians' independent yeoman—were dirt farmers. These writers considered livestock growers as primitive, passing, and inferior to the superior and more permanent plant growers. The epitome of this whole attitude can be found in the words of the most distinguished living Turnerian.

> Far below the yeoman farmers in the South's social scale [wrote Ray Allen Billington] were the poor whites who, as "crackers," "hillbillies," or "sandhillers," were scattered in small communities through the poorest southern lands: the Georgia pine barrens, the sandy-woods section of southern Mississippi, the piney forests of Alabama, and the worn-out soils abandoned by cotton planters. Most of them made a pretense of planting a crop but lethargy overcame them once the seed was in the ground. They depended for food less on their weed-choked fields than on omnipresent hogs who cared for themselves and on game they brought down with their long rifles. Unkempt, illiterate, shiftless, and lazy, these miserable byproducts of the plantation system were condemned to their squalid existence by more fortunate neighbors who pushed them onto unproductive lands, then kept there by the ravages of the parasitical hookworm which left them lethargic and listless. Yet they too defended slavery, largely because they subconsciously realized that this artificial barrier alone kept them from the very bottom of the social scale.[18]

A special word needs to be added about Sam Bowers Hilliard's excellent recent work on the southern food supply, *Hog Meat and Hoecake*. Hilliard is often brilliant and sometimes profound, and as a result of his diligent labors we know a great deal more about the raising and consumption of livestock (especially hogs) in the antebellum South than we ever knew before. But he, too, is caught up in the Phillips-Turner trap. He recognizes that enormous quantities of hogs were raised but vacillates between believing that they were incidentally raised by plant growers who aspired to become planters, à la Phillips, and by frontiersmen who were being pushed ever westward or toward "internal frontiers," à la Turner and Owsley. Only now and again does Hilliard depart from a two-character model of southern society (that is, "subsistence farmers" and the people they aspired to become, slaveowning cotton planters)

[18] Billington, *Westward Expansion: A History of the American Frontier* (4th ed., New York, 1974), 315.

and note that there may have been a third "class" of antebellum southern whites, namely herders.[19]

In 1962 Eugene D. Genovese subjected what he regarded as the Owsley "thesis"—and what, more properly, can be regarded as some suggestions Owsley made—to a harsh critique. But Genovese missed Owsley's point and inadvertently supplied information supporting the point we propose to make about the importance of livestock drovers in the antebellum southern economy. Genovese addressed himself toward proving that the great slave plantations—whether planting tobacco, rice, sugar cane, or cotton—produced far from enough livestock even for plantation consumption and that what they did produce was of inferior quality. He pointed out that hogs slaughtered in Chicago in 1860 averaged 228 pounds—as against a southern average, *determined by study of the records of twenty-four southern plantations,* of a mere 140 pounds. Indeed, Genovese says, the 140-pound figure is inflated by "inclusion of the heavier hogs bought from drovers to be slaughtered on the plantations."[20]

That is just it: the raising of livestock was a function performed not only by yeoman farmers and the operators of plantations but also by people who raised cattle and hogs as their principal occupation and who did so out of both tradition and choice. In 1840 a traveler in southern Mississippi noted that "The people are for the most part pastoral, their herds furnishing their chief revenue." This trade in animals, he concluded, "has enriched many people . . . ." A resident of northeastern Texas stated in 1850 that many of his neighbors raised livestock for sale in Louisiana: "Two thousand head or upwards [of cattle] are annually shipped to New Orleans." During the antebellum period, a preacher recalled, "most of the people [of northern Florida and southern Georgia] . . . lived by raising stock." And in 1848 a visitor reported: "The principal revenue of the people [of East Tennessee] . . . is derived from the business of raising cattle."[21]

Though additional research is needed to determine exactly who

[19] Hilliard, *Hog Meat and Hoecake,* 9, 40–45, 56–59, 92–140, *passim.*

[20] Genovese, "Livestock in the Slave Economy of the Old South—A Revised View," *Agricultural History,* XXXVI (July 1962), 143–49.

[21] John F. H. Claiborne, "A Trip Through the Piney Woods," Mississippi Historical Society, *Publications,* IX (1906), 514–38 (quotations on pages 515 and 522); *Patent Office Report, 1850,* p. 189; Simon P. Richardson, *The Lights and Shadows of Itinerant Life: An Autobiography* . . . (Nashville and Dallas, 1901), 26–27; Charles Lanman, *Letters from the Alleghany Mountains* (New York, 1849), 153; see also William Faux, *Memorable Days in America: Being a Journal of a Tour to the United States* . . . (London, 1823), 135, 143–45; Frederick W. C. Gerstaeker, *Wild Sports in the Far West* (London and New York, 1854), 166, 214–17, 284, 293; [J. Goldsmith], *The Present State of the British Empire in Europe, America, Africa and Asia* (London, 1768), 323, 361, 373; Charles W. Janson, *The Stranger in America* . . . (London, 1807), 186; François A. Michaux, *Travels to the West of the Allegheny*

these livestock growers were and where they came from, there is enough available information to make some fairly confident suggestions. Lewis C. Gray as well as Percy Wells Bidwell and John Ironside Falconer print maps and other data that show the geographical distribution of cattle and swine, as reflected in census figures; *Hog Meat and Hoecake*, along with several studies of agriculture in particular states, offers valuable (if often misunderstood) information; and studies of migration, both from Europe to America and inside the South, afford enough material to warrant a few general observations.[22]

At the outset it must be understood that the raisers of livestock in the Old South were not one group but three—each with countless gradations both in the extent of their specialization and the volume of their business. Abundant evidence indicates that many planters kept herds, though, as Genovese notes, they tended to be small and of less than first-rate quality and though, as E. Merton Coulter says, many planters disdained to raise swine on the ground that it was beneath their dignity.[23] Second, there were the yeoman farmers, growers of plants, who almost universally kept some hogs and often raised sizable herds. Third, and possibly most important, there were drovers, whose main or sole occupation was that of herding, and who, when they raised any crops at all, did so only incidentally or for fattening their stock.

Mountains . . . (Paris, 1804), 236–37, 239, 257; Frederick L. Olmsted, *A Journey in the Seaboard Slave States with Remarks on Their Economy* (New York, 1856), 65–66, 100, 271, 709; John F. D. Smyth, *Tour in the United States of America* . . . (2 vols., London, 1784), I, 161; David B. Warden, *A Statistical, Political, and Historical Account of the United States of North America* . . . (3 vols., Edinburgh, 1819), II, 215, 221, 339, 362, 390, 391; III, 18, 149–50, 257, 341.

[22] Gray, *History of Agriculture*, II, 831–57; Bidwell and Falconer, *History of Agriculture in the Northern United States, 1620–1860* (Washington, 1925), 387, 388, 398, 438, 440; Hilliard, *Hog Meat and Hoecake*, 92–140; Moore, *Agriculture in Ante-Bellum Mississippi;* Herbert Weaver, *Mississippi Farmers, 1850–1860* (Nashville, 1945); Blanche H. Clark, *The Tennessee Yeoman, 1840–1860* (Nashville, 1942); Cornelius O. Cathey, *Agricultural Developments in North Carolina, 1783–1860* (Chapel Hill, 1956); James W. Thompson, *A History of Livestock Raising in the United States, 1607–1860* (Washington, 1942); James G. Leyburn, *The Scotch-Irish: A Social History* (Chapel Hill, 1962); Marcus L. Hansen, *The Atlantic Migration, 1607–1860: A History of Continuing Settlement of the United States* (Cambridge, Mass., 1940); Ian C. C. Graham, *Colonists from Scotland: Emigration to North America, 1707–1783* (Ithaca, 1956); Barnes F. Lathrop, *Migration into East Texas, 1835–1860: A Study from the United States Census* (Austin, 1949).

[23] Coulter states that although planters "kept some hogs, in many parts of the Lower South many people had a prejudice against raising swine, probably because they thought it was not dignified." Coulter, *The Confederate States of America, 1861–1865* ([Baton Rouge], 1950), 246. It would be foolish to raise livestock, an Alabama planter thought, "for cotton at 10 to 12½ cents per pound is much more profitable." And a Mississippian claimed that planters "could, were we not so absorbed in cotton raising, raise hogs enough for our own meat. A few sensible old farmers do this, but the most of us abandon every thing for the sake of cotton, and so we depend almost entirely upon the more northern States to furnish us with this most essential commodity." *Patent Office Report, 1850*, pp. 301–302, 187–88.

Many of the American drovers of both the eighteenth and nineteenth centuries came from the Celtic areas of the British Isles, meaning the southwestern, western, and northern parts of England, the Scottish Lowlands and Highlands, and most especially the "Scotch-Irish" plantations of Lowland Scots in Ulster, northern Ireland. Not all Celts were drovers, and not all drovers were Celts, of course, but if one tracks down where the Scotch-Irish went in their great migration that began soon after 1715, involved perhaps half a million souls, and did not abate until after the panic of 1837, one has pinned down important antebellum livestock country. They went to Philadelphia, thence to the uplands around that city, and thence to the uplands of the Pennsylvania valleys. From there they moved in two general directions: westward along the Ohio Valley, on both the Ohio and Kentucky sides of the river, and southwestward down the several valleys of Maryland and Virginia, back up to Virginia's Southside, down through the Piedmont of the Carolinas, and then into Tennessee and northern parts of Georgia, Alabama, and Mississippi, and ultimately into Arkansas, northern Louisiana, and Texas. Throughout, from 1715 to 1837 and beyond, as the Scotch-Irish went they took their cattle-and-hog culture with them.[24]

Moreover, the migration of the Scotch-Irish was attended all the way by what, when they reached the Great Plains, was called the "open-range system." Thanks to Billington, Walter Prescott Webb, John Wayne, and a host of movies and television shows, every schoolboy knows about the open range: the cattle barons of the Great Plains reaped fortunes by grazing their herds on public lands until the hated sheep farmers and the grubby plowmen began to fence the ranges in the 1880s. Rather less known is that the open

[24] Leyburn, *The Scotch-Irish*, and Lathrop, *Migration into East Texas*, provide much information on this pattern of movement. In 1790 Scots and Scotch-Irishmen (including those from outside Ulster) already constituted just under a fourth of the total white population of the South, and they may well have formed a majority in those parts of the South emphasized in the text; extrapolated from "Report of Committee on Linguistic and National Stocks in the Population of the United States," American Historical Association, *Annual Report, 1931*, I (Washington, 1932), 107–408, but especially 206–70. The geographical distribution of the Scots and Scotch-Irish in 1776 can be inferred from the religious maps in Charles O. Paullin, *Atlas of the Historical Geography of the United States*, edited by John K. Wright (Washington, 1932), plates 82–88; virtually all of the Presbyterians and many of the southern Baptists were of Scots background. The maps for 1860 are suggestive but less conclusive. Customarily, at least until the Tennessee frontier was reached, westward and southwestward migration was not a generalized movement of the whole Scotch-Irish population with existing frontiersmen leading the way. Rather, the latest arrivals moved farthest out on the frontier. Highland Scots followed a different pattern: they headed straight for the interior of North Carolina and were much less mobile.

range had been part of the tradition of the antebellum South for some decades, and of the British uplands for some centuries before that, and had in fact been the indispensable condition of Celtic livestock tending for a long, long time.

A quick survey will illustrate the point. Land tenure in the Lowlands and in Ulster until 1715, and in the Highlands until late in the eighteenth century, implicitly or explicitly contained a provision that grazing and foraging rights pertained to every person who lived on the land, no matter how high or low his station; the lowliest cotter could graze his hogs on the uncultivated lands of the most lordly landholder. The enclosure movement, which had had profound effects upon English farming in the preceding two centuries, now hit the Scots, but its meaning was different, for the Scots were primarily drovers who disdained to be mere tillers of the soil.[25]

When the Lowlanders and the Scotch-Irish made their exodus to America they carried their habitual ways with them. Moreover, colonial and state laws protected them in those ways. Gray indicates that it was not until the mid-1830s that Virginia passed its first laws permitting fencing on an extremely limited basis and another decade before South Carolina followed suit; until then, and to a considerable extent afterward, anybody owning cattle and hogs could graze them in the pastures and woods of any planter, excepting only land that was both fenced and in crops—to the chagrin of Edmund Ruffin and many another "progressive" planter. Indeed, Ruffin labored for twenty years before being able to obtain in 1858 a special act of the Virginia legislature permitting planters in Prince George County to limit the open-range rights of drovers by erecting fences around entire estates or adjoining estates—which attests to the numbers and political strength of the herdsmen. This "reform & revolution in this heretofore fixed policy of Va," Ruffin hoped, might soon be extended to other counties—despite what he called the "pig-headed" opposition of men like J. B. Cocke—and if so, it would be "almost as great a benefit for the agricultural interests of Virginia, as I had before rendered in any other way."[26]

[25] R. A. Gailey, "Agrarian Improvement and the Development of Enclosure in the Southwest Highlands of Scotland," *Scottish Historical Review,* XLII (October 1963), 105–25; James E. Handley, *Scottish Farming in the Eighteenth Century* (London, 1953); Leyburn, *The Scotch-Irish;* T. C. Smout, *A History of the Scottish People, 1560–1830* (New York, 1969).

[26] Gray, *History of Agriculture,* II, 843; William K. Scarborough, ed., *The Diary of Edmund Ruffin* (1 vol. to date, Baton Rouge, 1972–), I, 150, 358.

What actually evolved in Virginia was what amounted to a local-option system: landowners in particular counties could by special acts of the legislature acquire the right to fence their property. Meanwhile, North Carolina had long since made it criminal to interfere with livestock grazing on any land not under cultivation and fenced no matter who owned the land or the animals, and that law remained on the books long after the Civil War; the open range or commons was the norm in Louisiana and Mississippi throughout the antebellum period; Tennessee did not pass laws permitting the fencing of entire farms until late in the nineteenth century; the local-option system continued in Texas and Louisiana until after World War II; practice in Florida, whatever the law, retained common grazing and foraging rights as late as the 1950s; and local-option laws remained in force in Georgia until 1957, when a statewide law ended the open range after a prominent businessman, Walter Candler, was killed when his car hit a cow that was asleep in the road.[27]

And yet Owsley, for all his perceptiveness, was able to write: "By 1840 the better agricultural lands in the older states and in many parts of the newer ones had been sufficiently settled by farmers to interfere with grazing upon the open range, and the herdsmen had largely disappeared from such lands." And in 1972 Hilliard could echo: "The herder either was pushed out by the farmer and the planter or, more likely, joined their ranks. In discussing former occupations of early settlers, many writers of the postwar period referred to the 'old-timers' as being cattlemen. Apparently they were cattle herders during the early years and shifted to crops later."[28]

Obviously, the variety of livestock that could be raised by the traditional Celtic method—if simply allowing one's animals to run wild and root for themselves on just anybody's land can be called a method—was limited or determined by the available natural food supply. The Scotch-Irish had long raised hogs and cattle indiscriminately, for the two get along well enough together; for

[27] Michaux, *Travels to the West of the Allegheny Mountains*, 236–39; Gray, *History of Agriculture*, II, 843; Cathey, *Agricultural Developments in North Carolina*, 51*n*; Moore, *Agriculture in Ante-Bellum Mississippi*, 62–63; Olmsted, *Journey in the Seaboard Slave States*, 709; Edmund C. Burnett, "Hog Raising and Hog Driving in the Region of the French Broad River," *Agricultural History*, XX (April 1946), 95; interview with Valton G. Midgett, Rodanthe, Outer Banks, North Carolina, August 28, 1974; Charles P. Roland to the authors, June 26, 1974; interview with John Henry Cassidy, Walton County, Florida, March 1974; James C. Bonner to the authors, July 19, 1974. E. Merton Coulter, *The South During Reconstruction, 1865–1877* ([Baton Rouge], 1947), 228, traces the gradual development of local-option laws after the Civil War.

[28] Owsley, *Plain Folk*, 34; Hilliard, *Hog Meat and Hoecake*, 117.

a surprising reason, to be related below, sheep and goats were not acceptable. In America the same pattern held, but the predominance of woodland over open pasture east of the Mississippi dictated that swine would fare better than cattle, and so it was. In southern and central Indiana and Illinois, in the Nashville Basin and the bluegrass region of Kentucky, and on the Gulf coastal plain cattle were as important as hogs, and once the Scotch-Irish penetrated the Prairie Plains and then the Great Plains cattle became far more important. But in most of the Old South the hog was king.

The Celtic herdsmen's way required little expenditure of either labor or money. In many areas of the South natural vegetation was so abundant that, as one contemporary noted, "They [sheep] require no feed, summer or winter . . . ." "We raise our hogs by allowing them to range in our woods, where they get fat . . . on acorns . . . ," insisted a South Carolinian. "The cost of raising cattle amounts to nothing more than the time consumed in marking and branding," claimed a man from northeastern Texas. "Cattle require no feeding. In spring and summer, the grass upon the prairies furnishes excellent grazing, and the wild rye, cane, and winter-grass in the bottoms, furnish food during the winter. . . . Hogs are never fattened upon corn, from the fact that they fatten themselves in the woods, upon acorns, which, of course, is the cheapest method of producing pork and bacon. Bacon and pork fattened upon acorns is considered by many as being sweeter and better flavored than that fattened upon corn."[29]

The herdsmen's life-style had another peculiar attribute as well: the wealth of the grazers was largely invisible to outside observers. From James Boswell's account of his travels through Scotland with Samuel Johnson in the eighteenth century until Frederick Law Olmsted's account of his travels through the South in the 1850s travelers uniformly reported scenes of poverty and squalor among the open-range herdsmen. All saw the cattle and hogs roaming the woods but noted them only incidentally or in passing; Olmsted, typically, saw only poverty by day and ate good pork every night. To this day there are "poor farmers" from west Florida to Colorado who appear, to the untrained eye, to be quite impoverished, but whose wealth in animals foraging the woods is such that the authors—and most of our readers—would readily exchange net worths with them.

Finally, there was, complementary to the commons or open-

[29] *Patent Office Report, 1850,* pp. 260, 233, 189.

range system, a tradition of driving great herds over long distances to market—a tradition antedating the Chisholm trail by centuries. The origins of the cattle and hog drives were in thievery; for several centuries prior to the Act of Union in 1707 many Highland and several Lowland clans had made their livelihood by going south, stealing stock, and driving herds long distances to secluded and well-protected places. (It was mainly for that reason that the prejudice against sheep and goats developed; those animals were noisy and difficult to drive at night and thus harder to steal than the more tractable cows and pigs.) Over the years the rustlers' trails were worn into roads, and when England and Scotland were merged, the same roads were used to drive animals long distances to markets in the Midlands, London, and the south of England.[30] By the middle of the eighteenth century, when the Scotch-Irish and the Scots were arriving in America in large numbers, the long drive to market was an established norm. By 1800 drives originating in the Carolina uplands terminated in Savannah, Charleston, Norfolk, and Philadelphia; animals were being driven from the Shenandoah Valley to Richmond and Baltimore; and herds were driven from Tennessee and Kentucky to Pittsburgh, Baltimore, and Philadelphia. After the War of 1812 drives were extended to the rapidly expanding lower South.[31]

By the 1830s the "industry" had become regularized into a pattern that was to prevail for a half century or more and had begun to be specialized as well. As farmers joined the herdsmen in populating a particular area the two became complementary: that is, far from displacing the herdsmen, or ranking above them as the Turner and Phillips schools maintained, many farmers were dependent upon the drovers as their principal market and geared their production to the drovers' needs by producing corn for fattening the livestock just before marketing. The principal farm crop raised by the sturdy yeoman of North Carolina, Mississippi, and Tennessee thus came to be not cotton but corn; indeed, more than half the cultivated acreage in the South in the 1850s was devoted to

[30] Archibald R. B. Haldane, *The Drove Roads of Scotland* (London and New York, 1952), 2–46, 199–201. An additional reason for the prejudice against sheep and goats, as many historians have observed, was the southerner's habit of keeping hunting dogs. A Virginian also reported that wolves ate the sheep in his area, but a Georgian stated that the people in his region were unwilling to raise sheep on a large scale, "owing to the depredations of dogs," and a North Carolinian, who had lost sheep to dogs, wished for "extermination of the whole canine race." *Patent Office Report, 1850,* pp. 367, 395, 369.

[31] Data regarding drives are from travel accounts, such as Johann David Schopf, *Travels in the Confederation, [1783–1784],* translated and edited by Alfred J. Morrison (2 vols., Philadelphia, 1811), II, 108–10, and those cited in note 21. A map showing the main droving routes is in Hilliard, *Hog Meat and Hoecake,* 194.

raising corn, first and foremost for feeding to animals, mainly hogs, just before and during the drives. "For the want of a market," noted a Kentucky farmer, "we are compelled to feed our grain to horses, mules, cattle, and hogs, and thus we realize about 20 cents per bushel for corn, which is a profit of about 100 per cent on the cost. Our grasses and clover yield about the same profit in live-stock."[32]

Fortunately, we have one excellent account of what the great antebellum southern pig drives were like—and from a most unexpected source. Edmund Cody Burnett, the distinguished editor and historian of the Continental Congress, grew up in the Scotch-Irish area of the French Broad River of eastern Tennessee, and toward the end of his life he wrote up and published an account of hog driving in his home area. His own memories went back to the 1870s, he had interviewed oldtimers who could remember the 1850s, and meticulous research carried him back another twenty years—and to the conclusion that methods had remained fundamentally the same throughout the nineteenth century.[33]

The French Broad River (now largely flooded by the Douglas Dam in the TVA system) meandered for twenty-five to thirty miles between Newport and Dandridge, and its bottom lands were of varying width. In that area 20,000 to 30,000 hogs were fattened for market every year, which means *a thousand hogs a mile.* Hog drives originating there and in the surrounding countryside went along the French Broad Road to Asheville, North Carolina, a distance of about fifty-five miles, and involved 150,000 to 160,000 hogs a year. Many hogs were butchered in Asheville, but many more were driven on elsewhere, for Asheville was a gathering place from which drives were continued to Savannah, Charleston, Norfolk, and the plantations in between.

Burnett also provides information about how the business had become specialized by mid-century and how the dirt farmers fitted into the larger scheme of things. East of the mountains, for example, the people who conducted the drives were called drovers, for herdsmen there took their own stock to market. In the west the drives were conducted by people who specialized in that function and were called drivers, as opposed to the drovers who "raised" the animals in the traditional way. Hog drives normally took place between August and November (cattle drives, at least in the Ohio

[32] Gray, *History of Agriculture*, II, 837; Clark, *Tennessee Yeoman*, 126; *Patent Office Report, 1850*, pp. 266–67.

[33] This and the three following paragraphs are derived from Burnett, "Hog Raising and Hog Driving," 86–103; see also the same author's delightful, "The Hog Drivers' Play-Song and Some of Its Relatives," *Agricultural History*, XXIII (July 1949), 161–68.

country, began when the hog drives ended). Drives were in herds of 300 to 2,000 hogs, the average being about 400. Normally there was one "pigboy" for every hundred head of swine, plus a manager for every herd. Hogs could be driven eight to ten miles a day; they stopped at night at stock stands or hog "hotels." The best-known stand in the area—famous "from Cincinnati to Charleston"—was that at Alexander, some ten miles north of Asheville, built about 1828 by Captain James Mitchell Alexander, a Revolutionary War veteran, and operated fifty years later by his descendants. The Alexander stand contained stores and a variety of manufactories, and could accommodate 4,000 hogs and fifty men at a time.

There were fifteen hog hotels on the fifty-five-mile road from Big Creek to Asheville, and their practices were fairly uniform. It took eight bushels of corn per hundred hogs per day on the drives —meaning 25,000 bushels a year for the hogs driven on the French Broad Road—and most of the corn was supplied to the standkeepers by neighboring farmers. The standkeepers paid the farmers fifty cents a bushel and charged the drivers seventy-five cents a bushel. The drivers paid either in due bills or in lame hogs at the South Carolina market prices. Hog prices, in turn, hinged on cotton prices, roughly at a ratio of one to two. That is, if cotton was at fourteen cents a pound, hogs were seven cents on the hoof. (Presumably, the price of hogs was geared to the price of other staples elsewhere.) The driver obviously took some chances in buying hogs from the drovers, for staple prices did fluctuate during the driving season. Too, he had to reckon both on the cost of boarding his animals and on the weight losses on the drives: from Big Creek to Asheville, over the mountains, 200-pound hogs would lose on the average twelve pounds, but from Asheville to South Carolina markets they would hold their weight or even gain weight.

There is every reason to believe that Burnett's account of the French Broad region is applicable to so many areas in the South as to constitute a virtually universal pattern. Gray points out that in the late 1830s and throughout the 1840s as many as 55,000 hogs passed over Point Mountain, North Carolina, that upwards of 80,000 were driven through Cumberland Gap (the "Kaintuck Hog Road"), 60,000 apiece through Buford's Gap and on the Kanawha route, and 40,000 to Alabama and Georgia, from Kentucky alone. Patterns of the drives began to shift somewhat by the 1850s, with the development of packinghouses in Louisville, Cincinnati, Nashville, Gallatin, and a number of other places on navigable rivers. But the drives themselves continued and grew greater every year.[34]

[34] Gray, *History of Agriculture*, II, 840–41; *Report of the Commissioner of Patents, for the*

Because livestock, and especially hogs, constituted such an important product of the antebellum South—though neither contemporary observers nor later historians have been fully aware of this fact—it behooves us, we believe, to consider some of the implications thereof. The first implication, for historians, is that we and our graduate students should be turned loose to forage the sources even as the hogs were turned loose to forage the oak ridges and the piney woods. Doubtless, there are in the publications and manuscripts of small, local historical societies reminiscences as valuable as Burnett's, and there must be other sources that are equally valuable—as a perusal of Owsley's and Hilliard's footnotes suggests.

Another implication is that the history of southern land laws and land-tenure practices, and perhaps those of the entire United States, needs thorough restudy, despite the tons of ink that have been spilled on the subject. Walter Webb once said that an enterprising graduate student could make quite a reputation for himself by doing a history of the law of riparian rights in America. Such a student could do even better by doing a study of grazing rights, fencing laws, and related matters.

Still another set of implications has to do with the importance of droving in assessing the economic and social impact of the Civil War and Reconstruction. The capital losses in the form of animals destroyed by both Confederate and Union troops during the war were as important to the drovers, relatively, as were the capital losses to the planters that resulted from emancipation. In South Carolina, for example, the hog population was reduced from 965,000 in 1860 to possibly no more than 150,000 at war's end. In describing the "devastation" of South Carolina by the Federal army, one observer noted that "the larger portion of the Country . . . [has been] utterly stript of its Stock . . . ." Eight years after the war there were still only 332,000 hogs in the state.[35]

Year 1847 (Washington, 1848), 531–34. About one-fourth of all the hogs slaughtered by packinghouses were processed in or around Cincinnati.

[35] James Chesnut, Jr., to Jefferson Davis, March 15, 1865, Jefferson Davis Papers (Duke University Library, Durham, N. C.); Francis B. Simkins and Robert H. Woody, *South Carolina During Reconstruction* (Chapel Hill, 1932), 258. On the theft and destruction of livestock by Union and Confederate forces in states other than South Carolina see Nimrod Porter Diary, January 16, 19, 23, February 15, March 5, 16, 22, 26, 27, 1865 (Southern Historical Collection, University of North Carolina Library, Chapel Hill, N. C.); John Houston Bills Diary, July 10, 12, September 26, October 19, 26, November 29, December 3, 10, 1863; January 20, March 7, May 1, July 4, 20, August 8, October 18, 1864, John Houston Bills Papers (Southern Historical Collection); Bayside Plantation Record, May 3, 1863 (Southern Historical Collection); S. L. Norwood to Walter W. Lenoir, April 24, 1865 (typed copy), Lenoir Family Papers (Southern Historical Collection); Bell I. Wiley, *The Plain People of the Confederacy* (Baton Rouge, 1944), 21–23.

The recovery of grazers in most other parts of the South seems to have been equally slow despite their life-style, which required little in the way of cash capital, land, or labor. In 1860 the South had raised two-thirds of the nation's swine, but in 1880 it raised less than half. And these figures tell only part of the story. Eight of the former slave states produced some 2,600,000 fewer hogs in 1880 than they had in 1860. Only in southern states with relatively small black populations and where there had been little fighting during the Civil War were there significant gains in the number of hogs between 1860 and 1880.[36]

Though these statistics are suggestive, more research is needed to determine exactly what happened to the herdsman and his way of life in the decades after the Civil War. It has long been a cliché that the "poor white"—by which, it should now be clear, is often meant herdsmen—oppressed blacks as intensely as they did because blacks were the only people beneath them on the social scale, and the poor white intended to keep them there. Yet another reason also seems plausible, at least as far as herdsmen were concerned. The freedmen threatened the open-range system far more seriously than had the likes of Edmund Ruffin; they foraged widely and stole and butchered the hogs and cattle they found roaming the woods. "We cannot raise a turkey, chicken, or a hog," reported James H. Clanton of Alabama in 1871. He had quit raising livestock "in consequence of the stealing by the negroes" and was paying twenty-five cents a pound for bacon that had sold for five cents before the war because "We dare not turn stock out at all."[37] In 1868 a Freedmen's Bureau official noted that livestock owners in his South Carolina district "still complain that their hogs and hens disappear; and, during my official term of fifteen months, I procured the liberation of, perhaps, twenty negro thieves from jail, . . . while at least as many more were sentenced by the courts . . . ." Liberation was usually contingent upon the accused leaving the area. "Andy [a freedman who] had stolen a pig . . . was in jail, awaiting trial," observed this same official; "but the sheriff was willing to release

[36] *Report on the Productions of Agriculture as Returned at the Tenth Census (June 1, 1880)* (Washington, 1883), 4–5; *Agriculture of the United States in 1860*, pp. 184–87. In 1880 every former slave state except Arkansas, Delaware, Florida, Missouri, and Texas had fewer hogs than in 1860. The big gainers were Missouri (over 2,000,000), Texas (nearly 580,000), and Arkansas (nearly 400,000). The big losers were Virginia (nearly 133,000, without counting the 511,000 hogs credited to West Virginia in 1880); Georgia (565,000), North Carolina (430,000), Alabama (496,000), Mississippi (381,000), South Carolina (338,000), Tennessee (187,000), and Kentucky (105,000).

[37] Quoted in Walter L. Fleming, ed., *Documentary History of Reconstruction* (2 vols., Cleveland, 1907), II, 279.

him on condition that he would take a [labor] contract out of the State . . . ."[38]

Complaints against black thieves were widespread throughout the Reconstruction period.[39]

All in all, [admitted Vernon Lane Wharton, a liberal scholar] the source of the great majority of the Negro's trouble with the law from 1865 to 1890 was his penchant for petty thievery. . . . With the coming of freedom sheer poverty and hunger gave an added incentive for such forays. The Negro found himself surrounded by temptation. Effective fences were rare, and hogs, sheep, turkeys, and cattle wandered untended in the uncultivated stretches of almost every plantation. The theft of such livestock, frequent enough in ordinary times, increased to alarming proportions in years of poor crops.[40]

In 1867, for example, the Federal army commander in Mississippi reported: "The crop . . . having been gathered, the freedmen are now idle, and without, in a great majority of instances, means of support. The result is great complaints from every section of the state of depredations being committed on live stock, hogs, sheep and cattle." Exasperated owners of animals sought ways to protect their property. A newspaper editor wrote: "Our advice to hog-raisers is, if a man is found under very suspicious circumstances in the woods, drop him, and let the buzzards hold an inquest over his remains." Wharton concluded that "The result of such agitation was the passage by the first Democratic legislature of a bill which declared the theft of any property valued at more than ten dollars, or of any kind of cattle or swine, regardless of value, to be grand larceny, subjecting the thief to a term up to five years in the state penitentiary. This was the famous 'pig law,' which was largely responsible for an increase in the population of the state prison from 272 in 1874 to 1,072 at the end of 1877."[41]

To move to a somewhat grander plane, the persistence and the importance of the drover suggests that he may have had a great deal to do with shaping that elusive but quite real quality known as the southern character. Indeed, we believe that Phillips's famous aphorism—that it was "the inescapable presence of the Negro"

[38] J. W. De Forest, "The Man and Brother," *Atlantic Monthly*, XXII (September and October 1868), 344, 415.

[39] See for example Porter Diary, January 22, March 23, August 20, 26, September 15, 26, October 15, December 7, 1865; January 12, September 24, 1866; Bills Diary, August 21, 1863; October 25, 1866; Everard Green Baker Diary, April 20, 1867 (Southern Historical Collection).

[40] Wharton, *The Negro in Mississippi, 1865–1890* (New York, Evanston, and London, 1965), 236–37.

[41] *Ibid.*, 237.

that made the South what it was—may be in want of revision, for the ineradicable presence of the Scotch-Irish drover seems at least equally influential. The drover was an independent cuss, for his wealth was mobile, he had the use of the land of even the greatest planters, he was much less dependent upon the weather than farmers were, and there was always a demand for his product. His life-style encouraged leisure rather than the compulsive pursuit of wealth that dominated both the northern commercial man and (despite their protests to the contrary) most southern planters as well; to the outsider, caught up in the race for profits, the herdsman appeared to be both indolent and shiftless.[42] His unhurried pace was reflected in his manners, in his speech, and in the very way he walked. Courteous, modest, and even deferential, he could yet be deadly if provoked, and the readiest way to provoke him was to treat him or his kin disrespectfully; he never forgot or forgave an insult. Though far from class-conscious, at least in a Marxian sense, he was proud and possessed of strong ethnic and racial prejudices and was intensely clannish and suspicious of outsiders. His hostility to governmental restraint was as striking as his skill in the political arts.

Finally, a word is in order about "models" of southern society and of American society as a whole. By and large southern historians have been more wholesomely skeptical of artificial social models than other historians have been. But abstract models, those of U. B. Phillips and F. J. Turner, have also dominated the descriptions and understanding of southern society. Phillips's model of a society organized on vertical and ambitional lines is highly questionable; what is needed, instead, is an organic model that takes into account the fact that society was organized around symbiotic and functional relationships. Turner's horizontal model of "stages of development" in frontier after frontier is equally questionable. Much of what Turner and his disciples regarded as uniquely southern or uniquely American characteristics, bred on the ever-passing frontier, were actually Celtic characteristics that predated both the South and the American frontier by many centuries.

[42] A full (and typical) description of the "poor white" is in Simkins and Roland, *History of the South*, 138–39. If allowance is made for a bit of exaggeration and minor errors this account accurately captures many qualities of the southern herdsmen. They were not as a rule, however, either Anglo-Saxon or impoverished, as Simkins and Roland describe the poor white as being.

Black Militancy in Readjuster Virginia, 1879–1883

By JAMES T. MOORE

VIRGINIA'S READJUSTER MOVEMENT EXPERIENCED A STRIKING transformation during its brief existence. Originating during the depression-ridden 1870s, it drew its initial strength from white farmers in the Piedmont and mountain counties. These rebellious Grangers and Greenbackers demanded tax cuts and, in particular, a downward "readjustment" of the burdensome state debt. By the 1880s, on the other hand, the movement had drifted into the national Republican camp. A dynamic railroad magnate, General William Mahone, had taken charge of the revolt, and its program had expanded to include federal aid to education, protective tariffs, and civil rights. Racial tensions mushroomed, alienating the mass of rural whites, and the movement collapsed in 1883.[1]

Examining the causes of this evolution, historians have generally emphasized Mahone's aggressive leadership, his emergence as the undisputed party "boss."[2] Others have noted the intrigues of the national Republicans, anxious to break the Democratic "Solid South."[3] Oddly enough, however, scholars have almost totally ignored the activities of the black Readjusters. Most accounts have described them as mere pawns in the political game, as cogs in the Mahone "machine." Such terms as "credulous," "tractable," "gregarious," and "childlike" crop up repeatedly in analyses of

[1] Nelson M. Blake, *William Mahone of Virginia: Soldier and Political Insurgent* (Richmond, 1935; cited hereinafter as Blake, *Mahone*), 156–234; Charles C. Pearson, *The Readjuster Movement in Virginia* (New Haven, 1917), *passim.*

[2] Blake, *Mahone*, 192–93; Allen W. Moger, *Virginia: Bourbonism to Byrd, 1870–1925* (Charlottesville, 1968), 49–50; Pearson, *Readjuster Movement*, 151–59; C. Vann Woodward, *Origins of the New South, 1877–1913* ([Baton Rouge], 1951), 96–98.

[3] Vincent P. De Santis, *Republicans Face the Southern Question—The New Departure Years, 1877–1897* (Baltimore, 1959; cited hereinafter as De Santis, *Southern Question*), 133–80; Stanley P. Hirshson, *Farewell to the Bloody Shirt: Northern Republicans & the Southern Negro, 1877–1893* (Bloomington, 1962; cited hereinafter as Hirshson, *Bloody Shirt*), 94–122.

MR. MOORE is assistant professor of history at Virginia Commonwealth University.

THE JOURNAL OF SOUTHERN HISTORY
Vol. XLI, No. 2, May 1975

their behavior.[4] Even black historians have accepted this image of racial subordination.[5] As this study will show, however, the stereotype of the "machine Negro" is severely distorted. Instead, Virginia's 100,000 black voters played a crucial role in transforming the Readjuster revolt—reshaping it, in effect, in their own image.

Years of frustration touched off this flash of black political awareness. Economic conditions, of course, played a major role. In the 1870s the average rural freedman eked out only \$6 to \$10 a month from the soil. A relative handful managed to buy their farms, but the great majority were landless peasants caught up in an endless cycle of poverty and debt.[6] Urban Virginia offered greater opportunities, particularly for skilled craftsmen, but even in the cities life was frequently harsh and unrewarding. Jerry-built "niggertowns" proliferated; gangs of ragged children roamed the streets; competition with laboring-class whites aggravated racial hatreds.[7] The black mortality rate soared, prompting conjectures that the entire race would die out in a few generations.[8] The nationwide economic collapse from 1873 to 1879 only compounded the distress.

The repressive political climate of the 1870s also intensified black resentment. The Conservative party, a coalition of white-supremacist Democrats and Whigs, mountaineers and planters, dominated the state during most of the decade. This relentless machine hammered the blacks with poll taxes, gerrymanders, and election frauds, reducing the number of Negroes in the state legislature from thirty in 1870 to only five in 1878. County officials excluded blacks from jury duty; local school boards employed white teachers for black schools, rejecting the applications of qualified

[4] Blake, *Mahone*, 261–62; Richard L. Morton, *The Negro in Virginia Politics, 1865–1902* (Charlottesville, 1919), 107, 119; Pearson, *Readjuster Movement*, 154–55; William L. Royall, *History of the Virginia Debt Controversy. The Negro's Vicious Influence in Politics* (Richmond, 1897), 32; Charles E. Wynes, *Race Relations in Virginia, 1870–1902* (Charlottesville, 1961), 27.

[5] Luther P. Jackson, *Negro Office-Holders in Virginia, 1865–1895* (Norfolk, 1945), 78–79; James H. Johnston, "The Participation of Negroes in the Government of Virginia from 1877 to 1888," *Journal of Negro History*, XIV (July 1929), 255, 263; Alrutheus A. Taylor, "The Negro in the Reconstruction of Virginia," *ibid.*, XI (July 1926), 530, 534.

[6] For contemporary comments on Virginia's rural blacks see the letters from George William Bagby to Richmond *State*, June 30, 1879; May 14, 20, 21, 1880; January 10, 11, May 27, 1881.

[7] Letters from George William Bagby to Richmond *State*, June 23, 1879; July 23, August 10, 1880; January 10, May 10, June 22, 1881; Orra Langhorne, *Southern Sketches from Virginia, 1881–1901*, edited by Charles E. Wynes (Charlottesville, 1964), 17, 37–38; Nannie May Tilley, *The Bright-Tobacco Industry, 1860–1929* (Chapel Hill, 1948), 515–18.

[8] Letters from George William Bagby to Richmond *State*, June 7, 23, 30, 1879; May 26, 1880.

Negroes; Conservative judges ordered public whippings for black criminals; hundreds of freedmen were disfranchised for petit larceny and other minor offenses. Reflecting the rise of prejudice, moreover, patterns of segregation emerged in restaurants, hotels, and other public places. Political impotence paved the way for public humiliation.[9]

Completing this cycle of despair, the Negroes' traditional allies—the white Republicans—seemed unable or unwilling to protect them. The national Republican leadership set the pattern by virtually abandoning the blacks after Reconstruction. President Rutherford Birchard Hayes adopted a "southern strategy" in 1877 which ignored racial issues altogether. Instead, he sought to build a respectable party in the region, one which could command the support of the wealthier classes. His administration stressed reforms in the civil service, not civil rights.[10] At the state level, moreover, Virginia's white Republicans showed a similar indifference to Negro problems. Generally cautious and ineffectual, this clique offered only token opposition to the Conservative regime. In 1877 they failed to nominate a gubernatorial ticket, and the Republican State Central Committee practically ceased to exist for the next three years. The demoralized party soon degenerated into a haven for spoilsmen, a machine for distributing the federal patronage in Virginia. A handful of white carpetbaggers and "old Whig" scalawags scooped up the choicest patronage "plums" to the disgust and dismay of ambitious blacks. The Petersburg *Lancet,* a Negro newspaper, provided a terse but accurate appraisal. "The Republican party of the present," it declared, "is but a skeleton, a relic of the past."[11]

In spite of these depressing trends, however, the blacks still had cause for hope. Their white-supremacist opponents—no longer so concerned about "Negro rule"—began to quarrel among

[9] The following provide insight into the repressive racial climate of the 1870s: Jackson, *Negro Office-Holders,* 79; Wynes, *Race Relations,* 13, 27; Pearson, *Readjuster Movement,* 109; Jack P. Maddex, Jr., *The Virginia Conservatives, 1867–1879: A Study in Reconstruction Politics* (Chapel Hill, 1970), 189–91. For a divergent and more sympathetic interpretation of the Conservatives' racial attitudes see Robert R. Jones, "James L. Kemper and the Virginia Redeemers Face the Race Question: A Reconsideration," *Journal of Southern History,* XXXVIII (August 1972), 393–414. Jones argues that the Conservatives, although committed to white supremacy, avoided the more blatant extremes of overt racial repression. It should be noted, however, that their "paternalistic" approach to the Negroes effectively nullified black political power in Virginia in the 1870s.

[10] De Santis, *Southern Question,* 66–103; Hirshson, *Bloody Shirt,* 21–44.

[11] Petersburg *Lancet,* December 9, 1882; see also George Teamoh to John F. Lewis, March 1, 1881, William Mahone Papers (Duke University Library, Durham, N.C.); letter from Zachariah Hunt to Salem *Weekly Register,* April 1, 1881.

themselves. As the 1870s wore on, in fact, the ties of white unity showed signs of disintegrating altogether. Wealthy planters and businessmen dominated the Conservative organization, and their policies provoked widespread resentment. Committed to laissez-faire economics, these traditionalists ignored appeals from the mountain counties for Greenback inflation and protective tariffs. They manifested a similar attitude toward the state's 18,000 Grangers, blocking proposals to regulate the railroads and tobacco warehouses.[12] Most disastrous of all, they frustrated the popular demand for cuts in Virginia's massive public debt. Instead, the patricians insisted on repaying the bondholders even if it meant higher taxes and reduced expenditures for the public schools. They maintained that this approach was both morally sound and economically prudent, that it would preserve the state's "good name" and encourage investments by foreign capitalists.[13] These arguments proved convincing for many voters, especially in the towns and in the aristocratic eastern "tobacco belt." Thousands of others opposed this enforced austerity, however, and full-scale political revolt erupted in 1879. Abandoning the old Conservative machine, a large bloc of rebellious whites organized the Readjuster party, which was dedicated to a downward "adjustment" of the debt. Virginia's white-supremacist majority had fragmented. A new political era had begun.

This Conservative split offered great opportunities for the Negroes. Constituting almost a third of the electorate, they held the balance of power between the Readjusters and the debt-paying elite (popularly known as "Funders" because of their desire to protect the state credit). The freedmen distrusted both factions, however, and moved very cautiously. During the 1879 legislative race, in particular, they seemed hesitant, uncertain, unwilling to commit themselves. They generally favored the Readjusters' debt program with its promise of better schools and tax reform, but circumstances prevented a formal alliance with the new party. For one thing, the insurgent leaders deliberately avoided close ties with the Negroes. They welcomed a few blacks to their state convention, but

[12] For insight into the Conservatives' economic views see Maddex, *Virginia Conservatives*, 146–47, 172–73; and James T. Moore, *Two Paths to the New South: The Virginia Debt Controversy, 1870–1883* (Lexington, Ky., 1974; cited hereinafter as Moore, *Debt Controversy*), 31–35.

[13] The debt had been contracted during the antebellum years to finance state investments in railroads and other internal improvements, and by 1870 it had climbed to $45,000,000. The following sources shed light on this financial crisis and also analyze the response of the Conservative elite: Pearson, *Readjuster Movement*, 1–23, 35–84; Woodward, *Origins of the New South*, 92–94; Maddex, *Virginia Conservatives*, 233–55.

fear of alienating the "poor whites" prevented more substantive gestures.[14] Further impeding cooperation, the national Republicans intervened in the campaign. President Hayes announced his hostility to Readjustment, and he urged the Negroes to spurn all forms of financial "repudiation."[15] The Funders also contributed to this bewildering political climate. Desperate for votes, they lured the once-despised freedmen with rallies, handbills, and flattering editorials. Wealthy patricians shared platforms with blacks, urging the "best men of both races" to unite in defense of the state credit. The Readjusters countered with vague promises to protect Negro rights, and the campaign ended on an ambiguous note.[16] Torn by these conflicting appeals, the blacks scattered their support all across the political spectrum. Some endorsed the Readjusters; a smaller number, the Funders. Others, the majority, refused to join either of the white factions. Clinging to their traditional ways, they voted for the Republican candidates, regardless of debt views. As a result some twenty-six members of the previously moribund "Radical" machine captured seats in the legislature, a dramatic increase over the previous session. More important still, this Republican legislative bloc—which included fourteen Negroes—held the balance of power in the General Assembly. Indeed, the blacks alone could tip the scales in the House of Delegates.[17] Their influence was definitely on the rise.

The new legislature convened in December 1879 amid an atmosphere of doubt and intrigue. Attention focused on the pivotal Republicans, of course, and at first they seemed to be drifting into the Funder camp. President Hayes certainly sought such a result. His emissaries descended on Richmond, urging an alliance between the Virginia Republicans and the Conservative elite. The Funders needed little encouragement. Rumor had it that they were willing to elect a white Radical to the United States Senate in return for control of the General Assembly. Most of the white Republicans

[14] Black delegates came from New Kent and Halifax counties. See the Richmond *Daily Dispatch*, February 27, 1879; see also Morton, *Negro in Virginia Politics*, 107; and Wynes, *Race Relations*, 19.

[15] De Santis, *Southern Question*, 95; Robert C. Glass and Carter Glass, Jr., *Virginia Democracy: A History of the Achievements of the Party and Its Leaders in the Mother of Commonwealths, the Old Dominion* (3 vols., [Springfield, Ill.], 1937), I, 230-32.

[16] Blake, *Mahone*, 182; Pearson, *Readjuster Movement*, 127–29; Wynes, *Race Relations*, 19.

[17] Election returns are available in Richmond *State*, November 4, 5, 6, 10, 1879, and Richmond *Daily Dispatch*, November 19, 22, 1879. The results produced the following alignments in the 1879–1880 General Assembly: Senate—fourteen Funders, seventeen Readjusters, and nine Republicans (two blacks); House—forty-two Funders, forty-one Readjusters, and seventeen Republicans (twelve blacks).

welcomed this proposal, naturally enough, and the fourteen crucial blacks also appeared to be wavering.[18] At the moment of crisis, however, the Readjusters' General Mahone took charge. Weighing less than a hundred pounds, this diminutive former Confederate made up in energy what he lacked in size. He enjoyed a reputation as a legislative manipulator—he had won some vicious railroad charter battles—and he brought all of his lobbying skills to bear on the blacks. He met with them repeatedly, indicating his willingness to fight for improved Negro schools, the abolition of the whipping post, and a variety of other reforms. What was more, the little general promised the freedmen a voice in patronage matters, a share of the government jobs.[19] Such arguments proved convincing; Negro votes enabled the Readjusters to organize the General Assembly, and the insurgents responded by placing blacks in a variety of minor posts from legislative doorkeepers to official clerks. Capping the deal, Negro Republicans and white Readjusters elected General Mahone to the United States Senate.[20] The black lawmakers had taken a fateful step. By aligning themselves with the debt revolt they had defied their old leaders, even their President.

This Readjuster-Negro axis dominated the legislature until its adjournment in March 1880. Black votes provided the margin of victory on roll call after roll call, electing dozens of white insurgents to state offices and county judgeships. Black votes also enabled the new party to pass a bill cutting the debt by 40 percent, a bill which was stymied only by the veto of a Funder governor.[21] In spite of these evidences of cooperation, however, the Negro legislators never served as Mahone's "dupes" or "tools." Drawn from the emerging black middle class, they generally had considerable education and, in some instances, prior legislative experience. Most were landowning farmers or professional men, and they voted their convictions, particularly when Negro interests were at stake.[22]

[18] For evidence of this intrigue see the Richmond *State*, November 7, 8, December 2, 1879; see also Robert A. Richardson to Mahone, November 15, 1879; S. Bassett French to Mahone, November 25, 1879; John L. Freesley to Mahone, November 27, 1879, Mahone Papers.

[19] Richmond *Daily Dispatch*, December 6, 8, 1879; see also George F. Bragg, Jr., to Carter G. Woodson, August 26, 1926, *Journal of Negro History*, XI (October 1926), 677.

[20] Richmond *Daily Dispatch*, December 4, 1879; Richmond *State*, December 16, 1879; *Nation*, XXX (March 18, 1880), 204.

[21] Virginia, House of Delegates, *Journal, 1879–80* (Richmond, 1879), *passim;* Virginia, Senate, *Journal, 1879–80* (Richmond, 1879), *passim*. Cited hereinafter as Virginia, House, *Journal*, or Virginia, Senate, *Journal*, with the proper years of session.

[22] At least four of the black legislators had some formal schooling, and one of them, Richard G. L. Paige, was a graduate of Howard University. At least five members of the delegation had prior experience in the state legislature. Five of the blacks were farmers, and at least two of these owned their land. The delegation also included a doctor, a lawyer, two

Testing their new political power, for example, they continually demanded more state jobs for their race. Ross Hamilton, a ten-year House of Delegates veteran from Mecklenburg County, played a vital role in this respect. He kept a close watch on Readjuster patronage policies, ferreting out unfairness and pressing for reforms. Others took even more controversial stands. State senator Cephas L. Davis made an unsuccessful attempt to obtain a meal in one of Richmond's whites-only restaurants. Forced to leave, he protested vigorously against this discrimination. Cumberland delegate Shed Dungee also challenged the "color line," introducing a bill to reduce the penalties for racial intermarriage, while Norfolk's Richard G. L. Paige called for legislative action to discourage lynching.[23] These proposals proved too advanced for the time—they received virtually no white support—but the Negroes sustained them in the face of certain defeat.[24] Political activism and racial militancy went hand in hand.

Defying white opinion, therefore, the blacks maintained a measure of political independence. As the legislative session drew to a close, in fact, their ties with the debt revolt appeared to be loosening. Their assertive conduct had created a tense racial climate, a climate which both embarrassed and angered their white allies. Spurning the Negroes' controversial demands, insurgent legislators showed their pique in a graphic way: they voted to segregate the races in the House visitors' gallery.[25] The Readjusters also balked at opening their local meetings to blacks, largely because they were afraid of losing control to the aroused freedmen. Meredith Watson, a Nottoway insurgent, expressed these apprehensions in a letter to Mahone. "I entertain fears," he wrote, "if we invite them into a mass meeting with us that they will in every instance vote us down."[26] Perhaps most ominous of all, old political hatreds continued to generate mistrust. The mass of Readjusters had traditionally voted Democratic in national elections, while the blacks clung to their Republican allegiance. Consequently, the approach of the 1880 presidential campaign signaled a major crisis.

---

preachers, a merchant, and a teacher. See biographical entries in Jackson, *Negro Office-Holders, passim.*

[23] For evidence of the black legislators' assertive conduct see Richmond *State,* December 2, 9, 16, 1879; January 12, 21, February 26, 27, March 8, 1880; Richmond *Daily Dispatch,* January 22, 1880.

[24] Paige's attack on lynching was buried in committee by a vote of 69 to 12; Richmond *Daily Dispatch,* January 22, 1880. Shed Dungee's efforts to repeal the antimiscegenation law were defeated by a 77–10 margin; Richmond *State,* March 8, 1880.

[25] Virginia, House, *Journal, 1879–80,* p. 161.

[26] Watson to Mahone, February 6, 1880, Mahone Papers.

An old-line party battle would fragment the debt revolt, driving Negroes and whites into hostile camps. Reunion—particularly after a bitter contest—might prove impossible.

Seeking to avert this disaster, Mahone concocted an audacious scheme. He urged Virginia's Readjusters and Republicans to unite behind a fusion slate of unpledged presidential electors, in effect declaring their independence from the national parties. Both wings of the revolt could support this neutral ticket, and together they could smash the Funder Democrats. In a close national race, Mahone's Richmond *Whig* asserted, the unpledged electors "would be in a commanding position well worth striving for."[27] They might even be able to dictate terms to the winner, exacting patronage favors. Logical and bold in conception, the plan seemed ideally suited to the state's treacherous political terrain.

In spite of its merits, however, the unpledged electoral ticket soon ran into trouble. Negro reactions ranged from outright hostility to relative indifference. Almost all the black legislators opposed the scheme. It was one thing to defy their national party on the debt issue, but it was something else to endanger Republican control of the White House. Memories of the recent General Assembly session, of squabbles over patronage posts and civil rights, also sparked black skepticism. If Mahone was really their friend, they reasoned, he should be willing to support their party's presidential candidate. Most of the white Republicans expressed similar views. Their federal jobs depended on a victory by their national party, of course, and they demanded the election of a "straight-out" Republican ticket in Virginia.[28] Surprised by this hostile response, the little general attempted to woo the dissidents. Readjuster newspapers hinted that the unpledged electors would probably back the Republican nominees in order to break the "Solid South." Mahone also encouraged rumors that he supported the Negroes' favorite, Ulysses Simpson Grant, for the Presidency.[29] Such tactics proved only partially successful, and many blacks, including the prestigious Ross Hamilton, remained skeptical. Consequently, the Republican state convention rejected Mahone's plan, nominating instead an electoral slate which was pledged to their national ticket. Readjuster agents encouraged the black delegates to bolt the

[27] Quoted in Pearson, *Readjuster Movement*, 136; see also William C. Pendleton, *Political History of Appalachian Virginia, 1776–1927* (Dayton, Va., 1927), 338.

[28] The following provide evidence of Republican attitudes toward Mahone's proposal: Richmond *Southern Intelligencer*, February 9, 16, 23, 1880; editorial from Staunton *Valley Virginian*, quoted in Richmond *State*, April 2, 1880.

[29] Richmond *Southern Intelligencer*, February 7, 9, March 29, 1880; Richmond *Daily Dispatch*, December 11, 1879; Richmond *State*, April 2, 9, 1880.

meeting, but they refused.[30] Once again the freedmen had demonstrated their willingness to defy white leadership. Before they had challenged a President; now they spurned Mahone.

Battered by this Republican uprising, the general also faced a serious challenge from the Conservative elite. During the spring of 1880 the Funders launched a vigorous drive to regain the allegiance of the white masses. They nominated a Democratic electoral slate and urged all white Virginians, regardless of their debt views, to support the party of Jefferson and Jackson. The impact was devastating; thousands of Readjusters, anxious to elect a Democratic President, began to shift into the Funder camp.[31] Mahone had already lost control of the Republicans, and now his own organization appeared to be collapsing as well. Pressured from all sides, therefore, he abandoned the neutral, unpledged ticket. Readjuster delegates met in Richmond and fielded their own slate of Democratic electors.[32] The two debt factions thus carried their feud into the presidential race, and they fought each other much more furiously than they did the Republicans. Virginia politics bordered on chaos.

Maneuvering through this confusion, Mahone continued to court the Negro vote. He repeatedly urged the Republicans to withdraw their electoral slate. He even designed special ballots for use by the freedmen. These ballots would "accommodate the prejudice" of the blacks by leaving off the names of the national Democratic nominees and bearing only those of the Readjuster electors.[33] Such ruses, however, were foredoomed to failure. The Negroes continued to form (in Mahone's words) a "solid phalanx" for the Republican machine.[34] John J. Wise, an Accomac insurgent, provided a more caustic appraisal. "The niggers here," he declared, "will vote the Garfield [Republican] . . . ticket from top to bottom. We will get no help from them."[35] Similar conditions prevailed across the state; the freedmen reasserted their independence from Mahone.

[30] Richmond *Southern Intelligencer,* April 26, 1880; Richmond *State,* April 22–24, 1880; *Nation*, XXX (April 29, 1880), 317.

[31] Richmond *State,* March 11, 12, May 19, 20, 1880; see also Harrison H. Riddleberger to Mahone, April 25, May 30, 1880; S. Brown Allen to Mahone, June 11, 1880, Mahone Papers.

[32] Richmond *State,* July 7, 8, 1880.

[33] Mahone to James H. Williams, September 30, 1880, James Harrison Williams Papers (University of Virginia Library, Charlottesville, Va.); see also Mahone to H. H. Riddleberger, October 24, 1880, Harrison Holt Riddleberger Papers (Earl Gregg Swem Library, College of William and Mary, Williamsburg, Va.).

[34] Mahone to Lewis E. Harvie, November 5, 1880, Lewis Edwin Harvie Correspondence (Archives Division, Virginia State Library, Richmond, Va.).

[35] John J. Wise to John S. Wise, November 1, 1880, Wise Family Papers (in possession of Mr. John S. Wise of Charlottesville, Va.).

This Negro solidarity crippled the Readjusters' 1880 campaign, paving the way for disaster. Fears cropped up in the Mahone camp—fears that the Republican "phalanx" might actually carry the state. Large numbers of white insurgents began to question the wisdom of maintaining their own electoral ticket and splitting the Democratic vote. Suspicions focused on Mahone: perhaps he was a Republican agent, deliberately keeping the whites divided; perhaps he was engineering a Republican coup from behind the scenes. The national Democratic leaders shared these fears. As the campaign entered its final weeks, therefore, they moved decisively to hold the state. The party's national committee endorsed the Funder ticket and urged Virginians to support it.[36] Mahone defiantly kept his electors in the field, but his mass following melted away. Wholesale defections took place in many areas. The returns told the story: Funder Democrats, 96,449 votes; Republicans, 84,020; and Readjuster Democrats, 31,527. A poor third in a field of three, the insurgents had won only nine of Virginia's counties.[37] National politics, along with black militancy, had shattered the debt revolt.

This fiasco compelled Mahone and his aides to reevaluate their political strategy. Probing the causes of their defeat, they began to hammer out plans for the impending 1881 gubernatorial campaign. Their conferences, their conversation, their correspondence, all pointed to one inescapable conclusion: they had no chance of victory without the Negro vote. "[We] Will know better next time," the general argued. "We have been too sensitive I suspect of combination."[38] Change was necessary; risks were inevitable. "It is," one of Mahone's lieutenants noted grimly, "a case of neck or nothing."[39] As a result, the insurgents moved to liberalize their policies, to make their program more attractive to the blacks. Readjusters in the heavily Negro "Southside" led the way, declaring their willingness to give the freedmen a larger share of the government jobs. Party spokesmen all over the state blasted the "color line" and promised to repeal the discriminatory poll tax. Many of the local Readjuster clubs opened their doors to blacks.[40]

[36] Richmond *State,* October 22–23, 1880; *Nation,* XXXI (October 28, 1880), 297–98.

[37] The counties were Bland, Buchanan, Dickenson, Greene, Highland, Page, Russell, Smyth, and Wise. For election returns see Ainsworth R. Spofford, ed., *American Almanac and Treasury of Facts, Statistical, Financial, and Political, for the Year 1882* (New York, 1882), 262.

[38] Mahone to James H. Williams, November 15, 1880, Williams Papers.

[39] William E. Cameron to H. H. Riddleberger, December 27, 1880, Riddleberger Papers.

[40] The following provide evidence of Readjuster efforts to attract Negro support during the early phases of the 1881 campaign: form letter from Mahone to the Readjuster county chairmen, November 17, 1880, copy in Mahone Papers; William E. Cameron to H. H. Riddleberger, March 22, 1881, Riddleberger Papers; Richmond *Weekly Whig,* January 7,

Overshadowing these gestures, Mahone single-handedly obliterated the greatest obstacle to the alliance: he joined the Negroes' national party. Abandoning the "Bourbon" Democrats, he cast his vote with the Republicans in the United States Senate. During the spring of 1881, moreover, he established friendly ties with the new Garfield-Arthur administration.[41] Old political lines began to crumble, old loyalties to dissolve.

These developments set the stage for a workable Readjuster-Negro coalition, and the blacks responded enthusiastically. Mahone's new ties with the national Republicans, in particular, seemed to dissolve all doubts. "If such great men," a Richmond Negro insisted, "as Conkling, Dawes, Hoar, Logan, the Camerons, Garfield, Arthur, and Gorham . . . can afford to aid this [Readjuster] party, I cannot see why we little fellows down here who are suffering cannot do the same thing."[42] Many of Virginia's white Radicals remained hostile to the debt revolt, fearing that it would destroy their influence, but the freedmen brushed them aside. Indeed, the spring and summer of 1881 witnessed a full-scale black revolt against these recalcitrant spoilsmen. More than a thousand Lynchburg Negroes demanded the removal of federal officeholders in their town, and similar rebellions broke out in Alexandria, Portsmouth, and Elizabeth City.[43] Black politicians in Richmond went a step further, issuing a call for a Negro state convention to endorse the Readjuster movement. This gathering took place in Petersburg in March 1881, and it provided a major boost for the "coalition" drive. The delegates attacked the political "color line," censured the white Republicans, and announced their support for Readjustment.[44] Bludgeoned by this Negro defiance, the Radical bosses abandoned their opposition to the debt revolt. The two parties—Republicans and Readjusters—were rapidly becoming one. Eager for victory, the Negroes jostled for place on the Mahone bandwagon.

This "coalition" ground swell crested at the Readjuster state convention in June 1881. Delegates from every branch of the debt

April 1, May 13, 1881; see also announcements of local Readjuster meetings in Richmond *Daily Whig*, April 1, 23, 1881.

[41] Hirshson, *Bloody Shirt*, 95–109; De Santis, *Southern Question*, 141–55; George F. Howe, *Chester A. Arthur: A Quarter-Century of Machine Politics* (New York, 1934), 135–37.

[42] Letter from R. A. Paul, quoted in Richmond *Weekly Whig*, April 26, 1881.

[43] Salem *Weekly Register*, March 11, 1881; Richmond *Weekly Whig*, January 7, July 8, 1881; see also letter from Zachariah Hunt to Salem *Weekly Register*, April 1, 1881; letter from C. Epps to Richmond *Weekly Whig*, June 24, 1881; S. C. Dundas to William E. Cameron, June 29, 1881, Mahone Papers.

[44] Richmond *Weekly Whig*, March 4, 1881; Richmond *Daily Whig*, March 17, 1881; see also W. J. S. Bowe to Mahone, December 1, 1880, Mahone Papers.

revolt, a third of them Negroes, flocked to Richmond to spell out the terms of the new alliance. The need for compromise was evident, and a spirit of solidarity prevailed. Ticket balancing became a fine art; the politicos nominated a Petersburg Readjuster, William Ewan Cameron, for governor and a white Republican, John Francis Lewis, for lieutenant governor. This pragmatic approach also found expression in the party platform—a skillful blend of debt adjustment, Negro rights, and protective tariffs (a popular demand among western Virginia's miners and manufacturers).[45] Cementing their ties with the freedmen, moreover, the white insurgents proclaimed a new era of racial harmony. Rockingham congressman John Paul demanded an end to "the barriers of prejudice," while Mahone urged his followers to obliterate "all race distinctions" from Virginia law.[46] Gubernatorial nominee Cameron spoke along similar lines. "I don't propose to carry the war to Africa," he declared, "but to carry Africa into the war."[47] These statements were largely rhetorical bombast, of course, but they reflected one essential fact: the Readjusters were steadily drifting toward Republicanism—civil rights, protective tariffs, and all. "Coalition" had become a reality—on the Negroes' terms.

These events touched off one of the hottest gubernatorial races in the state's history. Lashing out at the new alliance, the Debt-Payers countered with a vigorous "white-supremacy" campaign. They nominated a prominent former Confederate, John Warwick Daniel, for the governorship, and they urged white Virginians to rally behind him. "It is not the principal of the debt," one of their newspapers argued, "but the principle of pure white Saxon government that we stand for; it is not the interest of the debt, but the paramount interest of our State and race that is now wavering in the balance . . . ."[48] The Conservative patricians called attention to these views by socially ostracizing their opponents. Duels resulted, along with occasional outbursts of mob violence. Warding off these attacks, however, the Readjusters continued to stress their popular debt views. Racial disputes rocked the alliance in some of the eastern areas, but Mahone worked night and day to restore harmony. As a result the insurgent groups clung together, electing their state ticket by a 12,000-vote margin. They held their own

[45] Richmond *State*, June 3, 1881; Staunton *Vindicator*, June 10, 1881; Richmond *Daily Whig*, June 27, 1881; *Nation*, XXXII (June 9, 1881), 398.

[46] Richmond *State*, June 2, 1881; Staunton *Vindicator*, June 10, 1881.

[47] Richmond *Weekly Whig*, June 24, 1881.

[48] Richmond *State*, September 27, 1881; see also Richmond *Conservative-Democrat*, October 22, 1881; Staunton *Vindicator*, November 4, 1881.

among the white mountaineers, and they swept the predominantly Negro Southside and Tidewater as well. Governor-elect Cameron carried twenty-eight of the thirty-two counties with black-voter majorities. The Readjusters also retained control of the legislature, where the returns boosted Negro membership to fifteen.[49] The "coalition" formula had succeeded magnificently.

This November 1881 triumph gave the insurgents the upper hand, and within weeks they moved to enact their program. They slashed the debt and reformed the state's tax structure, placing heavier burdens on railroads and other corporate interests. Most important of all, they poured funds into Virginia's struggling schools and asylums. Reaping the rewards of political activism, moreover, the Negroes shared in this windfall. They demanded (and received) a new state college and an up-to-date insane asylum, both located in Petersburg. Readjuster money had a similar impact on elementary education. The number of black schools more than doubled, while their enrollment skyrocketed from 36,000 in 1879 to 91,000 in 1883.[50] Alleviating a major grievance, the insurgents also acted to remove white teachers from Negro schools. Richard R. Farr, the state superintendent of public instruction, asserted his desire "to see every colored school . . . taught by a thoroughly competent colored teacher."[51] Consequently, the total of black instructors tripled, rising to almost 1,300.[52] The Readjusters capped these achievements by striking down racial discrimination in teacher salaries; they required county officials to provide equal pay for Negroes and whites under penalty of law.[53] A spirit of change, of new beginnings, pervaded the educational system.

This reform impulse soon swept into other areas, battering the old regime. The General Assembly put an end to the hated whipping post early in 1882, and a statewide referendum abolished the poll tax a few months later. Readjuster judges broke with precedent

[49] Three blacks won seats in the state Senate, while twelve were elected to the House of Delegates. Election returns are available in the *Warrock-Richardson Maryland, Virginia, and North Carolina Almanack for 1883* (Richmond, [1882]), 30; see also Richmond *Weekly Whig*, December 2, 1881.

[50] Virginia, Superintendent of Public Instruction, *Fifteenth Annual Report . . . 1885* (Richmond, 1885), 245, shows an increase in the number of Negro schools from 675 in 1879 to 1,715 in 1883. Black school enrollment rose from 35,768 to 90,948 in the same period. See also Virginia, General Assembly, *Acts and Joint Resolutions . . . 1881–82* (Richmond, 1882), 246–47, 283–86, 473–74.

[51] Virginia, Superintendent of Public Instruction, *Twelfth Annual Report . . . 1882* (Richmond, 1882), 59.

[52] Virginia, Superintendent of Public Instruction, *Fifteenth Annual Report . . . 1885*, p. 243.

[53] Virginia, General Assembly, *Acts and Joint Resolutions . . . 1881–82*, p. 37.

by allowing Negroes to serve on juries.[54] Keeping up the momentum, the insurgents also expanded patronage opportunities for their black followers. The freedmen took over state jobs as college professors, asylum physicians, and prison guards. Governor Cameron dramatized this trend by employing a Negro as his official messenger.[55] Mahone became involved as well, using his Senate influence to win the blacks a share of the federal "spoils." His activities resulted in the appointment of a Negro as Norfolk's assistant postmaster, while other blacks received a variety of lesser posts. The government bureaus in Washington began to hire black "Mahoneites," and the federal agencies in Virginia did the same. "My office looks [like] Africa," an Internal Revenue collector in Danville declared, "because I have so many colored people in it."[56] Given the racial climate of the time, these developments constituted a full-fledged civil rights revolution.

In spite of these reforms, however, Readjustment continued to offer something less than complete equality for the blacks. Mahone and his lieutenants remained white supremacists at heart, and they had no intention of endangering the main patterns of white rule in Virginia. Political expediency also led them to assume a cautious stance. Mahone was afraid of alienating his white supporters (approximately 30,000 strong), and he attempted to project a moderate, middle-of-the-road image on racial issues. As a result, the insurgent program was a curious patchwork of half-measures and compromises, of pro-Negro gestures cloaked in "white-supremacy" rhetoric. Although they expanded the black schools and asylums, for example, the Readjusters scrupulously maintained the segregated character of those facilities. Indeed, they denied any desire to break down social barriers between the races. "Our party . . . ," the Richmond *Whig* explained, "encourages each race to develop its own sociology separately and apart from unlawful contamination with each other, but under a government which recognizes and protects the civil rights of all."[57] Prominent Read-

[54] *Ibid.*, 213–14, 401; resolution of the Nansemond Republicans, Richmond *Weekly Whig*, September 15, 1882; Carter M. Louthan to Mahone, March 13, 1882, Mahone Papers.

[55] Bragg to Woodson, July 27, 1926, *Journal of Negro History*, XI, 673; Petersburg *Lancet*, September 9, 1882.

[56] Quoted in Morton, *Negro in Virginia Politics*, 120; see also W. N. Stevens *et al.*, *An Address to the Colored Voters of the State of Virginia: The Record of the Bourbon-Democratic and Liberal-Readjuster Parties Contrasted—What the Leading, Most Influential, Intelligent and Representative Colored Men of Virginia Have to Say to Their People* (n.p., [1883]), broadside in Baugh Family Papers (University of Virginia Library).

[57] Richmond *Weekly Whig*, September 21, 1883; see also Blake, *Mahone*, 261–62; James T. Moore, "To Carry Africa into the War: The Readjuster Movement and the Negro" (unpublished M.A. thesis, University of Virginia, 1968), 39–75.

justers underlined this stand with repeated denunciations of racial intermarriage.[58] Seeking to minimize fears of "Negro rule," the insurgents also soft-pedaled the blacks' new political power. They allowed the freedmen a larger share of the "spoils," as noted previously, but the major administrative and elective offices remained in white hands. No black rose above the rank of state senator during the Readjuster years. Gradual Negro progress under white tutelage was the order of the day, along with continued racial segregation. Only on such terms could the insurgents hope to retain enough white support to control the state. They walked a political tightrope, and their position was precarious at best.

Even with this careful planning, however, the "Mahoneite" racial strategy suffered from one disastrous defect: the general and his aides had grossly underestimated Negro ambitions. Having exercised the balance of power in Virginia politics, the freedmen were in no mood to accept a subordinate role. They had provided at least two-thirds of the votes for the Readjuster ticket in 1881, and they began to demand a proportionate voice in state affairs. During the next two years they demonstrated their spirit by calling for more of the government jobs and an increased share of the delegates at party conventions. In many of the eastern counties they virtually took over the Readjuster machine, nominating their own men for public office without regard for white wishes. Shocked by this upheaval, Mahone's lieutenants bitterly described the blacks as "arrogant" and "boisterous."[59] The freedmen scored their greatest breakthroughs in the heavily Negro "Southside," of course, where they took full advantage of their numerical superiority. Alfred S. Pryor, a black educator in Petersburg, celebrated this trend by listing his town's Negro officeholders. "We have . . . representatives," he announced, "on the School Board and City Council. We have a Clerk of the Market, City Physician, City Gauger, Keepers of the Hay Scales and Powder Magazine, which are positions of both profit and trust." Similar developments were occurring, he added, "all over the State."[60] In Danville black policemen walked through a downtown marketplace controlled by black merchants, while black justices of the peace settled legal dis-

[58] Richmond *Weekly Whig*, May 13, September 16, 1881; December 8, 1882; October 19, 1883.

[59] The Mahone Papers contain many complaints of this nature. For examples see John L. Hendrick to Mahone, July 23, 1883; James D. Brady to Mahone, July 31, 1883; William F. Jones to Mahone, August 7, 22, 1883; A. S. Mayo to Mahone, September 18, 1883.

[60] Petersburg *Lancet*, September 16, 1882.

putes.[61] In such places "Negro rule" was more than a slogan; it bordered on fact.

Spreading beyond politics, this Negro militancy soon permeated the atmosphere of Readjuster Virginia. Rural blacks became increasingly dissatisfied with the sharecrop system, and many of them threatened to seek the free homesteads of the frontier West.[62] This defiant mood swept through the cities as well, touching off a wave of civil rights activism in 1882 and 1883. Petersburg freedmen withdrew their children from the public schools to protest against inadequate facilities, while the town's black newspaper urged a boycott of discriminatory businesses. "Show your race pride," the Petersburg *Lancet* insisted, "and dont [*sic*] buy One Cents' [*sic*] worth of anything from those places who refuse you accommodation. In plain words dont [*sic*] buy even a stick of candy from a confectioner, who want [*sic*] sell you a glass of soda or a plate of cream. Dont [*sic*] be so foolish and humiliate your manhood as to cringe and fawn to these devils . . . ."[63] The Richmond *Virginia Star*, another Negro organ, adopted a similar tone. The newspaper prodded the whites to desegregate their churches, and it also attacked the state's law against racial intermarriage. "We want a good honest government," the *Star* editorialized, "that does not make a difference on account of the color of the skin."[64] Blacks in Lynchburg's tobacco factories joined this upheaval by striking for higher wages, while domestic servants in Danville found a more subtle way to express their views. "It is a very common practice," a group of angry whites complained, "for the negroes who are employed about our houses to allude to white ladies and gentlemen as *men* and *women*, and to negroes as *ladies* and *gentlemen*. This is a practice almost without exception with the negro women. They do it to imitate and throw contempt on the white race."[65] Old habits of subordination were dying; a new, more aggressive spirit had been born.

This increased racial consciousness severely weakened the Negroes' ties with the debt revolt. Dissatisfied with Mahone's

[61] Pearson, *Readjuster Movement*, 164; Morton, *Negro in Virginia Politics*, 119–20.

[62] Richmond *State*, January 2, 1880; Langhorne, *Southern Sketches*, 29; George William Bagby to Richmond *State*, May 14, 1880; S. P. Nottingham to Mahone, June 25, 1881, Mahone Papers.

[63] Petersburg *Lancet*, May 19, 1883; see also *ibid.*, July 15, September 2, 1882; October 13, 1883.

[64] Richmond *Virginia Star*, November 11, December 16, 1882.

[65] *Coalition Rule in Danville* (n.p., 1883), 3. A copy of this campaign pamphlet may be found in the Baugh Papers. See also Richmond *Weekly Whig*, April 6, 1883; W. Asbury Christian, *Lynchburg and Its People* (Lynchburg, 1900), 343.

moderate policies, black militants began to argue that Readjustment had accomplished little for their people. A few of them even attempted to revive the old "straight-out" Republican machine, this time under Negro control. Others showed their alienation by flirting with the hated Funders, by attending their rallies and voting their ticket in local elections.[66] These trends dismayed the white insurgents, naturally enough, and many of them called on Mahone to force the freedmen back into line. Recognizing political realities, however, the general knew that repressive tactics would only drive the Negroes away. Defeat would be the inevitable result. "It is to be remembered," he noted in an 1883 interview, "that the Readjuster party . . . is composed of about 110,000 colored and about 65,000 white voters."[67] Instead, he worked to regain the blacks' confidence. Deemphasizing "white supremacy," he moved to allow the Negroes a greater influence in Virginia politics and government than ever before. The Readjuster movement had entered its last and most radical phase.

Mahone launched this new drive with a series of carefully calculated gestures. He began in 1882 by attacking racial barriers within the Readjuster machine itself. Issuing directives to his lieutenants across the state, he demanded the inclusion of blacks in the local party leadership from precinct workers to county committeemen.[68] Later in the same year he took an even bolder step: he declared his willingness to support a Negro for the "Southside's" seat in the United States House of Representatives. "It is largely a Republican district," he argued in a letter to one of his aides, "and it is a black district. My judgment further is, that it would be politic to nominate a colored man—certainly we couldn't afford to defeat the nomination of a colored man. They are claiming it, and honestly they ought to be allowed it. It would help us with that vote not only there in the 4th district but all over the State."[69]

This proposal almost became a reality. Working to calm the black revolt, white insurgents in the "Southside" adopted the general's plan. They conceded "as a matter of course" that the Negroes

[66] For Readjuster responses to these black defections see Petersburg *Lancet*, August 1, 19, September 16, 1882; Richmond *Weekly Whig*, June 1, July 6, 1883; Woodstock *Virginian*, June 1, 1883; and *Funders Hugging Negroes! Political Cohabitation of White Bourbon-Funders with Colored Funder Straightouts* (n.p., 1883), broadside, Williams Papers.

[67] Richmond *Weekly Whig*, June 15, 1883.

[68] Bragg to Woodson, July 27, 1926, *Journal of Negro History*, XI, 674; Mahone, *Circular* (Richmond, 1882), broadside in Baugh Papers; see also the following in the Mahone Letterbooks (Duke University Library): Mahone to W. R. Watkins, August 21, 1883; Mahone to A. G. Kellam, September 8, 1883.

[69] Mahone to Lewis E. Harvie, July 3, 1882, Harvie Correspondence.

should choose the congressional candidate. The freedmen quarreled among themselves, however, and personal rivalries fragmented their strength. Unable to unite behind any of their own politicos, they wound up selecting a white man, Benjamin Stephen Hooper, as the party nominee.[70] Mahone's efforts had misfired, but the incident had allowed the Readjusters to show their concern for Negro rights. They received a similar opportunity in the spring of 1883. At that time state investigators discovered that the Richmond city school board had failed to take an oath required by law. The negligent officials were all Funders known for their conservatism on racial issues, and Governor Cameron exploited their mistake in a particularly dramatic way. He replaced them with a Readjuster board which included two Negroes. Angry whites wailed about "Africanization," but the insurgents refused to back down. Instead, they defended the move as an act of simple justice to the mass of urban freedmen.[71] Concession followed concession; reform followed reform.

This trend proved disastrous for the debt revolt. The general's tactics enabled him to placate the Negroes, but at the same time he alienated the overwhelming majority of white Virginians. The result was a massive public reaction against his program. Exploiting racial fears, the Funders argued that Readjustment would soon lead to integrated schools and "mixed" marriages. The "Mahoneites" attempted to counter this propaganda by stressing economic issues, especially protective tariffs and railroad regulation, but the impact was negligible. The whites continued to move into the Funder camp. The insurgents barely held their own in the 1882 congressional elections, and they lost most of the county and municipal races a few months later. The balance of power was shifting against them.[72]

These developments set the stage for the climactic 1883 legislative campaign. Discredited by their racial policies, the Readjusters were on the defensive all over the state, even in their mountain strongholds. The Funders, on the other hand, were welding the white masses into a superbly organized machine. Younger men took over the party leadership, and the elite adopted a much more flexible attitude toward the debt issue. Hammering away at "Negro rule," moreover, the patricians destroyed Mahone's last real chance

[70] Petersburg *Lancet*, August 19, 1882.

[71] Richmond *Weekly Whig*, May 18, 25, June 1, 8, July 6, 1883.

[72] Richmond *Daily Whig*, November 8–10, 1882; Staunton *Vindicator*, June 8, 1883; Woodstock *Virginian*, June 1, 1883; see also Blake, *Mahone*, 224; Moore, *Debt Controversy*, 113–14.

for victory; they suppressed the black vote in several of the closely contested areas. Powhatan Funders threatened to kill any freedman who voted against them, and armed thugs broke up an insurgent rally in South Boston. Aristocratic Richmonders carried their guns into the streets on election day.[73]

Taking even more drastic steps, conservative whites in Danville launched a ruthless drive to regain control of their town. They claimed that black influence in municipal affairs was excessive, and they appealed to whites all over the state to help them in their struggle against "Negroism" and "Readjusterism." Racial tensions mushroomed, naturally enough, and the results became evident a few days before the election. A pushing incident touched off the bloody "Danville Riot," a small-scale race war in which four Negroes were murdered by a white mob.[74] These brutal tactics paid off at the polls. The Funders carried the state by almost 20,000 votes, and they won sizable majorities in both houses of the legislature.[75] "White supremacy" had triumphed. Racial hysteria had shattered the insurgent regime.

The Readjusters' influence faded rapidly after this defeat. They lost control of the governor's mansion in 1885, and Mahone gave up his Senate seat the following year. The general made various bids to regain power, but he suffered repeated setbacks. He died in 1895, a broken and bitter man. The Negroes experienced a similar eclipse of political influence. Weakened by gerrymanders and election frauds, they were eliminated from the state legislature early in the 1890s. The 1902 state constitution severely circumscribed their right to vote, and they ceased to be a factor in Virginia politics. The future belonged instead to the conservative Democrats, the champions of white rule.[76]

Viewed in this perspective, therefore, the Readjuster period had been a crucial episode in the history of black Virginians. During the years from 1879 to 1883 they had functioned as an effective pressure

[73] The following letters in the Mahone Papers provide insight into these repressive tactics: M. F. Swann to Mahone, October 18, 1883; Henry F. Brooks to Mahone, October 29, 1883; G. W. Jackson to Mahone, October 31, 1883; see also William L. Royall, *Some Reminiscences* (New York and Washington, 1909), 201.

[74] *Senate Reports*, 48 Cong., 1 Sess., No. 579: Senate Committee on Privileges and Elections, *Report . . . [on] the Alleged Massacre of Colored Men at Danville, . . . Virginia . . .* (Serial 2178, Washington, 1884), *passim; Coalition Rule in Danville, passim;* Blake, *Mahone,* 226–27; Pearson, *Readjuster Movement,* 163–64.

[75] The Funders received 144,885 votes, and the Readjusters polled 126,951. See returns in Richmond *Daily Dispatch,* January 16, 1884; and Spofford, ed., *American Almanac, 1884,* p. 262.

[76] Blake, *Mahone,* 230–74; Moger, *Virginia,* 60–66, 181–202; Jackson, *Negro Office-Holders,* 81.

group, and they had scored important gains on issue after issue. Indeed, in the final analysis they had probably been too successful for their own good. Emboldened by their early triumphs, the freedmen had attempted to move too far and too fast in their drive for equality. They had infuriated white opinion, and the results had been devastating. A more cautious approach would almost certainly have paid dividends in the long run. A milder racial climate might well have enabled Mahone and his lieutenants to remain in office for decades, with incalculable benefits for the Negro cause.[77] This, of course, was not to be. Black votes had made the Readjuster regime possible; black militancy, in turn, had made the Readjuster collapse inevitable.

[77] The benefits might have extended beyond Virginia's borders, resulting in improved conditions for blacks in other areas as well. The national Republicans regarded the Readjuster-Negro alliance as the prototype for similar biracial political experiments in other states, especially in the upper South. The collapse of the debt revolt convinced them, however, to give up this drive. Instead, they resumed their gradual retreat from the region, abandoning the South to the overt racism of the white-supremacist Democrats. Disfranchisement and "Jim Crow" segregation were the inevitable results. A successful, politically potent Readjuster regime in Virginia might well have retarded or ameliorated these repressive trends. For an analysis of the national Republicans' interest in the debt struggle see Woodward, *Origins of the New South*, 99–106.

The Demise of the Colored Farmers' Alliance

By William F. Holmes

In assessing the impact of agrarian reform movements in the South upon blacks in the late nineteenth century historians have given little attention to the Colored Farmers' Alliance. That neglect results largely from the fact that the official records and newspapers of the organization have not survived so far as any historian has been able to determine. From what little is known about the Colored Alliance it is clear that it represented an important phase of agrarian protest in the South during the late nineteenth century and that it may have been one of the largest black organizations in American history.[1]

Founded in Houston County, Texas, in 1886, the Colored Farmers' Alliance soon spread into every southern state and at its height in 1891 boasted of a membership of 1,200,000. Like so many other farm clubs of that era, the Colored Alliance urged its members to learn new farming techniques, acquire ownership of their homes, and improve their level of education. It sponsored co-operative stores and in the ports of Norfolk, Charleston, Mobile, New Orleans, and Houston established exchanges through which members bought goods at reduced prices and obtained loans to pay off mortgages. It published newspapers and in some areas raised money to provide longer public school terms.[2] As did many other

[1] Officially the Colored Alliance was known as the Colored Farmers' National Alliance and Co-Operative Union. Acts of Incorporation, United States of America (Office of Recorder of Deeds, Washington, D.C.), Book IV, folio 354. For earlier accounts of the Colored Alliance see two articles by Jack Abramowitz: "The Negro in the Agrarian Revolt," *Agricultural History*, XXIV (April 1950), 89–95, and "The Negro in the Populist Movement," *Journal of Negro History*, XXXVIII (July 1953), 257–89; see also William W. Rogers, "The Negro Alliance in Alabama," *Journal of Negro History*, XLV (January 1960), 38–44; Floyd J. Miller, "Black Protest and White Leadership: A Note on the Colored Farmers' Alliance," *Phylon*, XXXIII (Summer 1972), 169–74.

[2] Richard M. Humphrey, "History of the Colored Farmers' National Alliance and Co-operative Union," in Nelson A. Dunning, ed., *The Farmers' Alliance History and Agricultural Digest* (Washington, 1891), 288–92; Washington *National Economist*, May 31, June 7, September 6, November 1, 1890; Raleigh *Progressive Farmer*, December 23, 1890; Houston *Daily Post*, January 3, 4, 1889; Richmond *Planet*, August 15, 1891; Kansas City

Mr. Holmes is associate professor of history at the University of Georgia.

The Journal of Southern History
Vol. XLI, No. 2, May 1975

black organizations of that era, the Colored Alliance urged its members to uplift themselves by hard work and sacrifice, thus demonstrating the philosophy that Booker T. Washington made famous at the close of the century.

At a time when the vast majority of Negroes lived in the South and made their living either as farmers or agricultural laborers the Colored Alliance attempted to help its members improve their position in American society. It failed to achieve that goal, however, for it began to deteriorate rapidly by 1891 and soon passed completely from the scene. By confronting the question of why the Colored Alliance failed, this paper will attempt to show what many blacks expected of the organization and why it proved unable to fulfill those expectations. An examination of the failure of the Colored Alliance will also afford insight into the state of race relations in the rural South prior to the era of the Populist movement.

From the time of its founding competition from rival black farm clubs weakened the Colored Alliance. In at least two states, Alabama and Tennessee, Negroes continued to maintain chapters of the Agricultural Wheel long after the parent organization merged with the Southern Alliance in 1888. Leaders of the Colored Wheel in Tennessee stoutly resisted overtures by Colored Alliancemen for a merger.[3] The most serious source of competition was the National Colored Alliance, an organization led by Andrew J. Carothers and organized in Texas about the same time as the Colored Farmers' Alliance. For three years it fought hard with its rival to win the support of black farmers and at one time claimed to have 250,000 members and chapters in every southern state. The leaders of the two colored alliances admitted that the rivalry between their organizations had "divided our churches . . . embittered our communities and created discord in our families." In 1890 the two groups agreed to merge, but the damage that had already been done by bitter rivalry was never repaired.[4] In 1891, when leaders of the Colored Farmers' Alliance tried to organize a cotton pickers' strike, Carothers emerged as a leading opponent of that scheme.[5]

(Kan.) *American Citizen,* July 26, 1889; Huntsville (Ala.) *Weekly Gazette,* January 11, 1890; Savannah *Tribune,* September 7, 1889; Indianapolis *Freeman,* August 30, 1890; July 25, 1891; New York *Age,* September 27, 1890; Nashville *Weekly Toiler,* March 6, July 31, 1889; Abramowitz, "The Negro in the Agrarian Revolt," 89–95.

[3] Huntsville (Ala.) *Weekly Gazette,* April 26, August 18, December 13, 1890; March 21, 1891; Indianapolis *Freeman,* January 23, 1892; Nashville, *Weekly Toiler,* July 10, September 11, October 17, 1889; May 28, 1890; October 14, 1891.

[4] Washington *National Economist,* January 25, 1890.

[5] Houston *Daily Post,* September 11, 1891; Memphis *Appeal-Avalanche,* September 11, 1891. Among the other Negro farm organizations in Texas with programs similar to those of

To weaken further the fabric of the Colored Alliance the leadership was divided between blacks and whites. Such men as J. J. Shuffer, the first president, and H. J. Spencer, the secretary, were black farmers who owned small tracts of land in East Texas.[6] Some whites also held important offices, the most notable being Richard Manning Humphrey, who served as general superintendent of the Colored Alliance.[7] Though he occasionally expressed a paternalistic view towards blacks, Humphrey did not subscribe to the harsh racism that became so prevalent among many whites by the late nineteenth century, and he worked hard in behalf of the Colored Alliance.[8] Yet, serious divisions occasionally appeared between him and black leaders. In most of his public utterances Humphrey carefully avoided offending whites; he frequently urged Negro farmers to support the programs of the Southern Alliance and to work in close cooperation with that order.[9] Perhaps it was because Humphrey tried so hard to conciliate whites during the early years of the Alliance that explains why he sometimes was not attuned to the demands of his black constituents. In 1890 the Colored Alliance and Southern Alliance met simultaneously at Ocala, Florida, and the Southern Alliance went on record as unanimously condemning the Lodge election bill, which promised federal protection to safeguard Negro voting rights. When a reporter asked Humphrey about the Colored Alliance's position on the measure, he replied that the members "do not complain that they are not

---

the Colored Alliance were the Colored Farmers' Association of Texas, founded in 1882, and the Colored Farmers' Home Improvement Lodge, chartered in 1887. Bernice R. Fine, "Agrarian Reform and the Texas Negro Farmers, 1886–1896" (unpublished M.A. thesis, North Texas State University, 1971), 81–82.

[6] Deed Record Books of Houston County (Office of County Clerk, Crockett, Texas), XIV, 193–94; XV, 263–64; XX, 392–93; XXVIII, 442–44; XXIX, 106–107; XXXVI, 33; LV, 231; LVI, 579–80.

[7] From the little that is known about Humphrey, he appears to have been an intriguing figure, one about whom we would like to know much more. Humphrey was born in Clarendon County, South Carolina, on February 14, 1836. He became a licensed minister in the Missionary Baptist church while in his teens and later attended Furman University from 1854 to 1858. For several years he served as a schoolteacher and minister in Alabama and Tennessee. During the Civil War he attained the rank of captain while serving with an Alabama infantry regiment. After the war he moved to Texas, where he farmed in addition to continuing his work as a teacher and minister. He was active during the mid-1880s in the Union Labor party, and in 1888 he ran for Congress as a Republican but was defeated by his Democratic opponent, William Harrison Martin. He died in Texas in 1906. Monticello (Miss.) *Lawrence County Press*, October 15, 1891; Miller, "Black Protest and White Leadership," 170–71; Ellis A. Davis and Edwin H. Grobe, eds., *The Encyclopedia of Texas* (2 vols., Dallas, n.d.), II, 648; Houston *Daily Post*, October 31, November 8, 1888; Ernest W. Winkler, ed., *Platforms of Political Parties in Texas* (Austin, 1916), 260–63.

[8] Washington *National Economist*, June 7, 1890; New York *Age*, December 13, 1890.

[9] Washington *National Economist*, July 26, 1890; Raleigh *Progressive Farmer*, August 26, 1890.

protected in the franchise" and went on to say that the Lodge bill would be unnecessary because through the Alliance movement the voting rights of all people would be protected.[10] Humphrey either spoke to please the Southern Alliance delegates or he did not know the views of his own membership on that issue, because the Colored Alliance strongly endorsed the Lodge bill.[11]

On other occasions Humphrey ignored the views of local Negro leaders and tried to impose his own policies upon the Colored Alliance. In Virginia, J. J. Rogers, a white, served as state superintendent until 1891, when a convention elected William H. Warwick, a black, to the position. So strongly did Humphrey and Rogers oppose the change that they circulated a petition among the Colored Alliancemen of Virginia charging that Warwick had been improperly elected. Warwick and other black leaders in Virginia retaliated by urging their members not to send dues to Humphrey as they had in the past. The black members stood behind Warwick.[12] In that same year, without consulting the Colored Alliance leaders in Georgia, Humphrey instructed J. L. Gilmore, a white Alliance lecturer, to address chapters of the Colored Alliance and recruit members. In 1892, when various farm and labor groups met in St. Louis to form the People's party, Humphrey ignored the urgings of Negro representatives from Georgia and allowed Gilmore to cast the state's eleven votes in behalf of a third party.[13]

A black-white division also doomed some economic enterprises and further contributed to the organization's demise. In 1889 a white Texan went to Marianna, Florida, organized chapters of the Colored Alliance, and persuaded the members to contribute funds for the establishment of a cooperative store. After local Colored Alliancemen purchased $1,200 in capital stock, the store opened with the white Texan serving as manager. Soon the black farmers discovered that prices at the cooperative store were as high as those at other stores; they stopped supporting it, and the store closed with a debt of over $600. Some believed the venture failed because the

[10] New York *Age*, December 13, 1890.

[11] Leavenworth *Advocate*, December 13, 1890; St. Paul *Appeal*, December 20, 1890.

[12] Richmond *Planet*, August 15, November 7, 1891; February 6, 1892; Richmond *Sun*, June 1, 1892.

[13] Atlanta *Constitution*, February 23, 1892; Atlanta *People's Party Paper*, March 17, 1892; Robert D. Lewis, "The Negro in Agrarian Uprisings, 1865–1900" (unpublished M.A. thesis, University of Iowa, 1938), 50–51. Other whites who held important positions in the Colored Alliance were F. A. Howell, who served as manager of the exchanges in Louisiana and Mississippi, and Harry McCall, whom Humphrey appointed to lead the order in Alabama. New Orleans *Weekly Pelican*, July 6, 1889; William W. Rogers, *The One-Gallused Rebellion: Agrarianism in Alabama, 1865–1896* (Baton Rouge, 1970), 142.

white Texan had worked only to advance his "own selfish ends."[14] Virginia Colored Alliancemen shared a similar experience in 1892, when they learned that J. J. Rogers, the former state superintendent, had managed the state exchange at Norfolk badly, and they stopped patronizing it. The collapse of the Norfolk exchange weakened the confidence of many in the Alliance and caused them to leave the order entirely.[15]

Some Alliance leaders claimed that the exchanges and cooperative stores throughout the South helped many blacks escape debt and become home owners, but there is nothing to support those claims. Although there is little information on the Colored Alliance's economic activities, it is safe to assume that most of its ventures, like those of other farm organizations of that era, failed.

As important as economic reversals and black-white conflicts in accounting for the eventual collapse of the Colored Alliance was the race question. Because blacks constituted such a large part of the region's agricultural population, some white agrarians came to realize that their organizations could not ignore them. "The fact is," the editor of a white farm journal noted, "that the law of self-preservation compels the southern white farmer to take the southern black farmer by the hand and hold him out of the clutches of the exploiter . . . ."[16] Despite the importance of cooperation between white and black farmers, racism proved to be a strongly divisive issue with which the agrarians never learned to cope effectively.

The Colored Alliance was founded partly because the farm organizations of that era either did not encourage blacks to join, as did the Grange, or specifically forbade black membership, as did the Southern Alliance.[17] An exception was the Agricultural Wheel, which spread from Arkansas into many southern states in the 1880s and achieved a membership of over 500,000. Although the Wheel maintained separate organizations for blacks and whites, some local chapters opened membership to both groups.[18] When rep-

[14] New York *Age*, November 2, 1889.

[15] Richmond *Sun*, June 1, 1892; William D. Sheldon, *Populism in the Old Dominion: Virginia Farm Politics, 1885–1900* (Princeton, 1935), 35–36.

[16] Washington *National Economist*, July 4, 1891.

[17] Theodore Saloutos, *Farmer Movements in the South, 1865–1933* (Berkeley and Los Angeles, 1960), 33–35; Lewis, "The Negro in Agrarian Uprisings," 19; Dunning, ed., *Farmers' Alliance History*, 62–64. In 1882 Texas State Alliancemen denied membership to Negroes because they believed blacks were undesirable social companions for their wives and daughters. William L. Garvin and S. O. Daws, *History of the National Farmers' Alliance and Co-operative Union of America* (Jacksboro, Texas, 1887), 35.

[18] Francis C. Elkins, "The Agricultural Wheel in Arkansas, 1882–1890" (unpublished Ph.D. dissertation, Syracuse University, 1953), 45, 105, 108, 149–50, 176.

resentatives of the Wheel and the Southern Alliance met at Meridian, Mississippi, in 1888 to arrange a merger of the two organizations, the issue of Negro membership proved to be the thorniest. The discussion of that question lasted for hours, and some delegates threatened to revolt. Alliancemen wanted to restrict membership to whites, but a minority of the Wheelers stoutly protested, arguing that each state should set its own policy regarding black membership. After much debate the Alliance leaders made a slight concession by permitting each state to establish rules for determining membership, thus making it possible for blacks and whites to form single chapters. But only white men could serve on the Supreme Council of the Southern Alliance.[19]

The Meridian agreement had little effect in bringing blacks and whites together in a single organization. Instead, the Southern and Colored Alliances continued to maintain their separate identities. Official spokesmen for the Southern Alliance always insisted that blacks could not join their chapters.[20] When the Southern and Northern Alliances met at St. Louis in 1889 the fact that the northerners permitted the blacks to join was a major obstacle preventing their merger.[21]

Although the Southern Alliance and Colored Alliance failed to unite, they did work together on some questions. Both advocated the abolition of the Louisiana Lottery, fearing it would lead farmers further into debt. In 1889 they joined forces against the Northern Alliance by opposing the Conger lard bill, a measure that attempted to impose high taxes and strict regulations upon the production of vegetable oil. Northern Alliancemen, some of whom were dairy farmers, supported the Conger bill, but southerners, both blacks and whites, wanted to buy vegetable oil at the lowest possible price.[22] The two Alliances also occasionally joined forces in attempting to improve their cooperative business ventures. The stores and exchanges of the Southern Alliance frequently encouraged Colored Alliancemen to do business with them. In 1890 the Southern Alliance formed the National Association of Business

[19] Nashville *Weekly Toiler*, December 19, 1888; Washington *National Economist*, March 14, 1889; F. G. Blood, ed., *Hand Book and History of the National Farmers' Alliance and Industrial Union* (Washington, 1893), 39; N. B. Ashby, *The Riddle of the Sphinx* (Des Moines, Iowa, 1890), 441–43; Elkins, "Agricultural Wheel," 239–40.

[20] Washington *National Economist*, September 14, 1889.

[21] Saloutos, *Farmer Movements in the South*, 82.

[22] Washington *National Economist*, October 11, 1890; Detroit *Plaindealer*, August 22, 1890; Cleveland *Gazette*, August 30, 1890; Huntsville (Ala.) *Weekly Gazette*, December 9, 1890; Herman C. Nixon, "The Cleavage Within the Farmers' Alliance Movement," *Mississippi Valley Historical Review*, XV (June 1928), 22–23.

Agents and State Exchanges, through which business agents for the state Alliances tried to work together and thereby achieve greater benefits for their members. The whites encouraged the Colored Alliance's business agents to join the National Association, for they knew their scheme might succeed better with the support of blacks.[23] They also called for many identical reforms, such as the abolition of national banks, the expansion of currency, and government ownership of railroads.[24]

At times spokesmen for the Southern Alliance and Colored Alliance claimed that by working for many common objectives their organizations were bringing about improved race relations. Many blacks, however, did not agree. Some worked against the Alliance movement for ideological and political reasons. The Colored Alliance's call for a third party and its support of radical reform programs caused some blacks to oppose it. At that time many Negroes were Republicans and considered the Alliance a threat to their party's power. They strongly opposed attempts by Alliance-backed candidates, and later by Populists, to unseat Republican incumbents.[25] In addition, many Negroes considered the Alliance reforms to be economically unsound, especially such measures as the subtreasury plan, the single tax, and government ownership of railroads.[26]

A number of black observers resented the discriminatory policies of the Southern Alliance. Noting that Negroes were not allowed equality of membership and were denied any representation whatever in the Southern Alliance's Supreme Council, they urged their fellow blacks to have nothing to do with agrarian reforms.[27] Some blacks insisted that the Southern Alliance was "composed in

[23] Washington *National Economist*, January 3, 1891; Abramowitz, "Negro in the Agrarian Revolt," 91; Nashville *Weekly Toiler*, October 10, 24, 1888.

[24] New York *Age*, December 13, 1890; April 4, 1891; Washington *National Economist*, June 7, December 27, 1890. The Colored Alliance did not merely rubber-stamp the Southern Alliance's reform program, for on several issues it took a stronger stand. When the two groups met simultaneously at Ocala, Florida in 1890, the whites called for a graduated income tax, but the blacks favored a single tax on land as a means of reducing the power of speculators. Some observers considered the single tax a more radical measure than the graduated income tax. At that time the black farmers also favored the formation of a third party, through which farmers and laborers could work for reform programs. The whites at Ocala refused to break from the Democratic party, the organization that had contributed so greatly to the maintenance of white supremacy since the end of Reconstruction.

[25] Leavenworth *Advocate*, May 3, October 25, 1890; Detroit *Plaindealer*, December 26, 1890; Indianapolis *Freeman*, January 24, September 12, 1891; June 25, 1892; Topeka *Times-Observer*, September 12, 1891; St. Paul *Appeal*, January 10, 1891.

[26] Kansas City (Kan.) *American Citizen*, August 14, 1891; Leavenworth *Advocate*, November 29, 1890; New York *Age*, March 14, 1891; St. Paul *Appeal*, December 6, 1890; June 13, 1891; Indianapolis *Freeman*, July 16, 1892.

[27] New York *Age*, August 2, 1890; St. Paul *Appeal*, June 13, 1891.

the main of former Democrats, and the colored man whose vote they had been in the habit of casting out in the good old days, now finds himself much sought after by both wings of the hoary old party of crime."[28]

While many articulate blacks had distrusted the Alliance movement from the outset and did not believe it was in accord with their interests, later events soon confirmed those suspicions and eventually persuaded many others to abandon the Alliance. Racism was at the core of these developments. When whites used violence to keep blacks in economic and political subjugation, an unbridged chasm rent the two alliances, and conflicts stemming from that rift finally destroyed the Colored Alliance.

Occasionally the Southern Alliance worked openly for policies to subjugate Negroes. The local Alliance chapter in Screven County, Georgia, issued orders in 1889 that no land could be leased to blacks; instead, Negroes should work for white farmers.[29] In 1890 the Alliance won control of a number of state legislatures in the South, and those legislatures under their control adopted anti-Negro laws. In 1891, for example, the Alliance legislature in Georgia passed a Jim Crow law for railroads, revived use of the whipping post, and provided that white and black prisoners could not be chained together. The Colored Alliance of Georgia protested these measures, but to no avail.[30] In Mississippi in 1890 the Southern Alliance became the chief driving force in calling a constitutional convention which disfranchised blacks by means of a poll tax and a literacy test.[31] Publications of the Southern Alliance frequently expressed strong anti-Negro views.[32] Considering the work of Southern Alliance politicians in Georgia and Mississippi and the anti-Negro views expressed in the order's newspapers, it is little wonder that blacks soon lost faith in the movement.

Several times when the Colored Alliance pursued policies designed to improve the economic position of blacks, whites retaliated by violently suppressing the movement, as was seen in Leflore County, Mississippi, in 1889. In that lowland Delta county cotton was the dominant crop, and during the preceding decade thou-

[28] Indianapolis *Freeman,* July 30, 1892.

[29] Savannah *Tribune,* December 7, 1889; New York *Age,* January 4, 1890.

[30] Clarence A. Bacote, "The Negro in Georgia Politics, 1880–1908" (unpublished Ph.D. dissertation, University of Chicago, 1955), 159–63.

[31] James S. Ferguson, "Agrarianism in Mississippi, 1871–1900: A Study in Nonconformity" (unpublished Ph.D. dissertation, University of North Carolina, 1953), 448–78.

[32] Raleigh *Progressive Farmer,* March 19, 1889; January 6, 1891; February 2, 1892; Clinton (N. C.) *Caucasian,* April 18, 1889; August 25, 1892; Nashville *Weekly Toiler,* December 26, 1888; May 4, 1892; Richmond *Sun,* October 19, 1892; Jackson *New Mississippian,* 1888, *passim.*

sands of Negroes had migrated there to work on the recently cleared plantations.[33] In the summer of 1889 Oliver Cromwell, a Negro, began organizing chapters of the Colored Alliance in the remote parts of Leflore County. He persuaded some blacks to stop trading with local merchants and to do business with a Farmers' Alliance cooperative store in Durant, a railroad town some thirty miles south of Leflore County. His work alarmed local planters and merchants, for it caused them to lose business and threatened their control over black tenants, many of whom depended upon merchants for advances in credit and supplies. Cromwell not only worked to make the blacks economically self-sufficient, but he also displayed his personal independence by occasionally delivering bold speeches to rally support for his cause. These speeches apparently worried the whites as much as did his economic policies. This man portrayed the Colored Alliance as a vehicle through which the Delta blacks might lift themselves out of their peasant status.[34]

Near mid-August 1889 whites tried to stop Cromwell by warning him to leave the county within ten days. In response, the Colored Alliancemen rallied to Cromwell's support and promised to defend him should the whites attempt to drive him from the county.[35] As word of the Colored Alliance's strong stand spread, whites from throughout Leflore and adjoining counties armed themselves and prepared to crush the Colored Alliance. Governor Robert Lowry sent three national guard units to Leflore to maintain order, but the troops remained on duty for only a short time.[36] After they withdrew a large posse, consisting of some two hundred armed whites, combed the countryside for two days, during which time they shot and hanged over twenty Negroes.[37]

The troubles in Leflore County demonstrate only too graphically why the Colored Alliance failed to survive. Soon after the posse completed its work many white planters held a meeting in which

[33] By 1890 blacks outnumbered whites in Leflore County 14,267 to 2,597. U.S. Census Office, *Compendium of the Eleventh Census: 1890* (3 vols., Washington, 1892–1897), I, 494.

[34] Jackson *Clarion-Ledger*, September 5, 1889; St. Louis *Post-Dispatch*, September 7, 1889; Jackson *New Mississippian*, September 4, 1889.

[35] Winona (Miss.) *Times*, September 6, 1889; Atlanta *Constitution*, September 2, 1889; New York *Tribune*, September 3, 1889; St. Louis *Post-Dispatch*, September 7, 1889.

[36] Mississippi, House of Representatives, *Journal, 1890* (Jackson, 1890), 594–97; St. Louis *Post-Dispatch*, September 7, 1889; Jackson *New Mississippian*, September 4, 1889; Natchez *Daily Democrat*, September 4, 1889.

[37] St. Louis *Post-Dispatch*, September 4, 1889; Atlanta *Constitution*, September 4, 5, 1889; Cleveland *Gazette*, September 21, 1889; Indianapolis *World*, quoted in Cleveland *Gazette*, November 9, 1889; Leavenworth *Advocate*, September 28, 1889; New York *Age*, December 28, 1889; Washington *Bee*, September 21, 1889.

they adopted resolutions declaring that the Colored Alliance "is being diverted from its . . . supposed purpose and is being used by designing and corrupt Negroes to further their intentions and selfish motives." They ordered the Durant Commercial Company, the Alliance store with which the blacks had been doing business, "to desist from selling goods or loaning money to the Colored Alliance or to any of its members." The planters also sent word to the editor of the *Colored Farmers' Alliance Advocate*, a newspaper published in nearby Carroll County, that he could no longer distribute his paper in Leflore County. Should the editor ignore the warning, he would face the wrath of a "united and outraged community."[38] With so many blacks killed and driven away and with so many of those remaining terrorized, the Colored Alliance in Leflore County collapsed.

Two years later, when the Colored Alliance called for a cotton pickers' strike, whites again used violence to suppress the blacks. Why the Alliance attempted such a bold scheme, which was unlike anything it had sponsored previously, is not completely clear. Much of the impetus came from white planters in the vicinity of Charleston, South Carolina, and Memphis, Tennessee, many of whom agreed not to pay cotton pickers over fifty cents per hundred pounds.[39] In response to those developments some members of the Colored Alliance persuaded Humphrey that their organization should take action to protect the pickers. Humphrey agreed to lead the movement, and during the summer of 1891, as he traveled throughout the South attending state meetings of the Colored Alliance, he quietly worked to organize cotton pickers for a strike the following fall.

Humphrey failed to persuade many Colored Alliancemen to cooperate, for some considered the scheme too dangerous, fearing it would "result in riot and bloodshed."[40] In addition, some members were farmers who either picked their own cotton or hired others to do it. Such men were not likely to support a pickers' strike.[41] After he encountered opposition to the strike within the Colored Alliance, Humphrey formed the Cotton Pickers' League. Practically nothing is known about the League, because it was a secret organization whose members refused to divulge its business. It did not charge an initiation fee but simply bound the members by an oath not to pick for wages lower than the League rec-

[38] Washington *Bee*, September 21, 1889.

[39] Houston *Daily Post*, September 6, 1891; Detroit *Plaindealer*, September 11, 1891.

[40] Houston *Daily Post*, September 11, 1891.

[41] Atlanta *Constitution*, September 9, 10, 1891; Houston *Daily Post*, September 12, 1891; Cleveland *Gazette*, September 19, 1891.

ommended.[42] Apparently, the Cotton Pickers' League, in contrast to the Colored Alliance, consisted solely of landless blacks who worked as field hands on cotton plantations in the Deep South. While Negro tenants had always formed a large part of the Colored Alliance, the organization had catered chiefly to the interests of landowners. Thus, the formation of the Cotton Pickers' League marked a radical change in the agrarian movement, for it attempted to improve the lot of landless black tenants by means of a strike.

Though the Alliance and the League were separate organizations, that distinction was never clear to the public, because the press generally credited Humphrey and the Alliance with sponsoring the strike.[43] Actually, the two organizations were closely related, since the League must have drawn many of its members from the ranks of the Colored Alliance and since Humphrey served as the chief spokesman for both organizations.

From the little that is known of the Cotton Pickers' League, it appears that the movement was doomed from the outset. Not only have farm laborers always been one of the most difficult groups to organize for collective bargaining, but the South—more than any other section—has always strongly resisted unionization. Nonetheless, Humphrey tried to bring off the largest agricultural strike in American history by organizing southern cotton pickers at a time when labor unions throughout the United States were notoriously weak. The Cotton Pickers' League lacked the local leaders and the means of communication necessary to bind its members into a united front. It is quite likely that the majority of cotton pickers never knew of the proposed strike. In addition, the League had no way to protect its members. When asked how the pickers would support themselves during the strike, Humphrey suggested that they find other jobs.[44] In the rural South of that era there were no alternative means by which blacks could support themselves. Thus, it is not surprising that the strike never materialized. Humphrey called for the strike to begin on September 12, 1891, but throughout the South pickers ignored his call.[45]

[42] Houston *Daily Post,* September 12, 1891.

[43] *Ibid.,* September 8, 11, 1891; Atlanta *Constitution,* September 8, 1891.

[44] Atlanta *Constitution,* September 13, 1891.

[45] Memphis *Appeal-Avalanche,* September 14, 1891; Atlanta *Constitution,* September 13, 1891; Detroit *Plaindealer,* September 18, 1891; Indianapolis *Freeman,* October 3, 1891; Washington *National Economist,* September 26, 1891. Only in South Carolina and Texas did some blacks attempt to strike. In Wharton County, Texas, one chapter of the Colored Alliance sympathized with the proposed strike, but it failed to get support of four other chapters in that county. Near Palestine, Texas, the pickers on one farm struck, but the

There was one notable exception. In late September a violent strike developed in the Arkansas Delta, a short distance from Memphis. Ben Patterson, a thirty-year-old black man from Memphis, led the strike. It is unknown whether he belonged to the Cotton Pickers' League, but chances are he was either a League member or was strongly influenced by Humphrey's call for a strike. He arrived in Lee County in early September—about the time the press first reported Humphrey's call for a strike—and during the next three weeks worked quietly, urging blacks to strike when he gave the word. He won the firm support of about twenty-five men. Patterson hoped that many others would join the strike once it had begun and thereby force the planters to pay a higher wage.[46]

The strike started on September 20, when some pickers working for Colonel H. P. Rodgers demanded that he raise their wages to seventy-five cents per hundred pounds. Rodgers retaliated by dismissing them and ordering them off his plantation. Throughout the following week the strike leaders traveled through wide parts of Lee County urging blacks to join the movement. It does not appear that they ever won a large following, because many blacks—out of apathy or fear or the conviction that the strike would fail—refused to support it. On September 25 a serious conflict developed when the strikers rode onto one plantation and demanded that the pickers join them; the pickers refused, and a fight ensued in which men, women, and children participated, "armed with hoes, sticks, knives and revolvers." Two pickers were killed.[47]

For several days prior to that fight local planters had been trying to catch the strike leaders. After the killing of the two pickers, the whites formed a large posse under the leadership of the county sheriff and began a manhunt for Patterson and his followers. During the last week of September they forcefully crushed the attempted strike; in the process they killed fifteen of the strikers—including Patterson—and imprisoned six others. At one point a band of whites seized nine of the strikers from a sheriff's deputy and lynched them.[48]

---

owner discharged them and "Matters immediately settled." Memphis *Appeal-Avalanche,* September 13, 1891; Houston *Daily Post,* September 13, 1891; George B. Tindall, *South Carolina Negroes, 1877–1900* (Columbia, S. C., 1952), 118–19.

[46] Houston *Daily Post,* September 28, 30, 1891; Memphis *Appeal-Avalanche,* October 2, 1891.

[47] Richmond *Planet,* October 17, 1891; St. Louis *Post-Dispatch,* September 27, 1891.

[48] St. Louis *Post-Dispatch,* September 27, October 2, 4, 1891; Memphis *Appeal-Avalanche,* October 1–7, 1891; Little Rock *Arkansas Gazette,* October 1, 2, 1891; Atlanta *Constitution,* October 3, 1891.

The cotton pickers' strike caused many blacks to reconsider their relations with the Alliance. The way Arkansas whites had ruthlessly suppressed the strike must have discouraged others who contemplated similar action. Albion Winegar Tourgée, who had served as a Republican judge in North Carolina during Reconstruction and who in 1891 remained one of the leading white advocates of full civil rights for blacks, believed that no group in the country needed higher wages more than cotton pickers. He noted, however, that some of the strongest opposition to the proposed strike came from the Southern Alliance. He hoped that Colored Alliancemen, who had tended to put great faith in the Alliance movement would now realize the "true spirit and purpose" of the whites. Blacks, he insisted, could expect little at the hands of the southern white farmers.[49]

In part, Tourgée was correct. The attempt to mobilize cotton pickers in 1891, more than any other single event, revealed a basic difference between black and white agrarians in the South. The Southern Alliance consisted primarily of cotton farmers, many of whom depended on blacks to pick their crops. The Colored Alliance, in contrast, was composed of many landless tenants who picked cotton for white farmers. When Humphrey tried to champion the interests of landless blacks by the radical means of a cotton pickers' strike he aroused the opposition of white farmers and discredited the Colored Alliance in their eyes. Opposition to the strike came from practically all segments of the white South, but spokesmen for the Southern Alliance were among the strongest opponents of the scheme.[50] In taking that stand the Southern Alliance reflected the harsh racial views that were then beginning to flourish in the South and that would become more prevalent in the region during the following decade.

The violence in Arkansas and Mississippi revealed that those blacks who joined the Colored Alliance expected it to serve, above all, as a vehicle through which they might improve their economic position. It also indicates that many whites were determined to maintain the system through which they exploited blacks. When Colored Alliance leaders tried to implement policies that threat-

[49] Detroit *Plaindealer*, October 2, 1891.

[50] Atlanta *Constitution*, February 23, 1892. The changed attitude of the Southern Alliance toward the Colored Alliance was best indicated by the *National Economist*, the official journal of the Southern Alliance. Until the cotton pickers' strike, the *Economist* had on a number of occasions expressed support for Humphrey and the Colored Alliance, but after the proposed strike the *Economist* gave no further attention to them. See also Raleigh *Progressive Farmer*, September 15, 1891; Atlanta *Constitution*, September 8, 1891; Houston *Daily Post*, September 11, 1891.

ened the whites' economic domination, they could expect determined and, quite likely, violent opposition. On other occasions in that era whites in the rural South used force to suppress Negro organizations that attempted to improve the economic lot of their members. In 1887 whites in South Carolina employed terrorist tactics to crush the Co-operative Workers of America, an organization that attempted to eliminate the dependence of blacks upon rural merchants. In that same year white sugar planters in Louisiana ruthlessly suppressed a strike by black workers.[51]

In the months following the abortive cotton pickers' strike the Colored Alliance began to decline rapidly, and by 1892 only a remnant of the organization remained. Like other farm organizations of the late nineteenth century it failed partly because of internal weaknesses and the collapse of its economic programs. The Colored Alliance also failed because it went beyond the self-help philosophy and attempted to improve the semipeasant status of many blacks by supporting programs designed to reduce economic exploitation by whites. It is possible that had the Colored Alliance adhered strictly to a philosophy of self-help and not challenged the caste system, it might not have encountered violent opposition from whites and might have enjoyed a longer existence. In fact, the Farmers Improvement Society of Texas, a Negro farm club founded in 1890, survived throughout the first half of the twentieth century, partly because it worked only for such conservative goals as encouraging its members to adopt improved farming methods and acquiring ownership of their homes.[52] The Colored Alliance dared to pursue bolder programs and died violently for its efforts.

[51] Tindall, *South Carolina Negroes*, 115–16; William I. Hair, *Bourbonism and Agrarian Protest: Louisiana Politics, 1877–1900* (Baton Rouge, 1969), 178–85.

[52] Jack Abramowitz, "John B. Rayner—Grass Roots Leader," *Journal of Negro History*, XXXVI (April 1951), 176–84; Carl Kelsey, *The Negro Farmer* (Chicago, 1903), 75.

Southern History in Periodicals, 1974: A Selected Bibliography

THIS SELECTIVE CLASSIFIED BIBLIOGRAPHY INCLUDES MOST SCHOLarly articles in the field of southern history published in periodicals in 1974 except for descriptive or genealogical writings of primary interest to a restricted group of readers. Since some journals were not published on schedule in 1973, articles from them were not included in the 1973 list published in the May 1974 issue of the *Journal.* The present listing includes these late journals with a bracketed notation that the article was published in 1973, or earlier if appropriate.

Entries under each heading are by author and are arranged alphabetically except for entries under "Military and Naval" and "Politics and Government," which are arranged chronologically.

GENERAL AND UNCLASSIFIED

F. N. BONEY. The South's Peculiar Intuition. *La. Stud.,* Winter [1973], 565–77.

BURTON A. BOXERMAN. Louis Patrick Aloe [St. Louis Jewish civic leader, 1867–1929]. *Bull. Mo. Hist. Soc.,* Oct., 41–54.

CHESTER D. BRADLEY. Was Jefferson Davis Disguised as a Woman When Captured? *Jour. Miss. Hist.,* Aug., 243–68.

WILLIAM E. COX. The Greens of Jefferson County, Mississippi. *Ibid.,* Feb., 77–103.

THEODORE J. CRACKEL. Custer's Kentucky: General George Armstrong Custer and Elizabethtown, Kentucky, 1871–1873. *Filson Club Hist. Quar.,* April, 144–55.

MARTIN CRAWFORD. The Great Georgia Railway Disaster Hoax [1856] Revisited. *Ga. Hist. Quar.,* Fall, 331–39.

ARCHIE K. DAVIS. The Veil of Humility [N. C. eulogized]. *N. C. Hist. Rev.,* Spring, 201–14.

PHILIP F. DUR. Jefferson Caffery [1886–1974] of Louisiana: Highlights of His Career. Part 1: 1911–1933; Part 2: 1933–1944. *La. Hist.,* Winter, 5–34; Fall, 367–402.

WALTER T. DURHAM. Wynnewood [Tenn. inn]. *Tenn. Hist. Quar.,* Summer, 127–56; Fall, 297–321.

ARLEN DYKSTRA. St. Louis Mourns the Untimely Death [1880] of Phelim O'Toole [firefighter]. *Bull. Mo. Hist. Soc.,* Oct., 32–40.

B. J. FETT. Early Life of [Texas gov.] Richard Coke [1829–1897]. *Texana,* No. 4 [1972], 310–20.

STANLEY J. FOLMSBEE. David Crockett and West Tennessee. *West Tenn. Hist. Soc. Papers,* 5–24.

Will D. Gilliam, Jr. Robert Jefferson Breckinridge, 1800–1871. *Reg. Ky. Hist. Soc.*, July, 207–23; Oct., 319–36.

Neal O. Hammon. The Legend of Daniel Boone's Cabin at Harrodsburg [Ky.]. *Filson Club Hist. Quar.*, July, 241–52.

John Henry Hatcher. [Chief Justice] Fred Vinson [1890–1953]: Boyhood and Education in the Big Sandy Valley [Ky.]. *Reg. Ky. Hist. Soc.*, July, 243–61.

Timothy C. Jacobson. Joseph Buckner Killebrew [1831–1906]: Agrarianism in the New South. *Tenn. Hist. Quar.*, Summer, 157–74.

C. Richard King. Margaret Borland [d. 1872]. *Texana,* No. 4 [1972], 321–27.

V. Paul Kramer. The Spanish Borderlands of Texas and Tamaulipas [1516–1848]. *Ibid.*, No. 3 [1972], 260–72.

David D. Lee, ed. Jesse Waugh [1832–1908?], West Virginian. *W. Va. Hist.*, Jan., 154–62.

Bernadette K. Loftin. A Woman Liberated: Lillian C. West [1884–1970], Editor. *Fla. Hist. Quar.*, April, 396–410.

William J. MacArthur, Jr. The Early Career of [Knoxville businessman] Charles McClung McGhee [b. 1828]. *East Tenn. Hist. Soc. Pub.*, No. 45 [1973], 3–13.

Robert M. McBride. Samuel Newell [1754–1841] of Sevier County. *Ibid.*, 14–24.

Pierre Marambaud. Colonel William Byrd I [1652–1704]: A Fortune Founded on Smoke. *Va. Mag. Hist. and Biog.*, Oct., 430–57.

Edwin E. Meek. Eugene Octave Sykes, Member and Chairman of Federal Communications Commission and Federal Radio Commission, 1927–1939. *Jour. Miss. Hist.*, Nov., 377–86.

Maurice H. Merrill. The Laws Which Have Governed Cleveland County [Okla.]. *Chron. Okla.*, Winter, 476–82.

Gary B. Mills. The Chauvin Brothers: Early Colonists of Louisiana. *La. Hist.*, Spring, 117–31.

Billie Beth Moore. The Forgotten Frontier [Red River area]. *Texana,* No. 3 [1972], 284–89.

W. Eugene Morse. "Judge" William Hemingway, 1869–1937. *Jour. Miss. Hist.*, Nov., 339–51.

Mary Ann Oglesby Neeley. Lachlan McGillivray [fl. 1736–1799]: A Scot on the Alabama Frontier. *Ala. Hist. Quar.*, Spring, 5–14.

Paul Pappas. The Question of Greek Independence in Kentucky, 1821–1828. *Reg. Ky. Hist. Soc.*, April, 143–70.

Thomas C. Parramore. The Bartons of Bartonsville [N. C.]. *N. C. Hist. Rev.*, Winter, 22–40.

William S. Powell. Carolana and the Incomparable Roanoke: Explorations and Attempted Settlements, 1620–1663. *Ibid.*, 1–21.

Frank C. Rigler. Logan Vandeveer [1815–1855], Forgotten Pioneer. *Texana,* No. 3 [1972], 203–25.

Philip Reed Rulon and Ronald Eugene Butchart. Henry Elijah Alvord, 1844–1904: Soldier, Scientist and Scholar. *Chron. Okla.*, Spring, 61–81.

EDWARD S. SHAPIRO. Donald Davidson and the Tennessee Valley Authority: The Response of a Southern Conservative. *Tenn. Hist. Quar.*, Winter, 436–51.

WILLIAM S. SIMPSON, JR. Dabney Carr [1744–1773]: Portrait of a Colonial Patriot. *Va. Cavalcade*, Winter, 5–13.

BROOX SLEDGE. A Postal History of Kemper County [Miss.], 1834–1964. *Jour. Miss. Hist.*, Feb., 69–75.

MRS. HUGH SMITH. LaFayette Hoyt DeFriese [1852–1928]: Alabamian of Fact and Fiction. *Ala. Rev.*, Oct., 243–62.

MIRIAM JANE SMITH. Forgotten Virginian—From British Merchant to Prominent Citizen: Thomas Rutherfoord 1766–1852. *W. Va. Hist.*, Oct., 50–62.

A. J. SOWELL. Ranger Relates Adventures of a Texas Frontiersman [George W. Evans, b. 1849]. *Texana*, No. 2 [1973], 188–96.

PHINIZY SPALDING. Myths and the Man: James Edward Oglethorpe [1696–1785]. *Ga. Rev.*, Spring, 52–57.

RICHARD J. STANABACK. Florida's Disrupted Mail Service, 1821–1845. *Fla. Hist. Quar.*, July, 66–73.

LOIS STONEHAM. Richard Andrews [1801–1835], First Martyr of the Texas Revolution. *Texana*, No. 4 [1972], 358–67.

R. STEPHEN TAYLOR. James Weir [1821–1906], First Citizen of Owensboro [Ky.]. *Reg. Ky. Hist. Soc.*, Jan., 10–19.

DANIEL TYLER. Governor [Manuel] Armijo [fl. 1820–1850] and the Tejanos. *Jour. West*, Oct. [1973], 589–99.

JAMES F. VIVIAN. Major E. A. Burke: The Honduras Exile, 1889–1928. *La. Hist.*, Spring, 175–94.

JOHN WALTON. Politicians and Statesmen: The Bristows [of Ky.] in American Government. *Filson Club Hist. Quar.*, Oct., 305–26.

ROBERT E. WATERMAN and THOMAS ROTHROCK, eds. The [Fontaine Richard] Earle–[Amanda] Buchanan [Earle] Letters of 1861–1896. *Ark. Hist. Quar.*, Summer, 99–174.

T. H. WATKINS. Discoverers of the Mississippi. *Am. West.*, March, 4–11.

LINDA WHITLEY. Benjamin I. Harper, [Battle of] San Jacinto Veteran. *Texana*, No. 4 [1972], 328–34.

LOUIS B. WRIGHT. Tribulations of a New Nation, American Style. *Va. Mag. Hist. and Biog.*, April, 131–43.

G. ALLEN YEOMANS. A Southern Segregationist [J. Thomas Heflin] Goes to Gettysburg [1913]. *Ala. Hist. Quar.*, Fall and Winter [1972], 194–205.

BIBLIOGRAPHY AND HISTORIOGRAPHY

Accessions Registry, 1973. Georgia Depositories. *Ga. Hist. Quar.*, Spring, 105–15.

ERIK ALLARDT. A Comment on [J. Rogers] Hollingsworth [and problems in theory construction]. *Hist. Methods Newsletter*, June, 245–48.

Baptist Biography and History in Periodicals, 1973. *Baptist Hist. and Heritage*, Oct., 247–50.

GEORGE S. BURSON, JR. The Second Reconstruction: A Historiographical Essay on Recent Works. *Jour. Negro Hist.*, Oct., 322–36.

ROBERT BUSH. Dr. [Edwin Anderson] Alderman's Symposium on the South [1903]. *Miss. Quar.*, Winter, 3–19.

EDWARD L. BYRD, JR. The Old South as a Modern Myth: An Interpretive Essay. *Red River Valley Hist. Rev.*, Spring, 55–65.

RANDOLPH CAMPBELL. Local Archives as a Source of Slave Prices: Harrison County, Texas, as a Test Case. *Historian*, Aug., 660–69.

LESTER J. CAPPON. Retracing and Mapping the [John and William] Bartrams' Southern Travels. *Proc. Am. Philos. Soc.*, Dec., 507–13.

JOHN W. CAUGHEY. The Insignificance of the Frontier in American History or "Once Upon a Time There Was an American West." *Western Hist. Quar.*, Jan., 5–16.

ISABEL V. CLARKE, comp., and PATRICIA A. ANDREWS, ed. Writings on Archives, Historical Manuscripts, and Current Records: 1972. *Am. Archivist*, July, 435–57.

THOMAS H. COODE and AGNES M. RIGGS. The Private Papers of West Virginia's 'Boy Senator,' Rush Dew Holt [1905–1955]. *W. Va. Hist.*, July, 296–318.

IRENE E. CORTINOVIS. Documenting an Event with Manuscripts and Oral History: The St. Louis Teachers' Strike, 1973. *Oral Hist. Rev.*, 59–63.

A Few Words About E. Merton Coulter [b. 1890]: Ellis Merton Coulter Begins His Third Career. *Ga. Hist. Quar.*, Spring, 6–23.

RICHARD J. COX. Public Records in Colonial Maryland. *Am. Archivist*, April, 263–75.

CHARLES W. CRAWFORD. Oral History—The State of the Profession. *Oral Hist. Rev.*, 1–9.

RICHARD O. CURRY. The Civil War and Reconstruction, 1861–1877: A Critical Overview of Recent Trends and Interpretations. *Civil War Hist.*, Sept., 215–38.

BLAISE C. D'ANTONI. The [Colonial] Church Records of North Louisiana. *La. Hist.*, Winter, 59–67.

DAVID BRION DAVIS. Slavery and the Post–World War II Historians. *Daedalus*, Spring, 1–16.

JAMES F. DOSTER. Tuscaloosa Historians. *Ala. Rev.*, April, 83–100.

L. TUFFLY ELLIS and BARBARA J. STOCKLEY, comps. and eds. A Checklist of Theses and Dissertations in Texas Studies, 1964–1974. *Southwestern Hist. Quar.*, Oct., 183–98.

LEROY H. FISCHER. Muriel H. Wright [b. 1889], Historian of Oklahoma. *Chron. Okla.*, Spring, 3–29.

Florida History in Periodicals. *Fla. Hist. Quar.*, July, 74–78.

Florida History Research in Progress. *Ibid.*, Jan., 309–17.

Florida Manuscript Acquisitions and Accessions. *Ibid.*, April, 423–29.

ERIC FONER. The Causes of the American Civil War: Recent Interpretations and New Directions. *Civil War Hist.*, Sept., 197–214.

GLORIA FRYE and BARBARA EDWARDS. A Decade of Publications, 1963–1973. *East Texas Hist. Jour.*, Spring, 17–22.

JAMES W. GEARY, comp. A Bibliography of Civil War Articles: 1973. *Civil War Hist.*, Dec., 329–63.

WILLIE D. HALSELL. A Bibliography of Theses and Dissertations Relating to Mississippi, 1973. *Jour. Miss. Hist.*, Feb., 105–11.

HUGH B. HAMMETT. Reconstruction History Before [William A.] Dunning: Hilary [Abner] Herbert [1834–1919] and the South's Victory of the Books. *Ala. Rev.*, July, 185–96.

J. ROGERS HOLLINGSWORTH. Some Problems in Theory Construction for Historical Analysis. *Hist. Methods Newsletter,* June, 225–44.

J. KAHK and I. D. KOVALCHENKO. Methodological Problems of the Application of Mathematical Methods in Historical Research. *Ibid.*, 217–24.

DENNIS KELLY. Linking Nineteenth-Century Manuscript Census Records: A Computer Strategy. *Ibid.*, March, 72–82.

JEFFREY L. KOZISEK. Manuscript Acquisitions of the Department of Archives and History, 1973. *Jour. Miss. Hist.*, Feb., 113–16.

DOLORES C. LEFFALL. The Black Experience in Africa, Latin America and the Caribbean: A Selected Bibliography of Articles Appearing in Periodicals 1973–1974. *Jour. Negro Hist.*, Oct. 352–95.

RICHARD P. MCCORMICK. The Comparative Method: Its Application to American History. *Mid-Am.*, Oct., 231–47.

ARCHIE P. MCDONALD. The Papers of the Texas Revolution, 1835–1836: An Appraisal. *East Texas Hist. Jour.*, Fall, 64–67.

RICHARD M. MCMURRY. The [Confederate Lt. Thomas Bennett] Mackall [1840–1915] Journal and Its Antecedents. *Civil War Hist.*, Dec., 311–28.

LOUIS H. MANARIN. A Building [Va. Public Records Office, 1748] . . . . for the Preservation of the Public Records. *Va. Cavalcade,* Summer, 22–31.

ALLAN R. MILLETT and B. FRANKLIN COOLING. Doctoral Dissertations in Military Affairs, Supplement II. *Mil. Aff.*, Feb., 12–16.

CLARENCE L. MOHR. Southern Blacks in the Civil War: A Century of Historiography. *Jour. Negro Hist.*, April, 177–95.

PHILIP R. MULLER. Look Back Without Anger: A Reappraisal of William A. Dunning [1857–1922]. *Jour. Am. Hist.*, Sept., 325–38.

MICHAEL O'BRIEN. Edwin Mims [1872–1954]: An Aspect of the Mind of the New South Considered. *Sou. Atlantic Quar.*, Spring, 199–212; Summer, 324–34.

JAMES S. OLSON. The Birth of a Discipline: An Essay on Chicano Historiography. *Soc. Studies,* Dec., 300–302.

PHILLIP S. PALUDAN. The American Civil War: Triumph Through Tragedy. *Civil War Hist.*, Sept., 239–50.

EDWARD C. PAPENFUSE. "A Modicum of Commitment": The Present and Future Importance of the Historical Records Survey. *Am. Archivist,* April, 211–21.

THOMAS C. PARRAMORE. Forging the Tremulous Link: The First Half-Century of the *North Carolina Historical Review*. *N. C. Hist. Rev.*, Autumn, 361–78.

WILLIAM W. PORTER II. William Bartram's [1739–1823] "Road to

Xanadu" on Modern Florida Maps. *Proc. Am. Philos. Soc.*, Dec., 514–18.

WILLIAM S. POWELL. North Carolina Bibliography, 1972–1973. *N. C. Hist. Rev.*, Spring, 215–23.

MORRIS L. RADOFF. The Maryland Records in the Revolutionary War. *Am. Archivist,* April, 277–85.

ROBERT REID. Changing Interpretations of the Reconstruction Period in Alabama History. *Ala. Rev.,* Oct., 263–81.

EARL M. ROGERS, [comp.]. Books on Agricultural History Published in 1972. *Agric. Hist.,* April, 305–12.

WILLIAM SAFFADY. Manuscripts and Psychohistory. *Am. Archivist,* Oct., 551–64.

MARTIN F. SCHMIDT. Early Prints and Maps of Kentucky, 1784–1850. *Antiques,* March, 556–60.

Southern History in Periodicals, 1973: A Selected Bibliography. *Jour. Sou. Hist.,* May, 245–78.

LALA CARR STEELMAN. Review of North Carolina Nonfiction, 1971–1973. *N. C. Hist. Rev.,* Spring, 161–69.

WALTER W. STENDER and EVANS WALKER. The National Personnel Records Center Fire [1973]: A Study in Disaster. *Am. Archivist,* Oct., 521–49.

JOHN H. THWEATT. The James K. Polk [1795–1849] Papers. *Tenn. Hist. Quar.,* Spring, 93–98.

CARL TYSON. A Bibliographical Essay: Politics in the American West. *Jour. West,* Oct., 117–22.

MILDRED MOTT WEDEL [ed.]. The [Jean-Baptiste] Bénard de La Harpe Historiography on French Colonial Louisiana. *La. Stud.,* Spring, 9–67.

MARVIN LAURENCE WINITSKY. Roger B. Taney [1777–1864]: A Historiographical Inquiry. *Md. Hist. Mag.,* Spring, 1–26.

ECONOMIC

BENNETT D. BAACK and EDWARD J. RAY. Tariff Policy and Income Distribution: The Case of the United States 1830–1860. *Explorations in Econ. Hist.,* Winter, 103–22.

FRED BATEMAN, JAMES FOUST, and THOMAS WEISS. The Participation of Planters in Manufacturing in the Antebellum South. *Agric. Hist.,* April, 277–97.

RICHARD M. BERNARD. A Portrait of Baltimore in 1800: Economic and Occupational Patterns in an Early American City. *Md. Hist. Mag.,* Winter, 341–60.

SUSAN SOKOL BLOSSER. Calvin J. Cowles's Gap Creek [N. C.] Mine: A Case Study of Mine Speculation in the Gilded Age. *N. C. Hist. Rev.,* Autumn, 379–400.

DAISY WADE BRIDGES. Carolina Gold and the U. S. Branch Mint in Charlotte. *Antiques,* Dec., 1041–46.

ALEXANDER CROSBY BROWN. The Guard Locks at Great Bridge [Va.]. *Va. Cavalcade,* Autumn, 70–79.

D. Clayton Brown. Sam Rayburn [1882–1961] and the Development of Public Power in the Southwest. *Southwestern Hist. Quar.*, Oct., 140–54.

Gary L. Browne. Business Innovation and Social Change: The Career of Alexander Brown [1764–1834] After the War of 1812. *Md. Hist. Mag.*, Fall, 243–55.

A. R. Buckalew and R. B. Buckalew. The Discovery of Oil in South Arkansas, 1920–1924. *Ark. Hist. Quar.*, Autumn, 195–238.

Randolph Campbell. The Productivity of Slave Labor in East Texas: A Research Note. *La. Stud.*, Summer, 154–72.

Powell A. Casey. Military Roads in the Florida Parishes of Louisiana. *La. Hist.*, Summer, 229–42.

Philip Coelho and James Shepherd. Differences in Regional Prices: The United States, 1851–1880. *Jour. Econ. Hist.*, Sept., 551–91.

Helen Bartter Crocker. Steamboats of Kentucky's Green River. *Antiques*, March, 570–75.

Stephen DeCanio. Productivity and Income Distribution in the Post-Bellum South. *Jour. Econ. Hist.*, June, 422–46.

Ralph Brown Draughon, Jr. The Ingenious John R. Remington [fl. 1840s], Alabama Inventor. *Ala. Rev.*, April, 139–51.

Lucius F. Ellsworth. Raiford and Abercrombie: Pensacola's Premier Antebellum Manufacturer. *Fla. Hist. Quar.*, Jan., 247–60.

Priscilla Ann Evans. Merchant Gristmills and Communities, 1820-1880: An Economic Relationship. *Mo. Hist. Rev.*, April, 317–26.

James E. Fickle. Management Looks at the "Labor Problem": The Southern Pine Industry During World War I and the Postwar Era. *Jour. Sou. Hist.*, Feb., 61–76.

Kenny A. Franks, ed. The California Overland Express Through Indian Territory and Western Arkansas [1860]. *Ark. Hist. Quar.*, Spring, 70–81.

David Galenson. The End of the Chisholm Trail [1885]. *Jour. Econ. Hist.*, June, 350–64.

Charles B. Garrison. Industrial Growth in the Tennessee Valley Region, 1959 to 1968. *Am. Jour. Agric. Econ.*, Feb., 50–60.

David B. Gracy II. Irrigation on the [Texas] High Plains—A Perspective. *Red River Valley Hist. Rev.*, Summer, 127–31.

Gerald Gunderson. The Origin of the American Civil War. *Jour. Econ. Hist.*, Dec., 915–50.

Lawrence R. Handley. Settlement Across Northern Arkansas as Influenced by the Missouri & North Arkansas Railroad. *Ark. Hist. Quar.*, Winter, 273–92.

Jay Higginbotham. The [Antoine] Chaumont Concession: A French Plantation on the Pascagoula [1719–1737]. *Jour. Miss. Hist.*, Nov., 353–62.

Robert Higgs. Patterns of Farm Rental in the Georgia Cotton Belt, 1880–1900. *Jour. Econ. Hist.*, June, 468–82.

Michael S. Holmes. From Euphoria to Cataclysm: Georgia Confronts the Great Depression. *Ga. Hist. Quar.*, Fall, 313–30.

E. L. Jones. Creative Disruptions in American Agriculture, 1620–1820. *Agric. Hist.*, Oct., 510–28.

THOMAS A. KELEMEN. A History of Lynch, Kentucky [coal company town], 1917–1930. *Filson Club Hist. Quar.*, April, 156–76.

CHARLES KENNER. The Origins of the "Goodnight" Trail Reconsidered. *Southwestern Hist. Quar.*, Jan., 390–94.

EDWARD F. KEUCHEL. A Purely Business Motive: German-American Lumber Company, 1901–1918. *Fla. Hist. Quar.*, April, 381–95.

RICHARD S. KIRKENDALL. Harry S. Truman: A Missouri Farmer in the Golden Age. *Agric. Hist.*, Oct., 467–83.

MARTIN M. LAGONDA. Greens, Grist and Guernseys: Development of the Florida State Agricultural Marketing System. *Fla. Hist. Quar.*, Oct., 146–63.

LESTER G. LINDLEY. Norvin Green [1818–1893] and the Telegraph Consolidation Movement. *Filson Club Hist. Quar.*, July, 253–64.

DANIEL F. LITTLEFIELD, JR., and LONNIE E. UNDERHILL. Timber Depredations and Cherokee Legislation, 1869–1881. *Forest Hist.*, April, 4–13.

FRENISE A. LOGAN. A British East India Company Agent [Thomas Bayles] in the United States, 1839–1840. *Agric. Hist.*, April, 267–76.

THOMAS C. LONGIN. Coal, Congress and the Courts: The Bituminous Coal Industry and the New Deal. *W. Va. Hist.*, Jan., 101–30.

CHARLES B. LOWRY. The PWA in Tampa: A Case Study. *Fla. Hist. Quar.*, April, 363–80.

JAMES L. MCCORKLE. The Louisiana "Buy-a-Bale" of Cotton Movement, 1914. *La. Hist.*, Spring, 133–52.

ROBERT H. MCKENZIE. Reconstruction Historiography: The View From Shelby [Iron Co., Shelby, Ala.]. *Historian*, Feb., 207–23.

ROBERT C. MCMATH, JR. Agrarian Protest at the Forks of the Creek: Three Subordinate Farmers' Alliances in North Carolina. *N. C. Hist. Rev.*, Winter, 41–63.

JAY R. MANDLE. The Plantation States as a Sub-Region of the Post-Bellum South. *Jour. Econ. Hist.*, Sept., 732–38.

KENNETH R. MARTIN. Wilmington's First Whaling Voyage, 1834–1837. *Del. Hist.*, Oct., 152–70.

ROBERT S. MAXWELL. One Man's Legacy: W. Goodrich Jones [1860–1950] and Texas Conservation. *Southwestern Hist. Quar.*, Jan., 355–80.

RUSSELL R. MENARD, P. M. G. HARRIS, and LOIS GREEN CARR. Opportunity and Inequality: The Distribution of Wealth on the Lower Western Shore of Maryland, 1638–1705. *Md. Hist. Mag.*, Summer, 169–84.

MINNIE DUBBS MILLBROOK. North from Dodge: Troubles Along the [Texas cattle] Trail. *Kan. Quar.*, Fall, 5–13.

DONALD J. MILLET. The Saga of Water Transportation into Southwest Louisiana to 1900. *La. Hist.*, Fall, 339–55.

DUNCAN GLENN MUCKELROY. History of El Capote Ranch [Gonzales Co., Texas]. *East Texas Hist. Jour.*, Fall, 3–21.

GARRY L. NALL. Dry-Land Farming on the [Texas] High Plains—A Perspective. *Red River Valley Hist. Rev.*, Summer, 122–26.

RUTH ANN OVERBECK. Texas Gets Out of the Mud. *East Texas Hist. Quar.*, Spring, 23–34.

JAMES C. PARKER. Blakeley [Ala.]: A Frontier Seaport. *Ala. Rev.*, Jan., 39–51.

HOWARD L. PRESTON. The Automobile Business in Atlanta, 1909–1920: A Symbol of "New South" Prosperity. *Ga. Hist. Quar.*, Summer, 262–77.

MILTON L. READY. Land Tenure in Trusteeship Georgia [1732–1752]. *Agric. Hist.*, July, 353–68.

JERE W. ROBERSON. The Memphis Commercial Convention of 1853: Southern Dreams and "Young America." *Tenn. Hist. Quar.*, Fall, 279–96.

———. The South and the Pacific Railroad, 1845–1855. *Western Hist. Quar.*, April, 163–86.

———. To Build a Pacific Railroad: Congress, Texas, and the Charleston [S. C.] Convention of 1854. *Southwestern Hist. Quar.*, Oct., 117–39.

THOMAS ROTHROCK. A King That Was [the Ark. red apple]. *Ark. Hist. Quar.*, Winter, 326–33.

STEPHEN SAYLES. Thomas Hart Benton [1782–1858] and the Santa Fe Trail. *Mo. Hist. Rev.*, Oct., 1–22.

MARTIN F. SCHMIDT. The Kentucky Stock Book: A Search for the Elusive. *Filson Club Hist. Quar.*, July, 217–27.

J. CHRISTOPHER SCHNELL and STEVEN W. STEWART. Sedalia [Mo.] as a Cattle Town [1866–1867]: The Long Drive. *Kan. Quar.*, Fall, 15–21.

THOMAS SCHOONOVER. El Algodón Mexicano y la Guerra Civil Norteamericana. *Historia Mexicana,* Jan.–March, 483–506.

———. Mexican Cotton and the American Civil War. *Americas,* April, 429–47.

JIMMY M. SKAGGS. Pecuniary Man: Attitudes of British Investors Toward the Western Range Cattle Industry. *Red River Valley Hist. Rev.*, Spring, 46–54.

——— and NORMAN L. WEED. Mercantilism in the Southwest: The Experience of the Texas Cattle Industry. *Kan. Quar.*, Fall, 23–34.

LYNDA WORLEY SKELTON. The Importing and Exporting Company of South Carolina (1862–1876). *S. C. Hist. Mag.*, Jan., 24–32.

STUART SEELY SPRAGUE. Alabama Town Production During the Era of Good Feelings. *Ala. Hist. Quar.*, Spring, 15–20.

———. The Canal at the Falls of the Ohio and the Three Cornered Rivalry. *Reg. Ky. Hist. Soc.*, Jan., 38–54.

LOUIS R. SMITH, JR. British-Indian Trade in Alabama, 1670–1756. *Ala. Rev.*, Jan., 65–75.

THOMAS A. STROHFELDT. Jacob Rizer [1785–1859]: A Bardstown [Ky.] Riflemaker. *Filson Club Hist. Quar.*, Jan., 5–15.

THOMAS E. TILL. Changes in Industries Located in the Nonmetropolitan South, 1959–1969. *Am. Jour. Agric. Econ.*, May, 306–309.

JOHN WAKSMUNDSKI. William McKinley and the Railway Workers: Insight into Political Strategy. *W. Va. Hist.*, Oct., 37–39.

ALAN D. WATSON. The Ferry in Colonial North Carolina: A Vital Link in Transportation. *N. C. Hist. Rev.*, Summer, 247–60.

BILL L. WEAVER. Louisville's Labor Disturbance, July, 1877. *Filson Club Hist. Quar.*, April, 177–86.

DONALD W. WHISENHUNT. Huey Long and the Texas Cotton Acreage Control Law of 1931. *La. Stud.*, Summer, 142–53.

DAVID H. WHITE. The Forbes Company in Spanish Florida, 1801–1806. *Fla. Hist. Quar.*, Jan., 274–85.

E. RUSS WILLIAMS, JR. Louisiana's Public and Private Immigration Endeavors: 1866–1893. *La. Hist.*, Spring, 153–73.

DOUGLAS C. WILMS. Georgia's Land Lottery of 1832. *Chron. Okla.*, Spring, 52–60.

GAVIN WRIGHT. Cotton Competition and the Post-Bellum Recovery of the American South. *Jour. Econ. Hist.*, Sept., 610–35.

WILLIAM LARRY ZIGLAR. Shipbuilding on the Pascagoula River. *Jour. Miss. Hist.*, Feb., 1–15.

MILITARY AND NAVAL
(Arranged chronologically)

ROBERT R. REA. Lieutenant Colonel James Robertson's Mission to the Floridas, 1763. *Fla. Hist. Quar.*, July, 33–48.

ROBIN F. A. FABEL and ROBERT R. REA. Lieutenant Thomas Campbell's Sojourn Among the Creeks, November, 1764–May, 1765. *Ala. Hist. Quar.*, Summer, 97–111.

ELIZABETH MEEK FELS. The Battle of Point Pleasant [W. Va.]: Its Relation to the American Revolution and to Tennessee. *Tenn. Hist. Quar.*, Winter, 367–78.

ROBERT L. KERBY. The Other War in 1774: Dunmore's War. *W. Va. Hist.*, Oct., 1–16.

KENNETH R. MACDONALD, JR. The Battle of Point Pleasant [1774]: First Battle of the American Revolution. *Ibid.*, 40–49.

NEAL O. HAMMON. Captain [James] Harrod's Company [in Ky.], 1774: A Reappraisal. *Reg. Ky. Hist. Soc.*, July, 224–42.

E. M. SANCHEZ-SAAVEDRA. "All Fine Fellows and Well-Armed": The Culpeper Minute Battalion. *Va. Cavalcade*, Summer, 4–11.

HARVEY H. JACKSON. The Battle of the Riceboats [1776]: Georgia Joins the Revolution. *Ga. Hist. Quar.*, Summer, 229–43.

WILLIAM M. FOWLER, JR. James Nicholson and the Continental Frigate *Virginia*. *Am. Neptune*, April, 135–41.

RANDALL M. MILLER. A Backcountry Loyalist Plan to Retake Georgia and the Carolinas, 1778. *S. C. Hist. Mag.*, Oct., 207–14.

DAVID A. H. CLEGGETT, ed. Hector McAlester's Plans for the Subjugation of Virginia, 1780. *Va. Mag. Hist. and Biog.*, Jan., 75–83.

HEARD ROBERTSON. The Second British Occupation of Augusta, 1780–1781. *Ga. Hist. Rev.*, Winter, 422–46.

LINDA ERICSON DEVEREAUX. The [Augustus W.] Magee–[Jose Bernardo] Gutierrez Expedition [into Texas, 1811-1813]. *Texana*, No. 1 [1973], 52–63.

LEE A. WALLACE, JR. The Petersburg Volunteers, 1812–1813. *Va. Mag. Hist. and Biog.*, Oct., 458–85.

James L. Morrison, Jr. Educating the Civil War Generals: West Point, 1833–1861. *Mil. Aff.*, Oct., 108–11.

Charles Merritt Barnes. Alamo's Only Survivor [Enrique Esparza]. *Texana,* No. 2 [1973], 175–88.

Michael L. Tate. Military Relations Between the Republic of Texas and the Comanche Indians. *Jour. West,* April, 67–77.

Linda Ericson Devereaux. The [Vicente] Cordova Rebellion [1838]. *Texana,* No. 4 [1972], 351–57.

Paul Laune. Reporter on the Spot: George Wilkins Kendall and the Ill-fated Texan–Santa Fe Expedition [1841]. *Am. West,* Nov., 4–11.

Claude H. Hall. Abel Parker Upshur: An Eastern Shoreman Reforms the United States Navy [1841–1844]. *Va. Cavalcade,* Spring, 29–37.

Walter T. Durham, [ed.]. Mexican War Letters to Wynnewood. *Tenn. Hist. Quar.,* Winter, 389–409.

Thomas H. Kreneck. The Neglected Regiment: East Texas Horsemen with Zachary Taylor [1846]. *East Texas Hist. Jour.,* Fall, 22–31.

Lester R. Dillon, Jr. American Artillery in the Mexican War 1846–1847. *Mil. Hist. Texas and Southwest,* No. 2 [1973], 109–29; No. 3 [1973], 149–71; No. 4 [1973], 233–50.

Peter W. Hairston, ed. J. E. B. Stuart's Letters to His Hairston [Family] Kin, 1850–1855. *N. C. Hist. Rev.,* Summer, 261–333.

Allan C. Hanrahan. The Portsmouth National Grays: From "Mutiny" to Glory. *Va. Cavalcade,* Autumn, 88–95.

Joseph L. Harsh. Battlesword and Rapier: Clausewitz, Jomini, and the American Civil War. *Mil. Aff.,* Dec., 133–38.

Jay A. Matthews, Jr. The Second U. S. Cavalry in Texas, 1855–1861. *Mil. Hist. Texas and Southwest,* No. 4 [1973], 229–31.

Richard W. Etulain [ed.]. A Virginian in Utah Chooses the Union: Col. Philip St. George Cooke in 1861. *Utah Hist. Quar.,* Fall, 381–85.

Richard A. Martin. Defeat in Victory: Yankee [Otis Little Keen's] Experience in Early Civil War Jacksonville [1861–1865]. *Fla. Hist. Quar.,* July, 1–32.

Maxine Turner. Naval Operations on the Apalachicola and Chattahoochee Rivers, 1861–1865. *Ala. Hist. Quar.,* Fall and Winter, 189–266.

Ronald B. Jager. Houston, Texas, Fights the Civil War. *Texana,* No. 1 [1973], 30–51.

Francis C. Kajencki. The Louisiana Tiger [Col. Valery Sulakowski and the Confederate Polish Brigade, 1861–1865]. *La. Hist.,* Winter, 49–58.

Val Husley. "Men of Virginia—Men of Kanawha—To Arms!" A History of the Twenty-second Virginia Volunteer Infantry Regiment, C.S.A. [1861–1865]. *W. Va. Hist.,* April, 220–36.

Richard P. Weinert, Jr. The Confederate Regular Cavalry [in Texas, 1861–1865]. *Texana,* No. 3 [1972], 244–59.

Kenneth W. Jones. The Fourth Alabama Infantry: First Blood [1861–1862]. *Ala. Hist. Quar.,* Spring, 35–53.

John O. Holzhueter, ed. William Wallace's [b. 1830] Civil War Letters:

The Virginia Campaign [1861–1862]; The Atlanta Campaign [1864]. *Wis. Mag. Hist.*, Autumn [1973], 28–59; Winter, 91–116.

J. S. Duncan. "[Texas Capt.] Martin Hart, Civil War [Union] Guerilla": Addenda [1861–1862]. *Mil. Hist. Texas and Southwest,* No. 2 [1973], 137–42.

Martin Hardwick Hall. A Nacogdoches Company in the Confederate Army of New Mexico [1861–1862]. *East Texas Hist. Jour.*, Fall, 45–50.

Tommy R. Thompson, [ed.]. Letters Home: From Private Thomas Henry Lochridge, 1861–1862. *Ark. Hist. Quar.*, Autumn, 239–51.

John A. Eisterhold. Fort Heiman [on Tenn. River]: Forgotten Fortress [1861–1865]. *West Tenn. Hist. Soc. Papers,* 43–54.

Martin Hardwick Hall. Captain John G. Phillips' "Brigands," C.S.A. [1862]. *Mil. Hist. Texas and Southwest,* No. 2 [1973], 131–35.

June I. Gow. Military Administration in the Confederate Army of Tennessee [1862–1865]. *Jour. Sou. Hist.*, May, 183–98.

Harry Forrest Lupold, ed. A Union Surgeon [John C. Gill] Views the War from Kentucky, 1862. *Reg. Ky. Hist. Soc.*, July, 272–75.

M. Foster Farley. [Commodore] Josiah Tattnall—Gallant American. *Ga. Hist. Quar.*, Supplement, 172–80.

Clarence E. Mitcham, contr. Civil War Letters [April 1862]. *Reg. Ky. Hist. Soc.*, July, 269–71.

Robert H. Joynt. Abraham Lincoln and the Capture of Norfolk. *Lincoln Herald,* Summer, 69–79.

Donald E. Reynolds, ed. A Mississippian in Lee's Army: The Letters of Leander Huckaby, Parts I–III [1862–1863]. *Jour. Miss. Hist.*, Feb., 53–67; May, 165–78; Aug., 273–88.

Dennis K. McDaniel. The 12th Wisconsin Infantry Regiment in West Tennessee [1862]. *Tenn. Hist. Quar.*, Fall, 255–64.

Mrs. W. H. Whitley, contr. Civil War Letters [Oct. 1862–Jan. 1863]. *Reg. Ky. Hist. Soc.*, July, 262–68.

George J. Winter. A Battalion of Sharpshooters [McGowan's Brigade, 1862–1865]. *Trans. Huguenot Soc. of S. C.*, 89–101.

Edwin C. Bearss. General John Hunt Morgan's Second Kentucky Raid (December, 1862). Part Four: Morgan, in a Hard Night March, Eludes the Trap. *Reg. Ky. Hist. Soc.*, Jan., 20–37.

Jerry O'Neil Potter. The First West Tennessee Raid of General Nathan Bedford Forrest [1862–1863]. *West Tenn. Hist. Soc. Papers,* 55–74.

Marjorie Logan Williams, ed. Cecilia Labadie [Galveston, Texas]: Diary Fragment, January 29, 1863–February 5, 1863. *Texana,* No. 3 [1972], 273–83.

Lowell H. Harrison. A Federal Officer [Samuel M. Starling] Pursues John Hunt Morgan [July–Aug. 1863]. *Filson Club Hist. Quar.*, April, 129–43.

Joseph E. Suppiger, ed. From Chickamauga to Chattanooga, the Battlefield Account of Sergeant John M. Kane [Sept. 1863]. *East Tenn. Hist. Soc. Pub.*, No. 45 [1973], 99–108.

Lary C. Rampp and Donald L. Rampp. The Civil War in the Indian

Territory: The [Col. William A.] Phillips' Expedition and Stalemate; Confederate Guerrilla Operations Intensify; Confederate Guerrilla Operations End. *Mil. Hist. Texas and Southwest,* No. 2 [1973], 77–108; No. 3 [1973], 173–95; No. 4 [1973], 251–80.

DAYTON KELLEY. The Texas Brigade at the Wilderness, May 6, 1864. *Texana,* No. 2 [1973], 103–23.

FREDERICKA MEINERS. [Confederate gen.] Hamilton P. Bee in the Red River Campaign of 1864. *Southwestern Hist. Quar.,* July, 21–44.

JOSEPH IOOR WARING, ed. The Diary [1864–1865] of William G. Hinson [1838–1919] During the War of Secession, Parts I, II. *S. C. Hist. Mag.,* Jan., 14–23; April, 111–20.

HARRY F. LUPOLD, ed. A Union Medical Officer [Dr. John C. Gill] Views the "Texians" [1864–1865]. *Southwestern Hist. Quar.,* April, 481–86.

JOHN E. DUNCAN, contr. The Correspondence of a Yankee Prisoner [Charles Davenport Duncan] in Charleston [S. C.], 1865. *S. C. Hist. Mag.,* Oct., 215–24.

ROYCE GORDON SHINGLETON, ed. South from Appomattox: The Diary of [Lt.] Abner R. Cox. *S. C. Hist. Mag.,* Oct., 238–44.

THOMAS C. LEONARD. Red, White and the Army Blue: Empathy and Anger in the American West [Indian wars]. *Am. Quar.,* May, 176–90.

DAVID E. KYVIG. Policing the Panhandle: Fort Elliott, Texas, 1875–1890. *Red River Valley Hist. Rev.,* Autumn, 222–32.

JOHN A. TURCHENESKE, JR. Arizonans and the Apache Prisoners at Mount Vernon Barracks, Alabama: "They Do Not Die Fast Enough!" *Mil. Hist. Texas and Southwest,* No. 3 [1973], 197–226.

THE NEGRO AND SLAVERY

MARTIN ABBOTT. Voices of Freedom: The Response of Southern Freedmen to Liberty. *Phylon,* Dec. [1973], 399–405.

DAVID WALLACE ADAMS. Illinois Soldiers and the Emancipation Proclamation. *Jour. Ill. State Hist. Soc.,* Sept., 406–21.

EDWARD N. AKIN. When a Minority Becomes the Majority: Blacks in Jacksonville Politics, 1887–1907. *Fla. Hist. Quar.,* Oct., 123–45.

HENRY E. BARBER. The Association of Southern Women for the Prevention of Lynching, 1930–1942. *Phylon,* Dec. [1973], 378–89.

ROSS W. BEALES, JR. [ed.]. An Incident at the Freedmen's School, Lexington, Virginia, 1867. *Prologue,* Winter, 252–54.

DONNIE D. BELLAMY. The Education of Blacks in Missouri Prior to 1861. *Jour. Negro Hist.,* April, 143–57.

ROBERT A. BENNETT. Black Episcopalians: A History from the Colonial Period to the Present. *Hist. Mag. Prot. Epis. Church,* Sept., 231–45.

ALLISON BLAKELY. Richard T. Greener [1844–1922] and the "Talented Tenth's" Dilemma. *Jour. Negro Hist.,* Oct., 305–21.

KATE BORN. Memphis Negro Workingmen and the NAACP. *West Tenn. Hist. Soc. Papers,* 90–107.

EVAN BRANDSTADTER. Uncle Tom and Archy Moore: The Antislavery Novel as Ideological Symbol. *Am. Quar.,* May, 160–75.

EDWARD E. CAHILL. Migration and the Decline of the Black Population in Rural and Non-Metropolitan Areas. *Phylon*, Sept., 284–92.

LAWRENCE O. CHRISTENSEN. Cyprian Clamorgan, *The Colored Aristocracy of St. Louis* (1858). *Bull. Mo. Hist. Soc.*, Oct., 3–31.

BARRY A. CROUCH. Black Dreams and White Justice [in the South]. *Prologue*, Winter, 255–65.

JUDY DAY and M. JAMES KEDRO. Free Blacks in St. Louis: Antebellum Condition, Emancipation, and the Postwar Era. *Bull. Mo. Hist. Soc.*, Jan., 117–35.

WILLIAM L. VAN DEBURG. Frederick Douglass [1817?–1895]: Maryland Slave to Religious Liberal. *Md. Hist. Mag.*, Spring, 27–43.

RALPH H. DESMARAIS. Military Intelligence Reports on Arkansas Riots: 1919–1920. *Ark. Hist. Quar.*, Summer, 175–91.

CHARLES B. DEW. David Ross and the Oxford Iron Works [Campbell Co., Va.]: A Study of Industrial Slavery in the Early Nineteenth-Century South. *William and Mary Quar.*, April, 189–224.

———. Disciplining Slave Ironworkers in the Antebellum South: Coercion, Conciliation, and Accommodation. *Am. Hist. Rev.*, April, 393–418.

MELVIN DRIMMER. [Scott] Joplin's [1868–1917] *Treemonisha* in Atlanta. *Phylon*, June [1973], 197–202.

WALTER EHRLICH. The Origins of the Dred Scott Case. *Jour. Negro Hist.*, April, 132–42.

PAUL D. ESCOTT. The Context of Freedom: Georgia's Slaves During the Civil War. *Ga. Hist. Quar.*, Spring, 79–104.

W. EDWARD FARRISON. Clotel, Thomas Jefferson, and Sally Hemings. *CLA Jour.*, Dec. [1973], 147–74.

DON E. FEHRENBACHER. Only His Stepchildren: Lincoln and the Negro. *Civil War Hist.*, Dec., 293–310.

MICHAEL FELLMAN. Theodore Parker and the Abolitionist Role in the 1850s. *Jour. Am. Hist.*, Dec., 666–84.

MILFRED C. FIERCE. Black Struggle for Land During Reconstruction. *Black Scholar*, Feb., 13–18.

DANIEL J. FLANIGAN. Criminal Procedure in Slave Trials in the Antebellum South. *Jour. Sou. Hist.*, Nov., 537–64.

MARVIN FLETCHER. The Black Volunteers in the Spanish-American War. *Mil. Aff.*, April, 48–53.

JOHN HOPE FRANKLIN. The Enforcement of the Civil Rights Act of 1875. *Prologue*, Winter, 225–35.

VINCENT P. FRANKLIN. Education for Colonization: Attempts to Educate Free Blacks in the United States for Emigration to Africa, 1823–1833. *Jour. Negro Educ.*, Winter, 91–103.

———. Slavery, Personality, and Black Culture—Some Theoretical Issues. *Phylon*, March, 54–63.

LAWRENCE J. FRIEDMAN. Life "In the Lion's Mouth": Another Look at Booker T. Washington. *Jour. Negro Hist.*, Oct., 337–51.

LUCIAN B. GATEWOOD. The Black Artisan in the U.S., 1890–1930. *Rev. Black Pol. Econ.*, Fall, 19–44.

WILLARD B. GATEWOOD, JR., ed. Arkansas Negroes in the 1890s: Documents. *Ark. Hist. Quar.*, Winter, 293–325.

RAYMOND GAVINS. Gordon Blaine Hancock [1884–1970]: A Black Profile from the New South. *Jour. Negro Hist.*, July, 207–27.

JAMES M. GIFFORD [ed.]. The Conscience of a Slaveholder [Anne Atkinson, fl. 1851]. *Research Stud.*, Sept., 185–87.

BRUCE A. GLASRUD. Jim Crow's Emergence in Texas. *Am. Stud.*, Spring, 47–60.

LARRY GROTHAUS. Kansas City Blacks, Harry Truman and the Pendergast Machine. *Mo. Hist. Rev.*, Oct., 65–82.

R. HALLIBURTON, JR. Origins of Black Slavery Among the Cherokees. *Chron. Okla.*, Winter, 483–96.

LOWELL H. HARRISON. Recollections of Some Tennessee Slaves. *Tenn. Hist. Quar.*, Summer, 175–90.

HOMER C. HAWKINS. Trends in Black Migration from 1863 to 1960. *Phylon*, June [1973], 140–52.

LINDA O. HINES and ALLEN W. JONES. A Voice of Black Protest: The Savannah Men's Sunday Club, 1905–1911. *Ibid.*, June, 193–202.

ROGER W. HITE. Voice of a Fugitive: Henry Bibb [d. 1854] and Ante-Bellum Black Separatism. *Jour. Black Studies*, March, 269–84.

CAROL E. HOFFECKER. The Politics of Exclusion: Blacks in Late Nineteenth-Century Wilmington, Delaware. *Del. Hist.*, April, 60–72.

WILLIAM F. HOLMES. The Leflore County [Miss.] Massacre and the Demise of the Colored Farmers' Alliance. *Phylon*, Sept. [1973], 267–74.

THEODORE R. HOVET. Christian Revolution: Harriet Beecher Stowe's Response to Slavery and the Civil War. *New England Quar.*, Dec., 535–49.

VICTOR B. HOWARD. Negro Politics and the Suffrage Question in Kentucky, 1866–1872. *Reg. Ky. Hist. Soc.*, April, 111–33.

JOHN T. HUBBELL. Some Reactions to the Desegregation of the University of Oklahoma, 1946–1950. *Phylon*, June [1973], 187–96.

LLOYD A. HUNTER. Slavery in St. Louis, 1804–1860. *Bull. Mo. Hist. Soc.*, July, 233–65.

W. SHERMAN JACKSON. The Collapse of the Peculiar Institution Through Military and Legal Action. *Ohio Hist.*, Summer, 183–91.

LEON JONES. Desegregation and Social Reform Since 1954. *Jour. Negro Educ.*, Spring, 155–71.

RALPH A. KELLER. Methodist Newspapers and the Fugitive Slave Law: A New Perspective for the Slavery Crisis in the North. *Church Hist.*, Sept., 319–39.

ANDREW A. KING. Booker T. Washington and the Myth of Heroic Materialism. *Quar. Jour. Speech*, Oct., 323–27.

BRUCE LEE KLEINSCHMIDT. The Phoenix [S. C.] Riot [1898]. *Furman Rev.*, Spring, 27–31.

SYLVIA H. KREBS. "Will the Freedmen Work? White Alabamians Adjust to Free Black Labor." *Ala. Hist. Quar.*, Summer, 151–63.

LESTER C. LAMON. The Black Community in Nashville and the Fisk University Student Strike of 1924–1925. *Jour. Sou. Hist.*, May, 225–44.

BILL LEDBETTER. Slave Unrest and White Panic: The Impact of Black Republicanism in Ante-Bellum Texas. *Texana,* No. 4 [1972], 335–50.

———. White over Black in Texas: Racial Attitudes in the Ante-Bellum Period. *Phylon,* Dec. [1973], 406–18.

ANNE S. LEE and GLADYS K. BOWLES. Policy Implications of the Movement of Blacks out of the Rural South. *Ibid.,* Sept., 332–39.

NATHANIEL H. LEFF. Long-Term Viability of Slavery in a Backward Closed Economy. *Jour. Interdisciplinary Hist.,* Summer, 103–108.

GERDA LERNER. Early Community Work of Black Club Women. *Jour. Negro Hist.,* April, 158–67.

RONALD L. LEWIS. Slavery on Chesapeake Iron Plantations Before the American Revolution. *Ibid.,* July, 242–54.

DANIEL F. LITTLEFIELD, JR., and LONNIE E. UNDERHILL. Black Dreams and "Free" Homes: The Oklahoma Territory, 1891–1894. *Phylon,* Dec. [1973], 342–57.

JACK P. MADDEX, JR. [Edward Alfred] Pollard's *The Lost Cause Regained:* A Mask for Southern Accommodation. *Jour. Sou. Hist.,* Nov., 595–612.

EDWARD MAGDOL. Local Black Leaders in the South, 1867–75: An Essay Toward the Reconstruction of Reconstruction History. *Societas,* Spring, 81–110.

CARL S. MATTHEWS, ed. Marcus Garvey Writes from Jamaica [1916] on the Mulatto Escape Hatch. *Jour. Negro Hist.,* April, 170–76.

JOHN MICHAEL MATTHEWS. The Dilemma of Negro Leadership in the New South: The Case of the Negro Young People's Congress of 1902. *Sou. Atlantic Quar.,* Winter, 130–44.

———. The Georgia [Railroad] "Race Strike" of 1909. *Jour. Sou. Hist.,* Nov., 613–30.

LINDA M. MATTHEWS. Keeping Down Jim Crow: The Railroads and the Separate Coach Bills in South Carolina. *Sou. Atlantic Quar.,* Winter, 117–29.

WILLIAM G. MCLOUGHLIN. Red Indians, Black Slavery and White Racism: America's Slaveholding Indians. *Am. Quar.,* Oct., 367–85.

BENJAMIN E. MAYS. Black Colleges: Past, Present and Future. *Black Scholar,* Sept., 32–37.

BERNARD MERGEN. The Pullman Porter: From "George" to Brotherhood. *Sou. Atlantic Quar.,* Spring, 224–35.

RANDALL M. MILLER [ed.]. Letters from Nashville [to Gen. William Harding from slave Susanna], 1862, II. "Dear Master." *Tenn. Hist. Quar.,* Spring, 85–92.

JOHN D. MILLIGAN. Slave Rebelliousness and the Florida Maroon. *Prologue,* Spring, 4–18.

GORDON D. MORGAN and PETER KUNKEL. Arkansas' Ozark Mountain Blacks: An Introduction. *Phylon,* Sept. [1973], 283–88.

PAUL DAVID NELSON. Experiment in Interracial Education at Berea College, 1858–1908. *Jour. Negro Hist.,* Jan., 13–27.

———. From Intolerance to Moderation: The Evolution of Abraham Lincoln's Racial Views. *Reg. Ky. Hist. Soc.,* Jan., 1–9.

EARL OFARI. Black Activists and 19th Century Radicalism. *Black Scholar,* Feb., 19–25.

JAMES S. OLSON and SHARON PHAIR. The Anatomy of a Race Riot: Beaumont, Texas, 1943. *Texana,* No. 1 [1973], 64–72.

WILLIAM H. PEASE and JANE H. PEASE, [eds.]. [David] Walker's [1785–1830] *Appeal* Comes to Charleston [S. C.]: A Note and Documents. *Jour. Negro Hist.,* July, 287–92.

HOWARD N. RABINOWITZ. Half a Loaf: The Shift from White to Black Teachers in the Negro Schools of the Urban South, 1865–1890. *Jour. Sou. Hist.,* Nov., 565–94.

DAVID C. RANKIN. The Origins of Black Leadership in New Orleans During Reconstruction. *Ibid.,* Aug., 417–40.

JOHN D. REID. Black Urbanization of the South. *Phylon,* Sept., 259–67.

JONG MO RHEE. The Redistribution of the Black Work Force in the South by Industry. *Ibid.,* Sept., 293–300.

HARRELL R. RODGERS, JR., The Supreme Court and School Desegregation: Twenty Years Later. *Pol. Sci. Quar.,* Winter, 751–76.

JOSEPH M. ST. HILAIRE. The Negro Delegates in the Arkansas Constitutional Convention of 1868: A Group Profile. *Ark. Hist. Quar.,* Spring, 38–69.

LOREN SCHWENINGER. John H. Rapier, Sr. [1808–1869]: A Slave and Freedman in the Ante-Bellum South. *Civil War Hist.,* March, 23–34.

GEORGE SHEPPERSON. The Afro-American Contribution to African Studies. *Jour. Am. Stud.,* Dec., 281–301.

ROBERT G. SHERER. William Burns Paterson [1849–1915]: "Pioneer as Well as Apostle of Negro Education in Alabama." *Ala. Hist. Quar.,* Summer, 121–50.

ROYCE GORDON SHINGLETON. The Trial and Punishment of Slaves in Baldwin County, Georgia, 1812–1826. *Sou. Humanities Rev.,* Spring, 67–73.

SUDIE DUNCAN SIDES. Slave Weddings and Religion: Plantation Life in the Southern States Before the American Civil War. *Hist. Today,* Feb., 77–87.

JOHN DAVID SMITH. The Recruitment of Negro Soldiers in Kentucky, 1863–1865. *Reg. Ky. Hist. Soc.,* Oct., 364–90.

PETER C. SMITH and KARL B. RAITZ. Negro Hamlets and Agricultural Estates in Kentucky's Inner Bluegrass. *Geog. Rev.,* April, 217–34.

W. WAYNE SMITH [ed.]. A Marylander in Africa: The Letters [1840–1846] of [ex-slave] Henry Hannon. *Md. Hist. Mag.,* Winter, 398–404.

DALE A. SOMERS. Black and White in New Orleans: A Study in Urban Race Relations, 1865–1900. *Jour. Sou. Hist.,* Feb., 19–42.

LOIS SPEAR. Negroes in Pre–Civil War History: New Myths in the Making. *Soc. Studies,* Dec., 310–13.

JOHN EDMUND STEALEY, III. Slavery and the Western Virginia Salt Industry. *Jour. Negro Hist.,* April, 105–31.

JUDITH STEIN. "Of Mr. Booker T. Washington and Others": The Political Economy of Racism in the United States. *Sci. and Soc.,* Winter, 422–63.

BETTYE C. THOMAS. A Nineteenth Century Black Operated [Baltimore] Shipyard, 1866–1884: Reflections upon Its Inception and Ownership. *Jour. Negro Hist.*, Jan., 1–12.

ROBERT PAUL THOMAS and RICHARD NELSON BEAN. The Fishers of Men: The Profits of the Slave Trade. *Jour. Econ. Hist.*, Dec., 885–914.

JERRY THORNBERY. Northerners and the Atlanta Freedmen, 1865–69. *Prologue*, Winter, 236–51.

BETTE B. TILLY. The Spirit of Improvement: Reformism and Slavery in West Tennessee. *West Tenn. Hist. Soc. Papers*, 25–42.

JOSEPH A. TOMBERLIN. Florida and the School Desegregation Issue, 1954–1959: A Summary View. *Jour. Negro Educ.*, Fall, 457–67.

PETER Z. W. TSONG. Changing Patterns of Labor Force Participation Rates of Nonwhites in the South. *Phylon*, Sept., 301–12.

CHARLES JACKSON TUCKER. Changes in Age Composition of the Rural Black Population of the South 1950–1970. *Ibid.*, 268–75.

WILLIAM M. TUTTLE, JR. [ed.]. W. E. B. DuBois' Confrontation with White Liberalism During the Progressive Era: A Phylon Document. *Ibid.*, 241–58.

KENNETH P. VICKERY. "Herrenvolk" Democracy and Egalitarianism in South Africa and the U. S. South [before 1936]. *Comp. Stud. in Soc. and Hist.*, No. 3, 309–28.

JANET K. WADLEY and EVERETT S. LEE. The Disappearance of the Black Farmer. *Phylon*, Sept., 276–83.

CAM WALKER. Corinth [Miss.]: The Story of a Contraband [slave] Camp. *Civil War Hist.*, March, 5–22.

EUGENE J. WATTS. Black Political Progress in Atlanta: 1868–1895. *Jour. Negro Hist.*, July, 268–86.

BETTY WOOD. Thomas Stephens and the Introduction of Black Slavery in Georgia [1738–1742]. *Ga. Hist. Quar.*, Spring, 24–40.

RANDALL B. WOODS. George T. Ruby [b. 1841]: A Black Militant in the White [Galveston] Business Community. *Red River Valley Hist. Rev.*, Autumn, 269–80.

POLITICS AND GOVERNMENT

(Arranged chronologically)

FRED LAMAR PEARSON, JR. Early Anglo-Spanish Rivalry in Southeastern North America. *Ga. Hist. Rev.*, Supplement, 157–71.

EUGENE LYON. The Enterprise of [founding] Florida [1563–1577]. *Fla. Hist. Quar.*, April, 411–22.

WARREN M. BILLINGS. The Growth of Political Institutions in Virginia, 1634 to 1676. *William and Mary Quar.*, April, 225–42.

WILLIAM S. PRICE, JR. A Strange Incident in George Burrington's Royal Governorship [1730–1734]. *N. C. Hist. Rev.*, Spring, 149–58.

ALAN D. WATSON. Henry McCulloh [fl. 1730s–1740s]: Royal Commissioner in South Carolina. *S. C. Hist. Mag.*, Jan., 33–48.

G. S. ROWE. The Legal Career of Thomas McKean, 1750–1775. *Del. Hist.*, April, 22–46.

ROBERT M. WEIR, ed. Two Letters by Christopher Gadsden, February 1766. *S. C. Hist. Mag.*, July, 169–76.

RONALD R. MORAZÁN. The Cabildo of Spanish New Orleans, 1769–1803: The Collapse of Local Government. *La. Stud.*, Winter [1973], 591–605.

JAMES LAVERNE ANDERSON. The Virginia Councillors and the American Revolution: The Demise of an Aristocratic Clique. *Va. Mag. Hist. and Biog.*, Jan., 56–74.

GEORGE C. ROGERS, JR. The Charleston Tea Party: The Significance of December 3, 1773. *S. C. Hist. Mag.*, July, 153–68.

JACK P. GREENE. The Political Authorship of Sir Egerton Leigh [1733–1788?]. *Ibid.*, 143–52.

JEAN H. VIVIAN. Thomas Stone [1743–1787] and the Reorganization of the Maryland Council of Safety, 1776. *Md. Hist. Mag.*, Fall, 271–78.

EDWARD J. CASHIN. "The Famous Colonel [George] Wells [d. 1780]": Factionalism in Revolutionary Georgia. *Ga. Hist. Quar.*, Supplement, 137–56.

NORMAN K. RISJORD and GORDON DENBOER. The Evolution of Political Parties in Virginia, 1782–1800. *Jour. Am. Hist.*, March, 961–84.

CHARLES T. CULLEN. Completing the Revisal of the Laws in Post-Revolutionary Virginia. *Va. Mag. Hist. and Biog.*, Jan., 84–99.

JOHN P. KAMINSKI. Controversy Amid Consensus: The Adoption of the Federal Constitution in Georgia. *Ga. Hist. Quar.*, Summer, 244–61.

NORMAN K. RISJORD. Virginians and the Constitution: A Multivariant Analysis. *William and Mary Quar.*, Oct., 613–32.

D. C. CORBITT and ROBERTA CORBITT, trans. and eds. Papers from the Spanish Archives Relating to Tennessee and the Old Southwest [March 1795]. *East Tenn. Hist. Soc. Pub.*, No. 45 [1973], 78–87.

DAVID H. WHITE. Commandant [Juan Vicente] Folch at San Fernando de las Barrancas [near Memphis], 1795–1796. *Tenn. Hist. Quar.*, Winter, 379–88.

JOHN B. BOLES [ed.]. Politics, Intrigue, and the Presidency: James McHenry to Bishop John Carroll, May 16, 1800. *Md. Hist. Mag.*, Spring, 64–85.

JAMES H. BROUSSARD. Regional Pride and Republican Politics: The Fatal Weakness of Southern Federalism, 1800–1815. *Sou. Atlantic Quar.*, Winter, 23–33.

ROYCE MCCRARY, ed. A Federalist View of Georgia Politics in 1808: A Letter by John Macpherson Berrien. *Ga. Hist. Quar.*, Winter, 447–49.

EDWIN W. EDWARDS. The Role of the Governor in Louisiana Politics: An Historical Analysis. *La. Hist.*, Spring, 101–16.

BRIAN G. WALTON. Elections to the United States Senate in Alabama Before the Civil War. *Ala. Rev.*, Jan., 3–38.

FRANK F. MATHIAS. The Turbulent Years of Kentucky Politics, 1820–1850. *Reg. Ky. Hist. Soc.*, Oct., 309–18.

D. L. A. HACKETT. Slavery, Ethnicity, and Sugar: An Analysis of Voting Behaviour in Louisiana, 1828–1844. *La. Stud.*, Summer, 73–118.

GRANT LYONS. Louisiana and the [Edward] Livingston [1764–1836] Criminal Codes. *La. Hist.*, Summer, 243–72.

BETTY LYNN BARTON. Stephen F. Austin's Arrest and Imprisonment in Mexico, 1834–1835. *Texana,* No. 1 [1973], 1–17.

WILLIAM H. ADAMS. The Louisiana Whigs. *La. Hist.,* Summer, 213–28.

EDWARD L. TUCKER, ed. The Attempted Assassination of President Jackson: A Letter by Richard Henry Wilde [Jan. 30, 1835]. *Ga. Hist. Rev.,* Supplement, 193–99.

JON L. WAKELYN. The Changing Loyalties of James Henry Hammond [1807–1864]: A Reconsideration. *S. C. Hist. Mag.,* Jan., 1–13.

JOHN A. NEUENSCHWANDER. Senator Thomas Morris: Antagonist of the South, 1836–1839. *Cincinnati Hist. Soc. Bull.,* Fall, 122–39.

DAVID RITCHEY. Williamson R. W. Cobb [1807–1864]: Rattler of Tinware and Crockery for Peace. *Ala. Hist. Quar.,* Summer, 112–20.

JOHN E. SIMPSON. Prelude to Compromise: Howell Cobb and the [U. S.] House Speakership Battle of 1849. *Ga. Hist. Quar.,* Winter, 389–99.

HELEN BARTTER CROCKER. J. Proctor Knott's [1830–1911] Education in Missouri Politics, 1850–1862. *Bull. Mo. Hist. Soc.,* Jan., 101–16.

JOHN C. SCHNEIDER. Riot and Reaction in St. Louis, 1854–1856. *Mo. Hist. Rev.,* Jan., 171–85.

WAYMON L. MCCLELLAN. 1855: The Know-Nothing Challenge in East Texas. *East Texas Hist. Jour.,* Fall, 32–44.

CRAIG L. KAUTZ. Beneficial Politics: John Slidell and the Cuban Bill of 1859. *La. Stud.,* Summer, 119–29.

JACK KELLY. John J. Crittenden and the Constitutional Union Party. *Filson Club Hist. Quar.,* July, 265–76.

FRANK L. KLEMENT. Ohio and the Knights of the Golden Circle: The Evolution of a Civil War Myth. *Cincinnati Hist. Soc. Bull.,* Spring–Summer, 7–27.

JOHN T. HUBBELL. Jeremiah Sullivan Black [1810–1888] and the Great Secession Winter. *Western Pa. Hist. Mag.,* July, 255–74.

LOWELL H. HARRISON. Governor [Beriah] Magoffin and the Secession Crisis. *Reg. Ky. Hist. Soc.,* April, 91–110.

JAMES L. BAUMGARDNER. Abraham Lincoln, Andrew Johnson, and the Federal Patronage: An Attempt to Save Tennessee for the Union? *East Tenn. Hist. Soc. Pub.,* No. 45 [1973], 51–60.

JAMES T. OTTEN. Disloyalty in the Upper Districts of South Carolina During the Civil War. *S. C. Hist. Mag.,* April, 95–110.

ROBERT W. DUBAY. Mississippi Political, Civilian, and Military Realities of 1861: A Study in Frustration and Confusion. *Jour. Miss. Hist.,* Aug., 215–41.

GARY L. WILLIAMS. Lincoln's Neutral Allies: The Case of the Kentucky Unionists. *Sou. Atlantic Quar.,* Winter, 70–84.

KINLEY J. BRAUER. [William Henry] Seward's "Foreign War Panacea": An Interpretation. *N. Y. Hist.,* April, 132–57.

JAMES W. MCKEE, JR., ed. Reflections of an East Tennessee Unionist [Maj. John Fouche Henry]. *Tenn. Hist. Quar.,* Winter, 429–35.

THOMAS SCHOONOVER [ed]. Documents Concerning Lemuel Dale Evans'

[1810–1877] Plan to Keep Texas in the Union in 1861. *East Texas Hist. Jour.*, Spring, 35–38.

PAUL J. ZINGG. John Archibald Campbell and the Hampton Roads Conference Quixotic Diplomacy, 1865. *Ala. Hist. Quar.*, Spring, 21–34.

JAMES A. BAGGETT. Birth of the Texas Republican Party. *Southwestern Hist. Quar.*, July, 1–20.

———. Origins of Early Texas Republican Party Leadership. *Jour. Sou. Hist.*, Aug., 441–54.

MICHAEL LES BENEDICT. Preserving the Constitution: The Conservative Basis of Radical Reconstruction. *Jour. Am. Hist.*, June, 65–90.

ARTHUR LEWIS GELSTON. Radical Versus Straight-Out in Post-Reconstruction Beaufort County [S. C.]. *S. C. Hist. Mag.*, Oct., 225–37.

WILLIAM C. HARRIS. The Creed of the Carpetbaggers: The Case of Mississippi. *Jour. Sou. Hist.*, May, 199–224.

GORDON B. MCKINNEY. The Rise of the [Leonidas Campbell] Houk [Republican] Machine in East Tennessee. *East Tenn. Hist. Soc. Pub.*, No. 45 [1973], 61–77.

JERRELL H. SHOFNER. A New Jersey Carpetbagger [George B. Carse] in Reconstruction Florida. *Fla. Hist. Quar.*, Jan., 286–93.

SARAH WOOLFOLK WIGGINS. Ostracism of White Republicans in Alabama During Reconstruction. *Ala. Rev.*, Jan., 52–64.

ARCHIE P. MCDONALD. Disloyalty and Punishment: Ex Parte Milligan. *La. Stud.*, Winter [1973], 607–15.

ROGER D. BRIDGES. John Sherman [1823–1900] and the Impeachment of Andrew Johnson. *Ohio Hist.*, Summer–Autumn, 176–91.

THOMAS W. HOWARD. Peter G. Van Winkle's [1808–1872] Vote in the Impeachment of President Andrew Johnson: A West Virginian as a Profile in Courage. *W. Va. Hist.*, July, 290–95.

HENRY I. KURTZ. The Impeachment of Andrew Johnson, Parts One, Two. *Hist. Today*, May, 299–306; June, 396–405.

JAMES C. PARKER. Tennessee Gubernatorial Elections, I. 1869—The Victory of the Conservatives. *Tenn. Hist. Quar.*, Spring, 34–48.

TOM DILLARD. To the Back of the Elephant: Racial Conflict in the Arkansas Republican Party. *Ark. Hist. Quar.*, Spring, 3–15.

PHILIP J. AVILLO, JR. Phantom Radicals: Texas Republicans in Congress, 1870–1873. *Southwestern Hist. Quar.*, April, 431–44.

J. STANLEY CLARK. The Career of [Okla. judge] John R. Thomas [1846–1914]. *Chron. Okla.*, Summer, 152–79.

OSCAR WALTER ROBERTS, ed. [Texas gov.] Richard Coke [1829–1897] on Constitution-Making. *Southwestern Hist. Quar.*, July, 69–75.

WILLIAM T. DOHERTY, JR. Berkeley's [Co., W. Va.] Non-Revolution: Law and Order and the Great Railway Strikes of 1877. *W. Va. Hist.*, July, 271–89.

ROBERT B. JONES. Tennessee Gubernatorial Elections, II. 1880—The Collapse of the Democratic Party. *Tenn. Hist. Quar.*, Spring, 49–61.

W. SILAS VANCE. The Marion [Miss.] Riot [1881]. *Miss. Quar.*, Fall, 447–66.

GILBERT CUTHBERTSON. The Jaybird–Woodpecker War [Fort Bend Co., Texas, 1886–1889]. *Texana,* No. 4 [1972], 297–309.

MYRA HIMELHOCH. St. Louis Opposition to David R. Francis in the Gubernatorial Election of 1888. *Mo. Hist. Rev.,* April, 327–43.

NICHOLAS C. BURCKEL. William Goebel and the Campaign for Railroad Regulation in Kentucky, 1888–1900. *Filson Club Hist. Quar.,* Jan., 43–60.

KARL LOUIS RODABAUGH. The [Farmers'] Alliance in Politics: The Alabama Gubernatorial Election of 1890. *Ala. Hist. Quar.,* Spring, 54–80.

CARL V. HARRIS. Annexation Struggles and Political Power in Birmingham, Alabama, 1890–1910. *Ala. Rev.,* July, 163–84.

ADRIAN ANDERSON. President Wilson's Politician: Albert Sidney Burleson [1863–1937] of Texas. *Southwestern Hist. Quar.,* Jan., 339–54.

D. ALAN HARRIS. Campaigning in the Bloody Seventh: The Election of 1894 in the Seventh Congressional District. *Ala. Rev.,* April, 127–38.

P. JOSEPH POWERS [ed.]. "Yours Very Truly, Thos. T. Crittenden": A Missouri Democrat's Observations of the Election of 1896. *Mo. Hist. Rev.,* Jan., 186–203.

CYNTHIA SHOOK. Richard Parks Bland [1835–1899]: Almost a [presidential] Candidate [1896]. *Ibid.,* July, 417–36.

HARRY PHILLIPS. Tennessee and the U. S. Court of Appeals for the Sixth Circuit. *Tenn. Hist. Quar.,* Spring, 22–33.

GEORGE O. CARNEY. Oklahoma's Territorial Delegates and Progressivism, 1901–1907. *Chron. Okla.,* Spring, 38–51.

CAL LEDBETTER, JR. [Ark. gov.] Jeff Davis [1862–1913] and the Politics of Combat. *Ark. Hist. Quar.,* Spring, 16–37.

DONOVAN L. HOFSOMMER. Oklahoma Railroad Maintenance Authority: An Example of Rural Pressure Group Politics. *Jour. West,* Oct., 108–16.

GARIN BURBANK. The Political and Social Attitudes of Some Early Oklahoma Democrats. *Chron. Okla.,* Winter, 439–55.

MELBA DEAN PORTER. Madeline McDowell Breckinridge: Her Role in the Kentucky Woman Suffrage Movement, 1908–1920. *Reg. Ky. Hist. Soc.,* Oct., 342–63.

WALTER A. SUTTON. Texas Congressmen and the Mexican Revolution of 1910. *Jour. West,* Oct., 90–107.

ORBEN J. CASEY. Governor Lee Cruce, White Supremacy and Capital Punishment, 1911–1915. *Chron. Okla.,* Winter, 456–75.

ALAN COLEMAN. The Charleston [S. C.] Bootlegging Controversy, 1915–1918. *S. C. Hist. Mag.,* April, 77–94.

SHERRY WARRICK. Radical Labor in Oklahoma: The Working Class Union [opposes W.W.I.]. *Chron. Okla.,* Summer, 180–95.

TED C. HARRIS. [Montana congresswoman] Jeannette Rankin [1880–1973] in Georgia [ca. 1919–1971]. *Ga. Hist. Quar.,* Spring, 55–78.

LEWIS L. LASKA. Mr. Justice [Edward Terry] Sanford [1865–1930] and the Fourteenth Amendment. *Tenn. Hist. Quar.,* Summer, 210–27.

ROBERT T. HAWKES, JR. The Emergence of a Leader: Harry Flood Byrd, Governor of Virginia, 1926–1930. *Va. Mag. Hist. and Biog.,* July, 259–81.

VON RUSSELL CREEL. Court in Peril: The [Okla.] Legislative-Judicial Struggle of 1927–1929. *Chron. Okla.*, Summer, 220–36.

W. RICHARD FOSSEY. The [Okla.-Texas] Red River Bridge Conflict [1931]: A Minor Skirmish in the War Against Depression. *Red River Valley Hist. Rev.*, Autumn, 233–47.

J. CHRISTOPHER SCHNELL. Missouri Progressives and the Nomination of F.D.R. [1932]. *Mo. Hist. Rev.*, April, 269–79.

ROBERT V. PARKER. The Bonus March of 1932: A Unique Experience in North Carolina Political and Social Life. *N. C. Hist. Rev.*, Winter, 64–89.

BRENT TARTER. A Flier on the National Scene: Harry F. Byrd's Favorite-Son Presidential Candidacy of 1932. *Va. Mag. Hist. and Biog.*, July, 282–305.

THOMAS WATSON. The PWA Comes to the Red River Valley: Phase I, Non-Federal Projects in Texas, June 1933–February 1934. *Red River Valley Hist. Rev.*, Summer, 146–64.

L. DAVID NORRIS. Pyrrhic Victory: The Campaign [1934] for Amendment Nineteen [limiting spending] to the Arkansas Constitution. *Ibid.*, Autumn, 248–68.

JOSEPH A. FRY. The Organization in Control: George Campbell Peery, Governor of Virginia, 1934–1938. *Va. Mag. Hist. and Biog.*, July, 306–30.

ROBERT E. JAKOUBEK. A Jeffersonian's Dissent: John W. Davis [1873–1955] and the Campaign of 1936. *W. Va. Hist.*, Jan., 145–53.

LIONEL PATENAUDE. Vice President John Nance Garner: A Study in the Use of Influence During the New Deal. *Texana*, No. 2 [1973], 124–44.

LAWRENCE J. NELSON. Oscar Johnston [1880–1955], the New Deal, and the Cotton Subsidy Payments Controversy, 1936–1937. *Jour. Sou. Hist.*, Aug., 399–416.

PHILIP A. GRANT, JR. Editorial Reaction to the [Byron Patton] Harrison–[Alben W.] Barkley Senate Leadership Contest, 1937. *Jour. Miss. Hist.*, May, 127–41.

ALVIN L. HALL. Politics and Patronage: Virginia's Senators and the Roosevelt Purges of 1938. *Va. Mag. Hist. and Biog.*, July, 331–50.

DAVID PORTER. Senator Pat Harrison of Mississippi and the Reciprocal Trade Act of 1940. *Jour. Miss. Hist.*, Nov., 363–76.

CLIFFORD E. TRAFZER, ed. Views from the Red River Valley: A "Liberal" Republican's [Waite Phillips] Philosophy [Nov. 1940]. *Red River Valley Hist. Rev.*, Spring, 70–77.

JACK B. MCGUIRE. Andrew [J.] Higgins [1886–1952] Plays Presidential Politics [1944]. *La. Hist.*, Summer, 273–84.

JOHN A. SALMOND. Postscript to the New Deal: The Defeat of the Nomination of Aubrey W. Williams [1890–1965] as Rural Electrification Administrator in 1945. *Jour. Am. Hist.*, Sept., 417–36.

NUMAN V. BARTLEY. Moderation in [Ga. gov. Lester G.] Maddox Country? *Ga. Hist. Quar.*, Fall, 340–48.

JAMES R. SWEENEY. The Golden Silence: The Virginia Democratic Party and the Presidential Election of 1948. *Va. Mag. Hist. and Biog.*, July, 351–71.

PETER R. HENRIQUES. The Organization Challenged: John S. Battle, Francis P. Miller, and Horace Edwards Run for Governor in 1949. *Ibid.*, 372–406.

DAVID PACE. Lenoir Chambers [1891–1970] Opposes Massive Resistance: An Editor Against Virginia's Democratic Organization, 1955–1959. *Ibid.*, Oct., 415–29.

LEAH BROOKE TUCKER. The First Administration of Mayor Lewis Cutrer of Houston, 1958–1960. *East Texas Hist. Jour.*, Spring, 39–50.

DALE C. SMITH and JAMES EVERETT VOYLES. New Coalitions in Alabama Voting Patterns: The Friends-and-Neighbors Phenomenon. *Ala. Rev.*, July, 197–212.

JAMES L. BARNIDGE. The Louisiana Constitutional Convention of 1973: The Road to Revision. *La. Hist.*, Winter, 35–48.

RELIGION

JOHN T. AMES. Cumberland [Presbyterian] Liberals and the Union of 1906. *Jour. Presbyterian Hist.*, Spring, 3–18.

DOROTHY C. BASS. Gideon Blackburn's [1772–1838] Mission to the Cherokees: Christianization and Civilization. *Ibid.*, Fall, 203–26.

DICKSON D. BRUCE, JR. Religion, Society and Culture in the Old South: A Comparative View. *Am. Quar.*, Oct., 399–416.

W. HARRISON DANIEL. The Effects of the Civil War on Southern Protestantism. *Md. Hist. Mag.*, Spring, 44–63.

———. Virginia Baptists and the Myth of the Southern Mind, 1865–1900. *Sou. Atlantic Quar.*, Winter, 85–98.

JOHN R. GUNDERSEN. Anthony Gavin's [1689–1750] *A Master-Key to Popery:* A Virginia Parson's Best Seller. *Va. Mag. Hist. and Biog.*, Jan., 39–46.

RHYS ISAAC. Evangelical Revolt: The Nature of the Baptists' Challenge to the Traditional Order in Virginia, 1765 to 1775. *William and Mary Quar.*, July, 345–68.

ALBERTA H. KLEMP. Early Methodism in the New Madrid [Mo.] Circuit. *Mo. Hist. Rev.*, Oct., 23–47.

MAX S. LALE. Trinity Episcopal Church: Marshall, Texas. *East Texas Hist. Jour.*, Spring, 3–16.

BENEDICT LEUTENEGGER, trans., and MARION A. HABIG, [ed.]. Report on the San Antonio Missions in 1792. *Southwestern Hist. Quar.*, April, 487–98.

WILLIAM G. MCLOUGHLIN. The Choctaw Slave Burning [1859]: A Crisis in Mission Work Among the Indians. *Jour. West*, April, 113–27.

DONALD G. MATHEWS. Religion in the Old South: Speculation on Methodology. *Sou. Atlantic Quar.*, Winter, 34–52.

HOWARD MEREDITH. Whirlwind [Indian day school]: A Study of Church-State Relationships. *Hist. Mag. Prot. Epis. Church*, Dec., 296–304.

DAVID T. MORGAN. Judaism in Eighteenth-Century Georgia. *Ga. Hist. Quar.*, Spring, 41–54.

JOHN L. MORRISON. The Centrality of the Bible in Alexander Campbell's [1788–1866] Thought and Life. *W. Va. Hist.*, April, 185–204.

JOHN M. MULDER. Joseph Ruggles Wilson [1822–1903]: Southern Presbyterian Patriarch. *Jour. Presbyterian Hist.*, Fall, 245–71.

Presbyterians and the American Revolution: A Documentary Account. *Ibid.*, Winter, 299–488.

TIMOTHY F. REILLY. Heterodox New Orleans and the Protestant South, 1800–1861. *La. Stud.*, Fall [1973], 533–51.

R. J. ROBERTSON, JR. The Mormon Experience in Missouri, 1830–1839, Parts I, II. *Mo. Hist. Rev.*, April, 280–98; July, 393–415.

PARKE ROUSE, JR. James Blair [1655–1743] of Virginia. *Hist. Mag. Prot. Epis. Church,* June, 189–93.

GEORGE EATON SIMPSON. Black Pentecostalism in the United States. *Phylon,* June, 203–11.

ARTHUR L. WALKER, JR. The Major [Harwell Goodwin Davis, b. 1882]. *Baptist Hist. and Heritage,* Jan., 40–47, 54.

SCIENCE AND MEDICINE

NANCY D. BAIRD. Asiatic Cholera: Kentucky's First Public Health Instructor. *Filson Club Hist. Quar.*, Oct., 327–41.

———. Asiatic Cholera's First Visit to Kentucky [1832]: A Study in Panic and Fear. *Ibid.*, July, 228–40.

JAMES O. BREEDEN. Thomsonianism in Virginia. *Va. Mag. Hist. and Biog.*, April, 150–80.

JOHN DUFFY. Nineteenth Century Public Health in New York and New Orleans: A Comparison. *La. Hist.*, Fall, 325–37.

JOHN H. ELLIS. Disease and the Destiny of a City: The 1878 Yellow Fever Epidemic in Memphis. *West Tenn. Hist. Soc. Papers,* 75–89.

WILLIAM ERNST. William Barton Rogers [1804–1882]: Ante Bellum Virginia Geologist. *Va. Cavalcade,* Summer, 12–21.

WAYLAND D. HAND. Measuring [of height] and Plugging: The Magical Containment and Transfer of Disease. *Bull. Hist. Med.*, Summer, 221–33.

PHILIP A. KALISCH. Lepers, Anachronisms, and the Progressives: A Study in Stigma, 1889–1920. *La. Stud.*, Fall [1973], 489–531.

LORENA S. WALSH and RUSSELL R. MENARD. Death in the Chesapeake: Two Life Tables for Men in Early Colonial Maryland. *Md. Hist. Mag.*, Summer, 211–27.

SOCIAL, CULTURAL, AND INTELLECTUAL

EMILY K. ABEL [ed.]. A Victorian Views Reconstruction: The American Diary of Samuel Augustus Barnett [1844–1913]. *Civil War Hist.*, June, 135–56.

CARL BERT ALBERT. Recollections of My Early Life [b. 1908]. *Chron. Okla.*, Spring, 30–37.

NANCY ALEXANDER. Looking West from Comanche: Robert T. Hill [1858–1941] Comes to Texas. *Southwest Rev.*, Winter, 1-16.

JOHN V. ALLCOTT. Scholarly Books and Frolicsome Blades: A. J. Davis [1803–1892] Designs a Library-Ballroom [Univ. of North Carolina]. *Jour. Soc. Arch. Historians*, May, 145–54.

BRENDA S. ARGO. Madame Octavia LeVert's [1810–1877] Tribute to Henry Clay. *La. Stud.*, Winter [1973], 631–38.

LeROY ASHBY. The Disappearing Dry: Raymond Robins [1873–1954] and the Last Days of Prohibition. *N. C. Hist. Rev.*, Autumn, 401–19.

REED A. BAIRD. Opie Read [1852–1939]: An American Traveler. *Tenn. Hist. Quar.*, Winter, 410–28.

W. DAVID BAIRD. The Reduction of a People: The Quapaw Removal [from Arkansas], 1824–1834. *Red River Valley Hist. Rev.*, Spring, 21–36.

T. LINDSAY BAKER, ed. and trans. Four Letters from [Panna Maria] Texas to Poland in 1855. *Southwestern Hist. Quar.*, Jan., 381–89.

WILLIAM J. BAKER. Thomas [Henry] Huxley in Tennessee. *Sou. Atlantic Quar.*, Autumn, 475–86.

BRUCE G. BEEZER. Arthurdale [Reedsville Experimental Community, W. Va.]: An Experiment in Community Education. *W. Va. Hist.*, Oct., 17–36.

WATT L. BLACK. Education in the South from 1820 to 1860 with Emphasis on the Growth of Teacher Education. *La. Stud.*, Winter [1973], 617–29.

F. N. BONEY. Nathaniel Francis [1805–1849], Representative Antebellum Southerner. *Proc. Am. Philos. Soc.*, Oct., 449–58.

———. The Southern Aristocrat. *Midwest Quar.*, April, 215–30.

JARED W. BRADLEY. William C. C. Claiborne [1775–1817], the Old Southwest and the Development of American Indian Policy. *Tenn. Hist. Quar.*, Fall, 265–78.

THOMAS ELTON BROWN. Oklahoma's "Bone Dry Law" and the Roman Catholic Church. *Chron. Okla.*, Fall, 316–30.

EDWARD E. CAHILL and HANNS PIEPER. Closing the Educational Gap: The South Versus the United States. *Phylon*, March, 45–53.

RANDOLPH B. CAMPBELL. Planters and Plain Folk: Harrison County, Texas, as a Test Case, 1850–1860. *Jour. Sou. Hist.*, Aug., 369–98.

LOIS GREEN CARR. "The Metropolis [St. Mary's City] of Maryland": A Comment on Town Development Along the Tobacco Coast. *Md. Hist. Mag.*, Summer, 124–45.

CARY CARSON. The "Virginia House" in Maryland. *Ibid.*, 185–96.

JAMES F. COOK. The [Ga. gov.] Eugene Talmadge–Walter [D.] Cocking [academic] Controversy [1941]. *Phylon*, June, 181–92.

THEODORE G. CORBETT. Migration to a Spanish Imperial Frontier in the Seventeenth and Eighteenth Centuries: St. Augustine [Fla.]. *Hisp. Am. Hist. Rev.*, Aug., 414–30.

IRENE E. CORTINOVIS. The Golden Age of [St. Louis] German Song [1840s–1900]. *Mo. Hist. Rev.*, July, 437–42.

JAMES W. COVINGTON. Florida Seminoles: 1900–1920. *Fla. Hist. Quar.*, Oct., 181–97.

E. T. Crowson. Samuel Stanhope Smith [d. 1819]: A Founder of Hampden-Sydney College. *Va. Cavalcade,* Autumn, 53–61.

Leonard P. Curry. Urbanization and Urbanism in the Old South: A Comparative View. *Jour. Sou. Hist.,* Feb., 43–60.

R. Bruce Davis. The Tornado of 1840 Hits Mississippi. *Jour. Miss. Hist.,* Feb., 43–51.

Kathleen A. Deagan. *Mestizaje* in Colonial St. Augustine. *Ethnohistory,* Winter [1973], 55–65.

Katherine B. Dehler. Mt. Vernon Place [Baltimore] at the Turn of the Century: A Vignette of the [John W.] Garrett [1820–1884] Family. *Md. Hist. Mag.,* Fall, 279–92.

Howard Dorgan. A Case Study in Reconciliation: General John B. Gordon [1832–1904] and "The Last Days of the Confederacy." *Quar. Jour. Speech,* Feb., 83–91.

J. P. Dougherty. Baroque and Picturesque Motifs in L'Enfant's Design for the Federal Capital [1791]. *Am. Quar.,* March, 23–36.

Ralph B. Draughon, Jr. A Honeymoon in 1850. *Ala. Hist. Quar.,* Summer, 164–66.

Andre Paul DuChateau. The Creek Nation on the Eve of the Civil War. *Chron. Okla.,* Fall, 290–315.

Maurice Duke. [James Branch] Cabell's and [Ellen] Glasgow's Richmond: The Intellectual Background of the City. *Miss. Quar.,* Fall, 375–91.

Arlen R. Dykstra. Rowdyism and Rivalism in the St. Louis Fire Department, 1850–1857. *Mo. Hist. Rev.,* Oct., 48–64.

Clement Eaton. Breaking a Path for the Liberation of Women in the South. *Ga. Rev.,* Summer, 187–99.

Ann W. Ellis. The Greek Community in Atlanta, 1900–1923. *Ga. Hist. Quar.,* Winter, 400–408.

O. B. Emerson. William Faulkner's Nemesis—Major Frederick Sullens. [editor, Jackson *Daily News*]. *Jour. Miss. Hist.,* May, 161–64.

Stanley J. Folmsbee. Campus Life at the University of Tennessee, 1794–1879. *East Tenn. Hist. Soc. Pub.,* No. 45 [1973], 25–50.

Kenny A. Franks, ed. Among the Plains Tribes in Oklahoma with [artist] Frederic Remington. *Chron. Okla.,* Winter, 419–38.

———. Political Intrigue in the Cherokee Nation, 1839. *Jour. West,* Oct., 17–25.

Angelo I. George. The Legend of Eleven Jones' Cave, Jefferson County, Kentucky. *Filson Club Hist. Quar.,* Oct., 342–59.

H. Roger Grant. The Society of Bethel: A Visitor's Account. *Mo. Hist. Rev.,* Jan., 223–31.

Ralph D. Gray and Gerald E. Hartdagen, [eds.]. A Glimpse of Baltimore Society in 1827: Letters by Henry D. Gilpin [1801–1860]. *Md. Hist. Mag.,* Fall, 256–70.

Albert J. Guerard. The View from the Persimmon Tree: Houston 1924–1972. *Sou. Rev.,* April, 286–306.

James William Hagy and Stanley J. Folmsbee, eds. The Lost Archives of the Cherokee Nation. Part III, 1777. *East Tenn. Hist. Soc. Pub.*, No. 45 [1973], 88–98.

ALVIN L. HALL. Charles Chaky De Nordendorf [1839–1884]: Soldier-Songster of the Confederacy. *Va. Cavalcade*, Summer, 40–47.

HAROLD B. HANCOCK. The Indenture System in Delaware, 1681–1921. *Del. Hist.*, April, 47–59.

MELVIN G. HERNDON. Samuel Edward Butler [1748–1809]: Revolutionary Patriot. *Ga. Hist. Quar.*, Fall, 349–56.

CHARLOTTE A. HICKSON. The Texas Gazette, 1829–1832. *Texana*, No. 1 [1973], 18–29.

CAROL E. HOFFECKER, ed. The Diaries of Edmund Canby, a Quaker Miller, 1822–1848. *Del. Hist.*, Oct., 79–131.

PATRICK G. HOGAN, JR. Humor of the Old Southwest vs. Southwestern Humor: A Problem of Transition and Definition. *Jour. Am. Stud. Assn. of Texas*, Vol. V, 29–34.

TOM HOLMAN. William G. Coffin [1811–1902], Lincoln's Superintendent of Indian Affairs for the Southern Superintendency. *Kan. Hist. Quar.*, Winter [1973], 491–514.

HARRY D. HOLMES and RONALD L. DAVIS. St. Louis: A New Look at an Old Western City, 1870–1910. *Jour. West*, July, 6–16.

W. STANLEY HOOLE, ed. East Florida in 1834: Letters of Dr. John Durkee [fl. 1830s]. *Fla. Hist. Quar.*, Jan, 294–308.

ARTHUR F. HOWINGTON. Violence in Alabama: A Study of Late Ante-Bellum Montgomery. *Ala. Rev.*, July, 213–31.

A. V. HUFF, JR. The Eagle and the Vulture: Changing Attitudes Toward Nationalism in Fourth of July Orations Delivered in Charleston [S. C.], 1778–1860. *Sou. Atlantic Quar.*, Winter, 10–22.

KENNETH R. JOHNSON. The Peabody Fund: Its Role and Influence in Alabama. *Ala. Rev.*, April, 101–26.

DONALD B. KELLEY. Intellectual Isolation: Gateway to Secession in Mississippi. *Jour. Miss. Hist.*, Feb., 17–37.

SUSAN CROCE KELLY. The Beginnings of the St. Louis Zoo [1910–1916]. *Bull. Mo. Hist. Soc.*, July, 268–78.

WILLIAM J. KIMBALL. The "Kentucky Tragedy [stabbing of Solomon Sharp, 1825]:" Romance or Politics. *Filson Club Hist. Quar.*, Jan., 16–26.

JOHN A. KOUWENHOVEN. Downtown St. Louis as James B. Eads [1820–1887] Knew It When the [Eads] Bridge Was Opened a Century Ago. *Bull. Mo. Hist. Soc.*, April, 181–95.

———. Eads Bridge [linking East St. Louis and St. Louis]: The Celebration. *Ibid.*, 159–80.

WALTER E. LANGSAM. Louisville [Ky.] Mansions from the Civil War to World War I. *Antiques*, April, 855–69.

A Letter from James McBride Regarding the Earthquake of 1811–1812. *Reg. Ky. Hist. Soc.*, Oct., 398–402.

EUGENE LEVY. "Is the Jew a White Man?": Press Reaction to the Leo Frank Case, 1913–1915. *Phylon*, June, 212–22.

Henry W. Lewis. Horses and Horsemen in Northampton [Co., N. C.] Before 1900. *N. C. Hist. Rev.*, Spring, 125–48.

William Henry Longton. The Carolina Ideal World: Natural Science and Social Thought in Ante Bellum South Carolina. *Civil War Hist.*, June, 118–34.

Royster Lyle, Jr., and Matthew W. Paxton, Jr. The VMI Barracks. *Va. Cavalcade,* Winter, 14–29.

Edgar E. MacDonald. [Ellen] Glasgow, [James Branch] Cabell, and Richmond [Va.]. *Miss. Quar.*, Fall, 393–413.

Douglas McReynolds. "Mysterious Names": Riddles in the Ozarks. *Bull. Mo. Hist. Soc.*, April, 205–207.

Jane Gaston Mahler. Our Huguenot Heritage; Homes, Houses of Worship, and Public Buildings. *Trans. Huguenot Soc. of S. C.*, 1–43.

Anthony V. Margavio and J. Lambert Molyneaux. Residential Segregation of Italians in New Orleans and Selected American Cities. *La. Stud.*, Winter [1973], 639–45.

P. Richard Metcalf. Who Should Rule at Home? Native American Politics and Indian-White Relations. *Jour. Am. Hist.*, Dec., 651–65.

George L. Miller. A [Md.] Tenant Farmer's Tableware: Nineteenth-Century Ceramics from [Moses] Tabb's Purchase. *Md. Hist. Mag.*, Summer, 197–210.

Sara Sprott Morrow. Adolphus Heiman's [1809–1862, architectural] Legacy to Nashville. *Tenn. Hist. Quar.*, Spring, 3–21.

Gary E. Moulton. Chief John Ross [1790–1866] and Cherokee Removal Finances. *Chron. Okla.*, Fall, 342–59.

Raymond E. Myers. The Story of Germanna [Orange Co., Va.]. *Filson Club Hist. Quar.*, Jan., 27–42.

Mark E. Nackman. Anglo-American Migrants to the West: Men of Broken Fortunes? The Case of Texas, 1821–46. *Western Hist. Quar.*, Oct., 441–55.

Charles T. Nall, ed. A Letter from [François Xavier Dupont] Petersburg, Virginia, January 10, 1789. *Va. Mag. Hist. and Biog.*, April, 144–49.

Julia Neal. Shaker Industries in Kentucky. *Antiques,* March, 603–11.

Ralph D. Nurnberger. The Great Baltimore Deluge of 1817. *Md. Hist. Mag.*, Winter, 405–408.

Michael O'Brien, ed. A Correspondence [between Edwin Mims and Donald Davidson], 1923–1958. *Sou. Rev.*, Autumn, 904–22.

Frederick A. Olds. Historians and Art: An Oklahoma Case Study. *Chron. Okla.*, Summer, 196–206.

Fred Lamar Pearson, Jr. Spanish-Indian Relations in Florida, 1602–1675: Some Aspects of Selected *Visitas*. *Fla. Hist. Quar.*, Jan., 261–73.

Clifton Paisley. Tallahassee Through the [William P. Slusser] Storebooks: Era of Radical Reconstruction, 1867–1877. *Ibid.*, July, 49–65.

JOHN R. PLEASANT, JR. Ruffin G. Pleasant and Huey P. Long on the Prisoner-Stripe Controversy [1930]. *La. Hist.*, Fall, 357–66.

GEORGE E. POZZETTA. Foreigners in Florida: A Study of Immigration Promotion, 1865–1910. *Fla. Hist. Quar.*, Oct., 164–80.

GERALD A. REED. Financial Controversy in the Cherokee Nation, 1839–1846. *Chron. Okla.*, Spring, 82–98.

GRACE RICE. The Day [April 4, 1921] I Rode [my horse] Jargo: The Terror of a Red River Flood. *Red River Valley Hist. Rev.*, Spring, 66–69.

BETTY RING. Salem [N. C.] Female Academy [established 1772]. *Antiques*, Sept., 434–42.

NORMAN K. RISJORD. Early Virginia: A Prison with Opportunity [for Jacobite prisoners]. *Va. Cavalcade*, Autumn, 62–69.

WILLARD B. ROBINSON. Temples of Knowledge: Historic Mains of Texas Colleges and Universities. *Southwestern Hist. Quar.*, April, 445–80.

TOMMY WAYNE ROGERS. Oakland College [near Rodney, Miss.], 1830–1871. *Jour. Miss. Hist.*, May, 143–60.

PETER ROMANOFSKY. "The Public is Aroused": The Missouri Children's Code Commission, 1915–1919. *Mo. Hist. Rev.*, Jan., 204–22.

CATHERINE M. ROTTIER. Ellen Spencer Mussey [1850–1936] and the [founding of] Washington College of Law [1898]. *Md. Hist. Mag.*, Winter, 361–82.

PARKE ROUSE, JR. Dr. Bennett [Wood] Green [1835–1913] and His Word-Book. *Va. Mag. Hist. and Biog.*, April, 181–90.

———. Yorktown Centennial Celebration: 1881 Extravaganza. *Va. Cavalcade*, Autumn, 80–87.

MATTIE U. RUSSELL. Devil in the Smokies: The White Man's Nature and the Indian's Fate [William Holland Thomas and the Cherokee]. *Sou. Atlantic Quar.*, Winter, 53–69.

DOROTHY SCURA. [Ellen] Glasgow and the Southern Renaissance: The [Southern Writers] Conference at Charlottesville [Va., Oct. 1931]. *Miss. Quar.*, Fall, 415–34.

NANCY B. SEDERBERG. Antebellum Southern Humor in the *Camden* [S. C.] *Journal:* 1826–1840. *Ibid.*, Winter, 41–74.

ARNOLD SHANKMAN. [Amasa R.] Converse [1842–1885], *The Christian Observer* and Civil War Censorship. *Jour. Presbyterian Hist.*, Fall, 227–44.

ROBERT W. SHOOK. German Migration to Texas 1830–1850: Causes and Consequences. *Texana,* No. 3 [1972], 226–43.

———. Years of Transition: Victoria, Texas, 1880–1920. *Southwestern Hist. Quar.*, Oct., 155–82.

L. MOODY SIMMS, JR. Edward Caledon Bruce [1825–1901]: Virginia Artist and Writer. *Va. Cavalcade,* Winter, 30–37.

———. Richard Malcolm Johnston [1822–1898] on Rural Life in Middle Georgia. *Ga. Hist. Rev.*, Supplement, 181–92.

———. William Ludwell Sheppard [1833–1912]: Artist of the Confederacy. *Lincoln Herald*, Fall, 139–42.

LEWIS P. SIMPSON. The Southern Recovery of Memory and History. *Sewanee Rev.*, Winter, 1–32.

James M. Smith. Thomas Henry Huxley in Nashville [1876]. Parts I, II. *Tenn. Hist. Quar.*, Summer, 191–203; Fall, 322–41.

William R. Snell. Masked Men in the Magic City: Activities of the Revised [Ku Klux] Klan in Birmingham, 1916–1940. *Ala. Hist. Quar.*, Fall and Winter [1972], 206–27.

Peter A. Soderbergh. The South in Juvenile Series Books, 1907–1917. *Miss. Quar.*, Spring, 131–40.

Stuart Seely Sprague. Town Making in the Era of Good Feelings: Kentucky 1814–1820. *Reg. Ky. Hist. Soc.*, Oct., 337–41.

J. C. A. Stagg. The Problem of Klan Violence: The South Carolina Up-Country, 1868–1871. *Jour. Am. Stud.*, Dec., 303–18.

Gary C. Stein. A Fearful Drunkenness: The Liquor Trade to the Western Indians as Seen by European Travelers in America, 1800–1860. *Red River Valley Hist. Rev.*, Summer, 109–21.

———. "And the Strife Never Ends": Indian-White Hostility as Seen by European Travelers in America, 1800–1860. *Ethnohistory*, Spring [1973], 173–87.

Thad Stem, Jr. Absent with Leave, or How Musty Files [N. C. newspapers] Came Alive. *N. C. Hist. Rev.*, Spring, 170–82.

Garry Wheeler Stone. St. John's ["palace," St. Mary's, Md.]: Archaeological Questions and Answers. *Md. Hist. Mag.*, Summer, 146–68.

Ray Swick. Aaron Burr's Visit [1805] to Blennerhassett Island [Ohio]. *W. Va. Hist.*, April, 205–19.

Rex Syndergaard. The Final Move of the Choctaws [from Miss. to Okla.], 1825–1830. *Chron. Okla.*, Summer, 207–19.

Ferenc M. Szasz. Antebellum Appeals to the "Higher Law," 1830–1860. *Essex Inst. Hist. Coll.*, Jan., 33–48.

James C. Thomas. The Log Houses of Kentucky. *Antiques*, April, 791–98.

George B. Tindall. Beyond the Mainstream: The Ethnic Southerners. *Jour. Sou. Hist.*, Feb., 3–18.

Alicia V. Tjarks. Comparative Demographic Analysis of Texas, 1777–1793. *Southwestern Hist. Quar.*, Jan., 291–338.

Margret G. Trotter. A Glimpse of Charleston [W. Va.] in the 1890s from a Contemporary Diary. *W. Va. Hist.*, Jan., 131–44.

Edward L. Tucker, [ed.]. Philip Pendleton Cooke [1816–1849] and *The Southern Literary Messenger:* Selected Letters. *Miss. Quar.*, Winter, 79–99.

Daniel Tyler. The Mexican Teacher [1821–1848]. *Red River Valley Hist. Rev.*, Autumn, 207–21.

Walter N. Vernon. Early Echoes from Bloomfield Academy [for Chickasaw Indian girls]. *Chron. Okla.*, Summer, 237–43.

———. Thomas Ward Vernon [fl. 1837–1850]: Elk River [Tenn.] Pioneer. *Tenn. Hist. Quar.*, Spring, 62–69.

Willie T. Weathers. Judith W. McGuire [1813–1897]: A Lady of Virginia. *Va. Mag. Hist. and Biog.*, Jan., 100–13.

Bill Weaver. The [Mark] Twain–[George Washington] Cable Lectures in Kentucky, 1884–1885. *Reg. Ky. Hist. Soc.*, April, 134–42.

Hermann Wellenreuther. Urbanization in the Colonial South: A Critique. *William and Mary Quar.*, Oct., 653–71.

Donald W. Whisenhunt. The Transient in the Depression. *Red River Valley Hist. Rev.*, Spring, 7–20.

Ridley Wills, II, [ed.]. Letters from Nashville, 1862, I. A Portrait of Belle Meade [Plantation]. *Tenn. Hist. Quar.*, Spring, 70–84.

Charles R. Wilson. "Morons," Monkeys and Morality: Reactions to the [John T.] Scopes Trial in Texas [1925]. *East Texas Hist. Jour.*, Fall, 51–63.

W. Emerson Wilson, ed. Phoebe George Bradford [1794–1840] Diaries. *Del. Hist.*, April, 1–21; Oct., 152–70.

Carolyn Murray Wooley. Kentucky's Early Stone Houses. *Antiques*, March, 592–602.

Charles E. Wynes. Fanny Kemble's [1809–1893] South Revisited: The South [Reconstruction Ga.] as Seen Through the Eyes of Her Daughter, Frances [Butler]. *La. Stud.*, Fall [1973], 473–88.

Peter G. Yackel. Benefit of Clergy in Colonial Maryland. *Md. Hist. Mag.*, Winter, 383–97.

Annual Report of the Secretary-Treasurer

By Bennett H. Wall

In 1974 the Southern Historical Association, like other professional organizations, definitely reflected the national economic situation. Meeting attendance declined, hard-pressed publishers cancelled exhibits and placed fewer advertisements in the *Journal*, the cost of postage and supplies increased more than 25 percent, and the costs of printing the *Journal* continued to mount. On the staff, the only wage increase was granted to a person on an hourly rate.

On the other hand, the editor continues to donate much of his summer time to the *Journal*, for like most other members his salary is based on the academic year. (This last should not be, for our organization cannot expect such dedicated work to go largely unrewarded.) Rice University continues its sponsorship of the *Journal*, providing the time of the editor and the assistant editor, secretarial help, supplies, office space, furniture and equipment, telephone, postage, etc. Tulane University furnishes storage space, office space, furniture, telephones, and other things. Illustrative of this support is the fact that the Southern Historical Association has never paid a monthly charge for a telephone or a light, water, or heating bill, nor has it paid other than infrequent nominal sums for janitorial services. The secretary mentions the above to inform the members that we are still obligated to the editor and his staff, to the staff of the secretary, and to the two named institutions for making possible our continued operation with nominal dues charges. While by decision of the Executive Council, repeatedly made, this Association does not seek ever larger bank balances and growing investments as a backlog and has ever sought to keep dues low, it is only with such personal and university support that we are a going concern. In 1974 two members wrote the Tulane University president expressing personal appreciation for the continued support of the SHA by Tulane. This pleased the secretary, and he hopes that other members will do likewise for both Tulane and Rice.

Mr. Wall is secretary-treasurer of the Southern Historical Association and professor of history at Tulane University

The Journal of Southern History
Vol. XLI, No. 2, May 1975

Because of special features of the new SHA constitution spelling out the work of the Nominating Committee, it became necessary for that committee to meet in special session in Atlanta on February 7, 1974. Chaired by John Hebron Moore, with Michael Les Benedict, Carl B. Cone, Louis R. Harlan, and Allen W. Trelease as members, this committee met its March 1 deadline and nominated for vice-president Frank E. Vandiver of Rice University and for the Executive Council James C. Bonner of Georgia College, Ernest M. Lander, Jr., of Clemson University, and Hans A. Schmitt of the University of Virginia. There being no nomination by petition, the secretary declared the slate of the committee elected at the annual business session on November 7. Since the Moore committee made its nominations before March 1 and nominations had to be made at the same time in 1975, the Executive Council chose the 1974–1975 committee by mail ballot. John Hebron Moore was selected for a second term as chairman, and William D. Aeschbacher of the University of Cincinnati, John S. Ezell of the University of Oklahoma, Robert W. Johannsen of the University of Illinois, and Willie Lee Rose of the Johns Hopkins University were chosen to serve with him. Their nominees are listed in the Historical News and Notices section in this issue.

At the annual meeting the council changed one bylaw and made an addition to another. (Both changes are noted later in this report.) They also reappointed Bennett H. Wall of Tulane University as secretary-treasurer and Sanford W. Higginbotham as managing editor of the *Journal.* The council appointed William D. Aeschbacher of the University of Cincinnati chairman of the Nominating Committee for 1975–1976. Other members appointed are Doris Elizabeth King of North Carolina State University, Samuel Proctor of the University of Florida, James Z. Rabun of Emory University, and George R. Woolfolk of Prairie View A. & M. University. The council approved nominations by editor Higginbotham of Noble E. Cunningham, Jr. of the University of Missouri–Columbia and Richard Lowitt of the University of Kentucky to four-year terms on the Board of Editors. They replace E. David Cronon of the University of Wisconsin and Holman Hamilton of the University of Kentucky.

The council made no selection of a meeting site for 1982, deciding instead to await a report on the annual meeting being prepared by the secretary.

Bell I. Wiley, representative of the SHA on the National Archives Advisory Council, attended the council meeting and reported on problems confronting the Archives and the efforts being made to alleviate these. Wiley has served on this advisory council for seven years.

Program Chairman Richard M. Brown and his committee developed an excellent program for the Dallas meeting. A total of 1,026 persons registered, of which 354 were nonmembers. Additionally, 30 exhibitors and 73 spouses registered for a total attendance of 1,129. However, 23 exhibitors did not pick up their badges, and at least 150 other persons in attendance did not register. Some of the latter may well have been visiting from the Community College Social Studies Association that met in Dallas at the same time and that will meet on the same dates as the SHA in Washington and Atlanta in 1975 and 1976.

In January 1974 the Association had 5,160 members. On December 31 there were 4,867 members, a drop of 293 members. No chairman or committee ever labored harder or with more imagination than did Marvin W. Schlegel and his committee. That our membership did not drop even more is due to their efforts. A sign of the times was that 170 libraries ceased to subscribe to the *Journal* in 1974. On December 31, 1974, there were 4,867 members and libraries; 2,424 regular members, 409 new members, 137 life members, and 16 reinstated members. There were also 1,787 library subscribers and 94 exchanges. The entire membership committee deserves the plaudits of the Association for their fine work.

During the year the Association lost eight members by death: Stanley J. Folmsbee of Knoxville, Tennessee; Willie D. Halsell of Itta Bena, Mississippi; Thomas Robson Hay of Locust Valley, New York; Blaine S. Hollimon of San Antonio, Texas; Mary Elizabeth Massey of Rock Hill, South Carolina; Richard Lee Morton of Williamsburg, Virginia; Edward H. Phillips of Charleston, South Carolina; and Irvin G. Wyllie of Kenosha, Wisconsin.

At the annual business session the members unanimously endorsed a motion by J. Joseph Huthmacher to support H.R. 16902, a bill introduced by Representative John Brademas to create a national study commission on the disposal of all presidential records. By unanimous vote they also indicated support of the suit of the American Historical Association and other organizations raising questions about the disposition of the records of the Nixon administration and seeking to render null and void the so-called "Sampson-Knight agreement" of September 7, 1974. SHA members were asked to write their congressmen supporting the Brademas bill, and SHA officers were directed to support both motions in every way possible.

Before the presidential address on November 7 President Gilbert

C. Fite recognized Charles P. Roland of the University of Kentucky, who chaired the Charles Sackett Sydnor Award Committee. Roland announced that Thomas B. Alexander and Richard E. Beringer had won the Sydnor Award of $500 for *The Anatomy of the Confederate Congress: A Study of the Influences of Member Characteristics on Legislative Voting Behavior, 1861–1865*, a distinguished book in southern history. President Fite then recognized Carol K. Rothrock Bleser of Colgate University, chairperson of the Graduate Student Award Committee. Professor Bleser announced that Warren A. Ellem had received the award for his article "Who Were the Mississippi Scalawags?" published in the May 1972 issue of the *Journal*.

The 1974 meeting marked the first time there was a concerted, systematic effort to invite social studies high school teachers to attend our meeting. Quite a number came, and several joined the SHA later.

While in session the council added this section to Bylaw 5: "The Executive Council, at its discretion, may determine for each meeting both the total number of sessions and the number of sessions to be devoted to non–United States history. The program shall emphasize southern history, broadly interpreted, but should not exclude sessions on general American history. Neither the annual business session nor the annual presidential address shall be an occasion for the serving of meals."

The council also voted to enlarge Bylaw 2 by adding the following third paragraph:

"The *Francis Butler Simkins Prize* is awarded in odd-numbered years for a distinguished scholarly first book in the general field of southern history published during the two preceding calendar years. This prize is sponsored jointly by Longwood College and the Southern Historical Association. It carries a stipend of $200, which may be increased from time to time, and a framed certificate."

The council expressed its appreciation to member Thomas B. Alexander for his report, which alters Bylaw 5 to conform with the previously approved Grantham Committee report (*Journal*, XXXVII, 257–70). They also discharged with thanks the committee consisting of Merrill D. Peterson, chairman, and Charles P. Roland appointed to study the Simkins Prize proposal of Longwood College.

In 1974 the Association also received from the estate of devoted member Thomas Robson Hay its first gift by will. It should be noted also that several members returned reprint royalty checks to the Association as contributions.

FINANCIAL STATEMENT

December 31, 1974

BALANCE AS OF JANUARY 1, 1974:			
Investments:			
4 Savings Certificates, First National Bank of Commerce, New Orleans, La., @ $3,000	$12,000.00		
4 U. S. Savings Bonds, Series H, @ $1,000	4,000.00		
2 shares Standard Oil of New Jersey stock	152.00		
Interest accrued but not collected	4,768.00		
Total investments		$20,920.00	
Checking account, First National Bank of Commerce, New Orleans, La.		8,905.62	
Total		$29,825.62	
RECEIPTS, JANUARY 1–DECEMBER 31, 1974:			
Annual dues collected	$43,348.05		
Back numbers of *Journal* sold by office	221.65		
Back numbers and reprints sold by W. J. Johnson, Inc.	277.00		
Net advertising in program (less printing)	124.55		
Net convention receipts, program sales and exhibits (income from registration, exhibits, program sales less SHA meals, staff expenses, hall rental, guards and registration staff, travel and other charges)	1,997.69		
Advertising in the *Journal*	2,569.95		
Index sales	66.00		
Reprint cover payments	81.75		
Reprint royalty (less authors' share)	1,600.00		
Xerox Inc., microfilm sales	776.94		
Bobbs-Merrill Reprint Series	112.79		
Contributions	25.00		
Sale of membership lists	1,075.00		
Miscellaneous	108.97		
Interest on investments accrued but not collected, 1974	1,130.00		
Total receipts		53,515.34	
Total to be accounted for			$83,340.96

DISBURSEMENTS, JANUARY 1–DECEMBER 31, 1974:

Printing *Journal of Southern History:*		
February issue	$ 6,449.81	
May issue (overage)	4,348.50	
August issue	6,712.58	
November issue	8,078.91	
Reprints and offprints	489.41	
Total *Journal* printing		$26,079.21
Miscellaneous printing (Association letterhead, committee materials, dues forms, etc.)		940.00
Total printing		$27,019.21
Nonpersonal expenditures:		
Deposits, Tulane University for bulk mailing, IBM cards, prorated IBM machine and printer rental, supplies, etc.	$ 2,500.00	
Freight	15.00	
Advertising	79.00	
Telephone	613.44	
Office supplies	81.51	
Office equipment and maintenance (typewriter service contracts, etc.)	268.90	
Mailing back issues (William Byrd Press)	443.54	
Stamps and other postage	1,260.00	
Refunds	198.00	
Bank charges	92.10	
Exchange discount	4.07	
Sydnor Award	500.00	
Graduate Student Award	50.00	
Secretary's surety	50.00	
Southern Humanities Conference dues	10.00	
Insurance	82.00	
Moving to new storage and space conditioning	393.28	
Miscellaneous	25.00	
Total nonpersonal expenditures		6,665.84
Personal services:		
Secretary's stipend	$ 2,500.00	
Administrative assistant	7,500.00	
Membership secretary	5,443.00	

FICA	753.30		
Nominating Committee expenses	729.66		
Other committee expenses	246.99		
Travel and expenses (secretary and staff)	457.72		
Total personal services		17,630.67	
(Held in escrow until 1974 convention bill is presented)		1,000.00	
Total disbursements			$52,315.72
Balance as of December 31, 1974			31,025.24
Total accounted for			$83,340.96

DISTRIBUTION OF BALANCE, DECEMBER 31, 1974:

Investments:			
1 Savings Certificate, First National Bank of Commerce, New Orleans, La. @ $6,000	$ 6,000.00		
4 Savings Certificates, First National Bank of Commerce, New Orleans, La. @ $3,000.00	12,000.00		
2 shares Standard Oil of New Jersey stock	152.00		
Interest accrued but not collected, 1974	5,898.00		
Total investments		$24,050.00	
Checking account, First National Bank of Commerce, New Orleans, La.		6,975.24	
Total			$31,025.24

Book Reviews

Roll, Jordan, Roll: The World the Slaves Made. By Eugene D. Genovese. (New York: Pantheon Books, c. 1974. Pp. xxii, 823. $17.50.)

Eugene D. Genovese's *Roll, Jordan, Roll* is an inspired repudiation of all the facile moral judgments that have scarred so many works about American racial history and practice. A monument of research and interpretive commitment, this culmination of the author's numerous southern studies should revive a battered academic industry, providing scholars with new ideas for future elaboration.

Placing the southern "domestic institution" in the broad context of labor arrangements elsewhere in the nineteenth-century world, Genovese draws effectively from the works of Max Weber, Antonio Gramsci, Eric Hobsbawm, and many others in the European structuralist tradition. This indebtedness enriches the text without overpowering it. Instead, intellectual Marxism inspires but never orchestrates the central thesis: the interrelatedness of black accommodation and resistance in the authoritarian framework. Rather than serving as points of paradox or faint irony, slave acquiescence and self-assertiveness move rhythmically together throughout the work like a brooding, percussive line in a symphonic score. Nowhere is this dramatic theme more profoundly moving than in the analyses of slave weddings and burials, work habits and family exchange, and all the other rituals that lent black experience a meaning beyond the immediacy of bondage. Rejecting old and recent stereotypes of race behavior, Genovese honors such maligned figures as the black preacher, the household "mammy," the slave driver, as well as the ordinary members of families. Serving as mediators, sometimes as protectors against white overlordship, slaves assumed leadership as occasion or duty required but usually rejected outright rebellion so that they and their kindred could make the best of a sad existence.

Using the accommodation-resistance connection, Genovese describes slave religion, a creative mixture of African remembrance and Christian adaptation, as the means whereby blacks sustained familial integrity and sought release from the coils of subservience. With graceful sensitivity, he shows the mingling of weakness and bravery, deception and dignity, amoral practicality and supreme moral vision, servility and rectitude that a highly personal system of oppression extracted from every black soul. His conclusion is that, though far less bellicose and modernistic than we of more blessed times might wish, the antebellum black southerner, like William Faulkner's Dilsey, *endured*. While admitting that mere survival scarcely sets a stage for revolution, Genovese insists upon the epical significance of the struggle for autonomy. Eloquently, *Roll, Jordan, Roll* demonstrates how accommodation merged into resistance, and rebellion into acceptance of what could not be overturned, only modified, hour by hour.

Any work that aspires to comprehend so intricate a network of personal relations is bound to falter here and there. Neither master nor slave "could express the simplest human feelings without reference to the other," Genovese exclaims (p. 3). But white and black southerners thought more about traps and whiskey, visits and loves, for instance, than they did about hatreds and ambivalent affections across the racial chasm. Though suggestive about the psychic effects of a late antebellum shift from corporal to mental coercions, Genovese too often romanticizes the under class, finding overly abstract purposes in opportunistic black participation in a still savage culture. As he persuasively argues, Victorian masterhood burdened slaves with such cruel benedictions as shame, guilt, Christian gratitude for crumbs of kindliness as well as the tortures of lash and cottonshed confinement, methods never wholly abandoned. Yet, to expect from masters and slaves behavior more elevated than a grubby desire to escape unpleasant self-revelations is to nurse illusions. Forced into alien embrace and interdependency, all members of society, according to station and sphere, chiefly wished to be left alone, deceiving themselves and others to justify dishonesty and indifference in the presence of cruelty and palpable evils. Upon that simple proposition, the South seceded from an allegedly interfering republic, and the slaves often fulfilled demeaning roles to keep the white man at bay.

Genovese also credits southern rulers with unusual sensitivity to the dilemma of slaves being both inert property and morally responsible beings, particularly before the bench. As ever, the law had to resolve tensions in the social order, a function hardly unique to southern magistracy. Though reflecting both ancient, personal styles of justice and modern forms of equity, the slave codes gave only the most sophisticated jurist cause to ponder inner contradictions. Genovese almost suggests that in jurisprudence the master class felt pangs of guilt about ownership, a sensibility wisely denied elsewhere in his writings.

The most telling difficulty is a failure to evoke the totality of southern life. One misses, for instance, a deeper exploration of black linguistic and oral traditions and white racist exploitations of them. Moreover, the Marxian simplicities about "industrial" and "preindustrial" polarities seem quaint in the light of subtler distinctions to be appropriated from modern anthropology. "Paternalism," a catchword throughout for the complexities of the Southern Way, cannot sufficiently describe the two-century evolution of white social structure and ideology. We cannot understand why blacks acted the way they did until we know how *all* members of the society interacted and constructed their values and institutions. In the absence of that historical dimension, Genovese's attempt to relate slave experience at the close of the era to modern black nationalism is specious—a leap through a void. There is a defensive quality in the introduction, in the scattered quotations from Julius Lester, Imamu Baraka, and other angry black intellectuals, in the layers of similar illustrations, and in a curiously tacked-on appendix about Japanese paternalism, as if the author is worried that the evidence he offers of slave complicity in the social order might challenge his radical credentials.

Perhaps the times demand some mode of linking slavery to modern ethnic consciousness in a positive way. More than the author intends, however, we see modern blacks trapped in age-old patterns of resentment and acceptance of the white man's intractable world. Present-day belligerence may mask inner black fear of having no glorious myths from the servile past, as if heroics, like power, must be shot from guns. Is there not a connection between the slavery-imposed imperatives of deception, escape, random violence, thievery, and the like and the modern black proletarian experience—excesses that complement persistent white tyranny (now impersonal and bureaucratized), complacency, and contempt for black mores? Genovese concludes otherwise. Historians, with a last, forlorn optimism unique in the world of arts and letters, demand a happy ending. Romance, not reality, leads to such a conclusion.

Nevertheless, these criticisms seem very mean-spirited in the light of Genovese's outstanding achievement. In an age of doubt that desperately seeks utopian solutions to problems of order and freedom through violence, political fantasy, and leaden bureaucracies it is comforting to find a work that confronts hard questions in a spirit of splendid individuality and affirms the humanity of forgotten people, whose workaday heroism and self-recognition far transcend both the cant and merits of sloganeers of whatever partisan or racial coloration. Genovese's poetic memorial to the black American spirit, like that spirit itself, will endure.

Case Western Reserve University BERTRAM WYATT-BROWN

The National Archives and Urban Research. Edited by Jerome Finster. (Athens, Ohio: Ohio University Press, c. 1974. Pp. xii, 164. $10.00.)

This is the sixth volume in the National Archives Conferences series and consists of all but one of the papers delivered at a conference held at the National Archives in June 1970. Most of the contributions are apparently presented in their entirety, but the staff resource papers are not included, although a helpful list of them is appended to this work. Also missing are the observations of the commentators (with one exception).

Following the various preliminary statements are the keynote remarks of Sam Bass Warner on "The New Demand for Relevance in American History," suggesting that the primary responsibility of historians is to be relevant to their discipline—a concept of relevance that will be viewed as heretical in some quarters.

The bulk of this volume consists of the papers delivered by the members of four panels: on urban population; on housing; on transportation; and on the impact of federal activities on the cities. The apparent intention of the conference organizers was to include in the presentations of each panel a survey of the extant literature and one or more papers dealing with relevant archival materials which would support additional investigations. This format is adhered to in three of the panel presentations.

The essays of Richard O. Davies (housing), Glen E. Holt (mass transit), and William H. Wilson (federal impact) are competent bibliographical and conceptual surveys coupled with suggestions for further study. That of Davies is, perhaps, the best written; Holt's is certainly the most complete; while Wilson's, dealing with a largely unexplored field, is unusually able in identifying works in progress.

The papers dealing with archival materials were contributed by members of the staffs of the National Archives, the Library of Congress, or other federal agencies. The value of these presentations varies considerably—a circumstance largely conditioned by the quantity and quality of archival holdings available. Leonard Rapport, for example, in his very brief essay on "Urban Transportation Records in the National Archives" indicates several odd corners where investigators might not think of looking but frankly acknowledges that "a researcher's chances are better at home" (p. 106). Some of the other participants are less candid and occasionally give too much attention to records of dubious utility.

The panel on urban population deviates from the established pattern. Herbert G. Gutman's paper is not included because of prior publication commitments, but the brief remarks of Donald J. Bogue, who chaired this panel, are printed, and probably contain—in the form of his "ten happy hypotheses for the 1970s" (p. 13)—more provocative ideas than most of the longer contributions. Of the other two papers presented by members of this panel, that of Jerome P. Pickard is a routine manipulation of census data, and William E. Lind's is the least comprehensive of the archival surveys.

Some interesting opportunities for urban research and some potential archival support for that research are suggested by this volume. What the contributors do not point out, except by inference, is that the National Archives and federal agencies, except for the manuscript censuses and a few peripheral collections, have little material for research on urban topics earlier than the late nineteenth century.

The book can serve urban historians moderately well as a sketchy catalogue of literature and archival holdings in three topical areas. Whether it is worth the exorbitant price is a matter that each scholar will have to resolve individually.

University of Louisville LEONARD P. CURRY

Debtors and Creditors in America: Insolvency, Imprisonment for Debt, and Bankruptcy, 1607–1900. By Peter J. Coleman. (Madison: State Historical Society of Wisconsin, 1974. Pp. xiv, 303. $17.50.)

This is a formidable survey of debtor-creditor relations over three centuries covering fourteen eastern states. Professor Coleman's study is separated into chapters on colonial, national, and state relief and then into sections on New England, the Middle Atlantic states, and the South Atlantic region.

We learn that although most Americans have since earliest settlement been borrowers and lenders, "Our credit-oriented society has yet to devise cheap, efficient, equitable, and humane ways of enforcing contracts for debt" (p. vii). For the colonials, according to Coleman, constitutional and technical problems made relief legislation difficult. This was also true for state legislatures later, both in terms of the complexities involved in writing comprehensive and coherent relief laws and in the confusion of federal-state relations on this question.

Coleman narrates these differences fourteen times. And although we discover diversity of legal principle and style marking the evolution of relief laws in the respective states, the law of debtor and creditor in all the regions developed along broadly similar paths. Needless to say, this makes for very repetitious reading.

One wishes that Professor Coleman had supplied fewer but deeper analyses. This is especially true in light of several implied hypotheses which are only partially developed. For example, although Coleman demonstrates the obsoleteness of the debtor's prison and the practical need for better relief and bankruptcy laws, he does not substantiate his claim that laws or prisons would have come or gone on their own practical merits or demerits (p. 268). When Massachusetts, for instance, abolished the debtors' prison in 1857, the action may very well have been "more symbolic than practical" (p. 45). Coleman's own evidence, however, indicates that imprisonment had become rare by 1857, not only because creditors had found other and better ways to protect their interests but also because of the abolitionist effort. And his evidence for New York (pp. 117–22) indicates a crucial role for reformers in the abolition of debtors' prisons.

Coleman's own assessments in some places also seem contrary to his notion, expressed in other places, that reformers' efforts were unnecessary to overcome inertia in the area of relief legislation. Among other things, Coleman tells us creditors "feared that abandoning the traditional enforcement system would encourage recklessness and irresponsibility" (p. 13); and that "Most men were too conservative on so fundamental an issue to act more quickly . . . though they acknowledged the defects of the prison system . . ." (pp. 155–56).

In some circles the idea of imprisonment as punishment lingered on through the nineteenth century; in others there was a reluctance to admit that networks of alliances and associations based on mutual trust and preservation of reputation were no longer viable. Borrowers and lenders often recognized their mutual interests and acted accordingly, but often they did not. Apparently there were reasons other than technical complexities that held them back.

Professor Coleman claims that "By the 1820's only the larger debtors, or those suspected of fraud, commonly spent more than a month in jail" (p. 254). His evidence on the increasing of jail boundaries (sometimes to county lines), on the exchanging of property assignments for jail deliveries, and on the previous confusion over numbers arrested and numbers jailed clearly challenges the views of earlier students of this subject.

Despite some criticisms, historians will find the book useful. Coleman raises important questions, if not always clearly, and points in interesting research directions.

State University of New York
New Paltz GERALD SORIN

Sugar and Slavery: An Economic History of the British West Indies, 1623–1775. By Richard B. Sheridan. (Baltimore: Johns Hopkins University Press, c. 1973. Pp. xiv. 529. $22.50.)

Professor Sheridan's long-awaited book describes the growth and consolidation of trade, slavery, and sugar production from 1623 to 1775 in the British West Indian colonies. The breadth and scope of his research and his ability to compress arguments and illustrations force topics—sufficiently broad for monographic treatment in less skillful hands—into nineteen chapters divided into more than 170 two-to-three-page sections. Around these sections he places insightful career studies of merchants and planters which enliven his traditional analysis of the impersonal determinants of economic history—terrain, migrations, price fluctuations, and war.

This rigorous compartmentalization, which underlines differences rather than similarities among West Indian societies, helps lead the reader through great quantities of data, which are succinctly and lucidly illustrated by the text as well as by intelligible tables and fine outline figures and maps. The interpretation begins with very large but very basic issues—historiography, population growth and consumption patterns of tropical products in Great Britain, West Indian weather, settlement, and plantation politics—and proceeds to chapter-length studies of individual islands. There is a break midpoint in the study and a return to more general issues chiefly concerning trade and varieties of merchants, comparisons of London and the outports, and the role of the rum trade in the coming of the American Revolution. The last third of *Sugar and Slavery* is a chronological narrative concerning the relationship of business cycles and warfare to the inexorable growth, under "Hobbesian" conditions, of large-scale plantations, planter oligarchies, and monoculture. The central argument—that the Caribbean was a major impetus for British economic growth, and for an industrial revolution that came "from without inwards" (p. 475)—is unobtrusively infused with a sense of the tragic fate of this corner of humanity ensnared in "One of the truly vicious circles of economic history . . . in which slave-grown sugar yielded molasses, molasses yielded rum, and rum, in turn, served as currency for replenishing the plantations with forced labourers" (p. 344).

Professor Sheridan's sources are chiefly contemporary pamphlets, histories, and London Public Record Office documents (trade statistics and censuses as well as official correspondence). He has made much narrower use of the superior West Indian plantation records in English national and provincial archives, which are fuller than comparable mainland documents and contain diverse views of plantation life from the specialists in the rationalized chain of command—the town agents, attorneys, surgeons, resident managers, and occasionally overseers, bookkeepers and missionaries—that absenteeism required.

One of the few comparisons he makes in a hemispheric perspective is between "settlement" colonies (New England and the Middle Colonies) and "exploitation" colonies, all those from Maryland to Tobago (p. 448). But this distinction may be even more useful when limited to plantation societies. Mainland plantation colonies were organized by "settlers," who came with their families and usually lived among and directly supervised the slaves (which facilitated their acculturation); in contrast, the island colonies were organized by "exploiters," adventurers not settlers, who came into comparatively more dangerous disease and weather environments to make a quick fortune and to survive to spend their profits elsewhere as leisured absentees. Absenteeism in the West Indies often left slaves to take care of themselves and in doing so created a Creole culture more African in orientation than that in North America.

Judging West Indian colonies on their own terms, Professor Sheridan does not repeat the misleading views of Lowell Ragatz and more recent scholars who argue that British Caribbean societies were somehow incomplete and fragmented. Meanwhile, he corrects the Puritan and New England bias in much of the historiography of colonial North America by marshaling overwhelming data to demonstrate that plantation America was indeed the America British officials and entrepreneurs envisaged and that the major portion of English resources and expertise went to the colonies south of Delaware. The islands, particularly, repaid the English handsomely—nearly half of the official value of all colonial imports by about the middle of the eighteenth century came from the islands, which also accounted for nearly one-fourth of all exports to African, Eastern, and American markets.

Professor Sheridan's book, in providing an immensely informed, indispensable guide to the genesis and maturation of the most valuable colonies in the old British empire, should encourage scholars to look at mainland and island colonies comparatively.

California State University Sacramento — Gerald W. Mullin

Black Majority: Negroes in Colonial South Carolina from 1670 Through the Stono Rebellion. By Peter H. Wood. (New York: Alfred A. Knopf, 1974. Pp. xxiv, 346, viii. $10.00.)

This book is brilliant in conception, in execution, and in the use of methodologies that cross the disciplines. The author has proved that the inner life of those at the very bottom of society can be recovered if the historian is willing to assemble all the tools of the social sciences and then, after having been armed with the tools, examine every shred of literary evidence that remains. Thoroughness strengthened by patience is the fundamental demand, but a knowledge of medical science, statistics, and linguistics is almost equally imperative. This attempt to squeeze everything out of the facts is admirable, but at times zeal drives the author past common sense. Can one really evolve "cowboy" from the early black involvement in the control of cattle at the cowpens?

Everything has been done with style. The quotation from James Baldwin's *The Fire Next Time* etches for the reader a powerful opening mind-struct. The jacket-cover painting of a Negro by Géricault is handsome and intriguing (does the red jacket, often given to the faithful slave, indicate that this is the picture of a good slave or a bad slave?). The title makes the most powerful impact—*Black Majority.* By 1708 in South Carolina the blacks outnumbered the whites. This study is, therefore, of the most numerous part of the society, and one which the author insists made significant contributions. Black initiative was responsible for the form and success of the early cattle industry, the culture of rice, the building of a bridge between the languages, and even the outward thrust of the settlements. Blacks were pioneers too. Although Dr. Wood in a fundamental way has reformulated the questions that should be asked about the early history of black-white relations in Carolina, this reviewer doubts that sufficient proof has been presented by the author to buttress some of his findings. For example, did the blacks or the whites contribute most to the rice agricultural cycle? Dr. Wood explains that the blacks had been planting rice in West Africa: was not one section of that coast called the Rice Coast and another the Grain Coast! But has the author taken into consideration the numerous books on agriculture which were available to the English planter, books whose influence David L. Coon has set forth in his dissertation, "The Development of Market Agriculture in South Carolina, 1670–1785"? This reviewer might point out that rice was grown in the Po River valley of Italy for over two hundred years before the settlement of South Carolina. Thomas Jefferson certainly knew of this culture; perhaps the early English planters of South Carolina did also. This assumption and slight stretching of facts is certainly no greater than Dr. Wood's, in that he uses quotations from the years 1785, 1798, and 1840 to prove that Africans knew how to grow rice in 1700.

There are very few errors in this book. "David Ramsey" should have been spelled "David Ramsay." Some misunderstanding of the indigo process is expressed on page 75, where it is stated that the production of indigo "necessitated large amounts of water steeping in vats and stagnating behind dams." The last phrase is inexplicable. More alarming are the many uses of "may" and "might" at the points where the author is leaping to his generalizations. The take-off bases at these points must admittedly be weak and unsound.

The major theme is of growing black resistance which culminates in the Stono Rebellion of 1739. Here lies the one central weakness of this great book. Patterns of black resistance are lifted from the school of Kenneth Stampp (see note on page 288), and thus the basic assumption is that blacks in slavery were always saboteurs. This book is therefore a product of the historical stance of the 1960s. One would like to ask Dr. Wood how does one get from his book to that of Fogel and Engerman's *Time on the*

Cross. If Dr. Wood is correct, it could only have been accomplished by white repression after the establishment of the slave code of 1740. But a surer answer might be revealed after more probing of the role of religion and of the family and even of the work ethic—of the mutuality of the races rather than of the separateness. Then this work would be a volume of the 1970s and perhaps nearer the truth.

University of South Carolina GEORGE C. ROGERS, JR.

North Carolina Higher-Court Records, 1702–1708. Edited by William S. Price, Jr. *The Colonial Records of North Carolina*. [Second Series], Volume IV. (Raleigh: Department of Archives and History, 1974. Pp. xl, 533. $16.00.)

This volume, the fourth in the *Colonial Records of North Carolina*, is labeled Second Series in order to distinguish it from those edited by William L. Saunders in the past century. The contents come chiefly from the records of the General Court; records from the Court of Chancery constitute less than 10 percent of the volume, and the miscellaneous items fill only thirteen pages. The seat of government from 1702 to 1708 was the home of Dr. John Hecklefield, sometime captain and high sheriff, at Little River on the border between Pasquotank and Perquimans precincts. Hecklefield figured prominently in the litigation recorded in this volume, especially cases connected with debts.

These records reflect many phases of economic life in early North Carolina. Tobacco appears to have been an insignificant product. Hides and furs, primarily those of deer but also those of other animals, were important. Pork and corn, of course, retained a commanding position, but tar does not appear to have been very significant. Trade, however, began to assume considerable importance especially with the West Indies, New England, and England. Most notable of the traders was the New Pennsylvania Company, represented often by Micajah Perry, a London merchant whose numerous suits involved debts of cash and pork.

Other phases of colonial life are clearly delineated. The headright system of fifty acres per individual flourished, including fifty acres for reentry into the province, as, for instance William Maund, Sr., who "Imported himsilf four times in this province . . ." (p. 473). Indentured servants are also referred to frequently; the outstanding case concerns Margret Barrit [*sic*] from Ireland, who was sold first to William Richardson by the mate of the vessel transporting her, then to John Bennet, who sold her to Bengiman Tulle [*sic*] of Currituck on July 13, 1699. On April 27, 1701, she petitioned for her freedom and obtained it despite the specious reasoning of John Bennet. There is no evidence in this volume that the "order Granted by the . . . Court of Corrowtuck to free the aforesaide Servant Girle . . ." (p. 462) was ever rescinded. Then there was Susannah Evans, who was accused of "Diabolically and malitiously" (p. 65) bewitching Deborah Bourshier, and Martha Richardson accused of the same offense against William Parker. Both were cleared. Perhaps the women's liberation movement stirred in the mind of Winifrid Morris when she was given her choice of "Twenty one Stripes on her bare Back" or a fine of fifty shillings with costs "for haveing a Basterd Child" (p. 334).

Despite these old practices and the different world revealed in this volume, the struggle for property and position is very modern and up to date. Nothing could be clearer in this respect than the predilection of the notables of the day to marry wealthy widows. Annaritta Butler [*sic*] sought in a different manner to achieve distinction—by making a legal agreement with Daniel Leigh to teach her son "to read write and Cast Accompt to the end of the rule of Divesion" (p. 77). She sued Leigh when he failed to fulfill the agreement.

Though necessarily routine in nature these records are very human. They also reveal much concerning the development of colonial government and its connection with the mother country. The volume is well-nigh perfectly edited, and only the index may be mildly questioned.

Commerce, Texas NANNIE M. TILLEY

This Sheba, Self: The Conceptualization of Economic Life in Eighteenth-Century America. By J. E. Crowley. *The Johns Hopkins University Studies in Historical and Political Science.* Series XCII, No. 2. (Baltimore and London: Johns Hopkins University Press, c. 1974. Pp. xiv, 161. $8.50.)

This book deals with the intellectual and rational aspects of the evolution of a meaningful commercial life in eighteenth-century America. Writing in only the broadest terms and shunning traditional historical approaches, Crowley is uncompromisingly abstract, and, in fact, the book seems at times more a philosophical treatise than anything else.

The concentration in *This Sheba* is upon the Americans' public attitudes and expressions toward work, with particular emphasis upon the moral problem "concerning the relationship between the self and society" (p. 2). It is the task of the author to show how these values altered and shifted in the eighteenth century and to demonstrate the ambivalence in American thinking in these areas prior to, during, and even after the American Revolution.

Crowley addresses, as the heart of the matter, the separation of work from moral and community overtones to the final triumphant idea of the exploitative, amoral features characterized by more recent notions of the American economy. He has dealt, in other words, with the secularization of American economic life and thought. To Crowley, by the time of the Revolution we had developed a "market society" with strong implications for both the social and economic order. By 1770 idleness, as an example, once thought a sin against one's neighbor and community, had become simply a vice.

All of this is heady stuff and a tall order for a short book—a drawback of which no one is more keenly aware than Crowley himself. It would be quite unfair to expect the author to "prove" his contentions in the strict sense. What he does best is to present hypotheses that might offer guides to future study for the young historian interested in the evolution of colonial economic ideas and self-awareness.

It is particularly gratifying to see the author make use of what might well be the most overlooked sources for a full history of the southern colonies in the eighteenth century: the sermons delivered before the trustees of the colony of Georgia at their annual meetings in London. By closely limiting the options of the settlers the trustees did all in their power to prevent the nasty drift toward "the isolation of man as an economic being" (p. 20), and the defense of the trust's ideas is found in these long-neglected anniversary addresses.

The Georgia experiment, handled in considerable detail by Crowley, had social importance in that it dealt intimately with the structure of society as well as with the structure of the economy. What Crowley calls "the social vision" of the trustees was intended to fit in neatly and compactly with the other aspects of the Georgia scheme. His interpretation of what Georgia's leaders were about, though silent on the role of Oglethorpe, the most prominent trustee, acts as something of a corrective to the glib generalities of Daniel Boorstin. Though the informed reader might express some surprise at three citation errors to authors in back-to-back footnotes and to other slips and oversights, it may well be that the overall interpretation of the rise and decline of the colony is sound. Crowley seems more at sea concerning other southern colonies: North Carolina is viewed as Lubberland; Virginia suffers from an intellectual inferiority complex owing to her lack of commercial development; the thinking of the Charles Town mercantile elite is nowhere systematically addressed.

Crowley is more at home in the middle and northeastern colonies where he makes good use of the ideas of such persons as Benjamin Franklin and John Danforth. It is from the latter's fiery 1704 sermon that the author draws his intriguing title.

Crowley has attempted a book of the first importance. He does not quite pull it off. Still, he has set his goals high and has presented his reader with ideas that will be helpful in these busy days of the bicentennial as we try to determine what we are and how we got that way.

University of Georgia PHINIZY SPALDING

From Colony to Country: The Revolution in American Thought, 1750–1820. By Ralph Ketcham. (New York: Macmillan Publishing Co.; London: Collier Macmillan Publishers, 1974. Pp. xiv, 318. $9.95.)

From Colony to Country celebrates the American Revolutionary epoch which stretches from the Stamp Act to early nationhood and across the lifetimes of a couple of dozen leaders whose ideas Ralph Ketcham uses to tell his story. Conceived in the foreglow of the bicentennial, the book exudes a warm, Whiggish affirmation of the gestation period of American self-government. The explanation for change is the familiar one of "novelty, improvisation, and unexpected possibilities" (p. 34), and American developments are contrasted with a depiction of England's common people as "still semifeudal, primevally silent" (p. 8).

If there is a thesis to the book, it is that a search for a unique national identity accompanied the birth pangs of the American nation and stimulated a public discussion which shaped future values. Although this is a topic in intellectual history, there is no serious engagement with ideas or their relation to the social context. References to current scholarship on the period provide ornamentation rather than an occasion for analysis. The result is a succession of unexamined cerebral vignettes. Professor Ketcham's conclusions about the transformation of Britain's North American colonies into a constitutional republic appear to be that every group contributed to the process. Of the antagonists in the Great Awakening he says, "both sides of the religious debate lent substantial support to the movement for independence and nationhood . . ." (p. 50). Comparing Ezra Stiles and Thomas Jefferson, he finds that "The Puritan educator and the Enlightenment statesman were kindred spirits, impelled by their common citizenship in a new nation to find enlarged meaning in patterns of thought and receptive to the idea that men and society could be transformed" (p. 182). Similarly, events preparatory to the Revolution pointed in the same direction: "Every threat of arbitrariness, from the suppression of Leisler's Rebellion and Zenger's trial to the Parson's Cause and the Coercive Acts, found colonials echoing, elaborating, and then extending the doctrines of Algernon Sidney, Trenchard and Gordon, Benjamin Hoadly, and Joseph Priestley" (p. 74). Professor Ketcham does not ignore dissenting opinions, but their influence is consistently homogenized into a constructive force. The book gives ample evidence of Professor Ketcham's familiarity with eighteenth-century sources, the writing is excellent, and all one's favorite quotations are included.

San Diego State University JOYCE O. APPLEBY

Tennessee: The Dangerous Example, Watauga to 1849. By Mary French Caldwell. (Nashville and London: Aurora Publishers, c. 1974. Pp. xvi, 384. $11.95.)

Written in a colorful and enthusiastic style by an author of several books on Tennessee topics, this work is a collection of accounts of various incidents associated with the early history of the area. The author, inspired by the forthcoming bicentennial observance, has drawn from a variety of sources to compile a uniformly admiring chronicle of leaders in the development of the Volunteer State tradition. While the account does not follow a consistent theme throughout, it is generally chronological in its selection of topics and does give a vivid picture of the development of Tennessee from frontier to statehood. After following the usual outline of Tennessee history through its first years the book gives considerable space to Andrew Jackson and concludes with a collection of sketches of "Heroes in the Winning of the West," all of whom had at least a marginal connection with Tennessee.

Most of the deficiencies in this book are related to the sources used in its writing. Recent scholarly studies were generally neglected in favor of selected older accounts, many of which are highly partisan. The author's selection often results in the reader's getting a one-sided view of the controversial events she describes. But this procedure is not uniformly followed. For example, the pivotal rivalry between Andrew Jackson and John Sevier is glossed over so that they appear as separate heroes rather than opposing political leaders motivated by a divisive hatred.

There are some historical errors in the text, such as the dates of the last Indian attacks on Knoxville (pp. 206–207) and of the appearance of the Whig party (p. 322), but the most obvious deficiency of the work is not historical scholarship but its treatment of the Indians. If the information presented in this bicentennial book does constitute the complete and true account of them, they were indeed bloodthirsty savages who deserved the death and deportation they received from white Tennesseans.

Despite the shortcomings which some professional historians will find, this book is a well-written version of early Tennessee history that will provide interesting reading for an audience unacquainted with more scholarly studies. Furthermore, since this account includes material which is not available in any other single source, it deserves a place in the bibliography of Tennessee history.

Memphis State University CHARLES W. CRAWFORD

In the Common Cause: American Response to the Coercive Acts of 1774. By David Ammerman. (Charlottesville: University Press of Virginia, 1974. Pp. xiv, 170. $9.75.)

History has occasionally been described as the tricks that the living play on the dead. In this intensive study of the First Continental Congress, David Ammerman claims to have unearthed two very noteworthy tricksters who successfully reversed this process—Joseph Galloway and John Adams. At first glance they appear to be most unlikely choices. Over the years countless historians have relied on the writings of both men in their quest for the causes of the Revolution. This is precisely the point. The author contends that Galloway purposely and Adams inadvertently conveyed the mistaken impression that the First Congress was marked by divisiveness rather than unity. As a result, most historians have come to designate April 19, 1775, as the beginning of the countdown to the Revolution.

Ammerman's thesis is that the real seedbed of the Revolution lies in the formulation of the American response to the Coercive Acts between May 1774 and April 1775. Since there was scarcely a colonial grievance that these acts did not somehow inflame, they served to arouse widespread popular opposition to Britain and undermined the position of those who were sympathetic to the mother country. As a consequence, the First Continental Congress was able to commit the colonies to an equally firm response. When Britain countered with force at Lexington and Concord it was too late for the colonists to turn back.

The author seeks to substantiate his conclusion that the First Congress was "the high-water mark of American consensus" (p. 101) by examining the infrastructure of the resistance movement. He argues convincingly that it was the provincial committees of correspondence, which by 1774 had been established in eleven of the colonies, that were instrumental in spearheading the movement for an intercolonial congress. The hundreds of inspection committees that were established to enforce the Continental Association in the winter of 1774–1775 added thousands of men to the web of resistance.

Although there is much that is praiseworthy in this work, the thesis is deficient in several respects. In the first place, one cannot forecast the onset of the Revolution from the vantage point of April 1775 without distorting all that transpired in the ensuing fourteen months. The die may well have been cast in Britain by the fall of 1774, as Ammerman contends, but the achievement of consensus among the thirteen colonies was a more time-consuming and delicate task. Most of the delegates to the Second Continental Congress knew all too well that a hasty decision to secede from the empire could abort the entire revolution. It was only by means of skillful manipulation and patient prodding that the Middle Colonies were finally convinced to give up their stubborn hope of peaceful reconciliation and accept independence.

The author also overestimates the extent of colonial unity during the winter of 1774–1775. He does this by making light of the attempts by conservative Whigs and Tories in New York and elsewhere to disassociate their colonies from the program of the First Continental Congress and by ignoring the significant pamphlet campaign launched by Anglican clergymen like Samuel Seabury and Thomas Chandler.

Despite these interpretive shortcomings, this is an important book. The real contribution that this well-researched and highly readable volume makes to Revolutionary scholarship is in the fresh insights that it offers on the First Continental Congress and the infrastructure of the early resistance movement.

Carthage College JOHN A. NEUENSCHWANDER

Southern Indians in the American Revolution. By James H. O'Donnell, III. (Knoxville: University of Tennessee Press, c. 1973. Pp. xiv, 171. $8.50.)

Prior to the American Revolution Indian relationships with whites largely consisted of coping with various European threats and encroachments. Occasionally the foreign powers made war on each other, and usually Indians allied with one or another country while trying to keep from being caught in the middle. But the American Revolution presented quite another situation. The most vigorous antagonists here were land-seeking Americans, whose savage onslaughts into Indian villages were nearly always followed by treaty parties intent on turning battlegrounds into farmlands. In the crisis of the American Revolution southern Indians turned largely to European allies, mostly British, and made valiant efforts to stop slaughter and land absorption but in the end fell back before victorious Americans.

The Revolutionary era experiences of the four major tribes of southern Indians, heretofore largely unavailable in a unified detailed presentation except to the hardy researcher, is now ready for the bookshelves of general readers and historians alike in James H. O'Donnell's *Southern Indians in the American Revolution*. Clear writing based upon meticulous research and sound judgments characterize a much-needed book.

During 1775 newly formed American agencies attempted to establish peaceful relations with southern Indians and at the same time to negate similar and more experienced British efforts. Both impulses failed. Few Indians trusted American professions of friendship, and they did not support the British policy of amity and limited military opportunity. English superintendent John Stuart moved late in 1775 and early 1776 to ally Creeks and Cherokees against frontiersmen. The latter tribe responded, and the resulting Cherokee War of 1776 was one of the most disastrous for Indians in the total history of Indian-white relations. Delays and lack of coordination prevented early implementation of Stuart's plan. Cherokees took the initiative in June 1776 in a three-pronged effort against Watauga-Nolichucky folk, Holston–Carter's Valley people, and settlers in Georgia and the Carolinas. The Carolina frontiersmen felt red terror in June and July; attacks on the mountaineers in July were less severe only because forewarned people forted up in time. South Carolina was first to retaliate; a ten-day sweep destroyed numerous towns on the border. North Carolinians and Virginians organized too, and by September a three-part campaign was launched into the Indian country with devastating results. Forces from Virginia, North Carolina, and South Carolina left ashes and rubble in their paths. British efforts to enlist Creek aid for the Cherokees failed, and save for hold-out Cherokees under Dragging Canoe, who withdrew into the Chickamauga area, one tribal faction after another surrendered both tomahawks and lands—and memories of the bitter defeats affected the Cherokees and other tribes' will to fight Americans throughout the remainder of the war.

The years 1777 and 1778 were periods of treaty making and comparative peace, with inevitable losses of land and little gains for Cherokees. In 1779 British agents had some success organizing Creeks against Americans; some groups dissolved against impending Patriot action, but many were used in coastal raiding and scouting. The death of British superintendent of Indian affairs John Stuart made coordination of Indian military assistance extremely difficult, despite efforts of deputies Alexander Cameron and Charles Stuart. Despite some successes in obtaining aid from Cherokees and Creeks, the deputies were harassed by a sudden and substantial reduction in their budgets and by a stepped-up activity on the part of the Spanish, now openly in the war. Mobile fell, but assistance from a thousand Creeks helped save Pensacola. Late in 1780 and again in 1781 emboldened but misguided Cherokees moved against frontier settlements, but again and again Patriot and militia forces administered punishing retaliation. Valiant Choctaw action against Spanish forces was blunted by British indecision and vacillation. Finally, Pensacola was lost, and British efforts among southern Indians shifted eastward. American successes at Augusta and other points offered little hope of Indian-British alliances, and an uneasy era of tentative peace interspersed with continuing raids ensued. Cherokees and Chickasaws sought peace with the victorious Americans, though many of the latter still distrusted red men. Creeks aligned with Spaniards for the most part, and Choctaws wavered.

Professor O'Donnell's study encompasses a complex period of red-white relations. In places the very complexity of the subject is almost a quicksand for the reader, but such occasional miring is more than offset by exceptionally helpful chapter-end summaries of essential trends and developments.

Georgia State University HENRY T. MALONE

The New Country: A Social History of the American Frontier, 1776–1890. By Richard A. Bartlett. (New York: Oxford University Press, 1974. Pp. viii, 487. $15.95.)

With this book, Bartlett has achieved an exciting and rewarding new synthesis of frontier history. As the subtitle indicates, the emphasis is on social history. Topics of most concern are those reflecting basic needs and activities of frontiersmen. Thus, emphasis bypasses badmen and recreation to fall on social and ethnic characteristics of those peopling the unsettled wilderness; their work, which was largely agricultural; the exploitative effects of this work; and the means by which they reached "the new country." This synthesis rests upon a sure command of a vast field of secondary literature and reflects Bartlett's immense knowledge of the subject. Although his purpose is never to entertain with anecdotes from his abundant store, he presents in logical context some fascinating tidbits. For instance, how many specialists in southern history know that the Jew Abram Mordecai founded Montgomery, Alabama, in 1785 or that the Serb Djordje Šagić (as George Fisher) was not Houston's first mayor (as Bartlett incorrectly states) but was an early justice of the peace and alderman there?

Appropriately, pictures and maps accompanying this fresh approach to frontier history reflect the author's purpose. He not only selected them with great care so that they document his text and advance the argument, but he also uses his own photographs to ensure that they reinforce the narrative. Credit lines for photographs, prints, and maps show that the author conducted this research as carefully and extensively as that for the text. He provides pictures that relate specifically to the time and place of the narrative. The result is a satisfying integration that transforms the pictorials into documentation, lifting them out of the category of mere illustration. The publisher must be thanked for the pictures' fine reproduction and for printing them at logical places in the text.

In breaking away from the traditional treatment of frontier history, Bartlett offers insights on a wide variety of topics. His examination of the role of land speculators highlights their contributions to frontier development, presenting them in a more favorable light than usual. The mechanics of actually surveying public lands, as provided by the Ordinance of 1785, are explained in graphic terms. Bartlett assumes correctly that most readers of American history have no personal acquaintance with farm implements, so describes just how they worked. The book is especially strong in dealing with the empirical aspect of frontier agriculture. Only through trial and error could farmers in the new country determine how best to raise crops, for the procedures followed "back home" often proved unreliable. Farming on the frontier depended on animals, and Bartlett's explanation of the genetics of mule breeding and the relative merit and expense of oxen versus horses is informative and convincing. Similarly, after reading his description of building a sod house, one feels that he could undertake that task.

Because of the topical organization, some repetition and confusion exists. In the urban chapter, for example, considerable shuttling back and forth from one part of the frontier to another leaves little sense of organic development. Here Bartlett deals with Memphis and Vicksburg long after the frontier had passed from Dixie. There should be no confusion about the intended audience: the general reader. With the book's sophisticated concepts of organization and approach, its rewarding details, and its vivid and imaginative writing, it supersedes other social histories of the frontier.

University of Maryland WALTER RUNDELL, JR.

The Papers of Thomas Jefferson. Volume 19: *24 January to 31 March 1791*. Edited by Julian P. Boyd and Ruth W. Lester. (Princeton: Princeton University Press, 1974. Pp. xxxvi, 646. $22.50.)

Boyd covers nine weeks more here, a further reminder that this edition of Jefferson's papers, like the great cathedrals, may take centuries to complete. Once again the editorial notes, numbering eleven, make up a book within a book, running in combination to about 287 pages. Such essays as "Consular Problems," "The Judicial Appointment of Joseph Anderson," and "Experiments in Desalination of Sea Water" are conventional, if generous and stylish, headnotes to groups of related documents. The rest, however, are more chapters in Boyd's remarkable history of the United States under President Washington.

In "Locating the Federal District" Boyd adds new proof for the existence of a bargain between northeastern financial interests and the congressmen who represented Potomac districts of Maryland and Virginia.

He also advances a strong circumstantial case that George Washington deceived the citizens of the upper Potomac by pretending to consider several of their towns as sites for the federal district after he had really determined on a location which included his own favorite town of Alexandria—and that not so much for his own personal interest as to win over the antifederalist George Mason to the side of the new government by an appeal to *his* personal interest. "Death of Franklin: The Politics of Mourning in France and the United States" is still more original. With the essays on commerce and the fisheries in this volume and the essay on tonnage duties in Volume 18, this proves a clear division in the United States government between pro-French and pro-British factions during the First Congress.

Finally, in "Threat of Disunion in the West" Boyd resumes the theme of corruption in the Treasury, noting that Alexander Hamilton and Henry Knox arranged for the archspeculator William Duer to have the contracts for supplying Arthur St. Clair's army in the Northwest Territory. Then, while Knox and Duer should have been working on getting supplies to Ohio, they were in fact engaged in a gigantic land speculation in Maine, no doubt aided by the public money they had secured. Thus, speculation in the East was tied to the weakness and temporary failure of the federal government in the West. Kentucky grumbled and strained against its fragile tie to the Union, not because the leaders were agents of Spain but because the free planters desired an honest and effective government rather than subjection to a corrupt faction.

By means of private letters and public proclamations, Jefferson and Madison reassured the Kentuckians, who, in spite of St. Clair's defeat, remained in the Union. Jefferson's most decisive action was to secure the approval of Washington for a new policy toward Spain: rather than drift along with the accommodating temper John Jay had maintained with Diego de Gardoqui, the United States would now insist on its right to the free navigation of the Mississippi. Jefferson also acted to secure better overseas markets for American goods. He sent notes to Paris, Madrid, and Lisbon, informing our agents that the Second Congress could be counted on to pass a navigation act against the British and that the United States would welcome the cooperation of France, Spain, and Portugal in opening a new era of free trade in the Atlantic.

While Boyd agrees on the nature of certain episodes with the treatment given them in Dumas Malone's *Jefferson and the Rights of Man*, the overall views of the two deans of Jeffersonian history are strikingly different. Malone observes the continuity of Jefferson's thought and actions with his behavior in the 1780s and emphasizes how gradually and reluctantly Jefferson entered into partisan domestic politics while attempting to remain true to his principles. Boyd has created, here and in the book-length notes of Volumes 17 and 18, a forceful picture of ideals and interests ruthlessly pursued and irreconcilably opposed. In doing so Boyd falls into a familiar trap: he sees little but sordid avarice for money and power among the Hamiltonians and almost nothing but love of human liberty among those friends of Jefferson who were leading the westward movement. Yet Jefferson's friends in Kentucky carried the state and the region for slavery and were in a great hurry to relieve the Indians of their land. If the politics of proto-Federalists were tinged with corruption, so were those of proto–Democratic Republicans. Boyd's Claude Bowers–like Manichaeism is simply unacceptable. His ingenuity in uncovering significant new facts about this period, on the other hand, is amazing.

University of Illinois Urbana-Champaign ROBERT M. MCCOLLEY

And They All Sang Hallelujah: Plain-Folk Camp-Meeting Religion, 1800–1845. By Dickson D. Bruce, Jr. (Knoxville: University of Tennessee Press, c. 1974. Pp. xii, 155. $7.50.)

This brief book (136 pages of text) based entirely upon printed sources is, according to its dust jacket, a "challenging reinterpretation" of camp-meeting religion. Using the concepts of anthropology and folklore, Bruce examines the religious ideas and practices of plain folk on the southern frontier. His first two chapters summarize a handful of standard books to sketch the nature of southern society and to emphasize that the Baptists, Methodists, and Presbyterians were the denominations favored by the plain folk. Because the Baptists and Methodists were especially adept at adjusting to the needs of frontier society and prospered mightily, their denominations are labeled folk religions. In his third chapter Bruce discusses camp meetings, suggesting that their structure was analogous both to the divisions of southern society and the morphology of the conversion experiences spelled out in ministerial memoirs. Chapter Four is devoted to an analysis of spiritual choruses sung at revivals, supposedly to reveal what their religion really meant to camp-meeting participants. The final chapter summarizes the functions such religion served for the plain folk of the Old South: it offered an alternative to the secular world, offered a spiritual community, and offered hope for a better world to come. Other historians have, of course, described such functions as the result of the pietistic faith of the yeomen.

This book was the first winner of the James Mooney Award sponsored by the Southern Anthropological Society, so perhaps it is primarily intended for that audience. Certainly, those familiar with southern religious history will find little that is new. Description and labeling, though useful, hardly make for reinterpretation. The concept of folk religion was developed for, and is most applicable to, popular European religious practices. The attempt to fit the southern evangelicals into this kind of model, rather than showing the particular historical evolution of southern religion, distorts the story. Similarly, most will be disenchanted by Bruce's ahistorical analysis. He seizes upon the highly organized, more sedate, and carefully structured camp meetings à la B. W. Gorham's *Camp Meeting Manual* (1854) and then applies this structural model to his discussion of even the earliest camp meetings of 1800 and 1801. He chooses quotations from any point on the time spectrum at will, as though folk religion was frozen in time. Moreover, his almost complete reliance on printed, stylized hymn choruses to discover the beliefs of the revival participants is a needless self-restriction and results in misinterpretation. Manuscript sermons, diaries, memoirs, correspondence, church records, and hymns are available in southern repositories, and they greatly expand our understanding of what the plain folk believed. The author belabors the obvious on one hand, and on the other extracts elaborate interpretations that the evidence, it seems to me, simply will not bear. Social-science jargon mars the prose. Had this book been compressed into an article, its conclusions would have appeared less pretentious.

Towson State College JOHN B. BOLES

The Emancipation of Angelina Grimké. By Katharine Du Pre Lumpkin. (Chapel Hill: University of North Carolina Press, c. 1974. Pp. xvi, 265. $11.95.)

Central to the life of Angelina Grimké, Charleston-born gentlewoman whose religious dissent and abolitionism drove her from family, section, and creature comforts to the peripatetic life of an antislavery lecturer, is an inherently fascinating riddle. Why, if moral conviction and personal pride inspired her to address huge and occasionally hostile audiences, did she after only four years disappear almost completely from reform activity?

In *The Grimké Sisters from South Carolina* (1967) Gerda Lerner analyzed both sisters from the premise that rational judgments led them to reform careers and that external forces pushed them back to private existence. In short, after Angelina's 1838 marriage to Theodore D. Weld, they were trapped in domestic servitude to home and children just when antislavery infighting over feminism and political and religious action isolated them from the movement's mainstreams.

By contrast Professor Lumpkin's biography stresses emotions. In explaining Angelina's transition from proper Carolina girlhood to Quakerism and abolitionism the author emphasizes experiences similar to those of her own adolescent awakening: the struggle against an elitist family's false norms (*The Making of a Southerner,* pp. 99–108) and the shock of observing Negroes being whipped (pp. 127–37). Thus, the first section of *The Emancipation of Angelina Grimké* attributes Grimké's career to a revolt against family and regional values. Yet Anne Firor Scott's *Southern Lady* contends that many southern women bitterly criticized slavery, and the Grimké family was known for unusual social awareness. Angelina's distinguished brother Thomas supported temperance, peace, legal codification, manual labor schools, and religious instruction for blacks in the 1820s and 1830s. Similarly, Grimké women sustained the Ladies Benevolent Society, succoring Charleston's sick poor. Indeed one might argue that Angelina extended family practice as much as she revolted against it.

Lumpkin's description of Angelina's lecture career, although marred by research overly restricted to the Grimkés' letters and papers, nonetheless covers acceptably the central phase of her public life. By contrast the analysis of Angelina's married life is new. Like Lerner, Lumpkin explores Angelina's resentment of her older sister's maternal role in the Weld household. But Lumpkin probes that distress further to conclude that the first fifteen years of the Welds' marriage was blasted by Theodore's tormented personality and his inability to accept equality of the sexes in his own home.

It was not until 1854, when the Welds moved to the Raritan Bay Community and ran its Eagleswood School, that Angelina again came into her own. There family life gave way to communal existence; Angelina found in teaching the career she had contemplated in her youth, and sister Sarah ceased to threaten lives relieved of traditional family roles. The community's dissolution and the Welds' consequent move to Massachusetts failed to reimprison Angelina, for she maintained her independence by teaching.

Essentially then, as Lumpkin sees it, Angelina Grimké Weld's emancipation was from the restraints of family life—whether from her mother's Charleston mores or her sister's and husband's jealous domination. Abstract ideals of right and justice molded her reform actions from youthful denunciation of slavery to mature familial acceptance of her brother Henry's gifted black children. But her own personal fulfillment came in escaping woman's traditional role. *The Emancipation of Angelina Grimké* is biography developed on a rather traditional psychological framework. It contributes to the history of feminism, but it will not replace Lerner's work either as antislavery history or as biography.

University of Maine, Orono JANE H. PEASE

History of the Supreme Court of the United States. Volume V: *The Taney Period, 1836–64.* By Carl B. Swisher. *The Oliver Wendell Holmes Devise.* (New York: Macmillan Publishing Co.; London: Collier-Macmillan Publishers, 1974. Pp. xx, 1041. $30.00.)

This is an encyclopedic study of the Supreme Court in the Taney years. Swisher does not limit himself to a discussion of major constitutional decisions. He describes the capabilities of court clerks, the merits of reporters, the difficulties of finding suitable lodging in the Washington of the Civil War years, Justice Taney's favorite cigars, Justice Davis's arrangement with his wife as to how much liquor he could consume while away from home, congressional debates (fruitful and otherwise) concerning changing the circuits which the justices were required to ride, and the political experiences and inclinations of successful and unsuccessful nominees to the Court. All of this surfaces among the usually clear and revealing discussions of every major constitutional issue of the years 1836–1864. No one who wishes to understand the history of the Court in these years can afford to ignore this work, even if he cannot afford to buy it.

Of course, in 975 pages any reviewer is likely to find things to quarrel with, and in this book some flaws are important. Swisher's reading of secondary materials seems to have stopped before Arthur Bestor, Harold Hyman, Alfred Kelly, and Stanley Kutler began publishing. His failure to read Stanley Kutler's work on the Supreme Court in the Reconstruction period and on the Charles River Bridge case is especially unfortunate. Swisher seems unaware of the possibility suggested by Kutler that John Marshall might have agreed with the bridge decision on the basis of *Providence Bank* v. *Billings* instead of opposing it as Swisher suggests. He also adopts the view that the Dred Scott decision severely weakened the Court as an institution. Kutler could have helped Swisher distinguish between hostility to the Taney Court and hostility to the Court itself and its necessary role in society. Work by Hyman and Kelly would supply a necessary antidote to Swisher's contrast of the respect for law by the Court versus the concessions to military necessity by Congress and the President during the Civil War.

The entire book might have had a more complete perspective had Swisher incorporated the work of all these writers plus the efforts of Arthur Bestor in assessing the meaning of the opposition to judicial decisions. Although noting the force of Curtis's dissent in the Dred Scott case, the author still views opposition to this decision and to Taney's other proslavery opinions as abolitionist-inspired. He fails to understand the large spectrum of opinions which gathered in opposition to the Court's protection of slavery. This stark dichotomy reinforces Swisher's image of the forces of law and order on one side and the antilaw forces on the other. The obvious extension of this viewpoint is a step toward the disdain for nonlawyer democrats which, as Morton Horwitz has pointed out, pervades most of the historiography of the court in the pre–Civil War era. That Swisher shares this viewpoint is suggested by his description of debtor-creditor cases of the 1830s and 1840s in terms which make the Court into the "bulwark of order" because it supported creditors consistently.

Although Swisher views the Dred Scott decision as a disaster, thus implicitly recognizing that bad law may contribute to disorder, he seems to believe that law and order are in the vast majority of cases interchangeable terms. He laments any decline in the respect for the Court as a weakening of order. In a society so vitally concerned with law and legal institutions such may be the case, but we should first analyze more carefully than Swisher does the validity of the equation. After all, to paraphrase Justice Stone, courts are not the only institutions which should be presumed to have the capacity to govern.

Still, this book's biases hardly diminish its merit. On the contrary, Swisher's successes vastly exceed his failures. When he describes the major problems faced by Taney's Court in the prewar years his efforts are almost uniformly excellent. He has provided for all students of the Supreme Court an invaluable book. A sign of its great worth is that it triumphs over its assumptions.

University of Kansas PHILLIP S. PALUDAN

The Mexican War, 1846–1848. By K. Jack Bauer. (New York: Macmillan Publishing Co.; London: Collier Macmillan Publishers, 1974. Pp. xxii, 454. $14.95.)

Book review editors, I am sure, take great and sometimes malicious delight in sending a book to a person who has recently published on the same subject. And in this case, my work (with Odie Faulk) was misreviewed in another journal by Professor Bauer. But there will be presented here no attack and little criticism of Bauer's fine work.

This book deserves kudos in almost every area. It is thoroughly researched, skillfully written, well organized (with some understandable exceptions), and handsomely printed. The maps and illustrations are excellent; the index, relatively complete, and the bibliography, acceptable. (I noticed that a flagrant error in my bibliography managed to repeat itself in Bauer's.) Furthermore, with its approximately 180,000 words of text, it is the fullest treatment of the war to be published in many years. The great strength of the book is the detailed analysis of the military actions. In particular, the role of the navy in the war is skillfully analyzed. The treatment of Commodore Conner is balanced, and the handling of Stockton is sound. Bauer in a deft sentence disposes of the paranoid prewar "Polk-Stockton conspiracy."

He is equally judicious in his handling of the jealousies that ran rampant through the military corps during the war. Polk's political fears of his generals are explained well. Taylor's quarrel over support is temperately treated. Scott's occasional petulance is not allowed to detract from his genuine ability as a military leader. Pillow's court-martial is objectively handled. Bauer does not take sides in any of these controversies, but he does skirt around a few issues, such as the controversial actions of the Texas Rangers and the San Patricio battalion, which curiously is not listed in the index, although it is mentioned numerous times.

What Bauer does do and do exceedingly well is describe the military campaigns. Strategy is analyzed, and tactics are clearly explained. If he did not personally view all of the various battlefields, he must have examined topographic maps in detail. Among numerous fine examples of military chronicling, I would single out the Battle of Buena Vista, pages 209–18, and the capture of Chapultepec, pages 313–21. In this account the poor *niños* of Chapultepec are given but two sentences—a space appropriate for the part they played in the battle, perhaps, but not for their role in the Mexican heritage of the war. But this does point up an understandable aspect of the book. The campaigns are treated almost exclusively from the point of view of American strategy and tactics.

The book's major weakness is its treatment of politics and diplomacy both before and during the war. The delineation of the problem of Mexican politics is particularly skimpy. It is vague on the important Federalist-Centralist dichotomy in Mexico; it misses the intensity of Paredes's violent anti-Americanism; it fails to cover the opposition to the war in Mexico, especially by the Federalists. Above all, in spite of the book's general objectivity, it seems to accept the now exhausted and discredited interpretation that Polk's ineptness and/or greedy designs forced Mexico into the war. On this issue, my point of view is so diametrically opposite that it would be both inappropriate and futile to comment. One point, however, might be allowed. Contrary to the generally and erroneously accepted position, which Professor Bauer adopts, there was no controversy between the United States and Mexico over the Nueces River. Mexico consistently and unremittingly claimed all of Texas to the Sabine. Mexico did not dispute the territory between the Rio Grande and the Nueces—she disputed the annexation of Texas, which Centralist leaders considered an act of war by the United States. Yet Bauer follows countless other less informed historians to state unequivocally that the war was a "conflict with Mexico over the delineation of the common boundary" (p. xix).

Texas Tech University SEYMOUR V. CONNOR

The Memoirs of Henry Heth. Edited by James L. Morrison, Jr. *Contributions in Military History,* No. 6. (Westport, Conn., and London: Greenwood Press, 1974. Pp. lxxviii, 303. $13.95.)

A critic comparing this book's substantial introduction with Heth's sometimes inconsequential memoirs might wish that Professor Morrison had chosen to be a biographer rather than an editor. His illuminating sketch of Heth is critical and scholarly—as indeed are his notes to the memoirs. He has also supplied useful illustrations, an index, and one map (another of Virginia is needed). Yet he has lavished his editorial efforts on a manuscript that is disappointing in its coverage of the part of Heth's life likely to interest most readers. Heth's role as a Confederate major general was his principal claim to the attention of students of history, but his reminiscences of the Civil War years are relatively brief, episodic, and occasionally confused. Except for the portion on his relatively obscure campaigns in West Virginia, they offer few novelties. They are, however, refreshing in their acknowledgment of their author's military failures—his "signal disaster" (p. 164) and "awful blunder" (p. 185). One reaction to them is wonderment as to how many able officers lacking Heth's family and military connections were passed over in promoting this amiable, courageous mediocrity.

Whatever his deficiencies as one of Lee's lieutenants, Heth nonetheless had some virtues as a memorialist. His humorous recollections of West Point (from which he graduated at the foot of his class) reveal the social life which helped create the camaraderie so characteristic of his generation of cadets. Especially valuable is his portrayal of aspects of the life of Old Army officers: the omnipresence of Virginians and other southerners; the attention to drink, women, horses, and hunting (perhaps in that order); the attitudes toward Mexicans ("greasers," p. 54), Mormons, and Indians. Those interested in the relations between army and Indian will read with profit Heth's account of his experience on the Great Plains in the 1850s; when in isolated commands he alternately parleyed with and fought the original inhabitants. Heth's narrative throughout is unusually frank and appreciative of human foibles which he knew he shared. His style is anecdotal, with particularly memorable stories concerning Winfield Scott and Ambrose Burnside. In fact, parts of the memoirs re-create the atmosphere of one of those evenings Heth loved so well, when old friends drank after a bountiful dinner and matched each others' tales. With the editor at Heth's elbow offering his sober modifications, the reader may after all find these memoirs to be rewarding.

Kent State University FRANK L. BYRNE

Shiloh: Bloody April. By Wiley Sword. (New York: William Morrow and Co., 1974. Pp. xxiv, 519. $15.00.)

Military history written by a nonprofessional historian with a very appropriate name, *Shiloh* is done in a style strongly reminiscent of the Civil War works of Bruce Catton. This comparison is particularly fitting because the two men have essentially the same view of this famed encounter. Sword contends that the Battle of Shiloh marked a decisive turning point in Confederate fortunes in the West. It was a clash of arms that the South had to win in order to restore balance to a situation which had become unsettled by the northern victories at Fort Henry and Fort Donelson. The failure of the Confederacy's attempt to surprise and destroy the strong Union force based at Pittsburg Landing set the stage for the ultimate loss of the vital Mississippi Valley. The tragic death of General Albert Sidney Johnston only compounded the southern tragedy.

Setting the stage from first the northern and then the southern perspective, Sword painstakingly explains the Confederate preparation of a surprise attack virtually unparalleled in military history. From a clash between a Union reconnaissance patrol and the vanguard of a large, unsuspected, and already advancing southern army, a bloody fight rapidly developed, and the entire grisly story is captured in this exhaustively researched hour-by-hour account. Based almost exclusively upon primary sources and particularly upon the reports contained in *The War of the Rebellion*, the picture which emerges is an incredible one of miscalculation and misperception, cowardice and courage, blundering, and missed opportunities.

Certain matters of organization and style tend to distract from an otherwise notable work. Approximately the first third of the text prepares the stage, and the material in these chapters could have been better presented. Within the battle narrative itself, there are so many decisions and actions cited as important that it is difficult to determine the truly decisive ones.

Sources of information offer yet another problem. The reference notes are sandwiched between the bibliography and the index. In addition to their awkward location, they are so abbreviated that only the better-known sources can be identified without reference to the bibliography.

Such flaws, however, should not be allowed to overshadow the generally outstanding quality of this work. Enhancing its value are a noteworthy foreword by military historian S. L. A. Marshall, excellent maps, portraits of key figures, three very informative appendices, and a highly useful bibliography. Overall, *Shiloh* is a book which deserves more readers than its price probably will attract.

Carson-Newman College JAMES L. BAUMGARDNER

The Segregation Struggle in Louisiana, 1862–77. By Roger A. Fischer. (Urbana, Chicago, and London: University of Illinois Press, c. 1974. Pp. xiv, 168. $6.95.)

Roger A. Fischer traces race relations in Louisiana from the beginning of segregation in antebellum New Orleans through the full development of the Jim Crow system at the end of the nineteenth century. In antebellum Louisiana slavery effectively preserved the color line in rural areas, but whites used formal and informal segregation to separate the races in the unique, international city, New Orleans. During "The Interregnum, 1862–67," segregation became firmly entrenched in rural Louisiana, but New Orleans's Negroes were able to desegregate the city's streetcars. In 1868 the Reconstruction constitution gave Negroes "a monumental victory" by forbidding segregation in public schools and public accommodations and by requiring potential officeholders to pledge their "belief in racial equality" (p. 55). Unfortunately, implementation and enforcement of these provisions were spotty at best. Despite "impressive" civil rights acts in 1869 and 1873, the movement to integrate public accommodations was a failure.

The picture in public education was brighter. While virtually all country parish schools were segregated de facto, Republican administrators were able to establish many new, black, public schools. Except for the disruption caused by white mob violence in 1874 and 1875, black and white children attended New Orleans public schools from 1871 to 1877 in "a truly remarkable experiment in interracial coexistence" (p. 110).

Rejecting the thesis that the "Redeemers" continued Republican policies, Fischer shows how the Democrats moved quickly and decisively after 1877 to end desegregation in the New Orleans public schools. He concludes by tracing increasing segregation in many areas of society in New Orleans from 1877 to the early twentieth century.

This excellent monograph has a few weaknesses. In explaining "the South's capitulation to such rabid racism" after 1890, Fischer claims that scholars have slighted the "epic encounter . . . . the desperation of the struggle" (pp. 156–57) for desegregation in Louisiana. But he does not show that segregation was the deciding issue in any major election. There was no struggle for segregation in public institutions (except Louisiana State University) and "in the country parishes . . . school segregation had never been really challenged" (p. 137). In public accommodations the civil rights acts, which were seldom or never tested, had little effect in New Orleans and none outside it. Even the school desegregation in New Orleans affected only about 10 percent of the students of either race in the city. The cumulative picture was not of an epic, desperate struggle throughout Louisiana but of sporadic conflicts in New Orleans and in the legislature which caused minimal social change.

Despite Fischer's belief in racial equality, he does not adequately treat developments within the black community. Negroes seeking civil rights became a "black power movement" (p. 154). Fischer accepts the Elkins thesis but does not explain how these "Sambos" could serve well in legislatures and a constitutional convention. Describing the development of white private schools in some detail, he ignores the development of black private schools after 1867 and 1868.

Except for these flaws, this study is exhaustively researched, clearly written, and well organized. This book is an important source for students of the history of Louisiana, the South, and race relations.

Wiley College ROBERT G. SHERER

Nor Is It Over Yet: Florida in the Era of Reconstruction, 1863–1877. By Jerrell H. Shofner. (Gainesville: University Presses of Florida, 1974. Pp. x, 412. $12.50.)

Nor Is It Over Yet is exactly what it purports to be, a history of Florida in the Reconstruction era, not simply a political history of the process. Yet it is that too, with political traumas as the frame around which the total is built. Nor is it an attempt to put down, once again, the Dunning school of Reconstruction as represented by W. W. Davis's *Civil War and Reconstruction in Florida* (1913), but rather it is a distinct advance in historical investigation and understanding. The reader discovers, refreshingly, that Floridians of the period grappled with many other problems besides the "muddy pool" (p. 288) of politics, that individuals and factions were often more important than parties, and that so-called "carpetbaggers" failed to live up to their image by remaining in the state even after 1877.

Shofner successfully ushers the reader through a political maze that serves to emphasize the disunity of both Republicans and Democrats. He states (p. 172) that "Factional membership fluctuated and some individuals [in the Republican party] remained more independent than others . . . ." He also notes (p. 195) that "moderate Republicans . . . . preferred collaboration with the Conservative [Democratic] leaders." Finally, he asserts (p. 197) that "In appealing to the Conservatives the moderate Republicans resorted to destructive tactics . . . . [and the Republican party] was continually torn by intraparty strife which sapped its strength and prevented unity." Floridians struggled vainly to create a civil government during Lincoln's wartime reconstruction, vainly reconstructed the state under Johnson, squirmed under military rule, adopted a moderate constitution under congressional direction, ratified the Fourteenth Amendment, and rejoined the Union on July 4, 1868. After an election marked by litigation and fraud in 1876, the Redeemers took control of the state in 1877. Yet, "The only major policy shift between the Democratic administrations after 1876 and their Republican predecessors was in civil rights" (p. 344).

Blacks had little reason for optimism except for the few years of Republican rule between 1868 and 1877. The Freedmen's Bureau was ineffective before 1868 (there is an excellent chapter on the subject); white Floridians of the Ku Klux Klan and other groups such as the Young Men's Democratic Clubs terrorized blacks; and after 1877, with the disappearance of the Republican party, even faint hope for black political advance faded.

Shofner details the restoration and extension of Florida's embryonic rail network, discusses trade and industry, and observes that 70 percent of the work force remained in agriculture. As elsewhere, no real change in landownership patterns took place, and farm tenancy and sharecropping replaced slavery with a system just as depressing. The model for over a century, a segregated school system emerged in 1869. Both parties promoted Florida successfully, as the influx of population and capital proved. State financial irregularity, lawlessness and violence, and endless litigation are carefully explored.

Organized along basically chronological lines, the topical chapters are arranged so as to provide relief from the nearly endless political parade. Shofner relies on a wealth of primary sources for this balanced and objective narrative. The only weaknesses are footnotes lumped at the end of the book rather than where they belong and a regrettable absence of maps. Still, *Nor Is It Over Yet* is a fine addition to Reconstruction historiography. Shofner observes that he had no intention of quarreling with earlier historians but hoped to rediscover the past. He accomplished his goal.

University of Akron ROBERT H. JONES

The Juhl Letters to the Charleston Courier: *A View of the South, 1865–1871*. Edited by John Hammond Moore. (Athens: University of Georgia Press, c. 1974. Pp. viii, 391. $12.00.)

Charleston native Julius J. Fleming, minister, schoolteacher, newspaper publisher, lawyer, and minor politician, settled in Sumter, South Carolina, shortly before the Civil War. Following that conflict he wrote some two hundred letters to the Charleston *Courier* as its Sumter "correspondent," under the pen name "Juhl." Though Fleming himself made little impression on South Carolina's history, his letters provide firsthand insight into conditions in the South during Reconstruction.

At times trivial and gossipy, the letters assume considerable significance when describing race relations during Reconstruction. As "Juhl" progresses from relief that the war was over to dismay and disgust with corrupt, advantage-taking politicians, he reveals an adaptable white mentality concerning blacks. He accepts the reality of change wrought by the war and is as much concerned with equal legal treatment and education for blacks as he is for southern agriculture under contract labor and sharecropping. Nonetheless, he believes that black equality should be ensured by concerned southern whites instead of Freedmen's Bureau agents or self-seeking politicians.

Although "Juhl's" letters never fully penetrate the depths of black thought and feeling in the era, they do give support, oddly enough, to both the Woodward and Williamson theses on Reconstruction and race relations and also that considerable separation of the races occurred voluntarily through black withdrawal. The letters taper off in 1870 and end abruptly in 1871 as legal work demanded more of Fleming's time and the *Courier* underwent financial retrenchment.

The editorial work in the preparation of this volume was primarily compilation. There is a general introduction, highlighting Fleming's life, supplemented by short prefaces to the letters for each year. Unfortunately, editor Moore's style in these introductions is not as felicitous as "Juhl's"; it is burdened with too many parenthetical comments and too many sentences begun by conjunction. Explanatory notes throughout the letters are few and, when present, usually seem inadequate. Many identifications are made merely by bracketing first name or initials within the text—a more than adequate process where Thaddeus Stevens is concerned, but hardly beneficial with regard to Richard B. Cain or D. J. Simmon.

Finally, either production costs or hopeful eye appeal eliminated approximately the bottom third of the book, resulting in compressed type in an odd-sized volume which is awkward to handle. For the above reasons, the twelve-dollar price appears costly for this essentially "scissors-and-paste" work.

University of South Carolina
Aiken

W. CALVIN SMITH

College Life in the Reconstruction South: Walter B. Hill's Student Correspondence, University of Georgia, 1869–1871. Edited by G. Ray Mathis. University of Georgia Libraries, *Miscellanea Publications*, No. 10. (Athens: University of Georgia Libraries, 1974. Pp. xii, 265. Paper, $7.00.)

On July 3 [?], 1869, Walter B. Hill, a junior in Franklin College, the liberal arts college of the University of Georgia, wrote his mother, Mary Clay Birch Hill, "Do you save my letters? I believe you formerly did so; & I hope you will continue it. For I was thinking recently what a good history of my College life they will be . . . in [the] future" (p. 97). It is fortunate for those who may be interested in the history of the University of Georgia and/or student life in the South during Reconstruction that Mrs. Hill had already decided to preserve her son's letters. G. Ray Mathis of Troy State University, whose doctoral dissertation is a study of the chancellorship of Walter B. Hill of the University of Georgia from 1899 to 1905, has selected a representative sampling of Walter Hill's letters to his father, mother, and brother beginning with a communication written on January 15, 1868, when Hill began his collegiate career, and closing with one dated July 26, 1871, a few days prior to his receiving both the master of arts degree in modern languages and the bachelor of laws degree. (Neither Mathis nor the publisher explains the use of the dates 1869–1871 in the title.)

Although the majority of the letters are reproduced only in part, the selections constitute a charming, informative account of college life in the South after the Civil War. Mathis has carefully identified most of the unfamiliar proper names in the text in his helpful notes, which this reader was pleased to find at the bottom of the appropriate page. Walter Hill, like most of his fellow students in pleasant and peaceful Athens, took his room and board in a private home. Since he was the smallest man in his class, Hill was greatly concerned with improving his health and eagerly sought outdoor exercise. He informed his family of this on several occasions and also wrote regularly about his church attendance and his efforts in promoting the literary, religious, and social activities of the college. Hill strove constantly to attain academic honors, and each year he placed near the top of his class. News of these achievements and of the college's two rival oratorical societies make up a sizable segment of his letters. Hill was very proud to be a member of Chi Phi, one of Georgia's three social fraternities at the time, and acquainted his family with periodic accounts of campus politics.

For readers interested in the monumental problems of the Reconstruction era this book has little to offer. There are no references to national issues whatsoever and only a few relatively insignificant ones to the contemporary Radical regime in Georgia. Hill, who originally scorned the Republicans, began to moderate his views slightly by the time he was ready to join his conservative Massachusetts-born father in the practice of law. Although this is not an earthshaking book, it is delightful to read.

Spring Hill College HOWARD W. SMITH

Two Paths to the New South: The Virginia Debt Controversy, 1870–1883. By James Tice Moore. (Lexington: University Press of Kentucky, c. 1974. Pp. xiv, 167. $12.95.)

James Moore's book begins with an arresting study in counterpoint. He depicts the postbellum Virginia Conservatives as men caught by the past in a grip so tenacious that it controlled all their actions. Their desire to uphold an ancient state's honor even prompted a politically suicidal determination that Virginia pay her full debt. In contrast, Moore sees the Readjusters representing modernity because they rejected the past and attempted to forge a new state to deal with a new age.

Moore describes the Conservatives and Readjusters as following radically different visions. Like Jack Maddex, Moore pictures the Conservatives as a group closely tied to antebellum Virginia through family as well as social and political views. But while Maddex found the Conservative effort to industrialize Virginia to be a break with an agrarian past, Moore finds it an extension of the antebellum crusade that envisioned industrialism on a social and political base still dominated by a traditional, elite community.

The Readjusters, chiefly westerners, blacks, and new urban men, none of them part of the old regime in fact or spirit, demanded fundamental change. Moore says they cried for industrialization as they pressed for social change and realized that old values were dead. Their modern vision included substantially increased state services, rising per capita income, racial justice, democratization of politics—all opposed by the Conservatives. While Moore certainly will not make disciples of all his readers, he has suggested an interesting dichotomy.

When Moore turns to a narrative of the bitter political war between Conservatives and Readjusters, he is only partially successful. His account has its strengths, particularly his discussion of the malignant factionalism within the Readjuster movement. But weaknesses predominate. A distinct shortcoming is the lack of any full treatment of local Conservative and Readjuster organization. Moore talks a great deal about organization, about Conservative courthouse cliques, about how Readjusters overcame them, about dissolution of Readjuster organization. But never do we actually see these organizations and what made them work. This is all the more surprising because of his work in Virginia newspapers and his statement that the William Mahone papers are full on organization. Moore's account might be plagued by its brevity; perhaps in a book that has only 123 pages of text (with footnotes at the bottom of the page) he simply could not cover the ground. Here, I think more would have been better. Also Moore makes much use of a comparative biographical analysis of Conservative-Readjuster leaders, but nowhere does he explain how he chose these men.

Even though Moore's political analysis falls short, his fresh approach to the Conservative-Readjuster clash merits applause.

Louisiana State University WILLIAM J. COOPER, JR.

The Shaping of Southern Politics: Suffrage Restriction and the Establishment of the One-Party South, 1880–1910. By J. Morgan Kousser. (New Haven and London: Yale University Press, 1974. Pp. xviii, 319. $15.00.)

J. Morgan Kousser has written a valuable book on an important subject, the disfranchisement movement that prevailed in the eleven ex-Confederate states during the late nineteenth and early twentieth centuries. In this study the author develops a view of the post-Reconstruction South which closely parallels that of C. Vann Woodward, namely, that the South went through a period of transition which eventually ended in a harsher and more restrictive racial system. In the 1880s southern politics remained open and democratic with 64 percent of the eligible voters participating in elections and with 25 percent of them supporting the Republicans or independent parties. A distinct possibility existed that a real two-party system could develop. By the first decade of the twentieth century, after the enactment of disfranchisement statutes, the situation had drastically changed: then only 30 percent of the electorate voted, and a mere 10 percent supported the Republicans. The political system had changed from a democracy to a "broadly-based oligarchy" (p. 224).

In pursuing this subject the author read widely in the published and unpublished literature of the period. The most innovative part of his work consists of careful analyses of election statistics employing a technique that historians have rarely used—Leo Goodman's ecological regression method. That method enabled him to estimate "the percentages of blacks and whites who voted for each candidate, as well as the proportion who did not vote, in every presidential and gubernatorial election and in many primaries and referenda in the South from 1880 to 1910" (p. xiv). As a result, he has obtained the most accurate information to date on which political groups favored disfranchisement and how the restrictive laws affected the electorate.

This study offers new findings on a variety of subjects. Contrary to the views of many previous scholars, Professor Kousser found the poll tax one of the most effective devices for reducing the suffrage. Though many have hailed the secret ballot as a progressive reform, in the South middle-class whites implemented it to disfranchise illiterates. By keeping voters united within the Democratic party, white primaries helped the South retain its one-party system after black voting had ended. Many authorities have long insisted that whites living in the hills and in areas of low black density were the leading proponents of Negro disfranchisement. The author proves that black-belt Democrats, especially the affluent and well-educated, most strongly supported disfranchisement. They wanted to eliminate the voting of poor whites as well as blacks. Populists, Republicans, and blacks consistently opposed the new laws. Finally, Professor Kousser takes issue with V. O. Key, who argued that whites had disfranchised blacks prior to the adoption of new suffrage laws by means of violence, intimidation, and fraud. He insists that the suffrage laws themselves were important and demonstrates that they caused an average reduction in voter turnout throughout the South of 37 percent.

Some readers may question the author on a number of points. If Democrats used the secret ballot as a disfranchisement tool, why then did southern Populists support that measure so strongly? Although Professor Kousser correctly emphasizes the importance of the final restrictive laws, Key's thesis still has much validity. Well before the adoption of disfranchisement constitutions and amendments South Carolina, Alabama, Virginia, and Georgia had election laws that greatly reduced black voting. In Texas and Mississippi violence played a more decisive role in restricting suffrage than the author acknowledges. In presenting his findings on the leadership of wealthy, black-belt whites in securing the suffrage laws, Professor Kousser comes close to describing disfranchisement in terms of an economic class movement. Opposition to disfranchisement was definitely stronger in the white counties, but many Democrats from those sections did favor restricting the suffrage. Actually, Democrats in the hills and black belts appear to have held similar views on disfranchisement: both wanted to end black political participation; few Democratic leaders from the hills opposed the new laws because they took votes away from poor whites.

The above criticisms mainly reflect differences in interpretation and should not detract from the soundness of this study. For those who wish to gain insight into the political system that prevailed in the South during the first half of the twentieth century, this book will be indispensable.

University of Georgia WILLIAM F. HOLMES

Coming of Age: Urban America, 1919–1945. By William H. Wilson. (New York and other cities: John Wiley & Sons, c. 1974. Pp. xii, 221. $9.95.)

American historians have spent too much time and research on the obscure trivia of antiquated ages and ignored the world that presses in upon them. So few urban histories, particularly good ones, reach the public that their release is an event.

William Wilson's work covers the maturing of American cities between 1915 and 1945. Skyscrapers transformed the "low and squat" city, freeways replaced brick and macadam, black shoppers and employees reflected the great cityward migration, municipal government felt the impact of the council-manager ideology, and, most important, a revolution in thinking about cities took place. The migrant black in the northern and western cities (no attention is given to the black in southern cities) sought help through store-front churches, the numbers game, the UNIA, and the Harlem Renaissance in the face of disorganization, alienation within his own race, and surburban flight. The emerging auto suburbs were the promotional results of the J. C. Nicholses, but they were the bane of the inner city. Such change was inevitable, but it wedded America to motor vehicle dependence and a shortsighted rejection of rapid transit.

To deal with the debilitated downtown and corrupt council-mayor arrangement urban progressive reformers introduced the council-manager idea. "What they wanted was a centralized urban administration that would efficiently organize the city's services . . ." (p. 60). Unfortunately, in spite of innovations like proportional representation, reform was usually dependent upon a political reformer with charisma and ethnic consciousness. Just as the rural city of 1915 became politically unmanageable by 1945, so urban problems grew and forced the city to look to the federal government for aid and direction. The thesis of the book is this total reversal both in physical and political complexion and in the attitudes of sociologists, urban planners, novelists, and federal program writers. By 1945 the problems of the city were national in scope and indissolubly interwoven.

This is an excellent example of historical scholarship. William H. Wilson provides a thorough blending of the writings of sociologists, novelists, and city planners of the caliber of the realist Robert Moses and the utopian Frank Lloyd Wright. He has not concerned himself with the detailed physical changes between 1915 and 1945 so much as with the attitudes and intellectual contributions and adaptations. However, no attention is paid to the southern city, as though Atlanta, Memphis, and New Orleans did not exist. Actually, they do not fit as neatly into the thesis. The impact of the World War II on the city is also slighted. Attention is given to the Depression and the New Deal but not to the war.

The book is a masterful job of synthesizing, and its lucid and capable style makes it a significant contribution to the study of the American city.

Dalton Junior College THOMAS M. DEATON

The Democratic Party and the Politics of Sectionalism, 1941–1948. By Robert A. Garson. (Baton Rouge: Louisiana State University Press and London School of Economics and Political Science, c. 1974. Pp. xiv, 353. $12.95.)

British observers of American politics have often provided fresh insights into the party and governmental structures of this country. Lord Bryce and Denis Brogan, to name only two examples, contributed substantially to our understanding of the political process. Robert Garson of the University of Keele attempts to continue that tradition in this book, a revision of his dissertation written at the London School of Economics. Garson seeks to analyze the rise of sectionalism in the Democratic party in the 1940s by focusing on the political events which took place in Washington and how they influenced the style and content of southern politics.

Garson believes that in 1936 Democrats belonged to a unified party committed to the ideology of the New Deal and to Franklin Roosevelt personally. Southern Democrats seemed to have accepted the growing influence of the northern wing of the party, which was composed of liberal intellectuals, blue-collar workers, and blacks. This unity collapsed when first Roosevelt, and then Harry Truman, decided to abandon the Dixie conservatives in order to secure the votes of the "Roosevelt coalition." The alienated southerners resorted to sectional rhetoric rather than substantive debate to combat the growth of federal paternalism which resulted from this shift in presidential policies. When Roosevelt and Truman used the power of the executive branch to aid the CIO and civil rights organizations, Garson believes that the South had only two choices: forming a third party or joining the Republicans. The emergence of the Dixiecrats in 1948 was not then a "flash in the pan" but a basic departure in American politics with long-lasting consequences. In an epilogue Garson contends that the Dixiecrat revolt led to the Eisenhower victories in the South and the successes of Goldwater in 1964 and Nixon in 1968 and 1972.

The book rests on solid research at the Roosevelt and Truman libraries and on newspapers, published memoirs, House and Senate committee hearings, and unpublished dissertations. The bibliography lists only five interviews with those involved in the Dixiecrat campaign, an unfortunate circumstance considering the number of major figures alive and still active in politics, including George C. Wallace. More disconcerting is the failure to consult the works of political scientists Bernard Cosman on the sources of the Goldwater vote and Donald Strong on the growth of urban

Republicanism. The sequel to V. O. Key's work edited by William Havard was apparently not available to Garson.

This book would have been strengthened considerably by a review of the political-science literature on the South. Garson's assumption that a strong, united Democratic party existed in 1936 doesn't hold up in light of recent research. Further, his focus on labor, anti–poll tax, health-insurance, fair-employment-practice, and civil rights legislative efforts in Washington ignores massive social and economic changes taking place in the South from 1941 to the present. While the race issue undoubtedly contributed to southern opposition to the "Fair Deal," there were significant economic factors as well. Even without the Dixiecrat experience, survey research suggests that Atlanta and Birmingham suburbanites would tend to vote similarly to their northern counterparts. When Garson argues that Truman wrote the South off in 1948, he fails to explain why Alben Barkley was added to the ticket rather than a northern or western liberal. In addition, Garson constantly overemphasizes the dissident Democrats—Strom Thurmond, Harry Byrd, and Fielding Wright—without giving equal attention to the overwhelming majority of congressmen and senators from the South who remained loyal to the party. Some of these men supported at least part of the legislation which the Dixiecrats found so repugnant. Despite his emphasis on the race issue and narrow focus on Washington, Garson has added another dimension to the work of Key, Strong, Havard, and Alexander Heard.

University of Wisconsin, Milwaukee KEITH L. BRYANT, JR.

The Morrison Era: Reform Politics in New Orleans. By Joseph B. Parker. (Gretna, La.: Pelican Publishing Co., 1974. Pp. xiv, 154. $7.95.)

The author, a political scientist, in this short volume undertakes an examination of de Lesseps S. Morrison's durability as a reform mayor in New Orleans from 1946 to 1961. The unique nature of Morrison's accomplishment is underscored by a recital of unsuccessful reform efforts in New Orleans from 1877 to 1946. A pragmatic *modus operandi* is established as the basis for the longevity of municipal machines as contrasted with the transitory character of ideologically oriented reform administrations. The generality of reformers, including those in New Orleans prior to the Morrison regime, suffered from a failure to accomplish a synthesis of reform ideals and machine techniques. This, however, was Morrison's achievement. According to Parker, "Only with the coming of . . . Morrison and his successful fusion of reform language and programs with machine techniques was a reform administration able to hold political power locally over a period of time" (p. 20).

Utilizing an attractive and energetic personality, Morrison fashioned a machinelike coalition of widely diverse groups, which he controlled in the absolute manner of a political boss. The nucleus of this organization was the ward-based Crescent City Democratic Association (CCDA), which he dominated through a caucus of ward leaders. In addition to ward politicians, the Morrison machine comprised wealthy businessmen, women from the middle- and upper-income areas of New Orleans, politically ambitious young men, and blacks. So pervasive was Morrison's influence that his departure from office in 1961 to accept an appointment as ambassador to the Organization of American States resulted in the organization's collapse.

While the analysis of political structure in this study is impressive, the treatment of policy formulation and implementation is sketchy. Policy matters such as the proposal of a new city charter and the selection of administrative department heads are mentioned, but there is no adequate assessment of the reform character of these and other issues in the light of Morrison's "fusion of reform language and programs with machine techniques." The survey of New Orleans's politics from 1877 to 1946, which encompasses the Choctaw Club, the city's encounter with Huey P. Long during 1934 and 1935, and a cataloging of reform movements, illuminates the difficulty of municipal reform in the city. Nevertheless, the superficial nature of this material detracts from the focus on the Morrison era.

The author has made extensive use of interviews and of an impressive array of secondary sources. The book is well written, and the sections dealing with Morrison and the CCDA provide valuable insights into the organizational structure and functions of a modern municipal machine.

Northwestern State University of Louisiana — James L. McCorkle, Jr.

All God's Dangers: The Life of Nate Shaw. By Theodore Rosengarten. (New York: Alfred A. Knopf, 1974. Pp. xxvi, 562, xiii. $10.00.)

During the past decade proponents of both quantitative and oral history have criticized so-called "traditional history" for neglecting the lives of the "common people." This book ably demonstrates what one of these alternative approaches has to offer. It is the oral autobiography of an eighty-five-year-old illiterate black tenant farmer, the result of 120 hours of taped conversations with Theodore Rosengarten, a young Harvard Ph.D. candidate. After a perceptive and informative introduction, Rosengarten allows the man he calls Nate Shaw to tell his own story. Not only has Shaw a remarkable tale to tell, but he tells it with wit, insight, and as Rosengarten claims, a vocabulary "remarkably broad and inventive" (p. xxiv). Nor is this surprising, for, as we are reminded, "Shaw belongs to the tradition of farmer-storytellers" (p. xxii).

The son of former slaves, Shaw was born in east-central Alabama. Hired out at an early age by his father, who pocketed his earnings, Nate eventually left home to marry at age twenty-one. He began working halves on land owned by whites but soon saved enough to buy a mule and pay cash for the cotton land he rented. Shaw vividly depicts the many obstacles plaguing his attempts to better his condition. In addition to white hostility, there was the envy of his fellow blacks, poor land, insufficient fertilizer, fluctuating cotton prices, and the forces of nature which brought bad weather and a host of ravenous insects. The boll weevil in particular proved that "all God's dangers aint a white man" (p. 223). But Shaw prospered, thanks to the help of his wife (who kept the accounts), his own hard work, and his skills as farmer, blacksmith, hauler of logs, and maker of ax handles and baskets. Though the chicanery of whites prevented him from buying his own farm, at the peak of his success Shaw had close to $2,000 worth of property, including livestock, wagons, and two automobiles.

But as Shaw puts it, "I was climbin up in the world like a boy climbin a tree. And I fell just as easy, too" (p. 285). After joining the abortive Sharecroppers Union, Shaw single-handedly drove off with gunfire deputies trying to evict a fellow union member in 1932. His explanation was simple: "I knowed . . . I was goin to be next" (p. 306). Numerous statements indicate that Shaw had mastered the lessons of survival, but he had also learned that there were certain things worth fighting for. "I've taken every kind of insult and went on. In my years past, I'd accommodate anybody; but I didn't believe in this way of bowin to my knees and doin what *any* white man said do. . . . First thing of all—I care for myself and respect myself " (p. 545).

For his act of defiance, Shaw received a twelve-to-fifteen-year prison term. Once again the master of survival, Shaw was a model prisoner. "I went through prison just as quiet as a plank of wood" (p. 392). Most readers will be surprised by the treatment Shaw received. He found the housing and food better and the white officials fairer than on the outside. Toward the end of his term he was able to sell his baskets, enjoy conjugal visits, and go home on weekends.

Released from prison in 1945, "Shaw was a mule farmer in a tractor world" (p. xxii). Although his post-prison life is the second longest of the book's four parts (Youth, Deeds, Prison, Revelation), it is anticlimatic. Shaw continued to farm, remarried after his wife of forty-four years died, and finally purchased his own small house with the help of his stepdaughter. By then his eldest son, the only one of his nine children still farming, had become the family's success story.

What we have is a modern-day slave narrative. While Rosengarten does not take the liberties of abolitionist editors and ghost writers, his sympathies are clear: "Nate Shaw was—and is—a hero to me" (p. xix), a fact which probably influenced his selection of certain stories rather than others (see pp. xxiii–xxiv). The book has other problems inherent in the slave-narrative genre, including typicality and the intentional or unintentional distortion of the past by an aged subject. But there is no denying the overriding value of an insider's view of important topics central to the study of black and southern history, including the extent to which cotton controlled the lives of black tenants and white landlords alike, Negro migration, class and racial conflict, racial progress, the work ethic, and the impact of the federal government.

This book is open to many interpretations. Some will salute Shaw as the typical black tenant farmer; others will see him as an exception, using Shaw's own view of his fellow blacks as supporting evidence. No matter.

The work's chief value is the addition of its considerable weight to the currently developing picture of southern black life both before and after emancipation. Stated simply, this view acknowledges the brutal conditions under which blacks lived, but argues that some blacks had opportunities for initiative and improvement and were able to maintain their self-respect and a sense of their own importance.

Readers will eagerly await Rosengarten's future volume devoted to the rest of the Shaw family.

University of New Mexico HOWARD N. RABINOWITZ

The Southern Baptist Convention and Its People, 1607–1972. By Robert A. Baker. (Nashville: Broadman Press, c. 1974. Pp. xiv, 15–477. $11.95.)

In a Toynbee-like approach Professor Baker depicts the story of the Southern Baptist Convention on a wide canvas. Using the date 1607 as a starting point, based on the founding of Jamestown, struck this reviewer as somewhat artificial. Baptists had not yet appeared in England, and a Baptist church probably did not exist in the South until about 1696. Only in 1715 did Virginia have a church of this denomination. The weakest part of this solid study is the opening, where the story is pushed back to the Council of Whitby. This developed from the author's intent to pursue "A holistic approach to the Convention" (p. ix), which he did achieve. If the opening pages attempt too much and add little to the book, the same cannot be said for the remainder of the volume, for the author knows how to prune as well as to plant.

The author deserves strong commendation for a Southern Baptist history which successfully captures the denomination's social, economic, and political milieu, the lack of which has plagued much ecclesiastical history. In the 146 pages devoted to the rise of Baptists before the organization of the Convention, there are a few historical inaccuracies. It was Jefferson, not Madison, who first took the oath of office in the new capitol (p. 77); the threat of civil war in 1832 was exaggerated (pp. 119, 153); and the reference to "the original thirteen colonies" (p. 86) should read states.

The book is divided into seven chronological periods and follows a regional demarcation used by the United States Census Bureau. It is superbly organized throughout and supplies an abundance of meticulously researched statistical material which should be of use to mature students of the Convention.

One of the book's major themes is the problem which the Convention faced of uniting churches, each of which had a background of strong local autonomy, into an effective working denomination. The parent body from which the Convention sprang conducted its work in a highly decentralized manner, taking the "society approach" to its benevolent work. From its organization in 1845 the Southern Convention was more centralized but retained residual elements of what Baker often refers to as the "society approach." He presents a fine analysis of how the Convention overcame this problem after half a century of internal strain. He notes that some of the Convention's founding fathers favored a "judicious concentration" of power (p. 165). Opposition to this centralization crystallized into the important movement of Landmarkism, which is treated interestingly. Several "spin-off" issues of Landmarkism and the divisive effect they had on the Convention from 1877 to 1917 are also discussed.

Baker believes that the history of the Convention should be written in multiple volumes, but until this is done his study will likely remain definitive. Almost any reader can glean many good things from this monograph, which is marked by the author's mature insight. Among other topics, the volume discusses significant books written by Southern Baptist authors, the Convention's reluctance to publish books, and the final triumph of the publishing policy engineered by J. M. Frost. In light of the current insistence on a change of the Convention's name, it is interesting to note that some of its organizers believed the name Southern was too sectional.

Northwestern State University WILLIAM A. POE

A Century of Jewish Life in Dixie: The Birmingham Experience. By Mark H. Elovitz. (University, Ala.: University of Alabama Press, c. 1974. Pp. xii, 258. $10.00.)

Mark Elovitz has written the first substantial history of any southern Jewish community. Jewish settlement of Birmingham dates back to 1871, the year the city was founded. Nearly all of the Jews who came to the rapidly growing industrial center during its first two decades of existence were merchants of Germanic origin. Esteemed by their Christian neighbors for their integrity, business acumen, and generosity, most of these "German" Jews prospered, and several were elected to positions of public trust and responsibility. Even during the heyday of the Ku Klux Klan, when fully one-tenth of the population of Birmingham belonged to the hooded order, Jewish businessmen seldom reported harassment or loss of patronage. One outspoken lawyer, who decided to leave the city, admitted that "the Klan sent an emissary to me. . . . He urged me not to go, saying that I was not the kind of Jew they were after" (p. 86). Acceptance was not absolute, for regardless of their prominence in city affairs Jews were excluded from Birmingham's most prestigious social clubs.

After 1890 hundreds of Jews from Russia and Poland poured into the city, and these strange-looking newcomers profoundly embarrassed their "German" coreligionists. Unable to speak English and unwilling to give up their religious orthodoxy, the "Russian" Jews formed their own synagogues and fraternal orders. Not until the 1930s did the barriers finally crumble. Thereafter both groups found it advantageous to cooperate with each other.

In writing this history Mark Elovitz, rabbi of Birmingham's Temple Emanu-El, has employed a wide variety of primary and secondary sources. In particular, he is to be commended for making use of oral-history interviews with "old timers" and others knowledgeable about "the Birmingham experience." Moreover, non-Jewish readers will appreciate the glossary of Hebrew and Yiddish words that appears at the end of the volume.

Unfortunately, a few things prevent this good book from being an excellent one. First and foremost, Rabbi Elovitz occasionally shuns controversial subjects. He gives only minimal attention to the question of black-Jewish relations. He does not place the attempted bombing of a Birmingham synagogue in 1958 in its proper historical perspective, and the reader will finish the book with only vague ideas as to how Birmingham Jews reacted to George Wallace or to the civil rights revolution of the 1950s and 1960s. Second, Elovitz frequently overwhelms the reader with unnecessary data and long quotations that should have been summarized. These criticisms, however, are not meant to demean the value of this study. Historians have all too often assumed that the South was populated only by white Protestants and Afro-Americans and that of these two only the first really mattered. Rabbi Elovitz has shown that, at least in the case of Birmingham, the role of Jews should not be overlooked.

Emory University ARNOLD SHANKMAN

History of Mary Washington College, 1908–1972. By Edward Alvey, Jr. (Charlottesville: University Press of Virginia, c. 1974. Pp. xiv, 682. $10.00.)

In recent years there has been an emphasis on particular rather than general history. In the wake of a veritable tidal wave of black history there has followed less forceful, yet significant, strong currents of institutional and women's histories. The *History of Mary Washington College, 1908–1972* combines these last two in one lengthy volume.

Professor Edward Alvey, Jr., for many years dean of the college, defines the scope of the book as "the story of a college: its origin, its development, and its role as an institution of higher learning." Stressing that it contains more than "legislative enactments, board actions, and curriculum changes," the author sees his work as "essentially a record of people and their personalities" and their impact on the institution (p. ix).

After a brief, nine-page discussion of higher education for women with emphasis on Virginia, the author records in minute detail the development of the school from its founding as a normal school for white girls—the changes not only in physical plant and personnel but also in philosophy and purpose and its place in the educational system of the commonwealth—to 1972, when it became a separate entity with its own board of trustees, integrated and coeducational. Having written a history of a similar institution, this reviewer was impressed with the similarity of trends, and even events, in the two schools. This is undoubtedly due to the fact that both were reflecting the changes in public education and in the life-styles of and roles for women.

The chief virtue of the volume is its thoroughness. The author has used an impressive list of sources. Furthermore, his connection with the college from 1934 until his retirement in 1967 gave him an enviable perspective. The book is divided into thirty-five chapters, most of them dealing with short spans of time, seldom more than five years. For the reader who wants to know what happened at Mary Washington College at any one time, the information is here. Fortunately, there is a lengthy, twenty-five-page index.

The chief weakness is the total lack of analysis, evaluation, interpretation, or synthesis. The book could be shortened and strengthened appreciably by judicious use of summaries and generalizations. In style the book is a chronicle or annals rather than a history.

Dr. Alvey, out of his vast knowledge of higher education and long personal experience, has compiled a book that will find its most appreciative audience among the alumnae of and his former colleagues at Mary Washington College.

Montevallo, Alabama LUCILLE GRIFFITH

Pioneer-at-Law. By George Edwards. (New York: W. W. Norton and Co., c. 1974. Pp. 247. $7.95.)

A native Texan educated at Southern Methodist University, Harvard, and the Detroit College of Law, George Edwards has been a labor organizer, city official, and judge in Detroit, a member of the supreme court of the state of Michigan, and is now judge of the United States Court of Appeals in Cincinnati. *Pioneer-at-Law* is partially his autobiography, but mainly it is a memoir of his father.

For more than half a century George Clifton Edwards personified Louis Brandeis's ideal of the people's lawyer. Practicing in Dallas during a period that spanned the triumph of militant white racism, the hypernationalism of the First World War, the rise of the Ku Klux Klan in the twenties, the labor violence of the thirties, and the push for racial justice in the forties and fifties, the senior Edwards repeatedly went into court in behalf of people whose ideas and actions seemed to threaten the established order. Nominally an evolutionary socialist in the tradition of Eugene Debs, Edwards chose to work "within the system" for the gradual expansion of constitutional freedoms for dissenting minorities. Managing to provide a fairly comfortable living for his family, Edwards in most respects observed the canons of middle-class respectability. Although he resigned from the Socialist party because it opposed Franklin Roosevelt's interventionist foreign policy before Pearl Harbor, he was still a member of the Masonic Order at his death in 1961.

George Clifton Edwards was no radical, but within the prevailing political climate of the city of Dallas and the state of Texas he often appeared so. While he eventually won a kind of grudging respect from the Dallas power structure, he willingly remained an outsider—sometimes ridiculed as a crank and a fool, at other times denounced and even physically threatened for his opposition to local injustices. About as much as any man could be expected to, he kept the faith.

Judge Edwards's book makes generally absorbing reading. Writing in an easy, almost conversational manner, he wanders around a good deal and often neglects to orient the reader chronologically, but he does convey a good sense of what Dallas was like when it was a smaller, more tightly controlled, and more repressive place to live. *Pioneer-at-Law* will prove moderately useful for students of the political and social history of Texas in the twentieth century.

Ohio University CHARLES C. ALEXANDER

Catch the Vision: The Life of Henry L. Whitfield of Mississippi. By Bill R. Baker. (Jackson: University Press of Mississippi, c. 1974. Pp. x, 173. $7.95.)

Henry L. Whitfield, educator and politician, deserved the biography that Bill R. Baker was encouraged to do for a doctoral dissertation in Mississippi State University. The study rests on an impressive bibliography, including the oral or written opinions of 350 people who had known the subject.

In the first chapter, "State Superintendent of Education," the reader learns something of the family background of the subject and that at the time of his birth in 1868 the recent war had caused "untold hardships." The chapter includes the names of the rural schools he attended and of those in which he taught, beginning at the age of seventeen. After thirteen years of teaching in rural classrooms, he was appointed state superintendent of education by Governor Anselm J. McLaurin in 1898. Whitfield apparently should be credited with enriching curriculums, improving attendance and school facilities, and raising the qualifications of teachers and the financial support of schools. The author generally fails, however, to distinguish between his subject's aspirations and his achievements.

In June 1907 Whitfield was elected president of the Mississippi Industrial Institute and College (later Mississippi State College for Women). Under his leadership improvements and additions were made to the physical plant, academic standards were raised, and enrollment and state support both grew significantly. He provoked considerable criticism by emphasizing "practical" education and by failing, without explanation, to renew the contracts of four faculty members. He himself was dismissed in 1920 because of his refusal to support the candidacy of Lee Russell for governor.

Widely and favorably known during his tenure as state superintendent of education and president of Mississippi State College for Women, Whitfield was elected governor in 1923. The enfranchisement of women in 1920 and the enthusiastic support of hundreds of "his girls" were major reasons for his success.

The governor was prominently associated with economy in government, reducing the tax burden on property by levying taxes on drinks, tobacco, and amusements and by tripling the income tax rate to 3 percent. The attorney general was placed on a salary, and a state purchasing agent and a uniform accounting system were established. Whitfield led in efforts to attract out-of-state capital as a means of hastening economic diversification.

Unfortunately, Baker worked without the guidance of one of his Graduate School's mature scholars. Such assistance could have spared the book its sophomoric composition, its excessive pietism, and its mingling of the subject's aspirations and achievements. The University Press of Mississippi must have an editor, but neither his name nor his influence appear in this book.

Mississippi State College for Women (retired) — Ottis Clark Skipper

Book Notes

British Maps of Colonial America. By William P. Cumming. (Chicago and London: University of Chicago Press, c. 1974. Pp. xii, 114. $10.95.) British colonists in North America were ever dependent on charts and maps: to make their way safely along the coasts, to travel into the interior, to sustain their territorial claims, to carry on trade, and to wage war. For more than a century after Englishmen settled at Jamestown, their maps reflected both an ignorance of the continent and a lack of skill in mapmaking. Indeed, it was not until the middle of the eighteenth century that the Atlantic seaboard was mapped with precision. Only then did professional cartographers like Gerard de Brahm, Lewis Evans, Claude Joseph Sauthier, and Joseph Frederick Wallet Des Barres use triangulation, celestial observations, and expert draftsmanship to produce a variety of superb maps and charts.

In *British Maps of Colonial America* William P. Cumming has not merely sketched the history of British cartography in colonial America but also added to our knowledge of maps and mapmakers—particularly those of New England and of the Revolutionary War. He has done so in four learned, coherent, and handsomely illustrated essays that deal in turn with the cartography of the South, the North, the Atlantic coast, and the French and Indian War as well as the Revolution. Although Professor Cumming's enthusiasm for fresh information sometimes leads to digressions, and although his essays are marred by trivial errors, historians and connoisseurs alike will find this book as informative as it is attractive. [Ira D. Gruber, Rice University]

The Toll of Independence: Engagements & Battle Casualties of the American Revolution. Edited by Howard H. Peckham. (Chicago and London: University of Chicago Press, 1974. Pp. xvi, 176. $7.50.) In this volume Howard Peckham, with the assistance of a team of graduate students, has assembled a comprehensive, chronological list of battles fought by Americans during the Revolutionary War. For each battle he has provided a brief description and an accounting of Americans, killed, wounded, captured, missing, and deserted. Although he has uniformly excluded civilian casualties as well as engagements involving privateers and merchant vessels—although his figures represent "verifiable minimums"—he records 34,947 American casualties in 1,546 engagements. Indeed, he estimates that including those who died in camp or in prison more than 25,000 lost their lives in the Revolution (about 0.9 percent of the population in 1780). Peckham has not tried to interpret his data.

A Documentary History of the Negro People in the United States, 1933–1945. Edited by Herbert Aptheker. Preface by William L. Patterson. (Secaucus, N. J.: Citadel Press, c. 1974. Pp. xxiv, 607. $17.50.) This third volume by Professor Aptheker brings to completion a project begun in 1964, with the first volume covering the period to 1910 appearing in 1951 and the second on the years from 1910 through 1932 being published in 1973. The editor hints in an appreciatory note that his publishers have suggested a possible fourth volume.

The 106 numbered sections, some having several parts, cover many topics, including Angelo Herndon, the Harlem and Detroit riots, the National Negro Congress, the Pan-African movement, and the Negro in the New Deal and World War II. It emphasizes the outlook of W. E. B. Du Bois and, in the words of William L. Patterson's preface, "brings to the fore, in particular, the great impact of the 1917 Socialist Revolution upon Black freedom fighters. That revolution and its impact . . . provoked also new trends of thought among U.S. Black people . . ." (pp. ix–x).

Isaac Shelby: Kentucky's First Governor and Hero of Three Wars. By Sylvia Wrobel and George Grider. (Danville, Ky.: Cumberland Press, c. 1974. Pp. vi, 153. $8.95.) The title, while uninspiring, succinctly summarizes the scope and purpose of this brief work. The first chapter moves quickly but adequately through young Isaac's family background, early years, and first conflict, Lord Dunmore's War. From there the narrative flows through his involvement in the Revolutionary War, career as governor, role in the War of 1812, and death at the age of seventy-five. Interspersed is the story of his personal and family life. What emerges is a western version of the commonly held image of George Washington—a man who longs for the pleasures of home and family but who undertakes many varied military and civic assignments thrust upon him by his fellow citizens because his sense of duty will not allow him to refuse them.

The book's greatest appeal to the professional historian probably will be the annotated bibliography. The text, in reference to larger events, contains some factual errors and leaves a few misleading impressions. More annoying is the total absence of footnotes. Even direct quotations, which are highly visible because they appear in italics, are not so blessed, although their sources usually can be identified by reference to surrounding comments or to the bibliography.

To write for the scholarly community, however, perhaps was not the author's intention. The book's lucid, flowing style and subheaded chapters make easy, entertaining reading which will have appeal to the general reader with some interest in local, state, and regional history. Also attracted by the work will be those who have family ties extending to this era and place in our national history. Indeed, the success of this work probably will depend upon how well received it is by individuals in these categories, as well as upon the interest in this era generated by the bicentennial celebration. [JAMES L. BAUMGARDNER, Carson-Newman College]

The Harvest and the Reapers: Oral Traditions of Kentucky. By Kenneth and Mary Clarke; *Three Kentucky Artists: Hart, Price, Troye.* By J. Winston Coleman, Jr.; *Uncle Bill of Wildwood: Nineteenth Century Life in the Bluegrass.* By Frances Jewell McVey and Robert Berry Jewell; *Kentucky Moonshine.* By David W. Maurer; *John Wesley Hunt: Pioneer*

Merchant, Manufacturer, and Financier. By James A. Ramage. (Lexington, Ky.: University Press of Kentucky, c. 1974. Pp. [xii], 98; [x], 77; xxiv, 100; xviii, 134; [xii], 104. $3.95 each.) These are the first volumes to be issued in a projected fifty titles in the Kentucky Bicentennial Bookshelf, sponsored by the Kentucky Federation of Women's Clubs, over thirty Kentucky business firms, and the National Endowment for the Humanities. The series will feature almost every aspect of Kentucky history and life and will include volumes by outstanding historians as well as other scholars and writers. Each will be approximately 112 pages in length. Persons may become charter subscribers to the series by paying $98.75 for the first twenty-five books now. They will thereby be guaranteed that all books in the series will be sold to them at $3.95 cash regardless of increased costs. They will also be entitled to a free bonus book. These first volumes are handsomely printed and bound and provide some notion of the broad scope of the series. They have no footnotes, but some of them provide brief bibliographies.

Tennessee History: A Bibliography. Edited and compiled by Sam B. Smith and Luke H. Banker. (Knoxville: University of Tennessee Press, c. 1974. Pp. xlii, 498. $17.50.) Scholars will welcome this highly useful bibliography of Tennessee. It is prefaced by a twenty-one-page bibliographical essay by the late Stanley J. Folmsbee and then presents twenty-seven major categories of listings. After a general reference materials section it proceeds in a largely chronological fashion to Reconstruction and military history from 1898 to 1972. This is followed by large sections on economic history; political history; constitutional, judicial, legal, and legislative history; social and cultural history, with special reference to education, religion, and Negroes; natural history; literature; and a large section on the histories of the state's ninety-five counties. There are author and subject indexes. The bibliography includes material through 1972, and the editors have listed more than a thousand master's theses and dissertations relevant to Tennessee history.

The Era of Franklin D. Roosevelt: A Selected Bibliography of Periodical, Essay, and Dissertation Literature, 1945–1971. Compiled and annotated by William J. Steward. (Hyde Park: Franklin D. Roosevelt Library, [1974]. Pp. [vi], 360. Paper, $4.75.) F.D.R. buffs and serious scholars will welcome this revision of a 1967 edition which has been out of print since 1970. Noting that there has been no decline in scholarly interest in F.D.R. since his death nearly three decades ago, the compiler offers this enlarged edition as an aid to researchers as they seek out pertinent but difficult-to-locate periodical articles and dissertations.

The compiler has achieved his objective in most admirable fashion. The format—four sections entitled Franklin D. Roosevelt, New Deal, World War II, and Archives, Bibliography, Historiography—facilitates use of the guide, and inclusion of author and subject indexes adds value to an already useful research tool. Most of the items are annotated; no attempt at critical analysis is made, however. The guide is, nonetheless, an excellent contribution. [George T. Morgan, University of Houston]

Public Papers of the Presidents of the United States: Herbert Hoover; Containing the Public Messages, Speeches, and Statements of the President, March 4 to December 31, 1929. (Washington: U. S. Government Printing Office, 1974. Pp. xxxviii, 812. $13.30.) The National Historical Publications Commission in 1957 recommended systematic publication of the papers of the Presidents, and this began with President Truman and has since continued. The earlier compilation by James D. Richardson covered the Presidents from 1789 to 1897, and private compilations were made after that period. The present volume is the continuation of the effort to establish an official series of the public writings and utterances of the Presidents. It covers the first year of the Hoover administration, and additional volumes will be devoted to each of the remaining years. This will be a welcome addition to our published public records.

Guide to the Official Records in the Mississippi Department of Archives and History. Compiled by Thomas W. Henderson and Ronald E. Tomlin. (Jackson: Mississippi Department of Archives and History, c. 1975. Pp. vi, 115. Paper, $3.00.) This useful compilation updates and supersedes an earlier guide by Dunbar Rowland published in 1914. In making the new guide, the records were rearranged and renumbered by record groups, retaining, however, the basic division into provincial, territorial, and state records used earlier. In addition to the official state records, the guide includes sections on county, municipal, and federal records in the department.

Mississippi: Conflict & Change. Edited by James W. Loewen and Charles Sallis. (New York: Pantheon Books, c. 1974. Pp. x, 368. Paper, $6.95; cloth, $10.00.) This is a very different type of high school textbook in Mississipi history, produced by the collaboration of faculty and students of Tougaloo College and Millsaps College, the first predominantly a black institution and the second a predominantly white one. Without adopting a negative attitude, it presents a very fresh picture of the state's shortcomings as well as its advances, and it offers a biracial approach to the state's history. Profusely illustrated, it has many useful maps and charts.

Materials for the Study of Washington: A Selected Annotated Bibliography. By Perry G. Fisher. *GW Washington Studies,* No. 1. (Washington: George Washington University Division of Experimental Programs, c. 1974. Pp. 63. Paper, $2.50.) The publication inaugurates a series of monographic studies on Washington, D. C., to be prepared by members of the faculty of George Washington University. Copies may be obtained from the Division of Experimental Programs. Prices are reduced for orders in quantity: $2.25 each for orders of 16 to 49; $2.00 each for 50 or more. Roderick S. French is general editor of the series.

Index to Maps of the American Revolution in Books and Periodicals,

Illustrating the Revolutionary War and Other Events of the Period 1763–1789. By David Sanders Clark. (Westport, Conn., and London, England: Greenwood Press, 1974. Pp. xvi, 301. $15.00.) As the title suggests this lists maps published in books and magazines. It is arranged primarily by geographical area, but it has a subject and name index to map references as well as a list of the publications which have been indexed.

Virginia History in Documents, 1621–1789. By William H. Gaines, Jr. (Richmond: Virginia State Library, 1974. Pp. x, 84; and 14 facsimile sheets in a folder. Paper, $5.00.) The Virginia State Library has issued this folder of facsimile reproductions of ten significant documents in Virginia's early history along with an explanatory booklet which provides a description of the provenance and significance of each document. The booklet also reproduces the texts of the documents in type and furnishes a brief bibliographical essay. The documents include an ordinance and constitution for a council and assembly in Virginia, July 24, 1621; the declaration of the people against Sir William Berkeley, July 30, 1676; Patrick Henry's Resolution against the Stamp Act, May 30, 1765; the proceedings of a meeting of representatives in Williamsburg, May 30, 1774; Resolutions of the Virginia convention for independence, May 15, 1776; the Virginia Declaration of Rights, June 12, 1776; the Virginia constitution, June 29, 1776; the bill for establishing religious freedom, proposed June 12, 1779, passed January 16, 1786; resolutions for ceding lands to the United States, January 2, 1781; and the form of ratification of the Constitution, June 25, 1778. All are handwritten documents except for the bill for religious freedom, which is taken from a report published in Richmond in 1784.

Wilmington–New Hanover Safety Committee Minutes, 1774–1776. Edited by Leora H. McEachern and Isabel M. Williams. (Wilmington, N. C.: Wilmington–New Hanover County American Revolution Bicentennial Association, 1974. Pp. xxvi, 147. $8.95.) This volume includes a fourteen-page introduction by Lawrence Lee to put the minutes in context, ninety-two pages of the transcribed minutes, and four appendixes containing resolves of the Continental and Provincial Congresses relating to the committee, a list of vessels mentioned in the minutes, a proclamation of Governor Josiah Martin dated June 16, 1775, and a biographical list of persons referred to in the minutes. An index provides subject and personal entries.

A Vagabond Newsman. By Nelson Shipp. (Atlanta: Cherokee Publishing Co., 1974. Pp. xii, 230. $5.95.) Nelson Shipp, born in 1892, became an important journalist and political aide in Georgia, but almost all of this anecdotal autobiography is about his early life. About a third of the book describes incidents from Shipp's boyhood in Cordele in the "wiregrass country" of south Georgia. He calls the rural Georgia of the early twentieth century a "frontier," and his account clearly indicates the atmosphere of casual physical violence in the area. The second third is a detailed description of a brief period when the young Shipp was a hobo by choice, wandering in the Midwest; in passing he describes life among the railroad workers. The last third, consisting mostly of unconnected incidents in Shipp's early newspaper career in Savannah, Macon, Columbus, and Atlanta, offers some intriguing glimpses of the relationships between reporters and editors and between journalists and politicians. Shipp's own political career, as he mentions in an aside, included more than twenty years in which he "served five governors as writer, headed two departments, and served in various specialized positions" (p. 209), but there is practically nothing about it in the book. [THOMAS H. BAKER, University of Arkansas, Little Rock]

The Cameron Plantation in Central North Carolina (1776–1973) and Its Founder Richard Bennehan. By Charles Richard Sanders. (Durham, N.C.: The Author, 1974. Pp. viii, 79. $11.00.) Charles Richard Sanders, professor emeritus of English at Duke University, has written and published this account of a famous plantation and its founder. Richard Bennehan, a Virginian, began the plantation in 1776, and it was subsequently enlarged after his daughter Rebecca married Duncan Cameron. Their son Paul Carrington Cameron owned some 1,900 slaves and over 30,000 acres before the Civil War. The descendants of the family still own large acreages there today. Richard Bennehan was an important person in the founding of Raleigh and the University of North Carolina. His descendants have been significant leaders of the state since that time. Persons desiring copies should write Professor Sanders at 103 Pinecrest Road, Durham, North Carolina 27705.

The Gunsmith in Colonial Virginia. By Harold B. Gill, Jr. *Williamsburg Research Studies.* (Williamsburg, Va.: Colonial Williamsburg Foundation, c. 1974. Distributed by the University Press of Virginia. Pp. viii, 139. Paper, $4.50; cloth, $7.50.) This new title in the Williamsburg Research Studies provides three chapters on gunsmiths in colonial Virginia, in Williamsburg, and in the Revolution. Three additional chapters describe gunsmith's tools and accounts and provide an alphabetical list of Virginia gunsmiths from 1608 to 1800.

The Polish Pioneers in Virginia. By Sigmund H. Uminski. *The Poles in America,* Volume II. (New York: Polish Publication Society of America, c. 1974. Pp. xxiv, 139. $5.50.) This brief work includes eight chapters and two appendices relating to Poles in early Virginia. It emphasizes that some Poles arrived as early as 1608 and were among the glassmakers sent over by the Virginia Company.

Addresses and Public Papers of Robert Walter Scott, Governor of North Carolina, 1969–1973. Edited by Memory F. Mitchell. (Raleigh: Division of Archives and History, Department of Cultural Resources, 1974. Pp. xl, 770.) This official documentary volume includes the official speeches, statements, and releases of Governor Scott. His list of appointments is published as an appendix. Not considered a part of the official records is a biographical sketch by Russell T. Clay.

Rowan County: A Brief History. By James S. Brawley. (Raleigh: North Carolina Department of Cultural Resources, Division of Archives and History, 1974. Pp. xvi, 176. Paper, $1.50.) This is the fourth in a series of short histories of counties in North Carolina published by the North Carolina Division of Archives and History. The author is a member of the staff of the Salisbury *Evening Post* and published *The Rowan Story, 1753–1953* in 1953. The typewritten text is supplemented by numerous illustrations.

The North Carolina Division of Archives and History at Raleigh issued in 1974 a third revised printing of *North Carolina Governors, 1585–1974: Brief Sketches.* By Beth G. Crabtree. (Pp. viii, 189. Paper, $3.00.).

Florida Place Names. By Allen Morris. (Coral Gables: University of Miami Press, c. 1974. Pp. 160. $5.95.) This alphabetical listing of place names with accounts of their origin was compiled by a former newsman who is presently clerk of the Florida House of Representatives.

Yesterday's Florida Keys. By Stan Windhorn and Wright Langley. *Seemann's Historic Cities Series,* No. 12. (Miami: E. A. Seemann Publishing, c. 1974. Pp. 128. $7.95.); *Yesterday's Atlanta.* By Franklin M. Garrett. *Seemann's Historic Cities Series,* No. 8. (Miami: E. A. Seemann Publishing, c. 1974. Pp. 166. $9.95.) These two volumes present a number of photographs illustrating the changes in the cities and areas to which they are devoted. There are brief introductory comments at the beginning of the chronological chapters into which they are divided and informative descriptive material accompanying each photograph. Not history in any formal sense, they are, nevertheless, of interest to historians.

Alfred R. Waud: Civil War Artist. By Frederic E. Ray. (New York: Viking Press, 1974. Pp. 192. $16.95.) This volume has two parts. The first provides a sixty-page biography of Alfred Waud, famous for his Civil War drawings for the *New York Illustrated News* and *Harper's Weekly.* The second part reproduces 108 black-and-white drawings with extensive notes.

Tennessee During the Revolutionary War. By Samuel Cole Williams. With an introduction by Frank B. Williams, Jr., and an index by Muriel C. Spoden. (Knoxville: University of Tennessee Press, c. 1974. Pp. xxx, 290. $8.75.) This is a facsimile reprint of the text of the original volume published in 1944 and reviewed in the February 1945 issue of the *Journal* (XI, 107–108). Sponsored by the Tennessee American Revolution Bicentennial Commission, it has an introduction by Frank B. Williams, Jr., a bibliography of the author's writings compiled by Pollyanna Creekmore, and an expanded and corrected index by Muriel C. Spoden.

The Life of Andrew Jackson. By John Reid and John Henry Eaton. Edited by Frank Lawrence Owsley, Jr. *Southern Historical Publications,* No. 19. (University, Ala.: University of Alabama Press, c. 1974. Pp. xvi, viii, 9–425, xvii–cix. $17.50.) Noting that this life was published first in 1817 and then in a number of subsequent editions, Professor Owsley asserts (p. xiii) that "the 1817 edition is by far the superior historical account . . ." and has therefore been chosen for reprinting. The body of the book is therefore the facsimile reproduction of this edition. Professor Owsley has provided a brief introduction, a listing of the various editions, notes on the text, a forty-six-page section of bibliography and appendices, an index to the original volume, and an index to his critical material.

The University of Oklahoma Press at Norman published in 1974 new paper and cloth editions of two standard studies by E. Wilson Lyon: *Louisiana in French Diplomacy, 1759–1804* (Pp. [iv], 268. Paper, $3.95; cloth, $8.95.) was originally published in 1934 and was reviewed in the August 1936 issue of the *Journal* (II, 408–409); *The Man Who Sold Louisiana: The Career of Francois Barbe-Marbois* (Pp. xx, 240. Paper, $2.95; cloth, $5.95.) was first published in 1942 and includes a brief note in the second printing.

Colonial Pensacola. Edited by James R. McGovern. *Andrew Jackson and Pensacola.* Edited by James R. McGovern. *The Pensacola Series Commemorating the American Revolution Bicentennial,* Volumes I and II. (Pensacola: Pensacola-Escambia Development Commission, 1974. Pp. iv, 124; pp. iii, 110. Paper, each, $2.50; cloth, each, $5.00.) These are the first two volumes of a projected ten to cover Pensacola's history from 1559 through World War II. The present volumes are revisions of earlier volumes printed in 1971 and 1972 respectively. Each consists of documents and formal papers presented by various authors.

Slavery, Colonialism, and Racism. Edited by Sidney W. Mintz. (New York: W. W. Norton and Co., c. 1974. Pp. x, 213. $10.95.) This is a separate printing of the April 1974 issue of *Daedalus* and includes eleven essays by twelve scholars relating to slavery in America and the West Indies and to aspects of black history in Africa and the New World.

The United States and France: Civil War Diplomacy. By Lynn M. Case and Warren F. Spencer. (Philadelphia: University of Pennsylvania Press, 1974. Pp. xviii, 747. Paper, $8.95.) This makes available a paperback edition of a significant book reviewed in the November 1970 issue of the *Journal* (XXXVI, 609–10).

Six Days or Forever? Tennessee *v.* John Thomas Scopes. By Ray Ginger. (London, Oxford, and New York: Oxford University Press, 1974. Pp. [xii], 258. Paper, $2.95.) This is a reprint of a volume first published in 1958 and reviewed in the November 1958 issue of the *Journal* (XXIV, 529–31).

The Forest History Society of Santa Cruz, California, and the Appalachian Consortium of Boone, North Carolina, have recently republished Carl Alwin Schenck's book *The Biltmore Story,* which was published in 1955. The reissued volume is now entitled *Birth of Forestry in America* (Paper, $4.50; cloth, $10.95.).

Historical News and Notices

THE ASSOCIATION

NOMINATIONS FOR 1975: The Nominating Committee, consisting of John Hebron Moore of Florida State University, chairman, William D. Aeschbacher of the University of Cincinnati, John S. Ezell of the University of Oklahoma, Robert W. Johannsen of the University of Illinois, and Willie Lee Rose of the Johns Hopkins University, has made the following nominations for 1975:

For vice-president: Richard L. Watson, Jr., Duke University

For the Executive Council (three-year terms):

Richard M. Brown, College of William and Mary
Charles B. Dew, University of Missouri–Columbia
Anne Firor Scott, Duke University

For the Executive Council (one-year term):

E. David Cronon, University of Wisconsin, Madison (to fill unexpired term of Richard L. Watson, Jr.)

In accordance with Article VIII of the present constitution these nominations will automatically become effective following the annual meeting unless one hundred members present a petition by September 1. If such a petition is presented the secretary-treasurer will mail an official ballot by October 1, which shall indicate which persons have been nominated by petition. These ballots must be returned to the chairman of the Nominating Committee by October 20, and he shall report the results to the secretary-treasurer by November 1. For further details, see Article VIII of the constitution (*Journal,* XL, 109).

President Richard N. Current has announced appointments to the following committees for the 1975 annual meeting at Washington, D. C.: *Membership Committee:* Frank L. Byrne of Kent State University, chairman, Thomas H. Baker of the University of Arkansas at Little Rock, Palmer H. Boeger of East Central State College of Oklahoma, Jo Ann Carrigan of the University of Nebraska at Omaha, Martin B. Coyner, Jr., of the College of William and Mary, Jane Lucas De Grummond of Louisiana State University, Henry C. Dethloff of Texas A&M University, Charles Deusner of Hillsborough Community College, W. McKee Evans of California State Polytechnic University, Walter Fisher of Morgan State University, Robert G. Gunderson of Indiana University, James E. Haney of Vanderbilt University, Herman M. Hattaway of the University of Missouri at Kansas City, Ronald L. Hatzenbuehler of Idaho State University, G. Seldon Henry of the University of Florida, William C. Hine of South Carolina State College, Donald B. Hoffman of Phi Alpha Theta, A. William Hoglund of the University of Connecticut, John T. Hubbell of Kent State University, Sara D. Jackson of the National Historical Publications Commission, Everette B. Long of the University of Wyoming, Robert C. McMath of the Georgia Institute of Technology, David E. Meerse of State University College at Fredonia, New York, William H. Pease of the University of Maine, William Charles Sallis of Millsaps College, David L. Smiley of Wake Forest University, J. Barton Starr of Troy State University, Mary K. Tachau of the University of Louisville, Sarah Woolfolk Wiggins of the University of Alabama at Tuscaloosa, Richard D. Younger of the University of Houston, and Anne Y. Zimmer of Wayne State University; *Sydnor Award Committee:* V. Jacque Voegeli of Vanderbilt University, chairman, Steven A. Channing of the University of Kentucky, and Charles B. Dew of the University of Missouri at Columbia; *Graduate Student Award Committee:* David L. Smiley of Wake Forest University, chairman, H. Larry Ingle of the University of Tennessee at Chattanooga, and George C. Rogers, Jr., of the University of South Carolina; *Simkins Prize Committee:* Marvin W. Schlegel of Norfolk State College, chairman, L. Marshall Hall, Jr., of Longwood College, and Joe G. Taylor of McNeese State College.

PERSONALS

Maryland Historical Magazine: John B. Boles named editor.

National Archives and Records Service: Charles M. Dollar appointed director of the Machine-Readable Archives Division.

University of Texas, El Paso: Kenneth B. Shover named chairman of the department and Oscar J. Martinez codirector of the University Oral History Institute; Oscar J. Martinez appointed instructor; Edward C. Clark promoted to associate professor; Edward C. Clark on leave.

DEATHS

Mary Elizabeth Massey, president of the Southern Historical Association in 1972, died of heart and kidney ailments on December 24, 1974, at Duke Hospital at the age of fifty-eight, following an extended period of illness. Born in Morrilton, Arkansas, on December 25, 1915, she was a graduate of Hendrix College, whose Alumni Association in 1967 named her their first Distinguished Alumna. She received her M.A. (1940) and Ph.D. (1947) from the University of North Carolina at Chapel Hill, where she worked under Fletcher M. Green. She taught at Morrilton High School from 1937 to 1939 and was director of Hendrix College Training School from 1940 to 1942. Her college teaching career began at Flora Macdonald College, from which she moved to Washington College (Maryland) before coming to Winthrop College in 1950, where she spent the remainder of her career. At Winthrop she was chairman of the History Department from 1960 to 1964, selected Distinguished Professor in 1965, and elected faculty representative to the Board of Trustees in 1972. During her career she received research awards from the Guggenheim Foundation (1963–1964), the Southern Fellowships Fund (1956), and the Huntington Library (1963), as well as Winthrop College.

She contributed importantly to several historical groups, notably as a member of the Advisory Council to the National Civil War Centennial Commission (1961–1965) and as a member of the Board of Advisors to the National Historical Society since 1970. Her devotion to the Southern Historical Association was a central focus of her life. Her first major responsibility was as chairman of the Membership Committee (1955), where she made "far and away the greatest addition" that had been made by any membership chairman since the Association's founding, she was a member of the Executive Council (1959–1961), chairman of the Program Committee (1962), and chairman of the Nominating Committee (1965) before being named the third female president in the Association's history.

Her books and articles reflected her meticulous scholarship and her interest in people, rather than abstract principles and social theories. *Ersatz in the Confederacy* (1952) and *Refugee Life in the Confederacy* (1964) dealt with the Confederate homefront. She was the only woman and the only southerner asked to contribute to the fifteen-volume series on "The Impact of the Civil War," which resulted in her last book, *Bonnet Brigades* (1966). She wrote a chapter in *The Writing of Southern History: Essays in Historiography in Honor of Fletcher M. Green* (1965) and published many articles in state historical journals and the *Journal of Southern History*. Her last completed scholarly endeavor, a paper on Mary Todd Lincoln, was read for her before the National Historical Society in September 1974. The completion of that work despite many physical obstacles, as well as her perseverance in her presidential year in the Association, were characteristic of her devotion to duty.

Mary Elizabeth was noted for her ever-present sense of humor and her sensitivity to and love of people even more than for her scholarly production. Her passing leaves a unique void at future annual meetings of the Association.

Contributions in her memory may be sent to a scholarship fund at Winthrop College in care of the History Department. [THOMAS S. MORGAN, Winthrop College]

Stanley John Folmsbee, professor emeritus of history at the University of Tennessee at Knoxville, died September 6, 1974, at the age of seventy-four. Born in New York he received his bachelor's degree at Dickinson College and his master's and doctor's degrees at the University of Pennsylvania. After a three-year teaching stint at Pennsylvania, he joined the faculty of the University of Tennessee in 1928 and remained there until his retirement in 1971. An active researcher and writer, he published numerous articles on Tennessee history and several books: *Sectionalism and Internal Improvements in Tennessee, 1796–1845* (1939); (coauth.), *History of Tennessee* (1960); (coauth.), *Tennessee: A Short History* (1969); and (coed.), *A Narrative of the Life of David Crockett of the State of Tennessee* (1973). One of the earliest members of the Southern Historical Association, Professor Folmsbee was a member of the Board of Editors of the *Journal of Southern History* from 1952 to 1955, chairman of the Program Committee in 1957, and a member of the Executive Council from 1964 to 1966.

ANNOUNCEMENTS AND ACTIVITIES

The Birmingham Metropolitan Study Project of the Center for Urban Studies at the University of Alabama in Birmingham, with support from a grant by the Greater Birmingham Foundation, has been established to encourage serious scholarly investigation of the history and development of metropolitan Birmingham. The project will provide financial assistance for research on the Birmingham metropolitan area by advanced undergraduate and graduate students and by established scholars—with stipends of up to $1,000 per quarter or semester—and make the results of this research available to the public through the Birmingham Public Library and the publication of an annual journal. At least one-half of available funds will be granted for student research.

Each applicant must submit a formal research proposal, including a full statement of the topic and its significance; an explanation of the procedures and methodologies to be used and the sources to be consulted; a research schedule; and a justification of the need for financial assistance. Student applications must be supported by a letter of evaluation of the project from a faculty member, preferably the principal academic adviser or thesis director. All applications will be evaluated by the Center for Urban Studies and a review board composed primarily of faculty representatives for colleges and universities in the Birmingham area. Deadlines for applications are March 1, June 1, September 1, and December 1.

Applications, supporting materials, and requests for additional information should be directed to Blaine A. Brownell, Chairman, Board of Review, Birmingham Metropolitan Study Project, Center for Urban Studies, University of Alabama in Birmingham, University Station, Birmingham, Alabama 35294.

The History Department at the University of Delaware will conduct a workshop on "History Through Media," June 16–July 18, 1975. The participants will study the technical aspects of media presentations using resources from the National Archives. The workshop is open to faculty, graduate and undergraduate students, and others interested in the subject. There are limited scholarship funds available. For further information write Professor James C. Curtis, History Department, University of Delaware, Newark, Delaware 19711.

The Oral History Association will hold its Tenth National Colloquium in Asheville, North Carolina, October 23–26, 1975. The theme for the colloquium will be "Oral History Comes of Age: The Tenth National Colloquium on Oral History." Inquiries about the meeting should be addressed to Ronald E. Marcello, Secretary, Box 13734, North Texas Station, North Texas State University, Denton, Texas 76203.

Middle Tennessee University has established an undergraduate program in historic preservation under the direction of Professor James K. Huhta.

LIBRARIES AND ARCHIVES

The National Archives and Records Service Cartographic Archives Division has accessioned approximately 1,500 maps and related materials mainly from the southern and western United States compiled chiefly by the Sedimentation Division of the Soil Conservation Service between 1934 and 1943. In addition, the Audiovisual Archives Division has accessioned 35,000 additional photographs from the Forest Service of the Department of Agriculture, 1911–30. A data-process subject printout was received with the records enabling the researcher to locate all photographs for a subject made in a state or several states. In addition the Archives and CBS, Inc., have established an archives of television news broadcasts from the CBS Television Network. Videotapes will be available for research use at the Archives, its eleven regional branches, the six presidential libraries, and on specific request through cooperating interlibrary loan libraries.

The *Guide to the National Archives of the United States,* 1974, has been published by the National Archives and Records Service. Superseding the long outdated *Guide* published in 1948, the new volume describes official records as of June 30, 1970, regardless of where they are located (with the exception of the presidential libraries). This volume costs $12.30 and is available from the Superintendent of Documents, U. S. Government Printing Office, Washington, D. C. 20402.

Other National Archives publications include a list published by the Atlanta Branch of all microfilm materials available at the East Point Federal Archives and Records Center. The list is available without charge from Mr. Gayle Peters, 1557 St. Joseph Avenue, East Point, Georgia 30044. The Kansas City Branch has published a similar *Region Six Microfilm List,* describing the branch's holdings through August 1974. It is available from the Chief, Archives Branch, Federal Archives and Records Center, 2366 East Bannister Road, Kansas City, Missouri 64131.

New National Archives microfilm publications are: M970, Letters Received by the Department of Justice from the State of Mississippi, 1871–1884 (4 rolls); M979, Records of the Assistant Commissioner for the State of Arkansas, Bureau of Refugees, Freedmen, and Abandoned Lands, 1865–69 (52 rolls); and M980, Records of the Superintendent of Education for the State of Arkansas, Bureau of Refugees, Freedmen, and Abandoned Lands, 1865–70 (5 rolls).

Among the Regional Archives the Atlanta Branch has accessioned records from the Atlanta Regional Office of the War Assets Administration, 1941–50, dealing with surplus property in Alabama, Florida, Georgia, Mississippi, North Carolina, South Carolina, and Tennessee (713 cubic feet); records from the U. S. District Court for the Southern District of Alabama (Mobile) including admiralty, bankruptcy, civil action, and criminal case files, 1944–48 (36 cubic feet); and additional court book records from the Southern District of Florida, 1938–48 (120 cubic feet). It has also received the first 312 rolls of 1900 census microfilm covering the states of Alabama through Kane County, Illinois. The film is available for legitimate research at the archives with several carefully defined restrictions. Detailed information should be obtained by writing the Atlanta Regional Archives, 1557 St. Joseph Avenue, East Point, Georgia 30344.

The Kansas City Branch has received the War Manpower Commission records of the Kansas City Regional Office (Region IX), documenting activities in Arkansas, Kansas, Missouri, and Oklahoma, 1942–45 (48 cubic feet); and U. S. District Court files of the Eastern District of Missouri for divisions operating at St. Louis and Hannibal (92 cubic feet).

The Harry S. Truman Library has received additional papers of Eleanor Bontecou, attorney in the Civil Rights Section of the U. S. Department of Justice, 1933–45 (4 cubic feet).

The Amistad Research Center at Dillard University has recently received the papers of Alexander Pierre Tureaud (1899–1972), a black New Orleans attorney and NAACP activist. The Center has begun microfilming the archives of the American Home Missionary Society, amounting to some 750,000 items spanning the years from 1826 to 1907.

THE JOURNAL OF SOUTHERN HISTORY

AUGUST 1975
Vol. XLI, No. 3

Published Quarterly by the Southern Historical Association

The Journal of Southern History

Published Quarterly by

THE SOUTHERN HISTORICAL ASSOCIATION

New Orleans, Louisiana

Printed by WILLIAM BYRD PRESS,
RICHMOND, VIRGINIA

The present constitution of the Southern Historical Association is printed in the February 1974 issue of the *Journal of Southern History*, Volume XL, Number 1.

Contributions and correspondence relating to articles, book reviews, and any other editorial matters should be sent to the Managing Editor, *Journal of Southern History*, Rice University, Houston, Texas 77001.

The subscription rate is $10.00 a year for a regular membership, $12.00 for family membership, $5.00 for enrolled student, and $3.00 for retired members. Upon payment of $200.00 any person may become a life member of the Southern Historical Association. Single numbers of the *Journal* are available at $3.00 plus postage. Changes of address must be made six weeks in advance of the publication of an issue in order for the change to be effective with that issue. A charge of $2.50 will be made for forwarding copies returned because of incorrect addresses.

Subscriptions, membership applications, and orders for current issues of the *Journal* should be sent to Bennett H. Wall, Secretary-Treasurer, History Department, Tulane University, New Orleans, Louisiana 70118. *Notice of nonreceipt of an issue must be sent to the Secretary-Treasurer within sixty days following publication of the issue.* Inquiries concerning noncurrent back issues of the *Journal* should be directed to Johnson Reprint Corporation, 111 Fifth Avenue, New York, New York 10003.

The Southern Historical Association disclaims responsibility for statements made by contributors.

Second-class postage paid at New Orleans, Louisiana, and at additional mailing offices.

The Journal of SOUTHERN HISTORY

VOLUME XLI | AUGUST 1975 | NUMBER 3

Contents

Charles Colcock Jones and the Southern Evangelical Crusade to Form a Biracial Community
By Donald G. Mathews 299

Black Ironworkers and the Slave Insurrection Panic of 1856
By Charles B. Dew 321

The Commercial-Civic Elite and City Planning in Atlanta, Memphis, and New Orleans in the 1920s
By Blaine A. Brownell 339

The Black Family in Transition: Louisiana, 1860–1865
By C. Peter Ripley 369

Notes and Documents:

Andrew Johnson and Reconstruction: A British View
Edited by Eric Foner 381

Northern Institutions in Southern Financial History: A Note on Insurance Investments
By B. Michael Pritchett 391

Book Reviews 397

Book Notes 436

Historical News and Notices 438

Book Reviews

MORISON, *The European Discovery of America,* by John J. TePaske 397
WALSH and FOX, eds., *Maryland,* by Philip S. Klein 398
LEE, *Blackbeard the Pirate,* by Miles M. Merwin 399
DOSTER, *The Creek Indians,* by Milton L. Ready 400
ROGERS, *Empire and Liberty,* by Roy N. Lokken 401
ROGERS and others, eds., *The Papers of Henry Laurens,* Vol. IV, by Jack P. Greene 402
DAVIS, *The Problem of Slavery in the Age of Revolution,* by Carl N. Degler 403
BEEMAN, *Patrick Henry,* by Stuart Seely Sprague 406
HENDERSON, *Party Politics in the Continental Congress,* by Robert C. Detweiler .. 407
HURST, *A Legal History of Money,* by Walter T. K. Nugent 409
JOHNSON and others, eds., *The Papers of John Marshall,* Vol. I, by Phillip S. Paludan 410
SYRETT and others, eds., *The Papers of Alexander Hamilton,* Vols. XX, XXI,
by Noble E. Cunningham, Jr. 412
VIOLA, *Thomas L. McKenney,* by Reginald Horsman 413
DILLON, *The Abolitionists,* by Louis Ruchames 414
PEASE and PEASE, *They Who Would Be Free,* by Arvarh E. Strickland 416
DAVIS, *Breckinridge,* by Robert G. Hartje 417
FOOTE, *The Civil War,* by Alwyn Barr 418
BENEDICT, *A Compromise of Principle,* by Richard O. Curry and Harry S. Stout .. 419
TAYLOR, *Louisiana Reconstructed,* by LaWanda Cox 421
NORDIN, *Rich Harvest,* by Peter H. Argersinger 423
EKIRCH, *Progressivism in America,* by D. Alan Harris 424
LINK and others, eds., *The Papers of Woodrow Wilson,* Vols. 15, 16, 17,
by E. David Cronon 425
SZASZ, *Education and the American Indian,* by W. W. Newcomb 427
MORGAN, *The Making of the TVA,* by Wilmon H. Droze 428
ANDERSON, *The Wild Man from Sugar Creek,* by Alexander R. Stoesen 429
HYNDS, *Antebellum Athens,* by James P. Hendrix, Jr. 431
THOMAS, *Southern Methodist University,* by Donald K. Pickens 432
CAMPBELL, *Two Hundred Years of Pharmacy in Mississippi,* by Charles Stephen Gurr 433
DOROUGH, *The Bible Belt Mystique,* by Kenneth K. Bailey 434
PETTIT, *Mark Twain & the South,* by E. Stanly Godbold, Jr. 434

Charles Colcock Jones and the Southern Evangelical Crusade to Form a Biracial Community

By Donald G. Mathews

Charles Colcock Jones and William Lloyd Garrison had much in common. Both were Evangelical Christians and moral elitists who wanted a perfect society. Both devoted their lives to the problem of black-white relationships. At one time both wrote about the necessity of destroying African slavery. They developed, however, in different ways. Garrison personified the northern abolitionist movement; Jones represented the southern Christian mission to the slaves. Although historians know a great deal about Garrison's pilgrimage, they know little about Jones's. Identified with the efforts of antebellum southerners to vindicate their social system, the mission as a historical institution and idea has suffered from the sentimentality of conservatives and the righteous indignation of radicals. Awareness of class interest, religious self-delusion, and racial fears, however, should not prevent historians from considering the ironies and almost hopeless contradictions that bemired southern Evangelicals. If the mission was a movement to impose social control, it nevertheless sprang from some of the best inclinations of white southerners. And if the best was inadequate to deal with social problems, perhaps the monumental quality of the inadequacy is worth remembering.

Until the Great Awakening in the South race relations had been shaped by the whites' need to control an indispensable if potentially dangerous labor force and had been only haphazardly affected by religious institutions. As a movement attracting blacks as well as whites and emphasizing the moral bases of life, the Awakening demanded careful scrutiny of the master-slave relationship. This action, facilitated by Revolutionary ideals of egalitarianism, gave rise to a long controversy about the emancipationist implications of Evangelicalism. Although emancipationists failed in their ultimate

---

Mr. Mathews is professor of history at the University of North Carolina at Chapel Hill.

The Journal of Southern History
Vol. XLI, No. 3, August 1975

aim, they succeeded in making slaves the moral charges of whites, as blacks were slowly brought within the orbit of Protestant Christianity. In the 1820s and 1830s southern clergymen felt a new sense of urgency with the stirring of slaves in the South and radicals in the North. Insurrection and abolitionism joined with a national impulse for reform to provide an audience for a man who hoped to save his country and soul by persuading his fellow southerners to create a biracial community based upon Christian precepts.

Charles Colcock Jones (1804–1863) grew up in a world where men and women daily exercised power and responsibility with the fretfully persistent knowledge of their ultimate powerlessness and moral failing. He was raised in a slaveholding family whose religious inheritance was the stern moral discipline of Presbyterianism. His natal county, Liberty (Georgia), had been founded by descendants of Puritans who since 1630 had arrived from England by way of New England and South Carolina. The church and religious society, called Midway, still formed the nucleus of social life; the words of the pastor still brought the promise of eternal life: "I rejoice to hear that God has showed you your unworthiness & wretchedness, because I am persuaded that he is about to bestow on you remarkable Comforts."[1] This tension between original sin and eternal bliss—with its consequences of personal anxiety and self-discipline—was the religious context within which masters viewed their slaves. Wanting their slaves to hold the same views, masters brought them into Midway Church.[2] There young Charles could see black and white together and muse about the special obligation which masters owed their slaves.[3]

But Jones did not at once articulate that obligation. An orphan, he was apprenticed by his uncle and guardian to a Savannah countinghouse in 1819 until a serious illness sent him into a personal crisis that resulted in his religious conversion. Steadily, he thought through the problems of becoming a minister until in 1825 he went north to Phillips Academy, Andover, Massachusetts. After graduation he attended both Andover and Princeton theological seminaries, graduating from the latter in the autumn of 1830.[4] Dur-

[1] John Boggs to Mrs. ——— Jones, March 29, 1813, Charles Colcock Jones Papers (Tulane University, New Orleans, La.). The author wishes gratefully to acknowledge a grant from the National Endowment for the Humanities which made research for this article possible.

[2] See Murdock Murphy Diary, July 10, 1819 (Alabama Department of Archives and History, Montgomery, Ala.); James Stacy, *History of the Midway Congregational Church, Liberty County, Georgia* (Newnan, Ga., 1903), 208–39.

[3] See for example the report of planters' activities for their slaves in Robert Quarterman to Mary Jones, December 25, 1828, C. C. Jones Papers.

[4] Columbia (S.C.) *Southern Presbyterian,* June 4, 1863; Mary Jones, "Miscellaneous Remembrances of Charles Colcock Jones," C. C. Jones Papers. For a brief overview of C. C.

ing his last year in the North, he wrote some rather remarkable letters, in which he began to avow the obligation of white to black, an obligation that eventually made him one of the legendary saints of the southern churches. The letters expressed, as contrapuntal themes, the divine imperative of moral self-discipline and the "curse" of slavery. The first theme was common among young southern clergymen in the nineteenth century, but the second was quite uncommon, seldom appearing except as an anguished prayer of confession.

Jones shared his "anxious thought upon the subject of slavery" with his cousin and fiancée, Mary. "A violation of all the Laws of God and man at once," he wrote. "A complete annihilation of justice. An inhuman abuse of power, and an assumption of the responsibility of fixing the life and destiny of immortal beings, fearful in the extreme." Jones had been provoked into writing these words by a visit from Liberty County acquaintances, whose attitudes and assumptions disturbed him. Although slightly homesick, he was saddened and embarrassed by the contrast between southern society and the northern society he had come to admire. "There is a calmness, an order, a morality, a general sentiment of right & wrong, a justice, an equality, in this society which is not looked for in ours." In New England, but not in the South, men could freely discuss great social issues such as slavery. The difference between the two sections was shameful. Perhaps the young were not totally guilty for the evil that had been "entailed" upon them, but still, they had to act. Certainly he, Charles Colcock Jones, had to act, for his "conveniences of life" came from slave labor. Troubled, he could not decide what to do. Perhaps he should postpone marriage until he was freed of slave property or could move away from the South.[5]

Brave words from a pious young man to his fiancée are a special kind of expression. In the early nineteenth century they were often the exaggerated manifestation of romantic yearnings and were designed to demonstrate the moral sensitivity of the writer. The austere and intense Jones, however, was not posturing for his lady, whom he had known since they were children. He was genuinely disturbed by the differences between the two sections and their citizens. Northerners *ask* favors, southerners *demand* service, he complained, and attributed the difference to slavery.[6] To his

---

Jones's life see the preface to Robert M. Myers, ed., *The Children of Pride: A True Story of Georgia and the Civil War* (New Haven and London, 1972), 7–31.

[5] Charles Colcock Jones to Mary Jones, September 8, 1829, C. C. Jones Papers.

[6] Jones to Mary Jones, October 5, 1829; see also Jones to Mary Jones, October 24, 1829, *ibid.*

anguish, Mary replied that slaves needed the white man's discipline, for immediate emancipation would set loose a people "ignorant and fearless of the commands of God." Far better, she said, to "raise them first in the scale of moral excellence, by a different mode of treatment from what has been adopted hitherto—by treating them more as rational beings and trying to instill into them virtuous principles."[7]

Both Mary and Charles believed that everyone had to be raised "in the scale of moral excellence." Although he had a high opinion of educated, responsible, and pious persons like himself, he also carried the burden of his own "extreme guilt and abominable vileness."[8] Consequently, he mercilessly drove himself towards perfection through prayer, self-mortification, and discipline.[9] So intense was he in fasting, praying, and preaching that his friends, relatives, and fellow seminarians hoped for some relaxation, humor, or other significant sign of frail humanity.[10] With all his intensity and earnest striving to perfect his own life, he did not forget his duty to the slaves. Indeed, that obligation became part of his own private war with sin and guilt—and perhaps shame for lacking the moral courage to renounce slaveholding and slavery.

How he would meet the obligation, Charles had still to work out. At Princeton Theological Seminary he organized a "Society of Enquiry Concerning Africans," before which he delivered a paper urging the establishment of missions to the slaves of Georgia. The proposal, coming as it did from the depths of his soul, seemed to transform his cautious, well-ordered, and private piety into eloquent, proselytizing zeal. The agent from the Presbyterian Board of Missions wished him well, and the awesome Professor Samuel Miller asked, undoubtedly with beneficent humor, "Mr. Jones, why do you not always speak in that warm, animated manner . . . ?" Miller also asked if Charles feared he would be "*excommunicated*" in Georgia.[11]

Charles wondered himself. When he first organized his Society of Enquiry he had fretted about the caution required of anyone who wanted to accomplish something in the slave society. Too many

[7] Mary Jones to Jones, November 24, 1829; see also Mary Jones to Jones, October 16, 1829; Jones to Mary Jones, October 24, 1829, *ibid.*

[8] Jones to Mary Jones, October 5, 1829; see the same sentiments in Jones to Mary Jones, December 20, 1829; April 19, 1830, *ibid.*

[9] Jones to Mary Jones, December 8, 1829, *ibid.*

[10] Jones to Mary Jones, January 1, March 19, 1830; Mary Jones to Jones, February 16, 1830, *ibid.*

[11] Jones to Mary Jones, February 3, 1830; for further elaboration see Jones to Mary Jones, May 18, 1830, *ibid.*

ministers had aroused southerners with "injudicious speech and conduct" and had consequently accomplished nothing. Somehow, he had to find a way to secure the "best interests of the coloured population and the approbation of the whites."[12] But the way was not easy. He would still boldly write: "It is high time that our country was taking some measures of some sort, whose ultimate tendency shall be the emancipation of nearly three millions of men, women & children, who are held in the grossest bondage, and with the highest injustice. And where are the men to devise and execute these measures? No where."[13] Jones could not accept such an answer. He at least could be one of those men. Finally, the contrasts of South and North, of divine imperative and human pragmatism, of ignorant, exploited slaves and responsible, educated masters were resolved in Jones's view of the transforming power of personal piety. He would, he wrote Mary, become a missionary to the "poor degraded slaves.[14]

The decision was, of course, only one of many which made Charles Colcock Jones the "Apostle to the Blacks." Over the years other decisions and many more experiences would make him the admirable man that he was. The original decision, however, came at the end of a severe internal struggle, during which he put down on paper carefully and quite self-consciously a condemnation of slavery as an exploitative and dehumanizing system. He knew, therefore, that he must as a morally responsible person fight against it. But such knowledge was not purely received. The perspective allowed by being a thousand miles from Georgia, reading colonization pamphlets, possibly recalling blacks at worship in Midway Church, falling in love with free New England—all these pieces were fitted by the diminutive young man into a mosaic of Christian responsibility, which in turn was laid into the framework of his own social and personal inheritance of slavery. Why he brooded so intently over the problem is impossible to say. But throughout his life there seemed to be a special relationship between himself and blacks—a sense of obligation which he never quite wished to be free of.

Somehow he knew as a young man entering his lifework that he must fight against slavery to destroy it; that is what he clearly said. He just as clearly decided not to do so. He quite naturally turned his focus from the institution to the victims, *fellow* victims, as he saw them. For if slavery had brutalized the black, it had also in his

[12] Jones to Mary Jones, February 3, 1830, *ibid.*
[13] Jones to Mary Jones, May 18, 1830, *ibid.*
[14] Jones to Mary Jones, September 18, 1830, *ibid.*

view created a moral dilemma for whites. As the self-conscious disciple of Jonathan Edwards, he knew that the will was not free to make the choices it would have preferred. As the equally self-conscious disciple of Samuel Hopkins, he knew that the omnipotent God as Lord of fallen creation could make good come from evil. Jones also shared the Hopkinsian view that Christ had died for all men, not merely the elect. Intellectually, then, he was prepared to make the decision he did. It would be specious to conclude that guilt dictated that Jones would become a missionary to slaves. His piety and sense of obligation were such that no matter what decision he made, he would have felt morally incomplete, personally dissatisfied, and constantly in need of forgiveness. Slaveholding, which once caused such moral anguish, was to become for Jones simply the secular context within which he had to fulfill eternal obligations; he never again wrote as he had to Mary of the evil of the slave system and its imperative destruction. Perhaps he repressed that specific acknowledgement of his personal helplessness and moral culpability because he had, as had all consistent Hopkinsians, professed that he was indeed "willing to be damned for the glory of God."

Less romantic, but probably more to the point is the fact that the destruction of slavery was never the primary theme of Jones's writing on the subject. Even in his most "abolitionist" flights of rhetoric slavery was but the institutional expression of a more basic reality of the "depravity and wickedness of man." God had already solved the problem of demonic power through the life-death-resurrection of Christ Jesus. The abundant signs of evil were often painful and tragic beyond human endurance, and yet they were also mysterious, for Jones and his fellow pietists placed their trust in a God whom they would praise even as He smote them. A religion whose myths elevated pain and suffering to the central, redemptive process of salvation promised final victory not only at the end of life, but at once. The Evangelical emphasis on the Christian's citizenship in the "next" world did not create an "other-worldly" religion. The scope of action was limited to be sure, but it was indeed "this worldly." Jones expected himself and his fellow Christians to "yield" their whole personality to the discipline of the Christ. The process was not so passive as the verb "yield" might imply, but active, as the eager seminarian emphasized to Mary: "We must 'watch,' 'be vigilant' 'be strong' 'acquit ourselves like men' 'strive' 'work' 'pray without ceasing' 'deny ourselves' 'take up the cross.' It is all a 'race' a 'pilgrimmage' a 'fight' a 'war.' "[15] In that

[15] Jones to Mary Jones, September 8, 1829, *ibid.*

war Jones wanted victory so much for himself and his wife that it is not surprising he should have wanted it also for those to whom he felt an ultimate sense of duty. Loyalty to this goal was reinforced by the value which American Protestants placed upon missionary enterprise, which was after all the projection by Evangelicals of their own experience as a model for proper conduct and belief. In making his decision to preach the Gospel to slaves Jones became part of the missionary impulse which combined the need for ideological commitment in the confusion of rapid social change with Romantic optimism and Christian benevolence.

Jones spent the rest of his life working out the implications and demands of his mission. Briefly and fitfully supplying a pulpit in a Savannah Presbyterian church after graduating from Princeton,[16] Jones returned to Liberty County in November 1832 where he established himself as a planter and began to develop a theory and plans for a mission to slaves. Farmers in the area had already been interested in such a project, and the availability of a well-educated, slaveowning clergyman provided them with the leadership they required. The result of this happy combination was to make of Liberty County a laboratory in which Jones could test his theories about reshaping slaves according to a Christian view of human destiny. The process of theorizing, begun in seminary, had already resulted in a pamphlet published while Jones was pastor in Savannah. In that statement and almost everything he wrote thereafter he publicized the "religious instruction of the Negroes" and the utopia it was to achieve: a biracial southern community held together by mutual trust, self-discipline, and Christian piety.[17]

Jones's theory was based first of all on the threat to the southern social order created by the imperfect socialization of blacks. This statement of the South's most basic problem and its solution was much different from that discussed in his northern letters of only a few years before. Then the problem had been slavery and the solution, emancipation;[18] but prudence and piety altered his goal. The missionary ideal was not to challenge social systems but to transform individuals. Once the focus of reform shifted from system to

[16] See Eliza Roberts to Mary Jones, August 12, 1831: "I know his Black People occupy much of his thoughts and it would be very desirable if he could be situated . . . [to give them religious instruction]." See also Joseph Jones to Mary Jones, October 13, 1831, *ibid.* Jones spent eighteen months in Savannah, May 1831 to November 1832.

[17] Jones, *The Religious Instruction of the Negroes. A Sermon* . . . (Princeton, 1832); Jones, *Religious Instruction of the Negroes. An Address . . . December 10, 1861* (Richmond, 1862).

[18] See for example [Jones], *Report of the Committee to Whom Was Referred the Subject of the Religious Instruction of the Colored Population, of the Synod of South-Carolina and Georgia* . . . (Charleston, 1834), 26.

individual the explicit threat to the social order was removed, in the process removing also much of the tension between "divine" imperative and human capability. The character of the change is not at all surprising. The brave words and bold expectations of his younger years were tempered by the experience of multiplying responsibilities and subtle social interaction. Working against stubborn southern opposition could not of itself have worn him down; abolitionist attacks upon his society, class, and personal reputation probably affected him more than he admitted.[19] But certainly his management of plantations and slaves changed him even more. The daily disappointments and difficulties of working with slaves seem to have gradually diminished his hope for eventual emancipation. The institution that once *had* to be destroyed became one that *might* be destroyed; it then became a perpetual apprenticeship in civilization for blacks. And still, in his letters, especially as he railed against the helplessness of pious young black women before their white seducers,[20] he revealed that he understood personally what ideologically he could not admit.

The ambiguity inherent in his situation and understanding he resolved by focusing on the deviation of black servants from the values of white masters. The slaves were, as everyone said, a "degraded people": ignorant, superstitious, and licentious. Mentally, spiritually, and behaviorally bereft of inducements to self-discipline, they endangered the safety and happiness of society because they had no sense of solidarity with whites—they were a "distinct people." The adversary quality of master-slave relations resulted from the blacks' development of their own "brotherhood." Black religious leaders fused together their own ignorance, African and Islamic remnants, and the spiritual needs of slaves to develop principles that bound blacks together for common cause against whites. The threat transcended mere lying, stealing, and universal dissimulation, for it included insurrection as well. Although it was not a persistent theme in his writings, Jones pointed out three years after Nat Turner's rebellion that "no enemy should be despised."[21]

[19] See Jones's report of abolitionist seminarians having excommunicated him in his letter to Samuel Miller, February 11, 1840, Samuel Miller Papers (Princeton University, Princeton, N. J.). See also Jones to Mary Jones, November 5, 1835, from Charleston: "The greatest excitement here has been & now is on the Abolition question, and sorry am I to inform you that the Cause of Religious Instruction has been most seriously injured. . . . Nothing can be attempted until the fever cools . . . . As Mr Pinckney and others say, the State is divided into two parties, the *Religious & Infidel*." C. C. Jones Papers.

[20] Jones to Mr. ————, August 26, 1861, *ibid.*

[21] [Jones], *Report of the Committee to Whom Was Referred*, 16; see also *ibid.*, 3, 7, for further elaboration; Jones, *The Religious Instruction of the Negroes in the United States* (Savannah, 1842), 110–11.

The enemy's primary threat consisted of something much more subtle than physical violence, however, and that was moral influence. Slaves nursed, raised, cared for, and played with white children, Jones observed. If servants were allowed to remain in a morally degraded condition, he argued, their careless and licentious behavior would seduce white children from the Evangelical goal of a new generation of respectable, self-disciplined, and virtuous men and women.[22]

Jones's view of why slaves were different reveals that frustrating combination of profound sensitivity and class orientation which often characterizes the middle-class reformer. Furthermore, Jones as a propagandist more than a theorist never really probed as deeply as he might have the implications of his reformist ideas and actions. He could not distinguish in his own mind the black man from the slave, so completely did the two merge in his own experience. He wrote harshly of the way in which slavery had degraded blacks but saw very little difference between slaves and free Negroes, since neither had had proper instruction in Christian values. The effects of servitude and prejudice could not be sloughed off merely by emancipation, he believed; they must be counteracted by a process of acculturation that began in childhood and was continued throughout life. So thoroughly did he identify Christianity with the process of change that he ignored the implications of his charge that whites had "reduced" the black man to his low estate. The process of "reduction" presupposed a previous, high level of culture, but Jones's view of Africa was not Edenic. He shared with his fellow missionaries a disregard for African (pagan) and Islamic (heathen) "superstitions." Indeed, the division of southern society was partially due to the persistence of African beliefs and practices. Culturally inferior Africans had been enslaved; but their treatment as slaves perpetuated their inferiority. As he discussed these matters, however, Jones also challenged white "prejudice" against Negroes and especially that theory which defined them as a "distinct variety of the human family."[23] Their values and behavior patterns, so unlike those of whites, were attributable not to race, but to their African inheritance and present treatment.

To change blacks, Jones first had to change whites, whose attitudes towards slaves were benighted and self-serving. "Having reduced them to ignorance, and by our neglect of duty confirmed

[22] Jones, *Religious Instruction of the Negroes. A Sermon*, 1, 12; [Jones], *Report of the Committee to Whom Was Referred*, 6, 16; Jones, *The Religious Instruction of the Negroes in the United States*, 112–40, 153.

[23] Jones, *The Religious Instruction of the Negroes in the United States*, 101–53.

them in vice, we now quarrel with their stupidity and obduracy."[24] He seems never to have lost completely the belief, elaborated first in seminary, that blacks had been made what they were by the actions of whites themselves. The situation could be changed, he insisted, because whites themselves had sprung "From a people once as degraded as Negroes."[25] The change would come only with great difficulty because Jones had to win diverse and often hostile groups: Christian laymen and ministers, who were in the minority, and the vast majority of southerners, the unconverted. Himself suspended between the rarified moralizing of his seminary experience and the mundane responsibilities of a planter, he disclaimed accountability for creating or sustaining the master-slave relationship but insisted that masters were accountable for the manner in which the relationship was perpetuated. He tried to arouse in Christians a sense of guilt and in non-Christians a sense of self-interest, both of which could be transformed into a universal sense of obligation. Self-interest and guilt dictated that masters understand the extent to which their wealth and that of the nation was based upon the labor of servants. To have one's wealth at the mercy of adversaries whose values differed from those of the master class and who resented the unfairness, injustice, and inadequacy of their treatment was irrational. As morally accountable human beings, slaves would respond favorably to masters who acted in a manner dictated by Evangelical ethics. Observing masters under strict rules of accountability, slaves would more willingly submit to rules imposed by the master—or so Jones argued. He understood the master-slave relationship as a political as well as moral relationship and regarded the inability of the masters to fulfill the obligations of the absolute power entailed upon them as a moral as well as a political failure. Jones therefore reduced his appeal to a familiar formula: Treat your servants as you would wish to be treated if you were in their position.[26]

By evoking a sense of obligation, Jones hoped to entice masters into bridging the chasm which separated them from blacks. The adversary relationship between the two classes could be changed only if masters were made aware of the way in which their attitudes toward blacks had shaped it. Thinking of servants primarily as property "associated in [their] business and thoughts . . . with labor

[24] [Jones], *Report of the Committee to Whom Was Referred,* 23.

[25] Jones, *Religious Instruction of the Negroes. A Sermon,* 23.

[26] *Ibid.*, 8–10, 31; [Jones], *Report of the Committee to Whom Was Referred,* 3, 9–13, 19, 25, 32; Jones, *The Religious Instruction of the Negroes in the United States,* 155–70; also his *Suggestions on the Religious Instruction of the Negroes in the Southern States* . . . (Philadelphia, 1847), 31–32.

and interest and gain and wealth,"[27] he said, the masters simply dehumanized blacks through carelessness as much as brutality. If slaves were not expected to behave as responsible human beings, they would in fact not do so, since Jones believed that servants' views of themselves were largely responses to their masters' expectations. In expecting slaves to be different, masters pushed them beyond the discipline and intimate relationships of family and community. The masters' views and expectations, Jones believed, were the result of unreflective responses to daily difficulties and frustrations with blacks. In a sense, whites knew too much about servants, especially their vices, inferior station, and ignorance. In a larger sense, however, Jones insisted, whites knew too little of them as human beings.[28]

Obligation and knowledge—these were to provide the impetus for a process of social integration that would eventually create Jones's biracial community. White ministers had to be made to acknowledge their obligation to serve blacks, to visit, counsel, and discipline them with the same care and affection customarily reserved for whites.[29] Important as ministers were, only masters had the power to heal the division of society, and since they were unbelievers as well as believers and since Jones thought Christian instruction was the principal activity through which community solidarity would be achieved, he faced a dilemma. He often emphasized the need for Christians to repent of their sins; but unbelieving masters had to be approached differently. They must be made to see that their personal interests and the interests of society rested upon the perfecting of their role.

To perfect their role, argued Jones, masters must learn how to manage people effectively; and the first principles of management were respect for persons and reasonable discipline. In demonstrating respect, masters must be concerned not simply with the labor but with the entire life of slaves. Beginning with such simple matters as intonation of voice and manner of assigning tasks, the master should develop a manner with servants that expressed his concern for them. Kind words would accomplish nothing without supplementary actions. Masters should guarantee the integrity of black families by requiring formal weddings and refusing to separate parents and children and also by counseling those with

[27] [Jones], *Thirteenth Annual Report of the Association for the Religious Instruction of the Negroes in Liberty County, Georgia* (Savannah, 1848), 14.

[28] *Ibid.*, 13–15; Jones, *The Religious Instruction of the Negroes in the United States,* 106.

[29] Jones, *The Religious Instruction of the Negroes in the United States,* 222–39, 250–51, 262–63.

marital difficulties and providing separate accommodations for privacy. Jones also suggested that slaves be encouraged to grow their own crops, a privilege which would cultivate industry, thrift, and honesty. Reasonable discipline, too, was required of masters. Jones did not quarrel with the fact that masters possessed absolute authority over their servants. Indeed, he demanded that masters understand what absolute authority required of them. And in his discussion of this matter, the rigid Evangelical discipline he demanded of himself is evident. If masters were to fulfill the role expected of them, therefore, they must provide slaves with a demonstrably fair and just system of discipline that would preserve public order and educate the blacks' moral sense. The final result would be a self-imposed moral control of one's life much like that Jones exercised over his own.[30]

The whole scheme of bringing blacks and whites closer focused upon the act of religious instruction, through which blacks would discover their masters' deep concern for them. At this point Jones appeared to be asking unbelievers to lead blacks into belief; but he was really trying to convince unbelieving masters that the only way to create a sense of social solidarity was to have both whites and blacks join the Christian church. The mission to the slaves was therefore as much, perhaps, even more, a mission to masters, for Jones insisted that the best way to make blacks believe that masters were their friends was in fact to *be* their friends.[31] Such a remarkable change in master-slave relations conjured up a romantic vision of the master's leading his servants at family prayers each evening, catechizing black youngsters each week, and continuously and carefully guiding the moral decisions of his black and white families.[32] ". . . to benefit servants, evangelize the masters," Jones wrote; "to benefit masters, evangelize the servants."[33]

The evangelization of servants required a complete expurgation of pagan and "worldly" beliefs and practices, a formidable task even if the slaves had been literate. Since they were not, the only method Jones had available was "oral instruction," which he made the chief means of his crusade. In 1837 he published a catechism to

[30] *Ibid.*, 206–19, 101–103; [Jones], *Thirteenth Annual Report*, 16–19, 60, 61; Jones, *Religious Instruction of the Negroes. A Sermon*, 29; Jones, *Suggestions on the Religious Instruction of the Negroes*, 35–36.

[31] Jones, *The Religious Instruction of the Negroes in the United States*, 187.

[32] *Ibid.*, 240–41, 262–69.

[33] *Ibid.*, 217; see also [Jones], *Report of the Committee to Whom Was Referred*, 19–20.

explain his system.[34] Although designed for slaves, the catechism was addressed not so much to their servitude as their ignorance. Black children were so responsive to the question-answer format that Jones edited his catechism to employ more accurately their words and phrases.[35] The responsiveness was important to Jones, not only because he wanted to be personally rewarded, as do all teachers, with some sign of success, but also because he needed to have some guarantee that the process would ultimately create the kind of community he had in mind. Equally as important as the interaction was the message. But exactly what the message was is difficult to determine from simply reading the catechism. Also important were the sermons which elaborated upon the lessons, the phrases employed in pastoral counseling, and the immediate response of the white teachers to their black charges. In addition, Jones's expectations of the eventual results of his instruction should at least indicate the message that was sent to the blacks if not the one they actually received.

The intention of the whole program of religious instruction apparently was to provide blacks with the cosmic and moral framework within which one was to direct his private life with the aid of church and master. Thus, in his catechism Jones attempted first of all to provide knowledge of what the Bible says about God's attributes, the creation and subsequent fall of man, and the whole "plan of salvation" God erected in response to man's disobedience. Slowly and carefully, Jones led his charges through the Christian mythos as he understood it:

Q. Who only is perfectly good in himself, and does good to us and to all creatures?
A. God. . . .
Q. Tell me some of God's goodness to you.
A. He gives us father and mother, meat and drink, and clothes to wear; and when we are sick he makes us well.
Q. Is it not great goodness in God to make us live in a Gospel land, and to give us his holy word?
A. Yes. . . .[36]

The answer was inescapable. Jones was trying to evoke from the blacks a sense of gratitude for or at least satisfaction with their life

[34] Jones, *Suggestions on the Religious Instruction of the Negroes,* 18; Jones, *A Catechism, of Scripture Doctrine and Practice, for Families and Sabbath Schools, Designed also for the Oral Instruction of Colored Persons* (Savannah, 1837).

[35] Jones, *Catechism,* 4.

[36] *Ibid.,* 30.

in slavery. He hoped blacks could be made to see that their station in life was not important for determining their value as individuals—their station they could not change. What was indeed important was the quality of their lives, something they most assuredly could change.

The quality, of course, was judged by behavior and its "moral influence." The motto of Jones's scheme of religious instruction could very well have been the ideal by which he attempted to manage his own family; "*Life*," he wrote Mary, "*is nothing without system*."[37] And system meant completely ordering one's daily life so that sobriety, respect for others, and self-discipline became second nature. These qualities he preached with a humorless, almost deadly didacticism, which could make the story of Cain and Abel into a homily against losing one's temper. A biographical lecture on the Old Testament prophets could be transformed into a plea "to improve your short time." "Waste not an hour," he warned, "but begin now to live for eternity."[38] Every part of the Bible had a practical lesson, he believed, and was therefore wary of religious instruction that was too "elevated" and abstract. There must be "applications," he emphasized, which would make his servants as sober, respectable, and responsible as his children. He encapsulated life in the concept of duty which he urged on both masters and servants.[39]

The message of religious instruction, however, like the theory which made it possible, cannot be understood apart from the activities Jones engaged in and the institutions he shaped. When he wrote of religious instruction of the Negroes he was writing about himself and his own efforts in Liberty County, Georgia. When he dismissed arguments against his project based on the inability of blacks to understand Christianity, to be constant, or to become trustworthy under the influence of religious instruction, he could simply reply that it was not so in Liberty County. There he developed the model for the whole of southern society. Gradually, schools were attached either to churches or plantations; scholars

[37] Jones to Mary Jones, June 2, 1837, C. C. Jones Papers.

[38] See Jones, "Lectures to Negroes," *ibid.*

[39] Jones to Mary Jones, October 26, 1837, *ibid.*; see also a copy of a letter from Jones to his children, July 26, 1850, Joseph Jones Papers (Tulane University); Jones, *Catechism*, 17, 129–31.

were taught by lay women and men; black leadership was trained, guided, and given responsibility.

First and foremost, discipline was established. Black "watchmen" and pastors of both races reviewed the religious life of the black community each sabbath after the morning services, deciding the grave matters of who should be put on probation and who should be excommunicated. The watchmen themselves met frequently to reinforce their own resolve as leaders of the black congregation. Black leadership was as important to Jones as it was inevitable, and in the interests of social order as well as religious orthodoxy, he believed it should be composed of black Christians answering to white Christians. The central concept for establishing bonds between black and white was the same as for establishing the integrity of his own life: constant, systematic surveillance.[40]

Forbidding and austere as the interaction between black and white may appear to have been in Jones's utopia, its actual effect upon him was profoundly emotional. He frequently spoke of affection between the two races and was sinfully proud of his special relationship with black parishioners. Addressing the General Assembly which created the Presbyterian Church in the Confederate States of America, he characteristically pleaded with his colleagues to minister to blacks with the same kind of enthusiasm usually reserved for accepting calls to the South's most prestigious churches. The rewards would be great, he promised. A pastor of blacks could "become a star in the right hand of the Saviour before them, and they [would] rejoice in his light, and learn to sing his hymns and quote his precepts and authority, and argue by his knowledge, and take him to be their friend."[41] If Jones spoke passionately on this point, he was perhaps confessing his own needs and the way in which they were met by close association with blacks. The master of over one hundred servants, he was a strict disciplinarian, a vengeful protector of his slaves' persons, and their confessor, counselor, and guide. He knew the worst problems of plantation management and yet valued the admiration and respect of those over whom he had absolute authority. Their affection for

[40] "Mission Record Book" and "Minutes of Watchmen's Meetings for Midway Church . . . 1840," C. C. Jones Papers; [Jones], *Sixth Annual Report of the Association for the Religious Instruction of the Negroes in Liberty County, Georgia* . . . (Charleston, 1841), 5–6; [Jones], *Seventh Annual Report* . . . (Savannah, 1842), 11 and *passim;* [Jones], *Eighth Annual Report* . . . (Savannah, 1843), *passim;* [Jones], *Thirteenth Annual Report*, 5.

[41] Jones, *The Religious Instruction of the Negroes. An Address*, 23.

him was a sign of personal as well as social reconciliation. The hiatus between social classes, which he publicly condemned and attempted to bridge with his mission, was possibly a projection of that personal alienation which had earlier enabled him, the son of slaveholders, to see the destructiveness of slavery. The order he wished for his own life could only be achieved by bringing into an orderly and redemptive system slaves who symbolized alienation itself.[42]

Whatever the psychic rewards of religious instruction, they were tangential to the goal of a biracial community. Community connotes mutual respect, common values, intimate and affective relations based upon personal acquaintance, and a sense, if not the actuality, of kinship. Equality, however, is not a necessary aspect of community, and especially not in Jones's thought. He firmly believed that there were properly different classes of men, and he doubted if social distinctions could be ignored without unjustly demeaning the respectable Christian folk who were the backbone of society. Although resenting northern charges that a class of slaveholders controlled the South, he clearly and unashamedly supported the rule of the honest, genteel, educated, and responsible.[43] To rule most effectively and justly, the moral hierarchs would follow the dictates of the Christian Gospel, which required the resolution of white-black antagonism. In accomplishing this admirable end, it was not expected that the two classes would have the same tasks and roles; rather, they would perfect their God-given roles as indicated by the social system and Christian charity. Masters would have to learn that the limits of their power were set by the rights of the slave to his or her person, privacy, family, and soul. They owed their servants just treatment, good housing, adequate medical facilities, decent clothing, and religious instruction. In return, servants would internalize the value system of the dominant class and submit willingly to their role as efficient and productive laborers. This happy integration would place servants beyond the reach of designing men and create in them a respectability that would win the trust and regard of whites. Both races would thus be reconciled in a salvation at once temporal and spiritual.

[42] For Jones's repudiation of the charges that the South was controlled by a "slaveocracy," see his article on "The Princeton Review on 'The State of the Country,' " Columbia (S. C.) *Southern Presbyterian,* February 16, 1861.

[43] Jones, *The Religious Instruction of the Negroes in the United States,* 206–19.

Jones never deluded himself into believing that his utopia had been achieved, even in Liberty County. Even good, Christian folk seemed to like the idea of the mission better than the work itself; the prejudices against the blacks were too great, the "common sense" observations of black ignorance and perverseness too close to axioms to transform enough whites, let alone blacks, into people like Charles Colcock Jones. But he never quit. Even when accepting two brief professorships (1837–1838, 1848–1850) at Columbia (S.C.) Theological Seminary, he continued as publicist. And he accepted a position as corresponding secretary of the Presbyterian Board of Domestic Missions (1850–1853) to be able to develop his program into a large-scale project. But he was struck down by disease in 1853 and sent back to Georgia from Philadelphia, a frail, wasted shell of a man kept alive by his wife's devotion and his own grit and fantastic discipline.[44] Safe at home, he returned to his black parishioners to spend the rest of his life as a planter, man of letters, and minister to blacks. He did not cut himself off from the rest of the world to die alone and isolated; he followed with characteristic intensity the proud successes of his children and the sorry predicament of his section as it fought to maintain order and stability against the onslaught of faithless men who wished nothing but the "subjugation and humiliation of the South."[45] The Confederacy created to prevent such tragedy he greeted optimistically, but as war erupted and spread south of Savannah he soon found his world crumbling about him. Yankee gunboats were on the coast and in the river; neighbors were sending their slaves into the back country to prevent their running away; Lincoln had mischievously issued an Emancipation Proclamation—Jones's stable, ordered community was collapsing. And in the midst of it all he rode his horse through cold and rain to visit the sick, bury the dead, comfort the survivors. But he himself could not be comforted, brooding over the deaths of his parishioners and servants by typhoid, cholera, measles, pneumonia, and gunshot. Emaciated and weakened by years of fighting a disease that wasted him, disheartened by the deaths of so many people he knew, and threatened with the destruction of his world, he was finally unable to fight for life. On March 11, 1863, he

[44] Myers, ed., *Children of Pride*, 16–17.

[45] Jones, "The Princeton Review on 'The State of the Country,' " Columbia (S. C.) *Southern Presbyterian*, February 16, 1861.

told himself that he was going to die; his lungs simply would not work. He thereupon began to put his papers in order, and a few days later after tea with his sister and wife he retired for a brief nap and never woke up.[46]

Jones's life and work help to clarify thinking about southern society and especially the role of religion. There has been considerable speculation about the moral as well as social contradictions of the antebellum South. Familiar concepts of "travail," anxiety, and guilt, connected as they are with the conflicting themes of Liberalism, Christianity, and slavery, have been employed by skillful historians to create a most arresting picture of a tortured and anxious people. Equally familiar concepts of class interest and ideology, connected with the themes of social development and political conflict, have been employed by equally skillful historians to reveal a South controlled by a class becoming ever more aware of itself and its enemies. Evangelical religion in the first view becomes a channel for alleviating the anxiety and guilt created by social and psychological tensions. In the second view the South's Protestantism is seen as something of a problem for its "democratic" qualities, but its effect seems generally to have been to mold the "paternalism" of the master class. These two views are resolved in the person of Charles Colcock Jones. He exemplified in his personal life and the values he handed on to his children those assumptions of class hegemony and responsibility which were essential for supporting the slaveholders' world view. He progressively exemplified in his internal life and vocation the awareness of moral and social tension which he acknowledged as his guilt. There is a point, however, in the perpetual Christian confession of guilt where one ceases to be specific and projects a sense of obligations unfulfilled into all relationships. That is what Jones did. If he specified his guilt, therefore, it was not for owning slaves, but for not being a perfect master and pastor.

Jones's personal feelings, however, were less important than his public activities. And these are to be measured more in symbolic than actual terms, for in the latter sense he failed. He simply was unable to persuade enough clergymen of his own denomination, let

[46] Jones, Diary, 1861, 1862, *passim,* March 11, 1863, C. C. Jones Papers. See also his essay in the same place on the conduct of the enemy. The Yankees had, among other things, sacked private dwellings, employed captured slaves to raise cotton, exhibited coarseness of language and feeling, confiscated property, and trained slaves to fight against the South. See also "Biographical Sketch of the Reverend Charles Colcock Jones, D.D.," *ibid.*

alone others, to develop an adequate system of religious instruction. He was of course not alone in his efforts; William Capers among the Methodists and William Meade among the Protestant Episcopalians attempted also to broadcast the idea of religious instruction. But it was he who was the chief theorist of the entire movement; his book was its Bible, his catechism its guidebook, his county the ideal community, his theory the best articulated hope of evangelicals who wished to reshape their society. As the feeble Methodist missions spread beyond the South Carolina conference which had spawned them, and as Baptists, Episcopalians, and Presbyterians wrote to him for advice, he felt no sense of victory, for he realized that only one in two hundred black children was attending religious instruction. Even fewer were converted, and he felt very much "alone, forsaken, rejected."[47] Aside from Jones's feelings, however, the very obvious fact that the Christian churches of the South were never able to create the kind of community he wanted is evidence of his failure.

American reform movements have never been completely successful, for they have usually worked for a perfect goal in an imperfect society. They have been especially unsuccessful if relying primarily upon goodwill instead of aggressive self-interest to generate change. Jones truly appealed to self-interest, but he could not demonstrate convincingly that his plan would serve the interests of the master class; rather, he emphasized that the program could work only if the masters changed their attitudes radically—and at this point the appeal was to goodwill. The utopian tactics of making perfect individuals in order to make a perfect society, compatible as they may have been with the goal, were not competent to achieve it. Movements must be able to focus upon a clear enemy in order to mobilize the resentments and angers created by a dysfunction of the social system. Temperance crusaders fought "demon rum," women's rights advocates fought Man's laws and prejudices, abolitionists fought the slave power; in each case the movement could unite against the enemy. The way in which proponents of religious instruction of Negroes argued was ample demonstration that the "enemy" was the master—but he was called upon to change himself. To persuade him to do so as a class was clearly impossible; and there was no way within the antebellum South to

[47] Jones to John Hartwell Cocke, July 19, 1844, written on a circular of the Presbytery of Georgia for April 6, 1844, John Hartwell Cocke Papers (University of Virginia, Charlottesville, Va.).

create a constituency that could compel masters to change. The system could not suffer the necessary confrontation; the social division it would exacerbate was the very problem that Jones was trying to solve. So he had to rely upon personal goodwill and enlightenment, which were simply not sufficient to create the kind of controlled, redemptive biracial community that he advocated.

As Jones had not succeeded with whites, neither did he succeed with blacks. He and his disciples did create black congregations throughout the South—this is not at issue. But they did not create a biracial Christian community. The black man whom Jones wished to incorporate into his community was not so passive as to allow himself to be molded into a replication of the white. Jones must have understood this, especially after a black congregation walked out on him as he exhorted them to "obey their masters."[48] He was a young man then, but he never forgot the incident. Also it must be remembered that much as he wanted a community in which black and white lived together in harmony and to mutual advantage, his class and religious experiences limited him. Truly desiring justice and fairness for the black man to the extent of those limits, he was incapable of allowing black men to help make the community. It was to be imposed by a rigid but not surprising application of the ideology that had helped him become a mature man. Unappealing to many whites, it could not be made universally appealing to a people whose social condition could not support the rigid self-discipline required of them. The goals were not clear, the rewards too few. This is not to deny that forms of Protestant Christianity were used to create a means of social integration, leadership selection, and ideological expression. There is much evidence that they did.[49] But black religion was as much a creation of the slaves themselves as it was a gift of the white man. Jones could not create his biracial community because it expected too much of the white man and too little of the black.

There is much that is "unrealistic" in Jones's view of social action. He attempted to work within a system he had once condemned for placing on people limitations that were impossible to

[48] Mary Jones, "Miscellaneous Remembrances of Charles Colcock Jones," C. C. Jones Papers.

[49] Lawrence W. Levine, "Slave Songs and Slave Consciousness: An Exploration in Neglected Sources," in Tamara K. Hareven, ed., *Anonymous Americans: Explorations in Nineteenth-Century Social History* (Englewood Cliffs, N. J., 1971), 99–130.

overcome. He tried, in other words, to change people without changing institutions and laws. The fact that the logic of the system was more powerful than the devotion to Christian values is not at all surprising to us and was disastrous for him. Had there been thirty thousand Charles Colcock Joneses instead of merely one, his ideas might have begun to change the South significantly, but the thought is pure fantasy. It reinforces the hopelessness of Jones's mission. But if it was so hopeless, why did he and the few like him persist? In terms of his ideology the case was not hopeless. Like his abolitionist antagonists he believed the race was worth the running because it was morally invigorating, personally satisfying, and socially useful. "God requires of us," he would have said with the same confidence and words as abolitionists, "that we do our duty." Contradictory as may have been his goals and methods, confused as may have been his view of blacks and slaves, he nevertheless attempted to make his society better. This is not to say that he had no other choices; he could have freed his slaves and fled North; he could also have kept quiet. But he tried that most morally ambiguous and difficult of tasks: to reform from within. Such a commitment remains now as it was then a situation fraught with irony and tragedy.

What then *did* Jones create as the preeminent advocate of religious instruction of the Negroes? Certainly, he provided religious care for his own servants and those of his neighbors, and he formulated a theory for a generation of southern churchmen to try to shape into reality. Sensitive as antebellum southerners were on the subject of slavery, they could not deny the human needs of blacks, nor could they isolate themselves completely from the currents of reform emanating from the religious heritage they shared with the North. Furthermore, the hope of making blacks into approximate replicas of whites through indoctrination had obvious attractions. And even if all blacks were not converted nor all masters enlisted as teachers, the *hope* was important. It helped to symbolize the paternalism which was becoming so ideologically important in the twenty years before the secession crisis. It provided a contact with northerners who wished to be assured that abolitionist criticism was uninformed and unfair. The hope also became a way for southerners, who as northerners might have joined radical movements, to expend their energy in doing good. But it was not a way of bleeding off discontent so much as a combining of private philanthropy with public service. Churchmen offered to make southern society whole if southerners would accept Evangelical Christianity. Southerners, aside from a few true believers, accepted the offer only insofar as they needed a symbol of Christian paternalism to vindicate their social system. In the process, Jones became a minor figure in the southern pantheon. His personal fight and public activities evoked sentimental accolades, as if by celebrating him southerners could vindicate themselves. After the War for Southern Independence, Jones's work would be remembered as the best example of Christian responsibility, his home life as the best example of southern civilization.[50] He and his work had become vindication for a society he had tried to change.

[50] William P. Harrison, ed., *The Gospel Among the Slaves. A Short Account of Missionary Operations Among the African Slaves of the Southern States* (Nashville, 1893); Atticus G. Haygood, *Our Brother in Black: His Freedom and His Future* (New York, 1881); Robert Q. Mallard, *Montevideo-Maybank: Some Memoirs of a Southern Christian Household in the Olden Time* (Richmond, 1898); Mallard, *Plantation Life Before Emancipation* (Richmond, 1892).

Black Ironworkers and the Slave Insurrection Panic of 1856

By Charles B. Dew

"Exaggerated reports of excitement in Tennessee regarding anticipated negro insurrections are circulating in other States," noted the Nashville *Union and American* on December 20, 1856. "The excitement in question was limited to the Iron Works on Cumberland river and their vicinity, and to Sumner County [Gallatin]," the editorial continued. "At the iron works there is no doubt that the negroes had talked of insurrection, and of fighting their way to a free State." Letters published in the Louisville *Courier* on December 6, 1856, claimed that slaves at three Tennessee blast furnaces located just below the Kentucky border were preparing to cross the state line and lead a revolt in the Hopkinsville area. "The Negroes in Southern Kentuck are in a mutinous state . . . ," reported a Louisville correspondent of the St. Louis *Missouri Republican*, and Nashville steamers arriving in St. Louis during the first weeks of December brought news that some twenty-five blast furnaces along the Cumberland had stopped operations as a result of the insurrectionary plot and that ironmasters had the suspected leaders of the revolt in chains.[1]

These contemporary reports of undoubted revolutionary activity among black ironworkers in the upper South in 1856 are echoed in most of the recent studies that touch on the insurrectionary panic of that year. "The situation in Kentucky and Tennessee particularly seemed to involve authenticated stories of proposed insurrections,"

[1] St. Louis *Missouri Republican*, December 9, 1856; St. Louis *Daily Missouri Democrat*, December 16, 1856.

Mr. Dew is professor of history at the University of Missouri–Columbia, and he wishes to thank the Graduate Research Council of that institution for a grant which aided in the preparation of this article. He would also like to express his gratitude for a summer residency fellowship at the Robert S. Starobin Memorial Library in Hancock, Massachusetts, where this article was written, and to thank the American Council of Learned Societies for a grant-in-aid in support of his residency at the Starobin Library.

The Journal of Southern History
Vol. XLI, No. 3, August 1975

notes Harvey Wish in the most detailed scholarly discussion of the 1856 fear, and his views are shared by a number of other historians.[2] A close analysis of the events surrounding the terror of 1856 in Kentucky and Tennessee suggests, however, that the fright in the white community was probably groundless. This interpretation, like that of Wish and other scholars who think a revolt of some sort was planned, is admittedly difficult to prove, but the weight of available evidence seems to indicate that white hysteria rather than a black plot lay at the bottom of the bloody insurrectionary panic in the Cumberland iron district in 1856.

The first reports of large-scale slave unrest in 1856 occurred in Texas in September, but as the date of the presidential election drew closer, rumors of servile insurrection spread to other areas of the South. The Texas troubles, centered in Colorado and Lavaca counties in the southeastern part of the state, supposedly involved a slave-Mexican alliance and abolitionist agents from the North. Several lynchings and brutal whippings quieted white fears in Texas, but news of the events there was published widely in newspapers in the upper South.[3]

The Tennessee phase of the panic began in late October and early November in Fayette and Tipton counties just east and north of Memphis. On the morning of October 28 a slave girl belonging to an engineer at a steam mill near Lafayette Depot in Fayette County informed her mistress that one of the slaves in the mill had told her of a plot to revolt on election day. The white woman informed her husband, the two hid near the quarters that night to listen in on slave conversations, and they reportedly heard enough to convince them that an insurrection was being planned. The next day the engineer had all thirty-two slaves at the mill arrested, and after an examination the local magistrate committed twenty-three

[2] Wish, "The Slave Insurrection Panic of 1856," *Journal of Southern History*, V (May 1939), 222; Herbert Aptheker, *American Negro Slave Revolts* (New York, 1943), 347–49; Kenneth M. Stampp, *The Peculiar Institution: Slavery in the Ante-Bellum South* (New York, 1956), 138; Robert S. Starobin, *Industrial Slavery in the Old South* (New York, 1970), 89–90, 114–15; Robert E. Corlew, "Some Aspects of Slavery in Dickson County," *Tennessee Historical Quarterly*, X (December 1951), 359–62. Caleb P. Patterson, *The Negro in Tennessee, 1790–1865* (Austin, 1922), 49–50, thinks a rebellion was planned in Tennessee, but he mistakenly cites 1857 as the year of the revolt. The most recent studies dealing specifically with slavery in these two states, Chase C. Mooney, *Slavery in Tennessee* (Bloomington, Ind., 1957), 62–63, and J. Winston Coleman, Jr., *Slavery Times in Kentucky* (Chapel Hill, 1940), 107–10, are noncommittal on the genuineness of the 1856 insurrection. Clement Eaton, *The Freedom-of-Thought Struggle in the Old South* (New York, 1964), 99–102, is the most skeptical recent analysis of the supposed revolt.

[3] Wish, "Slave Insurrection Panic of 1856," 207–209; Nashville *Union and American*, November 23, 1856.

of the supposed conspirators to jail in the county seat of Somerville. The aroused white citizenry immediately put a "Vigilant Patrol" into the field and turned up a white man in a slave cabin who could not account for his presence there. He was also jailed. "The excitement was very great for several days, but it is now pretty much subsided," wrote a Fayette County man on November 5. "Facts were brought to light sufficient to satisfy all present, not only of the guilty intentions of some six or eight of the negroes arrested, but it was made clear to the minds of thinking men present, that the thing was not confined to this particular neighborhood," he warned, "but that they expected to act in concert with various others in the surrounding counties and States."[4] Shortly after the news of the Fayette County incident was published whites in neighboring Tipton County reported the discovery of a plot among slaves on several plantations there to stage an uprising that would coincide with the revolt in Fayette. The Memphis *Bulletin,* in describing the events in Tipton, editorialized that "rascally abolition emissaries" were undoubtedly behind this unrest, and if apprehended "they should be taught the virtue of hemp."[5]

In late November 1856 the Somerville *Star* outlined the disposition of the cases in Fayette County. Of the twenty-three blacks jailed earlier, seventeen had been freed on a writ of habeas corpus and taken home by their masters, although whippings had been administered before they left the custody of the law. The remaining six men were brought to trial before three judges and a regularly impaneled jury. The court found grounds for punishing five of the six with four whippings of thirty-nine lashes each to be carried out over the space of two weeks; an additional sentence required that the five men also "stand four times in the pillory—an hour each time. The sixth one, being an older man than the others, and for other considerations also, received but ten lashes." This newspaper account made no mention of the fate of the white man arrested earlier or of the disposition of the charges against the slaves in Tipton County.[6]

Given the nature of the supposed plot in these two counties, the sentences handed down by the Fayette court were light and suggest that, if anything, some loose talk was all that was involved in this revolt. In both counties local whites believed the slaves were plan-

[4] W. E. Eppes to Col. J. P. Pryor, November 2, 1856, Memphis *Daily Appeal,* November 5, 1856.

[5] Memphis *Bulletin,* quoted in Franklin (Tenn.) *Western Weekly Review,* November 14, 1856.

[6] Somerville (Tenn.) *Star,* November 29, 1856, quoted in New York *Herald,* December 11, 1856.

ning to "rise" on election day, kill the white women and children while the men were voting, seize money and arms, and then attack the unsuspecting men either at the polls or on their way home from the polling places. In the case of the Fayette County insurrectionists the next step called for them to commandeer cars on the Memphis and Charleston Railroad and make a rush on Memphis, "where they would find arms and friends from up the river to carry them off to the Free States if they did not succeed in taking this country."[7] If the Fayette court had uncovered any firm evidence of a plan of this nature, it seems highly likely that the gallows rather than the lash and the pillory would have figured in the judges' decision.

Two weeks after the news of these "plots" in southwestern Tennessee was published the insurrectionary panic broke out with full fury along the Cumberland River to the north. In many ways this region in northern Tennessee and southern Kentucky was ideally suited for a white panic over a possible slave revolt. "Through what is called the Iron District, on the Cumberland and Tennessee Rivers, there are from 8,000 to 10,000 slaves employed at the iron works. . . . congregated in large numbers, working in the various labors of making charcoal, digging ore, and tending the furnaces, in gangs, mostly by themselves, with a few whites for general overseers," an Evansville, Indiana, paper reported in early December. "There are many of these works situated within a few miles of each other, and in sections that have few white inhabitants."[8] This estimate of the number of slaves engaged in iron manufacturing in the Cumberland area was somewhat inflated, but the region certainly was characterized by a heavy concentration of slave industrial workers, as indicated by employment figures given in a list of Cumberland ironworks compiled in 1852:[9]

	White Laborers	Black Laborers
Nineteen blast furnaces	1,045	1,360
Nine forges	260	410
Two rolling mills	90	140
Total workers	1,395	1,910

[7] Memphis *Daily Appeal*, November 5, 1856; Franklin *Western Weekly Review*, November 14, 1856.

[8] Evansville (Ind.) *Journal*, December 6, 1856, quoted in New York *Herald*, December 12, 1856.

[9] "Manufacture of Iron on Cumberland River, Tennessee," *Hunt's Merchants' Magazine and Commercial Review*, XXVIII (May 1853), 644–45. A footnote to these employment figures states that they refer to "employees . . . engaged in manufacturing of Pig Metal, Blooms, and Iron. No estimate made of hands to raise corn and pork."

During the years immediately following this enumeration a marked expansion of the iron industry occurred in this district. Between 1852 and 1856 no less than twelve new blast furnaces were constructed, five older furnaces were rebuilt and returned to production, and two new forges were erected along the Cumberland and Tennessee rivers;[10] these installations probably raised the number of slave ironworkers in the area to approximately 3,000 men. Although whites outnumbered blacks in each of the counties that made up the iron district,[11] the substantial increase in the number of furnaces and forges in the four years prior to the panic, the introduction of even greater numbers of industrial slaves, and the relative isolation of many of the ironworks could easily lead to heightened fears of slave uprisings in a year of political turmoil and uncertainty and of widespread and well-publicized insurrectionary rumors. The proximity of this region to free territory also made it relatively easy for whites to believe reports of a black revolution, especially when these reports stressed, as they invariably did, that a mass flight to the North was a central feature of the rebellion. Adding even greater fuel to the explosive situation in northern Tennessee were memories of an earlier panic which had gripped Clarksville, the principal town in the district, in 1835. In December of that year white fears of a revolt by slaves employed at surrounding ironworks had led to the procurement of arms from state authorities in Nashville and the organization of a special vigilance patrol in Clarksville during the Christmas holidays.[12]

[10] J. P. Lesley, *The Iron Manufacturer's Guide to the Furnaces, Forges and Rolling Mills of the United States* . . . (New York and London, 1859), 128–37, 215.

[11] The census of 1860 gives the following population figures:

	White	Free Black	Slave
Counties in Tennessee:			
Dickson	7,774	7	2,201
Montgomery	11,235	106	9,554
Stewart	7,405	76	2,415
Counties in Kentucky:			
Calloway	8,409	14	1,492
Crittenden	7,838	19	939
Livingston	5,955	36	1,222
Lyon	4,167	46	1,094
Trigg	7,562	41	3,448
Totals	60,345	345	22,365

Source: Joseph C. G. Kennedy, *Preliminary Report on the Eighth Census. 1860* (Washington, 1862), 260–61, 281–82. The census of 1850 listed 50,416 whites, 387 free blacks, and 19,519 slaves in these counties; see J. D. B. De Bow, *Statistical View of the United States . . . Being a Compendium of the Seventh Census* . . . (Washington, 1854), 236, 242, 302, 308.

[12] Mooney, *Slavery in Tennessee*, 62.

Not surprisingly, the first reports of serious unrest among slave ironworkers in the Cumberland region occurred at a blast furnace near Clarksville. "Quite an excitement was occasioned on Sunday last [November 23] in the neighborhood of Louisa Iron Works, by the discovery of a plan of insurrection among the negroes," reported the Clarksville *Jeffersonian* on November 26, 1856. Some six or eight "ring leaders" had been arrested at the furnace, which was located in Montgomery County some twelve miles south of Clarksville, and had been incarcerated in the county jail. "We learn that several of them made confessions revealing a general and widespread scheme which was to have been carried into execution on or about the Christmas holidays," the report continued, "and that various divisions from all parts of the country adjacent to this place were to rise, carrying murder and devastation in their path, march upon this place, concentrate their forces, take the city, sack it, rifle the Banks and then proceed North." The same issue of the Clarksville paper also noted several other alarming events which undoubtedly contributed to heightened tension in the town and the surrounding countryside. A Englishman named James, a carpenter who had been working in the area for some weeks, had been hauled into the local court on November 25 and "charged with visiting negro cabins, and talking to the slaves about freedom." Since he was unable to post the $500 bond demanded by the court, he also went to jail. On November 24 a slave boy had been subjected to a public whipping in the Clarksville market "for having more pistols and other weapons in his trunk than the law allows," and on the same day the Clarksville court had found a black man guilty of "violating one of the commandments with an abandoned white woman . . ." and had ordered "Corrections intended to bring him to a sense of the enormity of his conduct, and the difference between white and black . . . ." In an editorial accompanying these reports the *Jeffersonian* warned "Cuffie" of "the power of the white race, and the swift and terrible retribution which would inevitably overtake him in any attempt at the forcible enfranchisement of himself or his fellows."

During the next week two conflicting reports appeared describing the supposed insurrection in the Montgomery County area. On November 27 the Nashville *Republican Banner* printed an account provided by "a gentleman just up from Clarksville," who claimed that the church at Louisa furnace had been mined with a keg of powder, "ready for the fatal match," that would have blown up the white population during worship services, and that "A large collection of arms and ammunition had also been discovered and seized."

The black "Generals and Captains" who were to lead the revolt were all under arrest. This secondhand report, which seems to have rested almost entirely on unsubstantiated rumor, was reprinted widely in other newspapers.[13]

The second account of the genesis of the Montgomery County revolt, an open letter signed by a number of white men at Louisa furnace, made no mention of these details, however. According to this description of events, which appeared in early December, the plot was uncovered on November 21 and found to embrace black laborers at three Tennessee ironworks, Louisa and O.K. furnaces in Montgomery County and Cumberland furnace in neighboring Dickson County. As soon as the plan was discovered, "the [white] people commenced the work of apprehending and punishing all the negroes whom they could find out, as having been cognizant of it," the letter went on. "Some of those negroes who were represented to be the most guilty, were lodged in the jails of Dickson and Montgomery counties." The only loss of life in these two counties came five days after the initial discovery of the supposed plot, and the circumstances surrounding this death suggest strongly that a white man's hysteria caused the killing. On the morning of November 26, a slave named Britton, belonging to one Solomon D. Raimey, "was heard just before day break, approaching Louisa Furnace as it seemed, making a great noise, and exclaiming at intervals 'Wake up Boys! wake up,' besides many other things, which could not be understood by those who heard him." When Britton entered the yard of William Nicks, who was "out on a patrolling expedition," and refused to obey orders from Nick's father-in-law not to approach the house, the white man shot and killed him. The Clarksville *Jeffersonian*, which published this letter on December 3, 1856, described the reaction of the other slaves at Louisa to this killing: ". . . some of the negroes at the Furnace, who had been under examination concerning the insurrection for several days, and had witnessed the high degree of excitement and indignation manifested by the whites, upon hearing this summary punishment of one of their fellows, immediately fled, under the impression that the excited whites had commenced a general and indiscriminate slaughter. They were soon retaken and quieted."

If an editorial which accompanied this report was indicative of the white mood in the area, the blacks at the Louisa works had good reason to fear "a general and indiscriminate slaughter" at the hands

[13] See Franklin *Western Weekly Review*, December 5, 1856; New York *Herald*, December 9, 1856; and Boston *Liberator*, December 12, 1856. Wish, "Slave Insurrection Panic of 1856," 210, accepts this account as a factual description of the events at Louisa Iron Works.

of their white masters. "The crimes contemplated should be atoned for precisely as though those crimes had been attempted and consummated," insisted the editor of the *Jeffersonian*. "Fearful and terrible examples should be made, and if need be, the fag[g]ot and flame should be brought into requisition to show these deluded maniacs the fierceness and the vigor, the swiftness and completeness of the white man's vengeance," the writer continued. "Let a terrible example be made in every neighborhood where the crime can be established, and if necessary, let every tree in the country bend with negro meat," he demanded. "Temporizing in such cases as this, is utter madness. We must strike terror, and make a lasting impression," the editorial concluded, "for only in such a course can we find the guaranties [*sic*] of future security."

Given the apparent degree of white anger and terror in the vicinity, it is remarkable that the Clarksville vigilance committee, which was organized in the wake of these reports, did not carry out summary executions of the black ironworkers who had been confined in the local jail. The members of the committee proceeded instead to examine the suspected leaders of the plot and to recommend a series of corrective measures dealing with past breaches of orderly slave discipline. City and county officials should prohibit all black meetings, "at frolicks, balls, benevolent societies, or at public worships, where negro preachers officiate . . . ." Owners of livery stables should not hire buggies or carriages to blacks on Sundays or any other days. Merchants should not trade with any slave without the express consent of the master, and guns and ammunition should not be sold to slaves under any circumstances. Bondsmen should no longer be permitted to hire their own time, and steamboat captains were specifically warned to discontinue their practice of hiring slaves without their owners' knowledge to load or unload cargo at night, since "The negroes invariably return to their masters next day, if not drunk, broken down and unfit for service." Extra care should be taken to keep whiskey out of the hands of slaves, and the committee advised that all saloons and liquor shops be closed until after the first of the year, "if not forever." White units should organize and ride regular patrols throughout the county as a precautionary measure, and extra day and night watches should stand guard in Clarksville. One resolution dealt specifically with black ironworkers: ". . . we call upon our city authorities to take strong measures to prevent negroes passing to and from the Iron Works from spending Christmas holidays in our town, and especially from staying a single night in the corporation, unless their masters reside here. In case, however, such negroes wives live in town, he will be permitted to stay here, provided he has a pass from his master, which is recognized or endorsed by the owner of his wife . . . ."

The most important report of the vigilance committee's activities, however, described the results of its investigation of the prisoners in the county lockup. "A great many negroes, suspected of having a hand in the damnable plot, were brought before the committee and examined but nothing of any importance was brought to light," the Clarksville *Jeffersonian* asserted. No mention was made of a powder keg under Louisa church, a secret cache of arms and ammunition, the English carpenter who had been visiting slave cabins, or any other elements of the "plot" that appeared in the panicky days after the first insurrectionary rumors surfaced in northern Tennessee.[14] No press notices appeared of executions in Dickson County, so presumably the slaves arrested in that jurisdiction were also freed.

Slave ironworkers just down the Cumberland in Stewart County, Tennessee, were not so fortunate, however. As in the case of the rumored revolt in neighboring Montgomery County, conflicting accounts of the Stewart County unrest appeared in area newspapers in early December. According to a letter from Clarksville dated November 28, 1856, and published in the Memphis *Daily Appeal* on December 5, the branch of the "revolt" centered at ironworks in Stewart and in the county seat of Dover came to light when a stock of five hundred arms was uncovered across the state line near Hopkinsville, Kentucky. The lash was applied to slaves in the Hopkinsville area, and confessions were extracted implicating blacks at Dover. Punishment inflicted on slaves in Dover produced information that black laborers at the nearby Cumberland Iron Works, a manufacturing complex consisting of several blast furnaces, a forge, and a rolling mill, were also in on the rebellion. "Some of the favorite servants, (at the Iron Works,) who have been greatly indulged . . . had to be whipped very severely before they would reveal any thing," the writer claimed, and one slave "received four hundred lashes before he would speak a word." The plot, to murder all the whites at the rolling mill, attack Clarksville, rob the bank, kill the whites there, burn the town, and then cut their way through to a free state, had been thwarted only because of the revelations that had been tortured out of the black participants, he believed.

A second version of the Stewart County developments appeared in the form of a letter dated December 13, 1856, and signed by a

[14] Clarksville *Jeffersonian*, December 17, 1856.

resident of Pembroke, Kentucky, southeast of Hopkinsville. This account, first published in the Canton, Kentucky, *Dispatch* and reprinted in a number of papers, gave a detailed and gruesome description of the results of this phase of the white panic. Just as the Clarksville letter of November 28 cited above traced the origin of the plot to Kentucky, this letter from a Kentuckian put the first stirrings of the Dover–Stewart County revolt in Tennessee. "Last Wednesday week [December 3] . . . news came here [Pembroke] that the negroes at the furnaces at Stewart county had rebelled, and that they had crossed the Cumberland river, and would attack Lafayette [Kentucky, southwest of Hopkinsville] that night, and with this came other rumors from Dover," the writer remarked. He saddled up and rode at once to Lafayette, where he found no attack imminent, but he did find "the town . . . in a state of perfect excitement upon the negro question," and a hastily formed vigilance committee was engaged in interrogating local blacks. "Tuesday [Thursday, December 4?] morning I went to Dover, and arrived there about 2 o'clock," he continued. "The people had hung four negroes at 11 o'clock that morning, and two more [were] then in town to be hung." The writer seemed pleased that he had gotten "to the place of execution in time to see the last one go off. . . . I learned that the men at the [Randolph] forge [part of the Cumberland Iron Works] were at work whipping the truth out of their negroes, so I rode out there that night, and was up with them all night," he went on. Some slaves had taken five hundred or six hundred lashes before admitting anything, and one of the blacks at the forge had died as the result of a severe whipping. These beatings had secured the details of a slave plot to rise on Christmas eve night, kill the white men and children at the forge, seize the white women as wives, and then link up with the slaves from the Cumberland rolling mill for a joint rush on Dover. At the rolling mill and at nearby Dover furnace, whippings had uncovered similar plans to murder the managers and take the white women, he asserted, and as a result one slave had been intentionally whipped to death at the mill and another had been lynched at the blast furnace. More executions would follow, he predicted, and he warned that one owner of a group of hired slaves who had succeeded in rescuing some of his men would probably "be mobed" if he returned and tried to claim his six or eight slaves who were still in the hands of the ironmasters.[15]

The final direct account of the events in Stewart County came

[15] T. M. Atkins to "Brother Henry," Canton *Dispatch*, quoted in Louisville *Courier*, December 29, 1856; see also Boston *Liberator*, January 16, 1857.

from an editor of the *Courrier des États-Unis,* a French-language newspaper published in New York, who happened to be steamboating up the Cumberland when the panic broke out. In letters from Dover and Clarksville dated Tuesday, December 2, and Wednesday, December 3, he described the atmosphere prevailing in the area at the height of the insurrectionary fear. "Before the only hotel in Dover are assembled excited groups of people, and from among them, horsemen, with revolver in hand and rifled [*sic*] slung across the back, start off frequently in all directions," he reported. "Here also meet, from distant places, numerous horsemen, whose animals covered with foam bear witness to the rapidity with which they have traveled." Most of the town's women and children were being guarded in the hotel and in several adjacent houses, and nine blacks were under arrest, four of whom, "the chiefs of the conspiracy," were to be hanged. Later that same day, the editor's steamboat stopped at the Cumberland rolling mill, and he heard further details of the supposed plot. Around November 22, a slave had attempted to escape from the Cumberland works but had been promptly recaptured. When taken, he had claimed that he had "fled from the persecution of his brethren in servitude who had threatened to kill him if he refused to take part in the conspiracy." As a result of his testimony almost eighty slaves had been arrested and interrogated, and sixty of these men were still under guard in the rolling mill and being whipped when the editor called at the works. The slaves' plan, which supposedly called for an uprising sometime between December 23 and December 26, "was to butcher the whites upon isolated farms and in the workshops . . . ," attack Dover, and then fight their way north to Indiana or Illinois. "Nothing less was contemplated than a general massacre," he assured his readers. In addition to the slave whippings, "three white Free-Soilers . . . [had] been arrested in Dover . . . ," been beaten for "exciting a revolt," and been warned to leave the state within thirty hours.[16]

Trying to sift a correct chronology of events from these various accounts is difficult enough, and determining the truth of the white charges of incipient rebellion is almost impossible, given the available evidence. Of the three reports cited above, the first, which traced the origin of the Stewart County revolt to the discovery of arms near Hopkinsville, is clearly in error. Letters from Hopkinsville and Lafayette published in the Louisville *Courier* during

[16] New York *Courrier des États-Unis,* December 11, 1856, quoted in Clarksville *Jeffersonian,* December 24, 1856.

December show that the panic in that area started with the rumor that blacks from three Stewart County works, Eclipse, Clark, and Lagrange furnaces, were marching on Dover and that the insurgents planned to sweep into Kentucky on their way to the Ohio River. The alarmed citizens of Lafayette organized a vigilance committee and issued a frantic call for help on the evening of December 2. The Hopkinsville sheriff and militia, 150 strong, responded the next morning but found nothing more than a frightened town when they arrived at Lafayette. Nevertheless, some thirty to fifty blacks in the Hopkinsville area were jailed, whipped, and forced to acknowledge a plot to rebel on Christmas Day.[17] When Christmas passed with no insurrection white fears subsided, and in mid-February all the slaves in the Hopkinsville jail were released.[18]

The second and third accounts of the Stewart County "rebellion" seem to offer the most trustworthy description of actual events, particularly their statements regarding executions of supposed black ringleaders. Numerous press reports confirmed that six or seven slaves were killed at Dover and nearby ironworks during the panic, including several men belonging to Senator John Bell.[19] There are, however, difficulties with the letter from Pembroke and the French editor's report. The editor laced his account with obvious rumors, which he presented as hard facts based on personal knowledge; among his more obvious errors was a tale that two hundred slaves had actually begun a march on Dover and that sixty of these insurgents had been arrested. The Clarksville *Jeffersonian*, commenting that "some wag was practicing upon his credulity," devoted its Christmas eve editorial to correcting this and numerous other errors and distortions in the report the French editor had filed earlier that month.

In the case of the account written by the man from Pembroke, his version of the panic in Lafayette is confirmed by newspaper reports, as is his description of the executions which were carried out in Dover. This letter accepts as legitimate, however, the rumors of a

[17] Louisville *Courier*, December 6, 10, 1856; see also New York *Herald*, December 9, 12, 1856.

[18] Louisville *Courier*, January 1, 1857; Covington (Ky.) *Journal*, February 21, 1857. The Hopkinsville correspondent of the *Courier* complained that it had, in fact, been a dull Christmas because boys were not permitted to shoot firecrackers and the town's black population had remained off the streets during the holidays.

[19] Clarksville *Chronicle*, December 10, 1856, quoted in Louisville *Courier*, December 13, 1856; Nashville *Daily Gazette*, December 18, 1856; Nashville *Patriot*, January 2, 1857. Wish, "Slave Insurrection Panic of 1856," 211–12, claims that nineteen blacks were hanged at Dover and that nine more were executed at the Cumberland Iron Works. These figures are based on early exaggerated press reports which were subsequently corrected.

planned uprising around Lafayette and Hopkinsville, but these rumors were later discounted by the release of all the black prisoners in the Hopkinsville jail. In addition, when he returned to Pembroke after visiting the panic-stricken Tennessee iron district, he found his home town in a state of uproar. His description of the situation there suggests strongly that he was willing to swallow a considerable amount of wild hearsay in his effort to justify the bloody suppression of the so-called plot and that he himself was a ready participant in the mob actions that figured so prominently in that suppression:

> We are at work here [Pembroke] to-day. We have one negro in chains, and will hang him, I think, certain; if the [vigilance] committee will not, the community are determined to do it. I think we will have quite an exciting time here before we get through. I have no doubt but that it is a universal thing all over the Southern States, and that every negro, fifteen years old, either knows of it or is into it; and the most confidential house servants are the ones that are to be the most active in the destruction of their own families. The negroes, everywhere they are examined, all agree that the men, [old] women and children, are to be slain, and that the young women are to be kept as wives for themselves, and a good many of them about Dover and the furnaces, went so far as to select their future companions.[20]

The section of this passage referring to the rebels' lust for white women would seem to offer more insight into the sexual fantasies and anxieties of the white males engaged in putting down the uprising than into the details of an actual plan of insurrection. Finally, what can one make of the information in this and other accounts which was gathered by ironmasters and vigilantes "whipping the truth out of their negroes"? Confessions secured by systematic and brutal torture constitute firm evidence only for the existence of white hysteria and reveal nothing concrete except the lengths to which some whites were willing to go in order to confirm their vision of the horrors of an incipient black rebellion.

When viewed against the background of events elsewhere in Tennessee, Kentucky, and throughout the South in 1856 the supposed insurrection in the Cumberland iron district emerges in all probability as simply another phase of the panic which gripped the slave states before and after the presidential election of that year. The white fear which began in Texas in September hit not only

[20] Canton *Dispatch*, quoted in Louisville *Courier*, December 29, 1856.

those sections of Tennessee already discussed—the Memphis area and the Cumberland region to the north; it also affected Nashville, Murfreesboro, Gallatin, Franklin, Columbia, Shelbyville, and Sparta, Macon and Perry counties in Middle Tennessee, and Obion County at the extreme northwestern tip of the state.[21] The panic contagion proved equally virulent in Kentucky, with insurrectionary alarms spreading down the Cumberland into Trigg and Lyon counties in the iron district and into half a dozen other widely scattered areas of the state.[22] By late December reports of budding slave rebellions were filtering out of Louisiana, Mississippi, Alabama, Arkansas, Missouri, Maryland, Virginia, South Carolina, Georgia, and Florida.[23] "The excitement in Tennessee and Kentucky, relative to the negro insurrection, appears to have nearly died out, but in other parts of the South it is as lively as ever," commented the New York *Herald* on December 15, 1856. "The negro plotting commenced down in Texas, near the Rio Grande, some three months ago," the editorial continued, "but every one was so absorbed at that time with the Presidential election, and the matter was passed over without comment. Since then it has developed itself in nearly every state," the editor wrote. "What is the cause of all this commotion?" The answer most frequently given by southerners to the *Herald*'s question was that the rise of the Republican party and the agitation of the slavery issue during the 1856 presidential campaign had produced a dangerous black revolutionary movement that threatened to engulf wide areas of the South in a bloody servile war.

"The present evils that affect us are mainly to be attributed to the late Presidential canvas[s]," proclaimed the Clarksville vigilance

[21] The fullest account of the spread of the panic in Middle Tennessee can be found in the Nashville *Daily Gazette*, especially December 2, 5, 7, 9, 11, 13, 16, 18, 21, 24, 25, 30, 1856; see also Nashville *Union and American*, December 5, 7, 23, 28, 30, 31, 1856; Franklin *Western Weekly Review*, December 12, 1856; Louisville *Courier*, November 24, December 15, 1856; New York *Herald*, December 10, 24, 1856; and Boston *Liberator*, December 12, 1856.

[22] Nashville *Republican Banner*, December 24, 1856; Nashville *Daily Gazette*, December 30, 1856; Louisville *Courier*, December 15, 27, 1856; Covington *Journal*, January 3, 17, 1857; New York *Herald*, December 18, 30, 1856; Baltimore *Sun*, December 19, 1856; Boston *Liberator*, January 2, 1857; see also Coleman, *Slavery Times in Kentucky*, 107–10, and Wish, "Slave Insurrection Panic of 1856," 214–15.

[23] The exchanges in the New York *Herald* furnish the most complete single contemporary record of the incidence of insurrectionary rumors in various areas of the South during these months; see December 11, 15, 17, 20, 30, 1856, January 3, 12, 1857; see also Baltimore *Sun*, December 4, 27, 31, 1856; Louisville *Courier*, November 24, 1856; Charleston (S.C.) *Daily Courier*, December 18, 1856; and Wish, "Slave Insurrection Panic of 1856," 215–21.

committee in early December; "we condemn the public discussion of all questions touching negro slavery, before crowds of people in the hearing of vast multitudes of negroes." The committee also railed against the "gross folly" of slaveowners who had permitted "their negroes to go to barbecues and other public gatherings, where public speakers for the one party or the other, discuss there delicate subjects of negro slavery . . . ."[24] Southern newspapers that commented on the slave unrest of 1856 frequently charged that the Republicans were primarily to blame for the disaster which had almost occurred in many parts of the South. "Unquestionably this discontent among the slaves is the result of the recent sectional contest," noted the Richmond *Enquirer*. "Excited by the incendiary operations of the Black Republican Party, emboldened by assurances of sympathy and promises of succor from the North, and stimulated, no doubt, by the secret suggestions of miscreants in our midst, they grew impatient of their subjection and eager for revolt." The plots which had recently come to light "admonish us of the calamities which the election of FREMONT would have brought upon the South," the editor warned, and he urged "Thinking men in the North" to "discountenance and suppress an agitation which threatens the country with such unspeakable calamities . . . ."[25] A number of southern editors also found local politicians, always of the opposition party, guilty of indiscreet comments before integrated political rallies. "The staple howl of the low and lying demagogues of the Pierce and Douglas school . . . during the canvass, was that the opponents of the 'Democratic party' were either abolitionists themselves, or the secret allies of abolitionists, who were waging a war up on the South, for the purpose of breaking down slavery and making the negroes equal to whites!" the St. Louis *Intelligencer* complained bitterly. "Thousands of negroes in

[24] Clarksville *Jeffersonian*, December 17, 1856.

[25] Richmond *Enquirer*, quoted in New York *Times*, December 18, 1856. Similar sentiments can be found in the Nashville *Union and American*, January 8, 1857; Richmond *Examiner*, quoted in Nashville *Patriot*, January 13, 1857; and New Orleans *Daily Picayune*, December 24, 1856; January 2, 1857. Another favorite scapegoat was the free black population of the South. A number of free blacks were whipped and driven out of Murfreesboro at the height of the Tennessee panic, and moves to expel the free black population were launched in Nashville, Tennessee, and Paducah, Kentucky; see Nashville *Daily Gazette*, December 5, 30, 1856; and Nashville *Union and American*, December 28, 1856. Editorials calling for added watchfulness over free blacks, tighter restrictions on emancipation, and the reenslavement of blacks already freed also appeared during the insurrectionary scare; see Staunton (Va.) *Vindicator*, quoted in New York *Herald*, January 9, 1857; New-Orleans *Delta*, December 3, 1856, quoted *ibid.*, December 11, 1856; and Richmond *Examiner*, quoted in Nashville *Patriot*, January 13, 1857.

the South heard these infamous harangues, and if they believed the howling 'democratic' knaves, they must have come to the conclusion that a large portion of the people in every State, (all, in fact, except the veritable *Buchanan* democracy,) were abolitionists, at heart, and ready to set the slaves of the South free!"[26] A stock Democratic reply to these charges was that the southern Know-Nothing press that printed such ravings was simply being an "*apologist* for 'northern abolitionists,' " and Democratic editors warned slaveholders against allowing such inflammatory sheets to come into their homes.[27]

What these charges and countercharges indicate most clearly is that the emergence of the Republican party as a major political force and the surprisingly strong showing of John Charles Frémont in the presidential campaign sent a tremor of fear through the South in the fall and winter of 1856. In mid-September the Clarksville *Jeffersonian* devoted most of its front page to a five-column letter signed by Jesse Daniel of nearby Louisa furnace explaining that he was abandoning his former allegiance to the Know-Nothing party because of reports of cooperation between northern Know-Nothings and Republicans in the forthcoming election. "There never was a more important crisis . . . in the history of the republic that so imperatively demands that the South should stand united than . . . the approaching contest," he wrote. Defeating Frémont was the only way to "rescue the fondly cherished rights and highly valued privileges of the South from the iron grasp and ruthless hand of the abolitionists that surround our Capital."[28] On November 26, when it published the first reports of unrest at Louisa furnace, the same paper admitted that "For many weeks past there has been an uneasy feeling in the popular mind in this section, and a good deal of apprehension has been excited by vague and undefined rumors of a proposed revolt of the negroes, and in some localities the excitement has been stimulated to a very high degree." The Louisa Iron Works may well have been one of the places where white apprehension ran highest. Blacks outnumbered whites at this installation by some eighty to fifty men,[29] and in

[26] St. Louis *Weekly Intelligencer*, December 9, 1856; see also Richmond *Whig*, quoted in Nashville *Patriot*, January 6, 1857; Louisville *Journal*, quoted in Nashville *Union and American*, January 11, 1857; and Clarksville *Weekly Chronicle*, March 6, 1857.

[27] Nashville *Union and American*, January 11, 1857; see also *ibid.*, December 11, 1856.

[28] Clarksville *Jeffersonian*, September 17, 1856.

[29] "Manufacture of Iron on Cumberland River, Tennessee," 644.

January 1856 a large-scale runaway attempt had occurred there. All eleven of Solomon D. Raimey's slaves hired to the works had tried to flee, including Britton, the black man shot to death at Louisa furnace on November 26. The men were all recaptured after five or six days,[30] but the event undoubtedly stuck in the minds of the white men at the furnace and probably took on added significance as the tension mounted during the fall political campaign. The stage seems to have been very well set for an insurrectionary panic at the Louisa works and the rest of the Cumberland iron district in the last months of 1856.

The whippings, shootings, and lynchings that followed the discovery of the supposed revolutionary plots of the Tennessee and Kentucky ironworkers were a bloody catharsis for the overwrought slave masters of the region. By late December all was quiet again on the Cumberland, and the editor of the Clarksville *Jeffersonian*, who earlier that month had called for the suppression of the insurrection by letting "every tree in the country bend with negro meat," could write smugly that there had been "no panic" in the aftermath of the first rumors. "Slave owners were alarmed lest the excitement and indignation against the negro should find vent in an indiscriminate massacre of the slaves and the *pocket nerve* throbbed fearfully," he quipped. "But the idea that they apprehended an uprising is without a shadow of truth."[31]

The Clarksville editor's confident assertion that "no panic" had occurred in the area in 1856 was not universally supported in Tennessee. In 1857 and 1858 the state supreme court heard arguments in a case involving the death of a slave who had been killed by three white men during the 1856 insurrectionary scare. The man who had owned the slave was suing the killers in order to recover the value of his lost property, and the court decided the case in the owner's favor. "The wild panic, and vague, undefined apprehensions about a 'rising or insurrection of the slaves,' at that time, cannot be allowed to save parties from liability for the destruction of their neighbor's property," the judges ruled. "This species of property, above all others, must be protected from *wanton* abuse." "Those who take it upon themselves, in these periods of groundless panic, to slay and destroy, without the sanction of the law, must do

[30] See the accounts for Brit, Charles, Alfred, Edmund, Jack, Sam, Peter, Wesley, Isaac, John, and George Raimey, Louisa Furnace Account Book, 1854–1860 (Southern Historical Collection, University of North Carolina Library, Chapel Hill, N.C.).

[31] Clarksville *Jeffersonian*, December 24, 1856.

so at their peril," the decision concluded. "Every description of mob-law, and reckless invasion of the rights of others, should be visited with the highest penalties."[32] A month before this decision was handed down the Tennessee legislature moved to prevent a recurrence of vigilante action in any future insurrectionary panics. A law passed in March 1858 required circuit or criminal court judges to open court immediately, impanel a grand jury to hand down indictments, and proceed at once with regular trials of any blacks accused of revolutionary activity. Guilt or innocence was to be decided by a jury of twelve men.[33]

In January 1857 the London *Times* picked up from its exchanges a copy of the resolutions of the Clarksville vigilance committee and proceeded to publish lengthy excerpts from the committee's proposals along with its own stinging editorial analysis. "The planters of Tennessee are about to try a great experiment in social legislation," the *Times* commented sarcastically. "A Committee of Safety at Clarksville has devised a coercive system of a stringency such as even our own Parliaments of former days would have hesitated to apply to Popish recusants or the Irish population in general."[34] In a reply to this rebuke the editor of the Clarksville *Chronicle* went to the heart of the white rationale for the bloody acts which had been carried out in his own and neighboring counties during the panic. "There is a natural antipathy between races of different colors . . . ," he wrote, "and the natural superiority of the white over the black will not tolerate equality of social and political rights . . . ."[35] In the overheated atmosphere surrounding the presidential election of 1856 sizable numbers of fearful and angry whites in the Cumberland iron region and in many other areas of the South were convinced that white lives were in danger and that white supremacy, embodied in the institution of slavery, was under direct assault from those who were being held in a position of permanent inferiority. Such a challenge demanded a swift and overwhelming response the whites believed, and the result was the brutal suppression of a black insurrection which seems to have existed only in the panic-stricken minds of white southerners in 1856.

[32] *Kirkwood* v. *Miller,* 5 Sneed 455 (April term, 1858).

[33] Tennessee, *Public Acts . . . 1858* (Nashville, 1858), 94–95.

[34] London *Times*, January 28, 1857. Another leading British newspaper also delivered a strong editorial indictment of the South's conduct during the panic; see Manchester *Guardian*, December 23, 1856, quoted in New York *Herald,* January 10, 1857.

[35] Clarksville *Weekly Chronicle,* March 6, 1857.

The Commercial-Civic Elite and City Planning in Atlanta, Memphis, and New Orleans in the 1920s

By Blaine A. Brownell

That upper- and middle-class business groups had heavy hands in many reform schemes of the early twentieth century and sought to further their own social and economic interests under a mantle of efficiency, economy, and businesslike methods is no longer a new or surprising revelation. It has become, in fact, a prevailing historical orthodoxy. Historians differ, of course, concerning the motives of the groups and precise character of this phenomenon; but whether it be attributed to unmitigated economic self-interest, to a sweeping conservative social view along the lines of "corporate liberalism," or to a "bureaucratic vision" of a "paradise of new-middle-class rationality," its significance can hardly be denied.[1]

The influence of urban business groups in promoting city-manager and city-commission forms of municipal government in the early twentieth century in order to consolidate their interests, expand their power, and ensure efficient urban administration on business principles is one of the more convincing demonstrations of the involvement of social and economic elites in reform activities.[2]

[1] James Weinstein, *The Corporate Ideal in the Liberal State: 1900–1918* (Boston, 1968), 3; Robert H. Wiebe, *The Search for Order, 1877–1920* (New York, 1967), 170. Most historians have divided early twentieth-century reform into various elements. Wiebe suggests (p. 176) that the urban reform movement was composed of two major groups: ". . . one group used the language of the budget, boosterism, and social control, [and] the other talked of economic justice, human opportunities, and rehabilitated democracy." Melvin G. Holli makes a similar distinction between "structural reform" and "social reform" in his *Reform in Detroit: Hazen S. Pingree and Urban Politics* (New York, 1969), 157–81.

[2] See especially James Weinstein, "Organized Business and the City Commission and Manager Movements," *Journal of Southern History*, XXVIII (May 1962), 166–82; Samuel P.

Mr. Brownell is associate professor of history and urban studies and chairman of the Department of Urban Studies at the University of Alabama in Birmingham. The author is indebted to a grant from the Penrose Fund of the American Philosophical Society and to the Institute of Southern History at the Johns Hopkins University, where he was a senior fellow, 1971–1972.

And the search continues for other, similar examples. Strangely, one of the most notable of urban "reform" efforts—certainly, among those which continued into the 1920s—has been all too frequently ignored. Leading commercial and civic groups were, in fact, apparently more prominent and influential in the early attempts to solve urban ills and direct future development through systematic, comprehensive city planning than they were in the revisions of municipal government. In most American cities chambers of commerce, merchants' associations, businessmen's clubs, and other major civic organizations were in the forefront of the city-planning movement, impressing it with their values, goals, and concepts and providing in many cases its initial talent and resources.

The first permanent, official city-planning commission in the United States was established in Hartford, Connecticut, in March 1907. Quickly, cities across the country moved toward planning as a means of alleviating blight, population density, poor transportation, and confusing patterns of land utilization. Many of these functions were not new: building restrictions of various kinds, park projects, and particular arrangements of public structures and streets dated back to the eighteenth and nineteenth centuries. The new element was the *comprehensive* plan, which ideally took virtually every phase of the city's life into account—including railroads, streets, housing, recreation, subdivisions, buildings, and civic art—and which by 1915 had become the fashion. An earlier emphasis on the "city beautiful," stressed by national spokesmen like Charles Mulford Robinson and by local women's groups and focusing on civic art, architecture, and amenities, was rapidly replaced by a concern for the "city efficient," for functionalism rather than aesthetics.

The essential dimensions and style of the modern comprehensive plan were evidenced in the impressive design for Chicago by Daniel Hudson Burnham and Edward Herbert Bennett from 1907 to 1909. Though it included many features of city beautification, such as extensive "pleasure parkways," it also emphasized efficient traffic circulation, a new system of freight handling, the consolidation of railroad facilities, building restrictions to protect property, the necessity for new subdivision regulation, and neighborhood schools. It also dealt with a large metropolitan area rather than simply a group of public buildings or a limited collection of parks. And by 1910 American city planners were highly interested in

Hays, "The Politics of Reform in Municipal Government in the Progressive Era," *Pacific Northwest Quarterly*, LV (October 1964), 157–69.

regulating patterns of land use through the adoption of European zoning schemes.[3]

Typically, local attempts at city planning were initiated by strictly commercial groups like chambers of commerce or by a number of voluntary business and civic bodies. Largely in response to these early efforts, an official or unofficial planning agency was established by the municipal government, its membership composed of unpaid, "public-spirited" citizens and, occasionally, a city-planning expert. After a suitable plan was devised the planning commission and the groups which originally sponsored it sought broad public support through a program of concentrated publicity. Invariably, the arguments advanced in support of city planning included efficiency, economy, businesslike management, functionalism, and an underlying theme of social control. Burnham's Chicago plan, for example, was developed under the auspices of the Commercial Club and, more specifically, with the aid and support of Charles Dyer Norton, an insurance executive, Frederic Adrian Delano, president of the Wabash Railroad, and Charles Henry Wacker, a wealthy merchant. According to one authority the city envisioned in Burnham's plan was "an essentially aristocratic city, pleasing to the merchant princes who participated in its conception but not meeting some of the basic economic and human needs."[4]

Commercial organizations quickly recognized that city planning was "directly connected" with "industrial and commercial work." Savings gained through managerial efficiency and new production techniques could be lost in congested streets and transportation foul-ups; unregulated land use could undermine property values and the security of investments; and inadequate facilities and amenities might not appeal to new industries and workers.[5] In addition, commercial and civic groups saw in city planning a chance to inspire new enthusiasm, larger memberships, and additional influence in urban affairs for themselves. As a former officer of the Pittsburgh Chamber of Commerce put it, city planning represented "to these leading industrial associations an opportunity to take a new and more commanding place for the benefit of their

[3] Burnham and Bennett, *Plan of Chicago,* edited by Charles Moore (Chicago, 1909); Benjamin C. Marsh, *An Introduction to City Planning: Democracy's Challenge to the American City* (New York, 1909); Mel Scott, *American City Planning Since 1890* (Berkeley and Los Angeles, 1969), 100–109.

[4] Scott, *American City Planning,* 101, 108 (quotation); Miriam I. Ross, "A Primer of City Planning Progress and Legislation," *American City,* XXVIII (February 1923), 131–33.

[5] George B. Ford, "Chambers of Commerce and City Planning," *American City,* X (May 1914), 448–49. Ford was a member of the city planning committee of the Merchants' Association of New York.

communities than has ever before been offered them."[6]

The significance of city planning for urban history, however, goes beyond this important connection between the local planning movement and upper-class economic concerns. It reveals in a particularly coherent way the responses of commercial and civic leaders to a specific historical situation and reflects their concepts of the urban community at a time when the twentieth-century American metropolis was being formed.

This essay concerns city planning in the urban South during the 1920s and focuses on the cities of Atlanta, Memphis, and New Orleans. The major characteristic of these cities as they approached the third decade of the century was growth, whether measured in population or territorial terms. Between 1900 and 1920 the populations of Atlanta, Memphis, and New Orleans grew by 123, 59, and 35 percent, respectively. Memphis more than doubled its land area through annexation in 1899 and expanded by another 59.3 percent in the next twenty years. Likewise, Atlanta's territory grew by 143.6 percent in the same period. By 1920 New Orleans remained the largest city in the region with a population of 387,219, while Atlanta (200,616) had displaced Memphis (162,351) as the second largest urban center in the Southeast.[7]

The 1920s was in some respects a crucial period for many southern cities. The frequent annexations of the late nineteenth and early twentieth centuries had swelled city boundaries and populations and escalated the demands on municipal authorities for streets, water and gas lines, sewers, police and fire protection, and streetcar service. Neighborhoods were uprooted or transformed, industries converged on residential areas, and business coveted desirable properties along heavily traveled thoroughfares. Growth by annexation was not usually "organic," in the parlance of the time, but was by the addition of seemingly indigestible chunks of land and people, some of which were organized into fairly autonomous communities.

This was urban growth on a grand scale, but it was often chaotic and without visible design. Most importantly, perhaps, southern cities were experiencing for the first time a confrontation between a still accelerating trend toward urban centralization and a new and growing capacity for decentralization provided by technological

[6] Richard B. Watrous, "The Responsibilities of Commercial Organizations in Furthering the Adoption of City Plans," *American City*, II (May 1910), 229–31; quotation on page 229.

[7] *Fourteenth Census of the United States . . . 1920*, Vol. III: *Population* (Washington, 1922), 222, 399, 970; Roderick D. McKenzie, *The Metropolitan Community* (New York, 1967), 336–38. The city of Birmingham, by contrast, experienced population growth in the same period of 365 percent and an expansion in land area of over 678 percent.

innovations. These contradictory tendencies, embodied in the skyscraper and the motor vehicle, promised unprecedented urban growth and social transformation and inspired attempts by southern urban elites to lay new foundations of social order and to deal, if only indirectly, with some troubling implications of growth and "progress." Members of the commercial-civic elite thus regarded comprehensive city planning as an essential tool to shape and order the twentieth-century metropolis.

The Memphis City Planning Commission pointed specifically to the annexations of 1899, 1909, 1913, 1917, and 1919 as reasons for a coherent program of orderly development. New Orleans commissioners, noting their city's status as the nation's fourth largest in terms of corporate area, complained of the "growing difficulty in the management of this vast territory in providing means for people to get around, in giving them suitable places in which they may live and work."[8]

It was not until the 1920s that a significant number of American urban areas contracted for comprehensive plans, and this was reflected in the South as it was in other regions of the country.[9] In January 1919 the North Carolina General Assembly passed legislation enabling municipalities to establish official planning bodies, and twelve towns and cities did so by 1930.[10] City-planning committees appeared in Atlanta and Memphis in 1920 and in Nashville a year later. In some cases mayors appointed advisory groups even before they received legislative approval. Thus, the first official commission in Nashville was not established until 1925, and legislative enactment followed rather than preceded the appointment of unofficial commissions in Atlanta and Memphis. Knoxville and New Orleans created authorized commissions in 1923, and the Crescent City committee was reorganized in 1927. Charleston established a City Planning and Zoning Commission in 1929. Though Birmingham failed to initiate a comprehensive plan during the decade, the city did create a zoning board and adopted a traffic plan recommended by an outside consultant in 1927.

While very much a part of the national planning trend, the South contained relatively few city-planning committees by the end of the

[8] Memphis City Planning Commission, *First Annual Report: City Planning Commission, Memphis, Tennessee, 1921* (Memphis, 1921), 2; New Orleans City Planning and Zoning Commission, *Major Street Report* (New Orleans, 1927), 8.

[9] The best overall survey of modern city planning in the United States is Scott, *American City Planning;* see especially pages 110–269.

[10] Kay Haire Huggins, "City Planning in North Carolina, 1900–1929," *North Carolina Historical Review,* XLVI (Autumn 1969), 391–92. I am grateful to Philip R. Muller for bringing this article to my attention.

decade. The U. S. Department of Commerce reported 786 official planning commissions throughout the country in 1930; but only 71 of these were located in the eleven former Confederate states. Massachusetts, New York, California, Ohio, and Pennsylvania together accounted for 447 city planning commissions, but Texas had only 17 (the largest number for a southern state), and Alabama and Louisiana had but two each. Nevertheless, by the end of the 1920s some 36 towns and cities in the South had enacted zoning ordinances, and Atlanta, Memphis, New Orleans, Knoxville, Mobile, and Charleston, among other regional cities, had active, official planning committees.[11]

In every major southern city commercial and civic organizations, especially chambers of commerce, were highly visible and important in the planning movement. Of the municipalities which formed planning commissions in North Carolina during the decade local chambers of commerce were extremely influential in at least seven. Members of the local elite were prominent in virtually every city-planning effort in the state.[12] Similarly, the Nashville planning committee was partly a product of discussions within the Exchange Club and the Chamber of Commerce, and Knoxville's Board of Commerce could justifiably take credit for the formation of an official planning body and the completion of a comprehensive plan for the city in 1929.[13]

Atlanta entered the twentieth century with a record of growth that was the envy of lesser cities throughout the region. But she also suffered from the accumulated problems attendant upon growth, including a dearth of parks and recreational areas and a maze of streets and railroads in the central business district. A plan initially proposed in 1909 by Haralson Bleckley, president of the Atlanta Architectural Arts League, to construct a downtown civic center and plaza of shops, restaurants, offices, and hotels above the railroad tracks in the city's core absorbed most of the energies of local civic bodies until 1917, when the idea was finally rejected by the State Road Commission.[14]

[11] Lester G. Chase, comp., *A Tabulation of City Planning Commissions in the United States* (Washington, 1931), 1–2, 7–39.

[12] Huggins, "City Planning in North Carolina," 389–90, 392–93.

[13] *Nashville This Week,* I (November 9–16, 1925), 5; Nashville City Council Minutes (Office of the Metropolitan Clerk, Nashville, Tenn.), August 18, 1925, XXII, 360–61; *Nashville Review,* III (September 15, 1921), 9; Lyndon E. Abbott and Lee S. Greene, *Municipal Government and Administration in Tennessee* (Knoxville, 1939), 27–28; Knoxville *Journal and Tribune,* March 25, 1920.

[14] Thomas M. Deaton, "Atlanta During the Progressive Era" (unpublished Ph.D. dissertation, University of Georgia, 1969), 405–407; Walter G. Cooper, *Official History of Fulton County* ([Atlanta], 1934), 441; *City Builder* (Atlanta), I (January 1917), 9; V (May 1920), 22–24; Robert R. Otis, "Atlanta's Plan, 1909–1932" (mimeographed diary, Georgia State

Organizations like the Presidents' Club, composed of chief executives of Atlanta's civic groups, continued to discuss the matter, however, and the Chamber of Commerce, with a membership of 2,890 in 1920, did not relax its efforts for city planning. William J. Sayward, who had recently opened his architectural practice in the Gate City, headed a chamber committee devoted to urban planning and housing conditions in 1919 and consistently promoted the formation of an official municipal planning body. In an address to a chamber gathering in December 1919 Mayor James Lee Key asked the members of the organization, "as representing the public and commercial interests of the city," to help achieve a city plan. As a result of this meeting the first full-scale Atlanta city-planning commission was formed early the following year. "This Commission will be composed of men and women who are thoroughly representative of all interests of the city . . . ," the chamber magazine announced. "The job they have been asked to do is just about the biggest and most important that was ever asked of an Atlanta committee."[15]

Composed of twenty-four members—eight appointed by the president of the Chamber of Commerce, eight by the mayor, and eight by the Fulton County Board of Commissioners—the planning committee elected John William Grant, a former alderman and chairman of the city finance committee, as chairman. Louis P. Marquardt, an attorney and labor representative, and Mrs. Samuel Lumpkin, a prominent civic leader, were designated vice-chairmen. Kendall Weisiger, who headed the efficiency department of the Southern Bell Telephone Company, was named secretary. All but Marquardt were appointed to the commission by the original twenty-four members in an obvious effort to secure leadership with extensive ties to the city's civic and political elite. Other members included Mell R. Wilkinson, the permanent head of the Presidents' Club and a former president of the Chamber of Commerce; two other former presidents and several past officers of the chamber; representatives from the three daily papers; the president of the Rotary Club and a member of its Board of Directors; the head of the Georgia Automobile Association; a former president of

---

Library, Atlanta), 1, 4–5. My account differs somewhat from Deaton's, which relies primarily on Franklin M. Garrett, *Atlanta and Environs: A Chronicle of Its People and Events* (3 vols., New York, 1954), II, 684–86.

[15] Cooper, *Official History of Fulton County*, 802–803, 386; *City Builder*, IV (May 1919), 8; Atlanta *Constitution*, January 6, 1920. The chamber's announcement of the commission and Mayor Key's remarks are in *City Builder*, IV (January 1920), 5–6. A good general presentation of business ideology in Atlanta relating to city planning and other subjects is Charles P. Garofalo, "Business Ideas in Atlanta, 1916–1935" (unpublished Ph.D. dissertation, Emory University, 1972).

the Atlanta Real Estate Board; a city alderman; and two women civic leaders. All in all, fifteen of the commissioners were members of the Chamber of Commerce, and the planning body was immediately endorsed by all leading commercial and civic organizations. In its first meeting the new commission elected the mayor, the chairman of the Fulton County Board of Commissioners, and Eugene Robert Black, president of the Chamber of Commerce, as ex officio members. No blacks were appointed to the commission.[16]

Given responsibility for studying problems of housing, schools, street paving, crosstown thoroughfares, the water system, and city traffic, the unofficial commission began its work in an atmosphere of optimism. However, the commission lasted barely six months. Its large membership proved "unwieldy" and "unworkable," it lacked funds to hire consultants, and its meetings apparently suffered from considerable absenteeism. In August 1920 the state legislature approved an official planning commission for Atlanta, and on October 12 Mayor Key appointed six prominent local citizens to the new committee.[17]

Robert R. Otis, builder and manager of the Peachtree Arcade, a large enclosed shopping mall which opened in 1918, and a former president of both the Atlanta Real Estate Board and the Rotary Club, was elected acting chairman of the commission. The appointment of United States Senator Hoke Smith, secretary of the interior under Grover Cleveland and twice governor of Georgia, obviously heightened the potential political influence of the new planning body. Smith's background in local affairs corresponded closely, however, with that of most other members. A lawyer and financier, he had considerable real estate interests in Atlanta, most notably the Piedmont Hotel. He was a member of the Chamber of Commerce, a director of the Fulton National Bank, and a member of the Atlanta School Board after returning to Atlanta in 1921.[18]

Perhaps the most notable member of the commission, and certainly one of Atlanta's most remarkable citizens, was Joel Hurt. Arriving in the city in 1875 at the age of twenty-five, Hurt established a real estate and insurance business, organized and managed the Atlanta Building and Loan Association in 1879, the Atlanta Home Insurance Company in 1882, and the East Atlanta Land

[16] *City Builder,* IV (February 1920), 5, 7; Atlanta Chamber of Commerce, *List of Members* (Atlanta, 1918); Atlanta *Journal,* February 11, 14, 1920.

[17] Atlanta *Constitution,* February 10, 1920; *City Builder,* V (February 1921), 23; Otis, "Atlanta's Plan," 6; Garrett, *Atlanta and Environs,* II, 777.

[18] Dudley Glass, ed., *Men of Atlanta* (Atlanta, 1924), pages unnumbered; Garrett, *Atlanta and Environs,* III, 95; Atlanta Chamber of Commerce, *List of Members* (1918).

Company in 1886. A man of seemingly boundless energies and ambition, Hurt has usually been credited with constructing the South's first skyscraper (the Equitable Building) in 1891–1892 and with developing Inman Park, Atlanta's first residential suburb, and Druid Hills, an even more ambitious outlying residential community. His final accomplishment, completed at the time of his death in 1926, was the Hurt Building.[19]

Other members of the commission were Charles A. Wickersham, president of the Atlanta and West Point Railroad and the Western Alabama Railroad; Frank A. Pittman, secretary and treasurer of the Pittman Construction Company and a former municipal building inspector and city councilman; and Fred J. Terry, who, according to one newspaper account, was "prominently identified with the labor interests of the city." In 1921 Robert Harvey Whitten of Cleveland was engaged as a planning consultant to the commission, and a year later Otis began a series of brief newspaper articles to educate the citizenry on the principles of planning and to draw attention to planning efforts in other cities, especially St. Louis, Cleveland, and Detroit.[20]

The membership of Atlanta's major planning committees reveals a pattern consistent with the experience of other large southern cities. Though efforts were made to include prominent female civic leaders and at least one representative of "labor," the majority of commissioners were affiliated with the white, male, commercial-civic elite. Moreover, they were often associated with real estate development, construction, transportation, and banking—endeavors with more then an incidental interest in the physical development of the city. The financial and social connections of the overwhelming majority of commissioners were primarily local and were concentrated both in the central business district and, actually or potentially, in subdivisions on the urban periphery. Urban planning commissions in the South, in other words, drew most heavily on those local individuals and groups who had considerable ex-

[19] Garrett, *Atlanta and Environs*, III, 572–73; Elizabeth Anne Mack Lyon, "Frederick Law Olmsted and Joel Hurt: Planning the Environment in Atlanta, 1892–1894" (unpublished paper presented to the Southeast American Studies Conference, Atlanta, April 27–29, 1972), 2–3, 5; Rich Beard, "Hurt's Deserted Village: Atlanta's Inman Park, 1885–1911" (unpublished paper presented to the Southeast American Studies Conference, Atlanta, April 27–29, 1972), 6, 11, 23–24. I am indebted to Dana F. White for providing me with copies of the papers presented at the conference. For an exhaustive survey of commercial buildings in Atlanta, see Elizabeth Anne Mack Lyon, "Business Buildings in Atlanta: A Study in Urban Growth and Form" (unpublished Ph.D. dissertation, Emory University, 1971).

[20] Garrett, *Atlanta and Environs*, III, 127; *Atlanta City Directory, 1920* (Atlanta, 1920); Atlanta *Journal*, October 12, 1920; Raymond W. Torras, "City Planning Commission," Atlanta *Tribune* (August 1929), 36; Otis, "Atlanta's Plan," 17–18.

perience in finance, transportation, and land development and who were most interested in the consequences of a comprehensive urban design. Conflict of interest was never mentioned and probably was never seriously considered; the backgrounds of such men and women were thought to be positive advantages in promoting the urban welfare. Members of the commercial-civic elite certainly considered themselves "public spirited," and it would never have occurred to them that they might not be capable of representing the interests and concerns of the entire city.

The leading commercial and civic groups in Memphis also demonstrated significant interest in city planning by 1919. The Memphis City Club created a number of standing committees to deal with specific aspects of city planning and recommended that various civic groups join to promote the appointment of an official planning commission. The Engineers' Club adopted a resolution on December 1 supporting a comprehensive plan and forwarded it to the City Club for consideration. Such a plan seemed necessary, the resolution concluded, for "relief from increasing street congestion, solution of transportation problems between various portions of the city, prevention of [the] erratic spread of business enterprise, stabilizing of property values and proper co-ordination among the various interests which constitute city life and growth . . . ." City Club committees also met with similar groups from the Lions Club, the Kiwanis Club, the Rotary Club, the Engineers' Club, the Memphis Art Association, the Nineteenth-Century Club (a large women's organization), and the Chamber of Commerce.[21]

In the same year the chamber—which boasted 3,821 members in July and more than thirty standing committees, many of which dealt with aspects of city planning—established an active City Planning Committee of more than twenty members drawn from various civic organizations, thus, in the chamber's view, "making it representative of [the] entire City." Under the leadership of Wassell Randolph, a local attorney and businessman, the chamber committee initiated a number of meetings with the mayor and the city commissioners. Soon thereafter, on March 30, 1920, a nine-member City Planning Commission was established by municipal ordinance. A year later the commission was "constituted" as an official city agency by state law, the original commissioners being reappointed to staggered three-year terms.[22]

[21] City Club of Memphis, *Bulletin*, November 4, 25, December 30, 1919.

[22] Memphis Chamber of Commerce, *Annual Reports, 1919–1920* (Memphis, 1920), 33; Memphis Chamber of Commerce, *Journal*, II (January 1920), 294; III (May 1920), 108; City Club of Memphis, *Bulletin*, February 3, March 2, 1920; Memphis Board of Commissioners Minutes (City Hall, Memphis, Tenn.), Book G, 78.

"It may be said with becoming modesty," Randolph wrote, "that this [Chamber of Commerce City Planning] Committee is the forerunner of the City Planning Commission—that through the activities of this Committee resulting in several conferences with the City Commissioners, the Commissioners were influenced to give the City Planning Movement careful consideration, with the result that the need for a City Planning Commission became a conviction . . . ." The new commission in its first annual report attributed its origins to the election in 1920 of "a new administration of progressive business men" who had been "elected on a business administration platform," and who "drew largely from the civic organizations which had City Planning Committees" in determining the planning commission's membership. Indeed, Randolph was not only chairman of the new commission but also a former president of the City Club and an active member of the Chamber of Commerce Board of Directors. His civic and business activities included management of his father's properties, especially the Bishop Building, and membership on the University of Tennessee Board of Trustees in 1927.[23]

Other commissioners included Charles J. Haase, a real estate and insurance broker, financier, and president of the Home Building and Loan Association; Edward B. LeMaster, a major realtor and developer who helped organize the Memphis Real Estate Board in 1910 and served as its first president; Samuel Evan Ragland, president of the First National City Bank, founder of the Southern Trust Company (a real estate mortgage firm), and former president and largest stockholder in the Memphis *News-Scimitar;* Dan Wolf, owner of a commercial printing company and former labor editor of the Memphis *Commercial Appeal;* and Walk Claridge Jones, a prominent local architect who designed some two dozen of the city's major buildings. The two female commissioners were Mrs. Irby Bennett, a civic leader especially active in the Nineteenth-Century Club and wife of a prominent Memphis broker; and Mrs. Eleanor O'Donnell McCormack, one of the first presidents of the Nineteenth-Century Club, a former county superintendent of schools, president of the Tennessee Federation of Women's Clubs, Red Cross director, law school graduate, wife of a Memphis cotton dealer, and adviser to important figures in state and local govern-

[23] Randolph's comment is contained in Memphis Chamber of Commerce, *Annual Reports, 1919–1920*, p. 33; and the origins of local planning are traced in Memphis City Planning Commission, *First Annual Report,* 9. See also the Biographical Files (Memphis Room, Memphis Public Library); and "Memphis, the South's Paris," Memphis Chamber of Commerce, *Journal,* VII (October 1924), 31.

ment. Serving as ex officio members were the city engineer, the chairman of the Park Commission, and two city commissioners whose responsibilities included public utilities and streets. The commission contained eight members of the Chamber of Commerce and five members of the City Club.[24]

The commission contracted with Harland Bartholomew of St. Louis for a comprehensive city plan in November 1920, and in April of the following year the members created two principal committees, one for streets and traffic and one for zoning. As the Memphis Chamber of Commerce *Journal* explained it, "The phenomenal growth and expansion taking place in Memphis demanded the services of a body of public spirited men to plan for the future, and correct present defects in our past growth."[25]

In New Orleans the story was very much the same. The Association of Commerce, which claimed a membership of 4,709 in March 1920, appropriated $7,500 for city planning in 1917. Since most planning consultants were involved in war work, however, it was not until 1919 that the organization's Civic Bureau, headed by Charles Allen Favrot, a socially prominent engineer and architect descended from one of Louisiana's oldest families, was able to engage Philadelphia planner Milton Bennett Medary, Jr., to prepare an initial survey and publicize the importance of city planning. Medary's series of fifty-two articles began appearing in the Sunday issues of local papers in August 1919. In addition, the Civic Bureau completed surveys on schools, juvenile delinquency, and business and industrial properties to assist the consultant in his work.[26]

Finally, in January 1923 the Association's City Planning Committee met with the New Orleans Commission-Council and shortly thereafter submitted an ordinance creating an official municipal planning body. In February the Commission-Council eliminated the ex officio memberships of various city officials (a move which apparently aroused some minor opposition), declared that all members "shall be real property taxpayers" and serve without compensation, and determined that commissioners should be appointed

[24] Biographical Files (Memphis Room, Memphis Public Library); Memphis Chamber of Commerce, *Classified List of Members, Business Mens' Club, Chamber of Commerce, 1916–1917* (Memphis, 1917).

[25] Harland Bartholomew and Associates, *A Comprehensive City Plan: Memphis, Tennessee* ([Memphis], 1924), 5; Memphis City Planning Commission, *First Annual Report*, 3; Memphis Chamber of Commerce, *Journal*, V (October 1922), 23.

[26] New Orleans Association of Commerce, *News Bulletin*, II (October 12, 1920), 10; II (June 21, 1920), 1; II (March 29, 1920), 3; John S. Kendall, *History of New Orleans* (3 vols., Chicago and New York, 1922), II, 790.

primarily from the city's commercial and civic organizations. The ordinance became law in May. The Association of Commerce took credit for most of these developments; it had expended close to $20,000 on city-planning projects and promotions between 1917 and 1923.[27]

As required by the ordinance, thirteen of the twenty members of the New Orleans City Planning and Zoning Commission were appointed as representatives of designated "leading commercial and civic organizations," including the Association of Commerce, the Board of Trade, the Cotton Exchange, the Contractors and Dealers Exchange, the Real Estate Agents Association, the New Orleans Federation of Clubs, the Young Mens' Business Club, and the Central Trades and Labor Council. (The New Orleans Real Estate Board had merged with the Association of Commerce in 1921.) Each of the designated thirteen organizations submitted a list of three names to the mayor, who then forwarded one name to the Commission-Council for approval. The ordinance also provided that seven representatives (including three women) were to be appointed at large. The commission's work was initially funded by contributions from local individuals and interested groups. Favrot was named chairman of the commission, and General Allison Owen, an architect and builder who belonged to most of the city's major civic clubs and served as president of the Association of Commerce in 1927 and 1932, was named vice-chairman. By 1927 the commission had included among its members (who were appointed for staggered five-year terms) fifteen members of the Association of Commerce and a number of engineers, real estate developers, and contractors. Virtually all of the seven commissioners appointed by the mayor were drawn from the city's commercial-civic elite.[28]

The annual reports of the commission provide an unusually rich source of information concerning its growing activities. During the first year it compiled all city ordinances relating to zoning, introduced a zoning enabling act into the state legislature, completed preliminary work on a zoning plan, held nine public hearings and fourteen general meetings, and received a $250 monthly operating allowance from the Commission-Council and an anonymous private gift of almost $2,000. Harland Bartholomew was engaged in

[27] New Orleans Association of Commerce, *News Bulletin,* V (January 16, 1923), 1; V (January 23, 1923), 2; V (February 6, 1923), 1, 8; V (July 24, 1923), 1; New Orleans *Item,* May 2, 4, 1923.

[28] New Orleans Association of Commerce, *News Bulletin,* V (May 8, 1923), 1, 4; New Orleans *Times-Picayune,* May 2, 1923; New Orleans City Planning and Zoning Commission, *Major Street Report* (New Orleans, 1927) 8; New Orleans Association of Commerce, *Red Book of New Orleans* (New Orleans, 1925); Kendall, *History of New Orleans,* II, 1191–93.

1926 to prepare a comprehensive plan, and the city increased its annual appropriation to $20,000. On June 6 the commission was reorganized by the municipal government: its membership was reduced to fifteen, and representatives of various government agencies were appointed. At the same time the city's annual financial support rose to $30,000, largely to cover Bartholomew's fees and expenses, and work proceeded on the preparation of maps and tables for the major street plan.[29]

The second official New Orleans planning commission retained seven members from the original body and added eight commissioners. Favrot and Owen continued as chairman and vice-chairman, respectively. The new commission's membership included two engineers, two architects, a banker, a real estate and mortgage broker specializing in city property, and one woman, the wife of the city purchasing agent. Ten of the commissioners were also members of the Association of Commerce.[30]

Emphasis on the city efficient was attributable not only to the functionalist movement among planners themselves but primarily to the interests and priorities established by their clients. "City planning," the Memphis *Commercial Appeal* observed in 1922, "really is given to making things useful, efficient and convenient." Rather than focusing on civic decoration, "real" city planning dealt with streets, zoning, and "many other things connected with the economy of population in the mass." Perhaps William J. Sayward of Atlanta said it best: "The city beautiful . . . is a very commendable ideal and one which should be assured its place; but we must not forget that the city beautiful must absolutely be founded on the 'city practical;' otherwise, there is no justification for any procedure along this line."[31]

In facing the consequences of rapid urban population and territorial growth established southern commercial and civic interests apparently had become by the 1920s less enamored of the boom-and-bust enthusiasm that vaulted small towns into great metropolises and more concerned with protecting property or consolidating gains in the mature city. This was no little transition; the business and civic groups that had emerged in the late-nineteenth-

[29] See mimeographed annual reports of the City Planning and Zoning Commission for July 17, 1923–August 31, 1924; September 1, 1924–June 30, 1925; July 1, 1926–June 6, 1927 (City Archives, New Orleans Public Library).

[30] New Orleans City Planning and Zoning Commission, *Major Street Report*, 5; New Orleans *Times-Picayune*, June 7, 8, 1927; New Orleans Association of Commerce, *Red Book of New Orleans* (1925).

[31] Memphis *Commercial Appeal*, February 18, 1922; Sayward, "City Planning Committee Urges Survey," *City Builder*, IV (January 1920), 12.

century urban South and had formerly gloried in all forms of growth and expansion simply had too much to lose and too little to gain from chaotic development in the early twentieth century. The development of the city and the forces and problems it spawned led to different notions of what the city should be and how its leaders should respond. The 1920s was a period, at least in the urban South, when commercial-civic elements began to look upon rampant growth as a potential problem rather than an invariable panacea, to consider the urban community as more delicate and vulnerable to dislocation and disorder.

This perception was not simply one of narrow economic interest; commercial-civic spokesmen did not, in fact, separate their concerns into social, economic, and political categories. The kind of city they envisioned secured property and facilitated their economic ambitions, but it also appealed to others in the city who were neither socially prominent nor economically prosperous. To attribute the conceptions of the urban community held by this elite solely to economic concerns or to defenses of free-enterprise capitalism would be a grievous error, similar to the defining of general social class interests in purely economic terms. With their faith in efficiency, organization, applied science, and businesslike methods and their interest in retaining a dominant role for themselves in urban society, members of the commercial-civic elite were appalled by the haphazard waste and potential dangers they saw in unregulated growth. At least some of them were disturbed that many municipalities took their basic shape, not from the decisions of enlightened community leaders, but from the meanderings of Indian trails and cow paths: ". . . instead of being laid out by the highest rate of intelligence . . . ," Sayward complained, the modern city "has in most cases been laid out, strange as it may seem, by the most primitive of minds." Commercial-civic spokesmen increasingly began to emphasize not only growth but "the economic value of a well ordered city."[32] Growth retained a hallowed place in the commercial-civic lexicon, but by the 1920s the principal challenge seemed to be to achieve a city that was both stable and expansive.

Matters of street transportation and zoning dominated the planning movement in the urban South, and most of the rest of the country, during the decade.[33] They formed the bulk of those com-

[32] Sayward, "City Planning Committee Urges Survey," 12–13.

[33] A questionnaire sent to the members of the New Orleans Association of Commerce in 1919 elicited a response that accorded higher priority to paving and street improvements than to the addition of new industries. New Orleans Association of Commerce, *News Bulletin*, I (June 16, 1919), 1.

prehensive plans drawn by Harland Bartholomew. Beginning his highly successful career in 1912 as an assistant engineer for the Newark, New Jersey, plan directed by Ernest Payson Goodrich and George Burdett Ford, Bartholomew became the engineer for the City Plan Commission of St. Louis in 1916 and started his private consulting practice three years later. His firm, Harland Bartholomew and Associates, was exceptionally active during the 1920s, completing comprehensive plans for thirty-two cities, including Kansas City, Pittsburgh, Toledo, and—in the South—Memphis, New Orleans, Chattanooga, Knoxville, and Orlando. His Memphis plan of 1924 became the prototype of his later efforts. Housing and "social" concerns were largely eliminated from his plans during the decade according to one writer, "leaving . . . a planning portfolio confined to the more acceptable objectives of the community's physical and functional reordering." Bartholomew later recalled that he "was not at complete liberty to introduce unusual new ideas and concepts in city planning, nor were the city plans produced exclusively my own work. We made a practice of having members of the city plan commissions participate extensively in the preparation of the comprehensive plan." Consequently, "the technical level of most plans was limited to what we could get the members of planning commissions to accept."[34]

The two major documents of the Memphis City Planning Commission prepared by Bartholomew reflected the principal concerns of the commercial-civic elite. A forty-two-page *First Annual Report* issued in 1921 contained a preliminary major-street plan, a transit proposal, and initial zoning studies; and Bartholomew's *Comprehensive City Plan* of 1924 was organized with attention to major streets, transit, transportation, recreation, zoning, and civic art, with the most detailed and extensive portions dealing with streets and zoning. Likewise, the 1922 annual report of the Atlanta City Planning Commission listed zoning as the top priority of

[34] Norman J. Johnston, "Harland Bartholomew: His Comprehensive Plans and Science of Planning" (unpublished Ph.D. dissertation, University of Pennsylvania, 1964), 7–24, 98–99, 122, 144, 154–55, 158, 181–82 (quotations on pages 158, 181–82). Johnston also notes (pp. 143, 150) that the commercial and civic influence on early city-planning efforts prevailed among other Bartholomew clients. In Wichita, Kansas, city planning was initiated through the efforts of the Board of Commerce and the Rotary Club, and the first planning studies in Hamilton, Ohio, were subsidized through subscriptions from the Chamber of Commerce. Bartholomew's firm accounted for almost a quarter of all comprehensive plans drawn in the nation in the first six years of the 1920s, and he served as the sixth president of the American City Planning Institute (the forerunner of the American Institute of Planners) from 1927 to 1929.

business, followed closely in importance by a general traffic plan.[35]

The street system was usually designated, as in Memphis, "the fundamental element" of the city plan, the "skeleton or framework of the city structure." A viable street network would include "main arterial thoroughfares" to carry the heaviest loads of motor traffic, "secondary (crosstown) thoroughfares" to funnel traffic into the main arteries, and "minor streets" to serve specific areas. A primary goal was to widen existing streets and construct new links between them. As the Atlanta planners put it, the "central business section of the city should have an approximate rectangular street layout, every street constituting the central portion of a main arterial thoroughfare." Bartholomew in his New Orleans plan emphasized that streets were by no means equal but served diverse and specialized functions. The main emphasis, he suggested, should be placed on the principal arteries. "Almost all metropolitan centers find it necessary," he wrote, "to designate major streets and devise plans for bringing them into coordinated use."[36]

Major-street plans in this period were aimed at increasing efficient traffic flow and vivifying the urban core. The downtown business district would be a "focal point" linking the main traffic arteries. Bartholomew was concerned, for example, that the locus of principal streets in New Orleans was somewhat removed from the central business section. "The aim," he noted, "is to create a series of wide, direct and well paved arteries radiating from this primary objective." Indeed, the planning metaphors of the 1920s were well chosen to reflect the conceptions of the modern metropolis which existed at the time. "The circulation of the urban body must be kept alive. Structural weaknesses in the arterial system, whatever their cause, bring about disorders which affect every phase of city life."[37]

[35] Memphis City Planning Commission, *First Annual Report;* Bartholomew *et al.*, *A Comprehensive City Plan: Memphis;* Atlanta City Planning Committee, *Annual Report . . . 1922* (Atlanta, 1922), 5. As the decade wore on Bartholomew gave greater emphasis to streets and motor-vehicle transportation. The basic framework established in Memphis was retained in his comprehensive plan for Knoxville in 1929, but a chapter on "Parking and Traffic Problems in the Business District" was added. See Johnston, "Harland Bartholomew," 171; Harland Bartholomew and Associates, *A Comprehensive City Plan: Knoxville, Tennessee* ([Knoxville, 1929]).

[36] Memphis City Planning Commission, *First Annual Report,* 11, 19–28; Atlanta City Planning Commission, *Annual Report . . . 1922,* p. 6; New Orleans City Planning and Zoning Commission, *Major Street Report,* 56.

[37] New Orleans City Planning and Zoning Commission, *Major Street Report,* 56. Special street-transportation studies were also completed by outside consultants for Atlanta, Birmingham, Memphis, and New Orleans during the decade. See John A. Beeler, *Report to the City of Atlanta on a Plan for Local Transportation, December, 1924* (Atlanta, 1924); Ross W. Harris, "Traffic Survey on the Vehicular and Street Railway Traffic Situation of Birmingham" (unpublished manuscript, 1927, City Clerk's Office, Birmingham, Ala.);

The ideal street system facilitated travel toward the central city, centralized the patterns of urban mobility, and vitalized the downtown business district. It was also calculated to promote expansion, especially into previously undeveloped areas. Here the contradictory tendencies of the time, centrifugal and centripetal, were resolved in the paved street, which linked the center with the periphery; and the automobile became the means whereby each could reinforce the other. New Orleans planners, for example, were particularly interested in using the major-street system to exploit regions on the urban outskirts as well as "underdeveloped" areas near the city's core. Bartholomew discovered that the principal area of New Orleans contained 28,000 acres of land, of which only 12,000 were sufficiently developed. Of the remainder, 14,000 acres suffered from "incomplete drainage, sewerage and water services." He suggested that initial concern had to be with correcting past faults in the system, but the street plan should look toward the eventual development of these areas, toward a decentralization of population over a larger territory.[38]

Commercial-civic elements seemed to be quite concerned that the expanding populations of their cities and the accompanying commercial and industrial enterprises would simply compound the confusion that large numbers of people and motor vehicles had already created in the central city. It was through a coherent street plan that such consequences were, at least in part, to be avoided. With the eventual adoption of the Memphis plan, the commissioners fully expected in 1921 that "orderly development will have been made certain for the future. The ultimate in city progress, which in January of 1920 was merely discussed, will have become a reality."[39]

Zoning was a fundamental feature of city planning during the 1920s and was usually the first coercive power obtained by local planning bodies. Many communities, in fact, such as Birmingham, adopted a zoning ordinance and created a zoning board in the

---

Memphis Board of Commissioners Minutes, Book G, 46; John A. Beeler, "Report to the Commissioner of Public Utilities, City of New Orleans on the Street Railway Situation, 1923" (unpublished report, City Archives, New Orleans Public Library); Miller McClintock, "The Street Traffic Control Problem of the City of New Orleans" (mimeographed report, 1928, City Archives, New Orleans Public Library).

[38] New Orleans City Planning and Zoning Commission, *Major Street Report*, 36–37.

[39] Memphis City Planning Commission, *First Annual Report*, 10. Bartholomew's comprehensive plan for Des Moines, Iowa, in 1928 reflected a declining emphasis on minor streets and the addition of "by-pass streets." See Johnston, "Harland Bartholomew," 166–67. These would, of course, become especially prominent in the traffic designs of the 1930s and result eventually in the massive circumvential freeways of the interstate highway system of the 1950s and 1960s.

absence of any efforts toward a comprehensive plan. Zoning in the urban South was much more than the preservation of residential districts against the influx of commerce and industry, though this was obviously one of its avowed purposes. It was in a very real sense a principal tool for stabilizing and fashioning the metropolis, for fixing spatial arrangements, protecting investments and property values, easing the blight and confusion of "transitional" and "mixed" areas, segregating the races, and encouraging the orderly expansion and decentralization of the urban population while maintaining the vitality of the downtown business district.

The Memphis zoning law drawn by Bartholomew went into effect in November 1922 without great difficulty. But in New Orleans and Atlanta zoning ordinances were held up in the courts. New Orleans obtained zoning authority in the Louisiana constitution in 1921, but it was not until July 1923 that the city won the first major court test of its powers. Not until 1929, after two years and seven months of public hearings, was Bartholomew's revised statute adopted by the Commission-Council. In Atlanta the first zoning ordinance, passed in April 1922, was successfully challenged in the courts on the ground that it was an illegal interference with private property rights. An amendment to the state constitution was ultimately required to grant zoning authority to Georgia municipalities. Finally, in December 1928 a zoning law based upon the earlier ordinance was approved by the City Council.[40]

Real estate interests initially opposed zoning efforts in some cities, especially Atlanta, but a majority of real estate spokesmen in the urban South praised planning and zoning for guarding land investments. The Memphis City Planning Commission, for example, argued that "Areas now occupied or expected to be occupied for residential purposes . . . should most certainly be given the protection essential to their permanency of development through exclusion of industrial or commercial intrusions." The social and economic chaos of changing neighborhoods and the uncertainty of unregulated development were to be avoided if at all possible. And those members of the commercial-civic elite who sat on city-planning commissions were not loath to contemplate some restrictions on the prerogatives of private property, nor were many of

[40] New Orleans City Planning and Zoning Commission, "Handbook to the Comprehensive Zone Laws for New Orleans, Louisiana" (mimeographed volume, 1929, City Archives, New Orleans Public Library), Chap. IV, 3–4, 7–8; New Orleans City Planning and Zoning Commission, "Report on Factors Involved in Carrying out the City Plan," 29; Bartholomew *et al.*, *A Comprehensive City Plan: Memphis*, 117–21, 127; Wassell Randolph, "Municipal Zoning; Proposed Ordinance," Memphis Chamber of Commerce, *Journal*, V (May 1922), 37–38; Garrett, *Atlanta and Environs*, II, 839; Robert Whitten, "Atlanta Adopts Zoning," *American City*, XXVI (June, 1922), 541–42; Atlanta *Constitution*, December 22, 1928.

those voluntary groups which provided the initial impetus for planning. As Randolph observed, the "modern view" of city planning "is that the public can control the private use of realty as to prevent an owner making a use of his lot which will depreciate the value of his neighbors' lots." Zoning might "interfere with the plans of individuals," the Memphis Chamber of Commerce *Journal* commented in 1922, "the same as other phases of city planning will temporarily discommode some of the people whose property is affected. But this is the cost of progress, and today's loss, in any program of permanent improvement, is compensated by tomorrow's gain." City planning was likened to the process in "every large industry" of "logically planning the arrangement of its plant and equipment . . . ," and zoning was "merely the common sense application of this same universal principle of orderly arrangement to the development of our city."[41]

The Memphis plan zoned older residential areas on the edges of commercial and industrial regions for both single-family dwellings and apartments in order to "fix the character of these transitional districts." These intermediate areas could also serve as buffer zones between heavily business sections and the low-density residential regions at some distance from the urban core. The idea was to "give stability and character, as well as encouragement, to the proper development of the city."[42]

Spatial stability in the South also meant racial segregation. Like most American cities southern urban areas reflected informal patterns of spatial separation along racial lines. Randolph observed that most black neighborhoods in Memphis were found "in the lower ground bordering on the drainage courses." The rule "is that the colored population is found exclusively in the cheaper, less desirable sections of the city. Thus, we have a sort of natural zoning of the races."[43] However, these informal boundaries had a tendency to float with the tides of urban growth and change.

[41] Memphis City Planning Commission, *First Annual Report*, 15–16; Randolph, "Municipal Zoning; Proposed Ordinance," 37; Memphis Chamber of Commerce, *Journal*, V (August 1922), 51; (September 1922), 27; Johnston, "Harland Bartholomew," 163–64, 199. Also see Huggins, "City Planning in North Carolina," 392. Johnston maintains (p. 158) that by the time of the 1924 Memphis plan, "the whole idea-concept of community over private right as expressed by Bartholomew's earlier reports is obscured." Johnston is misled here by his reliance on Frederick Lewis Allen's portrait of the decade, for such an "idea-concept" is indeed found, even in southern business publications and in Bartholomew's plans for southern cities. The point is that the reordering and structuring of the city, the prevalence of community over private rights, was made to conform to commercial-civic interests, concerns, and priorities.

[42] Bartholomew *et al.*, *A Comprehensive City Plan: Memphis*, 123 (first quotation); Memphis City Planning Commission, *First Annual Report*, 16 (second quotation).

[43] Memphis City Planning Commission, *First Annual Report*, 7. For information on infor-

The first zoning law in Atlanta changed informal Jim Crow arrangements into a formal pattern of residential segregation. Residential areas were divided into white, black, and undetermined zones, while black servants' quarters in white neighborhoods and white property ownership in black sections were legally sanctioned. The plan, devised by Robert Whitten, was, according to *Survey* magazine, "the first to embody in an outspoken form segregation along the line of social composition of the population" and constituted a potential precedent for separating immigrants and other ethnic groups in northern and western cities.[44] Whitten defended the concept on the grounds that it was neither undemocratic nor antisocial. The creation of "colored districts" provided "adequate areas for the growth of the colored population" and encouraged blacks to develop "a more intelligent and responsible citizenship." Separation lessened the possibility of race riots and social upheaval, he claimed, and stabilized property values in transitional racial areas. "Hundreds of acres of land were left undeveloped or poorly developed in various parts of the city," he observed, "because of uncertainty . . . ." Whitten also repeated a maxim of most planners of the time: ". . . wherever you have a neighborhood made up of people largely in the same economic status, you have a neighborhood where there is most independence of thought and action and the most intelligent interest in the neighborhood, city, state and national affairs."[45]

Zoning had been recognized for some time as a tool for fixing existing spatial arrangements, but it was not an arbitrary imposition of a static pattern. It was also a method for promoting urban expansion, of extending the city into surrounding territory and encouraging economic development. Height restrictions discouraged the rise of skyscrapers since, according to the planning theory of the time, such structures were "uneconomical" and "injurious to the community." By limiting building heights population density would be

mal and statutory residential segregation in Birmingham, see Carl V. Harris, "Reforms in Government Control of Negroes in Birmingham, Alabama, 1890–1920," *Journal of Southern History*, XXXVIII (November 1972), 571; *Zoning Ordinance of Birmingham, Alabama* (Birmingham, 1926), 12–15; Birmingham *News*, June 15, 1926; Blaine A. Brownell, "Birmingham, Alabama: New South City in the 1920s," *Journal of Southern History*, XXXVIII (February 1972), 29.

[44] "The Atlanta Zoning Plan," *Survey*, XLVIII (April 22, 1922), 114–15. Separation of population groups by zoning was not unprecedented before the 1920s. California municipalities employed crude zone districts to segregate Chinese immigrants in the 1880s. See Sam B. Warner, Jr., *The Urban Wilderness: A History of the American City* (New York and other cities, 1972), 28–29.

[45] Robert Whitten, letter to the editor, *Survey*, XLVIII (June 15, 1922), 418–19. According to the Atlanta City Planning Commission's *Annual Report . . . 1922*, p. 4, residential segregation was adopted for "the promotion of public peace, order, safety and general welfare . . . ."

lessened and urban residents dispersed over a larger area. Planning committees also sought through subdivision ordinances to direct the development of the city into peripheral sections, even beyond the municipal limits. In his Memphis plan Bartholomew wrote that "the primary purpose of city planning and zoning is to regulate and distribute the population of a city for the protection of health, safety and general welfare . . . ." Planners in New Orleans were particularly anxious to populate those regions of the city which had only recently been rendered habitable by sewer and drainage improvements, and Atlanta planners devised their zoning ordinance to promote "the spreading out of the population" and prevent "excessive over-crowding in the tenement house areas . . . ." In addition, sizable tracts were allocated for industry, and the major thoroughfares were zoned for commercial use, creating a ribbon pattern of business expansion throughout the city.[46]

The preparations involved in the Memphis zoning plan were fairly typical: an extensive survey of existing tendencies in land use was followed by the drawing of use, height, density, and land-value maps, as well as other specific studies. The emphasis, as one newspaper said of the New Orleans plan, was on "dividing the city into the zones with as little change as possible and with an eye to the natural growth of each activity." Order was the key word, though its substance was often attempted through the preservation of older patterns of land utilization. Thus, traditional habits of mixed land use in New Orleans were reflected in a plan that resembled less a streamlining than a crazy quilt of various zones. The extensive area south of the business district in Memphis, containing railyards, terminals, factories, and warehouses, was designated industrial and unrestricted; large blocks in the downtown area and along the major streets were zoned commercial; and most of the areas two to four miles outside the central section were set aside for residential use, primarily single-family dwellings. The heights of buildings tapered off abruptly the farther one moved away from the business district. This was essentially, of course, the land pattern of the twentieth-century metropolis, which zoning plans fully accepted and encouraged. As far as the planning commissioners were con-

[46] Bartholomew *et al.*, *A Comprehensive City Plan: Memphis*, 124, 126; New Orleans City Planning and Zoning Commission, "Handbook to the Comprehensive Zone Laws," Chap. II, 2; New Orleans City Planning and Zoning Commission, *Major Street Report*, 34; Atlanta City Planning Commission, *Annual Report . . . 1922*, p. 4; Johnston, "Harland Bartholomew," 163–64. Johnston writes that securing approval for any type of zoning during the 1920s meant "buying off the business interests and the boosterism of their confident expectations of the times."

cerned, the city was endangered by such patterns only when they were uncontrolled and without direction.[47]

Comprehensive city planning obviously involved more than major streets and zoning, though these elements received by far the greatest emphasis. Recreational areas were exceptionally sparse in Atlanta and also to some extent in Memphis and New Orleans. Intensive land use in downtown New Orleans placed most parks in areas of low population density, thus underlining the advantages of urban decentralization. In Memphis, Bartholomew proposed a number of community centers, playgrounds, and small neighborhood parks and planned a major downtown park on "The Island," a small strip of land directly across the Wolf River from the central business district. Boulevards and scenic parkways were also included in his overall scheme. The riverfront areas in both Memphis and New Orleans, which were choked with railroad tracks, warehouses, and shipping docks, also received the planner's attention. Bartholomew's most ambitious vision, perhaps, entailed a totally renovated Memphis waterfront, with modified Greek temples at the river's edge rising dramatically to what has been described as "an acropolis effect on the bluffs." Some features of the city-beautiful emphasis were also retained, with plans in New Orleans for additional trees and monuments, the preservation of the Vieux Carré, and the elimination of billboards, sidewalk obstructions, and overhead electrical wires.[48]

Significantly, few of these proposals were ever acted upon. A successful Vieux Carré Commission was organized in New Orleans to protect the architectural character of the French Quarter, but such protection obviously had important economic as well as aesthetic advantages. Action came almost solely with respect to streets and zoning. Matters of housing, particularly for lower-income groups, were virtually ignored, even though dwelling shortages plagued most regional cities in the first years of the decade. The solutions offered for this problem were along the lines of increased mortgage capital and additional private construction. Parks and street improvements were concentrated in the central business district and

[47] Bartholomew *et al., A Comprehensive City Plan: Memphis*, 118–19, 116; New Orleans *Item*, July 17, 1923; New Orleans City Planning and Zoning Commission, "Handbook to the Comprehensive Zone Laws," Chap. V, 29; Randolph, "Municipal Zoning; Proposed Ordinance," 37–38.

[48] New Orleans City Planning and Zoning Commission, *Major Street Report*, 45, 40; Bartholomew *et al., A Comprehensive City Plan: Memphis*, 93–115, 132–33; Virginia Phillips, "Rowlett Paine, Mayor of Memphis, 1920–1924," West Tennessee Historical Society, *Papers*, XIII (1959), 103 (quotation); New Orleans City Planning and Zoning Commission, "The Plan for Civic Art" (mimeographed report, April 8, 1931, City Archives, New Orleans Public Library), 31.

in white neighborhoods, ignoring many crucial needs of the significant black populations in these cities. Finally, in the press of their more immediate concerns, southern city-planning commissions never seriously considered plans for schools, waterworks, and other important municipal facilities, though a series of bond issues in Atlanta, Memphis, and New Orleans generally recommended the expansion of such services. Planning commissions did, however, make recommendations on street-railway routing.

The city planning adopted with such alacrity by the urban commercial-civic elite was hardly an unqualified success. It was fraught with problems and difficulties that deepened during the 1920s and into the depression years. Municipal governments and state legislatures were often reluctant to grant power or autonomy to city-planning bodies, and the advocates of city planning were themselves soon caught up in the policy wrangles which accompanied ambitious schemes of this sort.

City-planning commissions were usually empowered to survey urban conditions, draw up plans and recommend ordinances, review street projects and land subdivisions, and in some cases act as review boards on the zoning statutes. The Atlanta commission's authority extended to an area six miles beyond the city limits. The actions of the commissions, however, were completely subject to the approval of the municipal governments, without which none of their decisions had the force of law. Bartholomew noted in his Memphis plan that without politically astute leadership on the planning commission neither the general public nor elected officials would abide by the substance of the comprehensive design. Similarly, the New Orleans commission warned that without "general acquiescence" in planning policies "individual and local interests will gradually bring about changes and amendments for selfish reasons until the entire scheme has been vitiated." And this, of course, was "the very sort of practice that has brought American cities to their present state of physical deficiencies." To preclude this possibility the commission recommended the formation of voluntary citizens' committees to support actively and publicly the comprehensive plan and its enforcement.[49]

Atlanta never adopted a comprehensive plan during the decade, though local planning advocates did achieve a zoning ordinance and a new street-numbering system. In a letter to the mayor in late

[49] See Bartholomew *et al.*, *A Comprehensive City Plan: Memphis*, 137–39; *The Charter and Ordinances of the City of Atlanta. Code of 1924* (Atlanta, 1924), 132–33; New Orleans City Planning and Zoning Commission, "Report on the Factors Involved in Carrying out the City Plan," 26–27.

1931 Robert Otis complained that Atlanta, "in the absence of sustained effort, fixed policy and sufficient funds, is still without a definite Plan for its growth." Bartholomew lamented in 1939 that the Gate City lagged twenty years behind other urban areas in the progress of its planning efforts. Planning commissions complained constantly of inadequate funding, public misunderstanding, and the intransigence of public officials. Carrying out the major features of the street plans, and especially the time-consuming and politically delicate enforcement of zoning laws, drained many planning bodies of their energies and prevented a genuinely comprehensive approach to urban ills. From the beginning Atlanta's commission "became immersed in zoning matters," according to Otis, "which forced a separation of the two into distinct boards." Long-range planning gave way, in other words, to immediate, piecemeal changes. Even in Memphis, where Bartholomew completed a major revision of his plan in 1940, many provisions were left unfulfilled. A newspaper study in 1947 found fifteen of the city's streets significantly improved as Bartholomew recommended, but twenty others were virtually unimproved, and thoroughfares that ran east and west had received more attention than those which ran north and south. The formation of city-planning commissions had been heralded throughout the urban South, at least among spokesmen for the commercial-civic elite, as ushering in a "new epoch" in city development, but these expectations were not to be fulfilled during the 1920s.[50]

One principal reason for the sudden collapse of many local planning activities at the end of the decade was, of course, the arrival of economic depression. Bartholomew's contract with the New Orleans commission was terminated in January 1930, and a year later the commission's annual budget was reduced from $20,000 to $7,500. The Commission-Council appropriated $6,000 in 1934 for printing the zone handbook and planning surveys, but this was never done. Likewise, the Atlanta commission's 1931 proposal for the extension and widening of over seventy streets at an estimated cost of $3,600,000 came at a most inopportune time.[51]

Though city planning during the 1920s was not entirely successful, it did reveal in its expressed purposes and policies the aspirations and concerns of the commercial-civic elite who fashioned and

[50] Otis, "Atlanta's Plan," 19, 20; Garrett, *Atlanta and Environs*, II, 820; Atlanta *Constitution*, December 13, 1939; Memphis *Press-Scimitar*, October 6, 1947; New Orleans *Times-Picayune*, June 22, 1923.

[51] See mimeographed annual reports of the New Orleans City Planning and Zoning Commission (City Archives, New Orleans Public Library), for 1930, 1931, and 1933; Otis, "Atlanta's Plan," 24–25.

supported it. Cities, "like all living organisms," Bartholomew wrote in the Memphis plan, "must either progress or decay." This familiar maxim of urban boosterism, linking progress and population growth, was very much alive in large southern cities, but the members of city-planning commissions were also apprehensive lest unregulated growth, given the complexities of the modern metropolis, lead ultimately to deterioration. Unless cities provided adequate facilities for traffic, education, recreation, and public health, the Atlanta *Journal* feared, "its very progress will become a penalty. Material expansion is worthwhile only to the extent that it is accompanied by inner civic advancement."[52]

Unbridled individualism was equated in planning reports with anarchy, and a state of "disorderly development" that may have been tolerable in the early stages of a city's life became unacceptable in the mature metropolis. Atlanta's "pioneering days are over," Sayward wrote, "its future is assured and its continued commercial supremacy cannot be doubted. This is the time for Atlanta, as it has been for all progressive cities, to take stock of herself with particular regard to those values which exist beyond the mere supply of bread and butter for our stomachs or clothes for our backs." Earlier necessities had dictated a chaotic urban arrangement that had "not kept pace with our commercial progress." All of which somehow led Sayward to the question: "Shall we permit ourselves to go down in history as a nation of traders simply like the Phoenicians or the Carthaginians, or shall we aspire to something like the measures of Athens and Rome?" References to antiquity aside, the principal concerns of commercial-civic spokesmen and their planners in the 1920s were precisely those of bread and butter and social order. They had come to believe, as Bartholomew wrote in his Memphis plan, that "Uncontrolled growth invites chaos and economic disaster."[53]

Planning commissions in Atlanta, Memphis, and New Orleans sought to achieve both stability and expansion, attract new industry and populations, ensure property values, curtail threats to the established order (whether social discontent or chaotic growth), and continue control of urban affairs in the hands of the commercial-civic elite. All this could presumably be achieved through the application of scientific expertise and businesslike methods under the

[52] Bartholomew *et al.*, *A Comprehensive City Plan: Memphis*, 137; Atlanta *Journal*, February 13, 1920.

[53] New Orleans City Planning and Zoning Commission, "Handbook to the Comprehensive Zone Laws," Chap. I, 2; comment by Sayward, *City Builder*, III (May 1918), 13; Bartholomew *et al.*, *A Comprehensive City Plan: Memphis*, 6.

aegis of enlightened local civic leadership. City-planning commissions were thus called upon, like voluntary commercial and civic groups, "to correlate and to harmonize the various interests of the city"—as the Atlanta *Constitution* put it—"and to bring them together in a working whole in pursuit of a definite general plan, concurred in by all, whereby to bring the city up to the required standard of efficiency in all of its departments and activities."[54]

In assessing the historical significance of city planning, at least in three southern cities during the 1920s, several points seem obvious. First, local planning efforts were dominated throughout the decade, not by housing reformers or academicians or even by professional planners, but by the commercial-civic elite. Spokesmen for business groups and voluntary civic associations regarded urban planning as a logical extension of the philosophy and methods employed in running large, complex, corporate economic enterprises, and they tended to emphasize notions of efficiency, economic growth, and social order. Secondly, commercial-civic spokesmen readily acknowledged the need to restrict private property rights in the public interest. They pointed specifically to the chaos proceeding from unregulated land use and equated it with a state of virtual anarchy. But if they were willing to limit the *rights* of property, it was primarily for the purpose of enlarging the *security* of property in a rapidly changing urban environment. Property was not only a source of income and social status but a major bulwark of social stability and economic order. Clearly implied in all their statements and policies was the proviso that the "public interest" was best determined and advanced by persons like themselves, by those with a significant and tangible stake in the city. Thirdly, commercial-civic elements were eager to engage municipal governments in the planning movement. They believed that without statutory authority and the approval of local government city planning would be severely limited in its impact. Thus, commercial and civic groups began their initiatives for planning by promoting the idea of official commissions operating as agencies of municipal government. Rather than looking upon this as a threat to the private sector, they supported a useful partnership between city government and local economic interests and civic leadership as necessary to carry out the purposes of city planning.

Finally, plans concerning the physical development of the city, which commercial-civic representatives helped to fashion, contained elements of social control. These elements derived from a

[54] Atlanta *Constitution*, February 10, 1920.

general perception of the urban situation and the notion that the efficient and orderly functioning of the physical city would significantly reinforce social order. The stability of property values, the racial segregation of residential areas, the improvement of local transportation, and the provision of recreational facilities were obviously calculated in part to remove sources of urban discontent and cope with some of the troubling consequences of "progress." The concept of social control as a motive is, of course, subject to abuse just as other themes and interpretive rubrics are susceptible of distortion. But members of the commercial-civic elite were obviously not interested in radical alterations of the existing order, and the plans they approved were deemed desirable precisely because they promised to secure the fruits of that order and revitalize it.

One question remains to be answered: If commercial and civic groups which included some of the most influential local citizens uniformly supported the idea of city planning, why did city-planning commissions not accomplish considerably more than they did during the 1920s? Some of the answers to this query are rooted in fact, others in conjecture. For one thing, members of the commercial-civic elite were hardly disinterested. City planning was fine, but when it came to specific policies individual property owners were likely to appeal a zoning ruling that did not suit them. Municipal governments were equally likely, if one can believe the complaints of many planning commissioners, to grant exceptions to the zoning law. City planning and zoning thus tended to break down at their most vulnerable level—the widening of a specific street, the zoning of a particular block. To know the full story would entail monumental labors in obscure and incomplete records, but it is reasonable to assume on the basis of known facts that the problem existed.

Planning advocates complained most often about a lack of funds, even in those cities where comprehensive plans were subsidized out of city treasuries. Municipal authorities were reluctant to devote large amounts of scarce resources in a total commitment to city planning, especially when public approval of bond issues for expanded city facilities was difficult to obtain. Furthermore, city planning never enjoyed a ground swell of popular support. Its advocates among the commercial-civic elite were legion, and virtually no citizens or group opposed it, yet it never assumed the status of a major issue and was rarely submitted to a public referendum. The massive publicity drives launched in its behalf and the hearings held on zoning provisions stirred some public interest, to be sure;

but a continuing commitment to planning required, as the planning advocates themselves admitted, a fairly significant degree of popular enthusiasm. Planning commissions accomplished enough in the urban South during the 1920s to warrant continued commercial-civic support, but their functions were far too complex to engender general public enthusiasm, and their achievements were not so grand as to justify the huge outlay of resources that might have produced more impressive results.

Perhaps the principal burden under which these city-planning commissions operated during the decade was simply the weight of the work itself as well as the limits of time, energy, and, to some degree, of financial support. The tasks which these commissions and their advocates set for city planning were simply too enormous and the expectations too great; and just as some initial successes were achieved the depression diverted public attention and resources elsewhere.

Many reform efforts of the early twentieth century were fundamentally elitist; they were calculated to preserve the existing order and often ignored the concerns of the great masses of people who would feel their impact most directly. (On the other hand, many such reform attempts failed because they were not supported by coalitions of varied interest groups.) Charges of elitism have been leveled with considerable accuracy at city planning. Later generations have been especially appalled by the emphasis during the "business decade" on streets, zoning, and efficiency and by the neglect of housing, unemployment, poverty, and human needs. Certainly, city planning in the urban South rested on commercial-civic conceptions of the urban community that were narrow and simplistic: the city, after all, was not a business corporation. The planning movement also failed to confront fully the issue of growth, continuing to harbor the notions that growth was an essential measure of urban success and that the city which failed to expand would surely die.

Criticisms of commercial-civic purposes, priorities, and economic policies have not, however, always extended to the *methods* of planning employed during the 1920s. The advocates of city planning held some terribly easy assumptions concerning the curative powers of skilled municipal management. Their belief that technology and improved communications and physical facilities, if properly arranged and directed, could maintain urban unity and allow continued growth without serious problems simply ignored the complex patterns of human life upon which technology was to be superimposed. Social and economic order, and the future of the city, depended on far more than matters of street layout, zoning, and additional facilities. No matter how often the planners resorted to the organic metaphor, one suspects that their principal conception of the city in this first decade of the automotive age was decidedly mechanistic.

City planning was an idea whose time had come by the 1920s, but as a tool of social control or of radical urban renovation it required considerable sharpening. Some of the classic planning problems and dilemmas of the twentieth century appeared at the beginning: Who should fashion the plans, and in whose interests? What is the nature of the urban community, and which of its features should be preserved? What is the potential of technology, and how can its impact on the complex urban fabric be anticipated and controlled? Should the function of planning be rooted in the neighborhood, the municipality, the metropolitan area, or the region? The art and science of planning have become immensely more sophisticated in concept and method since the 1920s, but many of the lessons of that decade apparently have yet to be learned.

The Black Family in Transition: Louisiana, 1860–1865

By C. Peter Ripley

Much has been written concerning the debilitating effect of slavery on the family and interpersonal relationships in general. Without question families were broken up by sales; daughters, wives, and sisters were subject to carnal calls of white males; parents were forced into strict obedience which affected the parent-child relationship. E. Franklin Frazier's conclusion that "even under the most favorable conditions . . . the exigencies of the slave system made the family insecure in spite of the internal character of the family"[1] is still basically true. At its worst the slave family was subject to the economic needs and personal whims of white masters.

Despite the obvious negative effects inherent in an institution which allows man to own man as chattel (and in part because of concentration on those effects) there are still important questions to be answered: To what extent did the slave family exist and thrive despite the institutional restrictions; and more specifically, what, if any, was the positive role of the master, what was the effect of the Civil War, what was the role of the United States military, and finally what was the role of the master-turned-employer on the black family in Louisiana?

Prior to the Civil War many slaveholders not only acknowledged slave marriages but encouraged them within the limits of the institution.[2] Nor was this practice inconsistent with paternalistic slaveholding and with good plantation management. To many

[1] Frazier, "The Negro Slave Family," *Journal of Negro History*, XV (April 1930), 259. For additional information with some differing conclusions see Robert W. Fogel and Stanley L. Engerman, *Time on the Cross: The Economics of American Negro Slavery* (Boston and Toronto, 1974), 126–44; and Eugene D. Genovese, *Roll, Jordan, Roll: The World the Slaves Made* (New York, 1974), 444–523, both of which appeared after this article was in process of publication.

[2] The information in this section is limited by the scarcity of primary material. It is therefore subject to greater speculation than the section dealing with the effects of Federal occupation, where more substantive and quantitative information is available through Federal

Mr. Ripley is a lecturer in history at Yale University and associate editor of the Frederick Douglass Papers.

The Journal of Southern History
Vol. XLI, No. 3, August 1975

masters conjugal relationships among slaves meant something more than merely pairing them off by sex to produce offspring for the plantation and to achieve greater tranquillity in the quarters. On the plantations of William J. Minor "marriages" and "divorces" were serious matters. Minor instructed his overseers that "marriages must not take place until after a month's notice . . . [and] divorces can only take place after a similar notice." Changes in mates were discouraged for "parties once divorced can not remarre [*sic*] without agreeing to receive 25 lashes well laid on unless they have agreed to take that for the privilege of parting."[3] The one-month waiting period before either marriage or divorce and the twenty-five lashes assessed for a second marriage would indicate that Minor took slave marriages seriously. There is no reason to believe that his slaves took their marriages any less seriously.

Minor was perhaps exceptional for the controls he exercised over slave relations, but the same cannot be said for his paternalism and the importance he placed on marriage. It was not uncommon for the slave marriage ceremonies to be major events on plantations. At one held in Terrebonne Parish the bride wore a white dress and a turban of white swiss, pink tarlaton, and orange blossoms; and the groom had a black suit, white gloves, and beaver hat. More common than fine attire was the celebration following the wedding.[4] No matter how racist or paternalistic the intent of masters, such activities did go on and were a significant part of slave life. The ceremony and the socializing were departures from everyday existence, and this made the slave marriage a notable event.

The breaking up of slave families by sales notwithstanding, some planters took their obligations to the black family seriously even beyond the convenience of the plantation. When an estate in Iberville Parish was being divided, an exchange was worked out with a second plantation to prevent the separation of husbands and wives.[5] Another example indicates both the commitment of a slave to his wife and also how a bondsman by aggressive action and an appeal

---

sources. For an excellent look at the slave family see John W. Blassingame, *The Slave Community: Plantation Life in the Antebellum South* (New York, 1972), 77–103.

[3] Southdown Plantation Journal, 1861, William J. Minor Family Papers (Louisiana State University Archives, Baton Rouge, La.). This depository will hereinafter be cited as LSU Archives.

[4] Prucilla M. Bond Diary, January 4, 1862 (LSU Archives); L. E. Power Diary, April 29, 1862 (Southern Historical Collection, University of North Carolina, Chapel Hill, N. C.).

[5] Statement of P. K. Owen and C. D. Craighead, September 20, 1862, Edward J. Gay Papers (LSU Archives). This transaction took place under the threat of advancing Federal troops.

to planter paternalism could exercise some control over his family. Prince's master was considering his sale to a speculator. Prince informed his master that he did not wish to leave, and he went to his wife's master stressing his desire to keep his family together. Prince was thereupon purchased by his wife's master.[6] Such experiences reflect paternalistic concern and action, but more significantly, they reflect the slave's own concern for his wife, his family, and his marriage.

There was in fact an interaction between planter and slave which influenced both and worked to strengthen the family. A reading of almost any southern antebellum newspaper reveals runaway slave notices stating that a particular fugitive might be heading for a specific location to rejoin his or her family. While this indicates that many families were indeed broken up by sales, it also indicates an interaction between the slave's strong commitment to his family and the master's awareness of that commitment. The mechanics of good plantation management also reflect this interaction, in that they were often family oriented. Marriages were a recognized means to greater slave contentment; slave quarters were equally family houses; garden plots were likewise family plots; food, although often rationed individually, was prepared for the family; and women were occasionally allotted time for cleaning the family cabin and mending the family clothes.[7] Thus, the desire for greater profit often worked to aid the black family.

When masters encouraged the black family through plantation organization and paternalism, they contributed to a stronger sense of family than was warranted under slavery. And since the life-style of the slaves centered around the family unit, this in turn had a reciprocal effect on masters. Not uncommon were planters who thought of their slaves in terms of family units rather than in the more common categories of the number of male hands, female hands, and children. For planters with over one hundred slaves to think of their slaves as husbands, wives, and children testifies to the strength of slave families, as least on those plantations.[8]

Yet it is inaccurate to conclude that the planters were primarily concerned with maintaining the idea of the family among their slaves. No doubt the concept of family was often present in spite of the planters. It is suggested, however, that a strong sense of family

[6] Sarah Lois Wadley Diary, August 27, 1863 (Southern Historical Collection).

[7] See for example Dr. Robert Collins, "Essay on the Management of Slaves," *De Bow's Review*, XXXII (January-February 1862), 155–57.

[8] See for example Cresant Plantation Journal, 1853, George Marshall Family Papers (LSU Archives) and Ellendale Plantation Journal, 1863, Andrew McCollam Papers (LSU Archives).

did exist under slavery and that planter paternalism, economically sound plantation organization, the slave's own strong commitment to his family, and the interaction between bondsmen and master all played contributing roles.

During the war the planters, the Confederate States government, and Federal authorities did much to weaken the black family through separation and dislocation. With the outbreak of hostilities slave controls became tighter. Marriages outside the plantation, always frowned upon, were discouraged even more after 1860. This limited the selection of potential partners, which must have been burdensome, particularly for bondsmen of smaller slaveholders. The marriages that did exist between servants of two masters were subjected to greater restrictions.[9]

The Confederate government's policy of hiring and impressing slave labor for the military effort also had a negative effect. One-fifth to one-half of the male slaves were subject to such duty, and the government exercised its prerogative widely in Louisiana. When the male was impressed, he went alone—no provision was made for his family. Separation by this method was common from the beginning of the war, and it increased after a Federal army arrived in southern Louisiana in April 1862.

With the coming of the blue-clad liberators the process of dislocation and separation was accelerated, particularly when Union troops made excursions into the interior of the state. With each new piece of Federally controlled territory, more planters fled deeper into the state or into Texas or Mississippi. A British traveler near the Louisiana-Texas border in the spring of 1863 reported, "The road to-day is alive with negroes, who are being 'run' into Texas out of [General N. P.] Banks's way. We must have met hundreds of them . . . ." The same was true to a lesser extent of the Mississippi-Louisiana border.[10] "Running" slaves to Texas and Mississippi was devastating for the slave family.

"Running" was for survival, and that meant mobility. Male slaves were more valuable and moved faster; they went with the planter. Women and children along with planter paternalism and slave family groupings were often discarded along the road. Women and children were simply left to survive as best they could. This usually entailed avoiding Confederate raiders (who, ironically,

[9] Joseph Embree to Henry Marston, August 10, 1861, Henry Marston Papers (LSU Archives); Lafayette Parish Police Jury Minutes, June 3, 1861 (LSU Archives).

[10] Sir Arthur J. Fremantle, *Three Months in the Southern States: April–June, 1863* (New York, 1864), 85 (May 10, 1863); your bro[ther] to Albert, April 28, 1863, Cummings-Black Family Papers (Hayes-Tilton Memorial Library, Tulane University, New Orleans, La.).

would probably have taken them to Texas) and finding their way to Union lines. There they posed a problem for Federal officials, who complained of having to issue rations to women and children because most of the men had been taken to Texas and could not provide for them.[11] The extent to which this situation was common is reflected in the records of contraband camps established by Federal authorities to care for the migrants. At one camp over 70 percent of the adult arrivals in one month were females.[12]

Increased contact between Union authorities and slaves had varying effects on black families. Where relations were close and constant, much the same type of interaction that had existed between slaves and planters developed between Federals and Louisiana blacks. But regulations protecting the black family were slow to emerge, and early policies governing contrabands, labor, and military recruitment did considerable damage before they were corrected.

When Union troops made their initial contact with bondsmen, many of them were impressed by the slaves' concern for their families. Blacks asked constantly whether they were free to join their wives or husbands.[13] Some military commanders shared the slaves' concern and made a conscious effort not to separate families. When the commander of the District of Western Louisiana ordered a cavalry sweep of a hostile area for horses and mules, he included the bringing in of male "Negroes without families" but cautioned that "no negroes who have families dependent upon them for support . . . [should] be taken."[14] There is some question, however, as to how closely such orders were followed.

As blacks evaded Rebel raiders and made their way to Union lines or followed troops back from excursions into the interior, Federal authorities were forced to deal with them. The routine that developed was to gather freedmen at contraband colonies es-

[11] Robert Gaskill to Henri Robinson, October 19, 1864, Letters Received, Bureau of Civil Affairs, Department of the Gulf, Records of the United States Army Continental Commands, 1821–1920, Record Group 393 (National Archives, Washington, D. C.; hereinafter cited as LR, BCA, DG); Thomas Calahan to Thomas W. Conway, October 2, 1865, Letters Received, Assistant Commissioner, Records of the Bureau of Refugees, Freedmen, and Abandoned Lands, Record Group 105 (National Archives; hereinafter cited as LR, AC, BRFAL); Winslow Roberts to E. G. Beckwith, September 23, 1863, LR, Provost Marshal General, DG.

[12] Register of Contraband, Greenville Colony, January 1863, Vol. CLXIX, BRFAL, La.

[13] Albert O. Marshall, *Army Life; from a Soldier's Journal . . . 1861–64* (Joliet, Ill., 1884), 398; George H. Hepworth, *The Whip, Hoe, and Sword; or the Gulf-Department in '63* (Boston, 1864), 141–42.

[14] W. B. Franklin to A. L. Lee, October 25, 1863, *The War of the Rebellion: A Compilation of the Official Records of the Union and Confederate Armies* (70 vols. in 128, Washington, 1880–1901), Ser. I, Vol. XXVI, Pt. I, 775.

tablished by the Bureau of Negro Labor. From there able-bodied males were either enlisted into the army or sent to work on fortifications, public works, or plantations. Only a portion of the men sent to labor on plantations were able to remain with their families. Most women and children either remained at the home colonies or went to plantations without husbands and fathers.[15] Except for those few who went to plantations together, families were separated indiscriminately, and despite any rhetorical concern on the part of authorities in the Department of the Gulf, the need for black laborers and black troops took precedence over the matter of black families.

Unfortunately, as the Union commitment to black troops increased, the situation for black families worsened. The squads of soldiers (often black) who made up recruiting parties had a wholesale disregard for the families of men they were enticing to join the army of liberation. Not infrequently blacks were taken off the streets and out of the fields and "enlisted" into the army at bayonet point. Many were not given time to notify their families before being marched to recruitment depots.[16]

Not all Federal officials were as callous as some of the recruiters, and not all ex-slaves tolerated such treatment. Thomas W. Conway of the Bureau of Negro Labor wrote an organizer of two black brigades that the troops had requested him "to keep a record of their wives [and] children . . . [in order] to prevent such a separation as will result in their not knowing where their families are." To that end, Conway, more sensitive than most to some of the blacks' needs, began a tour of plantations, making a registry of families of black soldiers.[17] That program continued throughout the war. In the fall of 1864 the bureau announced that it had compiled a register of all laborers on plantations and asked commanders of black troops to advise their men of its existence. The register had a twofold purpose: to establish mail communication between soldiers and their families; and to obtain certificates for the families so they might receive the rights and protection due them. The bureau acknowledged that there was a need for such a service because of the early methods of recruitment. The postal service was widely

[15] S. B. Holabird to J. W. McClure, May 17, 1863, Generals Papers, Records of the Adjutant General's Office, Record Group 94 (National Archives; hereinafter cited as GP, AGO); John S. Clark to Norman Leiber, October 23, 1862, LR, DG.

[16] Plantation Journal, October 9, 11, 1863, William T. Palfrey Family Papers (LSU Archives); William J. Minor Diary, September 29, 1863, Minor Family Papers; Thomas W. Conway to Daniel Ullman, May 15, 1863, GP, AGO.

[17] Conway to Ullman, May 15 (quotation), 27, 1863, GP, AGO.

used, and teachers assigned to black regiments spent considerable time writing letters to families of illiterate soldiers. It is difficult, however, to evaluate its success. When the war ended the bureau had failed to locate the addressees of some four hundred letters, and no doubt a portion of that number represents families which were not reunited.[18]

Because of crude recruitment methods and the "frantic" state of many wives as their men were marched away some new recruits did not wait for the bureau to reestablish their contact with their families; they took their own leave of the army and rejoined them in person. This practice was common enough to force the military to place guards over recruits to prevent their escape.[19] Federal authorities, in attempting to meet military needs, showed little respect for black families until black soldiers by their own actions sensitized many of the whites to their concerns.

Much the same was true for black laborers on plantations. Abandoned plantations run by the Treasury Department for the profit of the government received the best laborers not taken by the army. But even agents of those plantations were reluctant to accept the added responsibility of providing for laborers' families until forced to do so. Finally, Treasury officials in Louisiana were informed that unless provisions were made immediately "to support the families of said laborers on the plantations . . . they [the laborers] must be returned."[20] Not surprisingly, much the same methods had to be used to force planters to care for their laborers' families. While this threat was in part a means of shifting and designating responsibility for the care of women and children, it also reunited families, and as the practice became policy, it prevented additional separations.

Throughout the war years probably the greatest crisis confronting the black family resulted from married males serving in the army. Problems arose because of their absence and because families of black soldiers became subjects of white abuse merely because they were families of black soldiers. Even with efforts to reestablish contact with separated military families the question

[18] New Orleans *Tribune*, November 16, 1864; Thomas D. Howard Diary, 177, Howard Family Papers (Southern Historical Collection); New Orleans *Black Republican*, April 15, 1865.

[19] Lawrence Van Alstyne, *Diary of an Enlisted Man* (New Haven, 1910), 193 (October 16, 1863); Marshall, *Army Life*, 398; Wadley Diary, November 11, 186[3]; Robert Tyson Diary, April 13, 1864 (LSU Archives); untitled, undated diary, Edmund Kirby-Smith Papers (Southern Historical Collection).

[20] J. S. Clark to B. Rush Plumly, October 27, 1863, Records of Civil War Special Agencies of the Treasury Department, Record Group 366 (National Archives; hereinafter cited as CWSATD).

as to who would care for them still remained. Many planters simply forced wives and children off plantations once husbands and fathers were in the army. The military frequently returned these dependents and informed planters that the returned blacks had served them as slaves and that they should now care for them.[21] This policy met with limited success. Enforcement was difficult, and many planters refused to assume the responsibility. Women and children were forced out of plantation cabins and out of deserted houses which by law they were entitled to occupy. As a result they abandoned garden plots, animals, and what few possessions they had accumulated in a lifetime of labor. Others were allowed to stay but were issued no rations or were charged for those provided. Although by the fall of 1864 families of soldiers were permitted to draw rations from the Army Quartermaster Deparment, the program was not a cure-all.[22] A wife had to present a certificate proving she was married to a Union soldier before she was eligible for rations. The widespread separation of families made that difficult and often impossible despite the coordinating activities of the Bureau of Negro Labor relating to the certificates. Nor was this service of the bureau widely available except in the New Orleans area or near military posts of some size.

Despite letters of protest by black soldiers and their commanders and despite action by the Bureau of Negro Labor, abuses continued. What should have been a simple matter of black soldiers and civilians visiting their wives and children on plantations was often an ordeal. Overseers and planters particularly resented visits by black troopers because of their reputedly bad effect on laborers. Many soldiers were turned away at gun point, and blacks not in uniform fared even worse. At least one man was hanged as a result of a visit to his wife; beatings, arrests, and imprisonments were more common.[23]

Those black families not separated by planters, Confederate labor policies, Federal recruiters, or the dislocation of wartime society struggled to stay together as best as they could. Ghettos

[21] Winslow Roberts to E. G. Beckwith, September 23, 1863, LR, PMG, DG, notations.

[22] George Hanks to J. T. Tucker, July 21, August 14, 1863, LR, BCA, DG; W. Maston to Captain Stearns, August 23, 1864, LR, PM, St. Mary Parish, DG; J. M. White to Captain Stearns, August 24, 1864, *ibid.*; F. M. Frisbie to Thomas W. Conway, September 18, October 2, 1865, LR, AC, BRFAL; E. G. Beckwith to Lt. Col. Crosby, May 16, 1865, LR, BCA, DG; Thomas W. Conway to Henri Robinson, September 17, 1864, LR, PMG, DG.

[23] George Converse to George Cozzens, June 15, 1864, CWSATD; Waterloo Plantation Journal, April 10, 1865, Minor Papers; statement concerning the hanging on Mr. LeSepps' Plantation, [June 1862], George F. Shipley Papers (Maine Historical Society Library, Portland, Maine); George Hanks to N. P. Banks, April 18, 1863, LR, BCA, DG.

Table 1
REASONS FOR PREVIOUS SEPARATION OF SLAVE COUPLES REMARRIED IN CONCORDIA PARISH, LOUISIANA, 1864–1865

Reasons for Separation	*Total Separations*	*Number of Separations by Length of Previous Marriage in Years*					
		0–5	6–10	11–15	16–20	21–25	26–40
Death	234	108	62	29	18	8	9
Force	162	92	47	12	6	3	2
Mutual Agreement	31	21	9	–	–	–	1
Desertion	20	16	2	1	1	–	–
Moral Reasons	7	4	3	–	–	–	–
Totals	454	241	123	42	25	11	12

sprang up near urban areas. A settlement near Gretna and Algiers, Louisiana, reported housed "700 black families," grocery stores, boardinghouses, houses of prostitution, and other services mirroring white society.[24] While some came as families, the flow of blacks to towns and military posts was often as much a search for lost families as it was a desire to leave the plantation and to test new freedoms. Once reunited, many families stayed. A majority of the freedmen, however, remained on the land. They stayed on plantations abandoned by their masters, living in their quarters and working their garden plots in order to keep their families together. In other cases they were able to lease small plots of land.[25] Most laborers and their families found themselves working on large plantations again. A reading of plantation journals and labor contracts indicates that a great many blacks were hired in family units, but in some instances the contracted families were kept together only at the expense of forcing the women and children to work for lower wages than they would otherwise have received.[26]

A more quantitative indicator of the nature of the black family is provided by Federal materials relating to marriages. Data from certificates of marriage performed in Concordia Parish, Louisiana, in late 1864 and early 1865 give strong testimony to the stability and importance of slave marriages and indicate the existence of certain social norms in slave society (see Table 1). Of a large number of ex-slaves married at that time, 454 acknowledged a "previous connec-

[24] William Dougherty to Captain Hayden, January 31, 1866, LR, AC, BRFAL, La.

[25] M. Hawke to Bagley, August 22, 1865, and R. K. Diossy to C. R. Strickney, September 1, 1865, Vol. XL, BRFAL, La.

[26] For example of family contracts see Greenwood Plantation contract, March 1866, David Weeks Family Papers (LSU Archives); for example of contracts made with families and wage discrimination against wives see Fairchild and Smith contract, February 1865, PMG, DG.

tion" during slavery and gave a discernible reason for the dissolution of that "connection."[27]

Data from these certificates provide interesting insights: 35.7 percent of the couples were separated by force, indicating that planter paternalism vis à vis slave marriages was not universal and that slave marriages of many years' duration were obliterated by the whims and needs of masters. Equally significant, however, is the fact that a majority (64.3 percent) of the marriages were terminated for reasons beyond the planter's immediate control, which indicates that many masters acknowledged and to an extent protected the slave family.

Even more important are the 87.2 percent of the couples who remained with one mate until events or conditions not of their making (death and force) ended the partnership. This would certainly indicate that stability and faithfulness characterized these marriages; conversely, the low percentage (.044) of desertions would indicate the same thing. Perhaps equally revealing of slave society are the separations resulting from what are designated moral reasons by traditional Judeo-Christian standards. This .015 percent contradicts the concept of promiscuousness in the slave quarters. On the contrary, that any slave marriage should be ended by one partner because of the adulterous relationship of the other partner suggests that a moral code existed in slave society and that at least some members lived by it.

Black religion during the slave period was without doubt a significant factor in strengthening the moral code. Churches for Louisiana blacks existed in all areas of the state both in towns and on plantations. More than forty black churches existing at the end of the Civil War were still operating well into the twentieth century.[28] Other churches with mixed congregations, usually made up of masters and their slaves, also served to reinforce morality in slave society. For example, one black member of the Hepzibah Baptist Church was recommended for expulsion because of "immoral conduct"; the transgression was dancing.[29] Many slaves were confronted with social standards which a vast majority of white society could not have met. The predominance of strict Baptist and Methodist doctrine in Louisiana and the widespread inclination to give slaves religious training in both black and mixed churches

[27] Marriage Certificates, BRFAL, La.

[28] See for example Church Archives (LSU Archives), which are Historical Records Survey materials of the Works Projects Administration.

[29] Hepzibah Baptist Church Record Book, April 12, [1859], Hepzibah Baptist Church Records (LSU Archives).

were factors in reinforcing the moral code and thus the family structure in slave society.

Much of the same stability and commitment evident in the certificates is reflected in the register of contrabands received at one of Louisiana's home colonies. In January 1863 over 50 percent of the adult arrivals considered themselves married, and 73 percent of the married males arrived with their wives.[30]

Strong, stable, and long-lasting commitments developed in slave marriages as did a supportive moral code. The Concordia Parish marriage certificates indicate that these values persisted as the ex-slaves progressed from contrabands to freedmen to citizens. The same conclusion is reinforced by the orders, reports, and comments of provost marshals, regimental chaplains, and Freedmen's Bureau agents who were empowered to perform marriage ceremonies.[31]

The freedmen were quick to respond to the opportunity to sanctify their marriages by the white man's standards. The 478 ceremonies in Concordia Parish can be supplemented by numerous other examples—56 marriages on two occasions in June 1864 in Iberville Parish, 12 in St. John the Baptist Parish the previous month, and 28 in St. Mary Parish in January 1865 were performed by authorized military personnel, justices of the peace, priests, and white ministers.[32] But no group was more adamant about having their slave marriages recognized by white society than black soldiers. The chaplain of a New York regiment wrote General Nathaniel Prentiss Banks that black soldiers frequently asked him to legalize the unions they had made in slavery, and he wanted assurance that it was within his power to do so before proceeding. Ex-slaves they may have been, but they recognized the importance white men placed on formally validating the obvious, and they were reluctant to be separated from their wives because they feared their women and children would have no legal claims in the event they were killed. Subsequent events proved their fears correct; wives needed proof of marriage even to draw the rations made available to soldiers' families. Banks assured the chaplain that

[30] Register of Contraband, Greenville Colony, January 1863, Vol. CLXIX, BRFAL, La.

[31] James Bowen to George Darling, April 14, 1864; Bowen to H. J. Foster, April 14, 1864; Bowen to Grover, April 14, 1864, LR, PM, DG; W. H. Vanarman to Thomas W. Conway, August 1, 1865, LR, PM, DG, notation.

[32] Marriage certificates, Edmund Gay Family Papers (LSU Archives); Daley to George Bowen, May 13, 1864, MR, PMG, DG; E. E. Sheppard to F. A. Starring, August 31, 1865, LR, PMG, DG; J. S. Clark to Thomas W. Conway, August 13, 1865, LR, AC, BRFAL; Reverend C. W. Hilton Diary, October 12, 1865 (Hayes-Tilton Memorial Library, Tulane University).

the marriages would be legal and issued a special order authorizing any minister to marry blacks free of charge.[33]

In summation, slave marriages with strong commitments existed in antebellum Louisiana; a significant percentage spanned a considerable number of years, buttressed from the outside by planter paternalism and plantation organization and from the inside by a pragmatic subcultural code. The abuses properly ascribed to slavery and inherent in the institution made these marriages even more significant.

The war, which eventually alleviated many of the negative effects of slavery, brought a new set of problems for the black family. Confronted by a hostile advancing army, many planters became refugees, abandoning homes, crops, and more often than not their paternalism. When time and circumstances permitted, all movable property was taken along by fleeing planters; when survival dictated, slave families were separated, wives and children being abandoned and the husbands and fathers going to Texas. Confederate military impressment of slave labor had a similar effect on slave families.

Escape to Federal lines or liberation by an advancing army was no guarantee of family security, for in the eyes of Federal officials black men were soldiers and laborers first, husbands and fathers second. A shortage of labor meant a constant demand for laborers on public works, fortifications, and plantations. Such laborers were frequently moved about with little regard for their families. Recruitment of black troops, which often approximated shanghaiing in the purest sense, produced wholesale separations, and the recruits protested with pen and paper, voices, and feet. Individuals and agencies eventually modified abusive Federal policies and attempted to compensate for past errors but with varying degrees of success. Union officials were never able to protect or provide adequately for families of black soldiers.

Despite these circumstances it is clear that slaves and freedmen had strong commitments to their families. They alternately proved it by running away and by remaining on plantations; they proved it by the length of their slave marriages and their eagerness to legalize those marriages when free; they proved it by protest and by action and concern for their families when separated by military duty; and they proved it many times in spite of planters and liberators alike.

[33] Job G. Bass to Banks, June 17, 1864, LR, DG, notations; see also Anonymous Papers (LSU Archives); marriage certificates, BRFAL, La., in which 31 percent of the males married in Concordia Parish were in the military service.

Notes and Documents

Andrew Johnson and Reconstruction: A British View

Edited by Eric Foner

Like almost every other phase of nineteenth-century American history, Reconstruction fascinated contemporary observers overseas. It is well known that foreign journalists, of whom Georges Clemenceau was the most conspicuous, produced insightful commentaries on Reconstruction politics. But the equally interesting comments on internal American affairs contained in the dispatches of foreign diplomats based in Washington have generally been neglected by historians of the period.[1] The two documents reprinted below, letters from the British minister Sir Frederick William Adolphus Bruce to George William Frederick Villiers, fourth Earl of Clarendon and his government's foreign secretary, contain some noteworthy and controversial observations on the policies of President Andrew Johnson during the "critical year" of 1866.

Bruce, a career diplomat who had served in such far-flung posts as China, Egypt, and Bolivia, was appointed minister to the United States in March 1865.[2] Among other assignments he was instructed to seek an improvement in Anglo-American relations, which were at low ebb because of Britain's pro-Confederate leanings during the

[1] A recently published exception is Thomas Schoonover, "The Mexican Minister Describes Andrew Johnson's 'Swing Around the Circle,' " *Civil War History*, XIX (June 1973), 149–61.

[2] *The Dictionary of National Biography . . . from the Earliest Times to 1900* (21 vols., London, 1949–1950), III, 97.

Mr. Foner is associate professor of history at the City College of the City University of New York. He wishes to thank the American Council of Learned Societies for financial assistance and the Earl of Clarendon for permission to reprint letters from the Clarendon Deposit, Bodleian Library, Oxford University.

The Journal of Southern History
Vol. XLI, No. 3, August 1975

Civil War and the depredations of the English-built southern ship *Alabama*. The activities of the Fenian Brotherhood, the Irish-American nationalist organization which was openly recruiting for an "invasion" of Canada, further strained relations. The British understandably objected to Fenian activities, while the Johnson administration, anxious not to alienate Irish-American voters, particularly at a time when it needed all the support it could muster for its Reconstruction policies, refused to take any decisive action against the group.[3]

Despite these obstacles, Bruce did establish a friendly personal relationship with Secretary of State William Henry Seward[4] and with the conservative Republican senator from Connecticut, James Dixon. Dixon, one of the few Republican senators who wholeheartedly supported Johnson's policies in early 1866, was a man who "exerted next to no influence"[5] in Republican circles, but he did serve as a liaison between Bruce and the President. On February 9, 1866, three days after Congress approved the Freedmen's Bureau bill and ten days before Johnson's veto, which marked the first open break between the President and congressional Republicans, Dixon arranged for Bruce an interview with President Johnson.

Bruce's report of this interview is an interesting indication of Johnson's outlook during this period of political flux and tension. Johnson's comments on Irish-American politics, the Fenians, Mexican affairs, and his view of the Radical Republicans, all stated with his characteristic candor, conform to what is known from other sources. Johnson's opposition to Negro suffrage is also well known, but what are truly astonishing are the President's belief "that the right of voting in this country requires to be raised not lowered" and his suggestion that "moral," "educational," and property qualifications be instituted for white voters. For if there is one thing upon which Johnson's admirers and his critics have agreed, it is his sincere commitment to political democracy (for whites). Johnson's comments on the virtues of rural voters and his distrust of "town voters of the poorer classes" support Kenneth M. Stampp's analysis

[3] The most recent study is Brian Jenkins, *Fenians and Anglo-American Relations During Reconstruction* (Ithaca and London, 1969), especially 23–25, 34–38, 47, 128–29.

[4] Glyndon G. Van Deusen, *William Henry Seward* (New York, 1967), 497. Van Deusen made use of a number of Bruce-Clarendon letters in Chapters 30 and 31 on Seward's role in Reconstruction and also in his chapters on foreign relations.

[5] Eric L. McKitrick, *Andrew Johnson and Reconstruction* (Chicago, 1960), 283.

of his social outlook: he "still romanticized the self-sufficient yeoman farmer, still regarded cities as centers of moral decay." But in view of Johnson's belief that the franchise should be restricted, one wonders if the President can still be regarded as, in Stampp's phrase, "The Last Jacksonian."[6] Or perhaps Johnson's view is simply another example of the distressing tendency in American history for men to alter their democratic belief in equality for whites when forced to confront the implications of extending that principle to blacks.

Two months after this interview the foreign secretary requested Bruce to furnish him with a more detailed analysis of Reconstruction politics, particularly with regard to the rights of the freedmen. "People here are watching American affairs with intense interest," Clarendon wrote, "and the feeling, as far as I can judge of it, is all for the President because he is thought to be politically wise and personally plucky." Yet "some of our philanthropists" were dissenting from this general feeling, arguing that if the South were quickly restored to the Union, "the condition of the Negro would be as bad as ever and that he would have no security for social rights of any kind." "I wish you would let me know," the foreign secretary concluded, "whether these opinions are justified as I have a great respect for some of the persons who hold them."[7] The "philanthropists" mentioned in Clarendon's letter were the leaders of the freedmen's assistance movement, a continuation of the British antislavery tradition, which attracted support from "the more religiously minded of the upper middle class." These benevolent reformers, as Clarendon noted and Christine Bolt's recent study has confirmed, were increasingly anxious over the status of the freedmen under Johnson's policies.[8]

Bruce's letter of May 6, 1866, the second document printed below, is an extended summary and analysis of the motivations and rationale of Johnson's policies. Less than a month earlier, on April 9, Congress had overridden Johnson's veto of the Civil Rights Act, which established the national citizenship of the freedman and offered federal protection for black civil rights, short of suffrage.

[6] Stampp, *The Era of Reconstruction, 1865–1877* (New York, 1965), 50–82, especially 54.

[7] Clarendon to Bruce, April 21, 1866, Clarendon Deposit, c. 142 (Bodleian Library, Oxford University, Oxford, England).

[8] Bolt, *The Anti-Slavery Movement and Reconstruction: A Study in Anglo-American Co-operation, 1833–77* (London, New York, and Toronto, 1969), 63–70, 74–78; quotation on page 63.

Johnson's veto had isolated him from the great majority of Republican congressmen, and Bruce's letter, probably based on continuing contacts with Seward and Dixon and via them with the President, is a fair summary of Johnson's perception of the Reconstruction issue at this crucial point. Bruce was not, it should be noted, a completely disinterested observer. For a variety of reasons, including his belief that the South, if quickly readmitted to the Union, would be unlikely to sympathize with Fenian activities or with an active prosecution of the *Alabama* claims, Bruce personally sided with Johnson against his Radical critics.[9] In addition, he may well have shared the color prejudice which Christine Bolt has shown was increasing in Great Britain in the 1860s.[10] On the other hand, Bruce, as a British aristocrat, seems in the letter to look with disdain on the racial prejudice of Johnson and his class of "mean Whites."

Among the more interesting of Bruce's comments is his observation that Johnson had "entirely . . . abandoned the agrarian ideas, which he apparently entertained at first." "Agrarian," of course, in this mid-nineteenth-century context, referred to proposals for social leveling, especially the redistribution of property. Why Johnson decided to move away from his intention of May and June 1865 to drive the planter class from power in the South has always been something of a mystery. Various historians have suggested that Johnson decided that northern capitalists were more of a danger to the southern yeoman than the planter aristocracy, that he needed the planters' support in a projected national conservative party, and that what he really desired was the personal satisfaction of the aristocrats supplicating for individual pardons during the summer of 1865.[11] Bruce's letter suggests another consideration—that Johnson believed that only the plantation aristocracy possessed the moral authority to control the labor and "civilize" the behavior of the freedmen. He therefore could not accept the idea of "turning the Negroes into small proprietors."

Clarendon apparently found his minister's lengthy analysis con-

[9] Jenkins, *Fenians*, 60–61, 130.

[10] Bolt, *Anti-Slavery Movement*, 141–70.

[11] Stampp, *Era of Reconstruction*, 65–71; McKitrick, *Andrew Johnson and Reconstruction*, 139, 144–49. A recent study suggests that Johnson's policy always aimed at resuming southern political life under the aegis of the South's traditional leadership. Michael Perman, *Reunion Without Compromise: The South and Reconstruction: 1865–1868* (Cambridge, England, 1973), 66–69.

vincing, for a few weeks later he wrote to Bruce, thanking him for his "very clear and interesting letter respecting the irrepressible Negro. It has made me understand the President's policy much more clearly than I have yet done." Clarendon now believed that Johnson's policy was "founded on justice and common sense as well as knowledge of black and white natures, the objects of parties and the ultimate welfare of the country."[12]

FREDERICK W. A. BRUCE TO EARL OF CLARENDON[13]

February 9, 1866

MY DEAR LORD,

In conformity with my understanding with Mr. Dixon, we called on the ladies at the Whitehouse last evening, and after a short time the President joined us

He made me sit down beside him, and expressed his satisfaction at having an opportunity of talking with me in a frank and informal manner. He alluded in a very friendly spirit to my conduct in the Osbourne flotilla affair, and said that my position as a friend to this country was thoroughly understood and appreciated, that he himself was anxious to see friendly relations existing with England, and did not wish to rely exclusively on reports of what passed between me and the Secretary of State.

After some general remarks, I alluded to the proceedings of the Fenians in this country, and to the preparations, as if for a state of War, that they obliged us to keep up on the frontier of the Provinces. He said with some emphasis, that this movement met with no sympathy on the part of the Govt., which on the contrary was anxious to discourage it, that he was much dissatisfied with the imperium in imperio, the Irish wished to create in this country, that the attempt to combine particular nationalities on this continent, was contrary to American interests, and inconsistent with their duties as American citizens, that he did not think the Fenian affair so formidable as was supposed, and that it would die out for want of fuel. He dwelt on the inconsistency of the Irish, who, while invoking aid on their own behalf as an oppressed race, were themselves the most bitter opponents of all attempts to improve and elevate the condition of the Negro in the United States. As my object was simply to discuss the question in its general bearings, and to draw the attention of the President to its importance, I thought it better not to suggest specific measures of repression, as such a course might excite the susceptibilities of Mr. Seward.

[12] Clarendon to Bruce, May 26, 1866, Clarendon Deposit, c. 142.
[13] Bruce to Clarendon, February 9, 1866, *ibid.*, c. 90.

In alluding to the Emperor's speech, he said he was not so satisfied, as others seemed to be with his declarations about Mexico. (This was meant at Seward, who professes to consider the question as satisfactorily arranged.) That he did not consider that the position was materially altered by it, and that its terms were ambiguous.

I told him that it must be recollected, that the Emperor had to consult the susceptibilities of the French nation, that I felt sure the expedition was undertaken in the belief (instilled into him by refugees) that elements existed in Mexico of order and good government which would come to the surface, if temporarily assisted, but with no intention to take permanent footing on this continent. That when the task proved more difficult than had been anticipated the idea of the Latin race was put forward to reconcile the French to the sacrifices it imposed. That the great characteristic of the Emperor, was his ability in getting out of difficulties, and that he would find means of withdrawing from this enterprise. The President fully admitted his ability, and said that the collapse of the rebellion would no doubt materially change his views. But I can see he is not fully re-assured as to the course he may eventually take.

On the internal policy of the country, the President appears to be quite settled in his views, and confident that they will be ultimately successful. He said there are a few extreme Radicals who are bent on pushing theories to extremes, and that the way to deal with them is to allow them to lay their plans fully before the people, who will decide against them.

He remarked on the inconsistency of those who, while advocating in the Freedmen's Bureau bill provisions for the maintenance & tutelage of the Negro, which could only be justified on the ground of his helplessness and inability to take care of himself, wished at the same time to confer on him the right by means of suffrage of taking part in the Govt. of the country. He gave it as his opinion that the right of voting in this country requires to be raised not lowered. He said that in the towns it had become a source of corruption and that voters were publickly bought and sold without any regard to the publick interests. The only remedy he saw was to provide that after a certain time a qualification should be required, perhaps a moral & educational qualification for the electors of the lower Houses, and a small freehold qualification for the electors of Senators &c. He said, you can depend on the morality of the rural voters, but not on that of the town voters of the poorer classes. That the rural voter, however poor, felt that he had an interest in the country, and identified himself with it, but not so the poor class of townfolk. Such a change would be beneficial to us, for you may recollect that in a letter I enclosed from a Mr. Perrie [?] in the West, he mentioned that the country-Irish took little part in the Fenian movement, and that it was chiefly confined to the town-Irish, and was taken up by politicians in order to gain their votes.

Every reflecting person I have talked to concurs in thinking that the successful working of this Govt. depends on the preponderance of the land being maintained in the electoral body.

Our conversation lasted about half an hour, during the latter part of it Mr. Stanton came in, and I thought it better to turn it upon general topics.

On leaving the President he expressed himself as much pleased with the interview, and added, that though all business must go through the Department of State, he should be glad to see me at any time, and hear any suggestions which I might wish to offer. I shall be very cautious in availing myself of this permission, as Mr. Seward's jealousy might be easily aroused. I told him I had seen the President, and had had a pleasant conversation with him, and he appeared pleased at my appreciation of him.

There is a singular charm in the President's manner. He is evidently a man of strong convictions and much thought, combined with tenderness of heart. He expresses himself with much clearness, and with an absence of anything like Americanism in his language and accent.

I shall learn through Mr. Dixon the impression my visit produced upon him.

I remain with the highest respect

Your Lordship's faithful Servt.

FREDERICK W. A. BRUCE

FREDERICK W. A. BRUCE TO EARL OF CLARENDON[14]

BRITISH LEGATION,
WASHINGTON
May 6, 1866

Private

MY DEAR LORD,

The question put in your last letter, as to the position of the Negro in the Southern States, supposing the President's policy of re-establishing State-rights to be carried out, is one of great interest & of great difficulty. I cannot speak on the subject with confidence, amid the conflicting reports I hear of Southern sentiment.

It does not however admit of doubt, that the freedom of the Negro is accepted in the South. The State Legislatures have sought to give it effect, and have generally recognized his civil rights in all cases where he is concerned. In some instances they refuse to admit his evidence where white men only are concerned.

[14] Bruce to Clarendon, May 6, 1866, *ibid.*

But the question between the President & the majority in Congress is not fairly stated, if it is represented as being solely a question of the more or less protection to be afforded to the Negro. There is a much wider issue involved. "How is a minority, consisting of an ignorant & despised race, to exist & be protected in the midst of a dominant and haughty Race who yesterday knew them only as Slaves & Chattels?"

The President, a Southern man, knowing the state of opinion in the Southern States, and the condition of the Negro, says in substance; that the existence and safety of the Negro Race depends on their position being harmonious with, and not antagonistic to, the Whites. He maintains, that they will be the victims of the hatred & suspicion engendered by any attempt to support them by unconstitutional Legislation and by Northern influence, against the opinion of the South. He asserts, that there is no feeling of hatred or revenge in the South against them; that their well-being is essential to the interests of Southern cultivators; that these interests are safer guides in dealing practically with the question, than the theories of ignorant Northern sentimentalists; that if left alone, (under the menace of interference, if acting unjustly), the Southern States will establish relations beneficial to both races, and that at all events the experiment ought to be tried before tampering with the Constitution of the country. Finally he does not hesitate to say that the sympathy professed by the Radical majority in Congress for the Negro, is insincere, & that their real object is to use him as a means to prolong their tenure of power.

Moreover he objects to the Radical plan of action, that it is impracticable. He denies the possibility of extending over the vast country known as the Slave States, any effectual protection based on the assumption that the resident Whites are hostile to the Negro. He is in favour of accepting the Constitution as it is, and of legislating, if necessary, for *proved*, not for *presumed* evils. He is as anxious that the Negro should become a useful member of society, as that he should be secured in the enjoyment of the rights of Man; and if he is unequal to the exigencies of his position in an industrious community, he is indifferent to his fate. In this view of the case he represents, I believe truly, American sentiments in its cooler moments, though the hostility to the South produced by the War, shows itself at present in an artificial sympathy for the Negro. The Negro is not an ideal being, except perhaps in New England, where he is as little known as he was in Old England at the period of emancipation. In the other Free States he is looked upon, as Punch describes, not as a Brother, but as a Bother, and there is no disposition to make sacrifices to save him from destruction, if he is too idle and improvident to take care of himself. The Irish particularly hate him, as a probable competitor in the lowest description of labour, which has hitherto been exclusively their field.

You will never get out of the heads of men, like Johnson, (himself originally a mean White) the idea, that the Negro is an inferior Being, totally inapt for the higher developments of civilization. The objections entertained by his class to Slavery, were political, and proceeded largely from the feeling of envy to the rich proprietors which republican institutions tend to produce. This class were the severest task-masters in the South, and they are now the negro's worst enemies. The badge of Slavery was the only distinction between them and the Black man, and their pride of Race is severely mortified, now that it is done away.

It is remarkable how entirely the President has abandoned the agrarian ideas, which he apparently entertained at first. I think he now perceives that, if his policy of re-construction is to be carried through, and the Southern States are to be restored to their autonomy, the interests and safety of the Negro will be best protected by the large proprietors. He has no faith in the plan of turning the Negroes into small proprietors, and thus depriving them of the care and civilizing influence of dependence on the White Man. He believes, that if they become squatters they will become idle, thievish, and dissipated. They will be exposed to the hostility of the Whites, and through bad usage and improvidence will soon disappear altogether. He wishes them to become a necessary link in the chain of Southern industry, and that can be only effected by a combination between their labour, and the capital and intelligence of the Whites. It is only in this way that the Negro can hope to escape the fate that has overtaken the Red Indian. Indeed if, as many suppose, White labour can be substituted for Black, in the raising of cotton, he will soon be driven for subsistence to the rice-swamps of South Carolina, and the sugar-plantations of Louisiana.

If therefore I am right in this statement of the views of the President and his adherents, it is evident that he looks upon the fate of the Negro, as dependent on *economical laws* not on *direct legislation*. He will therefore oppose to the utmost all revolutionary changes in the Constitution of the U. States, not only because of his reverence for it, but because he does not think the object of the philanthropists will be thereby attained. He will not refuse to consider any specific measure intended to meet a specific necessity, once that necessity is proved to exist. But he will resist all à priori legislation, which is based on the idea that the Negro must be put under the tutelle of the Federal Govt., as unconstitutional, and as prejudicial to the interests of the Negro himself. The question between him and the Radicals, is not one of humanity, but of sagacity, in dealing with this most difficult problem, and I think, though I speak with diffidence, that the President's plan will work more favourably for the Slave than any scheme which his opponents have hitherto been able to elaborate. I do not enter upon the political objectives & schemes which will render necessary a quasi-military occupation of the South, and which will give to the South the support on Constitutional grounds of a large party in the North itself. But it is impossible to consider that question fairly without taking into account the constitution of this Govt., which is not a Republick one & indivisible, but is an agglomeration of separate Republicks under a Federal Head, the powers of which are jealously specified and circumscribed.

I remain with the highest respect

Your faithful Servt.

FREDERICK W. A. BRUCE

Northern Institutions in Southern Financial History: A Note on Insurance Investments

By B. Michael Pritchett

The supposed domination of northern capital over southern financial affairs has been the subject of frequent debates, and some have found this domination to be chiefly responsible for the South's relative economic backwardness. A recent study of the financial history of the life insurance industry has produced data bearing on this issue and offers a case study with probable application to the actions of other financial intermediaries as well.[1]

In the early years of the twentieth century many southern states considered legislation to restrict northern financial domination by controlling the location of the investments of insurance companies. One of the most outspoken antagonists of the insurance industry was Fitz Hugh McMaster, insurance commissioner of South Carolina. Holding a sectionalist point of view, he asserted: "I believe it may be stated . . . as an axiom, that there is no other single agency in the United States comparable to life insurance making for the concentration of wealth in certain centers and putting the control of money in so very few hands."[2] He also observed that "Such states as Massachusetts, New York, Connecticut, Pennsylvania and New Jersey . . . have laid the whole country under tribute to them . . . . If the other states of the Union are content

[1] For methodological details and implications of the financial history beyond those reported here see B. Michael Pritchett, "A Study of Capital Mobilization, the Life Insurance Industry of the Nineteenth Century" (unpublished Ph.D. dissertation, Purdue University, 1970).

[2] McMaster, *In Consideration of Requiring Local Investments by Life Insurance Companies* (Columbia, S. C., 1911), 1.

Mr. Pritchett is assistant professor of economic history at Brigham Young University.

The Journal of Southern History
Vol. XLI, No. 3, August 1975

Table 1

REGIONAL RESERVES AND INVESTMENTS COMPARED

Group	Reserves	Investment	Ratio of Investment to Reserves
Northwestern	$ 70,978,674	$ 144,847,826	204%
Middle Atlantic	550,438,080	898,775,257	163%
Southwestern	141,010,733	175,778,501	124%
Pacific	65,933,495	81,314,499	123%
Central Northern	267,828,893	304,850,890	114%
South Atlantic	91,534,649	101,769,061	111%
Gulf and Mississippi Valley	103,711,638	101,417,762	98%
New England	129,490,576	80,335,014	62%
Totals	$1,420,926,738	$1,889,088,810	

forever to pay tribute to a handful of states and not require the capital which is collected in those states to be invested in the securities of the state in which it originates, then all that I have to say is that these states are altruistic to the point of folly . . . ."[3]

Ideas of this type were challenged by men like Robert Lynn Cox, general counsel and president of the Association of Life Insurance Presidents. A leading defender of the industry, Cox noted that "For several years it has been a common belief that life insurance companies were causing a depletion of the wealth of certain states . . . . This belief has been particularly common in the Southern and Western portions of the United States."[4] He responded with the observation that "It will certainly be conceded that a comparison of reserves with investments under this grouping will determine whether or not any considerable section of the United States has been seriously discriminated against or has been impoverished even temporarily by the operation of life insurance companies."[5] He then presented figures on the geographical distribution of life insurance investments and reserves (see Table 1) and concluded that no region of the country had been significantly injured by life insurance operations.[6]

[3] McMaster, *Life Insurance Companies Should Be Compelled to Invest in the Securities of Those States in Which the Funds Originate* (Columbia, S. C., 1914), 12.

[4] Cox, *The Geographical Distribution of the Investments of Life Insurance Companies* (New York, 1909), 1.

[5] *Ibid.*, 12.

[6] *Ibid.*

The conclusions of McMaster and Cox were colored by the particular financial yardsticks that they chose for comparative purposes. McMaster compared the total cash drawn from his state by the various companies with the typically smaller amount of investments made therein and concluded that only local insurance companies did not produce a net cash outflow in the state where the policies were sold. In marked contrast, Cox chose to ignore all that part of insurance company income used to pay company expenses, and he thereby compared with regional investment only that portion of insurance company income which became reserves. This device made it possible for him to assert that virtually all regions had net gains in their experience with the life insurance industry.

Most of the earlier data on life insurance financial operations have relied heavily on companies registered in New York and therefore have a potential regional bias.[7] Furthermore, the aggregation process used in other studies has systematically suppressed the details necessary to a regionalized study. It was therefore necessary to generate a new, more detailed financial history of life insurance companies to measure their impact upon interregional capital flows.

The present evaluation is based upon the detailed reports of all companies known to have conducted legal reserve life insurance business in the nineteenth century. The income and individual investments of each of these companies was determined yearly by state (the records of 321 companies were used).[8] The data for the states were then consolidated into two regions defined so as to be compatible with the figures presented by Cox: the South Atlantic (Virginia, West Virginia, North Carolina, South Carolina, Georgia, and Florida) and the Gulf and Mississippi Valley (Alabama, Mississippi, Tennessee, Kentucky, and Louisiana). Investment data were obtained from 1843 to 1900, but the reports filed before 1874 did not generally require regional detail on income. Such detail was gathered for companies where it existed, but it was not found on a basis general enough to permit as reliable a comparison as it was possible to prepare for the years after 1873. Table 2, therefore, presents a comparison of interregional flows of funds related to life insurance companies in the two southern regions for the years 1874–1900.

[7] Institute of Life Insurance, *The Historical Statistics of Life Insurance in the United States, 1759 to 1958* (New York, 1960), 18–21.

[8] For a complete list of all the companies included in each year see Pritchett, "A Study of Capital Mobilization," 348–85.

As noted above, the conclusions of McMaster and of Cox were dramatically altered by the way they defined the dollar concepts that they chose to compare. In order to minimize that problem in this study, the dollar amounts of the flows are not presented, but the comparisons are made on the basis of percentages. By doing this, attention is not directed specifically to the question of the net amount of money entering or leaving a region but rather to the question of the relative extent to which the South yielded life insurance revenues versus the relative extent to which it received life insurance investments.

The decision to compare the percentage of total domestic life in-

Table 2

RELATIVE CAPITAL FLOWS COMPARED

	South Atlantic		*Gulf and Mississippi Valley*	
Year	*% of Total Premiums Paid*	*% of Total Investment Received*	*% of Total Premiums Paid*	*% of Total Investment Received*
1874	.65	.39	1.81	.41
1875	.78	.34	2.00	.40
1876	.95	.35	2.25	.41
1877	1.20	.29	2.73	.60
1878	1.40	.44	2.84	.46
1879	1.62	.38	2.93	.41
1880	1.83	.38	3.15	.46
1881	1.90	.39	3.15	.49
1882	1.95	.74	3.13	.55
1883	1.99	.72	3.40	.68
1884	1.97	.84	3.67	.81
1885	2.15	.79	4.01	1.16
1886	2.16	1.08	4.23	1.36
1887	2.18	1.20	4.26	1.33
1888	2.38	2.04	4.28	1.66
1889	2.18	2.12	4.30	2.40
1890	2.17	1.86	4.43	2.06
1891	2.61	1.45	4.52	2.22
1892	2.83	1.59	4.40	2.45
1893	3.02	1.70	4.62	2.39
1894	3.18	1.75	4.74	2.42
1895	3.44	2.08	4.81	2.92
1896	3.78	1.97	4.90	2.93
1897	3.73	2.23	4.74	3.12
1898	4.18	2.43	4.86	2.87
1899	4.23	2.60	4.96	2.67
1900	4.33	2.81	5.05	2.90

surance premium income arising in the South with the percentage of total domestic life insurance investments it received, of course, ignores the income from death benefits; or, more precisely, it assumes that the mortality tables were constant among regions in the period 1874–1900. Further, only those investments with a potentially "regional nature" were included on the investment side, specifically, real estate, mortgages, stocks, and most bonds. Such items as United States bonds and cash on hand were excluded from the investment figure.

Since the state of origin was available in the company records, regionalization of premium income was a matter of simple arithmetic, but this was not the case for investments. Real estate, mortgages, state and local bonds, and the stocks and bonds of intrastate companies were fairly easy to assign geographically, and this was done yearly by state. The value of the stocks and bonds of interstate companies, however, had to be assigned on some appropriate basis among the states within which the company operated. This involved, chiefly, railroad and canal companies. In each year the dollar value of each life insurance company's investments in companies of this type was allocated among the states involved in each investment item on the basis of the proportion of track or canal mileage of the individual transportation companies within each state. The state data was then aggregated into the two regions defined above.

The findings in Table 2 agree with those in Table 1 in the sense that both reveal that the South Atlantic and Gulf and Mississippi Valley regions benefited less from early life insurance operations than the country generally. However, it bears repeating that the ratio of reserves to investments selected as a criterion by Cox is of questionable appropriateness as an indicator of net flows of funds, since it ignores the very substantial portions of insurance industry income going to purposes other than amassing reserves.

On the simple criterion of the proportion of total domestic life insurance premiums paid versus the proportion of total domestic investment received, it appears that the South Atlantic States and, more especially, the states of the Gulf and Mississippi Valley region were disadvantaged by life insurance operations when compared to the nation generally, at least in the period for which the data were analyzed.

If the tendencies evidenced in the life insurance industry are also characteristic of the operations of other financial intermediaries and especially if conditions were no better in the antebellum period than these later tendencies would indicate, then the historical charges of northern capital domination of the South may well have been true.[9]

[9] The author is continuing an attempt to clarify the applicability of this argument to the antebellum period. Preliminary efforts have shown that estimates of the trends in the base data of this paper can be made which are of sufficient statistical significance to permit extrapolation of those series with some confidence. Extrapolation of the investment and income series suggests that the relative share of investments received by the two southern regions was less than the relative share of income they provided well into the antebellum period. This indication must be regarded as tentative, however, until confirmed by a completion of the data development for the earlier period or, at a minimum, by comparison with appropriate benchmark information. To date no such confirmation has been completed for the income series, but data have been developed for portions of investment. Complete series of life insurance holdings of stocks and bonds have been prepared for the period 1874–1943. This information was developed by region using the approach described earlier. The statistical trends in these two types of investment were found to be consistent with those in the extrapolated series.

Book Reviews

The European Discovery of America: The Southern Voyages, A.D. 1492–1616. By Samuel Eliot Morison. (New York: Oxford University Press, 1974. Pp. xviii, 758. $17.50.)

Over twenty years ago Samuel Eliot Morison advised young historians: "'Be free, all worthy spirits, and stretch yourselves!' Bring all your knowledge of life to bear on everything you write." At eighty-eight Morison is still stretching himself to his fullest, offering of both his vast talents as a historian and his experience, humanity, maritime expertise, and great zest for life. Even more than in *The Northern Voyages*, he has created a magistral work.

The Southern Voyages is a narrative history of sixteenth-century exploration, encompassing the area from the Gulf of Mexico and California in the north to Cape Horn in the south. Among Morison's explorers there are far more heroes than villains, since he profoundly admires the spirit, curiosity, persistence, and endurance of his central characters and tends to excuse or tolerate their faults and foibles. Columbus may have been humorless, aloof, stubborn, and a bad administrator, but he had "an indomitable will and stubborn persistence despite neglect, poverty, and ridicule" (p. 267). In addition, he was a superb navigator, determined at all odds to get to the East by sailing west. Amerigo Vespucci emerges as a "genial faker" for the way he trumped up a 1497 voyage that never occurred in order to get credit for explorations carried on by others. Vespucci's reward? The amiable liar gave his name to America, proving perhaps that sometimes prevarication pays. Even more of a sailor than Columbus, Ferdinand Magellan was the greatest mariner of his day. Not only was he the first to negotiate the treacherous straits which now bear his name, but he and his crew also had to endure the terrible vicissitudes of the seemingly endless voyage across the Pacific, surviving on rotten biscuits smelling of rat urine, the rats themselves, and guanaco hides. Although Magellan died at the hands of the natives in the Philippines—stupidly in Morison's view—his feats far surpassed those of Columbus or Vasco de Gama. Another major figure, Francis Drake was more than just the scourge of the Spanish Main; he was an excellent sailor, solicitous of his men, and humane in his treatment of Indians.

Columbus, Vespucci, Magellan, and Drake are well known to most schoolboys, but Morison describes a host of others of lesser repute. Pedro Alvares Cabral helped give Portugal its American foothold. Juan Ponce de León, Pánfilo de Narváez, Álvar Núñez Cabeza de Vaca, and Hernando de Soto did the same for Spain in Florida and the Gulf of Mexico. To Alonso Álvarez de Pineda, however, goes the credit for discovering the Mississippi. Although not exactly household names, Pedro Sarmiento de Gamboa, Simón de Alcazaba, Juan Rodríguez Cabrillo, Francisco de Ulloa, Juan Fernández Ladrillero, Cortés Hojea, Oliver DeNoort, Georges Spilbergen, Isaak Le Maire, Willem Schouten, Thomas

Cavendish, and others also get their due in Morison's chatty, brilliant prose.

This is exploration history writ large. Like *The Northern Voyages* Morison uses Justin Winsor's technique of following each chapter with an extensive bibliographical essay. These provide delightful commentary not only on the chroniclers and historians from whom Morison fashions his narrative but also on the frauds they have perpetrated on us. Copious numbers of plates and photographs complement the text, but even more significant are the brilliantly drawn maps of Vaughn Gray. Following Magellan's tortuous route through Tierra del Fuego, one can almost feel what his crew had to endure. In the end one can only be thankful that God was willing to let Morison write *The Southern Voyages*, an epic work of true grandeur.

Duke University JOHN J. TEPASKE

Maryland: A History 1632–1974. Edited by Richard Walsh and William Lloyd Fox. (Baltimore: Maryland Historical Society, 1974. Pp. xvi, 935. $12.50.)

Writing state history poses special and difficult problems for the historian. Authors of national histories cannot deal directly with sources because of their sheer volume, but they have an abundance of sound secondary books at their disposal. Local historians can go back directly to the sources because their bulk at the town or county level is manageable. But the sources for state history are too vast over several centuries to be examined by one person, and secondary materials exist mainly in the form of minor articles or unpublished master's theses and doctor's dissertations.

Given these problems, the publishers have produced a book which is a model of its kind, solving the major difficulty by dividing the state's history into ten segments, each a chapter written by a different author. The multiauthor technique achieves a probing of the sources and a depth of analysis which could never be accomplished by a single author, for no one lives long enough to perform such a gargantuan task. But the editors, who also served as authors of chapters, by dividing the labor and skillfully directing the whole have achieved their objectives with singular felicity.

Unlike most state histories, this one is copiously documented—and with footnotes, not the too common and much less useful endnotes. The editors have provided a sane and instructive scheme of organization with chronological units which tie in with topical emphasis. The book is printed in large, easy-to-read type on substantial paper. Nearly seventy full-page illustrations are happily scattered throughout, at places where they enhance the adjacent text—a measure of good sense which is scarcely believable in a day when publishers commonly dump all pictures together in a separate section. But the volume is so big (four pounds avoirdupois) that holding it to read becomes tiresome, and the back binding is not quite up to what is demanded of it. Two volumes would have avoided these difficulties but would also have altered the present bargain price of $12.50.

The coeditors, William L. Fox and Richard Walsh, have done an excellent job in harnessing the talent needed to produce this book in the short time between the period of its inception and its publication in 1974. One might expect a hodgepodge of stylistic forms from ten different authors, but this does not come to pass. The several contributions blend smoothly, and transitions are well conceived. There is some repetition, but very little considering the scope of the project. I would have been glad to see the name of each author attached to his work in the table of contents. This does appear in the chapter headings—Aubrey C. Land for the provincial era; Editor Walsh for the Revolutionary era; James S. Van Ness for the social history of the Middle Period; W. Wayne Smith for the politics of the Middle Period; Richard R. Duncan for the Civil War era; Eleanor Bruchey for post–Civil War industrialization; Editor Fox for post–Civil War social development; James B. Crooks for Maryland progressivism; Dorothy M. Brown for Maryland, 1919–1941; and Franklin L. Burdette for modern Maryland. Each of these chapters is sustained both by footnotes and by a generous bibliographical essay, and the whole is concluded by a thirty-page index.

This is state history with the modern look—the way it ought to be done. It is appropriately dedicated to Harold R. Manakee, one of its initiators, who died in 1974.

Pennsylvania State University PHILIP S. KLEIN

Blackbeard the Pirate: A Reappraisal of His Life and Times. By Robert E. Lee. (Winston-Salem, N.C.: John F. Blair, Publisher, c. 1974. Pp. viii, 264. $8.95.)

Professor Lee's book should be read with caution. The author's preface is indicative of the work: "This history is intended for those who desire to read, against a historical background, true accounts of daring deeds of personal courage" (p. v). The deeds are those of one of the most notorious pirates of the early eighteenth century, Edward Teach or, under the descriptive name he chose, Blackbeard. Teach, in common with others who took to piracy, began his career as a merchant seaman. During the later years of Queen Anne's War he shifted to privateering. Restless with the cessation of hostilities, bored at the prospect of the low-paid round of ocean trade, Teach turned to piracy in 1716. As Blackbeard he attacked shipping in the Caribbean and off the coasts of Virginia and North and South Carolina. In June 1718 the pirate surrendered and accepted under a royal act of grace a pardon from Charles Eden, the proprietary governor of North Carolina. Despite the pardon, and supposedly in collusion with Eden and Tobias Knight, secretary, chief justice, and collector of the colony, Blackbeard returned to piracy. His activities, coupled with pleas from trading interests in the colony and the testimony of captured crew members, provoked the royal governor of Virginia, Alexander Spotswood, into sending a land and naval expedition against the "Prince of Villains." In November 1718 Blackbeard was killed in an engagement at Ocracoke Inlet.

The core of the study is concerned with the last five months of Blackbeard's life. Lee challenges accepted interpretations of the roles played by Eden, Knight, and Spotswood during that time period. He successfully questions Knight's direct involvement in piratical activities. But for the most part the author's contentions are lost in a maze of contradictions and legalistic quibbling. For instance, he emphasizes the legality of the condemnation proceedings brought against a French merchantman seized by Blackbeard in August 1718. Few historians would deny that Eden and Knight, acting in a vice-admiralty capacity, could claim salvage awards. But Lee obscures the fact that in such proceedings the value of the vessel is also considered. In this case the vessel was not examined, and Eden allowed it to be destroyed. In the chapter entitled "Dispute over Jurisdiction" Lee argues that Spotswood had no authority to enter North Carolina. The evidence he cites in Appendix C (pp. 239–42) can be used to support Spotswood's claim to legal jurisdiction over admiralty matters arising in Virginia, North Carolina, and the Bahama Islands. Finally, the merit of the work is compromised by genealogical and descriptive digressions of the worst scissors-and-paste sort.

General readers and students of North Carolina history will find some points of interest in Lee's book. It should be read in conjunction with Captain Charles Johnson, *A General History of the Robberies and Murders of the Most Notorious Pyrates* (1724), and Hugh F. Rankin, *The Golden Age of Piracy* (1969). For the historian there is little treasure to be found in *Blackbeard the Pirate*.

University of Santa Clara MILES M. MERWIN

The Creek Indians and Their Florida Lands, 1740–1823. By James F. Doster. (2 vols. New York and London: Garland Publishing, 1974. Pp. 296; 301. $42.00 the set.)

Until the creation of the Indian Claims Commission by the 1946 Claims Act, no tribe could bring suit against the United States without special permission of Congress. By that act Congress hoped to settle once and for all the centuries-old claims of the Indians. All the nation's aboriginal tribes had five years within which to file their claims before the commission. In a significant limitation, the commission could return only a money judgment in favor of the tribes. No land would ever be given back to the Indians.

The resultant battles before the Claims Commission produced a national mini-debate on the problems of Indians in American life. James Doster's two-volume study of the Creek Indians and their Florida lands from 1740 to 1823 is part of the scholarly fallout from that litigation.

By the 1740s the Creeks were moving into the areas of the present state of Florida, displacing or absorbing the various tribes already settled there. As a composite tribe or a loosely knit confederacy the Creeks seemed to have a penchant for locating on debatable lands. The Upper Creeks resided on lands claimed by France, England, and, later, the United

States, Georgia, and Alabama. The Seminoles, really Florida Creeks, fixed upon the land around the 31st parallel, a much-contested area between England, Spain, France, the United States, and the Creek nemesis, Georgia.

The problem of land claims was further complicated by clan rivalries, prior treaties, the American Revolution, the lack of a Creek central government before 1823, and the bitterness over the murder of William McIntosh, a literate half-breed chief, on April 30, 1825.

It can comfortably be said that the volumes will serve as a handy work of reference on the treaty history of the Creeks from 1740 to 1823. Still, they have scholarly limitations which will qualify their use. There is no index, and footnote references are to petitions and exhibits used in the hearings rather than to the primary sources themselves. The two volumes are more a lawyer's background brief than a scholarly work, but they are nonetheless valuable as a well-written summary of Creek history from 1740 to 1823.

University of North Carolina Asheville — MILTON L. READY

Empire and Liberty: American Resistance to British Authority, 1755–1763. By Alan Rogers. (Berkeley, Los Angeles, and London: University of California Press, 1974. Pp. xiv, 205. $8.95.)

Alan Rogers, employing the currently fashionable liberty-power dichotomy in colonial-British imperial relations, develops upon a thesis, partly explored by Bernhard Knollenberg a decade ago, that the origin of the American Revolution lay in American resistance to British authority during the Great War for Empire. Rogers finds that the war brought into sharp focus the long existing divisions between imperialists and anti-imperialists in colonial politics and that from 1754 to 1763 colonists in various ways defended their liberty from the encroachments of British power. The colonies wrecked the Albany Plan of Union in 1754 on the ground that it would be destructive of colonial liberty. When the crown placed responsibility for Indian affairs in appointed superintendencies, colonial assemblies openly resented crown invasion of their prerogatives. When colonial voluntary enlistments in the British army declined after 1756, British efforts to impress colonial men, horses, and wagons for military service aroused colonial hostility. Colonists opposed the British policy of quartering troops in privately owned accommodations as violative of their liberty. British wartime restrictions on colonial trade, designed to prevent trading with the enemy, antagonized colonial merchants because of the ideological implications of such restrictions. Colonial assemblies, dominated by anti-imperialist politicians, were generally uncooperative. The postwar imperial crises from 1763 to 1775 only reiterated the problems of the war years: quartering of troops, trade regulations, impressment, and the need for additional revenue.

Rogers's well-organized analysis will render easier further studies of the wartime origin of the American Revolution. Unfortunately, the colonial liberty–British power antinomy hypothesis, which controls Rogers's analysis, has caused him to ignore or belittle salient facts that contradict his hypothesis. William Johnson, for example, was a better superintendent of Indian affairs than Rogers indicates, and, while Sir Jeffery Amherst was clumsy in his handling of the Pontiac uprising, he did not cause it. The colonists' greed for western lands occupied by Indian tribes, faulty colonial Indian policies in the past, and the influence on the Indians by Frenchmen living in the Illinois country and the Fort Detroit area are unmentioned. In his account of the Albany conference of 1754 Rogers does not mention the colonists' concern about the French threat in the interior. If the French had won the Great War for Empire, what would have happened to colonial liberty? The quartering of troops during the war would not have been a problem if colonists had constructed sufficient barracks. Rogers's argument that there was little colonial illegal trade with the French after 1759 and that in the writs-of-assistance case Boston merchants were motivated by ideological abstractions rather than their material interests is not convincing. It does not appear that Rogers has done sufficient research to disprove entirely the conclusions of George L. Beer, Lawrence Henry Gipson, and Virginia Harrington that colonial illegal trade with the French enemy was extensive.

Rogers's bibliography indicates research in good source materials, but unfortunately he did not consult the valuable manuscript collections at the William L. Clements Library, and he does not appear to have researched at the Public Records Office in London. He lists Public Records Office microfilms, but there is no substitute for being there.

East Carolina University ROY N. LOKKEN

The Papers of Henry Laurens. Volume IV: *Sept. 1, 1763–Aug. 31, 1765*. Edited by George C. Rogers, Jr., David R. Chesnutt, and others. (Columbia, S.C.: Published for the South Carolina Historical Society by the University of South Carolina Press, 1974. Pp. xxvi, 720. $25.00.)

Like its three predecessors, the fourth volume of *The Papers of Henry Laurens* is superbly edited and produced. Thoroughly annotated, it is set out in a handsome and usable format. It covers exactly two years and contains over 650 separate documents (presumably all of the known material relating to Laurens for the period), including around 600 letters written by Laurens. These materials reveal the same basic personality traits Laurens had manifested in his earliest surviving correspondence. He was patient, self-disciplined, and hard working, one of those "carefull Active Men who" strived "by every Laudable measure in their power to get a livelihood & make some figure in business" (pp. 5–6). A man of great public spirit, he had enormous respect for law and was willing, when necessary, to sacrifice his "private Interest" to the "public good" (p. 672). And he was a quintessential moderate who abhorred excess in private and public life.

This volume finds Laurens in a "middle state of Life retreating . . . from that bustle & hurry that my attention to commerce had unavoidably led me into . . ." (p. 295). In a letter to a friend he had not seen in twenty-two years he reviewed his "former annals & future intentions" (p. 296). Both in family and business life, he thought, things had turned out "upon the whole to my advantage, far beyond my merrits & more than adequate to my most Sanguine hopes" (p. 295). He did not "pretend or affect to be very Rich," but he had "enough to procure contentment" (p. 419) so that he could afford to draw his "business . . . within a very contracted sphere" (p. 393). Thus, he had "in general declined the Affrican business . . ." (p. 167) which he had earlier found so lucrative and had limited his commission business to a few "particular old friends in England." He did "not mean wholly to retire" but merely "to draw a little of my attention from the *Busy World*" of commerce so he could devote more time to his family, "some duties that I owe to my Country, the necessary improvements of my Lands in & near Charles Town, [and] a few Vessels in which I am concerned or own . . ." (p. 296).

The documents teem with rich materials concerning many other facets of eighteenth-century Anglo-American life in which Laurens was involved: the prosperous state of the South Carolina economy, including the bullish markets in slaves, rice, indigo, naval stores, and money; the organization of internal and external trade; the vast and intricate networks of overseas commerce into which merchants such as Laurens were bound; the rhythms, risks, and rewards of trade; the external requirements of rice and indigo plantations; the attitudes of a husband and father towards his wife and children; the uncertainties and anxieties of life in an unhealthy environment; local politics and the impingement of British politics on colonial consciousness; and slavery, including the planters' ethnic preferences in slaves, modes of social control, and, in one superb document detailing the "good qualities" and "bad" of a "Negro Man named Abram" (pp. 298–99), the character of interracial relations and perceptions.

Johns Hopkins University JACK P. GREENE

The Problem of Slavery in the Age of Revolution, 1770–1823. By David Brion Davis. (Ithaca and London: Cornell University Press, 1975. Pp. 576. $17.50.)

In his previous volume, *The Problem of Slavery in Western Culture,* David Brion Davis brought the intellectual history of antislavery doctrine down to the middle of the eighteenth century, having canvassed it from antiquity and in Britain, France, and the New World. In this volume the span of time is barely fifty years, and the range of countries is confined to the United States, Britain, and France, and even then the last receives only brief attention. Some of the issues raised and conclusions advanced in this volume, however, are sharper and more profound than in the earlier volume.

On one level the presentation is quite straightforward. The book tells the story of the rapid growth of antislavery argument and action in Britain, the United States, and France during a period of political and economic revolution. It is worth noting that the Industrial Revolution, in Davis's view, is by far the most important of the four revolutions; the second most important is the successful uprising of St. Domingue blacks under Toussaint L'Ouverture. But, as in Davis's first volume, the delineation of a development is only the beginning. For the arguments of the pamphleteers and writers are not only summarized and related to one another, they are also cogently and imaginatively analyzed as to their meanings and implications. Davis is careful to show, to cite but one of several examples, that it was not necessarily inconsistent to argue for the freedom of Americans from British slavery, real or potential, while holding hundreds of thousands of blacks in actual slavery. Yet at the same time, he points out, that superficial conflict in practices is central to understanding the special way Americans defined and perceived freedom. He devotes two chapters to analyzing the impact of the antislavery agitation in both Britain and the United States on the law and on the interpretation of the Bible. In passing he reveals the ingenuity of the antislavery advocates by showing why the biblical support for slavery did not invalidate, in their eyes, the divine basis of the Bible, and why, again in their view, antislavery, far from being a threat to traditional law or the established order was actually a means of extending the rule of law—to Africans. Always, Davis is alert to the role of contingency in history and to the ways in which ideology and interest shape and limit each other. He refuses to let himself be trapped into choosing between interest or ideology as primary explanations for social motivation.

Despite the length of the volume, a large portion of the corpus of American abolitionist literature is not discussed. Part of the reason is that the closing date of the study excludes the great age of abolitionist literature in the United States. But certain aspects of antislavery agitation even when they fall within the terminal dates of the book are also omitted. The Missouri debates over slavery are not analyzed at all. Thus, Davis's discussion of antislavery in America is largely confined to the age of the American Revolution, the debates over the Constitution, and the old, if ever fascinating issue of Jefferson's ambiguous commitment to antislavery. Although Davis does not indict Jefferson as personally, that is, sexually, as Winthrop Jordan did, his bill of particulars against Jefferson is more devastating. Nor was Jefferson alone, Davis points out, in finding it difficult to follow out his antislavery views while living in and profiting from a slave society. The Jamaican Bryan Edwards and the French colonial Moreau de Saint-Méry were similarly compromised by their class positions. (Davis does suggest that the English and French colonials seemed to have liked Negroes personally more than Jefferson did, but he does not pursue the point.) He goes on to observe, too, that it was the very social diversity of the slave South—many nonslaveholders with political power—that caused the South to develop the most sophisticated and ultimately persuasive proslavery argument of all. And although Davis does not make the point, that same social diversity goes far to explain why the South alone developed a racial defense of slavery.

That the book does not deal with all or even most of the abolitionist literature in the United States certainly needs to be noted, but that limitation does not constitute a serious defect. The truth is that the achievement of this book does not lie in the novelty or the breadth of its analysis of the American material. (Even the incisive probing of Jefferson's views on slavery was published earlier, in 1970.) It is the compellingly brilliant and subtle analysis of the British antislavery argument that makes this volume a major contribution to the history of ideas. This is the second and more profound level on which the book proceeds.

The large question that Davis addresses is: What was the relationship between the rise of antislavery in Britain and the emergence of a new social order? He rejects Eric Williams's thesis that the successful movement against the slave trade was provoked by the changing economic interests of Britain in the world economy. If Davis is too subtle to settle for such a gross economic determinist position, he is also too honest and open-minded to deny the remarkable temporal coincidence of the two developments. Nor can he, for the same reasons, ignore the coincidence between the outpouring of antislavery literature and the dramatic emergence of a literature concerned with controlling and disciplining free labor. (It needs to be said, however, that this second body of writings is referred to but neither described nor analyzed—an undoubted weakness in the book.) Out of these coincidents arises the old question: Why were these antislavery people so concerned about blacks in remote places while they were so unconcerned about the many whites held in wage slavery all around them? Davis's answer rightly eschews the easy explanation of status anxiety, social displacement, or psychological deviation. Forthrightly, he accepts the humanitarian impulses of the abolitionists as fundamental; their efforts he refers to at one place (p. 42) as "a momentous turning point in the evolution of man's moral perception, and thus in man's image of himself." His own answer is that antislavery agitation emerged when it did because, to a new class and new social order then coming into dominance, slavery was the exact opposite of all that they stood for. Slavery as external coercion, rather than internalized control, was the ultimate violation of a system of values in which a man's freedom was defined, to use C. B. Macpherson's words, as the "proprietorship of one's own person." Davis seems to be saying that what began with Locke in the seventeenth century as a theory became a philosophy of a class and eventually of a whole society by the end of the eighteenth century. Yet he is so circumspect in advancing this interpretation that it is not always clear that he wants to assert it. Indeed, his subtlety of approach throughout is so pronounced that he often omits simple causal connections. Thus, he points out that many English writers like Malthus, Burke, Romilly, and Bentham, who were deeply concerned about social order, were also strong abolitionists, but he refrains from saying there was a causal connection. In another place he puts the connection obliquely, as in this passage: "This ideology emerged from a convergence of complex religious, intellectual, and literary trends—trends which are by no means reducible to the economic interests of particular classes, but which must be understood as part of a larger transformation in attitudes toward labor, property, and individual responsibility" (p. 82).

He further suggests that in an age of intense social oppression, opposition to slavery relieved the tension in those sensitive English men and women who perceived the oppression around them but who could not countenance the social disruption that the lifting of that oppression would entail. This is not the same as saying, he cautions, that manufacturers or other advocates of the new emerging industrial order were using antislavery to distract attention from their own forms of exploitation. Yet, he goes on, there was some connection, even though he will not spell it out other than to suggest the effects: "If British abolitionists could express horror over the iron chains of the slave trade, their acts of selectivity and definition helped to strengthen the invisible chains being forged at home" (p. 456).

One is tempted to say that there is a Marxist struggling to be recognized in this book. Yet for all of Davis's emphasis upon class interest and class control over individual idealism, he stops short of traveling the full Marxian route to a self-conscious ruling class. The men and women of the antislavery cause were not, as Davis reads the evidence, pressing for a conscious triumph of the new economic and social order, however profoundly they may have been influenced or their cause shaped by its needs and demands. For at bottom the process was dialectical. Not surprisingly therefore, it is Hegel, not Marx, to whom Davis makes acknowledgment. For the final point which he leaves with us is that one of the consequences of the abolitionists' concentration upon slavery is that they, along with historians, who have generally followed their lead, perceived slavery as a very special status instead of as a point on a continuum of human subordination and exploitation. For today we are still part of that social order which first emerged in Britain in the late eighteenth century and which perceived slavery as a form of subordination and exploitation that was outmoded and unique rather than ageless and a matter of degree. In that way Davis's intellectually stimulating book adds to, as it builds upon, recent studies like *Time on the Cross* and *Roll, Jordan, Roll,* which have emphasized the complexities and ambiguities of slavery as a system of exploitation and control. All these studies thus require us to see slavery as a critical issue not only in the history of politics and reform, but in the evolution of social thought and social organization in the modern Western world.

Stanford University CARL N. DEGLER

Patrick Henry: A Biography. By Richard R. Beeman. (New York and other cities: McGraw-Hill Book Co., c. 1974. Pp. xvi, 229. $9.95.)

Patrick Henry was an enigma both to his contemporaries and to past historians who have attempted to understand the man. He is remembered by nonhistorians through three phrases: "If this be treason, make the most of it"; ". . . give me liberty or give me death"; and "I am not a Virginian, but an American." Though these statements have come down in garbled and often misunderstood form, they have found their way into the pantheon of historical phrases.

The biographer who seeks to get inside Patrick Henry, to feel and act as that orator acted, finds his path blocked at every turn. Henry was no Adams when it came to preserving papers; his first biographer was William Wirt, a writer of the Parson Weems school, who preferred flavor and drama to accuracy. Henry's enemies included such formidable Revolutionary statesmen as Jefferson and Madison. Henry was primarily an orator, an art unappreciated in an era in which elocution means a trip to the dictionary.

Despite these obstacles, Professor Beeman succeeds in painting a Patrick Henry whose positions on public issues seem less contradictory than earlier studies have indicated. The author accomplished this feat not by out-detailing Robert D. Meade, but by asking new, relevant questions. "How does Patrick Henry fit into the world of eighteenth-century Virginia?" opens many locked doors. Leaning heavily upon Jack P. Greene and others who have studied the Revolutionary era's politics and society, Beeman strips away some of the garish paint brushed on by William Wirt in 1817. Stressing the normative aspects of Henry's rise into the ranks of the elite, this is a times-and-life biography in which the Virginian finds himself as often as not the dependent variable.

Many controversies from the Parsons' Cause to Henry's stand on the Constitution are seen as a product of localism and Henry's career experience. Professor Beeman's Henry is a phenomenal orator, whose family influence is equal to that of the Jeffersons and Marshalls; a man who through attention to land speculation and advantageous marital alliances moved into Virginia's remarkable ruling elite. Henry is a pragmatist who could fulminate against the British when it was to his advantage or keep his lips sealed when it was not; who could favor stronger government when he was a frustrated governor and yet oppose the Constitution when he felt it threatened his "country," western Virginia. As the author puts it, "Interests, not ideology, and instinct, not reason, tended to be the forces that guided his conduct" (p. 129). Where other students of Henry have emphasized uniqueness and twistings on issues, Beeman has emphasized similarity. It is a case of seeing the forest instead of individual trees.

Morehead State University STUART SEELY SPRAGUE

Party Politics in the Continental Congress. By H. James Henderson. (New York and other cities: McGraw-Hill Book Co., c. 1974. Pp. xviii, 475. $15.00.)

A rash of works treating the Revolutionary era is appearing as the nation's bicentennial nears. Few, however, achieve the high level of H. James Henderson's analysis of the Continental Congress. Henderson, who began this study under the direction of Richard B. Morris at Columbia University, has plowed through the rich documentation on the Congress to produce an astute appraisal. Although recognizing the frailties of the Congress, he stresses its durability by contrast with the impermanence of revolutionary assemblies elsewhere; he also asserts that its record of accomplishments "has rarely been equaled during a comparable time span in American legislative history" (p. 430). In only fifteen years the Congress managed to declare independence, conduct the military affairs of the Revolution, frame an alliance with France, conclude peace with the British, and organize the territorial system for settlement of the West.

Of course, others, including Merrill Jensen who covered much of the same ground as early as 1940 in *The Articles of Confederation*, have already argued that the Congress was not the impotent body of tradition. Henderson's contribution lies less in evaluating the success of the Congress than in exposing a concealed structure of partisan politics among the delegates to that body. A number of recent studies have examined partisan politics in the states, including Jackson Turner Main's *Political Parties Before the Constitution* (1973) and Van Beck Hall's *Politics Without Parties: Massachusetts, 1780–1791* (1972). Now Henderson has established the existence of sustained and fairly coherent parties at the national level as well.

Using a quantitative method similar to the Guttman scalogram, he analyzes 1,069 roll-call votes in the Congress for the period 1777 to 1786 and identifies a configuration of voting blocs. He sees these as rudimentary congressional parties, although they lacked the labels, platforms, electoral tickets, and grass-roots organizations we have come to associate with modern parties. Some readers may quibble with the use of the term *party*, and others will find the study tedious—there are some twenty-eight tables with scores of explanatory notes.

But Henderson makes a compelling case for the existence of partisan alignments in the Congress and establishes that the basic divisions were sectional rather than ideological. Alignments followed a North-South fault, with the delegates from the Middle States dividing or shifting from one regional coalition to the other. He suggests that this sectional configuration continued when the nation's first party system was formed in the 1790s and that the partisan struggles of the Continental Congress constituted a "germinal period" (p. xiv) for the development of national party politics. One wishes he had explored this view more thoroughly, although Mary P. Ryan's quantitative analysis of party formation in the United States Congress in the period 1789–1796 (*William and Mary Quarterly*, October 1971) bears out the essential sectional character of the early parties.

Despite his "effort to capture the temper as well as the structure of congressional politics" (p. xiv), Henderson is more convincing in documenting the existence of partisan divisions than he is in explaining the motives behind them. Perhaps his important study will stimulate other scholars to look even deeper into the issue of party politics before the first party system.

San Diego State University ROBERT C. DETWEILER

A Legal History of Money in the United States, 1774–1970. By James Willard Hurst. (Lincoln: University of Nebraska Press, c. 1973. Pp. xviii, 367. $9.50.)

Here is a book whose title fits. The title, the 205 pages of text, and the 128 pages of fine-print backnotes (followed by a list of sources and an index) all share several characteristics. They are accurate. They cover a very broad territory. They state what the author wants them to state, and omit, sometimes to the point of leaving to the reader's imagination, what he does not want them to state. They are terse, tightly organized, and temperate. This is a book definitely directed toward a scholarly readership, and while it will perhaps satisfy legal scholars more than it will "pure" historians because of its style as well as organization, its combination of ecumenicity and accuracy should nonetheless make it of considerable value to historians interested in the legal history of social and economic institutions. Such has been the case with earlier books on corporations, treason, "the conditions of freedom," and other subjects by James Willard Hurst, professor of law at Wisconsin. So should it be with this book, which as the title states is a legal—that is, not social or intellectual or financial or party-political—history of those critical substances which we call money, from the first Continental Congress to 1970.

The text consists of an introduction dealing with the 1774–1790 period, a first chapter called "Functions of Law and Functions of Money," and a second chapter called "Allocations of Control over the System of Money." A very useful analytical table of contents precedes the text. Both chapters range over the entire 1790–1970 period, but the second is subdivided chronologically at 1860 and 1908 and seems (to this historian) easier going than the first. Professor Hurst's sources are, principally, state and federal court decisions, state and federal statutes, federal executive and congressional reports, published writings by and about policy makers, beginning with Hamilton and Jefferson, and secondary scholarly works on legal and monetary history, whose variety is not exhaustive but evidently represents careful selection.

The introduction shows that shapers of policy in the Revolutionary period recognized money (and banking) as a legitimate governmental concern and at the Constitutional Convention a concern of the national government vis-à-vis state legislatures. Otherwise, events shaped what little policy there was. The first chapter traces the development of ideas (evidenced in statutes and decisions) about the areas where law might touch on money and its functions. Law could define a monetary system (standards, units, coinage; gradually, banking and nonspecie money); to some extent relate the money supply to resource flow; to a much lesser extent use money to change economic or social structures, certainly less so than taxation, especially in the twentieth century. Laws and treaties attempted or succeeded in defining international economic relationships, very poorly in the late nineteenth century and with considerable effectiveness after 1944. In this chapter the author is basically saying that law did not create, or even coherently recognize as possible, a monetary system which was to promote productivity or growth or broad wealth distribution. Policy developed almost negatively, in terms of national economic goals, in the nineteenth century and developed through the force of relatively short-range events even in the middle third of the twentieth century. As Hurst puts it (p. 74), "Typically this society [from the 1790s through the 1960s] dealt with its affairs in narrowly pragmatic fashion, making a philosophy out of crossing bridges when it came to them; open discussion of the grander purposes of money policy was perhaps of no poorer, but also it was of no better quality, than the handling of most questions of broad reach."

The theme of pragmatic, short- or middle-vision development of monetary law pervades Chapter Two even more insistently. Here Hurst is concerned, in the periods 1787–1860, 1860–1908, and 1908–1970, with three sets of issues involving control over allocation of power regarding money: federal versus state government; private commercial banks versus government regulation; government agencies versus each other and versus central bankers. Before 1860 legislative and administrative policy making was weak, and "public-interest functions of money supply [were readily delegated] to private organizations" (p. 174). From 1860 to 1908 Congress reacted to short-run pressures while the executive "uncritically accepted" the conventional wisdom that specie payments (in gold) was the main issue (p. 197); neither those branches nor the judiciary regarded specie as but one issue among many involving the real money supply, and thus none developed coherent goals or policy. After 1908 a national monetary policy did begin to cohere, and its sources and scope develop, but the arena of policy making and conflict was not the states, Congress, or the Supreme Court primarily, but the Treasury and the Federal Reserve (both FRB and FOMC) (pp. 199, 228, 237).

Hurst's arguments are of course much more refined than this summary reveals. I find no substantive disagreement and hardly any specialist's quibbles. Not a monetary history like Friedman and Schwartz's, not a history of statute law or of judicial decisions, it instead discusses over the whole history of the republic the development of actions on what should and should not be done regarding monetary law. I know of no other book that does that, or that so forcefully makes the judgment that Americans, with regard to money as with so many other things, have been the unknowing victims of dead political economists. Hurst seldom dwells explicitly on the context of monetary thought or rhetoric, which I would have liked, and the judgment is more what Hurst teaches me than what he explicitly says; but in his focus on executive, legislative, and judicial action he makes his case very well indeed.

Indiana University, Bloomington WALTER T. K. NUGENT

The Papers of John Marshall. Volume I: *Correspondence and Papers, November 10, 1775–June 23, 1788; Account Book, September 1783–1788*. Edited by Herbert A. Johnson and others. (Chapel Hill:

University of North Carolina Press in association with the Institute of Early American History and Culture, c. 1974. Pp. xlvi, 448. $17.95.)

Compiling and editing the papers of John Marshall is an important job, and this first volume of the Marshall papers meets the challenge superbly. It is all the more impressive an accomplishment since Marshall himself provided almost no help at all. He was not a careful record keeper, and so the editors have had to rely on people with whom Marshall came in contact and on public records which provide information on the future justice's activities from 1775 to 1788. The material here is wide in scope. It includes army records revealing Marshall's activities as lieutenant in the Continental Army, his studies as a law student, cases he tried as an attorney, and his efforts as a state politician, a private land speculator, and member of the Virginia convention called to ratify the Constitution. In addition, the editors have included Marshall's account book for 1783–1788. This last source reveals his personal life, his involvement in society, his enjoyment of gambling, and the growth of his law practice. There is material of use here for a social history of Virginia as well as study of Marshall himself.

Distinguishing this work are the excellent editorial notes which accompany the documents. The editors have done intensive work on the complexity of land purchase and speculation in the late eighteenth century. Their discussion of the Fairfax land case is especially helpful, as is their commentary on Marshall's Kentucky land speculation. Unfortunately, their commentary on some of the cases will be understood only by those with training in law. What, for example, would a nonlawyer make of the following: "It is not clear whether the heir-at-law is the heir of the life tenant or the heir of the testator; however, since there was a residuary clause in the will, normally the executor or residuary legatee of the testator would claim the slaves if they reverted to the testator's estate" (p. 187)? In fairness, it should be noted that at times they do seem conscious of the fact that nonlawyers are a part of their audience, but this concern does not prevail.

The most important contribution of this volume is to provide a picture of Marshall as a practicing lawyer and thus to reveal the nature of law practice in eighteenth-century Virginia. If anyone needed more proof that the future Chief Justice understood the law as well as most of his peers the evidence is here. He clashed in court with able lawyers like John Taylor and John Randolph and held his own. Marshall's argument in *Hite* v. *Fairfax*, though in a losing cause, still shows an able lawyer at work, and it is most useful to have it before us so that we can see Marshall on the other side of the bench.

Evidence here also shows Marshall to have been a member of the legal establishment of his time. His bias against untrained "County Court lawyers" who don't trust judges (p. 124), his anxiety over Shays's rebellion, his efforts to expand the judicial system of Virginia all demonstrate his belief "that these have truth on their side who say that man is incapable of governing himself" (p. 201). One hopes that readers of these words will also have in mind Morton Horwitz's warnings against taking such opinions of popular justice at face value. (*American Journal of Legal History*, XVII, 275.)

However one wishes to take Marshall's words, we now are beginning to have all of those words which are discoverable and to have them in a format that can only encourage interpretations which match the quality of this collection. The editors should be congratulated on performing a difficult and important task with great skill and diligence. Given the high quality of this volume the historical and legal professions should eagerly await the publication of the rest of the series.

University of Kansas PHILLIP S. PALUDAN

The Papers of Alexander Hamilton. Volume XX: *January 1796–March 1797;* Volume XXI: *April 1797–July 1798*. Edited by Harold C. Syrett and others. (New York and London: Columbia University Press, 1974. Pp. xviii, 597; xvi, 560. $17.50 each.)

Bringing together all of Hamilton's papers for the period covering the final year of Washington's administration and the first year of Adams's Presidency, these volumes establish with an authority not previously equaled the extraordinary influence that Alexander Hamilton, a private citizen, had in the highest levels of the government. Hamilton's influence has been often noticed, and there are no startling revelations here. But rarely have we been able to see so clearly how dependent Washington was upon his former secretary of the Treasury or so plainly how Hamilton operated while Adams was President. Included are the exchanges between Washington and Hamilton relating to Hamilton's role in drafting Washington's farewell address, Hamilton's outline and draft, and editorial notes tracing the drafting process. In the letter thanking Hamilton for his draft of the farewell address, Washington asked him to furnish materials for his address at the opening of Congress. Later he forwarded materials prepared by department heads for the message, and Hamilton supplied the draft which Washington incorporated with only minor variations into his last annual message to Congress. Washington regularly consulted Hamilton on foreign affairs and clearly valued Hamilton's judgment over that of Secretary of State Timothy Pickering. Although Hamilton corresponded some with Pickering while Washington was President, he directed his advice on foreign policy mainly to the President in letters that were not always flattering to the secretary of state. Volume XX contains considerable material relating to the contest in the House of Representatives over implementing the Jay Treaty and on Adet's notes during the election of 1796.

Once Adams became President, Hamilton's correspondence with Pickering increased, and the secretary of state urged Hamilton to continue to communicate his views to him. Hamilton also maintained his correspondence with Secretary of the Treasury Oliver Wolcott, who had regularly consulted his predecessor since taking over the Treasury post.

Most dependent upon Hamilton was Secretary of War James McHenry, who more than once sent directly to Hamilton communications from Adams asking for the opinions and advice of his cabinet; McHenry then used Hamilton's reply to respond to the President. Not content with this access to the inner councils of the executive branch, Hamilton built support for his policies by sending detailed memoranda to William Loughton Smith, chairman of the House Ways and Means Committee, and to Theodore Sedgwick, a leading Federalist in the Senate. In addition, Hamilton continued to write pieces for the newspapers and during the XYZ crisis published a series of seven articles on American relations with France. Volume XXI contains much material relating to the XYZ affair. As had been true since Hamilton's retirement from the Treasury, his continuing role in the government was not unsolicited intrusion. His advice was actively sought and in the case of McHenry, imploringly so. Hamilton also corresponded with the former President; Volume XXI ends with Hamilton urging Washington to use his influence to secure "Men of capacity & exertion" (XXI, 535) for high posts in the newly authorized provisional army.

Volume XXI also contains all of the material the editors could assemble on the Reynolds pamphlet, including Hamilton's draft and the printed version. An editorial note reports the editors' failure to find satisfactory answers to all of the questions posed by the Reynolds affair. While accepting much of the evidence presented by Julian Boyd, they are not persuaded that Boyd's suspicion that Hamilton fabricated the affair with Mrs. Reynolds to hide official corruption in the Treasury Department is supportable.

Maintaining the high editorial standards earlier established, these volumes provide further proof of the value of the type of comprehensive, scholarly editorial work that this series represents.

University of Missouri
Columbia

NOBLE E. CUNNINGHAM, JR.

Thomas L. McKenney: Architect of America's Early Indian Policy: 1816–1830. By Herman J. Viola. (Chicago: Swallow Press, c. 1974. Pp. xii, 365. $15.00.)

Thomas McKenney is a difficult subject for a biographer. Although he lived to the age of seventy-three, his main public career was concentrated in some fourteen years from 1816 to 1830 when he was, with a brief interlude, superintendent of Indian trade and head of the Office of Indian Affairs. After 1830 his only substantial contribution was the *History of the Indian Tribes of North America* with James Hall. In this book Herman Viola surveys the whole of McKenney's life, but the main concentration is on his public service; less than five pages are devoted to the years prior to 1816, and less than fifty pages to the prolonged twilight from 1830 to his death in 1859. The book then is in part biography and in part a study of McKenney and American Indian policy in the years from 1816 to 1830. This combination is not completely a happy one, although much is revealed by the thoroughness of the author's research.

There are three main sections of the book. The first is a discussion of McKenney's management of the government factory system and his fight to save it from the attack of private interests. Here, as in the long section discussing his management of the Office of Indian Affairs, the main strength is in revealing detail rather than in the overall conceptual framework. This strength of descriptive detail continues in the last section, where Viola considers McKenney's efforts to regain office, his publications, his lectures, and his decline. The author does not attempt any comprehensive analysis of McKenney's character, and, in spite of details on McKenney's opportunism, he views his subject charitably. McKenney in these pages is generally regarded as a good friend of the Indian.

Although Viola argues that McKenney "was a major architect of the civilization and removal programs" (p. 184), he devotes surprisingly little attention to the manner in which the removal policy evolved in these years, or even the manner in which McKenney eventually came to support it. The book's importance would have been enhanced if more attention had been devoted to the interconnection of McKenney's detailed management of Indian affairs with the main course of American Indian policy. Viola's evidence at times suggests that McKenney was at least as much a political and financial opportunist as he was a genuine friend of the Indian.

This book is effective both in depicting McKenney's day-by-day operation of the factory system and the Office of Indian Affairs and in showing his maneuverings after he was dismissed from office. It is less effective as a biography or as an analysis of how those responsible for the management of Indian affairs shaped or were shaped by federal and state demands on the Indians.

University of Wisconsin, Milwaukee REGINALD HORSMAN

The Abolitionists: The Growth of a Dissenting Minority. By Merton L. Dillon. *Minorities in American History*. (DeKalb: Northern Illinois University Press, c. 1974. Pp. xiv, 298. Paper, $3.00; cloth, $10.00.)

This history of the abolitionist movement is by a historian who has already made distinguished contributions to the study of the antislavery movement in biographies of Benjamin Lundy and Elijah Lovejoy and an excellent bibliographical survey of antislavery literature in the *Journal of Southern History* in 1969. As the title of his present work suggests, Dillon focuses upon the abolitionists, the proponents of "immediate emancipation" within the pre–Civil War antislavery movement. Yet his treatment is not a narrow one, for he sees the abolitionists within the context of the society of their day. To use his own words, "The changing relationship between the abolitionist minority and the rest of society, and the process by which a portion—but not all—of the abolitionist program gained northern majority acceptance are the main themes of this book" (pp. xii–xiii).

Dillon writes out of a sure knowledge of the secondary literature as well as the primary sources of abolition history. His presentation, moreover, breathes judiciousness and fairness as he discusses the quarrels, often based upon serious ideological and practical differences, between groups of abolitionists who were quite often bitterly opposed to one another. Garrisonians, non-Garrisonians and anti-Garrisonians, moral suasionists and pacifists, political abolitionists and the proponents of forceful and violent emancipation are treated with understanding and insight. Dillon thereby avoids the trap into which so many historians of the antislavery movement have fallen by becoming identified with one or another group of abolitionists, especially the anti-Garrisonians and the enemies of John Brown, and by exceeding their spiritual progenitors in bitterness, contempt, and vindictiveness. Dillon evaluates, judges, and, sometimes, takes sides. But he does so with a sympathetic appreciation of the complexity of the issues which faced the abolitionists and with respect for their sincerity and idealism even where he judges them critically.

There are several areas to which Dillon devotes more attention than have other antislavery historians: abolitionist activities during the late 1840s and especially the 1850s; the relationships between Garrisonians, Liberty Leaguers, and Republicans, with the shifting allegiances of large numbers from one to the other despite the steadfastness of a hard core of leadership in the former two; abolitionist activity during the Civil War and Reconstruction, in which he draws heavily upon James McPherson's work; and, finally, his emphasis upon the relationship between the abolitionists and later movements for equal rights for blacks and against racism. Most noteworthy, writing on Garrison's resignation from the American Anti-Slavery Society with the passage of the Thirteenth Amendment at the end of 1865 and his closing of the *Liberator,* Dillon makes abundantly clear, what has so frequently been misunderstood even by Garrison's biographers, that this did not mean an abandonment of the freedmen but a substitution of new forms of organization and struggle for what he considered outmoded organizations.

There are several areas of abolitionist history wherein this reviewer would take issue with the author. These include the role of the Protestant evangelical movement of the late 1820s and early 1830s in the rise of the abolitionist movement, the nature and uniqueness of Garrison's contributions, and the reasons for the Garrisonian attitude toward political activity, nonresistance, and disunion. The disagreements, rather than being fundamental, concern emphases in interpretation within each of these areas and merit consideration, but limitations of space prevent elaboration here.

A few minor errors which have crept into the text, perhaps through typographical mishaps, may be noticed. On p. 36: Garrison was twenty-four years old, not twenty-two, in 1829. On p. 126: Gerrit Smith ran for Congress in 1852, not 1842. On p. 134: Garrison's reference to the Constitution as "a covenant with death, and an agreement with hell" is based on Isaiah 28:18, not 28:28. These can easily be changed in a new printing.

In essence, in a field teeming with controversy and acrimony, Dillon has written a cogent and instructive volume.

University of Massachusetts, Boston LOUIS RUCHAMES

They Who Would Be Free: Blacks' Search for Freedom, 1830–1861. By Jane H. Pease and William H. Pease. (New York: Atheneum, 1974. Pp. xii, 331. $10.00.)

Fortunately, the authors of this important book decided not to write "a narrative of black abolitionism in the antebellum North" but rather "to analyze the perceptions, attitudes, values, goals, and means of those Northern Negroes who struggled within the abolitionist crusade—and frequently outside of it—to achieve a meaningful freedom for themselves and their brethren in slavery" (p. v). This conceptual focus took the authors beyond the several significant studies already available treating Afro-Americans in the abolition movement and the disabilities faced by free blacks in the North. Professors Jane H. Pease and William H. Pease have provided a systematic treatment of black thought between 1830 and 1860 that ranks in importance with August Meier's pioneering work covering the era of Booker T. Washington.

Other scholars have already demonstrated that abolitionism was not monolithic and that black abolitionists divided into factions along with their white colleagues. The authors of this book hold, and argue their point convincingly, that in addition to the other divisions, there was a "very basic racial split" among abolitionists, which led to "a distinct black abolitionism" (p. 3). Black abolitionists viewed freedom less abstractly than their white allies, and they formulated ideologies and tactics to better their condition in the North, while working to free their brethren in the South. Moreover, free blacks in the North were more flexible than white reformers in their ideological positions and more pragmatic in their methodology.

Basic to the existence of black abolitionism was the development of black consciousness or a black community, which began evolving long before 1830. The early stages of black consciousness were epitomized in the writings of David Walker and Henry Highland Garnet, in the work of Paul Cuffe, and in the development of separate institutional structures, especially the black church and the black press.

The main thesis of the book, that free blacks in the North were fighting the discrimination they faced while struggling to end slavery in the South, is developed in Chapters Six through Twelve. These chapters are largely topical in organization, treating dominant ideas and ideological divisions among Afro-Americans as they campaigned to improve economic conditions, to end segregation, to extend the suffrage, and to strike at slavery by aiding fugitive slaves. Ironically, the authors found that Afro-Americans, slave and free, made their most significant contribution to the coming of freedom with their militant resistance to the fugitive slave law of 1850, when, "Proudly and openly they put the law to naught" (p. 232). But, Afro-Americans did not see the 1850s as a "turning point." They believed things were getting worse, and many turned to emigration schemes as the only route to true freedom and equality.

Although this exhaustively researched and lucidly written book is largely a chronicle of failure, it is a valuable contribution to the study of black thought and black leadership. The authors viewed their major contribution to be the insights they provided on the question of why black abolitionists could not reach their goals "in a society whose dominant group avowedly espoused the values these goals embraced" (p. 297). Equally important to students of Afro-American life and history is their treatment of the origins and development of patterns of black thought and action that have become enduring components of the black American experience. No scholar should undertake to deal with protest, accommodation, black nationalism, or separatism and assimilationism in either the nineteenth or twentieth centuries without reading this book.

University of Missouri, Columbia ARVARH E. STRICKLAND

Breckinridge: Statesman, Soldier, Symbol. By William C. Davis. (Baton Rouge: Louisiana State University Press, c. 1974. Pp. xxii, 687. $17.50.)

Historians who have recorded this nation's issues and events for the quarter century beginning in 1850 have seldom considered Kentuckian John C. Breckinridge among its top leaders. In *Breckinridge: Statesman, Soldier, Symbol* William C. Davis gives new prominence to a man who served his country as congressman, Vice-President, and senator before casting his lot with the Confederacy, where he continued prominent service, first as a general and then as the South's last secretary of war.

In this fine study, Davis explores the life of his subject in three chronological periods which relate to three stages of personal development. He was statesman before the war—influential Democrat, southern conservative, a strict interpreter of the Constitution but persistent critic of slavery—a man destined for the Presidency until the war came.

He was soldier when his role as statesman ended with his enlistment in the cause of the Confederacy. As a general officer, he led troops in battle, first in the West and then in the East, sometimes with distinction, more often with his actions marked by mistakes. Stressing his leadership under General Braxton Bragg, but especially impressed by his victory at New Market, Davis commends Breckinridge's handling of troops, his improving understanding of military tactics, and his ability to size up battle situations. The general's military reputation suffers, however, from the mistakes he made—at Shiloh, Stones River, and Chattanooga—and in the criticism directed his way by General Bragg, criticism that affected negatively much of the historical interpretation of his career.

As symbol, the Kentuckian was a man without a country, an elder southern statesman who at war's end refused to return to his native land until he and others like him were exonerated of blame for the war in which they made such great sacrifices. He was symbol of the Old South, the Lost Cause, divided Kentucky, and of a people seeking understanding in a nation that seemed insensitive to their feelings.

Davis is at his best when he reviews and evaluates the man—"calm, methodical, cautious in forming his resolves, . . . and never giving in to emotional or 'rebellious' reactions" (p. 625), or when he offers more balanced judgments in criticism of his firm states' rights as "entirely out of touch with the needs and realities" of America at that time (p. 627). Sometimes the study is too detailed, especially in the accounts of the political phases of his career. Sometimes Davis is overly defensive of his subject. His appraisal of the personality of his subject is stronger than his analyses of his military actions.

Nevertheless, this is a first-rate biography—well written, well researched, and with good balance. Carefully and meticulously, Davis has woven the narrative of a Kentuckian through a turbulent life. This is a study of the human dimension in our history, of a person who endured in the face of calamity with dignity and courage, who emerged to continue a struggle for justice and honor. It is also more than biography—the story of Kentucky in the war period, the story of a state that attempted, as did its son John C. Breckinridge, to mediate in sectional disagreement only to fail and then suffer in the war that resulted.

Though some may contend that Davis may have placed his subject too high among the figures of prominent Americans of the past, few will take issue with the fact that at last John C. Breckinridge has found his biographer—and in the year in which Kentucky celebrated its own state bicentennial.

Wittenberg University ROBERT G. HARTJE

The Civil War: A Narrative. Red River to Appomattox. By Shelby Foote. (New York: Random House, c. 1974. Pp. [viii], 1106. $20.00.)

This is the third and concluding volume in a massive narrative history of the great sectional clash by Shelby Foote, a novelist who described his approach in the first volume. "Accepting the historian's standards without his paraphernalia, I have employed the novelist's methods without his license" (I, 815). Foote's account invites comparison with other recent multivolume histories of the war by Bruce Catton and Allan Nevins. Like Catton, Foote focuses upon the military events of the conflict but in greater detail and with more emphasis on the western campaigns, especially those in the Trans-Mississippi, than Catton or Nevins. Economic and social aspects of the war enter into Foote's narrative to a lesser extent, however, than in Nevins's. By emphasizing the attitudes of southern leaders and ignoring inflation and grass-roots peace movements, for example, Foote may overestimate the degree of unity behind the Confederate war effort in 1865.

Foote enlivens his wide-ranging narrative of both land and sea operations with colorful quotations and perceptive biographical sketches. The novelist displays his literary skill most clearly in descriptions of combat and especially in recounting the nightmare of the Bloody Angle at Spotsylvania. He explores with sensitivity the loss of comradeship and of historical significance experienced by some soldiers when the armies disbanded. In discussing disputes between generals, such as Kirby Smith and Richard Taylor, he usually strikes a reasonable balance. Yet a few debatable issues arise from his military account. Foote does not question the Confederate department system which fragmented command responsibilities and troop allocations in the West according to Thomas Connelly and Robert Kerby. Nor does Foote seem to share Connelly's doubt about the effectiveness of Confederate cavalry, which failed to disrupt Sherman's supply lines in 1864. No mention is made of the unnecessarily slow pace set by Sterling Price during his Missouri raid, which allowed Union pursuit to overtake and defeat his cavalry force. Occasionally, minor factual lapses occur, such as attributing the massacre of black troops at Poison Spring solely to the Indians in the Confederate command. Nevertheless, these points do not detract significantly from the military narrative, which seems destined for considerable acclaim.

When Foote turns to political affairs his grasp seems less sure, and he appears largely unaware of the revisionist studies of recent years. The term "Jacobins" is employed frequently to describe the Radical Republicans, although historians for over a decade have warned against such comparisons with the French Revolution. Foote makes no distinction between Sumner's state-suicide theory and the Wade-Davis bill as does Herman Belz. After Lincoln's last speech on Reconstruction policy Foote mentions only Radicals as having doubts about the President's position, ignoring several others who felt more hopeful of compromise and party unity. The trial of Henry Wirtz is criticized with little reference to conditions in Andersonville which led Ovid Futch to more subtle judgments in his thorough study of the prison and its commander. Looking ahead to Reconstruction, Foote sees only Republican corruption and greed, despite the critical studies of ex-Confederate Redeemers. Throughout Foote relies upon Hudson Strode's highly favorable biography to present Jefferson Davis as a tragic hero without many of the flaws attributed to him by other historians. Emphasizing Davis's unrepentant postwar career, Foote closes upon a different note from Nevins, who ends with a sense of hopeful nationalism. Thus, we glimpse again the differing life-styles and ideologies which led to the conflict.

Despite these limitations of the nonmilitary aspects of the volume, the more extensive military portions of this imposing narrative appear capable of standing well the tests of time and rereading.

Texas Tech University ALWYN BARR

A Compromise of Principle: Congressional Republicans and Reconstruction 1863–1869. By Michael Les Benedict. (New York: W. W. Norton and Co., c. 1974. Pp. 493. $18.95.)

This is an important book. In part it is a work of synthesis as Benedict effectively utilizes recent scholarship and agrees with historians such as Trefousse, Hyman, Kutler, Cruden, Belz, the Coxes, and numerous others "that 'Radical Reconstruction' was not very radical after all" (p. 13). In addition, most of the material contained in Benedict's earlier, innovative monograph, *The Impeachment and Trial of Andrew Johnson* (1973), is also utilized here. If, as Benedict argues, the Republicans impeached Johnson out of political necessity, why then was the President acquitted? Most important, perhaps, was the fact that by the time the Senate voted on impeachment, "impeachment had succeeded in its primary goal: to safeguard Reconstruction from presidential obstruction" (p. 311). As the sense of crisis waned, differences in Republican ranks on financial questions, the tariff, and internal improvements made Johnson's continuation in office a few months longer more palatable to some Republicans than the prospect of having Benjamin F. Wade in the White House.

Beyond impeachment and historical synthesis, this book is an innovative study in its own right that intelligently applies a quantitative voting analysis of the Thirty-eighth to Fortieth Congresses to the question of defining (and clarifying) the problem of factionalism within the Republican party. Indeed, Benedict presents one of the stronger cases made thus far for a legitimately integrative historical method that effectively harnesses quantitative techniques to the substantive problems of political motivation and behavior. If anything, Benedict's utilization of quantitative techniques is too modest as he relegates important discussions of procedure and technique to overly brief footnotes and appendices.

To provide both an empirical context and methodological prolegomenon for his study, Benedict concentrates much of his quantitative analysis in the book's opening chapter. Here Benedict employs standard statistical routines such as Guttman attitudinal scalings and strength of factional cohesion indices to examine congressional alignments and provide a systematic answer to the very basic question: "Who were the radicals?" Once establishing a valid set of roll calls that distinguish alternative factional and ideological alignments in the legislature, Benedict proceeds to categorize "consistent" Republican factions in both the House and Senate, Thirty-eighth to Fortieth Congresses. From the roll-call scale analysis Benedict identifies a coherent group of consistent "radicals" (38 in the House, 11 in the Senate) in contrast to the more numerous "nonradical" Republicans, labeled "centrists" and "conservatives" (32 in the House, 20 in the Senate). Because shifting factional alignments were especially "fluid" in these Congresses Benedict is left with a relatively small yet distinct group of clearly identifiable Republicans (101 in all) who, in Benedict's words, remained "beacons in a sea of shifting allegiances" (p. 27). Employing the 101 congressmen as attitudinal archetypes of alternative Republican attitudes towards Reconstruction Benedict convincingly demonstrates that "The groups that supported radical legislation never made up 50 per cent of either house of Congress, constituted the majority of the Republicans only half of the time, and never controlled an overwhelming majority of the Republican votes" (p. 27).

In view of the extensive quantitative evidence that Benedict musters in his opening chapter it may be improper to ask for more. Yet it is perhaps not too unreasonable to ask why a collective biographical profile of congressional Republicans (or at least the 101) could not have been compiled and then correlated with legislative performance. More than anything else, scale analysis and cohesion indices represent an attempt to penetrate attitudes—attitudes that may become even more clearly defined when examined under the lens of systematic biography. Beyond providing additional information, collective biography has the added advantage of restoring individual focus to legislators. Like all quantitative techniques voting statistics establish valid, empirical criteria for classification and generalization. While not without its advantages, as Benedict's work clearly attests, statistical generalization tends to lose sight of individuals in the group. Once the categories, consistency ratios, and "high" cohesion indices are set up, individuals become locked in mathematical space with the result that significant *intra*-categorical variations and individual differentials are sometimes lost. Collective biography represents one technique capable of systematically penetrating through to the individual cases.

Fortunately, the lack of complementary statistical techniques is more than offset by the thoroughness with which Benedict has carefully mined the collected papers, diaries, letters, and manuscript collections of individual congressmen. Indeed, it is through the integration of sound quantitative analysis with "traditional" historical inquiry that the full import of *A Compromise of Principle* becomes realized. In sum, Benedict's work deserves the widest possible reading audience—both from the methodological and substantive points of view.

University of Connecticut RICHARD O. CURRY
HARRY S. STOUT

Louisiana Reconstructed, 1863–1877. By Joe Gray Taylor. (Baton Rouge: Louisiana State University Press, c. 1974. Pp. xiv, 552. $20.00.)

The revolution in Reconstruction historiography, which had its beginnings in the 1930s and is still in progress, has only haltingly displaced the traditional "Dunning School" state histories of Reconstruction. Joe Gray Taylor's volume supersedes those of John Rose Ficklen (1910) and Ella Lonn (1918), and also that of Willie M. Caskey (1938). The author modestly identifies his purpose as that of retelling the story in the light of the research and interpretations of the last third of a century without the prejudices of an earlier generation.

Taylor has succeeded admirably in fulfilling his promise, and more. Of the secondary accounts cited in his bibliography and footnotes, a large preponderance have appeared since the Caskey volume, including many dealing specifically with Louisiana. Taylor has not overlooked the implications for the Louisiana story of revisionist writings focused on the national scene. Understandably, there are a few significant studies that have escaped his attention, and some that have appeared too recently to be incorporated into his account. Primarily a lucid, well-written synthesis of old and new scholarship, the volume also incorporates the results of the author's own examination of a considerable range of primary sources. These include local newspapers, legislative records, a substantial number of family papers, church records, and selected parish tax-assessment rolls. Particularly good use is made of the Henry Clay Warmoth papers.

The author's approach is even-handed, recognizing the crucial role of dominant white racial attitudes and violence without either attempting to justify white behavior or indulging in contrite censure. For Louisianians interested in their past, this volume by a native southerner and longtime resident of the state should bury whatever remains of the old myths and distortions that long made "Black Reconstruction" an apparently compelling justification for racial injustice and sectional resentment. They will find conclusions that may shock the sensibilities of those reared on entrenched misconceptions. For example, Ben Butler as military commander of New Orleans was "more humane than severe" (p. 18); Democrats had at least equal responsibility with Radical Republicans for the state's debt of the mid-1870s; under Warmoth, the first carpetbag governor, taxes "were not extraordinarily high" (p. 208). Warmoth's hated successor and fellow carpetbagger, William Pitt Kellogg, merited credit for political and social reform legislation and for initiating fiscal responsibility but could not surmount the white fury aroused by the large (not dominant) place he gave to blacks in his administration.

There remain aspects of the Louisiana story during Reconstruction which are not adequately explored by monographic works or Taylor's own research. He has called attention to the need for a study of Louisiana scalawags. The topic could usefully be enlarged to include all white racial accommodationists, beginning with the 1863 Free State men. Thirty years after T. Harry Williams's discovery of the Unification movement of 1873, it is surprising that so little has been done to pursue Williams's suggestion that the traditional picture of white attitudes during Reconstruction was in need of revision. A better understanding of the carpetbaggers, who figured so importantly in the state, would result from further research and a closer analysis than Taylor applies to their leaders. His characterization of the race attitudes of Warmoth and Kellogg may be accurate but is unconvincing on the basis of evidence presented. Other critical areas that invite more attention are black leadership, the black urban experience, and the manner in which Louisiana freedmen responded to emancipation. The need has been partly filled by studies published too recently for Taylor's consideration. The general outlines of economic change are well defined in his volume, but it is surprising to find still accepted without qualification Roger Shugg's questionable conclusion that the number of plantations increased dramatically in the 1860s and early 1870s. As cliometricians give increasing consideration to the post–Civil War decades, new insight and fresh controversies can be anticipated in explanation of the economy's failure to meet reasonable expectations.

Further researches will supplement rather than replace *Louisiana Reconstructed,* which should enjoy a long life as the standard account in its field. The volume will be indispensable for all who wish to make their way through the labyrinth of Reconstruction politics at the state level. It will also prove a useful introduction to nonpolitical aspects of the period, with two long chapters on the state's economy and another on social and cultural developments. The book is a worthy modern successor to the best of the Dunning studies.

Hunter College LaWanda Cox
City University of New York

Rich Harvest: A History of the Grange, 1867–1900. By D. Sven Nordin. (Jackson: University Press of Mississippi, c. 1974. Pp. x, 273. $12.00.)

Convinced that Solon J. Buck's classic *The Granger Movement* (1913) is both outdated and misleading, Sven Nordin attempts in *Rich Harvest* to put forward what he has elsewhere called "a revisionist interpretation" of the Patrons of Husbandry. Unlike Buck, Nordin focuses very narrowly upon the Grange alone and insists that it "was primarily a social and educational fraternity for farmers and their families rather than a medium for political and economic activities" (p. viii). The result is a massively researched, generally well written, very informative, but not altogether satisfying book.

Nordin's most interesting formulation is that there were actually two Granger movements. The first, the traditional subject of scholarly attention, centered in the West and South from about 1870 to 1880; the second Granger movement centered in the East and eastern Midwest from about 1880 to 1900. Easterners joined the Grange, Nordin maintains, to gain assistance in overcoming the competitive agricultural advantages enjoyed by Plains farmers, a frontier influence upon the Grange that Buck certainly neglected. Unfortunately, in examining Grange activities, Nordin does not differentiate between the two phases, thereby losing the analytical power he had found in the concept of two movements separated by time and region. Instead, he discusses general subjects common to *both* movements, such as basic social or educational concerns.

Thus, Nordin finds that prosaic, not protest, activities form the Grange's importance in rural history. He agrees with the recent historiographical de-emphasis of the role of the Grange in the passage of the "Granger laws," concluding that Patrons neither initiated nor dominated the movements for railroad regulation. In three very good chapters Nordin also impressively details Grange activity in educational matters, where Patrons significantly influenced institutions, curricula, and adult education. Socially, the Grange helped to break down traditional rural isolation and integrate farm communities.

Finally, however, Nordin is not fully persuasive. Declarations that social and educational activities were most important to Patrons are countered by observations that farmers regarded such a Grange as "sterile," for they sought an organization devoted to attacking monopolies and rural economic problems (pp. 129–31). Either most Grangers were not interested in Grange activities then or Nordin credits only some Patrons, defining away those who do not fit his "revisionist interpretation." Thus, Granger political activity is "illegitimate" (p. 175), and Patrons who favored protest actions "misunderstood the Grange's mission" (p. 122). Perhaps, had Nordin analyzed organizational developments and the changing social bases of Grange membership rather than describing routine activities, *Rich Harvest* might have provided more conclusive statements about the Grange and its mission. Ultimately, Nordin's work, though very suggestive, is as unbalanced as Buck's and can only complement not replace it.

University of Maryland Baltimore County — PETER H. ARGERSINGER

Progressivism in America: A Study of the Era from Theodore Roosevelt to Woodrow Wilson. By Arthur A. Ekirch, Jr. (New York: New Viewpoints, 1974. Pp. x, 308. Paper, $4.95; cloth, $10.00.)

Considering the number of studies on the "Progressive Era" which have appeared in the past twenty-five years, a synthesis of this material is in order. This is what Arthur A. Ekirch, Jr., attempts in *Progressivism in America*. Expanding on an idea he noted in *The Decline of American Liberalism* nearly twenty years ago, Professor Ekirch shows how the cross-fertilization of European and American liberal thought influenced the American reform impulse after 1900.

Ekirch sees the growth of a strong centralized national government in the United States as progressivism's response to problems created by industrialism at home and imperialism abroad. In the area of domestic reform, American progressives became convinced that by improving the environment in which people lived they could change human nature and create a utopian society. In their relations with other nations, the same conviction led them to support war as a means of creating a better world community. They seized upon the concept of strengthening American government as the means of achieving both ends.

Professor Ekirch finds that reformers on this side of the Atlantic were indebted to European liberals for many of their ideas. His investigation of the European roots of American progressivism begins with Darwinism. Especially important in the development of progressive thought was the concept of Reform Darwinism: once American intellectuals, influenced by the pragmatism of James and Dewey, accepted the premise that changing the environment could improve human nature, utopianism became practicable.

Ekirch contends that this utopianism enabled the American progressives gradually to turn "the Populist and Socialist ideas of the 1890's into an American version of state socialism or social democracy" (p. 34). American solutions for urban problems—the social-justice crusade, the movements for more efficient government and public ownership of utilities—evidenced strong ties between progressivism and European social democracy. The ideas of the socialists, often European in origin, introduced to the progressives the concept of the national state with its commissions and laws to regulate the economy and society. Both Democratic and Republican progressives, anxious to prevent socialism from gaining a place of major importance in American politics, adapted socialist ideas to their parties' programs and thus made centralization of power in the national government more acceptable to Americans.

The American public's acceptance of imperialism after 1900 offered further evidence of the intellectual interchange between American and European liberals. The ideas of A. T. Mahan and Elihu Root on naval and military policy, which bolstered the nationalist Progressives' tendency to centralize power in the state, culminated in Woodrow Wilson's shift to New Nationalism and his espousal of war as an instrument of international reform. Ekirch concludes that American progressives and European liberals erred in their belief that war was "the best way to institute social change . . ." (p. 274). While Wilson's determination to make World War I a crusade for democracy and a war to end wars marked the "apotheosis" of the progressive impulse, the American experience in the war brought about the "liquidation of the Progressive spirit" in the United States (p. 261).

Some historians will question Ekirch's conclusion that progressivism ended in 1918. Others may feel that he has slighted some groups who made significant contributions to progressivism, such as the Populists. Yet Ekirch's work is a substantial addition to the literature of the Progressive Era, and, as he observes, "A single book cannot do full justice to a movement so broad and diverse as American Progressivism" (p. x).

Old Dominion University D. ALAN HARRIS

The Papers of Woodrow Wilson. Edited by Arthur S. Link and others. Volume 15: *1903–1905*; Volume 16: *1905–1907*; Volume 17: *1907–1908*. (Princeton: Princeton University Press, 1973, 1973, 1974. Pp. xx, 608; xxii, 598; xxii, 647. $20.00; $20.00; $22.50.)

These three volumes in the continuing series under the general editorship of Professor Arthur S. Link cover the major part of Woodrow Wilson's service as the first lay president of Princeton University. They thus constitute without question the fullest and most useful body of source materials about this important but, until recently, comparatively little known period of Wilson's life. The documents brought together in these volumes amply demonstrate Wilson's significance as a major reform influence in American higher education, whose work changed Princeton from a complacent and rather undistinguished small Presbyterian college into a leading university. Although he was an acknowledged expert on public administration, Wilson began his presidency without any practical administrative experience or, it also seems clear, any well-defined educational philosophy. These volumes trace the development of both aspects of his innovative presidency of Princeton, with suggestive parallels to his later political career.

His apprenticeship year behind him, in 1903 Wilson began moving boldly to assert his leadership over all aspects of Princeton's affairs. He saw his role, as he told Thomas Nelson Page, as lying "midway between the autocratic presidency and the presidency which is a mere chairmanship of the Faculty" (June 24, 1904, Volume 15, p. 393). Taking advantage of his early honeymoon support, he shrewdly undercut the powerful and tradition-minded Curriculum Committee of the Board of Trustees by insisting that the appointment of new faculty members must in effect be lodged in his and the faculty's hands. There must be no repetition of his disappointment of the early nineties when the Board vetoed his efforts to recruit historian Frederick Jackson Turner because of his Unitarian faith. Determined to upgrade the quality of the faculty, Wilson dismissed the erratic but popular Arnold Guyot Cameron, holder of a named professorship in French, in what proved to be the most difficult and divisive act of his early presidency. For the first time he organized the faculty into eleven departments and four larger discipline-related divisions, thereby ending Princeton's previously haphazard and chaotic administrative structure. As chairman of the faculty Committee on the Course of Study, in 1903–1904 he pushed through a major overhaul of the undergraduate curriculum, intended like his reorganization of the faculty to bring about a much greater coordination and integration of undergraduate studies by, among other things, cutting down on the number of elective courses and requiring upper-class students to concentrate their work in a major department. Wilson was by no means the only critic of the currently popular free-elective system pioneered by Harvard in the last third of the nineteenth century, but under his leadership Princeton was one of the first universities to design a new curriculum aiming to correct its weaknesses.

Another significant educational reform of these years was the introduction of the preceptorial system, a Princeton version of the Oxford tutorial system. The plan called for adding half again as many faculty, in the form of a corps of enthusiastic and dedicated young scholar-teachers appointed on a rotating basis for limited terms, so as to provide closer contact between students and faculty in small classes and individual discussion. The obvious limiting factor was the high cost of such instruction, which Wilson surmounted by organizing the first systematic and broadly based fund raising drive among the alumni and friends of the university. He then scoured the country for fifty of the ablest young preceptors he could find, whose lively presence became a hallmark of the Wilson administration and revitalized the intellectual life of the campus. Wilson was determined to improve the physical plant as well as the academic program of the university, and accordingly spent considerable time in planning for needed new facilities. One of his most controversial schemes was his proposal in 1906–1907 for the construction of residential quadrangles which would create a sense of community and, incidentally, do away with the snobbish traditional upper-class eating clubs. The quadrangle plan immediately stirred up heated opposition from the outraged alumni of the eating clubs, leading the trustees eventually to withdraw their support and a chastened and humiliated Wilson to begin, though not complete, a shorthand draft of a letter of resignation. At the same time, the beginnings of his protracted dispute with Dean Andrew F. West over the nature and location of the proposed new Graduate School signaled that his last years at Princeton would be marred by mounting contention and frustration.

Apart from the richly detailed mosaic of academic life during one of Princeton's most eventful periods revealed in these volumes, there is also much new material on Wilson's health and personal life and his growing involvement in Democratic politics. In the spring of 1904 Mrs. Wilson and their daughter Jessie spent two months in Europe, and as usual during such separations the frequent long letters between husband and wife provide extensive coverage of day-to-day events, including interesting comments on the medical treatment prescribed after Jessie contracted diphtheria while in Italy. Wilson's own health problems (a serious stroke in May, 1906, and a lesser one late the following year, a hernia operation, and difficulties with phlebitis and arteriosclerosis) provide additional insights into the nature of medical care at this time. During these years Wilson's high visibility and generally conservative political views attracted the interest of Democratic politicians at both the state and national level, who saw him as a possible means of countering the continuing hold of William Jennings Bryan on the party leadership. Wilson, it now seems clear, took these early political overtures more seriously than we have hitherto assumed. He went so far as to prepare a Credo outlining his political views for a small group of New York Democrats presumably considering him as a 1908 presidential prospect, which stressed individual liberty and declared flatly that "the government should not undertake the direct supervision and regulation of business" (August 6, 1907, Volume 17, p. 337).

These volumes continue the high editorial standards established at the outset of this project: exhaustive research, scrupulous accuracy, and helpful but not obtrusive editorial notes, some of which are virtually small scholarly articles. Professor Link and his associates deserve high praise for this major scholarly undertaking. We await future volumes on Wilson's national service with mounting interest and anticipation.

University of Wisconsin, Madison E. DAVID CRONON

Education and the American Indian: The Road to Self-Determination, 1928–1973. By Margaret Szasz. (Albuquerque: University of New Mexico Press, c. 1974. Pp. xx, 251. $10.00.)

Indian education was once viewed as "civilizing" the savages; it was replaced by a supposedly more sophisticated but hardly more sympathetic attempt to coerce Indians into total assimilation into the mainstream society. Finally came partial recognition, aided by a now vocal and determined Indian minority, that Indians deserved a voice in, if not control of, their own education. Indian education is a complex subject and a delicate one, for it leads directly to some of the basic problems and controversies of our national life. Margaret Szasz has waded bravely into this tangled thicket to write a perceptive, well-balanced, and comprehensive analysis of American Indian education in the twentieth century.

The study begins with the famous Meriam Report of 1928, a product of a movement to reform the Indian Bureau that began soon after World War I, which is characterized by the author as "the symbol of definitive response to the failure of fifty years of assimilation policy" (p. 24). The following forty years were hectic ones, not only for the country, but for its Indians and for Indian education as well. The first commissioner of the bureau to respond to the recommendations of the Meriam Report was Charles J. Rhoades, appointed by President Hoover in the spring of 1929. But with the onset of the Depression and the election of Franklin D. Roosevelt to the Presidency action and new directions were the order of the day for the country and for Indians. John Collier, a charismatic reformer, was quickly appointed commissioner of Indian affairs, a position he held until 1945. Not surprisingly, the most interesting chapters in this book deal with this era, the plans that were made, the programs that were initiated, and the successes and failures of Collier and his dynamic education director, Willard Walcott Beatty.

The second half of *Education and the American Indian* deals with World War II and the postwar years. This is a complex period in Indian education and so close to the present that our perspective is apt to be distorted, but Dr. Szasz manages to carry the story with aplomb through the Kennedy Report of 1969 and on to the passage of the Indian Education Act of 1972 in an epilogue. The book, then, is oddly open ended, perhaps as it should be. Indian education has, in considerable measure, failed, but the struggle is ongoing, and success may lie in the future.

To relate the history of Indian education in the United States is to weave together the many strands that have affected it—shifting public attitudes, varying economic conditions, moods of Congress, inertia of an old bureaucracy, the abilities of commissioners of Indian affairs and their directors of education, to mention a few. On the one hand, such a recitation and analysis is apt to be descriptively ponderous, on the other, passionately partisan. While there are arid stretches in this volume, a tremendous quantity of data has been distilled effectively and with economy. That this is done with considerable detachment is remarkable, particularly as many of the people who are central to this history excite high feelings.

Texas Memorial Museum W. W. NEWCOMB

The Making of the TVA. By Arthur E. Morgan. (Buffalo: Prometheus Books; London: Pemberton Books, 1974. Pp. xvi, 205. $10.95.)

The Making of the TVA is Arthur E. Morgan's defense of his record as the Tennessee Valley Authority's first board chairman. Morgan wrote that the goals and purposes of the TVA were "exactly in line with my interests and experience and with my boyhood dreams of what I hoped would be my career" (p. 4). Morgan indicates that his goals were quite similar to those of President Roosevelt—that is, the upgrading of the quality of life of the people in the Tennessee River Basin. The physical transformation of the river by the construction of numerous dams, locks, and powerhouses was only a means to an end for Morgan. His real interest was in reordering society in the valley. Unfortunately, Morgan's altruism was not matched by an equal amount of political realism. His unwillingness to accept the real world of political give-and-take led to his dismissal as chairman.

Morgan has reassembled the much-aired arguments of 1938 when a joint committee of Congress found for Morgan's colleagues Harcourt A. Morgan and David E. Lilienthal. Although H. A. Morgan and Lilienthal are both severely criticized for their positions, stances which A. E. Morgan believed were not in the best interest of the TVA, it is Lilienthal who is clearly the villain. At one place or another Lilienthal is charged with trying to discredit Chairman A. E. Morgan (pp. 27, 35, 137, 168-69), with violating the no-patronage provision of the TVA Act (p. 30), with opposing President Roosevelt's program for the valley (pp. 56–57, 154–55), with protecting the interests of Alcoa at the expense of TVA (pp. 108–11), with calling board meetings without notifying Chairman Morgan, with lying to the President about A. E. Morgan's vacations (p. 115), with not informing Chairman Morgan of the developing power policy under Lilienthal's direction (p. 144), with giving primary emphasis to power development instead of navigation and flood control (p. 146), and with numerous other serious actions. According to A. E. Morgan, Lilienthal convinced the President and Senator George Norris that he (A. E. Morgan) "had gone over to the power boys, hook, line, and sinker" (p. 169). This was the reason for A. E. Morgan's dismissal by Roosevelt, argues the former chairman.

Morgan's case against Lilienthal is not convincing. The book had to be written though, for Chairman Morgan believed that the investigation of the board fight by a congressional committee in the summer of 1938 was not an objective hearing. The book was intended to serve the purpose of righting the historical record.

The book is interesting and will be a useful primary source for later analyses of TVA's history. Scholars will take exception to Morgan's use of asterisks instead of numbers for footnoting. Also, a properly placed bibliography would add to the book's value. The lengthy quotations tend to divert the reader's attention and encourage skimming. Morgan, now in his ninety-seventh year, must be admired for his contribution to the history of TVA.

Texas Woman's University WILMON H. DROZE

The Wild Man from Sugar Creek: The Political Career of Eugene Talmadge. By William Anderson. (Baton Rouge: Louisiana State University Press, c. 1975. Pp. xx, 268. $11.95.)

Discussion of the political career of Eugene Talmadge usually has centered on his irascible temperament and demagogic tendencies. He was often viewed in the press as an example of the worst in southern politics and a threat to democratic processes. Studies of the man and his era have lacked objectivity—a tendency encouraged by his spectacular political and administrative style. The usual recollection is of snapping red galluses, juice-spitting "wool hat boys," and an emphasis on personalities over issues, all of which were true to the form of Georgia politics in his day. Thus, it has been relatively easy to describe Talmadge and to exhibit approval or dismay, but efforts to understand the consequences of his actions have been lacking.

William Anderson vividly portrays Talmadge's actions, but he also presents Talmadge as the means by which Georgians moved from rural isolation and provincialism to the point where its people could more easily accept the world they confronted after 1945. Talmadge's efforts to hold down government expenditures and to preserve the "old way" and his belief in the independence of the "poor dirt farmer" and white supremacy gave Georgians a sense of holding onto their past and defying the outside world. But the Great Depression and World War II made change inevitable. What Talmadge provided was the satisfaction that voting for and supporting him meant being true to Georgia. After paying this homage, however, Georgians went on to vote for Franklin D. Roosevelt and, through necessity or desire, to accept change.

The focal point of Talmadge's politics after 1936 was opposition to the New Deal, which he saw as a threat to southern economic, social, and political values. He considered F.D.R. an "extreme radical" and sought to generate "grass-roots" opposition to increased federal power. Closely tied to this was Talmadge's ambition to gain a Senate seat and possibly to run for President. In the end, however, his bids for higher office proved abortive and demonstrated the willingness of Georgians to have Talmadge in the governor's mansion for their emotional needs while they supported men of a different quality for national offices. Talmadge was forced to accept these limitations and died shortly after winning his fourth campaign for governor in 1946. Between 1926 and his death Talmadge had served three terms as agriculture commissioner and three as governor. Few of his genre were more colorful or successful.

Anderson has clearly illustrated the Janus-faced nature of Georgia politics in the Talmadge era. Voters and leaders sought to retain their traditions while knowing that a future of greater responsibility, maturity, and physical comforts beckoned them. They opposed the increased power of the federal government, while they, including Talmadge, welcomed its largess. This condition was not limited to Georgia, but it was epitomized by Talmadge.

The absence of a major collection of Talmadge papers required the development of oral sources. Anderson has discriminatingly created these and carefully traced the changing nature of Talmadge's press support. The spirit of the man, the place, and his times exists in this successful political biography which presents a balanced view of Talmadge and his contributions to Georgia.

Guilford College ALEXANDER R. STOESEN

Antebellum Athens and Clarke County, Georgia. By Ernest C. Hynds. (Athens, Ga.: University of Georgia Press, c. 1974. Pp. viii, 200. $7.50.)

For Athens and surrounding Clarke County growth was steady but slow from the county's official founding in December 1801 through the 1820s. Development accelerated in the 1830s and peaked in the 1840s and 1850s, only to be stifled by growing sectional controversy and, finally, war. Agriculture was always the dominant occupation, but there was also considerable economic diversity in the county, with a number of manufacturing establishments emerging in the late 1820s and early 1830s. After 1841 a railroad served as a key economic stimulus.

Professor Hynds places a great deal of emphasis on the role of the University of Georgia in the development of the area. Athens, destined to become the county's largest city, was founded in 1801 concurrent with the choice of a site for the institution. The growth of this city and the county as a whole fluctuated in almost direct correlation with that of the university. This, in turn, was dependent upon such interrelated factors as legislative funding of the institution, the quality of leadership by university administrators, and general economic conditions.

The author, associate professor of journalism at the University of Georgia, has given us a book that is not without merit. The chapter on newspapers and periodicals and another one on "How the People Lived" are both interesting. These and other chapters are based upon considerable research in a variety of primary sources. Newspapers, court and tax records, and federal census returns have all been used extensively, and a few personal papers are cited. But it is in the area of secondary studies that this volume falls far short.

This monograph makes constant mention of potentially interesting topics. Agricultural and industrial slavery, the Second Party System, trends in education and other intellectual developments, manufacturing, experimentation in agriculture, sectional controversy, and general urban trends are among the many areas discussed. But even when allowances are made for this being a study of local history, any monograph dealing with the antebellum South that discusses such important subjects without any reference to such scholars as (to mention only a few) Stampp, Elkins, Starobin, Dew, McCormick, Eaton, Mitchell, Gray, Nichols, Freehling, Potter, or Wade continually frustrates the reader.

Because of the total lack of perspective, one must ask the inevitable: Who would benefit from reading such a book? It might prove to be an interesting footnote to the student of higher education, or even of urban development, in the Old South, but it is more probable that its use will be limited to those with only an antiquarian interest in Athens and the surrounding area. To know that one A. Brydie advertised for sale in 1834 "one of the biggest cakes ever made in the area" (p. 30) or to read a 290-word footnote debating in which tavern a meeting was held (p. 136) may be important information for a few readers, but not, I suspect, for most students of southern history.

Greenhill School JAMES P. HENDRIX, JR.

Southern Methodist University: Founding and Early Years. By Mary Martha Hosford Thomas. (Dallas: Southern Methodist University Press, c. 1974. Pp. xii, 224. $12.50.)

The ancient adage about not judging a book by its covers holds true in the case of *Southern Methodist University: Founding and Early Years.* Written by an SMU graduate as a Ph.D. dissertation (Emory University, 1971), this book was published by SMU. The situation was ideal for a gloss job, a nostalgic recalling of good old school days conducted by wise and all-knowing professors. Such books are tragically common in the history of higher education in the United States. On the other hand, Dr. Thomas's account is not an exposé, a muckraking enterprise revealing the "real" history of SMU.

Fortunately, she chose the middle way, praising and condemning in about equal parts. Her bibliography is very complete. She utilized Methodist church, school, and private records in telling the SMU story. It is a tale with a certain fascination, of how a group of men, both lay and clerical (the honor of the founding is the subject of a certain historiographic dispute), planned to move Southwestern University from Georgetown, Texas, to Dallas. The result was that Southwestern remained in central Texas, and a new school was established in north Dallas.

From the first the school and Dallas were bound together by financial ties and the desire for a first-class academic institution. As Thomas observes, this arrangement was both a strength and weakness of the new school. In her chapters one can find detailed information on the development of faculty and programs, often with a sharp observation or two. For example, she is quite critical of how SMU dealt with Henry Nash Smith, probably the best-known scholar ever to teach at the school, when he was unfairly attacked by the chairman of the Department of English. In addition, the football program drew some criticism from Dr. Thomas. The coach made $12,000 a year during the Depression, while the average faculty wage was $1,500. At the same time the Hilltop had a reputation as a "playboy" school, which Dr. Thomas believes was well founded. The situation changed because of Umphrey Lee's presidency, starting in 1939, and World War II. Of course, Dallas changed as a result of the war, and in time SMU followed.

For all its merits, and the book has many, a few mild criticisms must be noted. Given that the text is only 170 pages long, the narrative might have included Lee's presidency, which ended in 1954 when Willis Tate became president. And aside from a few observations about football, she ignores intercollegiate athletics in her text, a most tragic omission. She doesn't give the reason or the origin of why SMU teams are called the Mustangs! Shame!

These flaws however are not fatal. For anyone interested in the history of higher education, Professor Thomas has contributed a valuable study.

North Texas State University DONALD K. PICKENS

Two Hundred Years of Pharmacy in Mississippi. By Leslie Caine Campbell. (Jackson: University Press of Mississippi, c. 1974. Pp. xvi, 207. $10.00.)

The history of pharmacy in Mississippi is here revealed chiefly through the activities of the state's longest lived professional pharmacists' organization, the Mississippi State Pharmaceutical Association (MSPA). This work is basically a study of the MSPA's activities over the last one hundred years. The author does a worthwhile job in his treatment of this organization but betrays the expectations created in the book's title.

Chapter One, twenty-eight pages, gives us our entire view of the first one hundred years. For this period the book offers only a brief commentary on Indian herbal medicine and general conclusions about health problems and medical legislation in the state. This chapter draws on many of the standard studies of antebellum medicine in the South. The author should have considered beginning his study with 1871. The first hundred years really don't seem to merit a chapter.

With the founding of the MSPA in 1871 Campbell finds his handle and the source for his research. His decision to narrow his view to that of the MSPA results in limitations, but Campbell exercises judicious care in dealing with highly internal sources.

The author follows pharmacy through the MSPA within four roughly equal time periods. Problems and advances in education, commercial interests, public-health roles, relationships between pharmacy and the medical profession, public relations, legislation, and regulation of the field of pharmacy are considered for each period. Within this topical-chronological treatment are sketches of several individuals important to the MSPA and especially to pharmacy education since 1871.

Campbell should be credited for his ability to judge the motives behind the founding, organization, and work of the MSPA. There is no reluctance to admit the primacy of commercial instincts. Disputes with the grocer who sold patent medicines and with the physician who dispensed his own drugs are well revealed and honestly interpreted. Recognition, however, is justly given to the important role played by the MSPA in the advancement of pharmacy education and licensing within the state.

The author does a creditable job of weaving the profession's concerns and activities into the wider pattern of social, political, and economic trends in the nation and in Mississippi. An extensive and well-organized bibliography provides institutional and professional sources for Mississippi pharmacy as well as references to standard secondary sources and public documents relating to southern medical and pharmaceutical history. More illuminating insights might have resulted from a wider employment of these excellent sources.

Georgia Southwestern College CHARLES STEPHEN GURR

The Bible Belt Mystique. By C. Dwight Dorough. (Philadelphia: Westminster Press, c. 1974. Pp. 217. $7.95.)

This is a study of religion in the American South, but it also treats a number of figures and movements not particularly identified with the region—including Billy Graham, Oral Roberts, Marjoe Gortner, Aimee Semple McPherson, Asa Alonso Allen, the Jesus People, and modern faith healers. Four chapters deal primarily with the contemporary scene, and six with pre–Civil War rural antecedents. Urban influences are slighted, however, and the last half of the nineteenth century is virtually ignored. Near the end Dorough concisely states several conclusions and conjectures: He believes that southern Protestantism has helped spawn or strengthen a rugged individualism, a preoccupation with moralism, a special attachment for place, land, and family, "*a syndrome of violence*" (p. 196), a fervent commitment to white supremacy, and a general resistance to social change.

Dorough is at his best in portraying frontier revivalism, though he says little on the topic that has not been told already by William Warren Sweet, Walter B. Posey, Charles A. Johnson, and others. Throughout early chapters he fails to draw adequate distinctions between manifestations that were characteristic of the frontier and the West generally and those that were peculiarly (or primarily) southern; and in later chapters there is no adequate differentiation between attitudes and traits that relate to twentieth-century evangelical Protestantism generally and those that pertain particularly to Protestants in the South.

It is true that *Bible Belt Mystique* is not offered as a major original contribution, and the volume will undoubtedly appeal to many general readers. Scholars too will be interested in some of the material, particularly the author's personal insights and reminiscences about religion in the vicinity of Bonham, Texas, during his youth. Yet Dorough is right in anticipating annoyance on the part of that reviewer who "reads the notes first" (p. 15). Among a total of 258 notes, not one reference appears to the works of Rufus B. Spain, David E. Harrell, Jr., Samuel S. Hill, Jr., John L. Eighmy, Ernest T. Thompson, John B. Boles, or Ernest R. Sandeen, and there is otherwise no indication that the distinguished contributions of these writers were consulted or utilized in any way. This is distressing, even in an account directed toward a nonscholarly readership.

University of Texas, El Paso KENNETH K. BAILEY

Mark Twain & the South. By Arthur G. Pettit. ([Lexington]: University Press of Kentucky, c. 1974. Pp. [x], 224. $9.75.)

Books about Mark Twain are rarely dull, and this one is no exception. An intriguing essay worthy of the attention of historians, *Mark Twain & the South* contains a good deal of new information, especially about Twain's relationship with and attitude toward blacks. The only black person Clemens knew well was George Griffin, an ex-slave who served him as a butler for eighteen years and whose antics could put those of Nigger Jim to shame. One might argue, although Pettit does not, that Clemens based his fictional treatment of southern blacks on limited evidence. Nevertheless, Pettit does show clearly that Clemens "began his career as a segregationist, turned himself into a champion of interracial brotherhood, and ended his life as a prophet of racial war" (p. 9). Toward the end of his life, when letters from black beggars were received sympathetically while those from white beggars caused him to lapse into profane outbursts, his wife Livy suggested a "dern good" motto for him to follow: "Consider every man colored till he is proved white" (p. 127).

Southern whites are not ignored in this study, but they are scarcely given equal time. For Twain, most were bigoted, crude, ignorant, superstitious, immoral, and prone to violence. Even the higher types, such as Aunt Polly and the Widow Douglas, were locked into an immoral social structure dominated by the evil of slavery. Not miscegenation itself but the curse white southerners placed upon it was tragic, according to Twain, who believed that dark skin was more attractive than white. In an unpublished manuscript written during the most cynical last dozen years of his life, when Twain had become convinced that it would have been better if Noah had missed the boat, he created the mulatto superhero Jasper as the epitome of the white man's Satan and symbol of the eventual destruction of the white race. Such graphic proof that the South fought the Civil War for a foolish reason, according to Pettit, might have been the elderly Twain's final vindication of the young Clemens who deserted the Confederacy.

The value of this brief and excellent study for historians might have been increased if the author had given a more extensive analysis of Twain's objectivity as a social critic of the South. Twain's opinions about the South were as ambivalent as his personality and border-state heritage, a stance of inconsistency that Pettit seems to feel aptly symbolizes the history of the South. If Pettit's case for Mark Twain as a precursor of southern writing of the twentieth century is to be taken seriously, his enlightening essay needs to be placed in a broader context of knowledge of southern history and compared to the works of southern novelists who plowed the same ground. Pettit is a historian who understands that the literature of a people is an important part of their history and a key to unlocking the mysteries of a civilization. He places myth, symbol, and fact in a continuum, at any point of which the scholar might penetrate in his quest for historical truth.

Valdosta State College E. STANLY GODBOLD, JR.

Book Notes

Documentary History of the First Federal Congress of the United States of America, March 4, 1789–March 3, 1791. Volume II: *Senate Executive Journal and Related Documents.* Edited by Linda Grant De Pauw and others. (Baltimore and London: Johns Hopkins University Press, c. 1974. Pp. xviii, 574. $22.50.) The meticulously edited and carefully annotated executive journal of the First Senate fills 134 pages and is supplemented by 344 pages of related documents which the Senate had before it in acting in its executive capacity. The major subjects to which the documents relate include a consular treaty with France, Indian treaties, commercial relations with Great Britain, tonnage on French vessels, United States prisoners in Algiers, and the northeast boundary dispute. The approval of the appointments to federal offices under the new government was a major task of the First Senate, and the editors have supplemented the journal record with a most useful biographical directory of all nominees for office, civil and military, sent by President Washington to the First Senate. This is the second of eighteen projected volumes in this valuable series. [NOBLE E. CUNNINGHAM, JR., University of Missouri, Columbia]

Essays on Urban America. By Robert F. Oaks, Bruce I. Ambacher, Richard G. Miller, and Richard C. Wade. Edited by Margaret Francine Morris and Elliott West with an introduction by Constance McLaughlin Green. *The Walter Prescott Webb Memorial Lectures,* IX. (Austin and London: University of Texas Press, c. 1975. Pp. 147. $7.00.) This volume contains an introduction; a lecture on "The City Under Military Occupation: Philadelphia, 1777–1778," by Robert F. Oaks; one on "Urban Response to Jacksonian Democracy: Philadelphia Democrats and the Bank War, 1832–1834," by Bruce I. Ambacher; one on "Fort Worth and the Progressive Era: The Movement for Charter Revision, 1899–1907," by Richard G. Miller; and one on "Historical Analogies and Public Policy: The Black and Immigrant Experience in Urban America," by Richard C. Wade.

Slavery and Race Relations in Latin America. Edited by Robert Brent Toplin. *Contributions in Afro-American and African Studies,* No. 17. (Westport, Conn., and London: Greenwood Press, 1974. Pp. xiv, 450. $17.95.) This is an anthology of fourteen essays and an introduction by the editor, who also contributes one of the essays. Five essays on Brazilian slavery and race relations are offered by Colin M. MacLachlan, Robert Conrad, Robert Brent Toplin, Florestan Fernandes, and Arthur F. Corwin. William F. Sater provides a chapter on Chile; David L. Chandler and Norman A. Meiklejohn, one each on New Granada; William F. Sharp, one on Colombia; John V. Lombardi and Winthrop R. Wright, one each on Venezuela; and Thomas G. Mathews, one on Puerto Rico. Franklin W. Knight writes on Cuba in the nineteenth century, and Marianne Masferrer and Carmela Mesa-Lago on integration in Cuba to the present time. The editor cautions that race has different meanings to Latin America, but most of the writers have a "revisionist" attitude regarding the better treatment of slaves as compared with North America and of the absence of color prejudice in Latin America. He notes that a careful examination of "the complex interrelationships between class and color bigotry that give racial prejudice its strength . . . may develop a more sophisticated understanding of the problem in today's Latin America" (p. 11).

Historical Atlas of Alabama. By Donald B. Dodd. Cartography by Borden D. Dent. (University, Ala.: University of Alabama Press, c. 1974. Pp. xvi, 160. $10.00.) This presents a series of maps in twelve sections, most of them presenting statistical material in graphic fashion. A very few are conventional historical maps. The topical maps cover total population, black population, cotton, industry, education, personal wealth, and transportation, focusing on 1860, 1900, 1930, and 1970. Brief narrative introductions precede the maps.

The Yeas and the Nays: Key Congressional Decisions, 1774–1945. By Albert Castel and Scott L. Gibson. (Kalamazoo, Mich.: New Issues Press, Institute of Public Affairs, Western Michigan University, c. 1975. Pp. [iv], viii, 177. Paper, $7.95.) This book attempts to cover the period prior to the first publication of the *Congressional Quarterly* in 1945. It is divided into ten chronologically organized chapters with information and voting analyses on a wide variety of topics ranging from the Northwest Ordinance to the Alien and Sedition Acts, the Tariff of Abominations, the Crittenden Compromise, and a host of others to the ratification of the United Nations Charter.

A Guide to the Microfilm Edition of the Mordecai Gist Papers. By Richard J. Cox. (Baltimore: Maryland Historical Society, [1975]. Pp. [vi], 26. Paper, $2.50.) This is a guide to over seven hundred documents in two rolls of microfilm, covering the years from 1774 to 1792 of Mordecai Gist (1742/43–1792), Revolutionary officer and nephew of Christopher Gist.

Manuscripts on Microfilm: A Checklist of the Holdings in the Manuscript Division. Compiled by Richard B. Bickel. (Washington: Library of Congress, 1975. Pp. [ii], 82. Paper, $1.15.) This will be a useful aid for those wishing to make use of the materials in the Manuscript Division. There are entries for 839 bodies of material. It does not provide descriptions of the collections, although it does include references to sources providing information.

A new title in the Kentucky Bicentennial Bookshelf is *Tobacco and Kentucky*. By W. F. Axton. (Lexington, Ky.: University Press of Kentucky, c. 1975. Pp. x, 149. $3.95.).

Historical News and Notices

THE ASSOCIATION

The forty-first annual meeting of the Southern Historical Association will be held November 12–15, 1975, in Washington, D. C., at the Shoreham Hotel. On Wednesday evening W. Frank Craven will address a general session on "The American Centennial Observance."

The annual business meeting of the Association will be held Thursday afternoon, with President Richard N. Current presiding. On that evening he will deliver his presidential address.

In addition to the meetings noted above, there will be forty regular sessions. Twenty will deal with southern history, two with general United States history, seven with European history, five with Latin American history, and two each with teaching, editing, and the historical profession in general.

PERSONALS

Alabama State University: William Morris named instructor.

University of Alabama, Birmingham: Dan Bjork appointed assistant professor.

University of Alabama, University: Grady McWhiney named chairman and appointed professor; Robert E. Johnson and John S. Pancake on leave for fall semester.

Allegheny College: Richard W. Turk on leave first term 1975–76 and Paul A. Knights second and third terms 1976.

American University: James A. Malloy, Jr., promoted to associate professor; Jean T. Joughin and Ira N. Klein on leave.

Arkansas Polytechnic College: Gene W. Boyett promoted to associate professor; Michael A. Link on leave.

Arkansas State University: Edgar O. Kirk has retired.

University of Arkansas, Monticello: William L. Shea promoted to assistant professor.

Auburn University: Richard Glen Eaves promoted to associate professor.

Austin Peay State University: Susie Coleman on leave.

Cameron University: Charles W. Smith named director of humanities; Ralph E. Blodgett promoted to associate professor.

Catholic University of America: Jon L. Wakelyn named associate dean for undergraduate programs, School of Arts and Sciences; Maxwell H. Bloomfield promoted to professor.

Columbus College: O. Burton Adams, John R. McCreary, and John S. Murzyn appointed associate professors; Benjamin F. Bailey has retired.

The Correspondence of James K. Polk: Wayne Cutler named editor; Herbert Weaver has retired.

Duke University: Peter H. Wood appointed associate professor and Joseph N. di Corcia and Alan A. Stone assistant professors; Joel Colton and Martin A. Miller on leave for academic year and John R. Alden for fall semester; Frances D. Acomb has retired, and John R. Alden will retire at end of fall semester.

Eastern Kentucky University: Bert M. Mutersbaugh promoted to associate professor.

Emory University: Dan T. Carter appointed Andrew W. Mellon Professor and David W. Robson visiting assistant professor; John T. Juricek on leave.

Fayetteville State University: Valerie O. Edmundson appointed instructor.

University of Florida: Elizabeth Hoffman on leave for academic year and William Woodruff for fall semester.

Fort Valley State College: Donnie D. Bellamy promoted to professor, Donald L. Grant to associate professor, and Eva D. Adams to assistant professor.

Francis Marion College: Hugh C. Bailey named academic vice-president.

Georgetown University: Thomas K. Ricks and John J. Witek appointed assistant professors.

Georgia College: Frank B. Vinson promoted to associate professor; Donald M. McKale on leave.

University of Georgia: Joyce Louise Erwin on leave for academic year and Phinizy Spalding from January to June.

Grambling State University: Louis C. Goodwin named dean of graduate studies and Minnie Thomas Bailey head of the Department of History and Philosophy; Lawrence E. Garner and James D. Henderson promoted to associate professor.

Guilford College: James F. Gifford, Jr., on leave 1975–76.

University of Houston: Patricia A. Lewis appointed assistant professor; John H. Hill has retired.

Howard University: Lorraine A. Williams named vice-president for academic affairs; Vincent Peloso promoted to associate professor; Thomas C. Holt on leave.

John Hope Papers: Alton Hornsby, Jr., named editor.

University of Kentucky: Eric H. Christianson and Ellen G. Friedman appointed instructors; Holman Hamilton has retired.

Madison College: Caroline T. Marshall promoted to professor.

University of Maryland, Eastern Shore: Graydon A. Turnstall, Jr., appointed lecturer; Glenn O. Nichols on leave.

Mississippi State University: Robert I. Willman appointed assistant professor; Charles D. Lowery and Jimmie G. Shoalmire promoted to associate professor.

Missouri Southern College: Robert Emmett Smith, Jr., named head of Department of Social Science.

University of Missouri, Columbia: Richard H. K. Vietor and Rachel Vorspan appointed assistant professors; Charles B. Dew, Konrad H. Jarausch, Paul C. Nagel, Charles G. Nauert, Jr., Robert E. Ruigh, Arvarh E. Strickland, and Selwyn K. Troen on leave for academic year and David P. Thelen for fall semester.

University of Missouri, Kansas City: Herman M. Hattaway on leave for fall semester.

Morehouse College: Harry W. Benjamin named director of Afro-American studies; Tyrone Thomas appointed instructor.

Northeastern Oklahoma State University: Maxwell O. White named dean of the College of Arts and Sciences, V. Lyle Haskins, director of the Social Sciences Division, and Rudia Halliburton, Jr., chairman of the History Department.

Oklahoma Baptist University: James W. Marcum promoted to professor.

University of Oklahoma: Thomas Flory and Jerome O. Steffen appointed assistant professors; Max L. Moorhead has retired.

Old Dominion University: Heinz K. Meier named dean of School of Arts and Letters and Norman H. Pollock department chairman; Carl Boyd and Frances Diamond appointed assistant professors.

Rice University: Leslie Fishbein appointed visiting assistant professor; Albert Van Helden promoted to associate professor.

St. Bernard College: Paul J. Zingg named chairman and appointed assistant professor.

Saint Louis University: John W. Bush named chairman; Edward Burger appointed instructor; Fredrick J. Dobney promoted to associate professor; William B. Faherty, Joseph A. McCallin, and Edward R. Vollmar on leave for one semester.

University of South Carolina: Leon F. Litwack appointed visiting professor for fall term and G. H. L. LeMay for spring term; Edward S. Cox, Walter B. Edgar, and Jessica K. Ehrlich appointed assistant professors; Robert B. Patterson and Hilel B. Salomon on leave for the academic year, Charles W. Coolidge and John Scott Wilson for fall term, and Thomas L. Connelly for spring term.

Southeast Missouri State University: Charles Clifton Bonwell and Robert H. Skelton promoted to associate professor.

Southern Methodist University: R. Hal Williams named chairman and appointed professor; H. Ray Buchanan and Donald L. Niewyk on leave.

Spring Hill College: Doniver A. Lund appointed visiting professor; Howard William Smith on leave.

Stephen F. Austin State University: William J. Brophy promoted to associate professor.

Stetson University: Gilbert L. Lycan has retired.

Sul Ross State University: Earl H. Elam named vice-president for academic affairs and E. James Hindman, chairman, History Department, and director, Division of Social Sciences.

Sweet Briar College: Gerald M. Berg appointed instructor; Michael D. Richards on leave; Lysbeth W. Muncy has retired.

Texas Christian University: Spencer C. Tucker promoted to associate professor; Frank T. Reuter has returned to full-time teaching; William Curtis Nunn has retired.

Texas Tech University: C. Alwyn Barr promoted to professor and Robert Hayes and Harry A. Jebsen, Jr., to associate professor; Benjamin H. Newcomb on leave for spring semester 1975.

University of Texas, Arlington: Glenn A. May, Gary D. Stark, and Ronald Suleski appointed assistant professors; Elliott West promoted to associate professor.

University of Texas, Austin: Guy Howard Miller named assistant dean of the College of Social and Behavioral Sciences; Philip L. White promoted to professor, Richard H. Pells and Thomas L. Philpott to associate professor, and Michal R. Belknap, Jay F. Lehnertz, Janet A. Meisel, and Burton Spivak to assistant professor; Brian P. Levack, Richard A. Ryerson, and Edward I. Steinhart on leave for academic year, and Richard H. Pells for spring semester.

Thomas More College: Mary Philip Trauth named chairman; Raymond G. Hebert appointed assistant professor.

Towson State College: Dean R. Esslinger and Mark I. Whitman promoted to professor and Edwin A. Hirschmann to associate professor; Jean A. Scarpaci on leave; John W. McCleary has retired.

Trinity University: Linda Biesele Hall appointed assistant professor; Roger B. McShane promoted to professor.

Vanderbilt University: Keith A. Davies appointed assistant professor; Douglas E. Leach on leave for academic year, Kermit L. Hall, Melvyn P. Leffler, and Forrestt A. Miller for fall semester, and J. León Helguera for spring semester.

University of Virginia: William H. Harbaugh named member of the Center for Advanced Study; David A. Shannon appointed Commonwealth Professor of History and Edward E. Younger Alumni Professor of History, Carl M. Brauer, Fred V. Carstensen, Charles W. McCurdy, and Sarah N. Stever assistant professors, and Clifford W. Haury instructor; Joseph C. Miller promoted to associate professor; Norman A. Graebner and H. C. Erik Midelfort on leave.

Wake Forest University: Richard L. Zuber named department chairman; Richard C. Barnett on leave spring semester.

Washington University: Derek M. Hirst appointed assistant professor; Richard H. Helmholz promoted to professor.

West Georgia College: Robert H. Claxton promoted to associate professor.

William Woods College: William T. Partin appointed associate professor.

DEATHS

William T. Jenkins, member of the Southern Historical Association and professor of history at Southeast Missouri State University, died December 27, 1974, at the age of fifty-six. A native of North Carolina, he received the B.A. degree from Birmingham-Southern College, the M.A. from Vanderbilt University, and his Ph.D. from the University of Georgia. He served in the Air Force during World War II. After teaching at Snead College, Shorter College, and Birmingham-Southern College, he joined the faculty at Southeast Missouri State University in 1966. He specialized in southern and Negro history. A study of antebellum Macon, Georgia, was in progress at the time of his death. A memorial scholarship fund in his honor has been established at Southeast Missouri State University. [HAROLD H. DUGGER]

Floyd Seyward Lear, professor emeritus of history at Rice University, died on May 25, 1975, in Houston at the age of seventy-nine. Born in New York, he received his bachelor's degree at Rochester and his master's and doctor's degrees at Harvard. He taught at Rice from 1925 until his retirement in 1974.

ANNOUNCEMENTS AND ACTIVITIES

The National Historical Publications Commission has been redesignated the National Historical Publications and Records Commission by a law signed by President Ford on December 22, 1974. Commission activities will now include projects pertaining to the collection and preservation of historical records, including those of state and local governments and those held by private organizations. Two representatives of the Society of American Archivists and two representatives of the American Association for State and Local History have been added to the Commission, and the authorized annual appropriation has been increased from $2 million to $4 million for fiscal years 1975 to 1979.

Grants for research at the Lyndon Baines Johnson Library are awarded annually by the Lyndon Baines Johnson Foundation. Interested persons may obtain further information from the Executive Director, Lyndon Baines Johnson Foundation, 2313 Red River, Austin, Texas 78705. Applications must be submitted by December 31 of each year. During 1975 the foundation awarded research grants to the following: Harold F. Bass, Jr., Vanderbilt University; Monroe Lee Billington, New Mexico State University; the Chinese Historical Society of America; Yogesh C. Halan, University of Delhi; Kenneth E. Hendrickson, Jr., Midwestern University; Carolyn Jeanette Martin, Indiana University; Charles W. Mitchell, Jr., Southwest Texas State University; Velva Jeanne Osborn, University of Iowa; Philip R. Rulon, Northern Arizona University; Peter K. Tergeist,

Free University of Berlin; and George E. Urch, University of Massachusetts.

The General L. Kemper Williams Prize for the best published work in Louisiana history has been awarded to Roger A. Fischer for his book, *The Segregation Struggle in Louisiana, 1862–1877*. The prize carries a $500 stipend and a commemorative plaque. The prize for the best manuscript on Louisiana history by an unpublished author was won by Robert E. Snyder for "Huey Long and the Cotton Holiday Plan of 1931." This prize carries a $200 stipend and a commemorative plaque. The competition is sponsored by the Historic New Orleans Collection in cooperation with the Louisiana Historical Association. Entries for the 1975 prizes must be submitted in triplicate by February 1, 1976, to the General L. Kemper Williams Prize Committee, c/o The Historical New Orleans Collection, 533 Royal Street, New Orleans, La. 70130.

The Stuart L. Bernath Prize of the Society for Historians of American Foreign Relations has been awarded jointly to Frank D. McCann, Jr., of the University of New Hampshire for *The Brazilian-American Alliance, 1937–1945* and to Stephen E. Pelz of the University of Massachusetts for *Race to Pearl Harbor: The Failure of the Second London Naval Conference and the Onset of World War II*. The prize of $500 is awarded annually for the best book on American foreign relations. Presses and authors are invited to submit works for the 1975 prize to Frank Merli, Department of History, Queens College, Flushing, New York 11367.

The 1974 E. Merton Coulter Award for the best article on Georgia history appearing in the *Georgia Historical Quarterly* has been awarded jointly to Edward J. Cashin of Augusta College for " 'The Famous Colonel Wells:' Factionalism in Revolutionary Georgia" and to Betty Wood of Girton College, Cambridge University, for "Thomas Stephens and the Introduction of Black Slavery in Georgia."

Professor Walter Rundell, Jr., of the University of Maryland has won the first annual Webb-Smith Essay Award given by the Department of History at the University of Texas at Arlington for his essay "Webb the Schoolteacher," which will be published as part of the tenth volume of the Walter Prescott Webb Memorial Lectures.

Competition for the second Webb-Smith Essay Award is now open. Entries should be essays of ten thousand words or less on the topic of European revolutionary history. For further information write the Webb Lectures Committee, Department of History, University of Texas at Arlington, Arlington, Texas 76019.

Robert Starobin Memorial Library Fellowships have been awarded to Randall M. Miller of St. Joseph's College, Bernard Fuller of the State University of New York at Binghamton, and Harvard Sitkoff of Washington University.

Dewey W. Grantham, Jr., of Vanderbilt University delivered Guilford College's annual Rembert W. Patrick history lecture on March 20, speaking on "Southern Progressives and the Racial Imperative."

Competition for the 1976 Jamestown Prize awarded annually by the Institute of Early American History and Culture is now open. Only authors who have not previously published a book are eligible. The subject of the manuscript must pertain to America before about 1815 or to the related history of the British Isles, Europe, or the Caribbean. In addition to the cash prize of $1,500, the winning manuscript will be published by the University of North Carolina Press in conjunction with the Institute of Early American History and Culture as part of the Institute's regular publication program.

Manuscripts may be submitted between April 15 and November 15, 1975. They should be mailed to the Editor of Publications, Institute of Early American History and Culture, Box 220, Williamsburg, Virginia 23185, and a letter should be sent separately indicating that the manuscript has been submitted. The manuscript must be a ribbon copy that is entirely double spaced, including quotations and footnotes. Footnotes should be collected at the end of the manuscript and organized by chapter. The manuscript may not be a contender for any other award while under consideration by the Institute Prize Committee.

The Prize Committee will complete preliminary judging within two months of the receipt of a manuscript, returning immediately those submissions not selected for the final round of competition. Authors of manuscripts with unusual promise will be notified that they are in the running for the prize and that final action will be delayed pending the closing of competition on November 15. The prize-winning manuscript will be chosen before February 28, 1976, and the presentation of the award will be made at the Institute Council meeting in May.

A Southern Labor History Conference is being formed to bring together trade unionists, academicians, history buffs, and others interested in the history of organized labor in the South. The organization will hold its first meeting at Georgia State University in the spring of 1976. To submit session proposals or to receive further information write Dr. David B. Gracy II, Archivist, Southern Labor Archives, Georgia State University, Atlanta, Georgia 30303.

The sixth Gulf Coast History and Humanities Conference will be held in Pensacola, Florida, on October 2–3, 1975, on "The Cultural Legacy of the Gulf Coast, 1870–1940." Charles Hosmer, Ellen Beasley, Walter Beinecke, James R. McGovern, and George Demmy will speak. For further information and copies of the proceedings of the previous conferences, write to Dr. Lucius F. Ellsworth, General Chairman, Gulf Coast History and Humanities Conference, John C. Pace Library, University of West Florida, Pensacola, Florida 32504.

The University of Mississippi will present a symposium October 1–3, 1975, entitled "The Slave Experience in America: A Bicentennial Perspective." The speakers will be John W. Blassingame, David B. Davis, Carl N. Degler, Stanley J. Engerman, Eugene D. Genovese, William K. Scarborough, and Kenneth M. Stampp.

The Association of Historians of Eastern North Carolina was founded in May 1974 to promote the study and teaching of history. Officers for 1975–1976 are William B. Still of East Carolina University, president; William R. Dempsey of Fayetteville State University, first vice-president; Jacqueline R. Heston of Rocky Mount Senior High School, second vice-president; and Vernon O. Stumpf of Campbell College, treasurer.

The Southwestern American Indian Society has been created and will be concerned with the study of Native Americans in North and Central America. It will publish the *American Indian Quarterly* under the editorship of William L. Turnbull. The annual membership dues are $7.00 plus an additional $0.50 for Pan Americans. Correspondence relating to editorial matters should be addressed to the editor at P. O. Box 443, Hurst, Texas 76053. Membership dues and correspondence on similar matters should be sent to Carolyn C. Howell at the same address.

The Missouri Valley History Conference will meet in Omaha, Nebraska, March 11–13, 1976. Proposals for papers or sessions dealing with all fields of history should be sent to Professor Tommy R. Thompson, Department of History, University of Nebraska at Omaha, Omaha, Nebraska 68101.

The University of Illinois Press, Urbana, Illinois 61801 has for complimentary distribution reprints of "A New Era for the United States: Americans and the War with Mexico," the inaugural lecture given by Robert W. Johannsen as the first James G. Randall Distinguished Professor of History at the University of Illinois.

A bicentennial conference celebrating the March 9, 1776, publication of Adam Smith's *Wealth of Nations* will be held at Eastern Kentucky University in the spring of 1976. Scholars in history, economics, philosophy, political science, and other fields touching on Adam Smith's writings are invited to submit proposals for papers by October 1, 1975. Those interested should write to Robert E. Stebbins, Department of History, Eastern Kentucky University, Richmond, Kentucky 40475.

Beginning with the academic year 1975–1976 the Department of History of Wright State University will offer as an optional component of its master of arts degree in history a program in archival and historical administration. For a brochure and details write: The Chairman, Department of History, Wright State University, Dayton, Ohio 45413.

LIBRARIES AND ARCHIVES

The National Archives has recently published a *Guide to Materials on Latin America in the National Archives of the United States,* which supersedes the earlier *Guide* published in 1961; *Historical Materials in the John F. Kennedy Library; Regulations for Public Use of Records in the National Archives and Records Service,* General Information Leaflet No. 2, Revised; *Select Audiovisual Records—Negro Art from the Harmon Foundation,* General Information Leaflet, Revised; *Select Audiovisual Records—Contemporary African Art from the Harmon Foundation,* General Information Leaflet, Revised; *Preliminary Inventory of Records Relating to International Claims,* Preliminary Inventory No. 177; *Preliminary Inventory of the Records of the Office of Education,* Preliminary Inventory No. 178; *Audiovisual Records in the National Archives of the United States Relating to World War II,* Reference Information Paper No. 70; *Cartographic Records in the National Archives of the United States Relating to American Indians,* Reference Information Paper No. 71; and *Inspection Reports on Foreign Service Posts, 1906–1939,* Special List No. 37.

Records recently microfilmed by the National Archives include M848, War of 1812 Military Bounty Land Warrants, 1815–1858; M891, The Records of the United States Nuernberg War Crimes Trials, Case 5, United States of America *v.* Friedrich Flick *et al.;* M967, Letters of Application and Recommendation During the Administrations of Franklin Pierce and James Buchanan, 1853–1861; M968, Letters of Application and Recommendation During the Administration of Ulysses S. Grant; M969, Law and Appellate Case Files of the U. S. Circuit Court for the Eastern District of Pennsylvania, 1790–1847; M983, Reports and Correspondence Relating to the Army Investigations of the Battle at Wounded Knee and the Sioux Campaign of 1890–91; and M984, Navy Department General Orders, 1863–1948.

The Harry S. Truman Library has accessioned the following groups of papers: the President's Secretary's file, including correspondence, memorandums, notes, speech drafts, reports, minutes of conferences, appointment books, maps, newspaper clippings, publications, and information on most of the significant issues that came to the attention of the White House during the Truman Presidency; records dating from Truman's service as presiding judge of Jackson County; a speech file from his years as a U. S. senator; post-presidential files, 1953–1971; records of the architectural firm of Neild-Somdal, Associates relating to the construction of the library during the 1950s; diary, 1947–48, of A. L. M. Wiggins kept during his years as undersecretary of the Treasury; papers, 1917–54, of Joseph M. Mehl, relating to his service in the Department of Agriculture; and an oral history interview with David L. Cole, director of the Federal Mediation and Conciliation Service, 1952–53.

The Lyndon Baines Johnson Library has recently accessioned the records of the Lower Colorado River Authority and the papers of Luther Holcomb, former vice-chairman of the Equal Employment Opportunity Commission.

The Southern Historical Collection of the University of North Carolina Library in Chapel Hill has received the papers of Sam J. Ervin, Jr., covering his twenty years in the U. S. Senate, and preparation of an inventory is now in progress. These papers include material on the Watergate hearings and his service on the Armed Service, Government Operations, and Judiciary committees and on the subcommittees on Revision and Codification of the Laws and on Constitutional Rights. Papers relating to his earlier careers as lawyer, judge, and member of the U. S. House of Representatives will be added later.

The Manuscript Division of the Maryland Historical Society has recently accessioned the following collections: the business records (1818–1964) of Robert Garrett & Sons, Inc., an investment banking firm, MS. 2089; the Edwin Warfield papers (1880–1918), relating to his career as governor of Maryland, 1904–1908, MS. 2098; Baltimore and Ohio Railroad papers (1862–1877) relating to the recovery of equipment in the South following the Civil War, MS. 2090; the Shriver family papers (ca. 1820–1900), relating primarily to James Shriver (1794–1826), a surveyor, MS. 2085.1; the Conway Robinson papers (1790–1930), relating primarily to Robinson, William Leigh, and the Colston and Dandridge families, MS. 2099; the Baxley-Minifie family papers (1789–1891), MS. 2097; business papers (1852–1863) of the Barreda Company, a guano distributor in Baltimore, MS. 2101; and thirty-two letters (1933–1950) between H. L. Mencken and Kemp Malone, professor of linguistics at Johns Hopkins University, MS. 2100. Also accessioned were records (1880–1930) of the Drovers and Mechanics National Bank of Baltimore; Marsh family papers (1790–1840); the Civil War papers of Governor Thomas H. Hicks; the diary (1892) of Walter I. Dawkins; Tyson family papers (1800–1890); McKim family papers (1850–1856); two account books (1761–1770, 1793–1823) of the Shriver family; manuscripts relating to Philip Tilyard, a Maryland artist; correspondence (1950–1973) to F. Millard Foard relating to Baltimore City College; and manuscripts (1702–1833) of the Carroll-Rogers families.

The South Carolina Department of Archives and History has recently microfilmed selected records of Union and Lancaster counties. These items may be purchased for $15.00 per roll. A list of items for sale is available from the Publications Division, South Carolina Department of Archives and History, P. O. Box 11669, Columbia, South Carolina 29211.

Recent accessions of the archives include selected records of the Cemetery Board, 1957–69; the Department of Corrections, 1933–56; the Secretary of State, including recorded instruments, 1935–73, internal management records, 1950–73, and corporation charters, 1900–73; and the General Assembly, including Acts and Joint Resolutions, 1967–72, House of Representatives Committee on the Judiciary, 1971–74, and House of Representatives Committee on Labor, Commerce, and Industry, 1969–73.

THE JOURNAL OF SOUTHERN HISTORY

NOVEMBER 1975
Vol. XLI, No. 4

Published Quarterly by the Southern Historical Association

The Journal of Southern History

Published Quarterly by

THE SOUTHERN HISTORICAL ASSOCIATION

New Orleans, Louisiana

Printed by WILLIAM BYRD PRESS, RICHMOND, VIRGINIA

The present constitution of the Southern Historical Association is printed in the February 1974 issue of the *Journal of Southern History*, Volume XL, Number 1.

Contributions and correspondence relating to articles, book reviews, and any other editorial matters should be sent to the Managing Editor, *Journal of Southern History*, Rice University, Houston, Texas 77001.

The subscription rate is $10.00 a year for a regular membership, $12.00 for family membership, $5.00 for enrolled student, and $3.00 for retired members. Upon payment of $200.00 any person may become a life member of the Southern Historical Association. Single numbers of the *Journal* are available at $3.00 plus postage. Changes of address must be made six weeks in advance of the publication of an issue in order for the change to be effective with that issue. A charge of $2.50 will be made for forwarding copies returned because of incorrect addresses.

Subscriptions, membership applications, and orders for current issues of the *Journal* should be sent to Bennett H. Wall, Secretary-Treasurer, History Department, Tulane University, New Orleans, Louisiana 70118. *Notice of nonreceipt of an issue must be sent to the Secretary-Treasurer within sixty days following publication of the issue.* Inquiries concerning noncurrent back issues of the *Journal* should be directed to Johnson Reprint Corporation, 111 Fifth Avenue, New York, New York 10003.

Second-class postage paid at New Orleans, Louisiana, and at additional mailing offices.

US-ISSN-0022-4642

The Journal of
SOUTHERN HISTORY

VOLUME XLI NOVEMBER 1975 NUMBER 4

Contents

Protestantism and Afro-Americans in the Old South: Another Look
By Kenneth K. Bailey 451

Using the Testimony of Ex-Slaves: Approaches and Problems *By John W. Blassingame* 473

Southern Mountain Republicans and the Negro, 1865–1900
By Gordon B. McKinney 493

Notes and Documents:

Jefferson Davis Ponders His Future, 1829
Edited by Lynda J. Lasswell 517

A Note on Evidence: The Personal History of Madison Hemings
By Dumas Malone and Steven H. Hochman 523

Book Reviews 529

Book Notes 583

Historical News and Notices 589

Index 601

Book Reviews

EATON, *A History of the Old South*, by William K. Scarborough 529
STERNSHER, *Consensus, Conflict, and American Historians*, by Arthur A. Ekirch, Jr. . . 530
SCHNORE, ed., *The New Urban History*, by Thomas L. Haskell 531
ENGERMAN and GENOVESE, eds., *Race and Slavery*, by Forrest G. Wood 533
VAUGHAN, *American Genesis*, by Don R. Byrnes 534
BILLINGS, ed., *The Old Dominion in the Seventeenth Century*, by J. Edwin Hendricks 535
PAPENFUSE, *In Pursuit of Profit*, by Frank A. Cassell 536
PALMER, *The Way of the Fox*, by John D. Hayes 538
REARDON, *Edmund Randolph*, by Patrick J. Furlong 539
CRAVEN, *Rachel of Old Louisiana*, by Sarah McCulloh Lemmon 540
WILTSE and MOSER, eds., *The Papers of Daniel Webster*, Vol. 1, by Norman D. Brown 541
SISSON, *The American Revolution of 1800*, by George B. Forgie 542
DARGO, *Jefferson's Louisiana*, by Edward Dumbauld 544
COVER, *Justice Accused*, by George M. Fredrickson 545
WILSON, *Space, Time, and Freedom*, by Robert E. Shalhope 547
WELTER, *The Mind of America, 1820–1860*, by William G. Shade 548
HEMPHILL, ed., *The Papers of John C. Calhoun*, Vol. VIII, by Harry Ammon ... 549
HOPKINS and HARGREAVES *et al.*, eds., *The Papers of Henry Clay*, Vol. 5, by Charles G. Sellers 550
ALVAREZ, *Travel on Southern Antebellum Railroads*, by Ralph B. Draughon, Jr. . . 552
CRENSON, *The Federal Machine*, by Edward Pessen 553
OATES, *The Fires of Jubilee*, by Wilbert H. Ahern 554
SATZ, *American Indian Policy*, by W. David Baird 555
TRENNERT, *Alternative to Extinction*, by W. Stitt Robinson 557
BROWN, *Edward Stanly*, by Paul H. Bergeron 558
WILEY, *Confederate Women*, by Mollie C. (Davis) Abernathy 559
FRASSANITO, *Gettysburg*, by Hal Bridges 560
JENKINS, *Britain & the War for the Union*, Vol. I, by Norman B. Ferris 561
COOK, *The Alabama Claims*, by Peter T. Sherrill 562
TREFOUSSE, *Impeachment of a President*, by Richard N. Current 563
DECANIO, *Agriculture in the Postbellum South*, by Ronald L. F. Davis 564
CORINA, *Trust in Tobacco*, by Elisha P. Douglass 566
REEVES, *Gentleman Boss*, by Martin E. Mantell 567
BILLINGTON, *The Political South in the Twentieth Century*, by Numan V. Bartley . . 568
WOLTERS, *The New Negro on Campus*, by August Meier 569
HOLMES, *The New Deal in Georgia*, by James A. Hodges 570
OSBORN, *John James Tigert*, by J. Isaac Copeland 571
TINDALL, *The Persistent Tradition in New South Politics*, by Paul D. Casdorph . . 573
PEIRCE, *The Border South States*, by Willard B. Gatewood, Jr. 574
PINKOWSKI, *Pills, Pen & Politics*, by Donald E. Everett 575
HAAS, *DeLesseps S. Morrison and the Image of Reform*, by Lyle W. Dorsett 576
KENNETT and ANDERSON, *The Gun in America*, by Otis K. Rice 577
FRY, *Night Riders in Black Folk History*, by Jimmie L. Franklin 578
MATHIAS, ed., *Incidents & Experiences in the Life of Thomas W. Parsons*, by George W. Knepper 579
MATHIS, ed., *"Uncle Tom" Reed's Memoir of the University of Georgia*, by W. Calvin Smith 580
CHURCH and CHURCH, *The Robert R. Churches of Memphis*, by Ronald L. Lewis . . 581

Protestantism and Afro-Americans in the Old South: Another Look

By Kenneth K. Bailey

Scholars who deal with southern Protestantism rarely minimize the involvements of the churches in racial discrimination, and this has been the main concern of several admirable studies. A recent book provides a detailed analysis of anti-Negro manifestations among white churchmen over a period of more than a century. In another volume wherein such tendencies are delineated in the Baptist denomination a perceptive author explains that investigations like his turn out to be "largely an examination of how the prevailing secular values gained confirmation from a denomination that lacked institutional leadership capable of independent judgment and action." Appropriately, his volume is entitled *Churches in Cultural Captivity.*[1]

[1] H. Shelton Smith, *In His Image, But . . . : Racism in Southern Religion, 1780–1910* (Durham, 1972); John L. Eighmy, *Churches in Cultural Captivity: A History of the Social Attitudes of Southern Baptists* (Knoxville, 1972), 20. Other studies that give attention to the southern churches and race relations include Samuel S. Hill, Jr., *Southern Churches in Crisis* (New York, Chicago, and San Francisco, 1966); Donald G. Mathews, *Slavery and Methodism: A Chapter in American Morality, 1780–1845* (Princeton, 1965); David M. Reimers, *White Protestantism and the Negro* (New York, 1965); Andrew E. Murray, *Presbyterians and the Negro—A History* (Philadelphia, 1966); Rufus B. Spain, *At Ease in Zion: Social History of Southern Baptists, 1865–1900* (Nashville, 1967); David E. Harrell, Jr., *Quest for a Christian America: The Disciples of Christ and American Society to 1866* (Nashville, 1966); Walter B. Posey, *Frontier Mission: A History of Religion West of the Southern Appalachians to 1861* (Lexington, 1966); Ernest T. Thompson, *Presbyterians in the South* (3 vols., Richmond, 1963–1973); Kenneth K. Bailey, *Southern White Protestantism in the Twentieth Century* (New York, Evanston, and London, 1964); Hugh G. Anderson, *Lutheranism in the Southeastern States, 1860–1886: A Social History* (The Hague, 1969); Lewis M. Purifoy, Jr., "The Methodist Episcopal Church, South, and Slavery, 1844–1865" (unpublished Ph.D. dissertation, University of North Carolina at Chapel Hill, 1965); Stiles B. Lines, "Slaves and Churchmen: The Work of the Episcopal Church Among Southern Negroes, 1830–1860" (unpublished Ph.D. dissertation, Columbia University, 1960); Robert O. Fife, "Alexander Campbell and the Christian Church in the Slavery Controversy" (unpublished Ph.D. dissertation, Indiana University, 1960). Professor W. Harrison Daniel has published more than a half-dozen able articles on blacks and the southern churches, including "Virginia Baptists and the Negro in the Early Republic," *Virginia Magazine of History and Biography*, LXXX (January 1972), 60–69; and "Southern Protestantism and the Negro, 1860–1865," *North Carolina Historical Review*, XLI (Summer 1964), 338–59.

Mr. Bailey is professor of history at the University of Texas at El Paso.

The Journal of Southern History
Vol. XLI, No. 4, November 1975

Assessments relating specifically to the churches and slavery have been severe almost without exception. It has been noted, for example, that churchmen in the region rarely protested laws which virtually mandated black illiteracy (notwithstanding a traditional emphasis on Scripture reading), that they rarely demanded religious privileges for slaves beyond what slaveowners voluntarily allowed, that they did not generally administer marriage vows to slaves, and that they did not press for restrictions of property rights so as to preclude the breaking up of slave families through sales. Taking such failings into account, several writers have unfavorably contrasted the impact of Protestantism upon slavery in the United States with the influences of the Roman Catholic church upon slavery in Latin America.[2]

Most historians would no doubt agree that racial discrimination ought to be studied in southern Protestantism and elsewhere and that it ought to be deplored. And there is no denying the reality of the offenses and derelictions usually recited, or their enormity, or the guilt. Yet it is also true that a preoccupation with great shortcomings easily depreciates ameliorative and fraternal tendencies that deserve continuing acknowledgment. The intent of this essay is to deal with these happier aspects and to argue that the southern churches were not so comfortably aligned with the racial mores of their region during the slavery era as now seems to be believed.

First of all, there is no doubt that the spiritual redemption of blacks was an earnest concern in all the major Protestant denominations. Ministering to slaves and free persons of color was the principal pursuit of several hundred southern white preachers in the generation preceding the Civil War and a part-time responsibility

Much of the research on which this article is based was accomplished during a fellowship appointment from the trustees of the John Simon Guggenheim Memorial Foundation, to whom the author makes grateful acknowledgment.

[2] Slavery in the United States is compared unfavorably with slavery in Catholic Latin America in Frank Tannenbaum, *Slave and Citizen: The Negro in the Americas* (New York, 1947), 82–103; Herbert S. Klein, *Slavery in the Americas: A Comparative Study of Virginia and Cuba* (Chicago, 1967), 86–126; Stanley M. Elkins, *Slavery: A Problem in American Institutional and Intellectual Life* (Chicago, 1959), 68–77; and Winthrop D. Jordan, *White over Black: American Attitudes Toward the Negro, 1550–1812* (Chapel Hill, 1968), 198–99. Such interpretations are persuasively challenged in David B. Davis, *The Problem of Slavery in Western Culture* (Ithaca, 1966), 252–53 and *passim;* and in Carl N. Degler, *Neither Black nor White: Slavery and Race Relations in Brazil and the United States* (New York, 1971), 33–39. See also Kenneth M. Stampp, "Rebels and Sambos: The Search for the Negro's Personality in Slavery," *Journal of Southern History,* XXXVII (August 1971), 371; and Robert W. Fogel and Stanley L. Engerman, *Time on the Cross: The Economics of American Negro Slavery* (Boston and Toronto, 1974; cited hereinafter as *Time on the Cross,* I). As W. Harrison Daniel has pointed out, southern Protestant groups did protest some of the civil handicaps of the blacks during the Civil War; Daniel, "Southern Protestantism and the Negro, 1860–1865," pp. 351–55.

of a much larger number who served biracial flocks. It was a cause with which such well-known figures as Paul Trapier (Episcopalian), John Lafayette Girardeau and Charles Colcock Jones (Presbyterians), Robert Ryland and William H. McIntosh (Baptists), and William Capers, James Osgood Andrew, and Holland Nimmons McTyeire (Methodists) were intimately associated, and a cause repeatedly espoused by the highest ecclesiastical councils, particularly the Southern Baptist Convention and the General Conference of the Methodist Episcopal Church, South. During sessions of these bodies, when the more celebrated clergymen in attendance were assigned to conduct worship from pulpits in the host city, all-black congregations were commonly among those chosen for a visit. Though social control was obviously an objective of religious as well as secular leaders, this motive does not adequately explain frequent idealizations of that white shepherd who was willing (in the words of Bishop Andrew) "to be looked down upon by the rich and great about him as *a negro preacher* . . . ." How better to flout the conceits and comforts of this world? How better to authenticate the purity of one's faith? As Lewis McCarroll Purifoy, Jr., has observed, "Nothing was so often mentioned in the biographical sketches of deceased ministers as their work among the colored people and the esteem in which they were held by their fellow ministers as well as by their colored congregations." In keeping with this emphasis, a monument at the grave of Bishop Capers memorialized the departed leader as "THE FOUNDER OF MISSIONS TO THE SLAVES IN SOUTH CAROLINA."[3]

Nor was it of small import that southern Protestantism persistently proclaimed the common origin of all mankind. As succinctly explained by a contributor to the Southern Methodist *Quarterly Review*, the kinship of races was "so clearly presented in the Bible . . . that wherever and whenever the Scriptures have been received as a supreme authority . . . the universal brotherhood of man has at once prevailed as an admitted truth." In espousing this view, a Mississippi Baptist association acknowledged no doubts that "the soul of the black man is equally precious with our own . . ."; that "when redeemed by blood, and housed in that city of founda-

[3] Methodist Episcopal Church, South, General Conference, 1858, *Daily Christian Advocate*, May 15, 22, 29, 1858; Southern Baptist Convention, *Proceedings, 1855* (Richmond, 1855), 6; *ibid., 1857* (Richmond, 1857), 7–8; *ibid., 1859* (Richmond, 1859), 15–16; Andrew, "The Southern Slave Population," *Methodist Magazine and Quarterly Review*, XIII (July 1831), 321; Purifoy, "Methodist Episcopal Church, South, and Slavery," 126; William M. Wightman, *Life of William Capers, D.D., One of the Bishops of the Methodist Episcopal Church, South* . . . (Nashville, 1859), 490. Charles Colcock Jones's remarkable ministry among blacks is chronicled in Robert M. Myers, ed., *The Children of Pride: A True Story of Georgia and the Civil War* (New Haven and London, 1972).

tions, whose Maker and builder is God, they will swell the Anthem of Moses and the Lamb as loud, as long and as ardent as we"; that "the coronet of Kingship—the robe of Priesthood—will befit the brow, and adorn the person of the African as proudly, as beautifully, as [it will] the polite American; [that] the music of his harp will be as sweet, as tender, and as touching; and [that] the joys of that blessed life will thrill his heart with as intense a rapture as ours."[4]

Rhetoric can be empty, of course, and often it is. Yet there were earthly occasions when a shared faith took precedence over customary racial etiquette. Having observed whites and blacks going their separate ways in the crowded streets of New Orleans outside the Roman Catholic Cathedral, Harriet Martineau was impressed that skin color was of no apparent consequence inside the edifice. During the celebration of a Mass there in the 1830s, she saw communicants "of every shade of complexion" worshiping side by side, "from the fair Scotchwoman or German to the jet-black pure African" (a phenomenon that was not unusual in Catholic churches in New Orleans, as John W. Blassingame and others have pointed out). Though the like of this was apparently unknown in southern Protestantism either within New Orleans or elsewhere, other interracial familiarities did crop up. When the rite of confirmation was administered in Episcopal churches in the South, for example, officiating bishops summoned white and black candidates to kneel together at the same chancel rail. And in both Episcopal and Methodist churches it was not uncommon for blacks and whites to receive the Lord's Supper at the same altar at the same time. Handshakes between black and white believers were fairly common during Protestant ceremonials, as at Summit, Mississippi, when "Ben . . . the property of Mrs. Elizabeth Bonus presented a letter from the New Providence Church [and] on motion was received and the right hand of Fellowship extended to him." Now and then handclasps followed anomalies of a nature witnessed at a Dovesville, South Carolina, church. Upon hearing extemporaneous testimonials from two applicants for membership—one a slave man, the other a white woman—the Dovesville congregation recessed and reassembled "at the water's edge and the willing converts went down into the water and were both baptized. After services the right hand of fellowship was extended to them making them welcome to name and place with us." In similar fashion, members of the Owensboro, Kentucky, First Baptist Church ac-

[4] W. N. Pendleton, "The Parentage of Mankind," *Quarterly Review of the Methodist Episcopal Church, South,* N.S. IX (July 1855), 322; Cold Water (Miss.) Baptist Association, *Minutes, 1854* (Memphis, 1853 [*sic*]), 9, 22; see also Smith, *In His Image,* 152–65.

companied a biracial group of converts "to the River at the wharf where Elders John G. Howard and A. Taylor Baptized the candidates." Equally a curiosity to later generations were accounts of white involvements in episodes like that witnessed by a Scottish theologian in the 1840s. While attending services in an all-black church in Mobile, he heard a white minister intone fervent thanks that "in Christ Jesus there was neither black nor white, bond nor free, master nor servant, that all were one in him"; as the prayer was spoken, the congregation approvingly "burst forth in a voice of mournful joy, 'God be praised! Glory be thy name.' "[5]

As Frederick Law Olmsted rightly surmised, blacks experienced "a greater freedom to individual impulse and talent" in religious activities than was ordinarily allowed otherwise. It was a freedom within limits, of course, but one that afforded enlarged opportunities for self-expression and access to ego-enhancing roles. At Methodist love feasts and at other meetings individual blacks were encouraged to recount experiences of grace. At virtually all religious gatherings worshipers zestfully proclaimed their faith through the singing of hymns. Blacks also commonly led in public prayer and were commonly installed as lay officers. And some preached and exhorted.[6]

In no way were the status implications of religion more visible than in the apparel of black worshipers, particularly in towns and cities. One traveler told of black Charlestonians who indulged their "characteristic love of showy dress" at a Sunday service. Another was impressed by the tasteful attire of blacks in a Baltimore church. Still another detected no "meanly dressed person" among a group of Negro communicants in New Orleans; indeed, "the men's clothes appeared as new and shining as those of fashionables on Broadway, New York." In Savannah a white northerner mingled with Negro worshipers who were "well dressed; the women chiefly wore head dresses of Madras handkerchiefs, though many had bon-

[5] Martineau, *Retrospect of Western Travel* (3 vols., London, 1838), I, 259; Blassingame, *Black New Orleans, 1860–1880* (Chicago and London, 1973), 16; Lines, "Slaves and Churchmen," 88; William P. Harrison, ed., *The Gospel Among the Slaves* (Nashville, 1893), 261; Mars Hill Baptist Church, Summit, Miss., Minutes (microfilm, Southern Baptist Convention Historical Commission, Nashville, Tenn.), December 15, 1861; Black Creek Baptist Church, Dovesville, S. C., Minutes (microfilm, Southern Baptist Convention Historical Commission), July 5, 1863; Owensboro, Ky., First Baptist Church, Minutes (microfilm, Southern Baptist Convention Historical Commission), March 5, 1843; George Lewis, *Impressions of America and the American Churches: From Journal of the Rev. G. Lewis* (Edinburgh, 1845), 169. Outside New Orleans, Catholic worship in the South was apparently generally segregated.

[6] Olmsted, *The Cotton Kingdom: A Traveller's Observations on Cotton and Slavery in the American Slave States*, edited by Arthur M. Schlesinger (New York, 1953), 468.

nets, and most of them wore gloves." A visitor in Augusta witnessed a procession of church-bound blacks that included women in "black silk dresses, [with] white muslin shawls" and men with "fine hats and gloves, cane, and usually a watch and breast-pin." And a tourist who scanned Richmond's fashionable streets one Sunday saw "more well-dressed coloured than white people. Many of the women were dressed most expensively in the latest Parisian mode, and generally with taste."[7]

Nor did the deportment of worshiping blacks always conform to the wishes of decorous-minded whites. For one thing, overwrought blacks were prone to blurt out interjections during preaching and prayer (though such outbursts were by no means limited to blacks and were often encouraged by evangelical preachers). Another perennial irritant was tersely described in the minutes of a South Carolina congregation. It pertained to the "comeing [of blacks] in to the house continually during divine service, which is a great annoyance to the church and especially to the speaker." A Richmond pastor was so distracted by such comings and goings that he finally prevailed upon officers to lock the churchyard gates at the beginning of each sermon. Early-arriving blacks were not always quick to relinquish their seats to whites who came after the building was filled. As Basil Manly, Jr., awkwardly explained to his parents, he was accommodated at a North Carolina revival meeting only when "the negroes, who had taken possession of the gallery[,] having been ordered out by the minister of the church, room was made for all that came."[8]

Moreover, black communicants occasionally raised wearisome questions, protested, and explicitly disallowed church authority in a decidedly unservile manner. A group of Georgia blacks once pressed a Baptist association to enlighten them on these points: "Is it scriptural, that members, worthy of excommunication, should receive that censure publicly? and if it be, what scripture authorizes

[7] William Ferguson, *America by River and Rail; or, Notes by the Way on the New World and Its People* (London, 1856), 115; Friedrich L. G. von Raumer, *America and the American People*, translated by William W. Turner (New York, 1846), 434; Lewis, *Impressions of America*, 194; Richmond *Religious Herald*, June 7, 1855; Lillian Foster, *Way-Side Glimpses, North and South* (New York, 1860), 94; [John Dix], *Transatlantic Tracings; or, Sketches of Persons and Scenes in America* (London, 1853), 237. Citations are to the observations of the six travelers in the same order that the observations are mentioned above.

[8] Black Creek Baptist Church, Minutes, July 6, 1850; Robert Ryland, "Origin and History of the First African Church," Henry A. Tupper, ed., *The First Century of the First Baptist Church of Richmond, Virginia, 1780–1880* (Richmond, 1880), 257–58; John D. Long, *Religion and Education in America; with Notices of the State and Prospects of American Unitarianism, Popery, and African Colonization* (London, 1840), 346; Raumer, *America and the American People*, 434; Basil Manly, Jr., to parents, August 19, 1844, Manly Family Papers (Southern Baptist Convention Historical Commission).

that practice?" Another convocation toiled through an agenda that included a petition from Afro-Georgians begging reconsideration of an earlier ruling on the mode of administering the Lord's Supper (the plea was rejected). A group of blacks in Mississippi submitted this puzzler for clarification: "Is it gospel order for a Baptist Church to hold members in fellowship who have married relations nearer than Cousins?" After disciplining a Negro member, a Kentucky congregation received "a paper . . . read from Alex Field of the colored portion of the church, stating that a portion of the colored branch of the church felt ag[g]rieved in relation to action of the committee . . . ." The reaction of Phillis, an Alabama slave, was less formal but equally unsubmissive. Apparently, she might have continued as a member in good standing of a white-controlled congregation had she acknowledged her shortcomings and promised to refrain from profanity. But this price she was unwilling to pay, letting it be known that "she did not want to be in the church."[9]

Few examples of black indocility stand out so clearly as that of Stephen Finger, a Methodist exhorter in the Hickory Creek (Tennessee) Circuit. Perturbed by indications that Finger was not a teetotaler, the quarterly conference officially admonished him and asked for a pledge of future abstinence, refusing meanwhile to continue his appointment as an exhorter. But Finger would not promise to reform; instead, the conference was advised that "he prefer[r]ed giving up his license." Faced with this unusual intransigence (and perhaps also intrigued by an unusual display of candor), the conference reconsidered its earlier action and renewed his license. A few years later Finger's conduct again became a subject of particular scrutiny by the conference, this time when he appealed after being excommunicated by his local church. Upon reviewing the litigation, the conference directed that a new trial be held, a procedure that led to his reinstatement. Even then, however, the conference's troubles with Finger were not over. Subsequently, he was the defendant in a complaint "which is in substance [his] disagreeing with his fellow servants in the family at home." This time the exhorter at least agreed to make "satisfactory acknowledgements."[10]

[9] Savannah River (Ga. and S. C.) Baptist Association, *Minutes, 1813* (n.p., n.d.), 5; Sunbury (Ga.) Baptist Association, *Minutes, 1846* (Savannah, 1846), 5; Union (Miss.) Baptist Association, *Minutes, 1828* (Natchez, 1828), 6; Owensboro First Baptist Church, Minutes, October 6, 1849; Bethany Baptist Church, Burnt Corn, Ala., Minutes (microfilm, Southern Baptist Convention Historical Commission), entry for conference on the Saturday before the first Sunday of April 1855.

[10] Tennessee Annual Conference of the Methodist Episcopal Church, South, Hickory Creek Circuit, Minutes of Quarterly Conferences (Methodist Publishing House Library,

Though a majority of blacks who attended religious services in the South probably were not church members, approximately 400,000 did belong to the various Protestant denominations on the eve of the Civil War—including more than 170,000 Methodists (members of the Methodist Episcopal Church, South), more than 150,000 Baptists (members of churches affiliated with the Southern Baptist Convention), perhaps as many as 30,000 Presbyterians, about 10,000 Disciples of Christ, about 6,000 Episcopalians (communicants rather than those baptized), and about 1,500 Lutherans. Outside the upper South, a New Orleans congregation of the African Methodist Episcopal church constituted a virtually unique instance of affiliation by southern blacks with a denomination whose ecclesiastical machinery was actually controlled by their race—and whose hierarchy was almost exclusively northern. An African Methodist Episcopal congregation in Charleston had been dissolved in the early 1820s following the arrest of Denmark Vesey and others on charges of conspiracy.[11]

On some church rolls the names of members were inscribed with only minimal notations as to race. In other cases Negroes in a biracial congregation were enrolled as a special "branch" or "arm," signifying that they functioned as a unit apart but were subject to the control of whites in the parent body. Commonly, also, Negro missions or chapels were clustered with one or more predominantly white churches in a pastorate over which a white clergyman presided. Under still another scheme a white missionary was assigned to a group of all-Negro congregations; at the end of the antebellum period 327 of these missionaries labored under the auspices of the Southern Methodist church alone, administering to more than 66,000 black communicants. And, finally, virtually independent all-Negro churches—sometimes with Negro pastors—were tolerated here and there, occasionally with a status little different from that of predominantly white congregations. Though religious affairs were not administered precisely alike in any two localities, it is safe to say that black ecclesiastical power rarely ex-

---

Nashville, Tenn.), September 11, 1843; October 13, 1849; March 9, 1850; December 24, 1859.

[11] *Minutes of the Annual Conferences of the Methodist Episcopal Church, South, for the Year 1860* (Nashville, 1861), 293; Southern Baptist Convention, *Proceedings, 1859*, pp. 60–61; Thompson, *Presbyterians in the South*, I, 443*n;* Harrell, *Quest for a Christian America*, 94*n;* Lines, "Slaves and Churchmen," 241; Anderson, *Lutheranism in the Southeastern States*, 39; Donald E. Everett, "Free Persons of Color in New Orleans, 1803–1865" (unpublished Ph.D. dissertation, Tulane University, 1953), 256; Marina Wikramanayake, *A World in Shadow: The Free Black in Antebellum South Carolina* (Columbia, S. C., 1973), 123–28.

ceeded what the white establishment wished it to be.[12]

It is easier to generalize about Negro participation in intercongregational bodies—associations, conferences, presbyteries, synods, assemblies, and the like—than in the government of local congregations. Almost certainly, no southern black served before the Civil War as a delegate to a Presbyterian general assembly or synod, to a Lutheran synod, to an Episcopal diocesan convention, to a Methodist general conference or annual conference, or to a Southern Baptist convention or a statewide Baptist association or convention. It *is* certain, however, that a few Negro preachers and exhorters functioned as members of Methodist quarterly conferences and that some delegates to district Baptist associational meetings were black, and at least two Negro Presbyterian clergymen are known to have been members of presbyteries in the upper South.

Black participation in such councils was discussed briefly during the Southern Methodist General Conference of 1858 when a delegate inquired whether church rules did not mandate the acceptance of licensed Negro exhorters as members of quarterly conferences (the presiding bishop thought not). The query was highly significant, indicating as it did that the matter had not been settled to the satisfaction of all Methodists. Clearly, however, the entitlements of black Christians in church government was an issue that peculiarly perplexed the Baptists. In the Hephzibah (Georgia) Association, for example, a membership application from the all-black Franklin Covenant Church was narrowly approved in 1849. Though the defeated minority quickly forced a reconsideration, "after a very lengthy discussion, the Church was received." Dissidents were apparently placated when the association afterward promulgated a statement that "it is inexpedient to constitute Churches composed of colored members only . . . and [that] we do most earnestly recommend to our Churches not to grant, in future, letters [authorizing a transfer of membership] for this purpose." In Texas the Union Baptist Association curtly rebuffed a Negro congregation seeking representation in 1855, explaining that "the establishment of independent Churches among our colored population would be inconsistent with their conditions as servants, and with the interest of masters." In Kentucky a Louisville Negro Baptist church was enrolled in the Long Run Association in 1842, but

[12] Harrison, ed., *The Gospel Among the Slaves*, 325 and *passim*. Another standard treatment is Charles C. Jones, *The Religious Instruction of the Negroes in the United States* (Savannah, 1842); see also Richard C. Wade, *Slavery in the Cities: The South 1820–1860* (London, Oxford, and New York, 1968), 167–68.

with the stipulation that only whites from another congregation would be recognized as its spokesmen; when the disfranchised church demurred and begged that its own black pastor be seated as a delegate the next year, the association reacted with uncertainty. First, an effort to forgo debate failed by margin of thirty to thirty-five; then, "after much discussion," a motion to seat him was voted down (he was, however, allowed to address the body). The Virginia Portsmouth Association was more of one mind in 1838 when it was similarly confronted with a request "that both coloured churches of Petersburg, be privileged to participate in the deliberations of this body by a delegation from among themselves, instead of, as heretofore, from the Market Street [white] church. The motion was unanimously rejected." To forestall other efforts of this nature the Virginia association subsequently amended its constitution to require that all delegates be white males, an action also taken by a number of other such bodies. The Union (Mississippi) Baptist Association made known its position in a simple resolution declaring "that the peace and good order of the whole church require that its entire government should be confined exclusively to the white portion of the church."[13]

Though several blacks who were seated at such intercongregational convocations are explicitly identified as slaves, surviving records usually reveal little beyond the bare fact of attendance (and all black delegates are not identified by race in the records). Rarely is there anything to indicate whether the blacks made speeches, whether they voted, or whether their influence was otherwise exerted. In all but a few instances black attendance was not regular, but was, rather, a short-interval, now-and-then, or

[13] Methodist Episcopal Church, South, General Conference, 1858, *Daily Christian Advocate*, June 1, 1858; Hephzibah (Ga.) Baptist Association, *Minutes, 1849* (Penfield, 1849), 4–5; Union (Texas) Baptist Association, *Minutes, 1855* (Galveston, 1855), 5, 23; Long Run (Ky.) Association of Baptists, *Minutes, 1842* (Louisville, 1842), 9; *ibid., 1843* (Louisville, 1843), 7; Portsmouth (Va.) Baptist Association, *Minutes, 1838* (Portsmouth, 1838), 6; *ibid., 1842* (Norfolk, 1842), 16; Union (Miss.) Baptist Association, *Minutes, 1845* (n.p., n.d.), 4; see also Luther P. Jackson, "Religious Development of the Negro in Virginia from 1760 to 1860," *Journal of Negro History*, XVI (April 1931), 192–95. A statement appearing in the 1846 edition of *The Discipline* of the Southern Methodist Church stipulated that "Our colored preachers and [colored] official members shall have all the privileges which are usual to others in the quarterly conferences, where the usages of the country do not forbid it," but the entire section of which this statement was a part was deleted in 1854. Church regulations as they stood in 1858 merely designated exhorters and local preachers as members of quarterly conferences without mention of race. See *The Doctrines and Discipline of the Methodist Episcopal Church, South* (Richmond, 1846), 196; *ibid.* (Nashville, 1854), 259; *ibid.* (Nashville, 1858), 55. For references to black Presbyterian clergymen who were members of presbyteries in the upper South see *Minutes of the General Assembly of the Presbyterian Church in the United States of America, 1860* (Philadelphia, n.d.), 148 (Hiram R. Revels); *ibid., 1849* (New York, 1849), 282 (John F. Cook); and *passim* in General Assembly minutes for other years.

once-only phenomenon.[14]

Among the exceptions was the Methodist Hickory Creek Circuit (Tennessee) Quarterly Conference, in which there was some Negro representation during most years in the 1840s and 1850s. The Louisiana Baptist Association was another exception, as were three Baptist associations in Georgia: the Hephzibah Association, the Georgia Association (not to be confused with the statewide Georgia Baptist Convention), and the Sunbury Association. Evidently, the Louisiana Association was the only such body to elect a nonwhite as a moderator; when that body met for the first time in the early 1800s Joseph Willis, a mulatto, was chosen to preside, and he was active afterward for several decades. True to its word, the Hephzibah Association admitted no other all-black church after 1849, but Franklin Covenant was regularly represented until it withdrew after the Civil War. In the Georgia Association black delegates were more numerous, and they participated over a considerably longer period of time: five of forty-seven affiliated congregations were all-black in 1859, and one had belonged since before 1800.[15]

But the biggest anomaly of all was the Sunbury Association, organized in 1818 and embracing congregations in the coastal area between the Savannah and St. Marys rivers. At the outset this association included only two all-black congregations among a total of thirteen, but the proportion increased in subsequent years. By 1857 thirteen out of twenty-five affiliated congregations were all-black, and the remainder had large black memberships; at that time white members numbered only 537 in an aggregate of 6,507.

[14] See for example Pearl River (Miss.) Baptist Association, *Minutes, 1820* (Monticello, 1820), 3; *ibid., 1822* (Columbia, 1822), 2; *ibid., 1824* (Port Gibson, 1824), 3; Mississippi Baptist Association, *Minutes, 1819* (Natchez, 1820), 2; Union (Miss.) Baptist Association, *Minutes, 1828* (Natchez, 1828), 4; Concord (Tenn.) Baptist Association, *Proceedings, 1856* (Nashville, 1856), 14; Elkhorn (Ky.) Baptist Association, *Minutes, 1840* (Lexington, 1840), 2; Savannah River (Ga. and S. C.) Baptist Association, *Minutes, 1811* (n.p., n.d.), 4, and *passim* in minutes of this association for other years; Cahaba (Ala.) Baptist Association, *Minutes, 1864* (Marion, 1864), 4; Walter H. Brooks, "The Evolution of the Negro Baptist Church," *Journal of Negro History,* VII (January 1922), 13, 15–16; Daniel, "Virginia Baptists and the Negro in the Early Republic," 61–63; Hickory Creek Circuit, Minutes of Quarterly Conferences, *passim;* Methodist Episcopal Church, South, Harrodsburgh (Ky.) District, Quarterly Conferences Held in This District (Methodist Publishing House Library), *passim;* Nashville First Baptist Church, Minutes (microfilm, Southern Baptist Convention Historical Commission), July 19, 1854.

[15] Hickory Creek Circuit, Minutes of Quarterly Conferences, *passim*; Brooks, "The Evolution of the Negro Baptist Church," 13; David Benedict, *A General History of the Baptist Denomination in America and Other Parts of the World* (New York, 1855), 778–79; Hephzibah (Ga.) Baptist Association, *Minutes, 1866* (Augusta, 1866), 16, and *passim* in minutes of this association for previous years; Georgia Baptist Association, *Minutes, 1859* (Augusta, 1859), 3, and *passim* in minutes of this association for other years.

A constitution approved in 1823 discriminated in no way against Negroes: each congregation was to be represented "by a convenient number of Delegates"; except for constitutional changes, actions would be by vote of a majority of delegates attending; delegates were enjoined that "in all cases a due regard shall be exercised for the feelings of the members." As "Septimus" explained in the Macon *Christian Index,* "there is no difference between the white and colored churches—all meet together on the same platform in the [Sunbury] Association." Though no Negro apparently served as moderator or held any associational office, Negroes voted freely and participated otherwise in the proceedings; at some meetings a majority of the delegates were black. As if to advertise a color-blind attachment to brotherhood, constituent churches were not grouped by race in listings carried in the annual minutes. Rather, they were arranged according to seniority in the association, each church with its own pastor. A more drastic innovation is indicated in the minutes of 1843: an entry shows that several whites joined a previously all-Negro congregation, accessions that were possible under Baptist polity only if applications were made to, and approved by, the Negro members. "Happy would it be for the interests of our Zion," declared the Georgia State Baptist Convention in 1844, "if all the churches were as devoted and effective as is the little band that constitutes this [Sunbury] Association." Looking back after the Civil War, one commentator surmised that the Sunbury Association had been "as near the apostolic rule" in its commitment to evangelism "as any body of believers in modern times."[16]

Whether to admit blacks into the clergy was one of the most sensitive of all questions in the white-controlled denominations, for their entry into the Christian ministry was an obvious incongruity in a society so firmly committed to perpetual black subordination. Yet most Protestants believed that God called particular men to proclaim the Gospel, that those He elected for this special work did not always seem to be plausible choices, and that the failure to heed such a call was a sin of utmost gravity. And there were widely known examples of blacks who persisted in preaching despite dire punishments. In the midst of a brutal flagellation one celebrated

[16] Sunbury (Ga.) Baptist Association, *Minutes, 1823* (Savannah, n.d.), 4, 11–13; *ibid., 1843* (Savannah, 1843), 9, 12; *ibid., 1857,* (Savannah, 1857), 15, and *passim* in minutes of this association for other years; Georgia State Baptist Convention, *Minutes, 1844* (Penfield, 1844), 18; Macon (Ga.) *Christian Index,* November 4, 1857 ("Septimus" quotation); February 14, 1867 (quotation); Memphis *Baptist,* June 5, 1869. The two Negro congregations that were charter members of the Sunbury Association had previously belonged to the Savannah River (Ga. and S. C.) Baptist Association.

black preacher "held up his hands and told his persecutors, that he rejoiced not only to be whipped, but *would freely suffer death for the cause of Jesus Christ*"; he averred that cutting off his head was the only effectual means of silencing him. Though the matter was not one about which all white churchmen agreed, a substantial number must have reasoned like the Reverend Charles Colcock Jones, of Liberty County, Georgia. Jones did not "see, if we take the word of God for our guide, how we can consistently exclude an entire people from access to the Gospel ministry, as it may please Almighty God from time to time, as he unquestionably does, to call some of them to it '*as Aaron was.*' "[17]

At any rate—as has already been noted—Negroes did preach under southern Protestant auspices. Some were encouraged to do so without formal credentials, almost always to congregations of their race. Others were licensed to expound under the control of their pastors but not to celebrate the sacraments. This was the limited authorization that the Methodist Episcopal Church, South, normally conferred upon its black exhorters and preachers. Though Methodist black preachers were all *local* (that is, they were appointed by local quarterly conferences and did not hold membership in the annual conferences, with which most full-time white Methodist ministers were connected) and though the churchly responsibilities entrusted to most of them were only part time, a few were nevertheless regularly ordained. In rare instances, on charges not served by members of an annual conference, black Methodists were installed as "supply" pastors at chapels or churches with black memberships; and several are known to have preached with some regularity to predominantly white assemblages. A few blacks were also ordained as Baptist, Presbyterian, and Disciples of Christ ministers. Whatever the denominational auspices, administering the sacred ordinances (even more than preaching) was a prerogative curiously out of keeping with the life-style prescribed for a person of color. It should be emphasized, however, that the overall number of *ordained* black ministers was small at all times, perhaps never as many as forty.[18]

[17] David Benedict, *A General History of the Baptist Denomination in America* . . . (2 vols., Boston, 1813), II, 190–92; Jones, *Religious Instruction of the Negroes*, 157–58. The Reverend Andrew Bryan of Savannah is the persecuted black preacher to whom reference is made; see also New York *Times*, July 8, 1856.

[18] *Doctrines and Discipline of the Methodist Episcopal Church, South* (Richmond, 1846), 69–70; *Minutes of the Annual Conferences of the Methodist Episcopal Church, South, for the Year 1859* (Nashville, 1860), 97, 100, and *passim* (and *passim* in annual conference minutes for previous years); Mathews, *Slavery and Methodism*, 64–65; Benedict, *A General History of the Baptist Denomination in America* (1855), *passim*; Thompson, *Presbyterians in the South*, I, 442–43; Fife, "Alexander Campbell and the Christian Church in the Slavery

Though the records of the period provide only scant glimpses of black religious leaders, ordained or otherwise, the prestige and influence of a few stand out. When the Reverend Andrew Bryan died in 1812 Savannah's leading white clergymen officiated at his funeral, and the local Baptist association formally eulogized his "extensively useful and amazingly luminous" life. A monument erected at his grave proclaimed (as Olmsted later observed) that Bryan had "done more good among the poor slaves than all the learned Doctors in America . . . ". Henry Evans's funeral in Fayetteville, North Carolina, in 1810, was "attended by a greater concourse of persons than had been seen on any funeral occasion [there] before. The whole community appeared to mourn . . . ." In a gesture of near canonization, Evans's remains were interred beneath the chancel of the Fayetteville Methodist Church. When the pastor of the First African Baptist Church of Lexington, Kentucky, died in 1854, his funeral procession was larger than any previously seen in that city, except at the funeral of Henry Clay. Lillian Foster witnessed a similar outpouring of two thousand or more persons in Savannah in 1855 accompanying the remains of the deceased pastor of that city's Third African Baptist Church. Blacks were also feted at elaborate ordination ceremonies. Prior to his ordination in Nashville in 1853 Nelson Merry met with a council of white ministers in the residence of one of the group. Four white clergymen then participated in a public ritual at the First Baptist Church; the ceremony included an ordination sermon, a formal charge, and the presentation of a Bible. At the conclusion officiating churchmen and members of the congregation extended Merry the fraternal right hand of Christian fellowship. Macon, Georgia, was the scene of a ceremony of similar proportions when a black man was ordained there.[19]

Controversy," 122–24. There were no black Lutheran or Episcopalian preachers in the antebellum South. Lines, "Slaves and Churchmen," 76–77; Anderson, *Lutheranism in the Southeastern States,* 212–15. Of course, blacks of all denominations were prohibited by law from preaching in some states.

[19] [Samuel Boykin], *History of the Baptist Denomination in Georgia: With Biographical Compendium and Portrait Gallery of Baptist Ministers and Other Georgia Baptists* (Atlanta, 1881), 48–49; Savannah River (Ga. and S. C.) Baptist Association, *Minutes, 1812* (n.p., n.d.), 5; Olmsted, *Cotton Kingdom,* 176; Wightman, *Life of William Capers,* 129 (quotation on Evans's funeral); Posey, *Frontier Mission,* 209–10; Foster, *Way-Side Glimpses,* 109–10; Nashville First Baptist Church, Minutes, November 29, 1853; Macon (Ga.) *Christian Index,* April 8, 1864. Frederick Law Olmsted's depreciatory reports about black preachers in the South have had a major influence on subsequent interpretations. See for example his *A Journey in the Back Country* (New York, 1860), 206–19, and his *Cotton Kingdom,* 203. Olmsted's characterizations do an injustice to a considerable group of dedicated black clergymen who were regarded respectfully by both races.

Merry preached in Nashville more than thirty years, maintaining close ties with the white community amidst the trying vicissitudes of that era. Comparing Merry with two whites who preceded him as pastor of black Baptists in that city, a white contemporary conceded that he was "perhaps the ablest, the most judicious, and certainly the most successful, of the three." When he died in 1884 clergymen "of every denomination (except Roman Catholic) came to his funeral and testified to his exalted character, wisdom, and prudence." Writers in the 1850s also made respectful references to a "grey-haired, venerable" black preacher who had presided over a large group of Baptists in New Orleans for fifteen years; and in southwestern Louisiana Joseph Willis's career as a Baptist leader extended into the 1840s. In Louisville a black Methodist who "spoke good English, and quoted Scripture well" served a smaller congregation. Acknowledging another such figure in 1846, the Georgia Baptist Association announced that "Our beloved and venerable colored brother, JACOB WALKER, of Augusta, so long and so favorably known to this body, has fallen by the hand of death"; the association believed he had well exemplified "the character of the christian and the minister."[20]

No antebellum black was so much in the limelight in a major biracial religious body as the Reverend John Day, missionary to Africa for the Southern Baptist Foreign Mission Board from 1846 until his death in 1859 and superintendent of Southern Baptist missions in Liberia and Sierra Leone during the last years of his life. Day's artfully phrased reports were widely printed in the denominational press, were frequently quoted, and no doubt did much to stir Southern Baptist hopes for Christianizing the continent of his ancestors. One report told of African tribes that were "not only pacific, but indicate a desire to learn what they call 'God Palaver' "; another detailed Day's own assiduous efforts in "preparing mothers to raise their children in the nurture and admonition of the Lord, young kings to rule in righteousness, and a larger company to carry the word of the Lord abroad"; and another stressed the receptivity of rank-and-file Africans to the belief "that there is a God who controls the affairs of man . . . [and that] they are accountable to him and will appear before him to answer for their conduct here." "There has been much money spent, and may I say much

[20] "Early Baptists of Tennessee," Atlanta *Christian Index and South-Western Baptist*, August 15, 1867; Chase C. Mooney, *Slavery in Tennessee* (Bloomington, Ind., 1957), 97; Penfield (Ga.) *Christian Index*, April 26, 1855; Sir Charles Lyell, *A Second Visit to the United States of North America* (2 vols., New York, 1849), II, 213–14; Georgia Baptist Association, *Minutes, 1846* (Penfield, 1846), 9–10; see also Benedict, *A General History of the Baptist Denomination* (1855), 778–79.

good done," Day assured his sponsors in 1852. His superiors freely acknowledged that "Upon information received from him, and his judgment as to men and measures, the [Mission] Board have, to a considerable extent relied" in their West African program.[21]

The name of John Chavis was also known to many well-to-do whites. Before his assignment as an unordained Presbyterian missionary in Virginia and North Carolina in the early 1800s, he is thought to have studied privately at Princeton, and he preached to whites more than blacks. But his greatest distinction was as a schoolmaster. Two of his students became governors; at least one served in the Congress; and others rose to eminence in nonpolitical fields. Another black who preached in the antebellum South has received general attention in traditional historical treatments but for secular achievements after the Civil War. The Reverend Hiram Rhodes Revels, who served Presbyterian congregations in Baltimore and St. Louis in the 1850s, received worldwide attention in 1870 when the Mississippi legislature elected him to the United States Senate—the first member of his race so honored.[22]

There seems little doubt that the black pastor who was most revered in the South during the generation preceding the Civil War was Andrew Marshall, nephew of Andrew Bryan and his successor as pastor of the Savannah First African Baptist Church. Born a slave, Marshall overcame great obstacles during his rise to eminence, but he lived always with special uncertainties because of his race. Even after he had become a well-known public figure, he

[21] Quotations in this paragraph in the order given are from the *Southern Baptist Missionary Journal,* V (July 1850), 32; Southern Baptist Convention, *Proceedings, 1851* (Richmond, 1851), 26; *Proceedings of the Ninth Annual Meeting of the Board of Foreign Missions of the Southern Baptist Convention, 1854* (Richmond, 1854), 17–18; *Proceedings of the Seventh Annual Meeting of the Board of Foreign Missions of the Southern Baptist Convention, 1852* (Richmond, 1852), 21; Southern Baptist Convention, *Proceedings, 1859,* p. 44. See also Southern Baptist Convention, *Proceedings, 1885* (Atlanta, 1885), 46; and Richmond *Religious Herald,* November 13, 1856. It is worth noting that the Southern Baptist Convention appointed no black missionary to the position of superintendent in the post–Civil War era; in 1872 the Southern Baptist Foreign Mission Board publicly raised the question as to "whether the work in Africa can be accomplished without a resident Superintendent of our race," and a convention committee concluded in 1881 that it was "very desirable, not to say absolutely necessary, to have a white man to superintend each station . . . ." Also, whereas it had been "settled" denominational policy in the 1850s "to send to the stations on the coast [of Africa] no other than colored men," in the 1870s and 1880s the need for white missionaries on that continent was stressed. Southern Baptist Convention, *Proceedings, 1872* (Baltimore, 1872), 45; *ibid., 1881* (Cincinnati, 1881), 26, 45; *ibid., 1882* (Atlanta, 1882), 70; *Proceedings of the Seventh Annual Meeting of the Board of Foreign Missions of the Southern Baptist Convention, 1852,* p. 15.

[22] Edgar W. Knight, "Notes on John Chavis," *North Carolina Historical Review* VII (July 1930), 326–45; Margaret B. DesChamps, "John Chavis as a Preacher to Whites," *ibid.,* XXXIII (April 1955), 165–72; Murray, *Presbyterians and the Negro,* 39, 53–54, 135; Samuel D. Smith, *The Negro in Congress, 1870–1901* (Port Washington, N. Y., 1966), 12–25.

was sentenced to be flogged for certain business transactions that apparently violated a law (a punishment that was inflicted only nominally). A fellow clergyman observed that "His strength of character showed itself in his indomitable perseverance, his calm self-possession, his practical sagacity, and a discretion which never failed him."[23]

Marshall experienced a great ordeal in the church, beginning in 1832, when a council of white Baptists formally accused him of doctrinal deviations relating to the teachings of Alexander Campbell. The council's finding was quickly endorsed by the Sunbury Association, which then demanded his removal from his pastorate. Enjoining all faithful Baptists to dissociate themselves explicitly from Marshall, the association went on to resolve that "the First African Church, as a member of this Association, on account of its corrupt state be considered dissolved; and that measures be adopted to constitute a new [African] Church, as a branch of the [Savannah] White Baptist Church." This drastic proscription was coupled with a demand that other African congregations in that vicinity also be reconstituted as tributary branches of white-controlled churches. Nor was the effort to force a reorganization confined to ecclesiastical procedures alone. The association transmitted copies of its resolutions to the mayor of Savannah and to the state legislature and created a special committee to interpret its actions to civil authorities. Another Baptist committee approached the white board of trustees that held immediate legal jurisdiction over the African-church property, urging that Marshall and his congregation be barred from the premises.[24]

Marshall's church reacted to these challenges in a conciliatory spirit, soliciting the "aid and protection of our brethren, the [white-controlled] Baptist Church of Savannah" and respectfully consenting "to come under the supervision of a committee of your body . . . ." But it was careful to stipulate that disagreements between it and its new monitors must be dealt with by referees "whom we shall choose out of the [white-controlled] Baptist Church in Savannah, whose counsel we bind ourselves to follow, provided it not be con-

[23] William B. Sprague, *Annals of the American Pulpit; or, Commemorative Notices of Distinguished American Clergymen of Various Denominations, from the Early Settlement of the Country to the Close of the Year Eighteen Hundred and Fifty-five* (9 vols., New York, 1857–1869), VI, 251–64 (quotation on page 258); Carter G. Woodson, *The History of the Negro Church* (Washington, 1921), 113–17. It is surprising that Marshall is not mentioned in many of the better-known treatments of the American Negro and of Southern Baptists.

[24] Sunbury (Ga.) Baptist Association, *Minutes, 1832* (Savannah, 1833), 6–7 (quotation); *ibid., 1833* (Savannah, 1833), 6; Emanuel K. Love, *History of the First African Baptist Church, from Its Organization, January 20th, 1788, to July 1st, 1888* (Savannah, 1888), 21–22.

trary to the precepts of the Gospel." Despite soothing phrases, the positions of the blacks on two points were inflexible: they would not voluntarily relinquish the congregational autonomy that Baptist polity allowed, and they would not dismiss Marshall. Nor was the main intention of the whites negotiable, namely, to bring the black congregation under white control in all essentials. Meanwhile, as the haggling dragged on, Marshall continued as pastor.[25]

Five years elapsed before a reconciliation was achieved. Finally, in 1837, with Marshall still not deposed, the Sunbury Association announced the acceptability of recent doctrinal pronouncements expressed by him, a finding that led to a full reinstatement (the other black churches and their pastors had not been actually excluded from the association). It was a happy ending for the blacks and one not explained by doctrinal accommodation alone. Central to the outcome were the attitudes of the mayor and the legislature, who did not intervene as the association apparently hoped that they would (probably largely because of Marshall's influence). Nor did the trustees of the church property cooperate with Marshall's accusers. Rejecting overtures from the white Baptist committee, they not only refused to exclude the condemned flock from the meetinghouse; they also explicitly condoned Marshall's continuance as pastor, scornfully affirming "our united determination to prevent the *unauthorized attempts of others* from depriving a large number of our fellow beings of their religious privileges . . . ."[26]

One contemporary acknowledged that Marshall "was known in distant parts of the country, and even across the Atlantic," another that his fame was worldwide. Nor was it unnoticed that "almost every intelligent stranger" who came to Savannah during

[25] Love, *History of the First African Baptist Church,* 12 (quotations) and *passim.*

[26] *Ibid.,* 17, 21–22 (quotation on page 22), and *passim*; Sunbury (Ga.) Baptist Association, *Minutes, 1837* (Savannah, 1837), 6. At the meeting of the Sunbury Association in 1857 (its very first after Marshall's death) white delegates pushed through a motion creating an all-white committee to consider "whether any plan can be adopted by which an entire white representation can be secured this body, without doing violence to the scriptural rights of our colored brethren, whose presence as delegates it is believed is not in keeping with the usages, or in accordance with the sentiment of the denomination in the State and Country." The next year the association's constitution was changed so as to apportion representation and to differentiate between whites and blacks; each church would thereafter be allowed two delegates, plus an additional delegate for each fifty white members or for each five hundred black members. In 1859 the constitution was again modified, this time to require that "the delegates from the colored churches shall not in any case exercise the right of suffrage." *Ibid., 1857* (Savannah, 1857), 4; *ibid., 1858* (Savannah, 1858), 4–5, 8; *ibid., 1859* (Savannah, 1859), 9. The Sunbury Association dissolved in 1866, and a New Sunbury Association was organized without any all-black congregations. New Sunbury (Ga.) Baptist Association, *Minutes, 1867* (Savannah, 1867), 11.

Marshall's later years tried to see him.[27] Among the dignitaries who sought out the black pastor at his home was the Reverend George Lewis, a representative of the Free Church of Scotland, during an official tour of the United States in 1844. Whether the two conversed about theology was not reported. But another prominent churchman who called at the Marshall residence— the Reverend J. L. Kirkpatrick of Charleston, later a moderator of the Southern Presbyterian General Assembly—was gratified to hear "so clear and decided a testimony to the precious though unpopular [Calvinistic] doctrines of Grace." Alexander Campbell proclaimed after personal conversations with Marshall that "he takes more care of his flock, and has them in better condition, than any other Baptist Pastor in the country"; Campbell apparently concurred in the assessment that Marshall was "in truth, the ablest and best preacher in Savannah." Numerous tourists attended regular services at the First African Baptist Church, among them Sir Charles Lyell, the geologist. Lyell told of "a good sermon, scarcely, if at all, below the average standard of the compositions of white ministers," one rendered in "a fine sonorous voice," with no notes, "in good style, and for the most part in good English," and enlivened with vivid imagery. Nowhere in his vast travels, Lyell declared, was he impressed more highly with the capabilities of the Negro race. When Fredrika Bremer worshiped with the congregation in 1850, she wept as the preacher expounded on the wonders of Christian redemption. The Reverend John Overton Choules, pastor of the Second Baptist Church of Newport, Rhode Island, marveled at the "great sweetness and power" of Marshall's voice and at a moving pulpit oration which had "more points of power . . . than I have heard in any sermon for five years"—and which Choules ranked among "the discourses of great men." He knew of "no northern Doctor that can read [aloud] as well." But no one was more carried away by Marshall's performance than the Reverend John M. Krebs, pastor of the Rutgers Street Presbyterian Church in New York City. Though the service that Krebs attended continued almost two and one-half hours, neither boredom nor exhaustion were part of his recollections of the experience. He remembered that Marshall spoke "with clear articulation and with a strong voice," rendering a sermon that had "a clear, full, consistent vein of thought running throughout the whole" and that "was not for a moment deficient in force or devotion." Deeply touched both by the "stirring Gospel eloquence" and by the ritual of the Lord's Supper, Krebs sought

[27] Sprague, *Annals of the American Pulpit*, VI, 252; see also Richmond *Religious Herald*, June 7, 1855.

out the pastor after the benediction. In an emotional greeting at the front of the sanctuary, "speaking through tears . . . ," the two clergymen "exchanged the mutual prayer that it might be ours, with all the Israel of God, at our next probable meeting, to sit down . . . in the kingdom of God, at the marriage supper, when the Lamb Himself shall preside."[28]

Marshall did not often travel outside Savannah and its immediate environs, though during his career he did conduct services in Macon, Augusta, Milledgeville, Charleston, and New Orleans, and he once preached to the Georgia legislature. In the year of his death, however, he visited New York City and delivered sermons at the First Baptist Church and other white churches there. His forthcoming appearances were announced in the New York *Times* and the New York *Tribune*, and a report on one sermon appeared in the *Times*. The account noted that his "very fair doctrinal" presentation was delivered in a "sonorous and deep" voice to a large and attentive congregation.[29]

But these were highlights at the very end of an exceptionally long life. Marshall's health deteriorated in New York, and when he arrived at Richmond on his homeward journey he was too ill to go farther. There he was invited into the home of the Reverend Basil Manly, Jr., who was at that time president of the Richmond Female College; and there he expired after more than a month's confinement, on December 8, 1856—apparently at the age of 101. On the day of his funeral in Savannah, "an immense throng, without respect to color or condition," congregated inside and outside the church. "Hundreds, unable to gain admittance, were assembled in front [of] and around the church, while the street was completely blocked up with vehicles of every description." The main oration, "eloquent and impressive," was spoken by the Reverend Thomas Rambaut, president of Cherokee Baptist College (Cassville, Georgia).[30] A cortege about a mile long—and including fifty-eight carriages—accompanied the casket to the burying ground. "Not more than two or three Funerals . . . have witnessed so large a col-

[28] Lewis, *Impressions of America*, 129–31; Louisville *Presbyterian Herald*, July 17, 1856 (Kirkpatrick quotation); Bethany (Va.) *Millennial Harbinger* (1839), 188, quoted in Fife, "Alexander Campbell and the Christian Church," 123; Lyell, *A Second Visit to the United States*, II, 14–15; Bremer, *The Homes of the New World; Impressions of America*, translated by Mary Howitt (2 vols., New York, 1853), I, 354; Richmond *Religious Herald*, June 7, 1855 (Choules quotations); Sprague, *Annals of the American Pulpit*, VI, 261–63 (Krebs quotations).

[29] Sprague, *Annals of the American Pulpit*, VI, 257; New York *Tribune*, July 12, 1856; New York *Times*, July 8 (quotations), 12, 1856.

[30] Richmond *Religious Herald*, December 11, 1856; New Orleans *Daily Picayune* (afternoon edition), December 20, 1856 (quotations).

lection of people, in the course of the present century, in that city . . . ," a white admirer declared. An obituary in the minutes of the Sunbury Association referred to Marshall as "our aged and venerable 'Father of Israel,' " and he was eulogized at the Georgia State Baptist Convention as "a strong man, both in body and mind; also much devoted to the cause of Christ, which enabled him to perform much labor, and be abundantly useful." Even more honorific was the recognition William Buell Sprague accorded him in his magisterial *Annals of the American Pulpit,* which began publication in 1857. Volume VI of this series—the volume on Baptists—carried biographical sketches of 166 distinguished American Baptist clergymen from the beginning of the colonial era through 1856. Not only was Marshall among those treated; the more than twelve pages devoted to him exceeded in length the coverage given any other Baptist except one.[31]

Of course, Marshall was one of a kind, an exception that easily distorts the general picture. Yet who would minimize the significance of such extraordinary figures as Marshall, Day, Merry, Willis, Chavis, Revels, Evans, and Bryan—and a host of lesser religious leaders—to a race so deprived of opportunity and recognition? It is instructive to read Robert E. Perdue's recent account of the political roles assumed by a number of Savannah's black churchmen in the post–Civil War era and to recall that elsewhere black religious leaders often emerged as spokesmen for their newly emancipated people. At least the antebellum southern churches did not *altogether* exclude Negroes from positions of ecclesiastical power and distinction. In addition to the leadership experiences of an exceptional few, moreover, there was the widespread participation of rank-and-file blacks in services wherein they were called upon to look beyond their present degradations, to make choices, to articulate convictions, to contemplate eternity, to conceptualize as children of God. That southern Protestantism was powerfully shaped by nonspiritual forces in its region, that principles were compromised, that expedience often dictated policy: these are obvious truths. But it is equally obvious that accommodations to secular outlooks were less absolute than has been generally concluded. Had the churches in the Old South in fact been captives of their regional culture blacks would have had no place in the clergy,

[31] Sprague, *Annals of the American Pulpit,* VI, 251–64 (quotation on page 261); Sunbury (Ga.) Baptist Association, *Minutes, 1857,* p. 7; Baptist Convention of the State of Georgia, *Minutes, 1857* (Macon, 1857), 13. Sprague had not intended to include sketches of persons who died after 1855; Marshall's biography was included on the erroneous initial assumption that he died a year earlier than he did.

which was probably the area's most venerated vocation; the liberties of blacks in religious activities would have been more narrowly restricted; the punctilios that customarily governed white-black interactions would have been adhered to more scrupulously at religious gatherings; and the disfranchisement of blacks in church decision making would have been indelibly clarified before the 1840s and 1850s. Even amidst the sectional crisis of the late 1850s a Mississippi convocation did not forget that "Many of our servants are members of our churches, and equal [to us] in the same church covenant . . . ."[32]

[32] Perdue, *The Negro in Savannah, 1865–1900* (New York, 1973), 38 and *passim*; Cold Water (Miss.) Baptist Association, *Minutes, 1858* (Memphis, 1858), 9–10, 25–26. When noting avenues to distinction to which slaves had access and those from which they were excluded, Robert W. Fogel and Stanley L. Engerman surprisingly omit any reference to opportunities in organized religion. Fogel and Engerman, *Time on the Cross*, I, 38–39, 57–58, 152–53.

Using the Testimony of Ex-Slaves: Approaches and Problems

By John W. Blassingame

Historians of the South's peculiar institution have been engaged in a perennial debate about the reliability of various sources. Conceding the virtual impossibility of finding the completely objective observer, many of them insist that every class of sources should be investigated. Stanley M. Elkins presented the most convincing argument on this point in 1959 when he wrote that eyewitness accounts of slavery "were both hostile and sympathetic in nature. It is perhaps best that each kind be given equal weight, as evidence in the judicial sense must always be, and the best presumption probably is that none of these observers was lying about the facts as he saw them. Different facts impressed different people, of course. . . . Much is gained and not much is lost on the provisional operating principle that they were all telling the truth."[1]

Unfortunately, few historians have acted on the principles outlined by Elkins. While examining practically all kinds of accounts written by white eyewitnesses, they have largely rejected those accounts written by ex-slaves. Ulrich B. Phillips led the way in his *Life and Labor in the Old South* (1929) when he declared that "ex-slave narratives in general . . . were issued with so much abolitionist editing that as a class their authenticity is doubtful."[2] Most scholars have followed Phillips in refusing to read the accounts of former slaves. Only three of the sixteen state studies of plantation slavery published between 1902 and 1972 drew even moderately on slave testimony. Among the general studies of slavery, only Frederic Bancroft, in *Slave-Trading in the Old South* (1931), used the testimony of former slaves extensively.[3]

[1] Elkins, *Slavery: A Problem in American Institutional and Intellectual Life* (2d ed., Chicago, 1968), 3.

[2] Phillips, *Life and Labor in the Old South* (Boston, 1929), 219.

[3] Harrison A. Trexler, *Slavery in Missouri, 1804–1865* (Baltimore, 1914); Chase C.

Mr. Blassingame is professor of history at Yale University and editor of the Frederick Douglass Papers.

The Journal of Southern History
Vol. XLI, No. 4, November 1975

A number of scholars have challenged Phillips and contend that in order to understand slavery from the vantage point of blacks, one must carefully study black testimony and suggest ways it can be used.[4] Historians need to know, for example, how to analyze interviews that were conducted with former slaves in the twentieth century. Which of the published autobiographies can be verified by independent sources? Which of them are least reliable? What kinds of questions can and cannot be answered by resort to the accounts of former slaves? How many of the stories were written by the blacks themselves? Who edited the published narratives?

The fundamental problem confronting anyone interested in studying black views of bondage is that the slaves had few opportunities to tell what it meant to be a chattel. Since the antebellum narratives were frequently dictated to and written by whites, any study of such sources must begin with an assessment of the editors. An editor's education, religious beliefs, literary skill, attitudes toward slavery, and occupation all affected how he recorded the account of the slave's life.

Generally, the editors of the antebellum narratives were an impressive group of people noted for their integrity. Most of those for whom biographical data were available were engaged in professions (lawyers, scientists, teachers, historians, journalists, ministers, and physicians) and businesses where they had gained a great deal of prior experience in separating truth from fiction, applying rules of evidence, and accurately portraying men and events. Many of them were either antagonistic to or had little or no connection with professional abolitionists. This was especially true of Samuel Atkins Eliot and David Wilson. Eliot, the editor of Josiah Henson's first narrative, was a musicologist and essayist who had served successively as state legislator, mayor of Boston, and congressman (1850–1851). When Eliot voted for the Fugitive Slave Law he was denounced by abolitionists. Solomon Northup's editor, David Wilson, was a New York lawyer, state legislator, occasional poet, and former school superintendent. He had no relationship with abolitionists.[5]

Mooney, *Slavery in Tennessee* (Bloomington, 1957); J. Winston Coleman, Jr., *Slavery Times in Kentucky* (Chapel Hill, 1940); and Bancroft, *Slave-Trading in the Old South* (Baltimore, 1931), cited many interviews and narratives in their studies.

[4] Benjamin A. Botkin, "The Slave as His Own Interpreter," Library of Congress, *Quarterly Journal of Current Acquisitions*, II (November 1944), 37; Richard Hofstadter, "U. B. Phillips and the Plantation Legend," *Journal of Negro History*, XXIX (April 1944), 109–24.

[5] Josiah Henson, *The Life of Josiah Henson, Formerly a Slave, Now an Inhabitant of Canada. Narrated by Himself* [to S. A. Eliot] (Boston, 1849); Solomon Northup, *Twelve Years a Slave*, edited by Sue Eakins and Joseph Logsdon (Baton Rouge, 1968), ix–xiv; Claude

Often, whites edited narratives because their interest in slavery was aroused by sensational trials involving kidnapped or fugitive blacks. For example, Harper Twelvetrees, a London manufacturer, copied John Anderson's story almost verbatim from the stenographic report of a Canadian extradition hearing. Similarly, when the New York free Negro Solomon Northup was rescued from slavery in Louisiana, he attracted the attention of one of his neighbors, David Wilson.[6]

Five of the editors, William George Hawkins, Joseph C. Lovejoy, James W. C. Pennington, Thomas Price, and William Greenleaf Eliot, were noted ministers in the United States and England. The most famous of them was William G. Eliot. Ubiquitous reformer and philanthropist, Eliot served a long tenure as pastor of a St. Louis Congregational church, was president of the city's school board, and founded Washington University at St. Louis. During the antebellum period Eliot frequently castigated "fanatical abolitionists" and adhered rigidly to his belief in gradual emancipation.[7]

Many whites edited the narratives because of their interest in history. In fact, nine of the editors had published historical works before 1860. The editors who wrote one historical work during the antebellum period included Samuel A. Eliot, Pennington, and Price.[8] Other editors might properly be treated as amateur or professional historians and biographers. Numbered among them were James S. Loring, Henry Trumbull, David Wilson, Joseph C. Lovejoy, Charles E. Lester, and Charles Campbell.[9]

M. Fuess, "Samuel Atkins Eliot," *Dictionary of American Biography* (23 vols. and index, New York, 1928–1973; cited hereinafter as *DAB*), VI, 81–82.

[6] Twelvetrees, ed., *The Story of the Life of John Anderson, the Fugitive Slave* (London, 1863); Frederic Boase, ed., *Modern English Biography* (6 vols., London and Edinburgh, 1965), III, 1055; Northup, *Twelve Years a Slave,* edited by Eakins and Logsdon, ix–xiv.

[7] Lunsford Lane, *The Narrative of Lunsford Lane* . . . , [edited by William G. Hawkins] (Boston, 1848); William G. Eliot, *The Story of Archer Alexander from Slavery to Freedom, March 30, 1863* (Boston, 1885); *Appleton's Cyclopaedia of American Biography* (6 vols., New York, 1886–1889), III, 121; Charlotte C. Eliot, *William Greenleaf Eliot: Minister, Educator, Philanthropist* (Boston and New York, 1904), 126–51; Frank J. Bruno, "William Greenleaf Eliot," *DAB,* VI, 82–83.

[8] Price, *The History of Protestant Nonconformity in England from the Reformation Under Henry VIII* (2 vols., London, 1836–1838); Bruno, "William Greenleaf Eliot," *DAB,* VI, 82–83; A. Everett Peterson, "James W. C. Pennington," *ibid.,* XIV, 441–42.

[9] Trumbull, *History of the Discovery of America* (Brooklyn, [1810]); Chloe Spear, *Memoir of Mrs. Chloe Spear, a Native of Africa,* [edited by James S. Loring] (Boston, 1832); Robert Voorhis, *Life and Adventures of Robert Voorhis,* [edited by Henry Trumbull] (Providence, 1829); Loring, "The Franklin Manuscripts," *Historical Magazine,* III (January 1859), 9–12; Israel R. Potter, *Life and Adventures of Israel Ralph Potter (1744–1826),* [edited by Henry Trumbull] (Providence, 1824); Loring, *The Hundred Boston Orators Appointed by the Municipal Authorities and Other Public Bodies* . . . (Boston, 1852); Joseph C. Lovejoy,

One of the most prolific was Charles Edwards Lester. A Presbyterian minister, consul, and reporter, he published twenty-seven books during his lifetime and translated a number of French and Italian works into English. Lester's *The Life and Voyages of Americus Vespucius* went through several editions between 1846 and 1903.[10] Undoubtedly the most highly qualified of the historian-editors was a southerner, Virginia's Charles Campbell. School principal, newspaper editor, and essayist, Campbell edited the papers of Theodorick Bland, Jr., and the military records of the American Revolution and wrote a book on the colonial history of his state. One of Campbell's contemporaries characterized his work as "remarkable for its research and accuracy."[11]

Some of the abolitionist editors also had impressive credentials. This is especially true of those editors with considerable journalistic experience: Louis Alexis Chamerovzow, Isaac Tatem Hopper, and James W. C. Pennington. Chamerovzow had edited various journals and served as secretary of the British and Foreign Anti-Slavery Society before he edited the narrative of John Brown. Thomas Cooper's account was edited by Hopper, the implacable Quaker prison reformer who had served as coeditor of the *National Anti-Slavery Standard* and was one of the foremost penologists of his time. Pennington, the editor of J. H. Banks's narrative, was a former Maryland slave who had spent sixteen years as an editor and investigative reporter for several black newspapers.[12]

Many of the procedures the editors adopted are now standard in any biographical study or oral-history project. Generally, the ex-slave lived in the same locale as the editor and had given oral accounts of his bondage. If the fugitive believed that the white man truly respected blacks, they discussed the advisability of publishing his account. Once the black was persuaded to record his experiences for posterity, the dictation might be completed in a few weeks or be spread over two or three years. Often, the editor read the story to the fugitive and asked for elaboration of certain points and clarification of confusing and contradictory details. When the

Memoir of the Rev. Charles T. Torrey . . . (Boston, 1847); Owen and Joseph C. Lovejoy, *Memoir of the Rev. Elijah P. Lovejoy* (New York, 1838).

[10] Allan Westcott, "Charles Edwards Lester," *DAB*, XI, 189–90.

[11] Isaac Jefferson, *Memoirs of a Monticello Slave, as Dictated to Charles Campbell* . . . , edited by Rayford W. Logan (Charlottesville, 1951), 3–8; Edward A. Wyatt, IV, *Charles Campbell, Virginia's "Old Mortality"* (Charlottesville, 1935).

[12] Pennington, *A Narrative of Events of the Life of J. H. Banks, an Escaped Slave* . . . (Liverpool, 1861); John Brown, *Slave Life in Georgia* . . . , edited by Louis A. Chamerovzow (London, 1855); Hopper, *Narrative of the Life of Thomas Cooper* (New York, 1832); Rufus M. Jones, "Isaac Tatem Hopper," *DAB*, IX, 224; Peterson, "James W. C. Pennington," *ibid.*, XIV, 441–42.

dictation ended, the editor frequently compiled appendices to corroborate the ex-slave's narrative. The appendices consisted almost entirely of evidence obtained from southern sources: official reports of legislatures, courts, governors, churches, and agricultural societies, books written by southern whites, or newspapers edited by them. If any of those among the editor's friends who first heard the narrative doubted its authenticity, they sometimes interrogated the fugitive for hours.[13]

A comparison of the narratives with other works written by the editors reveals few essential differences between the techniques they employed. Charles Campbell approached Isaac Jefferson's narrative with the same detachment that he used in editing the papers of Theodorick Bland. The appendices, poems, and letters contained in Joseph C. Lovejoy's biographies of his brother and of the Reverend Charles T. Torrey are similar in character to those included in his edition of the narrative of Lewis and Milton Clarke. The same pattern prevails in various historical works and the narratives edited by Wilson, Lester, Loring, Price, and others.[14]

One indication of the general reliability of the edited narratives is that so few of them were challenged by antebellum southerners. The first exposé was of the narrative of James Williams, which Alabama whites proved was an outright fraud. The only other antebellum attack on a narrative involved the autobiography of Charles Ball. In Ball's case, however, the charges cannot be substantiated. A comparison of the narrative with antebellum gazetteers, travel accounts, manuscript census returns, and histories of South Carolina shows that Ball accurately described people, places, rivers, flora and fauna, and agricultural practices in the state. Since the only narrative included in U. B. Phillips's justly acclaimed *Plantation and Frontier Documents* was that of Charles Ball, it may have been more reliable than the antebellum critics were willing to concede.[15]

[13] Lewis G. and Milton Clarke, *Narratives of the Sufferings of Lewis and Milton Clarke* . . . , [edited by Joseph C. Lovejoy] (Boston, 1846), 129–41; Moses Roper, *A Narrative of the Adventures and Escape of Moses Roper* . . . , edited by Thomas Price (London, 1840), 121–84.

[14] See for example Solomon Northup, *Twelve Years a Slave,* [edited by David Wilson] (Auburn and Buffalo, 1853); Peter Wheeler, *Chains and Freedom: or, The Life and Adventures of Peter Wheeler* . . . , [edited by Charles E. Lester] (New York, 1839), v–20.

[15] Ball, *Slavery in the United States: A Narrative of the Life and Adventures of Charles Ball, a Black Man* . . . , [edited by Thomas Fisher] (New York, 1837); Edwin J. Scott, *Random Recollections of a Long Life, 1806 to 1876* (Columbia, S. C., 1884), 9–10, 31–32, 95–98; John M. Bateman, comp., *The Columbia Scrapbook, 1701–1842* (Columbia, S. C., 1915), 20, 31–34, 53; Helen K. Hennig, ed., *Columbia, Capital City of South Carolina, 1786–1936* (Columbia, S. C., 1936), 10, 67–70, 315, 374; Robert Mills, *Statistics of South Carolina* . . . (Charleston, 1826), 688, 713–14; John Drayton, *A View of South-Carolina* . . . (Charleston, 1802), 104, 111, 116–49; William G. Simms, *The Geography of South Carolina* (Charleston,

Of course, many of the more reliable narratives contain elements which cannot be attributed to the blacks. Certain literary devices which appear in the accounts were clearly beyond the ken of unlettered slaves. First, many of the narratives contain long dialogues which could only represent approximations of the truth. Sometimes it is obvious that the editors fleshed out the sparse details supplied by the fugitives to heighten the dramatic effect of the dialogues. Second, the abolitionist editors often included direct appeals to their white readers. Many of them also penned long digressions on the duplicity of northerners in maintaining slavery. Similarly, the most complicated philosophical, religious, and historical arguments were sometimes attributed to the slaves to show that bondage violated divine law and the natural rights of man.[16] On occasion a narrative contained so many of the editor's views that there was little room for the testimony of the fugitive. Sometimes the accounts were so romantic and focused so heavily on the flight from bondage that they were more akin to Indian-escape literature than slave autobiographies. These features are so prevalent in the narratives of Elleanor Eldridge, Sally Williams, Jane Blake, and others that they generally reveal few of the details of slave life.[17] There can be little doubt that the abolitionists interjected some of their own ideas into the narratives. Apparently, however, a majority of them faithfully recorded the factual details they received from the former slaves.

If it is conceded that many of the abolitionist editors were honest but biased men, the major task of the historian, then, is to find ways to separate their rhetoric from the sentiments of the slaves. The first step in this direction is to compare the antebellum narratives with some of the best autobiographies written by former slaves after the Civil War. Although they are sometimes rather romantic or devote few pages to their life on the plantation, the accounts published during the postbellum period are in many ways the most significant and reliable of the lot. The pain of the whip had generally faded enough for the former slaves to write about bondage with less passion than their antebellum predecessors.[18] Another way of identify-

1843), 122–27; Phillips, ed., *Plantation and Frontier Documents: 1649–1863* (2 vols., Cleveland, 1909), II, 59–67; James Williams, *Narrative of James Williams. An American Slave* . . . , [edited by John G. Whittier] (Philadelphia, 1838).

[16] Henry Box Brown, *Narrative of Henry Box Brown* . . . (Boston, 1849), 1–3.

[17] Blake, *Memoirs of Margaret Jane Blake* (Philadelphia, 1834); Eldridge, *Memoirs of Elleanor Eldridge* (Providence, 1838); [Sally Williams], *Aunt Sally; or, The Cross the Way to Freedom* (Cincinnati, 1858). Other unreliable narratives include Aaron, *The Light and Truth of Slavery* (Worcester, Mass., n.d.); Reginald Rowland, *An Ambitious Slave* (Buffalo, 1897); John H. Simpson, *Horrors of the Virginian Slave Trade . . . . The True Story of Dinah* . . . (London, 1863); and Smith H. Platt, *The Martyrs, and the Fugitive* . . . (New York, 1859).

[18] See Henry C. Bruce, *The New Man. Twenty-nine Years a Slave. Twenty-nine Years a Free Man* (York, Pa., 1895); Louis Hughes, *Thirty Years a Slave* (Milwaukee, 1897); Jacob

ing elements added by white editors is to compare the first edition of a narrative with each revised version. The first edition of most narratives is often the one with the fewest distortions.[19]

Even when one is able to identify and discount abolitionist rhetoric in the accounts of fugitive slaves, the "facts" supplied by the blacks may seem false. The only way such doubts can be removed is to try to verify the details of the account by examining independent sources. Fortunately, a plethora of antebellum sources enables historians to ascertain whether the abolitionist editors distorted the accounts of the fugitives. Several of the blacks, for example, made and wrote numerous speeches and letters antedating the publication of their narratives. When these records are compared with the published accounts, it is obvious that many of the editors tried to write the details of the fugitive's life as he dictated them. This is especially true of the narratives of Lewis and Milton Clarke,[20] Josiah Henson,[21] William and Ellen Craft,[22] and Henry Box Brown.[23] A number of scholars have investigated judicial proceedings, manuscript census returns, diaries and letters of whites, local records, newspapers, and city directories and have proven that the narratives of Solomon Northup, John Brown, Olaudah Equiano, and others were authentic.[24]

Many blacks who had purchased their freedom, been manumitted, or escaped from bondage wrote autobiographies without the aid of white editors. A comparison of the narratives of such well-known blacks as William Wells Brown, Frederick Douglass, Henry Bibb, Pennington, Jermain Loguen, Austin Steward, and Richard Allen with their antebellum letters, speeches, sermons, and books reveals so many similarities in style that there can be no doubt about either the authorship or authenticity of their accounts. Even

Stroyer, *My Life in the South* (Salem, 1889); Elizabeth H. Keckley, *Behind the Scenes* (New York, 1868).

[19] Josiah Henson, *An Autobiography of the Reverend Josiah Henson*, edited by Robin W. Winks (Reading, Mass., and other cities, 1969), v–xxxiv.

[20] Jean Vacheenos and Betty Volk, "Born in Bondage: History of a Slave Family," *Negro History Bulletin*, XXXVI (May 1973), 161–66.

[21] Robin W. Winks, *The Blacks in Canada: A History* (Montreal, New Haven, and London, 1971), 178–84, 195–204.

[22] Mifflin W. Gibbs, *Shadow and Light: An Autobiography* (Washington, 1902), 12–13; *Chambers's Edinburgh Journal*, 2d Ser., XV (March 15, 1851), 174–75; William Craft, *Running a Thousand Miles for Freedom* . . . (London, 1860).

[23] *Liberator*, June 8, 1849; July 11, 1850; Gibbs, *Shadow and Light*, 13–14; *Non-Slaveholder*, IV (May 1849), 107.

[24] Northup, *Twelve Years a Slave*, edited by Eakin and Logsdon; John Brown, *Slave Life in Georgia*, edited by F. Nash Boney (Savannah, 1972); Philip D. Curtin, ed., *Africa Remembered: Narratives of West Africans from the Era of the Slave Trade* (Madison, Milwaukee, and London, 1967), 60–98.

such obscure men as John Thompson, Noah Davis, Solomon Bayley, and G. W. Offley have left enough records to establish their authorship of their autobiographies.[25] Similarly, more than 90 percent of the sixty-seven narratives published after the Civil War were written by the blacks themselves.

Although most of them are authentic, the published narratives constitute a limited sample of the total slave population in a number of ways. First, there are many more accounts of slavery in the upper than in the lower South (and practically none for Florida, Arkansas, and Texas). Second, and most important, black women wrote less than 12 percent of the narratives. Third, the percentage of fugitives among the narrators was much higher than the percentage of blacks who escaped from slavery. While less than 5 percent of the bondsmen successfully followed the North Star to freedom, fugitives wrote about 35 percent of all narratives (the others were written by slaves who purchased their freedom, were manumitted, or were freed after the Civil War began). Finally, an overwhelming majority of the narrators were among the most perceptive and gifted of the former slaves.

Because of the high proportion of exceptional slaves among the black autobiographers, many scholars insist that more of the average slaves should be heard and point to the 2,194 interviews with ex-slaves compiled by the Works Progress Administration between 1936 and 1938 as the chief source for such testimony. Deposited in the Library of Congress, the collection was rarely used until Greenwood Press published it in 1972. Even before the interviews were published, Benjamin A. Botkin and Norman R. Yetman had made a convincing case for their use. George P. Rawick and Eugene D. Genovese have added their own enthusiastic endorsement of Botkin's and Yetman's views. According to these scholars the WPA interviews are much more representative of the total slave population, less biased, and less distorted than the published narratives of former slaves.[26] Since there are few systematic analyses of the interviews, it is difficult to assess the validity of their claims. One obvious shortcoming of any study based on the WPA data, however, is that few American historians have been trained to use

[25] See for example Wilson Armistead, *A Tribute for the Negro* (Manchester, 1848), 519–22; Bayley, *Narrative of Some Remarkable Incidents in the Life of Solomon Bayley* . . . (London, 1825).

[26] Genovese, "Getting to Know the Slaves," *New York Review of Books*, September 21, 1972, pp. 16–19; Yetman, "The Background of the Slave Narrative Collection," *American Quarterly*, XIX (Fall 1967), 534–53. Unless otherwise indicated, all references to the WPA interviews are to George P. Rawick, ed., *The American Slave: A Composite Autobiography* (19 vols., Westport, Conn., 1972).

interviews. Because of his traditional fascination with the written word, the American historian, when confronted with the oral lore represented by the WPA interviews, has no methodological tools which are applicable to them.

Social scientists have pinpointed several problems in interpreting oral lore which are especially evident in the WPA interviews.[27] The first and most important question one must raise about these sources is whether the interview situation was conducive to the accurate communication and recording of what the informants remembered of slavery. In this regard, it should be noted that black interviewers were virtually excluded from the WPA staffs in all of the southern states except Virginia, Louisiana, and Florida. Discrimination in employment led to a distortion of information; during the 1930s caste etiquette generally impeded honest communication between southern blacks and whites.

John Dollard, Hortense Powdermaker, Allison Davis, and many other social scientists who studied the South during the 1930s give vivid pictures of the milieu in which the WPA data were collected. In the context of the 1930s the oft-repeated declaration of WPA officials that they were not interested in "taking sides" on contemporary racial problems seriously limited their ability to obtain accurate information from southern blacks.[28] Traditionally, any white man who is not "with" black folks is inevitably viewed as being "against" them. Anyone who doubts this should read the essay by William R. Ferris, Jr., on the problems he encountered while collecting oral lore in Mississippi in 1968. During his interviewing Ferris found that

> it was not possible to maintain rapport with both Whites and Blacks in the same community, for the confidence and cooperation of each was based on their belief that I was "with them" in my convictions about racial taboos of Delta society. Thus when I was "presented" to Blacks by a white member of the community, the informants regarded me as a member of the white caste and therefore limited their lore to non-controversial topics.
>
> . . . .

[27] For suggestive critical essays see Lewis A. Dexter, *Elite and Specialized Interviewing* (Evanston, 1970), 119–62; *American Journal of Sociology*, LXII (September 1965), entire issue; Stephen A. Richardson *et al.*, *Interviewing: Its Form and Functions* (New York and London, 1965).

[28] Yetman, "The Background of the Slave Narrative Collection," 534–53; Allison Davis, Burleigh B. Gardner, and Mary R. Gardner, *Deep South: A Social Anthropological Study of Caste and Class* (Chicago, 1941); Bertram W. Doyle, *The Etiquette of Race Relations in the South: A Study in Social Control* (Chicago, 1937); John Dollard, *Caste and Class in a Southern Town* (New Haven and London, 1937); Hortense Powdermaker, *After Freedom: A Cultural Study in the Deep South* (New York, 1939).

> Blacks rarely speak openly about their society with Whites because of their vulnerability as an oppressed minority. . . . As the group in power, Whites can afford to openly express their thoughts about Blacks, whereas the latter conceal their feelings toward Whites as a means of self-preservation.[29]

The black man's vulnerability to white oppression was painfully evident in the Depression South. From 1931 to 1935, for example, there were more than seventy lynchings in the South; nine blacks who had committed no crime were killed, and twenty-five were lynched for minor offenses. Many of the black informants lived in areas where labor contracts were negotiated in jails, debt was perpetual, travel was restricted, and the threat of violence made peonage a living hell. Historian Pete Daniel, after an exhaustive study of southern peonage, concluded that "The violence that attended peonage sent tentacles of dread throughout the entire black community."[30] Since many of the former slaves still resided in the same areas as their masters' descendants and were dependent on whites to help them obtain their old-age pensions, they were naturally guarded (and often misleading) in their responses to certain questions. Frequently the white interviewers were closely identified with the *ancien régime*; on occasion they were the grandsons of the blacks' former masters.

The answers to many of the questions on the WPA interview schedule could neither be divorced from the dependent position of the aged blacks nor the contemporary state of race relations in the South. Since attitudes toward the past were often so intertwined with the present in the minds of both informants and interviewers, there was a high premium placed on giving the "right" answers to such questions as: "Was your master kind to you?" "Now that slavery time is ended, what do you think of it?" "Was your master a good man?" "Which was best, slavery or freedom?"[31] Not content with these and other leading questions indicating the kinds of replies they wanted, many of the interviewers refused, initially, to accept the "wrong" answers. This was especially the case when the former slaves described their masters as cruel and said that life on the plantation was characterized by unusually hard work. A

[29] Ferris, "The Collection of Racial Lore: Approaches and Problems," *New York Folklore Quarterly*, XXVII (September 1971), 261–62.

[30] Daniel, *The Shadow of Slavery: Peonage in the South, 1901–1969* (Urbana, Chicago, and London, 1972), 29; Charles S. Johnson, Edwin R. Embree, and W. W. Alexander, *The Collapse of Cotton Tenancy* (Chapel Hill, 1935); Arthur F. Raper, *Preface to Peasantry: A Tale of Two Black Belt Counties* (Chapel Hill, 1936); Charles S. Johnson, *The Shadow of the Plantation* (Chicago, 1934); Commission on Interracial Cooperation, *The Mob Still Rides: A Review of the Lynching Record, 1931–1935* (Atlanta, [1936?]).

[31] Rawick, ed., *The American Slave*, III, Pt. 3, pp. 237, 253–54; Pt. 4, pp. 82, 86; XVII, 41, 303.

Georgia interviewer, for example, was disturbed by the responses of Nancy Boudry to her questions:

> Nancy's recollections of plantation days were colored to a somber hue by overwork, childbearing, poor food and long working hours.
>
> "Master was a hard taskmaster," said Nancy. . . .
>
> "I had to work hard, plow and go and split wood jus' like a man. Sometimes dey whup me. Dey whup me bad, pull de cloes off down to de wais'—my master did it, our folks didn' have overseer.
>
> . . . .
>
> "Nancy, wasn't your mistress kind to you?"
>
> "Mistis was sorta kin' to me, sometimes. But dey only give me meat and bread, didn' give me nothin' good—I ain' gwine tell no story. . . .
>
> . . . .
>
> "But the children had a good time, didn't they? They played games?"
>
> "Maybe dey did play ring games, I never had no time to see what games my chillun play, I work so hard. . . ."[32]

The white staff of the WPA had mastered so little of the art and science of interviewing that many of them found it impossible to obtain trustworthy data from their informants. The whites disregarded a fundamental rule of interviewing which Ferris noted in 1968: "As a white collector, rapport with Blacks was particularly delicate and required constant sensitivity to the feelings of informants."[33] Many of the WPA interviewers consistently referred to their informants as darkeys, niggers, aunteys, mammies, and uncles. Reminiscent as these terms were of rigid plantation etiquette, they were not calculated to engender the trust of the blacks. Rather than being sensitive, the white interviewers failed to demonstrate respect for the blacks, ignored cues indicating a tendency toward ingratiation, and repeatedly refused to correct the informants' belief that the interviewer was trying to help them obtain the coveted pension. Not only did most of the whites lack empathy with the former slaves, they often phrased their questions in ways which indicated the kinds of answers they wanted.

Every recorded interview had two authors, the person who asked the questions and the one who answered them.[34] Often the white interviewer-author's actions and demeanor led to distortions and limitations of what the black informant-author told him. Many of the blacks played it safe; they claimed that they remembered very little about slavery and gave one- or two-page interviews. Even the

[32] *Ibid.*, XII, Pt. 1, pp. 113–14.

[33] Ferris, "The Collection of Racial Lore," 271.

[34] On informant-interviewer interaction see Lewis A. Dexter, "Role Relationships and Conceptions of Neutrality in Interviewing," *American Journal of Sociology*, LXII (September 1956), 153–57.

informants who gave the longest, most candid interviews refused to talk about certain things. One frustrated Kentuckian, for example, reported that "In interviewing the different negroes in this community I have not found a single negro that could admit[,] if I asked the direct question[,] that they are the least bit superstitious."[35] Sometimes it was impolitic (if not dangerous) for the ex-slave to tell all that he remembered. This is especially evident in the folk songs and tales. Although practically every intensive study of these cultural elements reveals much antiwhite sentiment, rarely does this attitude surface in the WPA collection. Many of the secular songs are lullabies or hunting songs; the white-hating trickster slave Jack almost never appears in the tales. The blacks were carefully editing what they told whites; generally, they told them only children's tales and songs. One indication of this is the difference between the tales recorded during the same period by the black folklorist J. Mason Brewer and those of the WPA. Taken from the same class of informants, the tales Brewer recorded have a relatively high antiwhite content and many Jack or John stories.[36]

A second weakness of the WPA interviews is that many of them are not verbatim accounts. The informants' stories were often edited or revised before they were typed and listed as official records. Even when the former slave's views are purportedly typed in his own words, the interview may have been "doctored," certain portions deleted without any indication in the typescript, and his language altered. Consequently, the interviews are not, as Norman R. Yetman claimed, "almost exclusively verbatim testimonies" in which blacks "describe in their own words what it felt like to be a slave." Indications of deliberate distortion and interpolation of the views of the WPA staffers pose a serious challenge to historians who rely on the interviews.[37]

The best evidence on the alteration of interviews appears in the records of Roscoe E. Lewis and a Georgia interviewer, J. Ralph Jones. In 1936 and 1937 Jones conducted five interviews which were returned to the state office of the WPA. Three of the five transcribed by the state office are virtually identical to the copies that Jones retained. The other two were significantly reduced in length and seriously distorted.[38]

[35] Rawick, ed., *The American Slave*, XVI (Kentucky), 99.

[36] Brewer, "Juneteenth," Texas Folklore Society, *Publications*, X (Austin, 1932), 9–54; Brewer, "John Tales," *ibid.*, XXI (Austin, 1946), 81–104.

[37] Yetman, ed., *Voices from Slavery* (New York, Chicago, and San Francisco, 1970), 1; Rawick, ed., *The American Slave*, I, xvii–xviii.

[38] Jones, "Portraits of Georgia Slaves," *Georgia Review*, XXI (Spring–Winter 1967), 126–32, 268–73, 407–11, 521–25; XXII (Spring and Summer 1968), 125–27, 254–57; Rawick,

Jones's interviews with Rias Body and Washington B. Allen were edited to delete references to cruel punishments, blacks serving in the Union Army, runaways, and blacks voting during Reconstruction. Jones had two interviews with W. B. Allen, and the second one is recorded in practically identical words in his record and the WPA typescript. The WPA typescript of the first interview, however, lists Allen's date and place of birth incorrectly and does not include 1,700 words which appear in Jones's record of the interview. About half of the section excluded from the WPA typescript referred to slave traders, the religious life of the slaves, the tricks they played on the patrollers, and the songs they sang. While the typescript refers to the kind treatment Allen received from his owners, Jones's records show that he spent a great deal of time talking about the hard work and cruel floggings characteristic of the plantation.[39] The WPA transcript gives the impression that Allen spoke in dialect, using such words as "fetched," "de," "dis," "chilluns," and "fokes." But in his records Jones observed that Allen "uses excellent English . . . ."[40]

J. Ralph Jones's experience was not unique. The same kinds of distortions appeared in the typescripts of the Virginia WPA. Nine of the Virginia informants included in the Library of Congress collection were also quoted in the 1940 publication, *The Negro in Virginia*. Roscoe E. Lewis, the editor, had the original report of the interviews in his possession, and seven of the nine informants he quoted presented views excluded from the typescripts of their accounts. According to the excerpts quoted by Lewis, between one and twelve hundred words of the original interviews were excluded from the typescripts of the accounts of Fanny Berry, Georgianna Gibbs, Charles Grandy, Della Harris, Mobile Hopson, Richard Slaughter, and Eliza[beth] Sparks. The typescripts are poor summaries of the ex-slaves' comments. Songs and religious sentiments were frequently left out of the WPA typescripts. Indications of cruel punishments, forced marriages, family separations, ridicule of whites, and the kindness of Union soldiers appeared in the records cited by Lewis but often do not appear in the WPA typescripts.[41]

---

ed., *The American Slave*, XII, Pt. 1, pp. 9–16, 86–90; Pt. 2, pp. 17–27; XIII, Pt. 3, pp. 14–15; Pt. 4, pp. 205–11.

[39] Jones, "Portraits of Georgia Slaves," XXI, 268–73, 407–11; Rawick, ed., *The American Slave*, XII, Pt. 1, pp. 9–16, 86–90.

[40] Jones, "Portraits of Georgia Slaves," XXI, 268–73; quotation on page 271.

[41] Writers' Program, Virginia, *The Negro in Virginia* (New York, 1940), 31–33, 57, 65–71, 82, 92–95, 143–44, 154–55, 170–71, 201–202, 302; Rawick, ed,, *The American Slave*, XVI (Virginia), 1–6, 15–16, 21–26, 31–41, 46–54. Lewis contributed a preface to *The Negro in Virginia*, but he was not formally designated editor of the volume.

Although the facts are not entirely clear, it is obvious that many of the WPA interviews were altered after the dictation ended. The national office of the WPA encouraged this in regard to the language patterns of the blacks when it urged state directors to record dialect uniformly. This may have accounted for dialect being ascribed to former slaves who spoke English perfectly. But how can one account for the discrepancies between the interviews Jones and others recorded and those the WPA staff typed? Were two out of every five interviews in Georgia and other southern states distorted in the same way? While there are no definitive answers to these intriguing questions, historians must ponder them when they try to use the WPA interviews.

A third factor which led to distortion of the WPA interviews was the average age of the informants; two-thirds of them were at least eighty years old when they were interviewed. And, since only 16 percent of the informants had been fifteen years or older when the Civil War began, an overwhelming majority of them could only describe how slavery appeared to a black child. Because all of the blacks were at least seventy-two years removed from slavery there was no sense of immediacy in their responses; all too often they recalled very little of the cruelty of bondage. A good way of determining the impact of age on the responses of former slaves is to compare the WPA interviews with the hundreds conducted by northern journalists, soldiers, missionaries, and teachers during and immediately after the Civil War. These informants were still close to bondage, and consequently they remembered far more of the details of slavery than the WPA respondents.[42]

Were the WPA informants, as Yetman claimed, representative of the total antebellum slave population? Apparently not. Since the average life expectancy of a slave born in 1850 was less than fifty years, those who lived until the 1930s might have survived because they received better treatment than most slaves. Taken at face value, there seems to have been a bias in many states toward the inclusion of the most obsequious former slaves. This is especially true when most of the informants had spent all of their lives in the same locale as their former master's plantation. Since the least satisfied and most adventuresome of the former slaves might have migrated to northern states or cities after the Civil War, the WPA informants may have been atypical of antebellum slaves. Geographically, the

[42] Yetman, "The Background of the Slave Narrative Collection," 534–53. For examples of interviews conducted by northerners during and immediately after the Civil War see Laura S. Haviland, *A Woman's Life-Work: Labors and Experiences of Laura S. Haviland* (Chicago, 1887), 439–49; and George H. Hepworth, *The Whip, Hoe, and Sword; or, The Gulf-Department in '63* (Boston, 1864), 152–59.

WPA collection is also a biased sample. Although 920,266 of the South's 3,953,760 slaves (23 percent) lived in Virginia, Missouri, Maryland, Delaware, and Kentucky in 1860, only 155 blacks from these states were included among the 2,194 published interviews (7 percent of the total). Consequently, the upper South (and especially the border states) is underrepresented. On the other hand, while Arkansas and Texas had only 293,681 or 7 percent of southern slaves in 1860, the 985 black informants in these states constituted 45 percent of all former slaves interviewed by the WPA.[43]

Most of the interviews are so limited in focus or are so short that it requires considerable skill to extract reliable information from them. In the South Carolina volumes, which contain some of the longest interviews, only 18 percent of the accounts are more than five pages long. Because of the brevity of the interviews it is often impossible to resolve internal inconsistencies, reconcile tone with "facts," separate rumor from direct observations, fathom subtle nuances, verify uncertain chronology, or determine the extent of "structural amnesia" and the manipulation of data to conform to the conditions existing in the 1930s. Since the major objective of the WPA project was to record folklore, other topics relative to plantation slavery often received little attention.

Although there are probably other weaknesses and limitations of the interviews which could be noted, the historian's major concern must be with determining ways to utilize them. One of the cardinal principles in interpreting oral lore is that the investigator must have an intimate knowledge of the informant's group, tribe, or race. According to the Africanist Jan Vansina, "members steeped in the culture itself, and sometimes only the more sensitive among them," are in the best position to study oral lore; "it is preferable that study of traditions be entrusted to people who belong to the society itself."[44] But whether black or white scholars study the WPA interviews is not as important as the approaches they take. They should begin by mastering the skills of the linguist and then systematically examine the internal structure of the interviews, the recurrence of symbols and stereotypes, the sequence of episodes, and the functions they serve.

Given the staffing policies of the WPA, some effort must be made to determine the relationship between the sex and race of interviewers and the reliability of the accounts. Generally, the stories are most revealing when the informant and the interviewer were of the same sex; black interviewers obtained more reliable information

[43] U. S. Bureau of the Census, *Negro Population, 1790–1915* (Washington, 1918), 57.

[44] Vansina, "Once upon a Time: Oral Traditions as History in Africa," *Daedalus*, C (Spring 1971), 456; see also Vansina, *Oral Tradition: A Study in Historical Methodology* (Chicago, 1965).

than white ones; and white women received more honest responses than white men. Fortunately, a majority of the former slaves in most states were interviewed by white women: 60 percent in North Carolina; 80 percent in Arkansas; and 90 percent in Georgia. The reverse, however, was true in South Carolina, where 78 percent of the former slaves were interviewed by white men.

There are also other important variations in the collections. Although the Arkansas staff interviewed more blacks than any of the others, a larger percentage of them had never actually been slaves. For example, about 40 percent of the Arkansas informants were born during or after the Civil War (many of them were in their forties or fifties in 1938). All things considered, the Georgia collection is one of the most reliable of the WPA volumes: most of the informants had actually been slaves (though not as old as the South Carolina blacks) and were interviewed by white women. The Georgia staff also made an effort to evaluate the interviews they collected. These evaluations were cautious and generally in accord with the data contained in the interviews. Louise Oliphant, for instance, asserted, "There are many ex-slaves . . . who have vivid recollections of the days when their lives were inseparably bound to those of their masters. . . . Mistreatment at the hands of their masters and the watchdog overseers is outstanding in the memory of most of them." On the other hand, Ruby Lorraine Radford discovered that "Out of about thirty-five negroes contacted[,] only two seemed to feel bitter over memories of slave days. All the others spoke with much feeling and gratitude of the good old days when they were so well cared for by their masters." Unlike most white interviewers, Radford did not accept such declarations as indicative of planter paternalism. Instead, she tried to correlate them with the average age of the informants and concluded that "Most of the slaves interviewed were too young during the slavery period to have experienced any of the more cruel punishments, though some remembered hearing tales of brutal beatings."[45]

The interviewing skill of the Georgians differed greatly from that of many other white southerners. Consequently, it is mandatory to compare the stories collected by black interviewers with those collected by whites. The key questions in this comparison are those which involve life in the quarters and the treatment of slaves (frequency of floggings, adequacy of food, character of masters, and so forth). The portrait given by South Carolina informants is a good example of those recorded by all-white interview staffs. According to South Carolina blacks most of them were well treated, bounti-

[45] Rawick, ed., *The American Slave,* XIII, Pt. 4, pp. 291, 309, 326.

fully fed and clothed, and rarely overworked by kind masters. Most of them longed for the old plantation days. Although a great deal of this can be attributed to the general propensity of man to view his childhood through rose-colored lenses, most of it was due to caste etiquette and the actions and attitudes of the white interviewers.

The former slaves who talked to black interviewers presented an entirely different portrait of their treatment from what they told white interviewers. Black scholars at Hampton Institute, Fisk University, and Southern University conducted approximately nine hundred interviews with ex-slaves between 1929 and 1938. The interviews they received run directly counter to the South Carolina image of planter paternalism. More important, none of the volumes of interviews conducted by whites reveal as much about the internal dynamics of slave life as these 882 accounts. The informants talked much more freely to black than white interviewers about miscegenation, hatred of whites, courtship, marriage and family customs, cruel punishments, separation of families, child labor, black resistance to whites, and their admiration of Nat Turner. If one begins with the testimony collected by the predominantly black WPA staff at Hampton, by John B. Cade in Louisiana, and by Ophelia Settles Egypt in Tennessee and uses them as the standard of accuracy, many of the general distortions in the WPA collection can be eliminated.[46]

In spite of the skewed sample, the distortions, and the biases, the WPA interviews reveal much about the nature of slavery. Given the average age of the informants when they were freed, for instance, their stories contain a great deal of information about the childhood experiences of slaves. And, given the interests of interviewers, they contain a large repository of folklore. Using only those slaves who were at least fifteen years old in 1860, it is possible to compile some limited statistics on the separation of families, the age at which children started work, the occupations of slaves, and the extent to which overseers and drivers were used. The most reliable information can be compiled by asking questions which differ from those asked by the white interviewers. In this way some of the distortions caused by the interview situation can be overcome. Since the memory of the harshness of the antebellum plantation was inversely related to the former slaves' geographical distance from it, it is necessary to compare the stories of informants still living on or near those plantations with those of blacks who had migrated and resided in other states. It is significant, for example, that former

[46] Ophelia Settles Egypt interviewed 100 former slaves; John B. Cade and his associates, 482; and Roscoe Lewis and Hampton Institute blacks, 300. Yetman, "The Background of the Slave Narrative Collection," 534–53 *passim.*

South Carolina slaves who were interviewed in Georgia had a far different view of bondage than those who were interviewed in South Carolina.[47] Such comparisons as this improve the accuracy of data compiled from the WPA interviews.

On certain topics the WPA interviews are incomparable sources. They probably contain, for example, more religious and secular songs than any other single source. Similarly, the interviews contain much genealogical data on black families not found anywhere else. The WPA collection is also a rich source of information on black speech patterns. There are, however, many problems involved in the use of such data.[48]

Uncritical use of the interviews will lead almost inevitably to a simplistic and distorted view of the plantation as a paternalistic institution where the chief feature of life was mutual love and respect between masters and slaves. A more sophisticated examination using the skills of the linguist, statistician, folklorist, behavioral scientist, anthropologist, and Africanist will uncover the complexity of life on the plantation. Such systematic studies of oral lore combined with critical examinations of published narratives will enable scholars to write more revealing and accurate portrayals of slavery.

Many scholars, while granting the desirability of studying both kinds of black testimony, still wonder which of them is the best kind of historical evidence. The WPA interviews are so numerous and now so much more accessible than the published narratives that at first glance they would appear to have the edge. On the other hand, the narratives, while part of the black oral tradition, are literary records and easier for most historians to study. Then, too, if all the narratives which have been published in newspapers, magazines, church minutes, and court records were collected, they would probably outnumber the WPA interviews. Actually, the two sources are complementary: the interviews include the women (50 percent of the total) and "average" slaves who did not publish their stories; the narratives include the blacks from the border states missing in the interviews; and the preponderance of WPA informants from Texas, Arkansas, and Florida makes up for the paucity of narrators from these states.

By and large, the topics covered in the interviews and the narratives are identical. Both kinds of testimony may be biased. The narrative has, however, three great advantages over the interview. First, the average narrator was twenty-eight years younger than the average WPA informant when their stories were recorded. Second,

[47] Rawick, ed., *The American Slave*, XIII, Pt. 3, pp. 127–31, 233–35, 288–94.
[48] *Ibid.*, I, 176.

an overwhelming majority of the narrators were over twenty years of age when they obtained freedom and could thus tell what slavery was like for adults as well as for black children. Third, all of the book-length narratives were far longer than the WPA interviews. As a consequence of these differences, personality traits appear in sharp relief in the narratives, while often being obscured in the interviews.

Although there can be no definitive answer to the question, there is a way to demonstrate some of the things mentioned above. One former Kentucky slave, Peter Bruner, wrote a narrative (1918) *and* was interviewed by the WPA (1936). A careful reading of the two stories reveals many of their similarities. But there are so many contradictions in the two accounts that it is obvious that (1) Bruner concealed some things from the interviewers, (2) the transcription was inaccurate, or (3) Bruner by 1936 had forgotten many of the details he included in his 1918 narrative.

In both the 950-word interview and the 54-page narrative Bruner recalled his cruel master, the floggings he received, and his numerous attempts to escape. But in the interview he revealed nothing about his parents or the development of his attitudes, character, or personality. In the interview Bruner and his master have a one-dimensional quality; both have complex personalities in the narrative. Besides these elements, Bruner's narrative includes many other things that he did not reveal to the WPA interviewer: his addiction to alcohol; blacks who helped runaways and resisted floggings; the amusements (gambling, drinking, dueling) of the planters and their oppression of poor whites; introspective revelations about his feelings about being enslaved; the development of his attitudes towards work, slaveholders, and poor whites; and the *Weltanschauung* of the slave.[49]

In the final analysis, the methodological skills possessed by the historian and the questions he wants to answer will determine whether he uses the narratives or the interviews. Where skills and interests intersect, he will use both. In either case, the approach must be a critical one and take into account the following declaration of Solomon Northup:

> There may be humane masters, as there certainly are inhuman ones—there may be slaves well-clothed, well-fed, and happy, as there surely are those half-clad, half-starved and miserable . . . . Men may write fictions portraying lowly life as it is, or as it is not—may expatiate with owlish gravity upon the bliss of ignorance—discourse flippantly from arm chairs

[49] *Ibid.*, XVI (Kentucky), 88–90; Bruner, *A Slave's Adventures Toward Freedom* (Oxford, Ohio, [1918?]).

of the pleasures of slave life; but let them toil with him in the field—sleep with him in the cabin—feed with him on husks; let them behold him scourged, hunted, trampled on, and they will come back with another story in their mouths. Let them know the *heart* of the poor slave—learn his secret thoughts—thoughts he dare not utter in the hearing of the white man; let them sit by him in the silent watches of the night—converse with him in trustful confidence, of "life, liberty, and the pursuit of happiness," and they will find that ninety-nine out of every hundred are intelligent enough to understand their situation, and to cherish in their bosoms the love of freedom, as passionately as themselves.[50]

If scholars want to know the heart and secret thoughts of slaves they must study the testimony of the blacks. But since the slave did not know the heart and secret thoughts of masters, they must also examine the testimony of whites. Neither the whites nor the blacks had a monopoly on truth, had rended the veil cloaking the life of the other, or had seen clearly the pain and the joy bounded by color and caste. The perceptions of neither can be accepted as encapsulating the totality of plantation life. Consequently, whether one focuses on the slaves or the master, one must systematically examine both black and white testimony. But, just as there are some topics on which only the masters can provide reliable information, there are some questions which only the slaves can answer. In this regard, scholars should always remember the perceptive observation of Frederick Douglass that a free man "cannot see things in the same light with the slave, because he does not, and cannot, look from the same point from which the slave does." Because of these differences in perceptions scholars who have studied a variety of sources have concluded that "There are questions about the slave system that can be answered only by one who has experienced slavery. How did it 'feel' to be owned? What were the pleasures and sufferings of a slave? What was the slave's attitude toward his owner, toward the white man's assumption of superiority, toward the white man's God? Did the slaves want to be free? Did they feel it was their right to be free?" The individual and collective mentality of the slaves, the ways they sought to fulfill their needs, the experiential context of life in the quarters and in the fields, and the black man's personal perspective of bondage emerge only after an intensive examination of the testimony of ex-slaves.[51]

[50] Northup, *Twelve Years a Slave*, [edited by David Wilson], 206–207.

[51] Douglass, *My Bondage and My Freedom* (New York, 1855), 339; Writers' Program, Virginia, *The Negro in Virginia*, 27.

Southern Mountain Republicans and the Negro, 1865–1900

By Gordon B. McKinney

The mountain Republicans of the upper South have been a riddle to southerners for more than a century. Located primarily in eastern Kentucky and Tennessee, northwestern West Virginia, southwestern Virginia, and western North Carolina, they are the only part of the white population of the South that has consistently supported the party associated with Reconstruction. During the period between the end of the Civil War and the beginning of disfranchisement of black voters around 1900 the coalition of blacks and mountain whites in the Republican party was a powerful political force in these five states.[1] The resulting conflicts and accommodations between the two racial groups reveal much about politics and race in the South during the Gilded Age. Two factors shaped their relationship: the relative lack of racial hostility between mountain whites and blacks and the dependence of the Republican party of the upper South on black votes. This biracial alliance proved to be more pragmatic than idealistic. Although mountain Republican leaders could proclaim that "We want no white man's party or colored man's party, but a party of principle; a party on whose banner is inscribed Liberty, Union and Equality before the law; a party that proposes to elevate mankind of all races and colors . . . ," the presence of a racially conscious lowland white population made this goal unattainable.[2] The Republican strategy

[1] There have been no studies dealing exclusively with mountain Republican racial policies, but the following accounts offer some useful information on the topic: Vincent P. De Santis, *Republicans Face the Southern Question—The New Departure Years, 1877–1897* (Baltimore, 1959); Helen G. Edmonds, *The Negro and Fusion Politics in North Carolina, 1894–1901* (Chapel Hill, 1951); Stanley P. Hirshson, *Farewell to the Bloody Shirt: Northern Republicans & the Southern Negro, 1877–1893* (Bloomington, 1962); Ross A. Webb, *Benjamin Helm Bristow: Border State Politician* (Lexington, 1969); Charles E. Wynes, *Race Relations in Virginia, 1870–1902* (Charlottesville, 1961); Carl N. Degler, "Black and White Together: Bi-Racial Politics in the South," *Virginia Quarterly Review*, XLVII (Summer 1971), 421–44.

[2] Thomas Settle, Jr., speech, March 1867, Thomas Settle, Jr., and Thomas Settle, III, Papers (Southern Historical Collection, University of North Carolina Library, Chapel Hill, N. C.).

Mr. McKinney is associate professor of history at Valdosta State College.

The Journal of Southern History
Vol. XLI, No. 4, November 1975

became one of offering their black following just enough to ensure their continued support while emphasizing issues that would attract greater numbers of white voters.

The mountain Republican parties of the upper South were created during the turmoil of Reconstruction. A few Republican votes were recorded in eastern Kentucky and northwestern Virginia in 1860, but the party did not really emerge as a potent force in the mountain regions until the end of the Civil War.[3] In both West Virginia and Tennessee the mountain politicians found themselves in control of the state government, and several of their leaders were elected governors and congressmen. North Carolina and Kentucky mountain Republicans had a voice in determining policy in their state organizations but were unable to dominate them to any extent. The mountain leaders in these two states were strong enough, however, to ensure that they controlled the party in their regions. Only in Virginia did the mountaineers fail to play a significant role in the Reconstruction party.[4] There were so few Republican voters in the area that the party leaders from counties and cities with large black populations dictated party policy.

The bitterness left by the war encouraged many mountain Republican politicians to support Congressional Reconstruction. The war had left the mountains devastated, and many mountaineers had opposed the Confederacy and wanted revenge on the lowland populations of their states for causing the war.[5] They enthusiastically supported measures that disfranchised former Confederates in order to ensure continued Republican control.[6] It

[3] F. H. Pierpoint to Waitman T. Willey, March 29, 1866; H. Hagan to Willey, April 11, 1866, Waitman Thomas Willey Papers (West Virginia Collection, West Virginia University Library, Morgantown, W. Va.): R. F. Walker to William Mahone December 10, 1867, McGill-Mahone Papers (University of Virginia Library, Charlottesville, Va.); W. C. Ken to B. S. Hedrick, March 22, 1867, Benjamin Sherwood Hedrick Papers (Perkins Library, Duke University, Durham, N. C.).

[4] F. B. Hart to William Mahone, April 22, 1869, McGill-Mahone Papers.

[5] Old Soldier to ———, July 24, 1865, Thomas A. R. Nelson Papers (McClung Historical Collection, Lawson McGhee Library, Knoxville, Tenn.); Leonidas C. Houk, *To the Voters of the 17th Judicial Circuit of Tennessee*, February 14, 1866, Leonidas Campbell and John Chiles Houk Papers (McClung Historical Collection, Lawson McGhee Library); G. M. Humphreys to W. T. Willey, March 7, 1867, Willey Papers; Statesville *American*, April 15, 1876; Winston (N. C.) *Union Republican*, August 10, 1876.

[6] Leonidas C. Houk, *To the Voters of the 2nd Congressional District of Tenn.*, August 1, 1865, Houk Papers; Alexander H. Jones to Thaddeus Stevens, January 4, 1867, James A. Padgett, ed., "Reconstruction Letters from North Carolina," *North Carolina Historical Review*, XVIII (April 1941), 191–92; William E. Stevenson to Arthur I. Boreman, March 8, 1869, William E. Stevenson Papers (West Virginia Department of Archives and History, Charleston, W. Va.); O. G. Schofield to William H. H. Flick, June 19, 1869, William Henry Harrison Flick Papers (West Virginia Collection, West Virginia University Library); William E. Stevenson to Francis H. Pierpoint, September 20, 1869, Francis Harrison Pierpoint Papers (West Virginia Collection, West Virginia University Library); James W. Patton, *Unionism*

soon became obvious that these measures alone would not be sufficient and that a new source of support was needed. The only available alternative was the Negro.

The decision to accept blacks as political allies was an agonizing one for mountain Republicans. Blacks were regarded as inherently inferior, and this attitude had been formed and accepted long before the Reconstruction period.[7] The John Brown episode had had a great impact on the mountaineers, indicating that many of them shared the South's fear of servile revolt.[8] In politics most mountain whites undoubtedly agreed with future Tennessee Republican leader William Gannaway Brownlow when he stated in 1861 that "if we were once convinced in the border Slave States that the Administration at Washington . . . contemplated . . . the *abolishing* of slavery, there would not be a Union man among us in twenty-four hours."[9] Although mountaineers may have disliked slavery as an economic system, they accepted and supported it as a means of social control.[10]

Despite their racial prejudice, mountain Republicans soon found that they had to deal with black voters. Negro suffrage was introduced into Virginia and North Carolina by the Reconstruction Acts of 1867, and by 1869 Kentucky and West Virginia mountain Republicans were forced to accept blacks as voters. Only in Tennessee did the Republicans enfranchise blacks voluntarily despite the protest of many East Tennessee Republicans, including future governor DeWitt Clinton Senter.[11] Mountaineers in other states were also upset by Negro suffrage, and some were angry enough to start the Civil War again.[12]

---

and Reconstruction in Tennessee, 1860–1869 (Chapel Hill, 1934), 101–102; E. Merton Coulter, *The Civil War and Readjustment in Kentucky* (Gloucester, Mass., 1966), 326.

[7] Recent historical scholarship has demonstrated that while there was some opposition to slavery in the mountain regions of the South, it was not accompanied by sympathy for blacks as persons. George M. Fredrickson, *The Black Image in the White Mind: The Debate on Afro-American Character and Destiny, 1817–1914* (New York and other cities, 1971), 20; Gordon E. Finnie, "The Antislavery Movement in the Upper South Before 1840," *Journal of Southern History*, XXXV (August 1969), 331–39.

[8] Frank Aglionby to ——— Aglionby, October 30, 1859, Frances Yates Aglionby Papers (Perkins Library, Duke University).

[9] Knoxville *Brownlow's Weekly Whig*, May 18, 1861; cited hereinafter as Knoxville *Whig*.

[10] Bryan Tyson to S. F. B. Morse, November 16, 1863; Bryan Tyson, *To His Excellency President Lincoln*, August 28, 1863, Bryan Tyson Papers (Perkins Library, Duke University); Arthur I. Boreman to Francis H. Pierpoint, February 27, 1863, Pierpoint Papers; H. Hagans to Waitman T. Willey, February 28, 1863; "Junious" to Willey, March 25, 1864; H. Dering to Willey, May 31, 1864, Willey Papers.

[11] John B. Brownlow to Leonidas C. Houk, February 8, 1867, Houk Papers.

[12] "Several gentlemen have said to me—'rather than permit free negroes to vote and hold office, we are ready for another war' I tell them, 'no'. Let us have peace. The last war nearly ruined us.—another will finish the job." R. M. Pearson to William L. Scott, July 16, 1868, William Lafayette Scott Papers (Perkins Library, Duke University).

These sentiments changed significantly as the first elections were held in the upper South under the new suffrage arrangements. The black voter proved to be a staunch Republican, allowing the party to win state elections in Tennessee, West Virginia, and North Carolina. Though blacks did not help the Republicans gain control in either Kentucky or Virginia, they at least made the party competitive and gave it hope for the future. In addition, there was little indication that blacks would challenge the white leadership of the party. This was particularly true in the mountain counties. One group of western North Carolina blacks told a Republican leader:

> We . . . wish to express to you our grateful thanks for the gratifying and praiseworthy way in which you spoke to us. Having so lately escaped from slavery, we know that our state and condition are backward, yet we are not so far back as to be ungrateful for kindness. We hope that 'ere long we may rise upward and testify to the friends of the colored man we are and have improved sufficiently to merit their praise. We venture to promise, that should you be nominated for Congress, we will not only give you our own humble support, but also that we shall make strenuous efforts to secure that of every other colored man in the County.[13]

This passive type of Negro Republican voter was an acceptable junior partner for most mountain Republicans.

Despite the general satisfaction with the Negro as a voter, his presence caused a major split within the mountain Republican parties. In West Virginia, Tennessee, and Virginia black suffrage came at a time when many ex-Confederates still could not vote. To the mountain Republicans this was unthinkable, and they started movements for complete manhood suffrage in their states.[14] Mountain Republicans in many cases could not justify denying the ballots to whites—even their political enemies—while blacks voted. There was editorial support for the movement in a black paper, indicating that some black politicians had joined the universal-suffrage movement.[15]

Though each of the state parties had somewhat different experiences with this movement, the result was always the same. In

[13] Alexander Gates *et al.* to William L. Scott, May 31, 1871, Scott Papers.

[14] R. F. Walker to William Mahone, May 16, 1869, William Mahone Papers (Perkins Library, Duke University); B. M. Kitchin *et al.*, *To the Republicans of Berkeley County*, 1870, American Political Broadsides Collection (Rare Book Collection, Perkins Library, Duke University); Spencer Dayton to William H. H. Flick, July 6, 1870; William P. Hubbard to Flick, April 19, 1871, Flick Papers; Knoxville *Whig*, June 13, 1869; Wheeling *Intelligencer*, September 1, 1869; Louisville *Commercial*, July 4, 1871.

[15] Maryville (Tenn.) *Republican*, October 23, 1869.

Virginia the Republican party split into Radical and Liberal wings, and each ran a candidate for governor. The Liberal or universal-suffrage wing ran Gilbert Carlton Walker in 1869 with the backing of the Conservative-Democratic party and some railroad interests. The mountaineers of southwestern Virginia, including the Republicans, were enthusiastic supporters of Walker, and he carried the region with over 70 percent of the vote.[16] Essentially the same thing happened in Tennessee. DeWitt Senter, interim governor, supported and implemented universal suffrage in the gubernatorial election of 1869 to help him defeat another Republican candidate, William Brickly Stokes. Once again the universal-suffrage candidate carried the mountain counties.[17] In West Virginia the universal-suffrage men seized control of the party and allowed all white males to vote.[18]

The mountain Republicans of North Carolina and Kentucky faced a different set of circumstances. In North Carolina the local Republicans had not disfranchised any of the former Confederates, and less than 10 percent of the white voters were prevented from registering by the Reconstruction laws passed in March 1867. Thus, it was dissatisfaction with Governor William Woods Holden's administration rather than the question of suffrage that led many mountain Republicans to support Democrats for the state legislature in 1870. The resulting Democratic victory brought the impeachment of Holden and the elevation of conservative mountain Republican Tod Robinson Caldwell to take Holden's place North Carolina Republicans now adopted a more conciliatory attitude toward the opposition and welcomed the Amnesty Act of May 1872 that restored full rights to most North Carolina Confederates.[19] Since Kentucky had not been reconstructed, universal suffrage already prevailed in that state. There was, however, a noticeable shift in party tactics in 1870 and 1871 which resulted in a virtual repudiation of Congressional Reconstruction. Avoiding race-related issues, Kentucky Republicans began to campaign on a platform of improved education and internal improvements. The response of mountain Republicans to the change was very

[16] *Enquirer Manual and Political Register for 1870* (Cincinnati, 1870), 109.

[17] *Congressional Globe*, 41 Cong., 2 Sess., 138 (December 15, 1869).

[18] S. H. Corn to William H. H. Flick, December 18, 1870, Flick Papers.

[19] William A. Russ, Jr. "Radical Disfranchisement in North Carolina, 1867–1868," *North Carolina Historical Review*, XI (October 1934), 281; *Tribune Almanac and Political Register for 1872* (New York, [1871]), 69; Asheville (N. C.) *Pioneer*, September 7, 1871; J. G. de Roulhac Hamilton, *Reconstruction in North Carolina* (New York, 1914), 537–58; Wilmington (N. C.) *Daily Journal*, May 23, 25, 1872.

favorable.[20]

The reaction against Reconstruction proved to be a political disaster for the mountain Republican parties. In each of the five states the Democrats were now in control of the state governments. It was equally important that the Republican party in these mountain areas split badly into competing factions.[21] By 1874 the Republicans were so disorganized that they failed to win a majority of the votes in any of the mountain regions—including formerly safe East Tennessee. Only the unexpected victory of John Daugherty White in a Kentucky mountain congressional district seemed to offer any hope for the future.[22]

At this point the mountain Republicans in each of five states seemed to reassess their situations and make dramatic changes in the party. Abandoning all issues, the mountain Republicans began to concentrate on organizational structure to save the party. The structure drew on the extensive Civil War experience of the mountaineers and resulted in a party organized much like the Union and Confederate armies. Each member of the party was assigned a military rank from private for the ordinary voter to general for leaders like Nathan B. Goff and William Mahone.[23] The voters were then organized into squads of ten with a captain to direct their voting on election day. The Houk machine in East Tennessee, for example, was so well organized that it had personal information on every voter in the Second Congressional District and could place 2,000 squad leaders in the field to ensure that every Republican voted.[24] Clear lines of authority were established; there was a careful structuring of personnel within the party; and power was centralized, usually in the hands of one man for the entire region.[25]

[20] *Tribune Almanac and Political Register for 1876* (New York, [1875]), 81; John D. White to John M. Harlan, June 2, 1875, John Marshall Harlan Papers (Law School Library, University of Louisville, Louisville, Ky.).

[21] Jacob M. Thornburgh to Oliver P. Temple, August 21, 1874, Oliver Perry Temple Papers (University of Tennessee Library, Knoxville, Tenn.); Charles G. Manning to Thomas Settle, Jr., November 22, 1875, Settle Papers; J. G. Ramsay to J. W. Douglas, December 4, 1874; Ramsay to U. S. Grant, January 8, 1875, James Graham Ramsay Papers (Southern Historical Collection, University of North Carolina); Maryville (Tenn.) *Republican*, September 22, 1874, supplement; Statesville (N. C.) *Landmark*, November 21, 1874; March 1, 1875.

[22] *Tribune Almanac, 1876*, pp. 74, 82; London (Ky.) *Mountain Echo*, April 30, May 7, 14, 1875.

[23] Richmond *Daily Whig*, October 13, 1882; George R. Underwood to John C. Houk, November 12, 1891, Houk Papers; P. H. McCaull to Mahone, October 17, 1886, Mahone Papers; Alfred Dockery to Thomas Settle, Jr., September 29, 1886, Settle Papers.

[24] John C. Houk to H. Clay Evans, March 28, 1892; J. M. Homer memorandum, September 22, 1894, Houk Papers.

[25] The most powerful of these men were John Daugherty White of eastern Kentucky, Leonidas Campbell Houk of East Tennessee, John J. Mott of western North Carolina, and Nathan Goff of northwestern West Virginia.

These organizations—often resembling big-city machines—proved to be quite effective, and by 1880 the mountain Republican parties were ready to win campaigns again. They did not do so immediately, but there was no chance that the mountain Republican parties would disappear.

One reason for their failure to be more successful in the late 1870s was a major shift in the national Republican party's southern policy. Starting with President Rutherford Birchard Hayes in 1877 the national party searched for a formula to win more southern white support.[26] Hayes attempted to attract former Whigs by appointing them to office, and this action deprived mountain Republicans of a large part of the federal patronage they expected to be theirs. West Virginia politician George Wesley Atkinson complained that this would "kill" the party in the southern mountains.[27] The situation did not improve much when Chester Alan Arthur became President in September 1881. He supported Independent Democratic movements such as the Readjusters in Virginia and the liberal antiprohibitionists in North Carolina, and like Hayes gave members of these groups federal positions that the mountain Republicans expected to control.[28] All this forced the mountain Republican politicians to depend on the resources the party had in the immediate area.

The most significant of these local resources was the black Republican. As Leonidas Houk, East Tennessee Republican leader, observed: "The more I have studied the matter, the more convinced I have become, that it would not only be good politics, but good Civil Service, and equitable Republicanism to distribute the appointments among all classes—Americans, Germans, Irish, and Colored people."[29] In the lowland regions of every state except West Virginia blacks formed the major portion of the party's voters. This meant that even if the mountain Republicans had wanted to ignore the blacks they could not have done so. Electoral failures, party reorganization, and political necessity required that the mountain Republicans work with black Republicans.

Much to their dismay mountain Republican politicians found that they were no longer dealing with a docile black voting popula-

[26] De Santis, *Republicans Face the Southern Question*, 71–85.

[27] Atkinson to William H. H. Flick, April 2, 1877, Flick Papers.

[28] Arthur hoped to attract independent Democrats to the party to offset Blaine's strength among regular Republicans in the South. For a more complete discussion of this point see Vincent P. De Santis, "President Arthur and the Independent Movements in the South in 1882," *Journal of Southern History*, XIX (August 1953), 346–63.

[29] Houk to Oliver P. Temple, April 30, 1883, Temple Papers.

tion. Knoxville Negro Henry Casper spoke for the new black political leaders when he announced: "We not only want to be nominated, but we want some assurance, that those who help nominate us are sincere and intend voting for us at the polls. We will not suffer that trick any longer. There are enough colored voters in Knox County to demand one or two good county offices every year if the Republican party would but give us what our numbers entitle us to."[30] Not only did the black Republicans make demands, but they did something about the discrimination they felt. William Yardley, an East Tennessee black leader, shocked the party in his state by running as a gubernatorial candidate in 1876.[31] Although he concentrated his campaign in West and Middle Tennessee with their large black populations, white East Tennessee Republicans were quite upset by his audacity. In the 1880s black protest meetings in Tennessee, Kentucky, and North Carolina demanded more equal treatment from the party leaders.[32]

Two incidents involving blacks and mountain Republicans during this period illustrate the problems the more aggressive black leadership created for white mountain Republicans. One problem was that blacks could act as the balance of power between competing white factions of the party. In 1882 in Tennessee's Second District a power struggle between Congressman Leonidas Houk and newspaper editor William Rule resulted in a desperate bargaining for black votes by both men. In 1881 Houk had induced blacks to protest Rule's appointment as postmaster of Knoxville.[33] This protest proved successful, and Rule was replaced with a Houk man. Rule was incensed by this action and announced that he was going to unseat Houk in 1882. His campaign was based in part upon an attempt to control the black vote.[34] Houk reacted to this quickly by making an alliance with black leader William Yardley. Later a campaign worker reported to Houk: "Yardley and Sam Anderson got all the colored people together at night and with locked doors, they passed resolutions endorsing you."[35] The response of the Rule forces was that "Yardley . . . is a notoriously cheap piece of

[30] Memphis *Appeal,* August 23, 1882.

[31] *Ibid.,* October 11, 1876.

[32] Knoxville *Tribune,* September 5, 1876; Louisa (Ky.) *Big Sandy News,* May 19, 1887, London (Ky.) *Mountain Echo,* May 19, 1882; Memphis *Weekly Appeal,* March 30, 1881; Nashville *Daily American,* March 9, 1884; Statesville (N. C.) *Landmark,* May 27, 1881; March 17, May 26, 1882; J. D. Alston *et al.,* minutes of meeting, April 2, 1881, William Woods Holden Papers (Perkins Library, Duke University).

[33] Memphis *Weekly Appeal,* March 30, 1881.

[34] J. L. Randle to Houk, June 29, 1882; W. H. Dietz to Houk, July 20, 1882, Houk Papers.

[35] Oliver P. Temple to Houk, July 12, 1882, *ibid.*

marketable material in every election."[36] The bitterness of the last remark clearly indicated that Rule had not been able to win the black vote and would be easily defeated by Houk. The significant point was that blacks were acting independently of white control in the mountain Republican party in East Tennessee.

West Virginia Republicans also encountered much dissatisfaction among black voters. Many black supporters seemed willing to leave the party in 1888 because they did not feel they were receiving fair treatment. The Colored Independent party made its appearance in July of that year. At that time one spokesman observed that there was increasing dissatisfaction with the Republican party among blacks.[37] Republican papers demonstrated a close connection between the new party and the Democrats, and this apparently negated most of its appeal.[38] Nevertheless, blacks had once more shown themselves willing to break from a mountain Republican organization, and they thereby forced the mountaineers to make adjustments.

The increasing black demands were being made on a group of men who still retained strong racial feelings. The editor of a West Virginia Republican paper probably expressed most mountain Republican feelings in the assertion that "They are just emerging from a purely animal existence and have their future to make out of very indifferent raw material."[39] Mountaineers expressed their prejudice in more than words. Throughout the late nineteenth century mountain men, like other southern whites, found lynching to be a suitable means of social control.[40] One East Tennessee Republican even justified the practice. "However deplorable lynch law may be I say that negroes lynched in the South for assaulting white women are not *lynched because they are negroes but because of the crime they have committed*. . . . I say it is the *unwritten* law of the South to lynch a brute who assaults a woman without regard to his race or color. If more negroes are lynched for this crime than white men it is not because they are negroes but because in the South more

[36] Clipping, 1882, William Rule Papers (McClung Historical Collection, Lawson McGhee Library).

[37] Wheeling *Intelligencer*, September 13, 1888.

[38] Weston (W. Va.) *Republican*, October 12, 1888.

[39] Wheeling *Intelligencer*, March 28, 1876.

[40] Typical lynchings of blacks in mountains are reported in Knoxville *Whig*, February 14, 1866; Wheeling *Intelligencer*, August 23, 1876; August 31, September 17, 1889; April 13, 1891; Statesville (N. C.) *Landmark*, October 19, 1883; September 19, 1889; October 1, 1891; Clinton (Tenn.) *Weekly Gazette*, August 4, 1892; Big Stone Gap (Va.) *Post*, February 2, September 28, 1893; Louisa (Ky.) *Big Sandy News*, February 10, 1893; Chattanooga *Daily Times*, February 12, 1894.

negroes commit the crime than whites in the North."[41]

This would seem to raise the question of how the mountain whites could work with the more aggressive black politicians. One answer appears to be demographic. There were few blacks living in the mountain counties, and this apparently freed the mountain whites of the fear of "Negro domination." The percentage of blacks in 1870 in the mountain regions ranged from a high of 14 percent in southwestern Virginia and western North Carolina to a low of less than 3 percent in northwestern West Virginia.[42] The average for the mountain counties in all five states was less than 9 percent. A more detailed statistical study of the relationship between white Republican voting in 1876 and the proportion of blacks in the population produced a correlation coefficient of −.70.[43] The negative correlation indicates an inverse relationship between the variables. As the percentage of blacks in the population rises, the percentage of whites voting Republican decreases; as the proportion of blacks in the population drops, the Republican share of the white vote increases. Thus, the small black population in the mountain counties made it easier for mountain Republicans to overlook their prejudice and work with blacks politically.

Despite the rapid increase in mining in the Appalachians in the upper South after 1880 and the increased presence of black miners, Republicans not only retained but increased their support among mountain whites. Table 1 will help explain why this does not represent a conflict with the previous analysis. Although the number of blacks living in the mountain counties was increasing rapidly during this period, they actually were declining in proportion to the rest of the population. In only 33 of the 147 mountain counties did the percentage of blacks increase faster than that of the total population.[44] Even this figure is misleading because the number of blacks involved was so small: for example, the percentage increase in Clay County, West Virginia, between 1870 and 1900 was 450 percent, but in actual numbers the change was from four blacks in

[41] John B. Brownlow to Oliver P. Temple, January 1, 1894, Temple Papers.

[42] *Compendium of the Eleventh Census: 1890* (3 vols., Washington, 1892–1897), I, 487–89, 499–501, 506–507, 512–14.

[43] Gordon B. McKinney, "Mountain Republicanism: 1876–1900" (unpublished Ph.D. dissertation, Northwestern University, 1971), 30–58.

[44] The mountain counties that had an increase in the percentage of blacks from 1870 to 1900 were: *West Virginia:* Barbour, Brooke, Cabell, Calhoun, Clay, Hancock, Harrison, Marion, Marshall, Ohio, Pocahontas, Randolph, Tucker, Tyler, Webster, Wetzel; *Kentucky:* Bell, Boyd, Harlan, Whitley, Wolfe; *Tennessee:* Cumberland, Hamilton, Morgan, Scott, Sullivan; *North Carolina:* Buncombe, Cleveland, Jackson, Rutherford, Transylvania; *Virginia:* Alleghany, Tazewell. *Compendium of the Eleventh Census,* I. 487–89, 499–501, 506–507, 512–14; *Twelfth Census of the United States: 1900, Population,* Pt. I (Washington, 1901), 540–41, 550–51, 556–57, 561–63.

TABLE 1

COMPARISON OF NEGRO POPULATION AND TOTAL POPULATION OF MOUNTAIN COUNTIES OF THE UPPER SOUTH, 1870 AND 1900

	1870		*1900*	
	Negro	*Total Population*	*Negro*	*Total Population*
Kentucky	8,621	211,232	11,178	449,975
West Virginia	7,715	324,440	16,154	695,363
Tennessee	36,238	327,035	65,387	625,971
North Carolina	29,673	207,318	53,145	424,579
Virginia	25,938	182,068	42,469	360,233
Total	108,185	1,252,093	188,333	2,556,121
Percent Negro	8.64%		7.37%	

Compendium of the Eleventh Census: 1890, I, 487–89, 499–501, 506–507, 512–14; *Twelfth Census of the United States: 1900, Population*, Pt. I, 540–41, 550–51, 556–57, 561–63.

1870 to a total of eighteen in a population of 8,248 in 1900.[45] In those few counties where there was a substantial increase in both percentage and numbers, like Hamilton County (Chattanooga), Tennessee, there was a noticeable decrease in Republican voting among whites.[46] Thus, this demographic variable was constant throughout this period. There were few blacks in the mountain counties, and this apparently allowed the mountaineers enough freedom to ignore racist appeals and work successfully with blacks in politics.

Another persuasive reason why white mountain Republicans were willing to work with blacks was that the arrangement was becoming increasingly successful. The southwestern Virginia Republican party, in fact, more than doubled its vote after Reconstruction. In the mid-1870s the Republican vote had nearly disappeared. Then in 1879 mountain Republicans, black Republicans, and poor Democratic farmers combined in a political coalition and formed the Readjuster party. Led by former Confederate general and railroad promoter William Mahone, the new party attacked the inequitable Virginia tax system. The issue

[45] *Compendium of the Eleventh Census*, I, 514; *Twelfth Census, Population*, Pt. I, 563.

[46] The white Republican share of the vote declined in Hamilton County from 35 percent in 1880 to 21 percent in 1900. These figures were computed using a method popularized by Allen W. Trelease in "Who Were the Scalawags?" *Journal of Southern History*, XXIX (November 1963), 445–68.

was a popular one, and the Readjusters won at the state level and in the mountain counties as well in the elections of 1879, 1881, and 1882.[47] Happy to be winning elections at last and to be sharing in the federal patronage that Mahone distributed, the Virginia mountain Republicans worked effectively with black Republicans. Their willingness was undoubtedly increased by Mahone's policy of placing black politicians in an obviously subordinate position.[48]

The 1883 local elections in Virginia provided a clear test of the mountain Republican's loyalty to his black allies. The revitalized Virginia Democrats ran a heavily racist campaign directed particularly at mountain Republicans.[49] Three days before the voting a widely publicized race riot took place in the city of Danville, and increased pressure was placed on white mountain voters.[50] The result was an increase in the Readjuster total in the mountain counties of more than 5,000 votes over the party's returns in 1882.[51] The reason for this somewhat unexpected result was as one mountain politician reported, "The Republicans, I am proud to say, stood to their guns like men—never saw them more determined, or united."[52] After surviving this experience, the mountain Republicans of southwestern Virginia were a potent political force.

Republicans in the other four mountain regions also enjoyed substantial successes as the party-army provided them with strengthened organizations. Not only were Republicans winning in the mountains—in 1888 eight mountain Republican congressmen were elected—but they were threatening Democratic hegemony at the state level as well. In North Carolina in 1886 Republicans and Independent Democrats won control of the lower house of the legislature.[53] This was a profound shock to the Democrats and led to the extension of outside aid from the Republican National Commit-

[47] The election returns for 1881 and 1882 were obtained from the Inter-University Consortium for Political Research, University of Michigan, Ann Arbor, Michigan, hereinafter referred to ICPR. The author wishes to acknowledge the aid the consortium extended him and the permission to use these data. The consortium should in no way be held accountable for the conclusions reached in this article. The close relationship between Readjusters and Virginia Republicans is demonstrated in William D. McIver to Mahone, December 3, 1882; Fred G. Rogers to Mahone, November 3, 1882; B. W. Clark to Mahone, March 28, 1882, Mahone Papers; Woodstock *Virginian,* May 19, 1882; Richmond *Whig,* October 13, 1882.

[48] John A. Brown to Mahone, March 29, 1888; Mahone interview, January 18, 1889, Mahone Papers; Richmond *Whig,* April 1, 1881; Memphis *Weekly Appeal,* August 10, 1882.

[49] *Coalition Rule in Danville,* Scrapbook, No. 31, p. 25, Mahone Papers.

[50] C. S. Wingfield to Mahone, November 2, 1883, *ibid.;* John T. S. Melzer, "The Danville Riot, November 3, 1883" (unpublished M.A. thesis, University of Virginia, 1963), *passim.*

[51] ICPR election data; Scrapbook, No. 32, p. 7, Mahone Papers. The percentage of Republican vote did decline as many peripheral voters were drawn to the polls by the sensational campaign.

[52] J. H. Ballard to Mahone, November 8, 1883, *ibid.*

[53] Statesville (N. C.) *Landmark,* January 6, 1887.

tee to North Carolina Republicans two years later.[54] Although the party failed to carry the state for presidential candidate Benjamin Harrison, three Republican congressmen were elected. This represented the party's best showing since Reconstruction. Kentucky Republican leader William O. Bradley was the party's gubernatorial candidate in 1887, and his energetic campaign reduced the normal 40,000 vote Democratic majority to 17,000. The next year these gains resulted in the election of three Republican congressmen from Kentucky. Tennessee mountain Republicans were cheered by the fact that businessman Henry Clay Evans carried the state's Third Congressional District for the Republicans, the party's first victory in that district in two decades.[55]

West Virginia Republicans in 1888 were even more successful, electing half of the state's four congressmen and a governor. Popular Republican congressman Nathan Goff had been persuaded to be the gubernatorial candidate, and he proved to be such an effective campaigner that the Democratic candidate refused to debate him.[56] When the returns were counted Goff had won by the slim margin of 110 votes. There were immediate protests of fraud, and an election contest conducted by a Democratic legislature eventually deprived Goff of his victory.[57] Still, West Virginia Republicans believed they were on the verge of a great breakthrough. Virginia mountain Republicans continued to enjoy success under Mahone's leadership. In 1886 the Republicans won six of Virginia's ten congressional seats, and in 1888 Harrison lost by only 1,500 votes out of more than 300,000 cast in the state.[58] The Republican party in the upper South was doing well, then, and was looking for some way to win control of their states.

rep. doing well

Since the major barrier to Republican success had been Democratic control of the election machinery, most mountain Republicans eagerly supported the idea of a federal election law.[59] They were significant leaders in trying to secure this legislation. Most mountain Republicans were positive that a federal election law would ensure party success in their states since it would

[54] Journal, J. Granville Leach Papers (North Carolina Division of Archives and History, Raleigh, N. C.).

[55] ICPR election data; Wheeling *Intelligencer,* February 4, 28, 1890.

[56] T. S. Riley to W. J. W. Cowden, September 13, 1888, Nathan Goff Papers (West Virginia Collection, West Virginia University Library).

[57] Wheeling *Intelligencer,* February 2, 12, 23, March 5, 13, September 9, 1889; Weston (W. Va.) *Republican,* March 16, 1889; February 8, 1890.

[58] ICPR election data.

[59] Winston (N. C.) *Union Republican,* April 25, 1889; Wheeling *Intelligencer,* December 31, 1889.

guarantee black voting as well as accuracy in the counting of votes.[60] Veteran mountain Republican congressman Leonidas Houk of Tennessee was the chief spokesman for the region in favor of the measure. During his first month in Congress in 1879 Houk endorsed the idea of federal control of elections, and he introduced a piece of legislation to do this in November 1889.[61] Although his own bill was dropped in favor of one proposed by Henry Cabot Lodge, Houk continued to support the idea. His position is stated clearly in a speech delivered in 1890: "In conclusion he urged that the colored people of the South should be given a fair chance. If the white people of the South would not take their hand off the Government must take it off. Let no man hold a seat on this floor who was returned by means of Winchester rifles, clubs and fraudulent ballot boxes."[62] In the floor debate on the Lodge bill Houk continued his enthusiastic support of the concept of federal intervention.[63]

Although Houk was probably the leading spokesman for a federal election law, there were many other mountain Republicans who supported Lodge's ideas. George W. Atkinson, congressman from West Virginia, proposed that criminal penalties be enforced if anyone interfered with federal elections.[64] Along the same lines, East Tennessee Republican congressman Alfred Alexander Taylor thought that the final version of Lodge's bill should be strengthened to ensure compliance with the law.[65] Kentucky mountain Republican congressman Hugh Franklin Finley was quite satisfied, saying, "I most cheerfully indorse the bill as the best election bill that has ever been offered to any Congress in this country . . . ."[66] Republican voters in the mountain regions also seemed to accept the measure according to Republican newspapers and meetings endorsing the Lodge proposal.[67] When the vote was taken in the House, seven of the eight mountain Republicans supported it and thereby allowed the measure to pass by a narrow margin.[68]

There was, however, another opinion of the legislation among mountain Republicans, and the leader of this point of view was

[60] *Cong. Record,* 51 Cong., 1 Sess., 6771 (June 30, 1890).

[61] Houk, *Freedom of Election in the South,* April 3, 1879, Houk Papers; Wheeling *Intelligencer,* November 7, 1889.

[62] *Ibid.,* March 6, 1890.

[63] *Cong. Record,* 51 Cong., 1 Sess., 6769–71 (June 30, 1890).

[64] Wheeling *Intelligencer,* May 24, 1890.

[65] *Cong. Record,* 51 Cong., 1 Sess., 6929 (July 2, 1890).

[66] *Ibid.,* 6774 (June 30, 1890).

[67] Weston (W. Va.) *Republican,* June 7, August 2, 1890; Johnson City (Tenn.) *Comet,* August 7, 1890; Wheeling *Intelligencer,* August 21, 1890; Winston (N. C.) *Union Republican,* September 4, 1890.

[68] *Cong. Record,* 51 Cong., 1 Sess., 6940–41 (July 2, 1890).

Congressman Hamilton Glover Ewart of North Carolina. Ewart maintained that "this election bill is as damnable, illogical, inequitable, and vicious a piece of legislation as was ever attempted to be placed upon the statute-books of this Republic."[69] He went on to explain his stand in the following terms: "Every year the Republican party in the States of Tennessee, North Carolina, and the two Virginias is becoming stronger and more aggressive. It is not acquiring this strength by making morbid appeals to the negro and by exciting their passions and prejudices, but by appealing to the sober judgement of the white voters of the South on the great issue of protection . . . ."[70] Nor was Ewart alone in this feeling. The Republican gubernatorial candidate in Tennessee opposed the bill, and Republican congressional candidates in North Carolina, Tennessee, and Virginia also attacked the Lodge proposal.[71]

When the Lodge bill did not pass in the United States Senate mountain Republicans found themselves in a difficult position. The legislation had alienated many white voters in their districts, and since it had failed, blacks had no more protection than before. As a result the congressional elections of 1890 were a real setback for mountain Republicans. In the elections they lost five of the eight seats they had held.[72] It is difficult to assess exactly how significant the election-law issue was in defeating the party. The Republicans were badly defeated everywhere in 1890, and it seems clear that mountain voters (like other voters across the nation) reacted to issues other than the Lodge bill. The election in the First Congressional District of Tennessee offers the best illustration of mountain Republicans' reactions to the Lodge bill. There, Alfred Taylor, a strong backer of the bill, was opposed by former congressman Roderick Randum Butler for the Republican nomination. After a hotly contested primary campaign both men claimed to be the regular party nominee.[73] The Democrats in this strongly

[69] *Ibid.*, 6688 (June 28, 1890).

[70] *Ibid.*, 6689 (June 28, 1890).

[71] D. C. Kelley to Will A. McTeer, September 29, 1890, Will H. McTeer Papers (McClung Historical Collection, Lawson McGhee Library); John C. Houk to Leonidas C. Houk, August 4, 1890, Houk Papers; Winston (N. C.) *Union Republican*, January 16, October 2, 1890; Statesville (N. C.) *Landmark*, July 10, October 9, 1890; Big Stone Gap (Va.) *Post*, August 22, September 26, 1890; Wheeling *Intelligencer*, September 15, 1890; Johnson City (Tenn.) *Comet*, September 25, 1890.

[72] Outspoken supporters of the Lodge bill, Taylor and Houk were reelected despite racist opposition. Clinton (Tenn.) *Weekly Gazette*, October 30, 1890; Chattanooga *Daily Times*, November 1, 1890.

[73] Johnson City (Tenn.) *Comet*, April 17, 1890.

Republican district decided not to run a candidate and to allow the two men to split their own party. In September Butler, in an obvious political maneuver, attacked the Lodge bill and federal control of elections.[74] Thus, the Republican voters of the district had a choice of candidates from their own party who took opposite positions on the issue. The election returns gave Taylor a narrow victory and indicated that he had won about 80 percent of the Republican vote.[75] It would be safe to conclude, then, that though there was substantial opposition to the Lodge bill among the mountaineers it was backed by a majority of mountain Republicans.

The failures of the 1890 campaign and further defeats in the 1892 election prompted a serious reevaluation of the party's position.[76] The Lodge bill was proving to be a serious political liability, and more and more mountain Republicans began to reject federal intervention in southern elections as a viable means of adding voters to the party.[77] The disenchantment with this approach to winning voters coincided with dissatisfaction with the bosses who had directed the party in the mountains during the 1880s. Between 1890 and 1894 all the old leaders were replaced by politicians who brought a new perspective to the party.

In each state the power struggle between the old and new leaders was relatively brief. John D. White, the eastern Kentucky mountain boss, was defeated by David Grant Colson in an attempt to win a congressional seat in 1894. Although the party was divided after Colson's election, White's reign was over.[78] In East Tennessee the powerful Houk machine disintegrated quickly after the death of Leonidas Houk in 1891, and by 1894 H. Clay Evans had become the dominant Republican in East Tennessee.[79] The Mahone machine simply lost control of the Republicans in southwestern Virginia. Mahone ordered the party not to run candidates in the elections of the early 1890s, but the mountain Republicans dis-

[74] *Ibid.*, September 25, 1890.

[75] ICPR election data. Using Lewis Baxter's vote as the Republican gubernatorial candidate and assuming that no Democrats would vote for the advocate of the Lodge bill, the Republicans divided approximately as follows: Taylor 11,500; Butler 2,200.

[76] For a description of this process at the national level see Hirshson, *Farewell to the Bloody Shirt*, 236–58.

[77] Augustus E. Willson, circular letter, November 4, 1892, Augustus Everett Willson Papers (Collections of the Filson Club, Louisville Ky.); D. M. Furches to Thomas Settle, III, July 29, 1892, Settle Papers; Weston (W. Va.) *Republican*, January 24, 1891; Winston (N. C.) *Union Republican*, June 11, 1891; Louisa (Ky.) *Big Sandy News*, October 21, 1892.

[78] J. K. Watkins *et al.*, circular letter, October 8, 1894, Scrapbook, David Grant Colson Papers (Southern Historical Collection, University of North Carolina Library); ICPR election data.

[79] Chattanooga *Daily Times*, August 23, 1894.

obeyed, and twice-elected congressman James Alexander Walker became the new leader of the party in the region.[80] Probably the quietest and least bitter change came in West Virginia. Machine leader Nathan Goff was being pressed by wealthy businessman Stephen Benton Elkins for control of the organization. In 1891 Elkins arranged to have President Benjamin Harrison offer Goff a federal judgeship, giving Goff a face-saving way to leave politics.[81] Elkins quickly took advantage of Goff's withdrawal and by 1892 had consolidated his hold hold on the party in West Virginia.

The same process occurred in North Carolina, but there were two separate stages to it. In 1889 and 1890 the boss, John J. Mott, lost control of federal patronage to John Baxter Eaves, who used his position as collector of internal revenue in the mountain region to take over control of the party.[82] Eaves maintained this position until 1894, when he resisted attempts to fuse the Republicans and Populists for electoral purposes.[83] At the state convention of that year Eaves was deposed, and a new group of Republican leaders emerged led by mountain Republican Jeter Connelly Pritchard.[84] The immediate success of fusion at the polls and election of Pritchard to the Senate ensured that the change in leadership would be permanent. Despite strenuous racist opposition from the Democrats in 1896 the fusion arrangement worked again, and the Populists and Republicans continued to control North Carolina.

The new leaders shared a common goal of bringing more white voters into the Republican party. They believed that the strategy of relying exclusively on blacks and former Unionists as the bosses had done could never make their party into the majority party in the upper South. The emphasis now would be exclusively on economic issues.[85] The advent of the "Democratic" depression of the 1890s made this a most fortuitous decision. In both 1894 and 1896 the Republicans elected most of the congressmen from the mountain districts, they elected governors in four of the five upper South

[80] Big Stone Gap (Va.) *Post*, December 6, 1894.

[81] Wheeling *Intelligencer*, December 17, 1891.

[82] Statesville (N. C.) *Landmark*, September 4, 1890.

[83] Eaves to Richmond Pearson, April 10, 1894; Marion Butler to Pearson, Richmond M. Pearson Papers (Southern Historical Collection, University of North Carolina Library); *Eaves to the Republicans of North Carolina*, June 8, 1894; H. L. Grant, circular letter, July 12, 1894, Settle Papers.

[84] Winston (N.C.) *Union Republican*, September 6, 1894.

[85] John W. Mason to Thomas E. Davis, August 6, 1892, Letterbook, John W. Mason Papers (West Virginia Collection, West Virginia University Library); Charles F. Ballard to Augustus E. Willson, February 29, 1892; Willson, circular letter, November 4, 1892, Willson Papers; Wheeling *Intelligencer*, June 4, 1891; Winston (N. C.) *Union Republican*, June 11, 1891: Clinton (Tenn.) *Weekly Gazette*, December 1, 1892; Louisa (Ky.) *Big Sandy News*, February 23, 1894; Big Stone Gap (Va.) *Post*, August 13, 1896.

states in the same period, and for the first time since the Readjuster period in Virginia four Republican senators represented the upper South in Washington.[86]

This successful new mountain Republican leadership tended to ignore the older groups in the party, particularly the blacks. Another significant factor was pushing the Republican leadership in the same direction. That was the rise of southern Negrophobia as a conscious intellectual and social movement.[87] Lynchings continued at an ever-increasing rate, and rigid segregation became the goal of many white southerners. Ominously for the Republican party, the program of the southern racial purists demanded an end to Negro suffrage. The mountain Republican politicians thus were caught between their need to retain black votes and the need to appeal to white, racist Democrats. Since the Democrats offered blacks so little, Republican politicians for the most part believed it safe to ignore the blacks.

Mountain Republican leaders now thought they had to convince whites that "the Republican party is not the negro party."[88] The result was an effort to construct a "lily-white" movement. Mountain politicians tended to avoid blacks in their campaign appearances and to deny them federal patronage, but their statements and campaign strategies contradict the idea that they wanted to end Negro suffrage. Black voters, despite their occasional challenges to the party leadership, were too valuable as allies to be disfranchised.

The new mountain leaders tried to ensure that black Republican voters had only a minimal voice in the party organization while they also sought to preserve the black right to vote. All white mountain Republicans seemed to agree that federal patronage should be distributed to whites only. One North Carolina black politician accurately observed that "the Republicans themselves don't think it wise for colored citizens to . . . fill state [or] federal positions . . . ."[89] Still, the appointment of blacks or promises of appointments were

[86] The Republican governors included Henry Clay Evans of Tennessee in 1894, who would eventually be denied his victory by the highly partisan work of a Democratic legislature; William O'Connell Bradley of Kentucky in 1895; Daniel Lindsay Russell of North Carolina and George Wesley Atkinson of West Virginia in 1896; William S. Taylor of Kentucky in 1899, who like Evans would be unseated by a Democratic legislature; and Albert Blakeslee White of West Virginia in 1900. The Republican senators included Jeter Connelly Pritchard of North Carolina elected in 1894 and 1896, Stephen Benton Elkins of West Virginia elected in 1894 and 1900, William Joseph DeBoe of Kentucky elected in 1897, and Nathan Bay Scott of West Virginia elected in 1898.

[87] Fredrickson, *Black Image*, 256–82.

[88] Clipping, 1879, Scrapbook, Willson Papers.

[89] M. N. Corbitt to Thomas Settle, III, July 26, 1892, Settle Papers.

made by mountain politicians when it was deemed necessary. The Elkins machine in West Virginia delayed giving patronage to black applicants in some cases to test their loyalty to the organization.[90] These tactics were quite successful in ending a revolt by blacks in West Virginia against Elkins in 1900.[91]

Even if a black did manage to secure a political job from mountain Republicans, he still had to contend with Republicans who thought he should not have the position. In March 1892 many white Republican Internal Revenue Service employees in the mountain counties in North Carolina refused to work with a recently appointed black worker and seriously disrupted the agency's operations.[92] A black deputy marshal in eastern Kentucky also found he had great difficulty performing his job because of the hostility of the mountaineers.[93] The dilemma faced by black appointees is well explained in the following letter from Charles M. Cansler, future educator and civil rights leader in East Tennessee. "I have recently been appointed to a position as substitute in the Railroad Mail Service for the line centering in Chattanooga Tenn. from the Civil Service examination of last August. Because of the existing prejudice on the part of the white clerks on these lines I have been unable to get such work as will enable me to secure a livelihood from this position."[94] It appears that for some mountain Republicans the assignment of even one office to a black Republican was too many.

Blacks were increasingly passed over as potential candidates for public office and were even discouraged from attending party conventions. Kentucky Republican gubernatorial candidate in 1895, William O'Connell Bradley, was apparently willing to make patronage commitments to blacks before he was nominated to ensure that blacks would not demand a spot on the state ticket.[95] Blacks were excluded from Republican state conventions as early as 1888, and by 1900 North Carolina Republicans could boast that their state meeting "was a convention not only dominated by white

[90] S. B. Avis to Elkins, April 27, 1900, Stephen Benton Elkins Papers (West Virginia Collection, West Virginia University Library).

[91] H. F. Gamble to Albert B. White, February 7, 1900; Daniel W. Shaw, *The Second Emancipation of the Negro,* August 16, 1900, Albert Blakeslee White Papers (West Virginia Collection, West Virginia University Library); H. C. Duncan to A. Brooks Fleming, March 10, 1900, Aretas Brooks Fleming Papers (West Virginia Collection, West Virginia University Library); H. M. Adams to Stephen B. Elkins, March 20, 1900; I. R. LeSage to Elkins, March 20, 1900; Phil Waters to Elkins, March 22, 1900, Elkins Papers.

[92] John W. Mason to W. W. Rollins, March 20, 1892, Letterbook, Mason Papers.

[93] Mt. Vernon (Ky) *Signal,* July 16, 1897.

[94] Cansler to Leonidas C. Houk, January 2, 1891, Houk Papers.

[95] Louisa (Ky.) *Big Sandy News,* August 2, 1895.

TABLE 2

VOTER REGISTRATION BY RACE IN KNOXVILLE, TENNESSEE, 1894

Ward	*White*	*Colored*	*Total*
1	454	39	493
2	192	84	276
3	212	141	353
4	165	35	200
5	224	419	643
6	407	95	502
7	756	678	1,434
8	385	270	655
9	836	252	1,088
Total	3,631	2,013	5,644

Clinton (Tenn.) *Weekly Gazette*, October 17, 1894

men, but composed of white men.[96] Moving increasingly toward segregation within the party, mountain Republicans became enthusiastic supporters of social segregation in churches, schools, public facilities, and on public transportation.[97]

Mountain Republicans used other means to give the appearance of eliminating the black man from politics while still striving to preserve his right to vote. One of the more effective ways to accomplish this was to gerrymander black voters to prevent their candidates from winning in local elections. Table 2 showing the ward populations of the mountain city of Knoxville, Tennessee, provides a good illustration of this tactic. While black voters made up 35 percent of the electorate, they were in the majority in only one of the city's nine wards. The contrast between the Fourth and Seventh wards is particularly instructive. In the former only 165 white voters formed a majority, while in the latter 678 blacks were in the minority.

TRIKS TO MIN. BLACKS

Another trick resorted to by mountain Republicans in an effort to minimize black participation in campaigns was to run candidates that seemed hostile to black interests. Southwestern Virginia mountain Republicans ran James A. Walker for Congress four times in the 1890s, although his record as a Confederate general and former

[96] Asheville *Citizen*, July 29, 1888; Winston (N. C.) *Union Republican*, May 10, 1900.

[97] Clipping, August 27, 1895, Scrapbook, William O'Connell Bradley Papers (University of Kentucky Library, Lexington, Ky.); Wheeling *Intelligencer*, February 20, 1892 Big Stone Gap (Va.) *Post*, October 18, 1894; Louisa (Ky.) *Big Sandy News*, August 30, 1895.

Democrat made him unappealing to blacks.[98] North Carolina mountain Republicans, reacting to the increasing racism of the opposition, supported Daniel Lindsay Russell for governor in 1896. He was quoted as saying that "The negroes of the South are largely savages."[99] The strategy behind Russell's nomination was explained by the candidate himself: "The Democrats will try the old dodge of trying the 'Color line' but it worries them to discover just how to do it. They have been preaching . . . that Russell is dead against the negroes, that he favors white supremacy and that he is opposed to even the mildest form of negro government. Now they will proceed to prove that he is in favor of compelling every white woman to marry a negro, and that he, himself is a mulatto. This is a rather heavy job for them, but not too big for them to attempt."[100] North Carolina black Republicans were so outraged by Russell's nomination that they called a convention to protest and demand a new candidate.[101]

Two other techniques were used to deemphasize the presence of blacks in the Republican party. Kentucky Republicans in the gubernatorial and state campaign of 1895 simply refused to acknowledge the existence of black Republicans. The party's campaign committee would not work with blacks and forbade candidates to mention racial matters.[102] Their advice seems to have been generally followed. Harvey Samuel Irwin, a candidate for state railroad commissioner, was asked in an open letter if he would vote to repeal the separate-but-equal railway coach law. Irwin refused to answer and continued his campaign as if the question had never been asked.[103] Gubernatorial candidate William O. Bradley withdrew from a series of joint debates with his Democratic opponent when racial issues began to dominate the discussions.[104] Negroes, angered by these snubs, formed the Kentucky Colored Democrat Club to force a change in the Republican campaign. Tennessee mountain Republicans developed the novel idea of voluntary black disfranchisement. In 1894 H. Clay Evans, the gubernatorial candidate, and his campaign manager, Newell Sanders, persuaded many blacks not to vote in the expectation that this would reduce the racial excitement and fraud perpetrated by

[98] Big Stone Gap (Va.) *Post*, September 6, 1894.

[99] Winston (N. C.) *Union Republican*, July 26, 1888.

[100] Russell to J. H. Ramsay, May 27, 1896, Ramsay Papers.

[101] James E. Shepard to Thomas Settle, III, May 19, 1896; M. N. Corbitt to Settle, May 27, 1896; *To the People of North Carolina*, June 6, 1896, Settle Papers.

[102] "The Republican Campaign of Kentucky, 1895," unpublished manuscript, George Davidson Todd Papers (Collections of the Filson Club).

[103] Clipping, June 30, 1895, Scrapbook, Bradley Papers.

[104] "Republican Campaign of Kentucky, 1895," Todd Papers.

the Democrats.[105] All these elaborate strategies were aimed at convincing white voters that the Republican party was a white man's party while at the same time preserving the Negro's right to vote.

Mountain white Republicans seemed willing to accept this solution to the racial situation within the party. The 1898 election in North Carolina offered the greater test of the willingness of mountain white Republicans to be identified with blacks as political allies. In this campaign the Democrats made a special effort to convince mountain voters of the evil results of black political advances made under the fusion government in that state.[106] Democratic state chairman Furnifold McLendel Simmons and Raleigh *News and Observer* editor Josephus Daniels directed the attack against black officeholders who had been elected since 1894. The two men launched a racist cartoon campaign in western North Carolina newspapers to ensure that even the illiterate would receive the message.[107] The climax of the bitter attack on fusion was a white man's convention at Goldsboro attended by more than 8,000 voters.[108] The mountain Republicans launched an equally racist counterattack that stopped short of demanding an end to black voting.[109] The percentages in Table 3 indicate that mountain Republican voters accepted their leaders' position. Although the Republican percentage of the vote did decline in western North Carolina in 1898, the decrease was relatively small and followed the general four-year pattern of the entire mountain region. North Carolina mountain Republicans simply refused to be frightened by continued Negro participation in politics.

Despite the efforts by mountain Republicans to conceal their dependence on black voters, Democratic attempts to disfranchise Negroes were successful in North Carolina and Virginia. The North Carolina legislature had framed a suffrage amendment to the state constitution in 1899 that would effectively eliminate most black voters. When the proposal was submitted to the voters in August 1900 the mountain Republican leaders vigorously opposed its approval.[110] Senator Pritchard and others concentrated their attack on the fact that despite the "grandfather clause" many poor

[105] Rufus Terral, *Newell Sanders: A Biography* (Kingsport, Tenn., 1935), 81–82; Benjamin W. Hooper, *The Unwanted Boy: The Autobiography of Governor Ben W. Hooper*, edited by Everett R. Boyce (Knoxville, 1963), 28.

[106] Statesville (N. C.) *Landmark*, October 4, 25, 28, November 1, 1898.

[107] *Ibid.*

[108] *Ibid.*, November 3, 1898.

[109] Winston (N. C.) *Union Republican*, September 1, 8, 29, October 13, 20, 27, 1898.

[110] *Ibid.*, January 11, 25, March 1, April 19, May 17, 24, 1900.

TABLE 3

PERCENTAGES OF THE REPUBLICAN VOTE IN THE MOUNTAIN COUNTIES OF THE UPPER SOUTH, 1896, 1898, AND 1900

	1896	*1898*	*1900*
North Carolina	51.1	49.3	52.2
Virginia	51.7	48.1	49.2
Kentucky	59.7	50.2	57.8
Tennessee	65.8	57.9	56.7
West Virginia	53.5	51.9	55.1

Computed from ICPR data

whites would lose the right to vote.[111] So effective was this approach that the Democrats had to call the legislature into special session a few weeks before the voting and modify the amendment to answer Republican criticism.[112] Nor did the mountain Republicans abandon the black voter. The leading Republican newspaper in the western part of the state printed an article written by black editor Timothy Thomas Fortune opposing the amendment.[113] Mountain Republicans were willing to allow the Democrats the right to prevent blacks from holding office—thereby ending the chance of "Negro domination"—but were unwilling to lose their Negro support at the polls.[114] This position apparently satisfied white mountain Republicans, who voted overwhelmingly against the suffrage changes.[115] Virginia Democrats saved themselves the trouble of a public debate and vote by having a constitutional convention declare that a new suffrage amendment was valid without popular ratification.

In the other three states of the upper South, the Negroes remained as voters, and the working relationship between mountain Republicans and blacks continued. In West Virginia the Republican party maintained control of the state until the depression of the 1930s with the black voter remaining a relatively loyal member of the party. Although the Republicans as a whole were in the minority in both Kentucky and Tennessee, mountain

[111] *Ibid.*, March 11, May 24, 1900.
[112] *Ibid.*, June 21, 1900.
[113] *Ibid.*, April 26, 1900.
[114] *Ibid.*, January 25, 1900.
[115] Statesville (N. C.) *Landmark*, August, 1900.

Republicans prospered in the years after 1900. Consistently winning congressional races in both mountain regions, mountain Republicans, blacks, and progressive Democrats combined to elect Progressive Republicans Benjamin W. Hooper of Tennessee and Augustus Everett Willson of Kentucky governors of their respective states. Even in the now lily-white electorate of southwestern Virginia mountain Republicans enjoyed some success. Campbell Slemp and his son Campbell Bascom Slemp constructed a Republican machine in the Virginia mountains that controlled the Ninth Congressional District for nearly two decades. In both Virginia and North Carolina, however, the old relationship between black and white Republicans was destroyed. With the black no longer a voter and still a competitor for federal patronage, mountain Republicans in those two states read the blacks out of the party.

The general position of white mountain Republicans on race relations within the party in the last third of the nineteenth century was determined by the power of the black man as a voter. The relationship that developed in each state was deeply influenced by two factors that remained relatively constant throughout this period. In comparison to other white southerners mountain whites did not live with a large black population, and this geographical and demographical fact made it possible for them to determine political affiliation on the basis of issues other than race. In addition, Negro voters proved to be extremely loyal to the Republican party and were too valuable as political allies to abandon. This did not mean that mountain Republicans viewed blacks as equals or that blacks necessarily had the right to run for and be appointed to office. But mountain Republicans did maintain that blacks had the basic right to vote—Republican. The men who had proposed to "elevate mankind of all races and colors" clearly had forsaken that goal and had turned instead to the elevation of their own political ambitions.

Notes and Documents

Jefferson Davis Ponders His Future, 1829

Edited by LYNDA J. LASSWELL

WRITTEN ON HIS BIRTHDAY IN 1829, THE FOLLOWING LETTER affords a rare personal glimpse of Jefferson Davis as a young man. Davis had just graduated from the United States Military Academy at West Point the previous summer and was beginning what was to be his first career. Before reporting for active duty, however, he had requested a six-month furlough to visit his home in Wilkinson County, Mississippi. On his trip southward Davis stopped for some time in Kentucky, the state of his birth. As a young boy he had returned to Kentucky to study at St. Thomas College near Springfield, and later he had attended Transylvania University at Lexington. It was the autumn of 1828 when he reached his home at Woodville. He had been away almost six years, during which time his father, Samuel Emory Davis, had died, as had an older brother and his youngest sister. Four older brothers and sisters had long since married and moved away, leaving Davis's mother, Jane Cook Davis, and his sister Lucinda and her family at Rosemont Plantation. Lucinda Stamps seems to have been Davis's favorite sister, perhaps because she lived the greater part of her life in the house Davis remembered from his childhood, the home where he said "my memories begin." This letter is believed to be the earliest of their surviving correspondence, the first of a series of letters which shows Davis's constant affection and concern for the welfare of the family.

Only recently ordered to Fort Winnebago (now Portage, Wisconsin), Davis explains his first assignment to the infantry school of practice—for basic training—at Jefferson Barracks near St. Louis, where he reported in January 1829. He was sent in March to the headquarters of the First Infantry at Fort Crawford (now Prairie du Chien) and was recorded as present for duty at Fort Winnebago in May. The new brevet second lieutenant, appointed acting assist-

MS. LASSWELL is a graduate student at the University of Tennessee at Knoxville and a former assistant editor of *The Papers of Jefferson Davis*.

ant commissary of subsistence for May and June, was not assigned to a company until August.

Davis also speculates on his future in this remarkable letter, considering careers in the army and the law, and ironically rejecting one in politics. It is unknown whether or not he received the law books he ordered from New York; he never served as a judge advocate while in the army, and he did not practice law as a civilian. He was to be disappointed in his hopes for a future assignment to a post near home, as he continued to serve in the Northwest until early 1833. Transferred to the newly organized dragoon regiment at Jefferson Barracks, he was then sent to Fort Gibson, Indian Territory, and was stationed there until his resignation in 1835. In fact, Davis never returned to Rosemont for any length of time after his 1828 visit. During his seven-year military career he was home only once—on a brief furlough in 1832. Soon after his resignation from the service, he married Zachary Taylor's daughter, Sarah Knox Taylor. They had planned to settle in Warren County on a substantial cotton plantation adjacent to the home of Davis's eldest brother, Joseph Emory Davis, who was one of the state's most successful planters. With Sarah Davis's sudden death in September 1835 Davis withdrew to his Brierfield Plantation and for the next eight years devoted himself to the cultivation of the plantation, living in virtual seclusion.[1]

Most of the material on Davis's early life was published in Volume I of *The Papers of Jefferson Davis,* but this letter was not discovered until 1972. It will be included in the final volume of the Davis papers along with other addenda. However, because of its unusually introspective nature, it has seemed desirable to make it available to scholars before that distant date. It is printed here for the first time, with the permission of the owners, Mr. and Mrs. Joseph P. Endris of Paris, Kentucky. It is most regrettable that Mr. Endris died June 28, 1975, before the letter appeared in print.

Part of a large collection of family heirlooms, the letter was discovered by Ernesto Caldeira and Percival T. Beacroft, who are researching the Davis family genealogy in conjunction with the current restoration of Rosemont Plantation. Mr. Endris's great-grandmother, Jane Stamps Alexander, was Jefferson Davis's niece, the eldest daughter of Lucinda and William Stamps. Jane Stamps

[1] All details of Davis's early career (to 1840) are found in Haskell M. Monroe, Jr., and James T. McIntosh, eds., *The Papers of Jefferson Davis* (2 vols. to date, Baton Rouge, 1971–1975), I, *passim.* The editor is grateful to Percival T. Beacroft, Ernesto Caldeira, Mary S. Dix, and James T. McIntosh for their assistance, and to Mr. and Mrs. Joseph P. Endris for permission to publish the letter.

was born in Mississippi but moved to Paris, Kentucky, when she married her cousin William W. Alexander in 1845. The Alexander descendants, especially Mr. Endris's mother, have continued to protect and augment the collection of furniture, documents, and other memorabilia still maintained in the Alexander home. Family tradition holds that Davis was close to the Kentucky branch of the Stamps family, visiting them frequently on his travels between Washington and Mississippi in thc 1840s and 1850s.

The four-page document appears as nearly like the original as possible. Spelling and punctuation are Davis's, with the exception that dashes marking the ends of sentences are changed to periods. An extended space is used where punctuation was omitted. Some words are added in square brackets for clarity or where the manuscript is damaged. Interlined words have been silently incorporated in the text, and word or phrase repetitions have been as silently deleted.

Addressed "Mrs. Lucinda F Stamps Woodville Mississippi" and postmarked "Prairie du Chien M. T. June 14 25 [cents]," the letter is endorsed in an unknown hand, "His style in youth or age still the same."

FORT WINNEBAGO OUISCONSIN PORTAGE MICH. T.
June 3d 1829

DEAR SISTER[2]

Shortly after my arrival here I wrote to you giving you some account of my trip and will now give you some account of my situation which is one of the most elevated in the country by which I do not mean that I am near the highest station of the nation but that the Portage is the summit level of the western and Eastern wateres the ouisconsin running into the Mississippi and the Fox into Green Bay which communicates with the lakes the Fort is on the Fox[3] the country around being prairie is now beautiful and being studded by islands of woods possesses by a variety in the scene an advantage over most Prairies the Fox is a sluggish and very crooked river its banks low and the grass grows to the waters edge which makes it look beautiful at a distance the water so clear that you see the fish swimming all through it and affording a fine opportunity for gigging, the officers of the Post are like those of the army generally men of light habits both of thinking and acting having little to care about and less to anticipate, promotion does not depend on merit at all and the duties being plain there

[2] Lucinda Farrar Davis Stamps (1797–1873), Davis's second eldest sister, was married to William Stamps and resided at Rosemont Plantation, near Woodville, Mississippi. *Ibid.*, 19.

[3] At this point in the text Davis drew a small diagram (½″ × 1½″) showing the location of the fort with respect to the Fox and Wisconsin rivers.

is but small inducement to study and as you readily suppose they like other men will not labour for the love of it. Their manners are genteel and as far as morality is deemed necessary in the intercourse of men of the world it is strictly observed dissipation less common than among the citizens of Mississippi and drunkards not to be found in the army at this time and as fast as young ones grow up they are dismissed from the service.

Yours of March 17th[4] arrived yesterday forwarded from Jefferson Bks. You cannot Dear Sister regret more than myself our more distant seperation but perhaps next year I may be stationed near you perhaps I may be sent further from you perhaps remain stationary but I think the first perhaps most probable. I cannot say that I like the army but I know of nothing else that I could do which I would like better your partiality for me has caused you to anticipate too much from me I believe that if I had returned home from Lexington[5] I might have made a tolerably respectable citizen but now I do not believe I could get along well with citizens for the four years I remained at west Point made me a different creature from that which nature had designed me to be I shall however endeavour to improve myself as much as circumstances will permit I have sent on to New York for some books among others some law Books which I intend to make when I can procure such a considerable part of my reading my means and situation in life prevent me from buying any thing like a course of professional books but I shall be stationed at some place when I leave this where they can probably be hired and returned if I should be suddenly ordered to another post. I was ordered to join the troops at Jefferson Barracks because that was the head-Quarters of the Infantry I was retained there because it was the school of Infantry practice and I did not belong to any Regiment I was afterwards assigned to the first Regiment of Infantry and ordered to report to it's head Quarters which was at Prairie Du Chien on my arrival at head Quarters I was ordered to this post because it was thought my services were most required here.

I Know you feel an anxiety to Know what I expect to do and if I had any definite plan I would most willingly unfold it[6] to you but as I have not I will give you a sort of composition the chief ingredient of which I am afraid you will say is nothing I intend to read with a view to acquire general information & to mix with general, legal reading if at anytime I should determine on a civil course of life I think I would prefer the practice of law to any other profession and [if] I should remain in the army a Knowledge of law [will qualify me?][7] the better for the duties of Judge Advocate whic[h] [is?][7] an honorable and frequently pleasing and profi-

[4] This letter has not been found.

[5] A reference to Davis's attendance (1823–1824) at Transylvania University in Lexington, Kentucky. He went directly from there to the United States Military Academy. Monroe and McIntosh, eds., *The Papers of Jefferson Davis,* I, lxxxv, 10–11.

[6] The words "unfold it" are written, struck out, then repeated.

[7] Manuscript torn.

ta[ble] duty. To day I am 22 years old[8] when I was a boy and dreamed with my eyes open as most do I thought of ripening fame at this age of wealth and power as I grew older I saw the folly of this but still thought that at the age of 22 I should be on the high way to all ambition desired and lo: I am 22 and the same obscure poor being that I was at fifteen with the exception of a petty appointment which may[9] long remain as small as it is at present[10]—and yet I am not dissatisfied for I behold myself a member though an humble one of an honorable profession one in which sychophancy though it may be beneficial is not necessary to success and the close of which will be a mere stoppage of the current, not attended by the maledictions which so often hang round the closing scene of the politician whose struggles begun in folly are closed in disgrace.

I fulfilled Mr. Stamps's[11] expectations in writing to him the second letter before I left Missouri[12] and hope to hear from him shortly. Miss Hooke's[13] marriage was regretted by some of the officers here who were acquainted with her as they said because she had married a man unworthy of her. Tell William[14] he must not forget me though I am far from him and that I hope to see him before he gets married unless he should be in a hurry in which case I do not wish him to wait for my arrival. When you write to me give me all the news of the family[15] and do not believe any thing which con-[c]erns you too small to interest me.

The diamond breast pin you gave me was universally admired by the Missouri girls and drew an attention in ball rooms which if I had been about four years younger might have made me vain but as it was I was disposed to believe they viewed it as the index of a Cotton plantation and if so the poor creatures would have been wofully dissappointed if enticed by

[8] Davis used June 3, 1807, as his birth date for some time. He later adopted 1808 as the year of his birth. This letter also shows the "J. F. Davis" signature which he used until the early 1830s. Members of his family continued to address and refer to him as Jefferson F. Davis as late as 1893. Monroe and McIntosh, eds., *The Papers of Jefferson Davis,* I, lxv*n.* and *passim.*

[9] The word "may" is repeated.

[10] Davis was brevet second lieutenant until March 1831 when he was appointed to a second lieutenancy in the First Infantry. He was not promoted to first lieutenant until May 1834. Monroe and McIntosh, eds., *The Papers of Jefferson Davis,* I, 182–83, 321–22.

[11] William Stamps, Jr. (1797–1878), Davis's brother-in-law, was a Kentucky-born planter and businessman who lived with his family at Rosemont Plantation. *Ibid.*, 275; family Bible owned by Joseph P. Endris, Paris, Kentucky.

[12] These letters, apparently written during Davis's brief stay at Jefferson Barracks, January–March 1829, have not been found.

[13] Identity unknown.

[14] Not a member of the known Davis family. Davis's nephew William Stamps was a small child in 1829. "William" may have been a neighbor or a servant. Monroe and McIntosh, eds., *The Papers of Jefferson Davis,* I, 520*n.*

[15] Members of the family believed living at Rosemont in 1829 included Lucinda and William Stamps; their four children—Jane Davis, Anna Aurelia, William, and Isaac Davis Stamps; Hugh Robert Davis, Lucinda's son from her first marriage; Jane Cook Davis, Lucinda's and Jefferson's mother; Ellen Mary and Jane Lucinda Davis, children of Davis's youngest sister who had died in 1824. *Ibid.*, 19, 22*n.*, 275, 282*n.*, 518–19.

the index they had examined the contents but I did not of course put myself to the trouble of telling them this. Remember me affectionately to Mother[16] and tell her I will [write] to her shortly

I hope some day to be permanently settled near you but if I never should if the distance between us should increase with time of separation still will my affections remain unchanged and unchangeable my reflections will often be about you and my greatest happiness consist in the Knowledge of your welfare and those who are to us an object of common anxiety. I feel something like the pain of leaving you but letters like meetings must have an end. You will doubtless think this one long enough.

Farewell your Brother
J. F. DAVIS

[16] Jane Cook Davis, widow of Samuel E. Davis, lived at Rosemont until her death at age eighty-four on October 3, 1845. *Ibid.*, lxviii, 22*n*.

A Note on Evidence: The Personal History of Madison Hemings

By Dumas Malone and Steven H. Hochman

On March 13, 1873, an obscure weekly newspaper in Waverly, Ohio, the *Pike County Republican*, published an autobiographical narrative of a former slave of Thomas Jefferson's named Madison Hemings. His story supported the allegation first circulated among Jefferson's political enemies and later by many abolitionists that he had kept a mulatto mistress and fathered mulatto children. Hemings claimed that his mother, Sally Hemings, was Jefferson's concubine and that he, Madison Hemings, was Jefferson's son, born in 1805 when that gentleman was President of the United States. How much attention this claim received outside south-central Ohio would be difficult to determine, but word of it reached James Parton, who was publishing a serial biography of Jefferson in the *Atlantic Monthly* at the time. Taking up the "Dusky Sally" story in his July 1873 installment, Parton stated politely that Hemings was "misinformed." In fact, said he, the father in question "was a near relation of the Jeffersons, who need not be named." A nephew of Thomas Jefferson, one of the Carr brothers, had been named in a letter Parton had received five years earlier from Henry S. Randall, but this was not published until 1951.[1]

The memoir of Madison Hemings appears to have remained in obscurity even longer. Credit for its rediscovery belongs to James H. Rodabaugh, formerly head of the Division of History and Science in the Ohio Historical Society. Through him John Dos Passos became acquainted with it by 1955. That author corresponded

[1] For Parton's comments see *Atlantic Monthly*, XXXII (July 1873), 28–29, and his *Life of Thomas Jefferson* (Boston, 1874), 568–70. Randall's letter of June 1, 1868, was published by Milton E. Flower in *James Parton: The Father of American Biography* (Durham, N. C., 1951), 236–39. An earlier letter implicating the Carr brothers, that of Ellen Randolph to Joseph Coolidge, Jr., October 24, 1858, was published in 1974 with relevant comments and references. American Antiquarian Society, *Proceedings*, LXXXIV, Pt. 1 (April 1974), 65–72.

Mr. Malone is working on the final volume of his biography of Jefferson at the University of Virginia. Mr. Hochman is his assistant. They wish to thank the staff of the Ohio Historical Society at Columbus, where research for this note was done.

with several scholars about it, though he himself made no literary use of it for some years. Meanwhile, in 1960, it was summarized in print by Merrill D. Peterson, who denied, however, that it proved Jefferson to have been the father of Madison Hemings.[2] That same year a critical examination of it was made by Douglass G. Adair, with whom Dos Passos had corresponded. Along with the memoir itself, Adair's study of "The Jefferson Scandals" was communicated to other scholars, but it remained unpublished until 1974, when it appeared in a posthumous volume of essays.[3] Without discrediting the sincerity of Madison Hemings, Adair rejected his claim and accepted Parton's explanation of his paternity. John Dos Passos in his account of Jefferson's Presidency cited this explanation approvingly in 1966, saying the "defamatory stories" circulated by James Thomson Callender "became part of the political mythology of the Jeffersonian era."[4] A few months before Adair's posthumous essay appeared, the article in the *Pike County Republican* was reprinted by Fawn M. Brodie under the title "Reminiscences of Madison Hemings." She has described this as "the most important single document" relating to the story of Sally Hemings, and except for a few minor inaccuracies she accepts it as factually correct.[5]

Apparently, neither she nor any of the other writers who have cited this document in recent years inquired into the circumstances of its original publication. Any document must be viewed by the historian in its actual setting of time and place, and there is all the more reason for him to do so if it deals with events that occurred long before it was written. This particular memoir refers to supposed happenings in Paris almost a score of years before the narrator himself was born. Our concern here, however, is with the circumstances of its appearance rather than its contents. In its published form it was a report of an interview by the editor of the *Pike County Republican*, S. F. Wetmore. Judging from its title, "Life Among the Lowly, Number One," he hoped it would create sympathy for the freedmen just as *Uncle Tom's Cabin* did for the slaves. That the treedmen needed sympathy and that the Republican party needed support at this particular place at that time be-

[2] John Roderigo Dos Passos Papers (Alderman Library, University of Virginia, Charlottesville, Va.); Peterson, *The Jefferson Image in the American Mind* (New York, 1960), 185–86, 482–83.

[3] Adair, *Fame and the Founding Fathers*, edited by Trevor Colbourn (New York, 1974), 160–91.

[4] Dos Passos, *The Shackles of Power: Three Jeffersonian Decades* (Garden City, N. Y., 1966), [vi], 153–55; quotation on page 155.

[5] Appendix in Brodie, *Thomas Jefferson: An Intimate History* (New York, 1974), 471–76; see also p. 30.

comes abundantly clear on examination of the local situation. Pike County was a Democratic bastion, and anti-Negro sentiment was very strong there, especially in Waverly.

The county seat was so hostile to black settlement that as late as 1888, according to the memoir of a leading citizen, a Negro had never been allowed to live within the town limits. It was said to be the only town in Ohio with a population above 2,000 of which this was true. Yet, as the memoir noted, many of the surrounding hills were "fairly infested with negroes."[6] When, in 1836, Madison Hemings first settled in the state, he lived in Pebble Township, directly west of Pee Pee Township which included Waverly. A skilled carpenter, he did extensive construction work in the town even though he was unwelcome as a resident. After about four or five years he moved north to Huntington Township. This was actually in Ross County, although his mailing address remained Pee Pee Township in Pike, apparently the nearest post office.

The editor and publisher of the *Pike County Republican*, S. F. Wetmore, was a native of Maine, who had lived in at least four other states before working for a Republican paper in Portsmouth, Ohio, at the end of the Civil War. From there he moved to Waverly and, "in hopes to be useful to the Pike County Republicans," revived their local party paper.[7] The opposing editor called him a carpetbagger, not only because he had invaded a Democratic stronghold but also because he was rewarded with federal patronage by the Republican administration of Grant.[8]

Since Waverly was strongly Democratic, Wetmore cultivated the rural districts of Pike and nearby counties. On his horse, "Old Ten Thousand," he rode through the countryside, visiting people both black and white and recording their circumstances in "Notes by the Way." On March 3, 1870, he began a series of biographical sketches of the oldest citizens of the county. He did at least thirty-two of these and made sure he mentioned numerous voters' names. Although the style was not wholly consistent, the interviews were generally presented as first-person narratives. In number one, answers to questions were given in the first person, but Wetmore noted that the daughter of the man interviewed had chanced to be at her father's house, and he had "learned from her facts that might have been overlooked." Clearly, the final article was Wetmore's

[6] M. J. Carrigan, ed., *Life and Reminiscences of Hon. James Emmitt, as Revised by Himself* (Chillicothe, Ohio, 1888), 285–87. For the general situation in Ohio see Eugene H. Roseboom, *The History of the State of Ohio*, IV: *The Civil War Era, 1850–1873* (Columbus, 1944).

[7] Waverly *Pike County Republican*, September 24, 1868.

[8] Waverly *Watchman*, April 1, 1873.

composition, even though the quotations in it appeared to be direct.

When, in 1873, he decided to begin a series on old colored residents of the area, his system of interviewing was well established. Before talking with Madison Hemings he could have consulted a life of Jefferson, though he sought to give the opposite impression, and he may probably be assumed to have asked leading questions. His Democratic rival, John A. Jones, editor of the Waverly *Watchman,* promptly published a reply to the story.

The contesting editors spoke for their political constituents as well as for themselves in the two documents that are printed below. Let us say in our own behalf that this note on evidence is intended as neither an attack on the sincerity of Madison Hemings, who appears to have been an estimable character, nor as a rounded critique of his story, which we find unacceptable in important respects for reasons not presented here. We would not exaggerate the significance of the fresh light we have shed on the circumstances of its appearance. But, quite clearly, the story was solicited and published for a propagandist purpose.

Editor's Introduction to "Life Among the Lowly"[9]

In our peregrinations in this and Ross counties, we have been made aware that a respectable portion of the population was made up of colored people, who came mostly from Virginia. In our visits among them we have picked up bits of personal history which we have thought the relation of would be entertaining reading. We this week commence a series of articles under the heading of "Life Among the Lowly." The subject is Madison Hemings, who claims to be a son of Thomas Jefferson, and who tells a straightforward story. While he never experienced many of the cruelties of slavery, we must say that the system was cruel, at best. To keep such a man as Madison Hemings, in the condition of a slave, however well treated in other respects, was a sin of very deep dye. He is an intelligent man, and understands himself well. If he had been educated and given a chance in the world he would have shone out as a star of the first magnitude. But he was kept under, by his own father, an ex-President of the United States, and a man who penned the immortal Declaration of Independence which fully acknowledges the rights and equality of the human race! This is but another instance added to millions

[9] Waverly *Pike County Republican,* March 13, 1873, on the front page without a heading. The second number of "Life Among the Lowly" did not appear until November 20, 1873. The third number, which seems to have been the last, appeared December 25, 1873. This one is an account of another former Jefferson slave, Israel Jefferson. It is reprinted in Brodie, *Thomas Jefferson*, 477–82.

justifying President Lincoln's proclamation of emancipation. It did not come a day too soon. Mr. Hemings is five feet ten inches in height, sparely made, with sandy complexion and a mild gray eye. And all this accords very nearly with the description given of Thomas Jefferson, except that he was six feet one and a half inch in height.

We might have referred to histories and woven into the narrative dates and circumstances going to confirm the statements of Mr. Hemings, but we have given the old man's story as he has given it to us. And in continuing this series of articles we shall allow the narrators to tell their own tales in their simple ways, without any attempt on our part to garnish their revelations. Some were well treated in slavery, others were badly used. The condition of a majority of those who emigrated to this region was that of nominal freedom, though a portion were slaves. As soon as we can we will give their humble stories to the public, in our columns, who must judge whether they are less entertaining and instructing than the information contained in a book written by Harriet Beecher Stowe of which our heading is a part of the title to "Uncle Tom's Cabin."

Reply of Rival Editor to "Life Among the Lowly"[10]

The editor of the "Republican" having nothing of a weighty character on his hands, has commenced the publication of a series of articles entitled, "Life Among the Lowly," or the Lives and Adventures of Illegitimate Sons of Illustrious Sires, the first installment of which appears in the last issue of that paper. Madison Hemings heads the list, claiming to be the natural son of Thomas Jefferson by an illegitimate daughter of John Wa[y]les, the father-in-law of Jefferson.

Hemings, or rather Wetmore, gives a very truthful account of the public and private life of the Jefferson family; but this no doubt, was condensed from one of the numerous lives of Jefferson which can be found in any well-regulated family library. We have no doubt but there are at least fifty negroes in this county who lay claim to illustrious parentage. This is a well known peculiarity of the colored race. The children of Jefferson and Madison, Calhoun and Clay far out-number Washington's body servants when Barnum was in the height of his prosperity. They are not to be blamed for making these assertions. It sounds much better for the mother to tell her offspring that "master" is their father than to acknowledge to them that some field hand, without a name, had raised her to the dignity of a mother. They want the world to think they are particular in their liaisons with the sterner sex, whether the truth will bear them out or not. This is a well-known fact to those who have been reared in those States where slavery existed, and with them, no attention whatever, is paid to these rumors.—If they were, the "master" would have to bear the odium of all the licentious practices that are developed

[10] Waverly *Watchman*, March 18, 1873.

on the plantation. The fact that Hemings claims to be the natural son of Jefferson does not convince the world of its truthfulness. He is not supposed to be a competent witness in his own behalf. He was no doubt present at the time of accouch[e]ment, but his extreme youth would prevent him from knowing all the facts connected with that important event.—Jefferson was over 62 years of age when Hemings appeared upon the sacred soil of Virginia, if we are to believe his biographer. The extreme age of Jefferson, coupled with his natural frigidity of constitution causes a doubt in our mind whether or not Hemings has been correctly informed about the author of his being. Solomon, (if we have been correctly informed) said, when he took his two hundredth wife, "it's a wise child that knows its own father."—The same is as true to-day as it was in days of Solomon. At all events, Jefferson is not here to put in a disclaimer, and we think it rather mean to take this advantage of the author of the Declaration of Independence.

A perusal of Hemings' autobiography reminds us of the pedigree printed on the numerous stud-horse bills that can be seen posted around during the Spring season. No matter how scrubby the stock or whether the horse has any known pedigree, the "Horse Owner" furnishes a full and complete pedigree of every celebrated horse in the country. One of these is copied, and the scrawniest "plug" rejoices in a descent that would put Sir Archy to shame. The horse is not expected to know what is claimed for him. But we have often thought if one of them could read and would happen to come across his pedigree, tacked conspicuously at a prominent cross-road, he would blush to the tips of his ears at the mendacity of his owner.

Book Reviews

A History of the Old Soutn: The Emergence of a Reluctant Nation. Third Edition. By Clement Eaton. (New York: Macmillan Publishing Co.; London: Collier Macmillan, c. 1975. Pp. xvi, 544. $12.95.)

At a time when many major works on southern history—especially those relating to the exotic subject of slavery—are emanating from scholars who have only a casual firsthand acquaintance with the region, it is refreshing to receive the latest product from the pen of one of our most distinguished native southern historians. Born in North Carolina, educated in the company of such luminaries as Thomas Wolfe at both Chapel Hill and Harvard, and for more than twenty years a professor at the University of Kentucky, Clement Eaton brings to the study of southern history a catholicity of interests and a sympathetic understanding rivaled perhaps only by C. Vann Woodward and David Donald among contemporary scholars.

First published in 1949 and revised in 1966, this book has long been utilized as a basic text in courses on the Old South. This latest edition, incorporating judiciously the fruits of the last decade of historical scholarship, will enhance its utility in this respect. There are few major changes. In keeping with current trends, there is additional material on southern women and a new chapter on "The Middle Class and the Disadvantaged." Recognizing certain organizational problems in the earlier editions, Professor Eaton has sought to eliminate them by restructuring the material in some chapters and giving more appropriate titles to others.

In response to new interpretations offered in recent books on slavery, the author has revised his views on various aspects of "the peculiar institution." Unfortunately, he seems to have been influenced most heavily by the much-heralded but now thoroughly discredited cliometric study *Time on the Cross,* though it should be noted that the most perceptive criticisms of that work had not yet appeared when Eaton's volume went to press. In particular, he accepts too readily the conclusions of Fogel and Engerman regarding the efficiency of slave labor, the extent of the interregional slave trade, and the number of black overseers. On the other hand, Professor Eaton's portrayal of slavery reflects more accurately the realities of life in the nineteenth-century South than do many other recent works on the subject. Thus, he doubts that the average southerner felt guilty about owning slaves. He observes correctly that southern slavery "was much milder than the laws indicate" (p. 243) and, in a thinly veiled allusion to Kenneth Stampp and Eugene Genovese, "warns . . . against accepting the neoabolitionist, Marxist stereotype of an institution that was actually composed of infinitely varied relationships" (p. 269).

On the equally intriguing question of Civil War causation Eaton concludes that the confrontation of 1860–1861 resulted from a combination of deep-seated cultural differences and the desire of southerners to preserve their "peculiar institution." And, quite correctly I think, he emphasizes the effect of both individual and sectional honor in driving the South reluctantly toward secession and independence.

Clement Eaton's version of antebellum southern history will not be received with universal approbation. Like each of us, he is a product of his own environment—in his case, the early-twentieth-century white South—and his writings, however unconsciously, reflect that viewpoint. It is ironic that more than a century after the Civil War historians are still influenced by many of the same sectional differences so brilliantly delineated by Eaton in his characterization of an antebellum southern way of life and its northern counterpart. Still, this book—well written, balanced, perceptive, and nonpolemical—conveys, perhaps more clearly than any other single volume, an understanding of that enigmatic and fascinating phenomenon in American history which was the Old South.

University of Southern Mississippi WILLIAM K. SCARBOROUGH

Consensus, Conflict, and American Historians. By Bernard Sternsher. (Bloomington and London: Indiana University Press, c. 1975. Pp. xiv, 432. $15.00.)

Consensus, Conflict, and American Historians is an ambitious book somewhat ambiguously titled. Sternsher explains that he is "interested not only in the idea of consensus but also in the question whether the idea is empirically true. That is why," he writes, "I distinguish between the consensus view and the fact of consensus, and why I depart at various points from written history to history itself, as well as to sociology, economics, and especially political science" (p. 4). The reader meanwhile may find it difficult to see the relationship of orthodox historiography and long summaries of monographs dealing with public policy.

In the matter of consensus history Sternsher gives particular consideration to the works of Louis Hartz, Daniel Boorstin, and Richard Hofstadter. Hartz is admired for his view that the historic American mission is still more a matter of ideology than of imperialism. Boorstin, in contrast, wins no praise for his skepticism about the importance of ideologies and the prospect of their export. Sternsher's analysis of each historian, it should be noted, leans heavily on essays by J. R. Pole, John P. Diggins, and Neal Reimer.

Hofstadter receives less attention than Hartz or Boorstin, although Sternsher does not question his inclusion among consensus historians. To the reviewer this seems dubious. Hofstadter's *American Political Tradition,* often pointed to later as a seminal work in consensus history, was hailed on its publication in 1948 as a book without heroes. Hofstadter's dismissal of certain reformers as conservatives or pseudoprogressives was less an exercise in consensus than good old-fashioned historical muckraking in the Progressive tradition. Among some of the consensus historians who were much influenced by Marxism in the 1930s there is a strong residual animus against the Old Left and its failure to move America more quickly toward collectivism via some sort of democratic socialism. But in the case of Hofstadter, unlike Boorstin, there is no reason to assume that a disillusioned liberal is necessarily a conservative or even consistently a consensus historian.

Sternsher makes a valiant effort to describe the modern reinterpretation of such key periods as the Jacksonian, the Progressive, and the New Deal eras. At the same time, he summarizes recent work in political science, particularly quantitative studies of political behavior on a state and local as well as national level. He seems to believe that these data, especially when correlated with statistics on degrees of economic affluence, provide important support for the consensus view of history.

Sternsher, though suspicious of their economic determinism, is not wholly unsympathetic to the New Left critics of consensus history. He admires their concern for the plain people and for society's losers among the poor and ethnic minorities. He also agrees with the belated attention to violence, if not to class conflict, as a factor in American life. But he does not accept the New Left's enthusiasm for Charles Beard's pathbreaking delineation of the contrast between appearances and realities in the conduct of American foreign policy.

A writer attempting to interweave so many varied themes may easily fail to achieve an intelligible synthesis, and this is indeed a major shortcoming of Sternsher's work. The determination to disregard conventional academic parochialism is commendable, but it is most worthwhile when it achieves a result that is truly interdisciplinary. Unfortunately, long sections devoted to paraphrasing and quoting from a single specialized book or article turn large parts of Sternsher's study into an anthology of selected monographs. Thus, a chapter entitled "Criticism of Tocqueville" is confined mostly to a digest of Edward Pessen s articles on the egalitarian myth in Jacksonian America.

Sternsher complains toward the close of his volume that historians frequently fail to take into account the findings relative to their field presented in the critiques by nonhistorians. Yet Hartz, a professor of government, has had great influence on historians, who have accepted with little dissent his argument that the United States has been governed by a monolithic liberalism derived from the political teachings of John Locke. And Sternsher himself cites extensively a broad sampling of political and social scientists as well as historians. This rich documentation is one of the strengths of the book which will enhance its value for the scholars for whom Sternsher writes. Even they would probably appreciate, however, a concluding chapter which is really a summary. Instead, Sternsher ends his work with a puzzling digression, inspired by Hartz's *The Founding of New Societies,* on the old question of whether Frederick Jackson Turner's thesis applies to others of the world's frontier areas.

State University of New York at Albany ARTHUR A. EKIRCH, JR.

The New Urban History: Quantitative Explorations by American Historians. Edited by Leo F. Schnore. Foreword by Eric E. Lampard. (Princeton: Princeton University Press, c. 1975. Pp. xii, 284. Paper, $8.75; cloth, $17.50.)

The subtitle of this book describes its authors as "historians," yet only four of the ten contributing essayists were trained in departments of history. The other six were trained primarily as economists or geographers. This is well and good, for the past belongs to anyone who can interpret it, regardless of institutional affiliation. But history departments should be aware that their presumptive monopoly on the past, and even the appellation "historian," is slipping. The nine papers in this collection stem from a 1970 conference sponsored by the Mathematical Social Science Board. MSSB is an interdisciplinary group of thirteen scholars who use a generous annual government grant to encourage the use of mathematical methods in the study of human affairs. This is the third volume in the MSSB's historical series, the first having been devoted to the dimensions of quantitative history, the second to the British economy after 1840, and a fourth volume to race and slavery in the Western Hemisphere. Economic historian Robert W. Fogel is editor of the series.

The essays collected here are as heterogeneous in subject matter and discordant in approach as the urban environment itself. The editor for the volume, sociologist Leo Schnore, artificially but usefully grouped them under the three headings: the growth and function of cities, accommodations to the urban environment, and economic analysis of urban-industrial phenomena.

Under the omnibus heading of growth and function, geographer Allan Pred presents some fascinating data on antebellum commodity flows and information diffusion, but his fine insights are almost hidden by a miserable prose style and needless reliance on professional jargon. In the volume's least successful essay, geographer Martyn Bowden tries to link the emergence of central business districts to thresholds of population, even though his own evidence plainly suggests that population is not the key variable. Historian Kenneth Jackson's unpretentious essay on suburbanization in the nineteenth century shows—unsurprisingly—that by any of six definitions of "urban deconcentration" the phenomenon is not unique to the twentieth century.

The most impressive paper in the section on accommodations to urban life is Kathleen Neils Conzen's study of patterns of residence in early Milwaukee. She employs factor analysis to construct a painstaking (though curiously inconclusive) description of a sudden crystallization of residence patterns, especially along ethnic lines, that occurred between 1850 and 1860. Zane Miller's examination of the black population of five southern cities, 1865 to 1920, provides only ambiguous support for his thesis—that blacks flourished in an urban environment—but the data he compiled are valuable in their own right. Gregory Singleton's belligerent claims for quantitative method are hardly justified by his tentative and unsurprising conclusions, but he too presents useful data showing that Fundamentalists in Los Angeles in the 1920s and 1930s were extraordinarily transient and generally alienated from the larger community.

Econometrics holds sway in the third section of the book. Readers of *Time on the Cross* will already be familiar with Claudia Goldin's contention that the declining population of urban slaves in the 1850s is attributable to the inelastic demand for slaves on plantations rather than to any inherent incompatibility between slavery and urban life.

The most exciting essay in the entire volume (published elsewhere in different form) is Robert Higgs's demonstration of a close correlation between inventiveness (patents) and levels of urbanization. Higgs attributes the greater inventiveness of urban population to the city dweller's lower costs of gathering and disseminating information. He suggests that this unintended consequence of urban concentration may explain the self-sustaining quality of urban-industrial development.

The final essay, by urban economists Joseph Swanson and Jeffrey Williamson, constructs a rarified model of firm location and optimal city size that is beyond my capacity to evaluate or even, in awe, to appreciate. By addressing themselves exclusively to their methodological peers, these two authors exemplify *fortissimo* a problem that runs through the whole collection: the contributors, each content with his own audience of specialists, are not even speaking to each other, much less to educated laymen. Eric Lampard in his witty and intelligent foreword pleads for a history that is rigorous but comprehensible to the general reader—to no avail. Though in many ways this is an admirable volume, in this important respect it fails.

Rice University THOMAS L. HASKELL

Race and Slavery in the Western Hemisphere: Quantitative Studies. Edited by Stanley L. Engerman and Eugene D. Genovese. (Princeton: Princeton University Press, c. 1975. Pp. xvi, 556. $20.00.)

This volume is the fourth in a series, *Quantitative Studies in History,* sponsored by the History Advisory Committee of the Mathematical Social Science Board. Nineteen of the twenty-one essays are modifications of papers first presented at a conference ambiguously entitled "An International Comparison of Systems of Slavery," held at the University of Rochester in 1972. The contributors were from the United States, Canada, and the United Kingdom, and they included social scientists as well as historians. The four main sections of the book deal with the slave trade, slave populations, urban blacks, and the post-emancipation response. The editors, who were also the organizers of the conference, point out that they "were more interested in the approach to problems and the methods employed than in the filling out of a preselected geographical or chronological pattern . . ." (p. xiii).

As is the case with any book by many authors, the quality of the selections is uneven, and there is little consistency in style. While each essay is interesting in its own right, there are wide—even extreme—variations in the degree to which the contributors employed quantification. Claudia Dale Goldin's statistical regression analysis of urban slavery makes extensive use of advanced mathematics, while Colin A. Palmer's review of religion among slaves in Mexico is a simple list of superstitions and makes one wonder why the editors included it in a volume concerned with quantification. Johannes Postma, discussing the Dutch slave trade, produced more pages of tables than he did of narrative, leaving the impression of overkill; while, conversely, Frederick P. Bowser, focusing on free blacks in Mexico City and Lima, was modest in his use of statistics but, because of his judicious integration of them into his narrative, was more persuasive. Generally, the historians employed the simplest statistical methods—some of it just plain counting—while the economists, predictably, seemed more comfortable with sophisticated mathematical data.

The editors' intentions are commendable, and the book is a solid contribution to both the study of slavery and the development of historiographic methodology. But there is no discernible common thread that runs through the essays (despite the editors' claim that there is); thus, the volume, while it does address itself to important issues, does not really come to grips with the overall significance of quantification in historical research. For example, the stated objective (p. xiv) of replacing commonly used but imprecise terms like "some," "more," and "less" with more exact mathematical references is undermined by the fact that these imprecise terms appear throughout the book. More fundamentally, the social and economic historian, even after exhaustive mathematical calculation, must still ask himself what it is he knows. It does not matter how good a researcher's tools are if his premise is not valid. An example is Richard Sutch's paper on slave breeding. Sutch's logic is convincing, but his argument is diminished by the fact that he was, by his own admission (p. 198), assessing slave breeding as a factor in a supply-and-demand model whose applicability to the slave economy he himself questioned (p. 176*n*). No one denies that slave breeders, whatever their extent, were responding to a demand. But was that demand a legitimate element in the competitive marketplace, or were slaveowners often buying slaves for such noneconomical reasons as social prestige? The answer to this question is crucial to an understanding of the slave market, but it is doubtful that the cliometricians will ever be able to answer it.

Nor is it likely they will even try. In commenting on three of the formal responses to the papers, Genovese agreed that "the most apparently technical questions cannot be answered outside a social and cultural context" (p. 535), and that, as George Shepperson argues (p. 106), some things are just not quantifiable. Perhaps Philip D. Curtin put it best: "Quantitative history, in short, is no substitute for nonquantitative history, it simply goes on where the other leaves off" (p. 108).

California State College, Bakersfield FORREST G. WOOD

American Genesis: Captain John Smith and the Founding of Virginia. By Alden T. Vaughan. (Boston and Toronto: Little, Brown and Co., c. 1975. Pp. xvi, 207. $6.95.)

Alden T. Vaughan has lived up to the usual high standards of *The Library Of American Biography* with his new study of John Smith, one of early America's spectacularly flamboyant characters. Oscar Handlin, the series editor, and Vaughan both consider the question of whether John Smith should be included in such a series and, fortunately for the teacher of colonial American history, answer in the affirmative. They could sustain their case by the fact that Smith is treated in both the *Dictionary of American Biography* and the *Dictionary of National Biography*.

The book itself is a brief but interesting chronological account of the deeds and misdeeds of its famous subject. It goes beyond some works in the series as it examines not only the man but also the question of the "American Genesis" and specifically the reasons for the initial British inertia in establishing an overseas empire. Smith was certainly the right man at the right time. His life bridged the period from the first halting efforts at colonization in the New World to the year 1631 when the Virginia and New England experiments were apparently successfully launched. Smith's own sense of history and his practice of the discipline furnished ample materials for the examination of the beginnings.

Vaughan is not concerned with breaking new ground; rather, he has chosen to present a synthesis of the treatment Smith has received from other scholars. The book is amply fortified with original source materials which are carefully woven into the narrative. Unfortunately, in keeping with the practice of the series, the reader is not furnished the luxury of utilitarian notes. This flaw is in part overcome by a note on the sources, which reveals the author's acquaintance with most if not all of the scholarly resources available for the treatment of Smith.

The book will probably have limited utility for experts in the period, but it will serve as a vehicle for presenting undergraduate students some understanding of John Smith, Virginia, the founding of America, and perhaps even the field of history itself.

Houston Baptist University DON R. BYRNES

The Old Dominion in the Seventeenth Century: A Documentary History of Virginia, 1606–1689. Edited by Warren M. Billings. (Chapel Hill: Published for the Institute of Early American History and Culture at Williamsburg, Virginia, by the University of North Carolina Press, c. 1975. Pp. xxiv, 324. Paper, $4.95; cloth, $12.95.)

This most recent addition to the Documentary Problems in Early American History series is a valuable contribution to the literature on seventeenth-century Virginia. The editing and writing are marked by the high standards which have long been characteristic of the Institute of Early American History and Culture. It will be useful to the scholar, student, and general reader interested in the history of the Old Dominion.

There is a mass of documentary material relating to the history of colonial Virginia, some published but much remaining unpublished, in archives, libraries, and other depositories. The editor has carefully selected more than two hundred documents, at least half of which have not appeared in print before, as a sampling of the materials available.

They are arranged in ten chapters covering broad phases of the colony's development. Each chapter begins with an interpretative essay which briefly discusses the historical segment covered by the documents and puts the documents in their proper setting.

The essays themselves are historical masterpieces. Alone, without the documents, they could stand as a concise history of Virginia from 1606 to 1689. They suggest the state of scholarship and interpretation in each topic covered and propose new avenues of research for the aspiring scholar. The language of the essays at times verges on the pretentious, but this mars but little their general excellence. The suggested readings which follow each essay provide a ready reference to the sources of historical interpretation.

The task of selecting documents to be included in such a collection as this is far more difficult than one might imagine. Even with a wealth of documents to work with, it is very hard to locate just the right document to illustrate each significant facet of the period and topic under consideration. On the whole, the editor has done his job well. Specialists in each field might quibble over documents or topics included or omitted. The democratizing effect of Bacon's Assembly and Bacon's Laws is slighted, for instance. But the documentary selection is generally concise and comprehensive.

For libraries, students, scholars, and devoted disciples of the Old Dominion this book is excellent.

Wake Forest University J. EDWIN HENDRICKS

In Pursuit of Profit: The Annapolis Merchants in the Era of the American Revolution, 1763–1805. By Edward C. Papenfuse. (Baltimore and London: Johns Hopkins University Press, c. 1975. Pp. xvi, 288. $12.00.)

Most of the current scholarship dealing with early American cities necessarily emphasizes population growth, economic development, and physical expansion. But what of the many towns whose ambitions of becoming a new Philadelphia or Charleston were never realized? Only a few historians, now including Edward Papenfuse, have turned their attention to those communities that lost out in the competition for trade and wealth. But as this book demonstrates, knowing why the process of urbanization failed in some places can illuminate the question of why it succeeded elsewhere.

Annapolis, the focus of Papenfuse's work, was ancient by American standards in the late eighteenth century. Established in 1684, Annapolis became the colonial capital of Maryland a decade later. The reorganization and expansion of the proprietary administration after 1715 assured the town of at least modest prosperity. The growing cadre of relatively affluent government employees together with gentlemen planters in the neighborhood created a demand for goods and services that sustained numerous craftsmen and some retail merchants. Despite its proximity to

Chesapeake Bay, the town did not generate significant transoceanic trade prior to the Seven Years' War. This resulted in large part from the town's inability to make itself a marketing center for the adjacent tobacco-growing areas and from the pervasive economic influence of the London commercial houses that effectively dominated trade in the region.

The year 1763 marked the beginning of a twenty-year period of growth and prosperity for Annapolis. A number of circumstances, including an increase in government personnel and high tobacco prices, combined to generate a rising level of personal wealth among the town's lawyers, placemen, and planters. This wealthy elite expended their riches in an orgy of conspicuous consumption. The building of immense and gracious town houses, many still standing, provided employment for the town's growing population of artisans, craftsmen, and laborers. The new wealth of Annapolis permitted the evolution of a small but important merchant group that not only controlled the local retail trade but also possessed sufficient capital to engage in direct trade with the West Indies and Europe. Indeed, during the 1770s Annapolis merchants were able to challenge British commercial houses successfully for control of Maryland's tobacco trade.

The era of the American Revolution proved a difficult time for the merchants of Annapolis. Blockades and the loss of the commercial connection with Great Britain reduced the flow of international trade. However, government contracts to house, feed, arm, and clothe American troops were a lucrative source of income for the town's businessmen. After 1779 and the American alliance with France the Annapolis merchants moved quickly to exploit the new opportunities for trade with continental Europe. The end of the war found Annapolis a thriving town whose merchants had extended their influence thoughout the entire region and established a flourishing international commerce. But dreams of greatness were quickly shattered by the economic realities of the post-Revolution years. The rise of Baltimore, a disastrous depression in tobacco prices, and quarrels among some of the leading merchants quickly terminated the golden age of Annapolis. By 1800 the town had returned to its former status as a sleepy village almost totally dependent on the payroll of the state government. Most of the men who had led the town through its great days either retired or migrated to Baltimore.

In writing this economic history of early Annapolis the author, now the archivist of Maryland, has fully explored the colonial and state records that are under his care. He has also utilized quantitative techniques to gauge the ebb and flow of economic activity in the town. The book bristles with tables detailing everything from the costs of building a mansion to the occupations of those making purchases at a retail store. While not all of this tabular material seems particularly relevant to the major themes of the book, Papenfuse has generally used his quantitative methodology effectively and judiciously. In sum, *In Pursuit of Profit* is a solidly researched volume that definitely contributes to the literature of Maryland in the Revolutionary and early national periods. It is a respectable addition to the list of scholarly publications now being produced by the Maryland Bicentennial Commission.

University of Wisconsin, Milwaukee FRANK A. CASSELL

The Way of the Fox: American Strategy in the War for America, 1775–1783. By Dave Richard Palmer. *Contributions in Military History,* No. 8. (Westport, Conn., and London: Greenwood Press, 1975. Pp. xx, 229. $12.50.)

The Way of the Fox presents a monographic analysis of Washington as a strategist. The author has no doubts that he was a good one, and neither will the reader after he or she finishes the book. The same reader, however, must wait until page 36 to learn that the term "fox" was created by British officers not Palmer. They used it derisively when chasing Washington; admiringly when he proved too slippery to catch.

Washington, however, was no Fabius. He used the offensive, both strategically and tactically, more often than the defensive; otherwise, the war could not have been won. Many historians have forgotten this military axiom and fail to give Washington full credit either as a strategist or an offensive tactician.

"The Old Fox" demonstrated these qualities amply in what Palmer calls the Christmas campaign of 1776. In ten days between December 25, 1776, and January 4, 1777, his demoralized army won two splendid victories (Trenton and Princeton), eluded a superior force, caused the British commander William Howe to evacuate New Jersey, and renewed its own pride and sense of purpose. The Revolution was saved.

Part One of the book, entitled "Strategy Essayed," treats in turn of strategy before Clausewitz, the impact on military thought of Frederick the Great, the significance of geography in America, and the view from London (no person in high office there had ever been to America). The two most important chapters in the book are in this section: "The Eternal Question," which analyzes the relations between Washington and the Continental Congress; and "Beyond the Horizon," which examines the little-realized war aim of territorial expansion.

Part Two, "Strategy Executed," defines how Washington handled four phases of the war, so distinct from each other that they were almost separate wars. These carry descriptive titles of their periods: "Run All Risques: April 1775–June 1776"; "A Choice of Difficulties: July 1776–December 1777"; "One Great Vigorous Effort, January 1778–October 1781"; "The Arts of Negotiations: November 1781–December 1783."

Palmer's style is easy but forceful. He analyzes the Christmas campaign of 1776 so: "Audacious it might have been, certainly daring, perhaps even desperate, but still calculated" (p. 133). He carefully chooses his words, such as "inspirit" instead of "inspire" (p. 162), and he depends heavily on striking metaphors: "Congress . . . foundered on the rocks of states' rights and sank in a sea of its own worthless paper money" (p. 73).

The six maps are too few, too simplistic, and on too small a scale for a strategic study of such depth. That for Yorktown should have been a nautical chart showing the significant hydrographic features of that amphibious campaign. The index is lamentably inadequate.

More than half of Palmer's notes refer to Fitzpatrick's *Writings of Washington,* showing the importance and the need for published source material. His first footnote to Chapter One acknowledges his debt to his mentors, Theodore Ropp and Jay Luvaas.

Texas City, Texas JOHN D. HAYES

Edmund Randolph: A Biography. By John J. Reardon. (New York: Macmillan Publishing Co.; London: Collier Macmillan Publishers, 1975. Pp. xvi, 517. $17.50.)

Edmund Randolph bore a great Virginia name and served both state and nation in high offices. Today he is remembered, if at all, as a puzzling figure of the great Revolutionary generation. In this scholarly biography, the first since 1888, his public services are fully described, but Randolph himself remains an enigma.

Edmund was trained in the law by his father John Randolph, the last colonial attorney general of Virginia, who fled to England in 1775. Edmund sided with his revered uncle Peyton Randolph, president of the First Continental Congress, and supported the rebellion. He served briefly on Washington's staff but returned to Virginia upon the death of his uncle late in 1775. Offices came easily to a Randolph in Virginia. He was quickly appointed an admiralty judge, then elected to the convention which declared for independence, and in May 1776 became the first attorney general under the new regime. He served briefly but unhappily in Congress, only long enough to acquire something of a continental view. The first great crisis of Randolph's public life came at the Constitutional Convention, where he introduced Madison's Virginia Plan, argued for it, and then moved into dissent on what seem minor points. He refused to sign the completed Constitution but refused also to oppose it, a confusing position then and now. After months of hesitation, and under strong pressure from Madison in particular, Governor Randolph became a chief advocate of ratification, arguing nobly with Patrick Henry at the ratifying convention. As the first federal attorney general Randolph's official duties were light, and he maintained a private law practice from financial necessity. He became a trusted political adviser to President Washington, taking, in Reardon's view, a vital middle ground in the growing struggle between Hamilton and Jefferson. When Jefferson resigned Randolph became secretary of state, although he lacked diplomatic experience or even significant interest in foreign policy. His middle ground lost its reason for being after Hamilton's resignation, and Reardon suggests that he thus lost his usefulness to Washington, who largely made his own foreign policy.

While Washington hesitated on the conditions for ratifying Jay's Treaty, with Randolph counseling delay, he came suddenly and fatally upon his second crisis. An intercepted French dispatch, conveniently provided by the British, suggested that Randolph had asked the French for money and had made several highly indiscreet revelations about American politics. Washington personally confronted him with the incriminating evidence, and Randolph, while protesting his innocence, broke down in anger and resigned immediately.

His efforts to vindicate himself turned into bitter recriminations against Washington and charges that he was the victim of a British plot. Reardon is not so partisan as to claim Randolph's complete innocence, but he makes little effort to explain how he could have blundered so terribly. Inexplicably, he fails to cite Julian Boyd's *Number 7* (1964), which convicts Hamilton of far greater indiscretions in his dealings with British agents while serving as secretary of the Treasury.

Reardon writes a readable traditional biography, with no effort to probe his subject's mind. Unfortunately, Randolph's thinking calls for some explanation, and the man remains a mystery to the end. His wavering on the Constitution, his motives in dealing with the French minister, and his repeated expression of dislike for the law, the only profession he ever attempted, all remain unexplained. Reardon recognizes that Randolph was often "filled with doubts and misgivings" (p. 185), but what lay beneath the surface is never considered. We have here a fine and well-researched account of what Randolph did but not why he did it. Strangely, the extensive bibliography ignores Jerald Combs's *The Jay Treaty* (1970), which contains an appendix on Randolph.

Indiana University, South Bend PATRICK J. FURLONG

Rachel of Old Louisiana. By Avery O. Craven. (Baton Rouge: Louisiana State University Press, c. 1975. Pp. xiv, 122. $6.95.)

Rachel Swayze Bell O'Connor's life spanned the antebellum period in Louisiana, and she helped to develop the cotton frontier of that state into a settled land of large plantations and numerous slaves. Based on an attic cache of some three hundred letters written by Rachel to her half-brother David Weeks and enriched by the author's lifetime of research in southern history, the account of her life and labor flows smoothly from the pen of Professor Craven.

The Old South and a woman's role in it are capsuled in Rachel's career. Marrying at fifteen, she was mother and widow at eighteen; marrying again at twenty-three in 1797 and starting a new life in a frontier parish with Hercules O'Connor, she bore him a son and lost both husband and son by the year 1822. From then until her death in 1846 Rachel managed the plantation and slaves, sometimes with the assistance of a white overseer, sometimes with none, until from their "very poor" beginning she amassed a thousand acres of land and eighty-one slaves producing nearly all of their living and around ninety bales of cotton per year.

Just as all southern planters had problems with careless overseers, so did Rachel. She was perhaps more conscious than male planters, however, of overseers who spent too much time in the slave quarters with "favorite misses" (p. 73). Just as many southern planters were plagued with lawsuits, so was Rachel, although more so because she was a woman in a man's world. The curse of disease and the hard labor of combining the tasks of plantation mistress with those of planter and of overseer caused Rachel, as it did many of her southern sisters, to seek refuge in piety and strength through prayer.

The gravest problem faced by southern planters was the reconciliation of humanity with business in the ownership of slaves. In Rachel, humanity dominated. She nursed the ill, took the babies into her home, trusted and loved them as her children, and apparently sold none. She was rewarded with loyalty and love, no revolts, no runaways. Yet she also conserved them as property, gloated over births, and passed them on to her heirs, deploring the evils of slavery but viewing the system as impossible to abolish.

Charmingly written, the book has provided the author with the opportunity to interject some of the fruitful conclusions of his long study, even as he prefaces each chapter with a pencil sketch illustrating yet another of his talents.

Meredith College SARAH MCCULLOH LEMMON

The Papers of Daniel Webster: Correspondence. Volume 1: *1798–1824.* Edited by Charles M. Wiltse and Harold D. Moser. (Hanover, N. H.: Published for Dartmouth College by the University Press of New England, 1974. Pp. xxvi, 518. $17.50.)

"I still live!" were the dying Daniel Webster's last words. They were in a sense prophetic. There are few American statesmen about whom more has been written than this congressional and constitutional giant, whose Washington career spanned the years from 1813 to 1852. Since 1966 alone four specialized monographs have appeared. Yet his scattered papers have been available only in fragmentary printed form. *The Papers of Daniel Webster* was planned as an integrated microfilm-letterpress project. In 1971 a microfilm edition of approximately 16,000 items prepared by Professor Wiltse was issued. The letterpress edition of "historically significant" documents has been planned in a total of fourteen volumes, of which seven are to be correspondence; three, legal papers; two, diplomatic papers; and two, speeches and formal writings. Each volume of correspondence includes a calendar of letters written in the same time period but not selected for publication. For each of these the microfilm frame is cited. Explanatory notes are interspersed with the correspondence to indicate what Webster was doing at a particular time or to clarify subsequent letters.

This volume covers Webster's life from his New Hampshire school days at Exeter and Dartmouth to the eve of his emergence as one of the congressional leaders of John Quincy Adams's administration. He early identified himself with the Federalist party, and after settling in Portsmouth,

New Hampshire, in 1807 to practice law, he launched an active political career. After serving two terms in Congress, 1813–1817, he moved to Boston to improve his prospects. The letters printed here acquit him of active disunionism during the War of 1812, although he approved Massachusetts's call for a New England antiwar convention and predicted that "if Peace does not come this winter [1814–1815], the Govt. will die in its own weakness" (p. 177).

Webster's arguments before the Supreme Court in the *Dartmouth College* case, *McCulloch* v. *Maryland*, and *Gibbons* v. *Ogden*—all decided during the period covered by this volume—brought him recognition as one of the country's leading constitutional lawyers. His election in October 1820 to the Massachusetts constitutional convention marked his debut as a Bay State politician. Early in 1822 he was sent to the General Court and later that year he was again elected to Congress. In the early 1820s he became known as one of the chief exponents of the "cause of humanity" because of his opposition in 1819 and 1820 to Missouri's admission as a slave state and his advocacy of American support for Greek independence. The correspondence in 1823 and 1824 details the efforts of the surviving New England Federalists to focus on a presidential candidate. After a long delay, Webster and his friends reluctantly supported John Quincy Adams, although they regarded him as a renegade for deserting to Jefferson at the time of the Embargo.

The editors' decision to put in letterpress only the "essential Webster" is to be commended. With publication costs rising sharply, more comprehensive letterpress projects seem certain to take many years to complete. Although few of that semimythical creature cherished by writers of jacket blurbs, "the general reader," are likely to peruse these volumes, the scholar of the times rather than of the man will find them satisfactory for most purposes. The Webster specialist will need the microfilm. It is hoped that someone will now undertake a full-scale biography.

University of Texas, Austin NORMAN D. BROWN

The American Revolution of 1800. By Daniel Sisson. (New York: Alfred A. Knopf, 1974. Pp. xviii, 468, vi. $12.50.)

Seeking to shift our understanding of politics in the 1790s, Daniel Sisson strongly criticizes the tendency of historians to see the turbulence of the period almost exclusively in terms of the development of the modern two-party system. The Founders, he writes, did not even understand—let alone accept—the concept of parties as legitimate institutions vying for power within a constitutional framework. Instead, they always adhered to the eighteenth-century understanding that a party was a group opposing the Constitution itself—obviously dangerous to the republic unless checked.

This healthy reminder stands at the beginning of what promises to be a richer and more complex view of the 1790s than now prevails, but the promise is not fulfilled. Sisson asserts that the election of Jefferson amounted to "the Revolution of 1800" and that preceding political crises are best understood as tending toward that event. His argument has its source in a letter Jefferson wrote to Spencer Roane in 1819. Sisson quotes from it: ". . . the Revolution of 1800 was as real a revolution in the principles of our government as that of 1776 was in its form . . ." (p. 437). Actually, Jefferson's letter begins with approving comment on some political "pieces" he had recently read. "They contain the true principles of the revolution of 1800, for that was as real a revolution in the principles of our government as that of 1776 was in its form . . ." (A. E. Bergh, ed., *The Writings of Thomas Jefferson* [20 vols. in 10, Washington, D. C., 1907], XV, 212). The letter quickly turns to tangential matters and does not return to the subject of revolution. By using the upper case where Jefferson did not, by omitting words without using an ellipsis, and by repeating the quotation several times, Sisson overdramatizes a comment arguably made in passing.

In different ways other writings of Jefferson and his contemporaries on revolution, on particular revolutions, and on the crises of the 1790s are arranged to support Sisson's idea, but so insistent is he, and so disparate are they, that nowhere does the revolutionary quality of the Revolution of 1800 come into focus. Consequently, the reader may variously infer that the transition was revolutionary because of the techniques used to achieve it, the principles vindicated by it, the shift in public opinion reflected in it, the policy accomplishments that resulted from it, or because it occurred at all; that the Revolution of 1800 was a repeat of, a continuation of, a completion of, or a return to the Revolution of 1776—or that it was a distinctly new phenomenon in history; and that the period between 1789 and 1800 was postrevolutionary, prerevolutionary, or simply revolutionary. None of these interpretations necessarily excludes any other one, but in the absence of attention to their precise relationships, the result is confusion.

Despite this conceptual disarray, from Sisson's ample narrative and quoted material the reader can form a clear picture of politics in the 1790s. Forever marked by their experiences in the Revolution and without the perspective of time to comfort them in using their new republican machinery, the leadership generation of the 1790s naturally tended to assess difficulties in apocalyptic terms. It was natural also that workaday politics should bring to the surface differences which the needs of fighting the Revolution and creating the Constitution had kept submerged. From these differences developed two groups, each seeing itself as sole possessor of republican truth, and each drawing upon the formulaic rhetoric of the Revolution to shape and express its perception that the other constituted a corrupt and devious party bent on replacing the Constitution with despotism. Resurrecting the familiar organizational and propagandistic techniques of the Revolution, both groups sought in the constitutional mechanism of presidential election to defeat the opposition (and hence, party itself) once and for all and restore the republic to its first principles. In the process they inadvertently demonstrated to future politicians that methods suitable to the revolutionary politics of the 1770s could be institutionalized for the more prosaic business of electing candidates to political office.

University of Texas, Austin GEORGE B. FORGIE

Jefferson's Louisiana: Politics and the Clash of Legal Traditions. By George Dargo. (Cambridge, Mass.: Harvard University Press, 1975. Pp. xii, 260. $15.00.)

The Louisiana Purchase, viewed by Jefferson as the acquisition of an extensive "empire for liberty," is generally regarded as his most important achievement as President. It was an action in keeping with his lifelong concern for the development of the West. He considered it sufficiently important that he was willing to suppress his constitutional scruples lest the French back out of the deal. In gaining this huge territory for the new nation, his purpose was to benefit Americans. The welfare of the inhabitants of the acquired area was secondary; in his opinion they were "as incapable of self-government as children." The need for defense against neighboring foreign powers or disaffected secessionists was constantly in his mind. One quasi-feudal plan he favored was to grant land to American migrants upon condition of two years' military service. This influx of defenders "would entitle the territory to become a state . . . and make it an American instead of a French state" (p. 144).

But the loyalty of the French "ancient inhabitants" was proved during the Burr conspiracy. It was the American carpetbaggers who supported Burr. Thereafter Edward Livingston and Daniel Clark lost favor; the latter was replaced by Julien Poydras as territorial delegate to Congress; the French party gained control of the local legislative bodies and adopted the digest (or so-called Civil Code) of March 31, 1808, prepared by James Brown and Louis Moreau Lislet. By this legislation the continued dominance of the civil law was guaranteed against efforts to replace it by the common law.

It should be noted, however, that the basic common-law constitutional safeguards such as habeas corpus and jury trial in criminal cases (which Jefferson described as "these first principles of freedom") were accepted by partisans of the civil law without opposition. In England all constitutional rights were common-law rights, which in America came to be viewed as natural rights of man. "Americans had a fixed, even dogged, belief that political liberty and common law rights were indissolubly linked" (p. 229). The Northwest Ordinance proclaimed "general principles of republican government, of which the common law was a major component" (p. 224). These fundamental civil rights, as well as the judicial machinery which was a familiar feature of the American system of government, were quickly established in Louisiana.

But the ancient inhabitants were allowed to retain the substantive law with which they were familiar. Governor W. C. C. Claiborne gave his approval to the digest, although he had on May 26, 1806, vetoed a bill recognizing the authority of the civil law. This situation represented a political compromise in which the national government accepted the civil law and the "population of Lower Louisiana finally accepted permanent American rule" (p. 173).

Dargo's main thesis is that the triumph of the civil law over the common law in Louisiana was not inevitable but was a result of the impact of the Burr conspiracy upon political alignments. He develops its ramifications with ability and portrays with clarity the course of events in that colorful locality.

The book is based on extensive research in many manuscript collections, newspaper accounts, and polemic pamphlets of the era. One chapter gives an excellent account of the batture controversy, in which Livingston claimed as private property the accretion of soil built up by the yearly inundations of the Mississippi River. In this dispute Claiborne and Jefferson supported the claim of the "ancient inhabitants" of New Orleans to public use of this deposit. Thus, this *cause célèbre* and the emotions which it aroused served to strengthen the rapport between the national government and the partisans of the civil law. "Burrism" and "Batturism" united in reinforcing Claiborne's willingness to gratify the popular preference for the civil law.

Perhaps Dargo's treatment overemphasizes to some extent Jefferson's zeal as a champion of the common law and his determination to introduce it uniformly throughout the new "empire for liberty." The President had too often admitted "the superiority of the civil over the common law code, as a system of perfect justice" and as an embodiment of natural reason (p. 218; such references could be multiplied from Jefferson's writings) to be characterized as an unconditional advocate of universal application of the English system of jurisprudence. If he could be convinced that the new territory gained for the American republic during his administration was no longer menaced by foreign intrigues or disunionist sentiment, if he could be satisfied of the political loyalty and capacity for self-government of its inhabitants, he could without misgivings recognize their autonomy and traditional preference with respect to the system of private law under which they chose to regulate their daily lives.

This excellent book is marred by more misprints than one would expect from an eminent university press, but they are obvious and do not mislead or confuse the reader.

Uniontown, Pennsylvania EDWARD DUMBAULD

Justice Accused: Antislavery and the Judicial Process. By Robert M. Cover. (New Haven and London: Yale University Press, 1975. Pp. xii, 322. $15.00.)

What does a judge do when he must decide a case arising from a law he believes to be unjust? Does he act like Captain Vere in Melville's *Billy Budd,* stoically performing a "duty" that violates his own conscience, or does he find some way to reconcile formal responsibility with his personal sense of justice? In this sensitive and beautifully written study, Robert M.

Cover demonstrates that the antislavery judiciary of the antebellum United States was forced again and again to play Captain Vere, with the black claimant to freedom as Billy Budd, the innocent man who must be condemned by an oppressive law.

The judges were in this unenviable position partly because of prevailing notions about judicial responsibility. Despite the persistence of the eighteenth-century conception of a natural law that transcends human law (and condemns slavery), judges did not consider themselves free to apply natural law except in cases where man-made or "positive" law was lacking or inconsistent. They were also reluctant to give even the appearance of usurping the legislative function, especially after Jacksonian advocates of codification and an elected judiciary had put judges on the defensive by accusing them of an elitist disregard of the popular will.

One of Cover's most important contributions to an understanding of antislavery thought is his recognition that the Garrisonian abolitionists understood and accepted this formalistic conception of the judicial role. They acknowledged that judges were bound by their oaths and professional commitments to defend a proslavery constitution and the laws implementing its provisions. But the Garrisonians went on to call upon antislavery judges to respond to the higher demands of conscience in the only honest and consistent fashion by resigning their offices. Other abolitionists argued either that the Constitution could legitimately be interpreted as an antislavery document or that the judge had a right to disregard positive law and base his decisions on natural law. The judges agreed with the Garrisonians in their narrow, formalistic conception of judicial responsibility but did not heed the call to resign because they in effect accepted the legitimacy of the legal and constitutional order in spite of their personal objection to its proslavery features.

In his close analysis of the decisions of four antislavery justices—Joseph Story, John McLean, Lemuel Shaw, and Joseph Swan—Cover shows the differing ways in which these men resolved what he calls a "formal-moral" conflict. The devices they used to resolve the dilemma in favor of formalism were (1) "Elevation of the Formal Stakes" (p. 229) by making it appear that a concession to antislavery morality in a fugitive-slave case would undermine the rule of law or even dissolve the social compact; (2) "Retreat to a Mechanistic Formalism" (p. 232), the fiction that the judge was a will-less instrument applying clear-cut rules and precedents; and (3) "Ascription of Responsibility Elsewhere" (p. 236), relying on the separation of powers to place the burden of antislavery action on the people and their elected representatives rather than on the judiciary.

Cover's argument seems to me convincing as legal history and at the same time very helpful to historians of antislavery in general. *Justice Accused* is the work of a lawyer, but it is addressed not merely to lawyers and legal scholars but to a jury of historians and social scientists. The legal jargon is kept to a minimum and the main points come through with exceptional clarity. I am also intrigued by the possible application of his conception of formal-moral conflict outside the realm of jurisprudence. The career of Abraham Lincoln, an antislavery politician with a lawyer's commitment to law and constitutionalism, can perhaps be further illuminated by an application of Cover's model. In short, this study expertly combines fine craftsmanship and theoretical resonance.

Northwestern University GEORGE M. FREDRICKSON

Space, Time, and Freedom: The Quest for Nationality and the Irrepressible Conflict, 1815–1861. By Major L. Wilson. *Contributions in American History,* No. 35. (Westport, Conn., and London: Greenwood Press, 1974. Pp. x, 309. $13.95.)

In his *American Historical Explanations* Gene Wise laments the fact that historians are more intent upon the gathering of data than they are concerned with its interpretation. It is in this regard that Major Wilson's book—which incorporates material from previously published articles—must be appreciated. He offers little new information; rather he presents a provocative analytic framework within which to interpret familiar material.

Wilson contends that three distinct formulations of the national idea of freedom—corporate, federative, and individual—provided initiative and shape to the political thought of the national period (1815–1861). Each of these dealt with the kind of freedom which gave meaning to the Union. Adherents of the corporate concept—embodied in the American System—believed American freedom developed qualitatively over time and placed a high premium upon ordered progress, economic self-sufficiency, and positive government intervention in society. This view dominated the period 1815–1828. Following Jackson's election, or more specifically after the nullification controversy, the ideology of Jacksonian democracy held sway. Jacksonians conceived of American freedom as developing quantitatively over space rather than qualitatively though time and thus believed in the goodness of an eternal present free from the prescriptive forces of past policies and future controls. These two views of freedom—corporate and federative—formed the basis of political discussion until the outbreak of the Mexican War, when free-soil ideology displaced them. Free-soilers did not recognize a debate over which kind of freedom should prevail; instead, they saw an irrepressible contest between freedom on the one hand and slavery on the other. Their emphasis upon the free individual disrupted the liberal dialogue over corporate and federative freedom. Indeed, Wilson believes that the free-soil consensus—a belief that the good of all arose from the unrestrained interaction of free men, each in the pursuit of his separate and short-term interests, with the federal government acting as a kind of genial broker dispensing the good things of the present with neither regulation nor restraint—presaged the Gilded Age.

Wilson has written an important book. Eugene Genovese, David B. Davis, Eric Foner, and many others have laid the groundwork for a work which takes up the irrepressibility of the Civil War from an ideological perspective. With an outstanding command of the very best of recent secondary literature and a thorough combing of congressional sources, Wilson provides us with just such a stimulating and thoughtful analysis. He has brought a fresh viewpoint to the timeworn idea of irrepressibility.

University of Oklahoma ROBERT E. SHALHOPE

The Mind of America, 1820–1860. By Rush Welter. (New York and London: Columbia University Press, 1975. Pp. xviii, 603. $14.95.)

A decade ago Rush Welter published a penetrating analysis of the problems inherent in most studies of American intellectual history and sketched the outlines of a possibly more fruitful approach based upon John Dewey's "transactional psychology," which portrays thought as "a continuous circular process of experiencing and augmenting experience." While that essay was strictly methodological, *The Mind of America, 1820–1860* represents an application of this approach to the intellectual history of the Middle Period. The bulk of the book deals with the years between 1820 and 1850 because Welter believes that "More than any other generation, the adult Americans who flourished . . . [during those years] gave the United States its distinctive character and direction" (p. vii).

In support of this proposition Welter examines four sectors of American thought: "History," "Society," "Politics," and "Free Institutions." In each he analyzes the development of certain basic concepts such as the American mission, equal rights, enterprise, constitutionalism, free religion, and free land, which he believes became the basic structural elements of the general American intellectual consensus that emerged by mid-century. The "bitterly felt" differences which had "existed between the parties" in the early years of this period "had largely disappeared by 1850. By then there was far more consensus than the echoes of earlier confrontations revealed." A concluding "interpretive essay" entitled "Consequences" focuses "on the ways in which the ideas of the Middle Period precipitated civil war . . ." (p. 333).

Although the dust jacket claims that this is "an exciting departure from traditional intellectual historiography" which gives "a clear picture of what the common man thought," it is difficult to find much that is new to the student of this period. Even more startling are the author's tendency to accept uncritically a number of the least tenable "Progressive" assumptions and his refusal to heed his own methodological advice.

Welter continues to view American intellectual development in terms of the progress of democratic ideals generated by an ongoing dialectic between "democratic" and "conservative" elements reflected in contemporary partisan conflict. Thus, he feels free to associate "democratic" beliefs with the Democratic party and "conservative" beliefs with the Whigs in ways totally unwarranted by the material and in conflict with the historiography of the past quarter century. Although he advised others to avoid all forms of reductionism, he follows his Progressive predecessors in ascribing materialist motives to "conservatives" and idealistic motives to "democrats." Whigs are invariably "apologists" for their "clients," and their "machinations" are described as "vacuous," "cynical," and "Machiavellian," while Democrats even in the midst of their most self-serving statements are portrayed as "purists" or "populist democrats" whose "convictions" were rooted in "principle" and expressed "America's most vigorous hopes."

Welter has struck upon one of the least exploited and richest sources for American political thought in the nineteenth century—the voluminous debates in the many state constitutional conventions. Yet he has failed to exploit this material adequately because he refuses to acknowledge that the ideas were cast in political rhetoric and must be understood within a specific historical context. Consequently, he often misunderstands the intent of political arguments and, as in the case of his handling of the Wilmot Proviso, incorrectly ascribes a causative role to propaganda devices.

Although he earlier argued that "ideas are interesting because they are held by men in groups," Welter pays little heed to describing with any precision the groups holding the ideas discussed here. This results in a great deal of confusion and allows Welter to manipulate individuals on the ground that he is "dealing with ideas rather than biographies." He can freely associate groups and ideas in any configurations he wishes. Erastus Root can be made to typify Democratic views, although he became a Whig; John Adams Dix speaks for those Democrats who joined the Republicans, although he remained a Democrat; and Alexander H. Stephens is portrayed as an exponent of "classic Democratic" convictions. Obviously, the ideas with which he deals were held in slightly different configurations by different individuals and different groups, but the reader has a right to ask for better assurances that something close to the ideas he describes were in fact subscribed to by historically specific groups of men.

Lehigh University WILLIAM G. SHADE

The Papers of John C. Calnoun. Vol. VIII: *1823–1824*. Edited by W Edwin Hemphill. (Columbia, S. C.: Published by the University of South Carolina Press for the South Carolina Department of Archives and History and the South Caroliniana Society, 1975. Pp. xlviii, 674. $25.00.)

Students of the political history of the inappropriately named Era of Good Feelings will find this most recent volume of *The Papers of John C. Calhoun* of particular interest. It is not just that it covers the crucial year of Calhoun's presidential candidacy, which collapsed in February 1824 when he failed to receive the nomination of the Pennsylvania convention, but this volume offers an unusual insight into the complex politics of the day. The correspondence (largely incoming as in the previous volumes) exposes the confusion resulting from the disappearance of the two-party system and the failure to develop a method of presidential nomination to replace the long-criticized caucus system. In the absence of party and without the prospect of party support once nominated, Calhoun and the other candidates had to seek allies within the states and participate in the direction of the campaign. Calhoun received a steady stream of reports on political trends from his backers as they constantly measured his strength and that of his rivals. Since his most enthusiastic supporters were younger men without commanding influence in state politics much of their data was speculative, intended to encourage the candidate as much as to inform him. As one reads these letters it is understandable why Calhoun was so optimistic thoughout 1823 about his prospects, when it is apparent (to historians at least) that he lacked a broad basis of support. Yet, in fact, neither he nor the other candidates had any real means of assessing the political situation.

Calhoun, like his rivals, turned to the press as the best means of advancing his candidacy and of establishing an image which would please as many as possible and not commit him to a narrow position. In a vein not uncommon among aspirants to national office, he told Lewis Cass on October 14, 1823 (and he repeated this to other correspondents): "I may boldly say, that my course has always rested on principles purely Republican, and on a policy truely national" (p. 312).

John Quincy Adams, whose diary still remains the great source for this epoch, has often been faulted for his hostility toward William H. Crawford, yet this was a passion which Calhoun and his supporters shared with equal fervor—and for much the same reason. They regarded Crawford as an intriguer totally without integrity. Indeed, Calhoun and his friends were so obsessed with Crawford that they consistently overestimated the threat to Calhoun posed by the candidacy of the secretary of the Treasury and failed to appreciate the very real strength of other candidates, notably Andrew Jackson. The political correspondence was hastily composed and is full of cryptic references, but these are amply clarified by the notes and by the lucid introduction of the editor.

As in the previous volumes covering Calhoun's years in the War Department, much of this volume is given to official correspondence. While these letters (many in abstract form) range over every phase of departmental business, those on Indian affairs are of the greatest interest. These letters expose prevailing attitudes both of the administration and of the public about the issues of civilizing the Indians and of removing them from their tribal lands. Because of the political implications of this issue, these letters have a double significance and well merit the extensive space allotted to them.

Southern Illinois University HARRY AMMON

The Papers of Henry Clay. Volume 5: *Secretary of State, 1826*. Edited by James F. Hopkins, Mary W. M. Hargreaves, and others. ([Lexington]: University Press of Kentucky, c. 1973. Pp. viii, 1096. $20.00.)

The mass of diplomatic correspondence produced during Clay's second year as secretary of state helps swell this volume to over a thousand pages, much of it filled with fine-print summaries of a majority of the letters and dispatches. The summaries, by the way, are full enough to serve in lieu of the literal documents for most purposes. While this comprehensive reproduction hardly makes for light summer reading, it does constitute an invaluable record of American diplomacy under Clay's direction and of Clay's personal and political life as well.

This was not a happy year for Clay. He smarted from the charges of "bargain and corruption" arising from his part in President Adams's election by the House of Representatives and his subsequent acceptance of the chief cabinet post from Adams. A coalescing congressional opposition launched the bitterest attack upon an administration that the country had seen in a generation, leading to a happily bloodless duel between the secretary and Senator John Randolph of Virginia. Clay's political base in Kentucky was threatened by the even more violent struggle between the Old Court and New Court parties, which he refused to help compromise and which led to a rupture with his former lieutenants Amos Kendall and Francis P. Blair. Clay's friends worried about his low spirits, and he suffered periodic bouts of illness through most of the year.

Yet Clay's political letters continued to express his characteristic sanguinity. True, Martin Van Buren had not yet moved unequivocally into the opposition, carrying the bulk of the Crawfordites with him, and proadministration candidates did hold up better than expected in some of the fall congressional elections. But President Adams's refusal to replace federal officeholders on political grounds was bringing cries of alarm from beleaguered administration supporters in many states, and Clay obviously failed to appreciate the power of the political disaffection that was coalescing already around the campaign to vindicate General Andrew Jackson in the presidential election of 1828.

The major diplomatic problems revolved around relations with the newly independent Latin American states and disputes with Great Britain over boundaries, claims, and American access to British West Indian trade. By the end of the year it was clear that Clay's diplomacy, by enlisting Russian support, had contributed to dissuading Spain from any attempt to reconquer its Latin-American colonies. Moreover, the danger of a Mexican-Colombian expedition to liberate the remaining Spanish colony, Cuba—with its threats of European intervention or slave insurrection—had been averted, though it is not so certain that American diplomatic efforts had produced this result. But Clay's greatest hope had been for his country to play a large role in the Panama Congress of American nations, and here he had been frustrated by congressional opposition and a series of accidents.

Meanwhile, the Adams-Clay hard line against Great Britain was proving totally unproductive, if not counterproductive. British policy had temporarily taken on a harsh anti-American tone. Even when the administration sent to London the country's most experienced diplomat, Albert Gallatin, the President and secretary worried mainly that Gallatin would be too accommodating to the British, and the American intransigence simply stiffened British resistance. About all Gallatin would be able to salvage was continued joint occupation of the disputed Oregon country.

Perhaps the strongest impression one gets from reading the diplomatic correspondence as a whole—comprising consular and legation dispatches from ports and capitals in most parts of the globe—is how totally committed the American government was, and probably had been for some time, to the support and expansion of American commerce. The State Department in its day-to-day conduct of diplomacy was already overwhelmingly an instrument of the American business community.

This volume continues the previously established standards of spare but meticulous editing, a style most appropriate for these materials.

University of California, Berkeley CHARLES G. SELLERS

Travel on Southern Antebellum Railroads, 1828–1860. By Eugene Alvarez. (University, Ala.: University of Alabama Press, c. 1974. Pp. xii, 221. $8.95.)

This study is a social history of railroads in the Old South seen primarily from the point of view of the passengers. There are digressions to discuss such matters as technological developments in southern railroading, but throughout most of the book the author confines himself to his topic. In describing the discomfort and danger which passengers on these early railroads encountered, he gives particular attention to the experiences of visitors from abroad who traveled on southern trains.

According to Alvarez, the South by 1860 had more railroad mileage than Great Britain, but southern trains were far more dangerous than those in England and France. The English and French used coal as a fuel, while most southern (and American) engines burned wood. These wood fires were less than satisfactory. They scattered sparks from the smokestack, started fires through the countryside, and burned holes in the unprotected passengers' clothing.

Almost every visitor to the United States commented on the rough democracy on American trains, but in both North and South Negroes and women were often segregated from white male passengers. The women were set apart as "a concession to their sensitivity" (p. 138), while the blacks were usually consigned to the baggage car or some other dismal accommodation. But blacks and women aside, there was on southern trains a certain rude equality which recognized no class or status. Europeans divided their trains into compartments; the long center aisle in American passenger cars was unique. The American arrangement encouraged sociability among the passengers, discouraged any aloof passenger who attempted to maintain his privacy, and disgusted visitors with the southern spectacle of chewing and spitting tobacco. Indeed, tobacco chewing was so prevalent that one railroad put up a sign which said, "GENTLEMEN ARE REQUESTED NOT TO SPIT ON THE STOVE" (p. 62).

Alvarez has extensively researched his book but relies most, and quite properly, on travel accounts. Nevertheless, the constant quotation from traveler after traveler sometimes becomes wearisome. The book is enlivened by some amusing incidental information. The reader learns, for example, that an incensed Englishman suggested that the American eagle be pictured holding a spittoon rather than the traditional claw full of thunderbolts. Alvarez also rescues from obscurity one Issac [*sic*] Dripps, who invented the most successful cowcatcher.

The book is excellently and extensively illustrated and can be recommended to all those interested in trains and southern social history.

University of Georgia RALPH B. DRAUGHON, JR.

The Federal Machine: Beginnings of Bureaucracy in Jacksonian America. By Matthew A. Crenson. (Baltimore and London: Johns Hopkins University Press, c. 1975. Pp. xii, 186. $10.00.)

In less imaginative hands this slim monograph by an associate professor in political science at Johns Hopkins could have been even slimmer. For, as Matthew A. Crenson makes clear at the outset, his aim was not to go over the vast ground covered in Leonard D. White's magisterial study of antebellum administrative history, *The Jacksonians* (New York, 1954), but rather "to examine and if possible explain the administrative changes that overtook the federal establishment during the tenure of Andrew Jackson" (p. 9). Mr. Crenson in fact focuses on two executive departments, the Post Office and the Land Office, not only because the reorganization proposals for these agencies "ran the full course from inception to enactment but because the agencies themselves were particularly important" (p. xi). His description of the main features in the reorganization of these departments covers perhaps twenty-five pages of Chapter 5. What fleshes out and gives special interest to Mr. Crenson's book is his discussion of the possible influences on and causes of these bureaucratic changes.

Mr. Crenson's interpretation relies heavily on Stanley Elkins's largely undocumented insight that social institutions in antebellum America were in a state of decay and Marvin Meyers's equally inspired reading that "The Jacksonians were intent on recalling 'agrarian republican innocence to a society drawn fatally . . . to the revolutionizing ways of acquisition, emulative consumption, promotion, and speculation. . .' " (p. 21). In Mr. Crenson's carefully drawn argument, Jacksonians instituted administrative reforms in the executive agencies in order to limit if not to prevent entirely the occurrence in the federal government of those lapses from the "traditional morality" that were ostensibly disfiguring the professions and the business community. The Jacksonian reorganizations, we are advised, were the work of men who "believed that [since] the actions of the government could have a direct effect on the morals of the nation. . . . It was essential, therefore, that the government and its officials do nothing that might lead the citizens toward vice" (p. 173). Jacksonian administrative reforms ostensibly created "a formal bureaucratic structure which was designed to produce mechanical adherence to some of the old standards of decency" (p. 164). If Mr. Crenson's attempt to explain the sources of Jacksonian administrative conduct is less than convincing, relying as it does on arid argument rather than historical evidence, it is made needlessly irksome by its seemingly endless repetition of the stale theme that the "declining social institutions" triggered the Jacksonian response.

Mr. Crenson's approach constitutes not simply a monocausal explanation of a complex historical phenomenon but in a sense a giant whitewash of some of the Jacksonian politicians, whose own misdeeds "triggered" a clamor for reform. Leonard White's no-nonsense explanation of Amos Kendall's Post Office reforms was that, in view of the caustic congressional appraisal of the department's operations under William T. Barry, "something had to be done" (*The Jacksonians*, p. 269). Mr. Crenson explains away the amazing defalcations of Samuel Swartwout, Andrew Jackson's unfortunate choice as customs collector for New York City, by the dubious suggestion that the customhouse was "beyond the reach of the secretary of the treasury" (p. 82). Just before Swartwout's crimes came to light Jackson rejected a proposal for the reorganization of the customs service that was supported both by Secretary of the Treasury Levi Woodbury and a committee of the House. Mr. Crenson also muffles the administration's "overlooking" of damaging evidence against Swartwout brought to the personal attention of the President by James A. Hamilton. In appraising the performance of Jackson, who urged violence against southerners choosing to receive northern abolitionist literature, and Kendall, for the latter's amazing suggestion that his subordinates owed a greater allegiance to an alleged higher law than to federal laws, Mr. Crenson finds they "halted the circulation of abolitionist literature . . . without any *glaring* disregard for legal obligations" (my italics, p. 151).

Mr. Crenson's knowledgeable comments about the nature and impact of the era's bureaucratic changes are unfortunately vitiated by his tortuous and tiresomely repetitive attempt to attribute these changes to alleged social developments that neither he nor anyone else has to date demonstrated were a reality. Interestingly, a somewhat similar attempt was made by a Jacksonian land examiner in Mississippi in 1837 several years after the reform of the Land Office had occurred. Discovering that the warm, personal friend who had been appointed to succeed a defaulting official was himself in arrears over $55,000, the investigator recommended that the man not be dropped; he had supposedly been corrupted by the example of his predecessor and "led away from his duty by a certain looseness in the code of morality . . ." (p. 85). Even then they knew that the Jacksonian who had his hands in the till was simultaneously yearning for a lost innocence.

City University of New York EDWARD PESSEN

The Fires of Jubilee: Nat Turner's Fierce Rebellion. By Stephen B. Oates. (New York and other cities: Harper and Row, Publishers, c. 1974. Pp. xvi, 187. $7.95.)

Few historical events rival Nat Turner's fierce rebellion for its dramatic and elusive nature. Efforts to tell the prophet's story have foundered on issues of evidence and perspective. The tempestuous nature of the event distorted or destroyed evidence about it; tensions of subsequent times warped efforts to re-create the episode. Despite (or because of) the stormy reception that met William Styron's fictional attempt, historians seemed reluctant to offer an alternative. Now, Stephen B. Oates has done so with notable success. His research in local sources, his intelligent use of the rich scholarship on slaves and slavery, and his graceful style have produced a compelling narrative.

Herbert Aptheker and Henry Irving Tragle demonstrated that research in local sources could add much to the main document, Nat Turner's *Confessions*. From their work, Oates went to the census records and the local archives to flesh out the personalities, both slave and free, comprised in this drama. While clarifying Nat's status as husband, father, and field hand and the reputation of such masters as Nathaniel Francis, this evidence still leaves much to the imagination. It allows Oates to describe who did what with more accuracy, but it is less clear on questions of motivation and significance.

A careful reading of the historical literature enables the author to address these broader issues. From the studies of John Blassingame, Eugene Genovese, and George Rawick, Oates convincingly portrays slavery and the slave community in which the prophet acted and from which he drew his strength. A discussion of the religious atmosphere of the time and place makes Nat's decision to rebel more understandable; an examination of the forces for slave control and alternative avenues of resistance explains the decision of most slaves not to join him. The analysis of the rebellion's legacy is largely derived from the secondary literature. Oates's focus on the personality of Governor John Floyd, however, provides a good view of the onset of the Great Reaction.

At first reflection, the new facts Oates unveils seem relatively insignificant. So much of his story is familiar or speculative. Yet in total his achievement is significant. He synthesizes important research on the antebellum South and slavery in a case study of an emotion-laden event. Moreover, he does so with literary grace. Eschewing qualifying phrases and employing imaginative dialogue, he gives life to this story without removing it to the realm of fiction. Nat Turner receives justice from the hands of this white southerner.

University of Minnesota, Morris WILBERT H. AHERN

American Indian Policy in the Jacksonian Era. By Ronald N. Satz. (Lincoln: University of Nebraska Press, c. 1975. Pp. xii, 343. $12.95.)

Historians in general and students of the American Indian in particular will welcome this study by Ronald N. Satz. A revision of the author's dissertation at the University of Maryland, *American Indian Policy in the Jacksonian Era* aims to provide a comprehensive analysis of federal-Indian relations between 1828 and 1852. Well researched and clearly written, it details the national debate which culminated in the passage of the Removal Act of 1830 and illustrates how the measure became a significant political issue in the campaign of 1832. Emphasizing the southeastern Indians, the study then describes how the government secured treaties of removal with the tribes and organized the emigration west of the Arkansas-Missouri border, demonstrating that poor administration, the use of contractors, widespread graft, and concern with economy compounded the plight of the dispossessed. Although federal officials had assured the Indians they would be sovereign in the West, the Jacksonians promptly proposed various territorial schemes that would facilitate policy implementation. Failing in these attempts, they turned instead to reorganizing the Indian Office and enacting a vigorous trade and intercourse law. Who ran the Office of Indian Affairs in Washington and how they shaped and implemented policy are carefully examined, as are the organization of the Indian field service, its duties, its opportunities for graft, and its wholesale politicization. Finally, the study chronicles how the Jacksonians having entered office committed to Indian removal to facilitate American expansion left office in 1852 convinced that further consolidations were necessary, promises to the contrary notwithstanding. This resulted because destiny beckoned and civilization of the Indian by means of education, Christianity, and private property had failed.

Aside from providing a volume that gives a useful overview of American Indian policy during these crucial years, Satz has made additional contributions. On several occasions he charts unknown waters. Particularly significant are his discussions of the removal act as a campaign issue in the Jackson-Clay-Wirt election of 1832, the Isaac McCoy–Lewis Cass territorial proposals of the early 1830s, the opposition to later, similar suggestions because of their implications for the free blacks, the apparatus of Indian policy administration, and T. Hartley Crawford's influence upon the course of Indian education. Moreover, his conclusions are both thoughtful and judicious. Convinced that the humanitarian rationale for removal was pragmatic rather than heartfelt, he nonetheless makes no moral condemnations of the Jacksonians. Their policy was defective primarily because it refused to concede that the cultural distinctiveness of the Indians was worth preserving.

Some students will wish, however, that Professor Satz had been more decisive in his conclusions. His admirable objectivity and his disciplined treatment of his subject leave some questions unanswered and raise others. Critical of policy that failed to recognize the Indian's cultural integrity, why should the author then fault the Jacksonians for insufficiently funding the civilization program that sought tribal acculturation? If Jackson and his colleagues erred in their Indian policy, was there a viable alternative? How did that policy affect the Indians of the Old Northwest and the upper Missouri? How, moreover, did the field agents of the Indian Office take advantage of their positions to increase their personal fortunes? In what ways were the tribes affected by the politicization of the Indian service? Such questions, though, only confirm the value of Professor Satz's study. Like all good books, it is at the same time a useful survey and tantalizingly suggestive.

University of Arkansas, Fayetteville W. DAVID BAIRD

Alternative to Extinction: Federal Indian Policy and the Beginnings of the Reservation System, 1846–51. By Robert A. Trennert, Jr. (Philadelphia: Temple University Press, c. 1975. Pp. xii, 263. $15.00.)

Formulation of Indian policy from colonial times to the middle of the nineteenth century represented a variety of experiments relative to land, trade, war, crime, and promotion of civilization and education. Based upon an ethnocentric assumption of the superiority of Anglo-American institutions, the policies sometimes provided for boundary lines between Indians and whites, including more specific areas with the removals of the 1830s. The alternative of removal with its general boundaries or barriers gave way to the creation of specific reservations following the Civil War. Their beginnings and philosophical origins, this study argues, came in the period from 1846 to 1851. For this era of Manifest Destiny and the acquisition of new territories in the Mexican War the author analyzes the motives behind the beginnings of the reservation system and seeks to identify the contributions to this idea by the officials at various levels of government. Part of the rationale for the volume is the conviction that this period has not been studied as thoroughly as the antebellum removals or the postbellum reservation system.

The acquisition of new territories made the mid-century a critical time in Indian affairs. In Texas the Rangers attempted to exercise control and perpetuate boundaries, while many Texans favored a policy of removal rather than a reservation system, particularly for the tribes which had migrated recently to the state. New Mexico witnessed extensive action by military forces, and by 1851 there was the beginnings of "a policy of separating the tribes on restricted lands" (p. 130). Other tribes along the emigrants' trails west of the Missouri River yielded territory in treaties of 1853 and 1854, while the Treaty of Fort Laramie in 1851 endeavored to protect the Oregon Trail with agreements with the most powerful tribes on the Central Plains—the Sioux, Cheyenne, and Arapaho. With definite areas provided for these and other tribes by the Treaty of Fort Laramie, the author views that treaty as "a landmark on the national path to a reservation system" (p. 193). Special attention is called to the early ideas of the reservation system as reflected in the annual report of 1848 by William Medill, commissioner for Indian affairs under President Polk, and by the advocacy of reservations by Luke Lea, who became commissioner in 1850.

This is a well-researched study with impressive use of manuscripts, particularly from the Office of Indian Affairs record group of the National Archives. The author notes the variety of motives for advocating the reservation system, including both the perpetual greed for land and idealistic arguments. The support from idealism, however, does not appear as widespread as it was for the removals of the 1830s or as it later emerged in support of the Dawes Severalty Act of 1887. The major thrust of the study focuses on ideas and proposals for reservations by government officials. It includes only limited information about Indian tribes and the impact of these policies on each group. While providing new information about Indian affairs at mid-century, the author sets forth no new major interpretations of Indian policy for the nineteenth century. The volume contains reference notes, bibliography, and index, but it would have benefited greatly from the addition of maps and appropriate illustrations.

University of Kansas W. STITT ROBINSON

Edward Stanly: Whiggery's Tarheel "Conqueror." By Norman D. Brown. *Southern Historical Publications,* No. 18. (University, Ala.: University of Alabama Press, c. 1974. Pp. x, 365. $10.00.)

Who is Edward Stanly? This question might well have been raised by nineteenth-century politicians or by twentieth-century historians. Apparently, there are no impressive answers to such a query; at least Professor Brown seems hard pressed to offer any. To be sure, the author assembles and presents a multitude of facts about Stanly, but they never take on much meaning.

This book is not a biography in the best sense of the word but rather a chronicle of Stanly's public career, which lasted from the 1830s through the 1860s. For those whose knowledge about Stanly needs refurbishing, it should be noted that he was a North Carolina Whig who served five terms (1837–1843, 1849–1853) in the United States House of Representatives. Believing his political career in his home state to be over, Stanly chose not to run for reelection in 1853 and instead moved to California. From then until his death in 1872 Stanly lived on the Pacific Coast, except when he returned to North Carolina in 1862 to serve an abbreviated stint as Lincoln's military governor. Stanly's absence from his native state and from the South during the critical period of the 1850s as well as his absence from public office make it quite difficult to agree with Professor Brown's claim about Stanly's significant role as a southern Whig Unionist.

In a book burdened with overstatements about Stanly, there is at least one notable understatement. In the preface Brown points out the paucity of Stanly manuscript materials and avers that the existence of some family letters "might have enriched his [Stanly's] portrait . . ." (p. vi). Surely they would have, for we learn next to nothing about Stanly's personal life. Tucked away in 332 pages of text and notes, for example, are no more than ten references to Stanly's two wives, Julia Jones (who died in 1854) and Cornelia Baldwin. Perhaps the author's inattention here is more deliberate than accidental, for Brown asserts that "The strongest single influence" upon Stanly was his father, John Stanly.

One searches in vain for evidence of Stanly's important contributions as a public servant. The tedious story of his lackluster years in Congress is relieved only by Stanly's penchant for fights and duels. His nine months as military governor of North Carolina in 1862 were pathetic and farcical. In California this "inveterate old line Whig" ran unsuccessfully as a Republican for the governor's chair in 1857, while in the presidential elections of 1864 and 1868 he worked for the Democratic ticket. After surveying Stanly's thirty-year public career, one cannot escape the conviction that he failed to make an enduring mark upon the history of the nation or region.

It is unfortunate that Brown, a talented scholar, decided to publish this warmed-over version of his 1963 dissertation, especially after making only a halfhearted effort to bring the research up to date. Brown is clearly a prisoner of his subject—a second- or third-rate figure. Presumably, one draws some consolation from the fact that there will not need to be another biography of Stanly.

University of Tennessee, Knoxville PAUL H. BERGERON

Confederate Women. By Bell Irvin Wiley. *Contributions in American History,* Number 38. (Westport, Conn., and London: Greenwood Press, 1975. Pp. xiv, 204. $10.95.)

Eminent historian Bell I. Wiley, adding to works by the late Mary Elizabeth Massey and others, stresses the role of women "in the bid for Southern independence" (p. xi). Containing an introduction worth reading, four chapters, notes, bibliographical note, index, and illustrations, this volume dispels the myth that southern women were inferior, weak creatures. Hardship, mental anguish, and ingenuity were required of Confederate women of all social classes. Most performed admirably. Women managed plantations and farms, operated businesses, and nursed the wounded; they showed strength in adversity while they encouraged their men. Wiley's work buttresses contentions that women during wars are required to substitute for men, shift roles, and support whatever causes the male-dominated society demands. In this sense, all wars are women's wars. Their bellicosity and support in this particular war might be explained by the prevailing nineteenth-century image of women as "ladies," who were expected to show admiration for military prowess, the symbol of masculinity.

Three chapters consider distinct types of elite women: Mary Boykin Chesnut, the intellectual of *Diary from Dixie* fame; Virginia Tunstall Clay, social butterfly, later suffragist; and Varina Howell Davis, "First Lady, Wife, and Mother." All, with husbands influential in prewar national and in pro-Davis Confederate social circles, were acquainted; all left diaries or other primary sources. Chapter Four on ordinary womenfolk balances the book. Wiley asserts that the "Failure of the Confederacy to alleviate the suffering of soldiers' families may have contributed more to Southern defeat than any other single factor" (p. 177). Other inequities expose Confederate priorities.

This book will attract historians of women in general and of the Civil War in particular. Mary Chesnut's inner rebellion against the restrictive southern society and her disgust for the system that devalued childless women are revealing. So is the easy acceptance of "women's place" by Varina Davis, who hated politics but yielded to her husband's wishes. Less revealing is the "Alabama belle," Virginia Clay, who appears stifled in the society which gave her little purpose.

Wiley concludes that the southern partriarchy diminished as a result of the war, but women lacked equal footing despite significant gains. He fails to emphasize that men lost confidence in defeat. Caught in ambiguity, men admitted women's value and still "contained" women of all classes in their efforts to regain economic, political, and social control. But this war remains pivotal for women's advancement.

Stories of wars are incomplete without consideration of women's roles. This book is important because readers normally uninterested in women's history will read it and perhaps be drawn to this exciting field. Certainly, readers will learn of the inflammatory-conciliatory role of women in the Davis-centered spats of the Confederacy.

Queens College, North Carolina MOLLIE C. (DAVIS) ABERNATHY

Gettysburg: A Journey in Time. By William A. Frassanito. (New York: Charles Scribner's Sons, c. 1975. Pp. 248. $12.95.)

This unusual book is a study, not of the Battle of Gettysburg, but of the photographs that were made of the battlefield and its dead after the fighting had ended. William A. Frassanito, who was educated at Gettysburg College and while there worked as a guide for three years at the Gettysburg National Park, explains that he "sought to uncover . . . every existing photograph of the Gettysburg battlefield taken between the year of the battle, 1863 (no images were ever recorded of the battle itself), and the year 1866, a span of time that includes all the significant views of the field when it looked basically as it did to the soldiers who fought there" (p. 17). In all, he examined more than 230 of these early photographs. The book presents his selections of the more important ones, together with his own photographs of key places on the battlefield, his maps of it, and his brief descriptions of the fighting.

His military history is rather sketchy. More important is his revisionist treatment of the photography at Gettysburg. Among the photographers who recorded the early scenes he identifies not only well-known figures such as Mathew Brady, Alexander Gardner, and Timothy O'Sullivan but also lesser-known artists such as Charles and Isaac Tyson of Gettysburg. After comparative study of the work of these men and further comparison of it with the physical battlefield, he offers convincing revisions in the authorship, date, and subject of a number of the photographs. With reference to ten dramatic views of dead soldiers he writes: ". . . the more famous have been individually labeled over the past century as showing Union dead at McPherson's Woods (near Lee's headquarters, to the west of town), Confederate dead on the first day's field, Union dead near the scene of Pickett's charge, and dead soldiers gathered for burial in the area known as the Wheatfield (to the far south of town). Yet a close study of the photographs shows, in fact, that they are views of the same bodies" (p. 198).

The bodies, Frassanito goes on to demonstrate, are those of thirty-four Confederate soldiers lying in "an out-of-the-way field adjoining the southwestern edge of the Rose Woods" (p. 199). Probably, the soldiers fell during the second day's battle. Gardner and his assistants photographed the bloated corpses from various camera angles on July 5, 1863.

University of California, Riverside HAL BRIDGES

Britain & the War for the Union. Volume One. By Brian Jenkins. (Montreal and London: McGill-Queen's University Press, 1974. Pp. x, 315. $12.50.)

For three decades E. D. Adams's magisterial *Great Britain and the American Civil War* has stood alone as the basic work in its field. The publication in recent years of such specialized studies as Frank Merli's *Great Britain and the Confederate Navy, 1861–1865* has only made more apparent the need for a thorough modern survey of Anglo-American relations during the Civil War years.

Brian Jenkins has embarked on the task of producing "the most comprehensive account yet to appear of Britain's role in the American Civil War." In this first volume he has indeed made an important contribution to the literature of Civil War diplomatic history.

His narrative covers roughly the first year of the conflict to the late spring of 1862 and emphasizes four main themes: (1) Confederate diplomacy toward Great Britain; (2) the role of Canada in Anglo-American relations; (3) British policy toward the North, the South, and Canada; and (4) the diplomacy of the United States government toward Great Britain. The discussion of Confederate diplomacy—especially of the personalities involved—is lucid and contains new insights and information not found in the pioneering books by J. M. Callahan and F. L. Owsley. The sections treating Canada are also detailed and well documented, providing a valuable supplement to the basic monograph by Robin Winks.

The discussion of the British role in the American Civil War is carefully researched and dexterously narrated, though perhaps unduly minimizing the roles in British cabinet decisions of "minor" officials like Argyll, Milner-Gibson, Lewis, Hammond, and Layard.

The thesis of those sections of the book devoted to United States diplomacy seems to be that Secretary of State Seward consciously adopted a policy of "bellicosity" as a "restraining factor" (p. 265) against British intervention in favor of the Confederacy. The author echoes the false assumption of Lord Lyons, the British minister in Washington, that Seward desired to annex Canada by force. It is unlikely that Seward intended, as the author asserts, to "perform the miracle of reunion with the healing nostrum of foreign complications" (p. 36). Jenkins takes "Poor Lyons" (p. 96) too seriously, when the "fearful" British minister worries about "Seward's insolent treatment of foreign powers" (p. 106). There was no "policy of intimidation" nor was Seward actually "bellicose" (pp. 112–13) as Lyons declared. The treatment in this book of events in Washington might have benefited from an investigation of government archives and manuscript repositories outside England and North America, although it is perhaps unreasonable in the light of Jenkins's laborious research in three countries to expect that he should have examined still more foreign source materials.

The narrative is documented mainly from primary sources, an extensive compilation of which appears along with a good selection of pertinent secondary works in an interesting bibliographical essay divided into four sections on the Confederacy, the Union, Canada, and Britain. It is particularly gratifying to find among the sources the Lyons papers at Arundel Castle, Sussex, England, documents far too long inaccessible to scholars of Civil War diplomacy.

Middle Tennessee University NORMAN B. FERRIS

The Alabama Claims: American Politics and Anglo-American Relations, 1865–1872. By Adrian Cook. (Ithaca and London: Cornell University Press, 1975. Pp. 261. $13.50.)

It is surprising that an issue which embittered Anglo-American relations for almost a decade has received so little attention from American historians. With the exception of several articles and a few chapters in works dealing generally with Anglo-American relations, there is no modern account of the settlement of the Alabama claims. Adrian Cook, an English scholar and visiting fellow at several American universities, has expanded his doctoral dissertation research and incorporated two of his articles into a monograph that helps fill the gap.

Cook begins his study with an account of the unsuccessful efforts of Charles Francis Adams and William H. Seward to resolve the Alabama claims in 1866 and 1867. He then describes, and to a lesser extent analyzes, the negotiations leading to the Johnson-Clarendon convention, which the U. S. Senate emphatically rejected. The greater part of the book concerns the determination of Secretary of State Hamilton Fish to bring about an agreement, the diplomatic efforts resulting in the Treaty of Washington, and the final argument over the indirect claims which almost undid the past accomplishments. Throughout the book Cook emphasizes the extreme sensitivity felt by the people of both countries toward the *Alabama* claims and the difficulties that an aroused public opinion caused in the negotiations.

Cook supports his study with a brief but satisfactory bibliographical essay. The primary sources include the pertinent records of the United States Department of State and the British Foreign Office and numerous private papers. Cook says he found the bulk of his evidence in the diary and letters of Charles Francis Adams, the Charles Sumner papers, and the diary and correspondence of Hamilton Fish. Extensive footnotes, properly printed on each page, also aid the reader.

There is little to criticize in Cook's study. He censures Secretary Fish's handling of the indirect claims, particularly the secretary's apparent waiving of the indirect claims in the negotiations leading to the Treaty of Washington. Subsequently, the British were dumbfounded when the Americans presented the indirect claims to the Geneva tribunal. Cook's criticism ignores the argument that there might not have been a Treaty of Washington nor any arbitration if Fish had not blurred the issue of the indirect claims, because the Senate almost certainly would not have approved the treaty if the Senate had believed that the administration was abandoning the indirect claims. Readers may also wish to compare Cook's account of the origins of the extrajudicial opinion which saved the Geneva arbitration with Charles S. Campbell's account in *From Revolution to Rapprochement.* Finally, Cook's study is heavily weighted with official United States records and the papers of American politicians, and the British side of the negotiations is not as thoroughly presented as the American position. However, these few criticisms do not detract from Cook's contribution. *The Alabama Claims* is a long overdue and worthwhile study of a major problem in Anglo-American relations.

University of Arkansas, Little Rock PETER T. SHERRILL

Impeachment of a President: Andrew Johnson, the Blacks, and Reconstruction. By Hans L. Trefousse. ([Knoxville]: University of Tennessee Press, c. 1975. Pp. xii, 252. $15.95.)

Were the Radical Republicans constitutionally justified in attempting to remove Andrew Johnson from the Presidency for reasons other than indictable offenses? Were they politically justified—that is, did they advance their cause by means of the impeachment? Michael Les Benedict has answered both questions in the affirmative in *The Impeachment and Trial of Andrew Johnson* (1973). Martin E. Mantell agrees with Benedict, at least with regard to the political justifiability, arguing in *Johnson, Grant, and the Politics of Reconstruction* (1973) that the impeachment was a success despite the acquittal, since the trial had the effect of lessening, if not eliminating, Johnson's obstructionism. But Hans L. Trefousse comes to quite the opposite conclusion in his latest book, *Impeachment of a President.*

According to Trefousse the removal attempt ended in frustration for the Radicals both because of their weakness and because of Johnson's strength. After the Democratic upsurge in the elections of 1867 the Radicals could no longer depend upon overwhelming popular support. They had the handicap of widespread Republican dislike for Benjamin F. Wade, the president pro tem of the Senate, who stood next in line for the Presidency. The impeachment managers bungled the case. And most of the Republicans felt serious doubts about the constitutionality of conviction on the grounds alleged (doubts that Trefousse himself seems to share). As for Johnson, he dealt with his foes far more shrewdly than historians have recognized. "So the great trial failed," Trefousse concludes (p. 179). "Johnson's policies of delay and defiance had been successful." It was a victory for racism. The consequence was the ultimate defeat of Radical Reconstruction.

For the most part Trefousse is retelling a thoroughly familiar story. Yet he tells it from a new perspective, and he freshens the account with unused quotations from manuscript sources. On the whole, he writes so smoothly, clearly, and interestingly that he may be forgiven a few dangling constructions. His argument is convincing.

Some of his observations along the way, however, might be questioned. Regarding the July 1866 law reducing the number of Supreme Court justices, he says (p. 43): "It is not clear whether this act was designed to prevent the President from filling vacancies, but it was later so interpreted." He cites Stanley I. Kutler, *Judicial Power and Reconstruction Politics* (1968), but Kutler provides no confirmation, saying instead (p. 52) that "the fact that he [Johnson] signed the reduction act must shake any interpretation of congressional reprisal against him." Kutler (p. 67) also contradicts Trefousse's statement (p. 62) that the *Milligan* decision "cast serious doubt on the constitutionality of the establishment of the military government in the South." It is hard to see how the Radicals held in common "a belief in an open economy based on free enterprise" (p. 19) when many of them were high protectionists.

University of North Carolina, Greensboro RICHARD N. CURRENT

Agriculture in the Postbellum South: The Economics of Production and Supply. By Stephen J. DeCanio. (Cambridge, Mass., and London: MIT Press, c. 1974. Pp. xiv, 335. $15.00.)

For economists interested in methodology and for historians interested in southern economic history Professor DeCanio's study should be required reading. Dividing his book into two major parts, the author, an economist at Yale, devotes nearly a third of his work to describing the inadequacies of traditional methods of historical research for resolving several central issues of postbellum southern economic history. The remainder of the book is a sophisticated statistical handling of the issues. By employing "powerful quantitative tests" (p. 120) and economic theory, the author strongly suggests that southern agricultural laborers were not exploited by their employers because their contracted wages equaled the marginal product of their labor; that cotton cultivation achieved for the South a relatively greater value of output when compared to alternative production possibilities; that differences in productivity associated with race seemingly involved locational fertility factors (soil differences) rather than human capital deficiencies (the effects of slavery) alone; and that southern farmers displayed a realistic grasp of their regional comparative advantages by rejecting crop diversification.

Although DeCanio's book may not be read by too many historians because of its elaborate statistical and theoretical format, those who do read it are likely to question both its methodology and conclusions. After one hundred pages of exposure to a "not-too-systematic survey" (p. 118) of the traditional methodology and the ambiguity of the "impressionistic evidence," the historian may wonder about the author's logic and understanding of the subject. The treatment of the "impressionistic evidence" is hopelessly out of its historical context and presented with little concern for the obvious question: Would a more systematic survey have changed the author's opinion of the sources or, more important, the author's approach to the problems under study? In view of this questionable straw-man technique, it is especially disturbing to find the results of the new methodology inconclusive and of dubious relevance. For example, DeCanio admits that his test of labor exploitation is limited to contractual stipulations possibly unrelated to the laborer's income. Some historians will surely question his definition of exploitation (wages not equivalent to the marginal product of the worker's labor), while others will wonder about the significance of a sophisticated statistical insight into something that may not have mattered. At another point (p. 13) DeCanio concludes that his tests undermine the naïve "legacy of slavery" notion that blacks as a group were deficient in human capital relative to whites as a group (since some blacks were more productive than some whites), but he then admits that his methodology is incapable of dealing with the other factors involved in productivity differences. Interestingly enough, when DeCanio attempts to deal with these other factors he employs traditional sources and methodology almost exclusively. Similarly, DeCanio may have missed the point about crop diversification by approaching it from the most convenient statistical standpoint of relative prices. Advocates of diversification possibly endorsed the idea not simply because of its greater income potential (which it may have achieved if the recent work of Roger Ransom and Richard Sutch on the price of merchant credit is correct) but also because they correctly understood that such cultivation would enable farmers to obtain a nonmarket self-subsistence conducive to independence both in their business and their way of life. To find that merchants would have accepted corn had it sold like cotton provides little insight into the historical motivation for the diversification idea.

But these problems, and others which are present throughout the book, should not cause historians to ignore this study. It is an important book, partly as an example of the problems of employing this type of methodology, but mainly because it deals with so many of the crucial issues of the postbellum southern economy. In fact, it is one of the few available book-length studies based upon the growing econometric literature on the period.

California State University
Northridge

RONALD L. F. DAVIS

Trust in Tobacco: The Anglo-American Struggle for Power. By Maurice Corina. (New York: St. Martin's Press, c. 1975. Pp. 320. $17.50.)

This volume is a narrative of the origins, development, combination, and interaction of the industrial giants that have dominated international tobacco manufacturing, chiefly the American, Imperial, and British-American tobacco companies.

After a sketchy introduction on the history of tobacco from the sixteenth to the late nineteenth centuries, Mr. Corina begins his narrative with the formation of the American Tobacco Company by James B. Duke and Duke's attempt to invade the British market. Damaging industrial warfare was averted when Duke and the leading British manufacturers agreed in 1901 to divide the world between them. The British group formed the Imperial Tobacco Company to dominate the industry in Britain and together with American established the British-American Tobacco Company to do the same for the rest of the world outside Britain and the United States.

So far the narrative would be quite familiar to students of American business history. Much more interesting is the account of combination and control of competition in the British industry from World War I to the present. Throughout this period Imperial had a virtual monopoly in the British market and maintained its position by price fixing, tie-in agreements, and other measures illegal in the United States at this time but apparently not so in England. Successive governments viewed these maneuverings with indifference until the Attlee Labor government, with great diffidence, established a Monopolies Commission in 1948.

Then (by American standards) came a long overdue investigation into Imperial. But so hesitant was the government to interfere with freedom of enterprise that a Restrictive Trade Practices Act was not passed by Parliament until 1956—sixty-six years after the Sherman Act became law in America. Imperial even after this time continued to hold 42 percent of the stock of its nearest competitor, Gallaher, Ltd. Paradoxically, some segments of business in Britain appear to operate with less governmental restraint in that nation's socialist climate than similar businesses in the capitalist climate of the United States.

Mr. Corina ends the book with an account of how American Tobacco Company, in a cloak-and-dagger operation, managed in 1968 to snap up 67 percent of Gallaher's stock and thereby fulfill Duke's original dream of entering the British market.

Because the book is not footnoted and has only a brief and entirely inadequate bibliography it is of no value as a reference work. A breathless style and emphasis on overdramatized detail indicate that it is pitched to the general reader, whoever he may be. As industrial editor of the *Times* of London, Mr. Corina apparently relies mainly on the files of his newspaper for source material. Devoting his attention primarily to combination and attendant financial arrangements, he virtually ignores other aspects of business history such as management, procurement, production, and accounting. Marketing and advertising receive some attention but not as much as these functions deserve. Company executives are characterized by personality idiosyncrasies, and no attempt is made to analyze their styles of management and roles in decision making. But these shortcomings are of value to the business historian because they indicate fertile areas in which further research and writing may be done.

University of North Carolina Chapel Hill — ELISHA P. DOUGLASS

Gentleman Boss: The Life of Chester Alan Arthur. By Thomas C. Reeves. (New York: Alfred A. Knopf, 1975. Pp. xviii, 500, xix. $15.00.)

For the student of nineteenth-century American politics, the most moving moment of Thomas Reeves's biography of Chester Arthur comes in the final pages, when Reeves describes Arthur's momentarily regaining strength on his deathbed and personally supervising the burning of most of his private papers. The value of what was thus lost to history must have been great, for as Reeves makes clear in this work Arthur was closely connected with many of the major political events of the Gilded Age. Despite this loss, Reeves has produced a detailed and comprehensive, "life and times" biography of the twenty-first President based on obviously exhaustive research. Following the traditional organization, it traces Arthur's ancestry back to his great grandparents on both sides and then follows a largely chronological organization to Arthur's death in 1886.

Over half the work is devoted to Arthur's prepresidential career. In this section Reeves writes less a biography of Arthur than a history of the complex struggles between the New York Stalwarts and their various opponents. Paralleling and complementing David M. Jordan's recent study of Roscoe Conkling (Cornell University Press, 1971), Reeves portrays Arthur during this period as a superb political technician and organizer, who performed well as customs collector in New York and generally enjoyed a good personal reputation. At the same time, Reeves believes that by the postwar period Arthur's early political idealism had been replaced by complete dedication to the interests of Conkling's New York Republican machine.

In the final third of the book Reeves studies Arthur's Presidency. His conclusion is that given the circumstances of his succession Arthur "was a good President at a period in our history when the American people neither expected nor sought great Presidents" (p. 423). While maintaining ties to the Stalwart Republicans, Arthur attempted to deal fairly with all wings of the party, enforced the Pendleton Act efficiently and effectively, and developed foreign policies that anticipated America's growing role in world affairs. Reeves believes that Arthur probably knew that he had Bright's disease as early as 1882, thus explaining the President's relatively short working hours and his lack of interest in renomination in 1884.

At times Reeves appears to be working overly hard to defend Arthur, but in general his assessment of the President's performance is a fair one.

However, this is not as great a reinterpretation as Reeves would have us believe, as other historians have reached very similar conclusions (see for example pp. 414–16 of Jordan's study of Conkling). So that while this work contains a well-developed narrative of events, it presents little in the way of new interpretation of Gilded Age politics. Reeves accepts the general assumption that the strongest force in politics was the drive for patronage. Thus, he believes that the Stalwarts supported Grant in 1880 because he was the only one they trusted to turn the patronage over to them (p. 177). But, if political expedience alone dictated their action, why were there for decades afterward reunions of the 306 "Old Guard" delegates who continued to vote for Grant even after Garfield's nomination was assured? This is but one indication of the intense political loyalties of the time, which, along with the high levels of political participation, indicate that forces other than the desire for immediate gain were important factors in Gilded Age politics. We still need a work that will describe those factors and relate them to the operation of national politics.

University of Arkansas
Pine Bluff
MARTIN E. MANTELL

The Political South in the Twentieth Century. By Monroe Lee Billington. (New York: Charles Scribner's Sons, c. 1975. Pp. xvi, 205. Paper, $3.95; cloth, $8.95.)

The Political South in the Twentieth Century is a clearly written and workmanlike survey of its subject. The book should prove extremely useful in courses dealing with recent southern history.

In the preface Monroe Lee Billington describes the work as an "interpretive account of southern politics in the twentieth century" (p. ix). Actually, aside from its emphasis on change rather than continuity and convergence rather than distinctiveness, the book is essentially an uncritical survey that offers little that is new and, indeed, ignores some of the recent literature about southern and American political developments. For the most part, it expands themes developed in Professor Billington's *The American South,* which was published in 1971.

The book is, however, a good student-level summary. It treats concisely and intelligently complex developments, and it achieves a nice balance, allotting adequate attention to both the South's role in national politics and to political developments within the region.

Billington devotes three chapters of the work to the pre–World War II period, stressing the influence of progressivism, World War I, and the New Deal. Progressivism "laid the foundation of democracy in later southern politics" (p. 9); World War I quickened the "pace of change" (p. 31); and the combined effect of the Depression and the New Deal made national issues relevant to southern politics. The next two chapters deal with the changing status of black southerners. Billington emphasizes the role of the Harry S. Truman administration in ensuring "the progress of civil rights for black Americans . . . toward victory" (p. 106). In the South,

Billington sees increasing black-voter participation as the single most important agent of social change.

The final portion of the work focuses on recent southern political developments, stressing the emergence of a two-party system. Billington is surely correct in faulting national Republican leaders, especially former President Richard M. Nixon, for showing greater interest "in winning presidential elections than in developing a two-party South" (p. 183). But despite this and other problems, Billington sees "a great deal of potential support" for Republicanism and suggests the gradual growth of a two-party politics based on economic interests, with southern segregationists lacking influence in either party. "One hundred years after Reconstruction," Billington concludes, "the South is far along the road back to the mainstream of biracial, two-party American national politics" (p. xiii).

University of Georgia NUMAN V. BARTLEY

The New Negro on Campus: Black College Rebellions of the 1920s. By Raymond Wolters. (Princeton and London: Princeton University Press, c. 1975. Pp. viii, 370. $15.00.)

This lucid and often absorbing account of incidents of protest at eight black colleges during the 1920s is on the whole adequately researched. The problem with it is that in seeking to establish generalizations the author, like some latter-day Procrustes, stretches and cuts the facts to fit his analysis.

A series of disparate incidents over a period of eighteen years (1914–1931) at only nineteen of the seventy-nine black institutions of higher education scarcely constitutes a "wave of rebellion," nor can it be said that such rebellions "engulfed most of the leading black colleges . . ." (p. 17). Indeed, one of the incidents described in detail, R. R. Moton's struggle against the all-white staff at the Tuskegee Veterans Hospital, is not a campus rebellion at all. Then, in several key respects the author misconstrues the social context in which these incidents occurred. The attempt to provide unity to the campus rebellions by attributing them in large part to the influence of Du Bois's prominence and militance is unwarranted. Secondly, Wolters inappropriately stresses the conflict between the advocates of industrial and higher education; actually, by the 1920s this debate had largely lost its salience, and in only two of the cases described does it genuinely emerge as an issue. Wolters is correct in emphasizing the rigid social regulations—including compulsory daily chapel attendance, the banning of fraternities, and highly limited contacts between the sexes—as important sources of student unrest; he errs in attributing their persistence so largely to white racist administrators and trustee-philanthropists. Actually, such regulations were, if anything, even more firmly entrenched in the fully-black-controlled schools; and the fact that they were an important source of friction at the A.M.E. church's Wilberforce University should have given the author pause. Nor does the author demonstrate any more than the most nebulous connections between campus rebellions and the New Negro movement of the 1920s. Thus, the issue of black control—the proximate cause of the struggles conducted by faculty and alumni at Howard University and Lincoln University, Pennsylvania—was an old issue, antedating the New Negro movement and lasting well beyond it; and in any case it was not central to most of the campus rebellions. Even in the case of Howard, where some of the faculty like Alain Locke and Dean Kelly Miller articulated the cultural pluralism of the New Negro ideology, the recognition of and the study of black culture and the black man's past were not the focus of protest. Indeed, since, as both men complained, black college students were dominated by white bourgeois values and aspirations, it can scarcely be said that the student rebels were a part of the New Negro movement. Finally, Wolters has failed to explore adequately the relevant structural aspects of the black colleges—both the fact that, as his analyses of the conflicts at Florida A. & M. College and Lincoln University, Missouri, demonstrate, racist public officials controlled black state colleges and the more important fact that both public and private Negro colleges were generally controlled by authoritarian and autocratic presidents. Most of the rebellions discussed—and nearly all of the others briefly referred to—involved revolt against the arbitrariness of college presidents, whether white or black, and this is true whether the protest came from alumni, from students, or from faculty. That, for example, the problems of the white president at Howard University, James Durkee, were not due primarily to his race, seems clear from the fact that his black successor, Mordecai Johnson, conducted a similar battle against administrative bureaucrats like Kelly Miller.

Three of the eight incidents described in detail have recently received scholarly attention elsewhere; still, used with care the volume will be useful to specialists.

Kent State University AUGUST MEIER

The New Deal in Georgia: An Administrative History. By Michael S. Holmes. *Contributions in American History,* Number 36. (Westport, Conn., and London: Greenwood Press, 1975. Pp. xii, 365. $14.95.)

Michael Holmes has written a single-minded but valuable book. Unfortunately for those who like exciting and lively narrative, the book does exactly what the subtitle promises. Eight chapters examine the New Deal agencies that the author contends most affected Georgia in direct ways that called for new administrative structures: the Federal Emergency Relief Administration (FERA); the Civil Works Administration (CWA); the Works Progress Administration (WPA); the Public Works Administration (PWA); the National Recovery Administration (NRA); the Agricultural Adjustment Administration (AAA); the Resettlement Administration (RA); and the Farm Security Administration (FSA). Each chapter tells how the federal government and Georgia administered the programs by describing organizational structure, project goals and disbursement of funds, and the key operational decisions. The chapters delineate the local political, social, and economic situations that hindered or helped the programs and offer judgments of overall achievements and failures of each of the agencies.

The cumulative effect almost, at times, anesthetizes a reader. Methodically, the chapters lay out the national law, the Georgia implementation, and the statistical result. Fortunately, an introductory chapter and a concluding chapter give good perspective to the agencies' organizational history. Holmes argues that too much emphasis has been placed on the national experience of the New Deal agencies, and what has emerged from such attempts generally is an examination *not* of a state's effect upon the New Deal but just the opposite. Holmes hopes to understand the workings of his New Deal agencies as affected by conditions in Georgia without any digression into state political, economic, or social conditions except as as they affected the agencies. The agencies, he discovered (not surprisingly), had success or failure as determined by three conditions. It was, he wrote, "the quality of the state administrative structure and personnel, the latitude they were given by the laws or by the federal administrations in adapting to meet local conditions, and the political, economic, and social environment facing them in the states which determined their achievements" (p. 307). He concludes that all the agencies had limited achievements but that the New Deal did not extract Georgia from the Great Depression.

There exist now numerous dissertations that examine aspects of the New Deal and state experience. Several are better written, more interesting, or as well researched as this book. Most adopt a broader narrative scope and ask more questions. None deal so intently with one question as does Holmes's study. He hopes that other historians will use his book as an introductory method to create a mosaic of state experience that will provide a more exact standard to measure the achievements of the New Deal. His bibliographical essay is constructed to guide other state researchers through the agency files in the National Archives, the principal source of his extensive research. Actually, his work fits neatly into what is already an emerging literature. Holmes's work will, as he writes, help scholars "understand what befell the New Deal once it left Washington and why it happened that way" (p. 14).

College of Wooster JAMES A. HODGES

John James Tigert: American Educator. By George Coleman Osborn. (Gainesville: University Presses of Florida, c. 1974. Pp. xvi, 544. $15.00.)

John J. Tigert retired in 1947 after a full career as college teacher and university president, with nineteen years devoted to the University of Florida. He was a native of Nashville, Tennessee, and attended Vanderbilt University, the institution with which his grandfather, Bishop Holland N.

McTyeire, had been so closely associated. As an undergraduate Tigert became a member of Phi Beta Kappa and a football player of considerable fame. These qualities, plus an obvious talent for leadership, led to his selection as a Rhodes Scholar.

Tigert's first academic appointment was to a professorship of philosophy at Missouri Central Methodist. Following this he became president of Kentucky Wesleyan College, then professor of philosophy and athletic director at the University of Kentucky. During World War I he joined the Army Education Corps and at the war's end returned to the University of Kentucky, where he remained until President Harding appointed him U.S. commissioner of education.

When Tigert became president of the University of Florida the institution had an enrollment of slightly more than two thousand students, an inadequate physical plant, and an academic program that was limited and in need of revamping. To his credit Tigert made tangible progress in the general upgrading of the university. Phi Beta Kappa and Sigma Xi established chapters on the campus, and course offerings on the undergraduate, graduate, and professional levels were expanded and strengthened. But perhaps Tigert found greatest satisfaction in the establishment of the General College, because it was a program for which he alone was largely responsible; also it reflected the strong influence that the Oxford years had had upon him.

All of the foregoing, and more, is recounted in too much detail. Tigert deserves a good, brief biography; instead, Professor Osborn has written one that is lengthy and dull. Little judgment was exercised in the choice of material, and even more disturbing is the lack of any real assessment of the man. For example, the paragraphs devoted to the history of Missouri Central College might well have been omitted, and the numerous speeches that are summarized or quoted in part could have been referred to more sparingly or omitted entirely.

The chapters on Tigert's work as commissioner of education are disappointing. Surely, he did more than travel and make speeches, and there is every reason to know that he stood for more than the American Legion's program of citizenship, with a flag in every classroom and a loyalty oath for teachers (p. 168). Unfortunately, the reader is left with no clear picture of his accomplishments or failures.

The Florida years were, of course, the important ones, and here we can wish that Tigert had emerged in sharper perspective. An undue amount of attention is given to football, the employment of football coaches, and college athletic associations. Certainly, these deserve mention, but it would have been more to the point to have discussed his relationship with the Southern Association of Colleges and Schools and his participation in its program.

Somewhere, somehow, the author let himself bog down in trivia and detail and failed to keep the larger story in mind. In addition, the writing leaves much to be desired.

University of North Carolina, Chapel Hill J. ISAAC COPELAND

The Persistent Tradition in New South Politics. By George Brown Tindall. (Baton Rouge: Louisiana State University Press, c. 1975. Pp. xvi, 72. $4.95.)

This slender volume is the published version of the 1973 Fleming Lectures at Louisiana State University in which George Brown Tindall examines three groups—Bourbons, Populists, and progressives—which have "dominated the story of post-Reconstruction politics" (p. xi). Following an insightful and penetrating review of the changing historiographical interpretations for each faction in the now-disrupted Solid South, the author concludes that a definite continuity ran throughout the social and political life of the New South era. Futhermore, he has drawn upon a Hegelian view of history to advance a well-thought-out and masterfully conceived argument that the Bourbons established a thesis, the Populists followed with an antithesis, and the progressives worked out a synthesis which determined the course of southern politics until the rise of meaningful opposition to one-party rule in the region during the second half of the twentieth century.

Although the Bourbons produced no philosophical giant such as John Locke or Edmund Burke, they were nonetheless able to dominate southern political life after 1876 in the author's view because of their ability to reconcile a deep-seated sense of community with a changing racial and economic order. They maintained power by not allowing the New South, with its pleas for industrial development and agricultural diversification, to interfere with a notion of life based on "an organic traditional community with its personal relationships, its class distinctions, its habits of deference to the squirearchy" (p. 22). In the 1890s, however, the stabiiity of the southern community with its underpinnings of white supremacy was challenged by the Populists, who sought to forge a new political coalition from the members of the "lower orders," both black and white, who did not share the world view of the Bourbons.

Tindall notes that while historians of southern populism have been much more adept at describing the origins of the movement than in indicating its long-term impact upon American politics, it was the threat to the traditional community imposed by the Populists that brought both their own destruction through a disfranchisement of the lower orders and the triumph of the Solid South. The progressives, on the other hand, with their emphasis on a wider-based democracy and more efficient government, were able to retain the southern sense of community by taking from the populists "their ideas of a more active government" (p. 61) while making their own reforms serve the New South creed. The southern progressive, moreover, kept the Solid South intact and became the legatee of the Bourbons by simply taking over disfranchisement and making it a "reform in the interest of good government" (p. 66).

This is solid history by a seasoned scholar, and while one might wish for longer, more detailed explanations of the various arguments presented, it is nonetheless must reading for the New South scholar.

West Virginia State College PAUL D. CASDORPH

The Border South States: People, Politics, and Power in the Five Border South States. By Neal R. Peirce. (New York: W. W. Norton and Co., c. 1975. Pp. 415. $12.95.)

Neal R. Peirce, a Washington-based political writer, originally planned to update John Gunther's *Inside U.S.A.* in a single-volume survey of changes in the United States during the past quarter century. Because of the vastness and complexity of the subject, he soon abandoned the idea of a single book and undertook instead a series of eight regional volumes. Of the six already published two deal with "people, politics, and power" in the South. The latest volume concerns the states (Virginia, North Carolina, West Virginia, Kentucky, and Tennessee) of the Border South, which is described as "America's Forgotten Region." The format is similar to that in other volumes in the series: the work opens with a general commentary on the region, noting in particular the significance of Appalachia, which at once constitutes the "most unifying force" and the most perplexing problem of the Border South; then each of the five states is treated in a separate chapter, which begins with a brief historical overview, followed by wide-ranging analyses of political and economic developments since World War II. A final chapter is devoted to the Tennessee Valley Authority, which the author views (p. 363) as "the finest program . . . of integrated regional planning" in the country, whose socioeconomic impact upon the Border South has been "nothing short of stupendous" (p. 367).

Peirce has faithfully followed Alexander Heard's advice (p. 361) to include in his books "the really meaningful *success* stories" of the South without skirting its problems and failures. Among many such stories included in this volume are those related to the democratization of Virginia politics in the wake of the Byrd machine's demise, the dramatic educational advances in Kentucky in the 1960s, and the establishment and successful operation of Metro government in Nashville, Tennessee. Despite evidences of remarkable progress in many areas, the picture is by no means devoid of what Peirce calls "gloomy indicators." The region has been and to a large extent remains economically sluggish, pointing up the difficulties of "prospering rurally" in twentieth-century America. Moreover, it has produced few outstanding political leaders, and its impact upon national politics has been relatively slight. The Border South lags far behind national norms in per capita income, standard of living, and education; it suffers from a high rate of out-migration and the predominance of low-wage, antiunion industries. Of the border states only Virginia approaches the national average in per capita income, a unique position explained by "the infusion of federal activity that has brought in many out-of-staters" (p. 17). Its neighbor, North Carolina, whose eastern half remains a vast underdeveloped area dominated by labor-intensive tobacco farming and plagued by a staggering out-migration of its black population, is gradually moving toward a diversified economy. But Peirce's analysis of North Carolina's low-wage industries and political inertia casts considerable doubt on whether the state can now justify its reputation for progressivism. In his opinion, however, West Virginia is "the saddest of all American states" (p. 151), because it suffers from a colonial-style coal economy, population drain, debased politics, devastated environment, and depression of the human spirit. Although Kentucky has many of the same problems, Peirce is far more optimistic about its future than about that of West Virginia. Despite an antiquated tax structure and other inadequacies, Tennessee, in his view is among the most progressive states in the region. Not only has Tennessee witnessed the emergence of a vigorous two-party system since the end of the Crump-McKellar era, but it is also "a regional rarity in that it has a very well balanced economy . . ." (p. 319).

This volume, like the one on the Deep South, provides a perceptive analysis of the political and economic situation in the five states of the Border South as well as a wealth of data on specialized topics ranging from Tennessee's Nashville Sound to Kentucky's horse racing. Based upon numerous interviews, firsthand observations, and research in a wide variety of printed sources, this highly readable book amply fulfills the author's aim to produce a work that would be useful to "all those curious about the American condition as we enter the last decades of the 20th century" (p. 11).

University of Arkansas WILLARD B. GATEWOOD, JR.

Pills, Pen & Politics: The Story of General Leon Jastremski, 1843–1907. By Edward Pinkowski. (Wilmington, Del.: Captain Stanislaus Mlotkowski Memorial Brigade Society, c. 1974. Pp. [ii], 172. $5.95.)

Son of a Polish émigré who studied medicine and married in France, Leon Jastremski was born in the chateau of the Count de Pontaut, Soulan. When his parents and older brother migrated to Louisiana, the infant Leon remained with maternal relatives until age six, when he joined his family in Vermilionville (Lafayette). Orphaned at thirteen, he served as a printer's devil before joining the Louisiana Volunteers at eighteen. Captured on three occasions, the prisoner-of-war life of the young captain is revealed through letters to his brother in Louisiana.

Jastremski and his brother opened a drugstore in Baton Rouge after the Civil War. As foreman of a fire company called upon to quell a polling-place riot Leon gained a measure of local fame and found himself in politics. In 1876 fellow members of the Knights of the White Camellia supported his election as Democratic mayor of Baton Rouge, an office he held for three terms. Active as a newspaper editor, Jastremski also served as state printer, a member of the 1879 constitutional convention, chairman of the State Democratic Committee, and a leading organizer of the United Confederate Veterans in Louisiana. In no one of these important roles does the subject receive more than superficial attention.

As United States consul in Callao, Peru, during Cleveland's second term, Jastremski attended to his duties in offices above those of the Grace

Brothers steamship company. It was while on leave early in McKinley's term that Jastremski read that the new President had appointed another to his post in Callao.

As the reform candidate for governor of Louisiana in 1904 Jastremski called for a Democratic party primary, secret elections, and the end of boss rule in New Orleans. Defeated, he ran again in the next gubernatorial campaign, but death took him before election day.

Ethnic considerations receive foremost attention in this volume. Other than his Polish name, however, this reviewer had difficulty in recognizing the paternal heritage of this Confederate officer, who wrote home in French. Numerous digressions refer to Polish immigrants in Louisiana and elsewhere, but the author did not demonstrate that they were friends of the subject. In fact, some readers may not be convinced that Jastremski had any particular dealings with others of Polish ancestry.

Historians may wish to turn to the appendix and review the 1903 and 1907 gubernatorial platforms of Jastremski and his position paper on labor. Each provides insights into the principles supported by this admittedly neglected political leader. Further research might reveal that he may have been Louisiana's leading proponent of what C. Vann Woodward called "Progressivism—For Whites Only."

Trinity University DONALD E. EVERETT

DeLesseps S. Morrison and the Image of Reform: New Orleans Politics, 1946–1961. By Edward F. Haas. (Baton Rouge: Louisiana State University Press, c. 1974. Pp. xiv, 368. $12.95.)

This is an unusually readable book for a revised dissertation. The author avoids pedantry and writes in a style that is clean and captivating. Rather than a biography of Morrison, this is a study of his political career within the framework of Louisiana and New Orleans politics. Although Haas devotes a few pages to Morrison's life before he became mayor and superficially describes his role as ambassador to the Organization of American States, the book is intended to be an investigation of his lengthy and eventful tenure as mayor of the Crescent City.

Relying upon manuscript collections—especially the Morrison papers—as well as interviews, newspapers, and government documents, Haas argues that "Although deLesseps Story Morrison maintained secret associations with members of the local underworld, sought to build his own personal political dynasty, and responded primarily to the stimulus of self-interest, he brought a sizable measure of reform to New Orleans. This reform, like the image, was hardly perfect, but it did embody undeniably constructive aspects that definitely benefited the port city" (p. 42). The evidence that Haas presents to support this thesis is impressive. My only quarrel with him is over Morrison's motives. It never occurs to Haas that Morrison might have loved his city and sincerely hoped to improve the quality of life for all its citizens. Instead, he assumes that every project for civic improvement (and there were many) was inspired by how many votes it would win for Morrison.

Despite his overly critical assessment of Morrison's motives, Haas has made an important contribution to the literature of urban politics. Scholars who are looking for in-depth voting analyses similar to the works by Bruce Stave, Joel Tarr, and John Allswang will be disappointed. However, for those who are interested in how an urban political organization functions from the decision-making and image-creating level this book will be most welcome. Like the modern studies of LaGuardia, Hague, Pendergast, and Pingree, this volume on Morrison documents how blurred the line is between "bosses" and "reformers."

University of Denver LYLE W. DORSETT

The Gun in America: The Origins of a National Dilemma. By Lee Kennett and James LaVerne Anderson. *Contributions in American History,* Number 37. (Westport, Conn., and London: Greenwood Press, 1975. Pp. x, 339. $12.95.)

Professors Kennett and Anderson have trained scholarly guns on the American experience with and attitudes toward individual possession and use of firearms and have richly illuminated the background for recent controversies over their control. They trace briefly the role of firearms in Europe from feudal times to the modern era and then turn to colonial America, where the prevalence of hunting and the need for defense against hostile Indians and foreign enemies gave the equipped militiamen an enduring esteem and made the rifle a revered possession. By the end of the colonial period the right of a citizen to own a gun had become so commonly accepted that it was later sanctified in the Second Amendment to the United States Constitution and thereby given a moral and philosophical, as well as a practical, basis.

The right to own firearms was further strengthened in the nineteenth century. On the trans-Mississippi frontier the gun played a significant role in Indian trade, defense of pioneers against hostile Indians, essential hunting, destructive sports, activities of outlaws and of vigilante organizations seeking to deal with them, and the belief that law-enforcement officers should be armed. In settled America new internal dangers were apprehended in Marxism, anarchism, strikes and labor unrest, agricultural discontent, and incidents associated with the New Immigration. These experiences reinforced the belief that the citizen had a right to arm for his own protection and for the common good.

Twentieth-century pressures for individual possession of firearms have generally originated with their manufacturers, organizations such as the National Rifle Association and sports groups, and those who contend that citizens need arms to combat organized crime and its use of the sawed-off shotgun and the submachine gun. Both world wars were followed by dramatic increases in the private ownership of guns and men skilled in their use. For example, between 1946 and 1968 Americans bought over 55,000,000 firearms.

Efforts at gun control have usually coincided with liberal periods of American history. The Progressive Era, with its emphasis upon conservation, criminology, and the new police science, brought passage of the Sullivan Law by the New York legislature in 1911. Through the efforts of Attorney General Homer Cummings and others, the New Deal produced the National Firearms Act of 1938. With the assassination of President John Kennedy and others fresh in the popular mind, the Great Society of Lyndon Johnson responded with the enactment of the Gun Control Act of 1968, which dealt with several facets of the gun problem but not with the sensitive issue of the "Saturday Night Special."

In treating firearms control in the broad context of the nation's history and development, Kennett and Anderson contribute to an understanding of the real depths of a dilemma peculiar to America. Fifty-six pages of notes and references for 256 pages of text attest the thoroughness of their research and their thoughtful contemplation of the question. In avoiding psychological and emotional arguments, they have shot straight from the academic shoulder. They offer no solutions to the problems, but they do demonstrate that a presentist approach to history, of which their work is a good example, may in some cases have genuine merit.

West Virginia Institute of Technology OTIS K. RICE

Night Riders in Black Folk History. By Gladys-Marie Fry. ([Knoxville]: University of Tennessee Press, c. 1975. Pp. xii, 251. $9.50.)

Professor Fry contends that in the past "formal" historians have neglected any serious consideration of the methods of psychological control of blacks by whites. This gap in our scholarship resulted from historians' "obvious preference for documented sources" (p. 57). Orally transmitted folk legends, upon which the author has heavily relied in this study, could afford an index to this unexplored area, and they could suggest "how the American Black viewed his own problems in the past, and how he explains his conduct and behavior in the present in accommodating to the dominant white culture . . ." (p. 10).

The dominant thesis of *Night Riders* is that during slavery and the post–Civil War period whites sought to control blacks through the use of the supernatural. The fraudulent ghost constituted the first in a gradually developed system of night-riding creatures. Neither harsh punishment nor rewards for good behavior proved successful in reducing the movement of slaves; thus, it was necessary to perfect a system which played upon fear and which utilized "scary creatures" possessed with omnipresence. Masters and slave patrollers were flesh and blood, but ghosts were "things" without limitation. The ghost technique as a psychological and social-control mechanism lost some of its effectiveness among blacks following the Civil War, for some of the freedmen were beginning to "catch on" to the practice. Consequently, whites had to find new solutions to what they considered a continuing problem—the control of blacks within the southern social order. The most effective features of the old system, the ghost garb and the mounted horsemen of the slave patrol, were used to form a new organization, the Ku Klux Klan. If some blacks had simply "played the game," feigning fear of the supernatural, they were indeed terrified of the living, armed men committed to white supremacy, who were capable of snuffing out their lives.

Whether whites tried to control blacks through the use of ghosts, the slave patrol, the KKK, or by weird stories of the hideous deeds of night doctors who trafficked in "living" victims, the ultimate intent, writes Fry, was to produce a climate of collective insecurity and disciplined obedience. Despite the general credibility of *Night Riders,* the book does have a few noticeable, if not major, weaknesses: (1) an inability to resolve successfully how widespread the belief in supernaturalism was within the black community, (2) the occasional assumption of the credibility of an informant a generation removed from an event without cumulative evidence, (3) a tendency to focus only on the South and to generalize about prevailing beliefs without an examination of the North, where more than 250,000 blacks lived in 1860, (4) failure to demonstrate adequately the relationship between the patrol system (Chapter 3) and supernaturalism, and (5) an indefiniteness about the transformation or change in attitudes of blacks resulting from the passage of time, education, and less need for specific kinds of controls.

These criticisms aside, *Night Riders* is a readable study of scholarly merit. Professor Fry is skilled in the techniques of her craft, and her folk history has a legitimate claim to the attention of folklorists and historians.

Eastern Illinois University JIMMIE L. FRANKLIN

Incidents & Experiences in the Life of Thomas W. Parsons from 1826 to 1900. Edited by Frank Furlong Mathias. (Lexington: University Press of Kentucky, c. 1975. Pp. xx, 210. $13.50.)

The image of America held by many citizens of the republic is a composite of grand generalizations learned in school and in fragmented life experiences. Even professional historians fall prey to the grand sweep of the frontier experience, the citizen soldier, and a thousand other alluring concepts. It is important, therefore, that the man-in-the-street and the professional each take the time occasionally to read about the experiences of very ordinary people attempting to cope with the forces that enmesh them. It brings the grand generalization down to earth, and it focuses the record of history on its basic datum—the individual.

It is within this context that we find the life of Thomas W. Parsons to be of interest and significance. He knew himself to be "*only one of many millions who have lived, labored and died 'unwept and unsung'* " (p. 1). He wrote these memoirs for the benefit of his descendants, but in the process he inadvertently provided the historian with a useful document that illuminates the sometimes dark recesses of our heritage.

Thomas W. Parsons, born in Virginia in 1826, moved with his parents to eastern Kentucky while still a very young boy. The great adventure of his early adulthood was soldiering in Mexico during the war of 1846 to 1848. He then returned to Kentucky, where he farmed and worked at a variety of short-term jobs. After marrying, he moved to west-central Indiana, where schoolteaching became his principal occupation. He returned to Kentucky in 1858 and resumed farming.

The last half of the narrative describes the onset of civil war; the incredible confusion in central Kentucky, where both Union and Confederate forces and their civilian sympathizers operated; the outright criminality of guerrilla bands and irregulars who used the war as an excuse to prey upon the civil population; and through it all Parsons's sporadic service with the Unionist Kentucky home guards. He survived captivity and the war, dying in 1915 at eighty-eight years of age.

Frank F. Mathias has edited the narrative with skill and attention. Some forty-three pages of closely printed notes attest to his interest, his diligence, and his ingenuity. He does not always consult the best sources, but there are few real errors, one glaring exception being the mislocation of prominent Mexican mountain peaks to the east of Vera Cruz (n. 42, p. 161) which would place them somewhere in the Gulf of Mexico. Another (n. 14, p. 167) claims excessively that spiritualism was "A major ingredient in all early 19th-century utopian movements . . . ." Useful maps appear on the endpieces; a short appendix is followed by an impressive bibliography. The book has been handsomely produced by the University Press of Kentucky.

University of Akron GEORGE W. KNEPPER

"*Uncle Tom*" *Reed's Memoir of the University of Georgia*. Edited with an introduction by Ray Mathis. University of Georgia Libraries, *Miscellanea Publications*, No. 11. (Athens: University of Georgia Libraries, 1974. Pp. xxx, 214. $10.00.)

Thomas Walter Reed entered the University of Georgia in 1885 at the age of fifteen. Immediately he fell in love with the university and the town of Athens and never left. Graduating with an M.A. in 1888 and LL.B. in 1889, he pursued careers in Athens as lawyer, journalist, and devoted alumnus. In 1909 he became registrar of the university and served until retirement in 1945. Thereafter, he wrote a history of the University of Georgia, comprising 4,100 pages of typescript, which were bound into nineteen volumes by the university library after Reed's death in 1950.

This edition of Reed's work consists of an excerpt from the years 1885–1889, when Reed was a student. Editing the volume, which might aptly be called, "The Best of Tom Reed's School Days," was no easy task because of Reed's repetitions and memory lapses, but Ray Mathis has done an excellent job. Errors are corrected, references to the typescript pagination provided, and the whole fully indexed.

Entertaining for the "old boys" is the appropriate phrase for much of the book. It is arranged in a fashion not unlike college yearbooks, with sections on students, faculty, and extracurricular activities, giving it appeal primarily for the general reader who is also an alumnus of Georgia. Yet, there is considerable social history of higher education in the late-nineteenth-century South, making the volume a useful source book. Reed's account of the classic college curriculum and his description of a faculty of Christian gentlemen filled with professorial dignity are noteworthy here.

General readers and specialists alike will benefit from the stories Reed tells, such as the wrathful reaction of the Georgia students when Athens lost the proposed school of technology to Atlanta. Reed's anecdotes and personal glimpses of the social and academic aspects of a small university community demonstrate the meagerness of health care, environmental convenience, and athletic programs in the old-style universities. At the same time, his accounts reveal the ingenuity with which students overcame this lack of modern facilities and made their lives at the college productive, whether by freezing out the cold with ice water on the windowsill or heated debate in the literary societies' halls.

The structure and content are, therefore, such as to render this volume a lively storybook of pre-annual-appropriations college days but not an objective university history of the Brooks, Hollis, or Powell type.

University of South Carolina, Aiken W. Calvin Smith

The Robert R. Churches of Memphis: A Father and Son Who Achieved in Spite of Race. By Annette E. Church and Roberta Church. (Ann Arbor, Mich.: The authors, 1974. Pp. xxii, 322. $9.50.)

One of the neglected topics in Afro-American history has been the role of blacks in the twentieth-century Republican party. This book traces the business career of Robert R. Church, Sr. Although born a slave, by the time of his death in 1916, through wise investments in Memphis, Tennessee, real estate, he was one of the South's first black millionaires. However, the focus is primarily on the political career of his son Robert R. Church, Jr. Preferring to work behind the scenes, Church, Jr., became one of the leading figures in Tennessee G.O.P. politics. Convinced that the ballot was the surest way for blacks to gain full citizenship, he campaigned vigorously to persuade the Republican party to accept its responsibility toward American Negroes when they were abandoning the G.O.P. for the Democratic party. Church lobbied for federal legislation against unfair employment practices, lynching, and the poll tax. By the end of World War II, however, Mayor E. H. ("Boss") Crump controlled Memphis and had politically isolated Church and his black supporters with a policy of fusion between "lily-white" Republicans and Democrats. In 1952 Church had made significant progress in a bid to recapture the Republican party machinery in Tennessee when a heart attack ended his life.

Based upon the Church family papers and an extensive number of newspaper accounts, this study can serve as a guide to the primary materials available to scholars. Unfortunately, the book is marred by organizational problems and conceptual obscurity. The most serious defect is the heavy reliance on direct quotations. At least two-thirds of the work consists of reproduced documents, family letters, and newspaper clippings. The role of the historian is to interpret his sources, not enumerate them. Because of its scrapbook presentation, which is often out of chronological sequence, crucial questions about the activities of Church in Memphis and national G.O.P. politics are left unasked and, therefore, unanswered. Throughout the study repeated references to Church, Jr., as a leader of "respectable" "Colored people" are both jarring and patronizing. Do these references suggest that blacks who did not agree with his approach were not "respectable"? Furthermore, there is little support for the claim that Church succeeded in sensitizing Republican policies toward the needs of black Americans. Far from affecting national G.O.P. policy, Church's symbolic and historical significance lies in his image as a lone courageous man fighting a lost cause in a political arena which respected his power but apparently cared little for the people for whom it was employed. No doubt many black Republicans, like the Robert R. Churches of Memphis, found themselves in this position, and they need the careful scholarly attention not found in this volume.

University of Delaware RONALD L. LEWIS

Book Notes

Representative Government and the Revolution: The Maryland Constitutional Crisis of 1787. Edited with an introduction by Melvin Yazawa. (Baltimore and London: The Johns Hopkins University Press, c. 1975. Pp. xii, 187. $10.00.) This volume presents a thirty-two-page introduction by the editor entitled "Representation and Constituent Instruction in the Maryland Assembly, 1776–1787: A Study in the Evolution of American Political Thought" and 150 pages of documents devoted to the question. A dispute over the emission of currency in 1787 precipitated a quarrel over the question of the instruction of the senators. This escalated into a sophisticated debate upon the nature of popular sovereignty and the limits upon its exercise. The editor notes that "The immediate issue of constituent interference was beyond resolution for the principal contenders . . . . [since] Each rejected the initial premises of the other. . . . Resolution, however, became tangential, for precisely from this disagreement a profound dialogue developed . . . . The discussions of the nature of government and society . . . transcended the solitary significance of the emission crisis" (pp. 28–29). This is a volume in the Maryland Bicentennial Studies.

A Bibliography of Printed Battle Plans of the American Revolution, 1775–1795. By Kenneth Nebenzahl. (Chicago and London: University of Chicago Press, 1975. Pp. xiv, 159. $12.00.) This bibliography, which was a by-product of research for a facsimile atlas of the Revolutionary War, lists and describes more than two hundred printed battle plans. All of the plans listed were first published between 1775 and 1795, usually in London or Paris. All contain military information, and nearly all are large-scale representations of engagements that took place in North America or the West Indies. Each individual entry includes not merely the size, scale, contents, and location of a plan but also an estimate of its military significance.

The Fate of a Nation: The American Revolution Through Contemporary Eyes. By William P. Cumming and Hugh F. Rankin. (London: Phaidon Press Ltd., 1975; distributed by Praeger Publishers. Pp. 352. $25.00.) This handsome volume interweaves selections from original documents with a basic narrative and supplements this text with numerous well-selected illustrations and maps. There are 278 illustrations in all, 38 of which are in color.

Biographical Directory of the Tennessee General Assembly. Volume I: *1796–1861.* By Robert M. McBride and Dan M. Robison. Edited by Robert M. McBride. (Nashville: The Tennessee State Library and Archives and the Tennessee Historical Commission, 1975. Pp. xiv, 889. $10.00.) This volume is the first of a projected four intended to provide biographical sketches of the members of the Tennessee General Assembly to the present day. Planned by the late Dan M. Robison, it is based upon the usual public sources plus information derived from questionnaires circulated through the state. The major portion of this volume is an alphabetical compilation of the biographies, but there is also a three-page addenda of information received after the manuscript had gone to press, a twenty-page bibliography, and a thirty-one-page index listing all persons mentioned in the sketches. The volume will be a treasure for scholars, local historians, and genealogists, and it is available at an astoundingly low price.

Indians of the Lower South: Past and Present. Edited by John K. Mahon. Gulf Coast History and Humanities Conference, *Proceedings*, Volume V. (Pensacola: Gulf Coast History and Humanities Conference, 1975. Pp. x, 158. Paper, $5.00; cloth, $7.95.) This volume reproduces the papers presented at the fifth Gulf Coast History and Humanities Conference, February 7–8, 1974. The first day considered "Teaching the Indian Past in History Courses," and the second was devoted to "Indians Who Left and Indians Who Stayed in the Southeast." Participants included Samuel Proctor, James A. Servies, John K. Mahon, Robert Ferguson, Jack Gregory, Rennard Strickland, John Peterson, Thomas LoGuidice, Adolph Dial, J. Anthony Paredes, Harry A. Kersey, Jr., Holátte Cvpvkke (C. B. Clark), Mary Young, and Angie Debo.

The Great American Frontier: A Story of Western Pioneering. Edited by Thomas D. Clark. (Indianapolis: Bobbs-Merrill Co., 1975. Pp. xlii, 334. Paper, $5.95.) This latest volume in the *American Heritage Series* follows the usual format of the series. It includes a brief bibliography, a twenty-two-page introduction by the editor, and seventy-two selections of sources presented in eleven chapters. The topics include trailbreaking, pioneering as an experience, life on the various frontiers, land questions, Indians, the rivers, the fur traders, the mine rushes, and the impact of the frontier.

Albert D. Kirwan. By Frank Furlong Mathias. (Lexington, Ky.: University Press of Kentucky, c. 1975. Pp. xiv, 190. $12.50.) This is a brief biography and anthology of the late Albert D. Kirwan, football coach, dean, president, and historian at the University of Kentucky for many years. Clement Eaton contributes a foreword, and the author provides a 64-page biography and a 111-page selection of Kirwan's writings and speeches.

Slavery and the Numbers Game: A Critique of Time on the Cross. By Herbert G. Gutman. *Blacks in the New World.* (Urbana, Chicago, and London: University of Illinois Press, c. 1975. Pp. xiv, 183. Paper, $2.95; cloth, $7.95.) This new addition to August Meier's series on *Blacks in the New World* is a slightly revised version of an essay review published in the January 1975 issue of the *Journal of Negro History* (LX, 53–227). Disclaiming any intention of denigrating quantitative history, properly used, Gutman rather effectively explodes the reliability of *Time on the Cross* as a study of slavery and the antebellum black. This is done in five major sections: "An Overview of T/C"; "Enslaved Afro-Americans and the 'Protestant Work Ethic' "; "Positive Labor Incentives and Slave Work Habits"; "The Slave Family, Slave Sexual Behavior, and Slave Sales"; and "An Archaic Historical Model." He argues that conclusions were based on inadequate data and faulty premises; and he attacks specifically the conclusions on punishments and the use of positive labor incentives; the statistics and conclusions on slave marriages and families, the effects of the slave trade, and particularly the number of "stable" families; and the conclusions on slave marital and sexual behavior. He finally concludes that *Time on the Cross* is particularly flawed by its implied assumption that slave behavior was simply a reaction to white initiatives.

Civil War Marine: A Diary of the Red River Expedition, 1864. Edited by James P. Jones and Edward F. Keuchel. (Washington, D. C.: History and Museums Division, Headquarters, U. S. Marine Corps, 1975. Pp. vii, 89. $1.65.) In a field literally awash with diaries and personal reminiscences, firsthand accounts of service by Marines during the Civil War remain exceedingly scarce. This, in the opinion of Professors James P. Jones and Edward F. Keuchel, makes the publication of the journal of Second Lieutenant Frank L. Church an unusual "find" for the military historian. The document covers a period from February 19 through May 25, 1864, and records the experiences of the twenty-one-year-old commander of a small Marine guard accompanying Admiral David Dixon Porter's flotilla on the Red River expedition. Most of the entries are relatively commonplace and shed little new light on Major General Nathaniel P. Banks's abortive advance upon Shreveport, Louisiana. Nevertheless, Lieutenant Church's diary seems likely to arouse some interest among enthusiasts and scholars for the rare personal glimpse it provides of at least one of the combat roles performed by the United States Marine Corps during the years 1861–1865. Professors Jones and Keuchel expand the narrative with a preface, an introduction, and an epilogue, in addition to thirteen pages of explanatory footnotes. Nineteen maps and illustrations are interspersed throughout the text, and a map of the "Valley of the Red River, La., from Mississippi River to Shreveport 1865," reprinted from the *Official Records of the Union and Confederate Armies*, is included. [BRUCE J. DINGES, Rice University]

The Presidial Press of Austin, Texas, has published three volumes which make available in book form articles previously published in journal or newspaper form. All are well bound, typographically attractive, and provided with useful maps and other illustrations. *The Civil War in the Indian Territory*. By Lary C. Rampp and Donald L. Rampp. (Austin, 1975. Pp. viii, 210. $9.95.) reproduces articles published earlier in the *Military History of Texas and the Southwest* (X, 29–42, 93–114, 249–72; XI, 77–108, 173–96, 251–80). *American Artillery in the Mexican War, 1846–1847*. By Lester R. Dillon, Jr. (Austin, 1975. Pp. xii, 120. $7.95.) reproduces four articles from the same journal (XI, 7–30, 109–30, 149–72, 233–50). *Sabers on the Rio Grande*. By Jerry Thompson. (Austin, 1974. Pp. [xiv], 235. $10.00.) is a revised reprinting of a series of articles appearing in the Laredo *Times* between September 27, 1973, and August 11, 1974. Handsomely illustrated with paintings by Bruce Marshall, it is intended to be the first part of a projected two-volume study of Laredo and Fort McIntosh.

The Civil War in Kentucky. By Lowell H. Harrison. (Lexington: University Press of Kentucky, c. 1975. Pp. x, 116. $3.95.) This is a new title in the Kentucky Bicentennial Bookshelf. Professor Harrison notes the limitations of space imposed by the series format and emphasizes that he is writing about the Civil War in Kentucky rather than Kentucky in the Civil War.

Public Papers of the Presidents of the United States: Richard Nixon: Containing the Public Messages, Speeches, and Statements of the President, 1972. (Washington: United States Government Printing Office, 1974. Pp. lii, 1161, A1–28, B1–21, C1–7, D1–3, E1–25, F1–2, I1–80. $18.55.) The documents in this volume reveal Richard Nixon at the height of his power, brilliantly orchestrating events at home and abroad to secure his reputation for statesmanship and, incidentally, his reelection. In quest of a generation of peace he made his historic trip to China in February, telling Chou Enlai, "There is no reason for us to be enemies" (p. 369). Three months later the President was in Moscow to sign agreements to curb competition in strategic arms. Events in Vietnam, meanwhile, were moving toward a climax. On May 8 Mr. Nixon announced the mining of North Vietnamese ports and proposed the terms of settlement that almost, but not quite, resulted in a truce on the eve of the election: return of U. S. prisoners, a cease-fire throughout Indochina, and complete withdrawal of U. S. forces. During the year he missed no opportunity to remind the electorate that he had brought a half million men home from the war since 1969.

In the realm of domestic policy Mr. Nixon kept the Democrats off balance with a shrewd mix of programs. Having appropriated in 1971 the demand of the Democrats for price and wage control, the President could take credit in the 1972 campaign for the slackening rate of inflation. He undercut the Democrats by proposing a Republican version of health insurance for everyone. He appealed to conservatives by vetoing the H.E.W. appropriations bill, securing passage of revenue sharing, and talking tough on crime. And he continued to court the votes of fearful whites by attacking the bussing of school children for purposes of racial balance. His aim, he said during the campaign, was to fashion a new American majority by basing policy on old-fashioned American principles.

The President's public utterances touched hardly at all on the subject of Watergate. Only when reporters pressed him at his infrequent press conferences did Mr. Nixon address this issue. On June 22, five days after the break-in, the President denied White House involvement but otherwise refused comment. On August 29 he assured reporters that White House Counsel John Dean had conducted a complete investigation and found no one presently employed by the White House "involved in this very bizarre incident." "What really hurts in matters of this sort is not the fact that they occur . . . ," he said. "What really hurts is if you try to cover it up" (p. 828). Finally, on October 5 Mr. Nixon said that the FBI investigation in the Hiss case "was basically a Sunday school exercise" (p. 957) compared to that agency's work on the Watergate case. Whether he knew, as he thanked the voters in November for his landslide reelection, how precarious was his victory, these documents, of course, do not reveal. [ALLEN J. MATUSOW, Rice University]

Louisiana: A Pictorial History. By Leonard V. Huber. (New York: Charles Scribner's Sons, c. 1975. $20.00.) The author provides a brief twenty-page historical introduction and then provides a wealth of illustrations with a brief textual comment organized into six chapters and covering aspects of the state's history from prehistoric times to 1974.

Early Georgia Portraits, 1715–1870. Compiled by the Historical Activities Committee, Marion Converse Bright, state chairman, for the National Society of Colonial Dames of America in the State of Georgia. (Athens: University of Georgia Press, c. 1975. Pp. xiv, 338. $25.00.) The portraits are arranged alphabetically by subject with two portraits per page. The accompanying text describes the size and the medium used, names the artist (if known), and gives the location of the portrait along with details on the subject. A separate thirty-four-page section on miniatures is alphabetized and described in similar fashion with three miniatures to the page. There is also a list of the artists, a list of unillustrated portraits, a list of patrons, and an index.

A List of References for the History of Black Americans in Agriculture, 1619–1974. Compiled by Joel Schor and Cecil Harvey. (Davis, Calif.: Agricultural History Center, University of California, Davis, 1975. Pp. vi, 116. Multilithed.) This is the fourteenth section of the comprehensive bibliography of American agricultural history being compiled and published in sections by the U. S. Department of Agriculture and the Agricultural History Center of the University of California at Davis. Copies are available free upon request to the Center at Davis, California 95616.

The Virginia State Library at Richmond issued in 1975 Numbers 39 and 41 of its *Publications.* Bound in paper, the titles in numerical sequence are: *More Virginia Broadsides Before 1877.* By Ray O. Hummel, Jr. (Pp. x, 106. $4.00.); and *The Music Books of Ruebush & Kieffer, 1866–1942: A Bibliography.* By Grace I. Showalter. (Pp. xii, 40. $2.00.). The first is a supplement to the Virginia section of *Southeastern Broadsides Before 1877*, published in 1971. It lists more than 900 Virginia broadsides not included in the earlier volume and brings the total of Virginia broadsides to nearly 3,400. There is an author, title, and subject index. The second lists the musical books published by the firm of Ruebush and Kieffer of Rockingham County, Virginia. Some two hundred titles were issued. There is a title index.

Society in Colonial North Carolina. By Alan D. Watson. (Raleigh: North Carolina Department of Cultural Resources, Division of Archives and History, 1975. Pp. [x], 93. Paper, $1.00.) This handsomely illustrated pamphlet is a new addition to a series of booklets issued over the years by the North Carolina Department of Archives and History. It is intended for school children and the general public.

North Carolina Troops, 1861–1865: A Roster. Volume V: *Infantry.* Compiled by Weymouth T. Jordan, Jr., with unit histories by Louis H. Manarin. (Raleigh: Division of Archives and History, 1975. Pp. xx, 678. $20.00.) This is the fifth in a projected thirteen-volume series. It covers the compiled service records of the 11th, 12th, 13th, 14th, and 15th regiments and the 13th Battalion of North Carolina infantry.

Tried by Fire: Washington Street United Methodist Church, Columbia, South Carolina. By Archie Vernon Huff, Jr. (Columbia, S. C.: R. L. Bryan Co., c. 1975. Pp. xii, 161. $10.00.) Methodist services were first held in Columbia, South Carolina, in 1787 by a circuit-rider, and a permanent church was established in 1804. In six chapters Professor Huff traces the history of the church to 1974. Two appendices list the ministers and the church officers over the years.

The Political Status of the Negro in the Age of FDR. By Ralph J. Bunche. Edited by Dewey W. Grantham. (Chicago and London: University of Chicago Press, c. 1973. Pp. xxxiv, 682. Paper, $7.95.) This is a paperback reprint of a book reviewed in the February 1974 issue of the *Journal* (XL, 156–58).

Historical News and Notices

PERSONALS

University of Alabama, Birmingham: Virginia V. Hamilton promoted to professor; John David Wortham on leave fall and winter quarters and David White winter and spring quarters.

University of Alabama, University: Forrest McDonald appointed professor.

American University: William Willard Wolfe appointed associate professor for 1975–76 and Janet Oppenheim Minihan assistant professor.

Arkansas Polytechnic College: Georgena D. Duncan appointed assistant professor for 1975–76.

Arkansas State University: Margrit A. Jay and Elizabeth R. Kindleberger appointed assistant professors and Robert L. Jones part-time instructor.

University of Arkansas, Fayetteville: Evan B. Bukey promoted to associate professor; Stephen F. Strausberg on leave fall semester and David A. Sloan spring semester.

University of Arkansas, Little Rock: Edward M. Anson, IV, Elizabeth J. Burns, and James E. Lester appointed assistant professors.

University of Arkansas, Pine Bluff: Sylvia M. Jacobs appointed assistant professor.

Austin Peay State University: Dean Rowley appointed instructor.

Birmingham-Southern College: William E. Nicholas, III, and Samuel N. Stayer promoted to associate professor.

Bowie State College: William J. Irwin promoted to associate professor and Barry A. Crouch to assistant professor.

Catholic University of America: Raymond F. Kierstead, Jr., appointed associate professor and Michael D. Metzger instructor; Joseph N. Moody has retired.

College of Charleston: Sister M. Anne Francis named chairman; Edmund Lee Drago and James C. Turner appointed assistant professors; Malcolm C. Clark promoted to professor and Paul A. Klevgard to associate professor; James W. Hagy on leave fall term and Malcolm C. Clark spring term.

Coker College: Fred R. van Hartesveldt appointed visiting assistant professor; Nancy Y. Ropp on leave for 1975–76.

Columbus College: O. Burton Adams, John R. McCreary, and John S. Murzyn promoted to associate professor; Benjamin F. Bailey has retired.

East Tennessee State University: Emmett M. Essin, III, promoted to professor.

Emory University: Jonathan D. Prude appointed assistant professor.

Florida Atlantic University: Otto L. Bettmann appointed adjunct professor; Tsung-I Dow promoted to professor; William F. Marina on leave for full year and A. Leslie Derfler for two quarters.

Florida State University: John Hebron Moore named chairman; Richard L. Greaves promoted to professor and Winston W. Lo and Robert J. Rubanowice to associate professors; David L. Ammerman and Jan K. Tanenbaum on leave for 1975–76 academic year.

Furman University: John Martin Block and Archie V. Huff, Jr., promoted to associate professor and William John Lavery and James B. Leavell to assistant professor.

George Mason University: Joseph L. Harsh named chairman; Marion F. Deshmukh and George Walker appointed assistant professors; Martin B. Cohen promoted to assistant professor; Ernest Cassara on leave 1975–76.

Georgetown University: Hisham B. Sharabi on leave fall 1975.

Georgia College: Martha L. Turner appointed assistant professor.

Georgia Southern College: C. Charlton Moseley promoted to professor; Julia F. Smith on leave.

Harding College: Thomas M. Howard on leave.

University of Houston: Bailey S. Stone appointed assistant professor, Barry J. Kaplan visiting assistant professor, and Francisco A. Rosales instructor; John O. King promoted to professor and Hyland B. Packard, Jr., to associate professor.

Institute of Early American History and Culture: Norman S. Fiering on leave for year beginning September 1, 1975.

Kentucky Wesleyan College: Lee A. Dew on leave for spring semester.

LaGrange College: James G. Johnson, Jr., appointed assistant professor.

Library of Congress, Manuscript Division: John C. Broderick named chief and Paul T. Heffron assistant chief; Roy P. Basler has retired.

Louisiana College: Thomas Howell named chairman; William Simpson appointed assistant professor.

Louisiana State University, Baton Rouge: Gary A. Crump and Patrick C. Lipscomb, III, promoted to associate professor; William J. Cooper, Jr., on leave.

Loyola College (Baltimore): Donald T. Wolfe named chairman.

Mars Hill College: John C. Crawford appointed to staff.

Mary Baldwin College: Jean Mather appointed instructor.

University of Miami: Bruce A. Lohof named chairman; Edward L. Dreyer, Andrew Handler, Bruce A. Lohof, John F. Reiger, and Robert M. Zaller promoted to associate professor.

Middle Tennessee State University: Sammy W. Clyatt appointed temporary instructor; John Morris on leave one semester.

Midwestern University: Kenneth E. Hendrickson, Jr., named acting vice-president of academic affairs and Forrest D. Monahan, Jr., acting chairman of the Department of History.

Mississippi College: James T. Currie appointed assistant professor.

University of Mississippi: Edward M. Walters appointed university archivist and assistant professor; David G. Sansing promoted to associate professor; James J. Cooke on leave spring 1976.

Mississippi University for Women: Kit C. Carter promoted to associate professor.

University of Missouri, Columbia: James P. Whittenburg appointed assistant professor and Samuel J. Berner, Michael J. Cassity, and Patrick J. Headen visiting assistant professors; Susan L. Flader promoted to associate professor.

University of Missouri, Rolla: Jack B. Ridley promoted to associate professor; Wayne M. Bledsoe on leave.

Morgan State University: Ernestein Walker named chairman; Kwang T. Kim promoted to associate professor; Charles Chikeka, Thomas R. Cripps, Roland C. McConnell, and Henry Shields Robinson on leave for 1975–76 academic year.

National Historical Publications and Records Commission: Frank G. Burke named acting executive director.

North Carolina Division of Archives and History: Robert E. Stipe resigned as director; Larry E. Tise named acting director.

University of North Carolina, Chapel Hill: Roberto Etchepareborda appointed visiting William Rand Kenan, Jr., Professor, William Lesko Barney, assistant professor, Persis Charles Hunt visiting lecturer, William Howard Beezley and James E. McClellan part-time visiting lecturers, and William Miles Fletcher, III, Sara Margaret Evans, George William Hopkins, and Linda Rose Skillen instructors; Carolyn D. Wallace appointed director, Southern Historical Collection and Manuscripts Department; Richard William Pfaff promoted to professor and Lawrence Devlin Kessler to associate professor; R. Don Higginbotham, Donald Gene Mathews, Joan Wallach Scott, and Joseph Samuel Tulchin on leave 1975–76, David Mark Griffiths and Joel R. Williamson for fall term 1975, Samuel Haskell Baron for calendar year 1976, and Lamar J. R. Cecil, Jr., Roger W. Lotchin, and Richard Allen Soloway for spring term 1976; J. Isaac Copeland has retired.

University of North Carolina, Charlotte: John E. Wrigley named acting chairman; Robert M. Mullins, Jeffery S. Rossbach, and Marian E. Strobel appointed lecturers; Dan L. Morrill promoted to professor; Paul D. Escott, Lyman L. Johnson, and Eric H. Monkkonen on leave for 1975–76; John O. P. Hall has retired and been named professor emeritus.

North Texas State University: William H. Wilson promoted to professor and Richard G. Lowe to associate professor; William E. Painter on leave for fall semester.

Oglethorpe College: J. Brien Key on leave for fall semester.

University of Oklahoma: Thomas R. Sykes appointed visiting assistant professor; Robert A. Nye promoted to associate professor.

Old Dominion University: Theodore A. Di Padova named assistant dean of graduate studies; Nancy T. Wolfe appointed assistant professor and Keith Burich instructor; John W. Kuehl on leave for fall semester.

Rice University: Richard Smith appointed visiting assistant professor; Thomas L. Haskell on leave for academic year, and Francis L. Loewenheim, Allen J. Matusow, and Albert Van Helden for the fall semester.

University of Richmond: The History Departments of Richmond and Westhampton Colleges have been combined, and Richard Barry Westin named chairman; Frances A. Underhill promoted to professor; W. Harrison Daniel and Frances A. Underhill on leave.

Saint Louis University: Martin G. Towey appointed assistant professor and Frederick J. Cowie and Ronald W. Jones part-time staff; John P. Willson on leave.

South Carolina Department of Archives and History: Charles H. Lesser named assistant director for archives and publications.

University of South Carolina: Harry D. Bralley appointed visiting professor; Richard D. Mandell promoted to professor; Thomas L. Connelly on leave.

Stetson University: Kevin J. O'Keefe appointed assistant professor; Marc H. Lovelace on leave.

University of Southern Mississippi: Orazio A. Ciccarelli promoted to associate professor.

Southwest Missouri State University: Dominic J. Capeci, Jr., Jere Krakow, and James C. Moyer promoted to associate professor; John L. Young on leave.

Southwest Texas State University: Ronald C. Brown, Claudine Ferrell, Aubrey H. Polser, Jr., Thomas W. Riddle, and Carl Zimmerman appointed instructors; Dennis J. Dunn promoted to associate professor; Dennis J. Dunn on leave fall semester.

Talladega College: Carl R. Stockton resumes chairmanship.

Tennessee State University: Phillip McGuire appointed to the staff.

University of Tennessee, Knoxville: Charles O. Jackson promoted to professor and John R. Finger to associate professor.

University of Tennessee, Martin: Charles F. Ogilvie promoted to professor and Ronald N. Satz to associate professor; John P. Wittenberg on leave.

Tennessee Wesleyan College: Durwood Dunn appointed instructor; Thomas J. Baker, Jr., promoted to associate professor; Robert L. Utlaut on leave for 1975–77.

Texas A&M University: Brison D. Gooch named associate dean of liberal arts and Allan C. Ashcraft acting head of department; Robert A. Calvert and W. James King appointed associate professors; Henry C. Dethloff promoted to professor, Larry D. Hill to associate professor, and Shirley J. Black to assistant professor.

Texas Christian University: R. David Edmunds appointed assistant professor; Frank T. Reuter on leave fall semester and Ben Procter spring semester.

Tulane University: Charles H. Carter named chairman of the university History Department and head of the Arts and Sciences History Department; Richard B. Latner and Colin MacLachlan appointed assistant professors; Sam C. Ramer on leave for academic year and Hugh F. Rankin for fall semester; Ralph Lee Woodward, Jr., was director of Tulane's Guatemalan Summer Institute and will be professor-in-charge of Tulane's Junior Year Abroad program in Paris this year.

Union University: Gay Semrau appointed instructor; Stan Ekrut promoted to assistant professor.

Vanderbilt University: Steven D. Crow appointed visiting assistant professor; George D. Sussman on leave for fall semester.

Virginia Commonwealth University: Marijean H. Eichel appointed assistant professor.

Virginia Polytechnic Institute and State University: Max H. Kele named director of humanities; Michael C. Hurst appointed professor. Max H. Kele associate professor, Thomas A. Dunlap assistant professor, and Charlotte Jean Shelton instructor; Homer E. Le Grand, Jr., and William L. Ochsenwald on leave fall quarter.

University of Virginia: Lewis A. Erenberg appointed visiting assistant professor for 1975–76.

Wake Forest University: Louise E. Hoffman appointed instructor; J. Edwin Hendricks and Richard L. Zuber promoted to professor.

Washington and Lee University: Robert W. McAhren promoted to professor and I. Taylor Sanders, II, to associate professor; Allen W. Moger has retired.

Washington University: Henry W. Berger on leave for academic year.

College of William and Mary: Thomas F. Sheppard named chairman of Department of History; Maurice W. Beresford appointed James Pinckney Harrison Professor of History for the 1975–1976 academic year, Dale E. Hoak associate professor, and Allan L. Kulikoff assistant professor; Anthony J. Esler on leave first semester and Ludwell H. Johnson, III, second semester.

Winston-Salem State University: Howard Barnes promoted to associate professor; Mrs. Linda Bland on leave 1975–76.

Winthrop College: Arnold Shankman appointed assistant professor; Thomas S. Morgan, Jr., promoted to professor and James A. Casada to associate professor; Ross A. Webb has returned to full-time teaching.

DEATHS

Robert Gunn Crawford, professor of history at East Tennessee State University, died June 6, 1975, at the age of fifty-seven. A native of West Point, Mississippi, he earned his bachelor's and master's degrees at Duke University and his doctorate at the University of Kentucky. He served in the navy during World War II and taught at the University of Tennessee before joining the faculty at East Tennessee State in 1947. He taught, on occasion, summer sessions at the University of Georgia and University of Alabama at Birmingham. After surgery for a brain tumor in January 1974, he returned to his classroom in September and taught until the last of April. He was especially effective in the classroom and around the seminar table, receiving the faculty award as Distinguished Professor in 1974. He published a number of articles, read papers, and served on panels in the professional associations. [FRANK B. WILLIAMS, JR.]

Hermann E. Schuessler, professor of history at the University of Maryland, died August 14, 1975, in Bottmingen, Switzerland. In addition to his book, *Georg Calixt, Theologie und Kirchenpolitik: Eine Studie zur Oekumenizitaet des Luthertums,* he published numerous articles and reviews. In this country he had taught at Boston College, Washington University, and Brown University, in addition to having held posts in Germany.

ANNOUNCEMENTS AND ACTIVITIES

The Tennessee American Revolution Bicentennial Commission and the Tennessee Historical Society invite the submission of article-length manuscripts on subjects relating to Tennessee during the era of the American Revolution, 1756–1796. Four prizes of five hundred dollars each are being offered, and the four winning articles will be considered for publication in the summer 1976 bicentennial issue of the *Tennessee Historical Quarterly*. Five copies of the manuscript should be sent no later than January 2, 1976, to James C. Kelly, Executive Director, Tennessee American Revolution Bicentennial Commission, 315 Capitol Towers, 510 Gay Street, Nashville, Tennessee 37219. Manuscripts should be typed double-spaced on 8½" × 11" paper, and the pages should be consecutively numbered, with the author's name, address, telephone number, and institutional affiliation (if any) on the title page. The manuscript should not exceed eight to ten thousand words in length.

The Forest History Society has announced that James E. Fickle has been selected as a cowinner of the 1974 Theodore C. Blegen Award for the best article in forest history. He published in the February 1974 issue of the *Journal of Southern History* an article entitled "Management Looks at the 'Labor Problem': The Southern Pine Industry During World War I and the Postwar Era." The other cowinner was Robert Peter Gillis for his article entitled "The Ottawa Lumber Barons and the Conservation Movement, 1880–1914," published in the February 1974 issue of the *Journal of Canadian Studies*. Mr. Fickle and Mr. Gillis will share a $250 prize and receive certificates. A certificate will also be presented to each of the publishing journals.

William C. Davis has received the fourth annual Jefferson Davis Award of the Museum of the Confederacy in Richmond, Virginia, for his book, *Breckinridge: Statesman, Soldier, Symbol*, a biography of John C. Breckinridge. The book, published by Louisiana State University Press, also won the press's 1973 Jules F. Landry Award.

The Society of American Historians has awarded the Allan Nevins Prize of one thousand dollars for the best-written doctoral dissertation on a significant theme in American history in 1974 to Gary A. May for "The China Service of John Carter Vincent," written at the University of California, Los Angeles, under the sponsorship of Professor Robert Dallek.

Gary B. Mills of Mississippi State University has been awarded the Louisiana Historical Association's Robert Brown Award for the outstanding article published in *Louisiana History* in 1974.

The Florida Historical Society has announced the recipients of its prizes for 1974–1975. The Rembert W. Patrick Memorial Book Award was presented to Jerrell H. Shofner of Florida Technological University for his *Nor Is It Over Yet: Florida in the Era of Reconstruction, 1863–1877,* published by the University Presses of Florida. The Charlton W. Tebeau Junior Book Award was given to Nancy Henderson and Jane Dewey for their *Circle of Life: The Miccosukee Indian Way,* published by Julian Messner of New York with photographs by David Pickens. Richard A. Martin received the Arthur W. Thompson Memorial Prize in Florida History for his article "Defeat in Victory: Yankee Experience in Early Civil War Jacksonville," which appeared in the July 1974 issue of the *Florida Historical Quarterly.*

William M. Tuttle, Jr., of the University of Kansas has won the Tom L. Evans Research Grant of the Harry S. Truman Library Institute for National and International Affairs for 1975–1976. Other grants have been awarded to Harold F. Bass, Jr., of Vanderbilt University, Lawrence S. Berman of Princeton University, Monroe L. Billington of New Mexico State University, Philip F. Cashier of Newing College of the State University of New York, Steven P. Gietschier of Ohio State University, Robert M. Hathaway of the University of North Carolina, John F. Karl of the University of Toronto, Karyl L. Kibler of the State University of New York at Stony Brook, Robert J. Maddox of Pennsylvania State University, Leo F. McCue, Jr., of Boston University, Robert A. Pollard of the University of North Carolina, David A. Rosenberg of the University of Chicago, Jerry P. Rosenberg of the University of Illinois, Solomon Slonim of the Hebrew University of Jerusalem, Marc J. Susser of Harvard University, Hal E. Wert of the University of Kansas, Lawrence S. Wittner of the State University of New York at Albany, and Allen L. Yarnell of the University of California at Los Angeles.

For information about the Tom L. Evans grant and the other grants write to The Secretary, Harry S. Truman Library Institute, Independence, Missouri 64050.

The National Historical Publications and Records Commission will continue its program of fellowships in advanced editing of documentary sources for American history and will award several fellowships for 1976–1977, each bearing a stipend of $11,000. Further information may be obtained from the Executive Director, National Historical Publications and Records Commission, Room 100, National Archives Building, Washington, D. C. 20408.

The Harvard University Graduate School of Business Administration and the Newcomen Society in North America announce a postdoctoral fellowship in business history in the amount of $13,000 to be awarded for twelve months' residence, study, and research at the Harvard Business School during 1976–1977. The fellow's doctoral degree may be in history, economics, or a related discipline such as sociology. The successful applicant may begin his twelve months' residence on either July 1 or September 1, 1976. Applications must be completed by April 1, 1976, and the fellowship will be awarded and all applicants notified by April 15, 1976. Inquiries concerning activities and goals of the program and application procedures should be addressed to Professor Alfred D. Chandler, Jr., Morgan Hall 207, Harvard University Graduate School of Business Administration, Boston, Massachusetts 02163.

The Office of Air Force History will award two fellowships to civilian graduate students who have completed all requirements for the Ph.D. except the dissertation and who have an approved dissertation topic dealing with U. S. military aerospace history. Each award carries a $4,000 stipend, and the deadline for applications is February 2, 1976. For further information and application forms, write to Chief, Office of Air Force History (AF/CHO), Headquarters USAF, Washington, D. C. 20314.

The U. S. Army Center of Military History will sponsor two $4,000 Dissertation Year Fellowships for qualified doctoral candidates researching in American military history in 1976–1977. Applications close on January 24, 1976. For further information write to the Chief Historian, Center of Military History, Department of the Army, James Forrestal Building, Washington, D. C. 20314, Stop 391. The visiting research fellows for 1975–1976 are Eric M. Bergerud of the University of California at Berkeley and John T. Crouch of the University of Wisconsin.

The Naval History Division of the U. S. Department of the Navy will award two $4,000 predoctoral fellowships for 1976–1977 to graduate students researching and writing in U. S. naval history. Applications will close on February 2, 1976. For further information write to the Director of Naval History, Washington, D. C. 20374.

The Department of History at the University of Tennessee, Knoxville, will sponsor a conference on the American Revolution on April 30, 1976. Speakers will be Alfred F. Young of Southern Illinois University, R. Don Higginbotham of the University of North Carolina, Chapel Hill, and Michael A. Kammen of Cornell University. For further information write to Milton M. Klein, Department of History, University of Tennessee, Knoxville, Tennessee 37916.

The fourth annual General Wilburt S. Brown Memorial Military History Conference will be held on January 24, 1976, at the University of Alabama Continuing Education Center. Participants will include Hugh F. Rankin of Tulane University, Forrest McDonald of the University of Alabama, William J. Morgan of the Naval Historical Center, John S. Pancake of the University of Alabama, and Charles R. Smith of the Division of Marine Corps History and Museums. For complete information write George M. Faulk, P. O. Box 2967, University, Alabama 35486.

The United States Air Force Academy will sponsor the seventh Military History Symposium from September 29 to October 1, 1976. Entitled "The

American Military on the Frontier," the symposium will include sessions on military explorers and the development of America, military life on the frontier, a comparison of military frontiers in the United States and elsewhere, and the influence of the frontier on the American military tradition. For further information write to Captain David Miles, Department of History, USAF Academy, Colorado 80840.

Norfolk State College and Old Dominion University invite urban specialists from all fields of social sciences to participate in the second annual Virginia Conference on Urban Studies to be held February 12–13, 1976, at Norfolk State College, Norfolk, Virginia 23504. The conference is entitled "The Urban South—Perspective '76." For further information write to Professor Jesse Pendleton, Department of Geography, Norfolk State College, Norfolk, Virginia 23504 or to Professor Carl Abbott, Department of History, Old Dominion University, Norfolk, Virginia 23508.

An Adam Smith bicentennial conference will be held at Eastern Kentucky University, March 24–26, 1976. The featured speaker will be Professor Kenneth Boulding of the University of Colorado. More than twenty papers dealing with Adam Smith's ideas and influence will be presented by historians, economists, political scientists, and philosophers. For further information and registration forms, which are due on March 17, 1976, write to Professor Robert E. Stebbins, Department of History, Eastern Kentucky University, Richmond, Kentucky 40475.

Professor Gary E. Moulton of Southwestern Oklahoma State University, Weatherford, Oklahoma 73096 is editor of The Papers of Chief John Ross and is seeking to locate documents relating to his subject. Those possessing such materials or having knowledge of them are requested to write Professor Moulton at the office of the project.

The Social Science History Association has been organized to further the interests of historians and social scientists concerned with the application of social-science theory and method in historical context. For information on charter, regular, and student memberships write to Jerome M. Clubb, Executive Secretary, SSHA, Center for Political Studies, University of Michigan, P. O. Box 1248, Ann Arbor, Michigan 48106. Robert Swierenga, Department of History, Kent State University, Kent, Ohio 44240 is editor of the association journal and is now accepting manuscripts for review for possible publication.

The University of Georgia Department of History is seeking to compile and maintain a current list of all theses and dissertations on Georgia history in progress. The list will be published annually in the *Georgia Historical Quarterly*. Professor F. Nash Boney is in charge of the project and requests that all persons having such information forward it to him. For each study he needs the name of the student, the title of his work, a very short summary if the title is vague, an indication of whether the work is a thesis or a dissertation, the name of the professor directing the work, and the approximate date of completion. Broader works which include Georgia as part of the Deep South or the Confederacy or some other regional entity may be included along with some indication of the extent of the Georgia material. For the first of these annual surveys studies officially completed as far back as June 1974 may also be listed. Rapid forwarding of the above information would be greatly appreciated.

LIBRARIES AND ARCHIVES

The Manuscript Division of the Library of Congress has recently acquired the following materials: the personal papers of Alexander Graham Bell, including laboratory notebooks (130,000 items); the Charles P. Taft Papers, containing several hundred pieces of correspondence with his father, William Howard Taft; additional John W. Draper family papers containing one hundred pieces of correspondence with General William T. Sherman; and the personal papers of Don Vincente Sebastian Pintado, assistant surveyor general of Louisiana and after 1803 chief surveyor of Spanish West Florida, containing fifty maps and plats of Spanish West Florida. The Harlan F. Stone, Harold Stephens, Peter Marshall, and pre-1940 George S. Patton papers and the diaries of William F. Leahy are available for use without special permission. The Library has published *Manuscripts on Microfilm: A Checklist of the Holdings in the Manuscript Division; Naval Historical Foundation Manuscript Collection: A Catalog; Manuscript Resources for Research on the American Revolution;* and *Hans P. Kraus Collection of Hispanic American Manuscripts.*

The Military Archives Division of the National Archives and Records Service has accessioned two volumes of communications from General Meade's headquarters, Army of the Potomac, from October 23, 1863, to May 24, 1864. The General Archives Division of the National Archives and Records Service has accessioned card indexes of the Bureau of Land Management pertaining to serialized cases processed through the Washington, D. C., office. They are of two types, an alphabetical name index, 1908–47, and a serial number index, 1908–65.

The National Archives has recently published *Preliminary Inventory of the Records of the National Mediation Board,* Preliminary Inventory No. 179, Record Group 13; *Preliminary Inventory of the Records of the International Military Tribunal for the Far East,* Preliminary Inventory No. 180, Record Group 238; *Records of the United States Strategic Bombing Survey—Inventory of Record Group 243,* Inventory Series No. 10; *Guides to German Records Microfilmed at Alexandria, Virginia No. 69—Records of German Field Commands: Divisions (189–218). Part IX; Select Audiovisual Records: Indians in the United States (Revised); List of Record Groups of the National Archives and Records Service, March 1975; Regional Branches of the National Archives* (General Information Leaflet No. 22 [Revised]); *Catalog of Machine Readable Records in the National Archives; Guide to Record Retention Requirements; Microfilming*

Records; and *Research Opportunities,* a description of the holdings of the Federal Archives and Records Center in Chicago.

Microfilm publications recently released include M800, Reports of Clerks and Bureau Officers of the Department of State, 1789–1911; M879, Index to Compiled Service Records of American Naval Personnel Who Served during the Revolutionary War; M880, Compiled Service Records of American Naval Personnel and Members of the Departments of the Quartermaster General and Commissary General of Military Stores Who Served During the Revolutionary War; M890, Records of the United States Nuernberg War Crimes Trials, Case 4, *United States of America* v. *Oswald Pohl* et al.; M901, General Orders and Circulars of the Confederate War Department, 1861–65; M926, Records of the Massachusetts Continental Loan Office, 1777–1791; M947, Letters Received by the Department of Justice from the State of South Carolina, 1871–84; M988, Admiralty Case Files of the U. S. District Court for the Eastern District of Pennsylvania 1789–1840; M938, Records of the Clerk of the Court, 1746–1932, and of the U. S. Commissioners, 1837–1860, of the U. S. District Court for the Southern District of New York; M990, Gorrell's History of the American Expeditionary Forces Air Service, 1917–19; M995, Papers and Minutes of Meetings of Principal World War II Allied Military Conferences, 1941–45; T1194, Minutes of Meetings of the State-War-Navy Coordinating Committee, 1944–47; T1198, Minutes of Meetings of the Subcommittee for the Far East, 1945–47; and T1197, Minutes of Meetings of the Interdivisional Area Committee on the Far East, 1943–46.

Among the recent accessions of the Dwight D. Eisenhower Library are the papers of Gordon Gray, President Eisenhower's special assistant for National Security Affairs, including material relating to the J. Robert Oppenheimer case and photocopies of correspondence with President Eisenhower, John S. D. Eisenhower, and Dillon Anderson.

The Lyndon B. Johnson Library has recently accessioned scrapbooks of Francis Eugene Worley, former Texas state legislator and federal judge; records of the United States–Mexico Border Development Commission; and papers of Welly K. Hopkins, former Texas state legislator.

The Special Collections Division of the University of Tennessee Library at Knoxville has recently acquired the following groups of manuscripts: the Lanman Papers, which consist of replies received from Tennesseans by Charles Lanman in the 1850s when he circularized all living past and present members of Congress for biographical information for his *Dictionary of the United States Congress;* the James B. Frazier Papers, containing his early twentieth-century gubernatorial and senatorial papers amounting to 25,000 letters, documents, and pieces of memorabilia; the John Jennings, Jr., Papers covering his career as U. S. representative from Tennessee's Second District from 1940 to 1950; the Howard and Irene Baker Papers, consisting of 60,000 pieces of legislative files, correspondence, speeches, bills, and clippings covering their careers from 1951 to 1964 as U. S. representatives from Tennessee's Second District; and the Herbert S. Walters Papers, consisting of 250,000 pieces of business, political, and personal correspondence and other papers covering Mr. Walters's career as a banker and contractor in Morristown and his year in the U. S. Senate to which he was appointed to fill the unexpired term of Estes Kefauver in 1963.

The South Carolina Archives has accessioned the following county records: those of the offices of the clerk of court, coroner, sheriff, magistrate, supervisor, and treasurer of Cherokee County, 1869–1973; the offices of the auditor, county commissioner, treasurer, and sheriff of Lancaster County, 1869–1973; and the offices of the clerk of court, sheriff, probate judge, auditor, treasurer, supervisor, board of education, magistrate, and coroner of Union County, 1790–1969. After the first of the year these records will be available on microfilm at $15 per roll and may be ordered from the Publications Division, South Carolina Department of Archives and History, P. O. Box 11669, Columbia, S. C. 29211.

Other accessions are records of the Department of Corrections, including accounts payable, 1962–68, general account, check registers, 1958–68, and payroll journal, 1938–67, and printed copies of the records of the General Assembly, including acts and joint resolutions, 1974, House of Representatives journal and Senate journal, 1974, reports and resolutions, 1974, and records of the secretary of state, recorded instruments, commissions and appointments, 1927–67.

Index

This index uses shortened titles of books to conserve space, and it does not include paperback reprints or anthologies and source books intended primarily for class use.

Abernathy, Mollie C. (Davis), comment by, 86; revs., 559–60
Abolition, 299, 300, 319; books on, revd., 259–60, 403–406; Henry Clay and, 43; Lincoln and, 44, 46, 50
Abolitionists, books on, revd., 414–17; and fear of 1856 slave insurrection, 335 ff.; and slave narratives, 474–79
Abolitionists, by Merton L. Dillon, revd., 414–15
Acadians, papers on, 70–71
Adair, Douglass Greybill, 523
Administrative history, books on, revd., 553–54, 570–71
Addresses and Public Papers of Robert Walter Scott, ed. by Memory F. Mitchell, noted, 288
Aeschbacher, William D., 234, 291; and nominating comm., 234
Africa, papers on, 67; antebellum sou. view of, 307; and Protestant missions to, 465–66
African Methodist Episcopal Church, 458
Agrarian reform, art. on Negro and, 187–200
Agricultural Wheel, 188, 191, 192
Agriculture, art. on antebellum sou., 147–66; book on, noted, 587; book on, revd., 564–65
Agriculture in the Postbellum South, by Stephen J. DeCanio, revd., 564–65
Ahern, Wilbert H., revs., 554–55
Alabama, book on, noted, 437; books on, revd., 120–21, 131–32, 278–79; paper on, 62; and livestock, 147, 152, 153
Alabama, C.S.S., 382, 384
Alabama Claims, by Adrian Cook, revd., 562–63
Albert D. Kirwan, by Frank F. Mathias, noted, 584
Alderson, William T., Jr., 88; sess. chmn., 87
Aldstadt, David P., paper by, 84
Alexander, Charles C., revs., 280–81
Alexander, Edward P., comment by, 87–88
Alexander, James Mitchell, 162
Alexander, Jane Stamps, 518
Alexander, Thomas B., receives Sydnor Award, 136, 236
Alexander, William W., 519
Alfred R. Waud, by Frederic E. Ray, noted, 289
All God's Dangers, by Theodore Rosengarten, revd., 275–77
Allen, Richard, 479
Allen, Washington B., 485
Allies for Freedom, by Benjamin Quarles, revd., 119–20
Almaráz, Félix D., paper by, 84
Alternative to Extinction, by Robert A. Trennert, Jr., revd., 557–58
Alvarez, Eugene, *Travel on Southern Antebellum Railroads*, revd., 552–53
Alvey, Edward, Jr., *History of Mary Washington College*, revd., 279–80
Ambacher, Bruce I., coauth., *Essays on Urban America*, noted, 436
American Artillery in the Mexican War, by Lester R. Dillon, Jr., noted, 585
American Colonization Society, 43, 52
American Genesis, by Alden T. Vaughan, revd., 534–35
American Historical Assn., 4, 7; comm. on teaching, 5
American Indian Policy, by Ronald N. Satz, revd., 555–57
American Problem in British Diplomacy, by Wilbur D. Jones, revd., 115–16
American Revolution, books on, noted, 283, 286–87, 289, 583; books on, revd., 250–55, 401–402, 407–408, 536–39
American Revolution of 1800, by Daniel Sisson, revd., 542–44
American Territorial System, ed. by John P. Bloom, revd., 100–101
Ames, Jessie Daniel, paper on, 80
Ammerman, David, *In the Common Cause*, revd., 252–53
Ammon, Harry, revs., 549–50
Amnesty Act (1872), 497

And They All Sang Hallelujah, by Dickson D. Bruce, Jr., revd., 258–59
Anderson, James LaVerne, coauth., *The Gun in America,* revd., 577–78
Anderson, John, 475
Anderson, Sam, 500
Anderson, William, *The Wild Man from Sugar Creek,* revd., 429–30
Andrade, A. Rolando, paper by, 71
Andrew, John Albion, 23
Andrew, James Osgood, 453
Andrew Jackson and Pensacola, ed. by James R. McGovern, noted, 290
"Andrew Johnson and Reconstruction: A British View," ed. by Eric Foner, 381–90
Anglo-American Politics, by Alison G. Olson, revd., 90–91
Annapolis, Md., book on, revd., 536–38
"Annual Report of the Secretary-Treasurer," by Bennett H. Wall, 233–39
Antebellum Athens and Clarke County, by Ernest C. Hynds, revd., 431
"Antebellum Southern Herdsman: A Reinterpretation," by Forrest McDonald and Grady McWhiney, 147–66
Antilon–First Citizen letters, book on, revd., 96–97
Antislavery, books on, revd., 403–406, 414–17, 545–47; and Henry Clay, 41–43
Appalachia, paper on, 77–78
Appleby, Joyce O., revs., 250–51
Aptheker, Herbert, ed., *A Documentary History of the Negro People . . . 1933–1945,* noted, 283–84
Arbena, Joseph L., paper by, 87
Archives, book on, noted, 286; book on, revd., 242–43
Argersinger, Peter H., revs., 423–24
Arkansas, paper on, 82; and interviews with former slaves, 488; and livestock, 147
Arming the Union, by Carl L. Davis, revd., 121–22
Arms, book on, revd., 121–22
Army, U. S., art. on La. blacks in Civil War and, 19–38; books on, revd., 128–29, 133–34; Jefferson Davis in, 517–21; Negro family in Civil War and, 372 ff.; and recruitment of blacks, 374, 380
Art, books on, noted, 284–85, 587
Arthur, Chester Alan, 177, 499; book on, revd., 567–68
Artillery, book on, noted, 585
Athens, Ga., book on, revd., 431
Atkinson, George Wesley, 499, 506, 510*n*
Atlanta, art. on city planning in, 339–68; book on, noted, 289; papers on, 69–70; SHA meeting in, 135–36
Axton, W. F., *Tobacco and Kentucky,* noted, 437

Bailey, Hugh C., 137; comment by, 63
Bailey, Kenneth K., "Protestantism and Afro-Americans in the Old South: Another Look," 451–72; revs., 434
Baird, Jay W., comment by, 72; paper by, 76
Baird, W. David, revs., 555–57
Baker, Bill R., *Catch the Vision,* revd., 281–82
Baker, Leonard, *John Marshall,* revd., 106–107
Baker, Robert A., *The Southern Baptist Convention,* revd., 277–78
Baker, Thomas H., 291; book note by, 287–88
Baker, Vaughan, paper by, 71
Ball, Charles, 477
Bancroft, Frederic, 473
Banker, Luke H., coed., *Tennessee History,* noted, 285
Bankruptcy, book on, revd., 243–45
Banks, J. H., 476
Banks, Nathaniel Prentiss, 372, 379–80; and La. Negroes, 34 ff.
Bannon, John Francis, sess. chmn., 84
Baptists, 156*n*; book on, revd., 277–78; papers on, 75–76; and Negro family, 378; Negroes and antebellum sou., 451 ff.; and slaves, 317
Barbé-Marbois, François, book on, noted, 290
Barbeau, Arthur E., coauth., *The Unknown Soldiers,* revd., 128–29
Barnard, William D., *Dixiecrats and Democrats,* revd., 131–32
Barney, William L., *The Secessionist Impulse,* revd., 120–21
Barnum, Phineas T., 527
Barr, Alwyn, revs., 418–19
Bartholomew, Harland, 350 ff.
Bartlett, Richard A., *The New Country,* revd., 255–56
Bartley, Numan V., sess. chmn., 69; revs., 568–69
Bateman, Fred, paper by, 75
Bauer, K. Jack, *The Mexican War,* revd., 262–63

Baumgardner, James L., book note by, 284; revs., 264–65
Baxter, Colin F., paper by, 83
Baxter, Lewis, 508*n*
Baylen, Joseph O., sess. chmn., 70
Bayley, Solomon, 480
Beacroft, Percival T., 518
Bebel, August, papers on, 77
Beck, Earl R., sess. chmn., 72
Becker, Carl Lotus, 11, 18
Bedichek, Roy, paper on, 61
Beeman, Richard R., *Patrick Henry*, revd., 406–407
Bell, John, 332
Bell, Rudolph M., *Party and Faction*, revd., 101–102
Bellamy, Donnie E., comment by, 86
Belz, Herman J., 57
Ben (a slave), 23, 454
Benedict, Michael Les, 234; *A Compromise of Principle*, revd., 419–21
Bennehan, Richard, book on, noted, 288
Bennett, Edward Herbert, 340
Bennett, Mrs. Irby, 349
Bergeron, Paul H., revs., 558–59
Bergquist, Charles W. comment by, 66
Beringer, Richard E., receives Sydnor Award, 136, 236
Berkeley, Dorothy Smith, coauth., *Dr. John Mitchell*, revd., 94–96
Berkeley, Edmund, coauth., *Dr. John Mitchell*, revd., 94–96
Berry, Fanny, 485
Berthrong, Donald J., revs., 91–92
Bibb, Henry, 479
Bible Belt Mystique, by C. Dwight Dorough, revd., 434
Bibliography, art. on, 201–32; books on, noted, 285, 286, 583, 587
Bibliography of Printed Battle Plans, by Kenneth Nebenzahl, noted, 583
Bickel, Richard B., comp., *Manuscripts on Microfilm*, noted, 437
Bidwell, Percy Wells, 155
Bierck, Harold A., Jr., sess. chmn., 87
Bigelow, Martha M., sess. chmn., 62
Billings, Warren M., ed., *The Old Dominion in the Seventeenth Century*, revd., 535–36
Billington, Monroe Lee, 135; *The Political South*, revd., 568–69; sess. chmn., 64
Billington, Ray Allen, and sou. agriculture, 153, 156
Biographical Directory of the Tennessee General Assembly, Vol. I, by Robert M. McBride and Dan M. Robison, noted, 583–84
Biracial worship, antebellum sou., 453–55, 458
Birmingham, 342*n*, 343, 356; book on, revd., 278–79
Birth of Forestry in America, by Carl A. Schenck, noted, 290
Black, Eugene Robert, 346
"Black Family in Transition: Louisiana, 1860–1865," by C. Peter Ripley, 369–80
"Black Ironworkers and the Slave Insurrection Panic of 1856," by Charles B. Dew, 321–38
Black Majority, by Peter H. Wood, revd., 246–48
"Black Militancy in Readjuster Virginia, 1879–1883," by James T. Moore, 167–86
Black troops, desertion of Civil War, 375, 380
"Black Violence and White Response: Louisiana, 1862," by William F. Messner, 19–38
Blackbeard the Pirate, by Robert E. Lee, revd., 399–400
Blacks and the Military, by Jack D. Foner, revd., 133–34
Blacks in Bondage, ed. by Robert S. Starobin, revd., 110–12
Blaine, James G., 499*n*
Blake, Jane, 478
Bland, Theodorick, Jr., 476, 477
Blassingame, John W., 454; "Using the Testimony of Ex-Slaves: Approaches and Problems," 473–92; paper by, 73–74
Bleckley, Haralson, 344
Bleser, Carol K. Rothrock, and Graduate Student Award comm., 136–37,236
Bloom, John Porter, ed., *The American Territorial System*, revd., 100–101
Boatright, Mody C., paper on, 61
Body, Rias, 485
Boeger, Palmer H., 291
Boles, John B., revs., 258–59
Bolt, Christine, 383, 384
Bonner, James C., 135, 234
Bonus, Elizabeth, 454
Booker T. Washington Papers, Vol. 3, ed. by Louis R. Harlan and others, revd., 125–26
Borden, Morton, revs., 109–110

Border South States, by Neal R. Peirce, revd., 574–75
Boswell, James, 159
Botkin, Benjamin A., 480
Boudry, Nancy, 483
Bowman, Albert Hall, *The Struggle for Neutrality,* revd., 105–106
Boyd, Julian P., coed., *The Papers of Thomas Jefferson,* Vol. 19, revd., 256–58
Brademas, John, 235
Bradley, William O'Connell, 505, 510*n*, 511, 513
Brawley, James S., *Rowan County,* noted, 289
Breckinridge, by William C. Davis, revd., 417–18
Breckinridge, John Cabell, 23; book on, revd., 417–18; paper on, 73
Bremer, Fredrika, 469
Bretos, Miguel A., paper by, 66
Brewer, J. Mason, 484
Bridges, Hal, revs., 560–61
Brierfield Plantation, 518
Britain & the War for the Union, Vol. I, by Brian Jenkins, revd., 561–62
British Maps of Colonial America, by William P. Cumming, noted, 283
Britton (a slave), 327, 337
Broadsides, book on, noted, 587
Brodie, Fawn M., 524; *Thomas Jefferson,* revd., 107–109
Brown, Henry Box, 479
Brown, John, 495; book on, revd., 119–20
Brown, John (slave), 476, 479
Brown, Letitia W., comment by, 65
Brown, Norman D., *Edward Stanly,* revd., 558–59; revs., 541–42
Brown, Richard Maxwell, 291; "The Fortieth Annual Meeting," 59–88; and program comm., 291
Brown, William Wells, 479
Brownell, Blaine A., 135; "The Commercial-Civic Elite and City Planning in Atlanta, Memphis, and New Orleans in the 1920s," 339–68
Brownlow, William Gannaway, 495
Bruce, Dickson D., Jr., *And They All Sang Hallalujah,* revd., 258–59
Bruce, Sir Frederick William Adolphus, 381 ff.
Bruner, Peter, 491
Bryan, Andrew, 463*n*, 464, 466, 471
Bryant, Keith L., Jr., revs., 273–74
Buchanan, James, 23, 336
Bureau of Negro Labor, U. S., 374–75, 376
Bureaucracy, book on, revd., 553–54
Burnett, Edmund Cody, 161–62
Burnham, Daniel Hudson, 340,341
Burts, Robert Milton, *Richard Irvine Manning,* revd., 127–28
Business, art. on sou. city planning and, 339–68
Business history, book on, revd., 566–67
Butler, Benjamin Franklin (1818–1893), and Lincoln's racial views, 56–58; and Negroes in La., 23 ff.
Butler, Mrs. Benjamin Franklin, 28
Butler, Roderick Randum, 507–508
Butler, Sylvia, paper by, 85
Byrne, Frank L., revs., 263–64; and membership comm., 291
Byrnes, Don R., 88; revs., 534–35

Cade, John B., 489
Caldeira, Ernesto, 518
Caldwell, Mary French, *Tennessee,* revd., 251–52
Caldwell, Tod Robinson, 497
Calhoun, John C., 527; book on, revd., 549–50
Callender, James Thomson, 524
Cameron, James Donald, 177
Cameron, Simon, 177
Cameron, William Evelyn, 178 ff.
Cameron, William Ewan: *see* Cameron, William Evelyn
Cameron Plantation, by Charles R. Sanders, noted, 288
Camp meetings, book on, revd., 258–59
Camp Parapet, 20, 26
Campbell, Alexander, 467, 469
Campbell, Charles, 475–76, 477
Campbell, Leslie Caine, *Two Hundred Years of Pharmacy,* revd., 433
Campus rebellions, book on, revd., 569–70
Candler, Walter, 158
Cansler, Charles M., 511
Capers, William, 317, 453
Carothers, Andrew J., 188
Carr, Peter, 523
Carrigan, Jo Ann, 291
Carter, Paul A., comment by, 76
Casada, James A., revs., 115–16
Casdorph, Paul D., revs., 573
Casper, Henry, 500
Cassell, Frank A., revs., 536–38

Castel, Albert, coauth., *The Yeas and the Nays*, noted, 437
Catch the Vision, by Bill R. Baker, revd., 281–82
Catechism, for slaves, 310–11
Century of Jewish Life, by Mark H. Elovitz, revd., 278–79
Chafe, William H., comment by, 81
Chaffin, Robert J., revs., 96–97
Chambers of commerce, and city planning, 341 ff.
Chamerovzow, Louis Alexis, 476
Channing, Steven A., 292
"Charles Colcock Jones and the Southern Evangelical Crusade to Form a Biracial Community," by Donald G. Mathews, 299–320
Charleston *Courier*, book on, revd., 267–68
Chase, James S., *Emergence of the Presidential Nominating Convention*, revd., 103–104
Chase, Salmon Portland, 24, 28, 30, 31
Chattanooga, black population of, 503; city planning in, 354
Chavis, John, 466, 471
Chesnutt, David R., coed., *The Papers of Henry Laurens*, Vol. IV, revd., 402–403
Choules, John Overton, 469
Church, Annette E., coauth., *The Robert R. Churches*, revd., 581–82
Church, Robert R., Jr., book on, revd., 581–82
Church, Robert R., Sr., book on, revd., 581–82
Church, Roberta, coauth., *The Robert R. Churches*, revd., 581–82
Church membership, statistics on Negro, 458
Churches, art. on race relations in antebellum sou., 451–72
City planning, art. on sou., 339–68
Civil Rights Act (1866), 383–84
Civil War, art. on La. blacks and, 19–38; art. on La. Negro family during, 369–80; books on, noted, 585, 586; books on, revd., 121–23, 263–65, 417–19, 559–62, 579–80; paper on 67; C. C. Jones and, 315, 316*n*; effect on sou. agriculture, 163–64
Civil War: A Narrative, Red River to Appomattox, by Shelby Foote, revd., 418–19
Civil War in the Indian Territory, by Lary C. Rampp and Donald L. Rampp, noted, 585
Civil War in Kentucky, by Lowell H. Harrison, noted, 586
Civil War Marine, edited by James P. Jones and Edward F. Keuchel, noted, 585
Clanton, James H., 164
Clarendon, George William Frederick Villiers, fourth Earl of, 381 ff.
Clark, David Sanders, *Index to Maps of the American Revolution*, noted, 286–87
Clark, John G., sess. chmn., 73
Clark, Thomas D., ed., *The Great American Frontier*, noted, 584
Clarke, Kenneth, coauth., *The Harvest and the Reapers*, noted, 284–85
Clarke, Lewis, 477, 479
Clarke, Mary, coauth., *The Harvest and the Reapers*, noted, 284–85
Clarke, Milton, 477, 479
Clarke Co., Ga., book on, revd., 431
Clarksville, Tenn., and 1856 slave insurrection panic, 325 ff.
Clay, Floyd Martin, 136
Clay, Henry, 464, 527; book on, revd., 550–52; influence on Lincoln of, 40–48, 55
Clayton, Bruce L., comment by, 86
Clemenceau, Georges, 381
Clemens, Samuel Langhorne, book on, revd., 434–35
Clergy, antebellum sou. Negro Protestant, 462–64, 466
Cleveland, Grover, 346
Cocke, J. B., 157
Coercive Acts, book on, revd., 252–53
Coker, William S., 88; sess. chmn., 79
Cole, Wayne S., comment by, 64
Coleman, J. Winston, Jr., *Three Kentucky Artists*, noted, 284–85
Coleman, Peter J., *Debtors and Creditors*, revd., 243–45
College Life in the Reconstruction South, ed. by G. Ray Mathis, revd., 268–69
Colleges, book on, revd., 569–70
Colombia, papers on, 66, 87
Colonial Pensacola, ed. by James R. McGovern, noted, 290
Colonial period, books on, noted, 283, 588; books on, revd., 90–94, 96–97, 249–50, 401–403
Colonization, Lincoln and, 43 ff.
Colored Farmers' Alliance, art. on, 187–200
Colored Farmers' Assn. of Texas, 189*n*

Colored Farmers' Home Improvement Lodge, 189*n*
Colored Independent party, 501
Colson, David Grant, 508
Colton, Joel, 137
Columbia, S. C., book on, noted, 588
Columbia (S. C.) Theological Seminary, 315
Coming of Age, by William H. Wilson, revd., 272–73
"Commercial-Civic Elite and City Planning in Atlanta, Memphis, and New Orleans in the 1920s," by Blaine A. Brownell, 339–68
Compromise of Principle, by Michael L. Benedict, revd., 419–21
Cone, Carl B., 234; comment by, 66–67
Confederacy, books on, revd., 417–18, 559–60; papers on, 73; C. C. Jones and, 315; and Negro family, 372–76
Confederate Women, by Bell I. Wiley, revd., 559–60
Confederates, and sou. mountain Repubs., 493 ff.
Confiscation Act, Second, 28, 31
Conger lard bill, 192
Congress, U. S., books on, noted, 436, 437; book on, revd., 419–21
Conkin, Paul K., *Self-Evident Truths*, revd., 97–98; comment by, 77–78
Conkling, Roscoe, 177
Connally, Ernest Allen, paper by, 71–72
Connor, Seymour V., revs., 262–63
Conrad, Glenn R., paper by, 70–71
Conscience Whigs, 45
Consensus, Conflict, and American Historians, by Bernard Sternsher, revd., 530–31
Conservative party, and Va. Negroes, 168 ff.
Constitutional history, books on, revd., 106–107, 260–61
Continental Congress, book on, revd., 407–408
Contraband camps, and migrant black families, 373–74, 379
Conway, Jill K., panelist, 82–83
Conway, Thomas W., 374
Cook, Adrian, *The Alabama Claims*, revd., 562–63
Cooper, Thomas (slave), 476
Cooper, William J., Jr., revs., 269–70
Cooperative movt., in Colored Farmers' Alliance, 187, 190 ff.
Co-operative Workers of America, 200
Copeland, J. Isaac, revs., 571–72
Corina, Maurice, *Trust in Tobacco*, revd., 566–67
Corn, in antebellum sou. agriculture, 160–61, 162
Cortinas, Juan N., 71
Cotner, Robert C., sess. chmn., 61
Cotton Pickers' League, 196–99
Cotton pickers' strike, 188, 196–99
Coulter, E. Merton, 155
Court records, book on, revd., 248–49
Cover, Robert M., *Justice Accused*, revd., 545–47
Cox, LaWanda, revs., 421–23
Cox, Richard J., *A Guide to the Microfilm Edition of the Mordecai Gist Papers*, noted, 437
Cox, Robert Lynn, 392–94
Coyner, Martin B., Jr., 291
Crabtree, Beth G., *North Carolina Governors*, 3d rev. ed., noted, 289
Craddock, Walter R., 137
Craft, Ellen, 479
Craft, William, 479
Craven, Avery O., *Rachel of Old Louisiana*, revd., 540–41
Craven, Wesley Frank, 438
Crawford, Charles W., revs., 251–52
Crawford, Robert Gunn, obituary notice on, 593
Crawford, William H., book on, revd., 112–13
Creek Indians, book on, revd., 400–401
Creek Indians and Their Florida Lands, by James F. Doster, revd., 400–401
Crenson, Matthew A., *The Federal Machine*, revd., 553–54
Crockett, Norman L., sess. chmn., 74
Cromwell, Oliver (fl. 1889), 195
Cronon, E. David, 135, 234, 291; revs., 425–27
Crouch, Barry A., paper by, 65
Crowley, J. E., *This Sheba, Self*, revd., 249–50
Crummell, Alexander, paper on, 86
Cullen, Joseph P., *The Peninsula Campaign*, revd., 122–23
Cumberland Iron Works, 329, 330, 331
Cumming, William P., *British Maps of Colonial America*, noted, 283; coauth., *The Fate of a Nation*, noted, 583
Cunningham, Noble E., Jr., 135, 234; book note by, 436; revs., 412–13

Current, Richard N., 135, 291, 438; revs., 563–64
Curry, Leonard P., revs., 242–43
Curry, Richard O., revs., 419–21

Dallas, Texas, SHA meeting in, 59
Daniel, Jesse, 336
Daniel, John Warwick, 178
Daniel, Pete, 482; comment by, 62
Daniels, Josephus, 514
Daniels, Roger, comment by, 82
Danville, Va., blacks and, 180, 181–82, 185, 504
Dargo, George, *Jefferson's Louisiana*, revd., 544–45
Davis, Allen F., panelist, 82–83
Davis, Allison, 481
Davis, Carl L., *Arming the Union*, revd., 121–22
Davis, Cephas L., 173
Davis, David Brion, *The Problem of Slavery in the Age of Revolution*, revd., 403–406
Davis, Ellen Mary, 521*n*
Davis, Hugh Robert, 521*n*
Davis, Jane Cook, 517, 521*n*, 522
Davis, Jane Lucinda, 521*n*, 522*n*
Davis, Jefferson, 29; art. on early career plans of, 517–22; paper on, 73
Davis, Joseph Emory, 518
Davis, Noah, 480
Davis, Robert R., Jr., revs., 119–20
Davis, Ronald L. F., comment by, 62; revs., 564–65
Davis, Ronald Leroy, sess. chmn., 81
Davis, Sarah Knox Taylor, 518
Davis, Samuel Emory, 517, 522*n*
Davis, William C., *Breckinridge*, revd., 417–18; paper by, 73
Dawes, Henry Laurens, 177
Day, John, 465, 471
Deaf Smith, by Cleburne Huston, revd., 115
Deaton, Thomas M., revs., 272–73
DeBoe, William Joseph, 510*n*
Debtors and Creditors, by Peter J. Coleman, revd., 243–45
Debtors' prison, book on, revd., 243–45
DeCanio, Stephen J., *Agriculture in the Postbellum South*, revd., 564–65
Degler, Carl N., revs., 403–406
De Grummond, Jane Lucas, 291
Delano, Frederic Adrian, 341
DeLesseps S. Morrison and the Image of Reform, by Edward F. Haas, revd., 576–77
Delpar, Helen V., comment by, 87
"Demise of the Colored Farmers' Alliance," by William F. Holmes, 187–200
Democratic party, books on, revd., 131–33, 270–74; paper on, 69; and 1856 slave insurrection panic, 336; in Ohio, 524–25; racial attitudes of, 41, 45, 49, 51, 54; and Readjuster movt., 167 ff.; and Sou. Alliance, 193–94; and sou. mountain Repubs., 493 ff.
Democratic Party and the Politics of Sectionalism, by Robert A. Garson, revd., 273–74
Democratic-Republican party, book on, revd., 542–44
Democrats and Progressives, by Allen Yarnell, revd., 132–33
Denison, George S., 29–30
DeNovo, John A., paper by, 74
Dept. of Agriculture, U. S., 147
Dept. of the Gulf, 23 ff., 374
De Pauw, Linda Grant, coed., *Documentary History of the First Federal Congress*, Vol. II, noted, 436
Depression, papers on, 82; and sou. city planning, 363
DeRosier, Arthur H., sess. chmn., 76
Desegregation, paper on, 65
Dethloff, Henry C., 291
Detweiler, Robert C., revs., 407–408
Deusner, Charles, 291
Dew, Charles B., 291, 292; "Black Ironworkers and the Slave Insurrection Panic of 1856," 321–38; comment by, 75; revs., 110–12
Dillon, Lester R., Jr., *American Artillery*, noted, 585
Dillon, Merton L., *The Abolitionists*, revd., 414–15
Dinges, Bruce J., book note by, 585
Diplomatic history, book on, noted, 290; books on, revd., 105–106, 115–16, 562–63; papers on, 64, 72, 79, 86–87
Disciples of Christ, Negroes and antebellum sou., 458, 463
Discipline, religion and slave, 309 ff.
Discovery, book on, revd., 397–98
Disfranchisement, book on, revd., 270–72
Dissent, papers on, 86
District of Western Louisiana, 373
Divorce, of slaves, 370
Dixiecrat party, book on, revd., 131–32

Dixiecrats and Democrats, by William D. Barnard, revd., 131–32
Dixon, James, 382 ff.
Dobie, J. Frank, paper on, 61
Dr. John Mitchell, by Edmund Berkeley and Dorothy Smith Berkeley, revd., 94–96
Documentary History of the First Federal Congress, Vol. II, ed. by Linda G. De Pauw *et al.*, noted, 436
Documentary History of the Negro People. . . 1933–1945, ed. by Herbert Aptheker, noted, 283–84
Dodd, Donald B., *Historical Atlas of Alabama,* noted, 437
Doherty, Henry L., paper on, 74
Doherty, Herbert J., Jr., revs., 112–13
Dollar, Charles M., comment by, 69
Dollard, John, 481
Dorough, C. Dwight, *The Bible Belt Mystique,* revd., 434
Dorsett, Lyle W., revs., 576–77
Dos Passos, John Roderigo, 523, 524
Doster, James F., *The Creek Indians,* revd., 400–401
Douglas, Stephen A., 335; and racial views, 40 ff.
Douglass, Elisha P., revs., 566–67
Douglass, Frederick, 39, 40, 47, 479, 492; paper on, 73–74
Dover, Tenn., fear of slave insurrection in, 329 ff.
Draughon, Ralph B., Jr., revs., 552–53
Dreifort, John E., paper by, 72
Drives, antebellum sou. livestock, 160–62
Droze, Wilmon H., revs., 428–29
Dugger, Harold H., obituary notice by, 442
Dumbauld, Edward, revs., 544–45
Dungee, Shed, 173
Durant Commercial Co., 196
Durden, Robert F., 88
Dye, Nancy Schrom, panelist, 82–83

Early Georgia Portraits, noted, 587
Eaton, Clement, *A History of the Old South,* 3d ed., revd., 529–30
Eaton, John Henry, coauth., *The Life of Andrew Jackson,* noted, 289–90
Eaves, John Baxter, 509
Economic history, art. on. sou., 391–96; books on, revd., 93–94, 249–50, 536–38, 564–65; papers on, 62, 72
Economy, art. on antebellum sou., 147–66
Editing, papers on, 73
Edmund Randolph, by John J. Reardon, revd., 539–40
Education, books on, revd., 123–24, 268–69, 279–80, 427–28, 571–72; papers on, 79, 85
Education and the American Indian, by Margaret Szasz, revd., 427–28
Edward Stanly, by Norman D. Brown, revd., 558–59
Edwards, George, *Pioneer-at-law,* revd., 280–81
Edwards, George Clifton, book on, revd., 280–81
Edwards, Jonathan, 304
Egypt, Ophelia Settles, 489
Ekirch, Arthur A., Jr., *Progressivism in America,* revd., 424–25; revs., 530–31
Eldridge, Elleanor, 478
Election of 1856, and fear of slave insurrection, 333 ff.
Election of 1879, Va., 170–71
Election of 1880, Va., 173–76
Election of 1881, Va., 176–79
Election of 1883, Va., 184–85
Election of 1948, book on, revd., 132–33
Eliot, Samuel Atkins, 474, 475
Eliot, William Greenleaf, 475
Elitism, art. on sou. city planning and, 339–68
Elkins, Stanley, M., 473
Elkins, Stephen Benton, 509, 510*n*, 511
Ellem, Warren A., receives Graduate Student award, 136–37, 236
Ellis, Richard E., revs., 104–105
Ellis, William E. paper by, 76
Elovitz, Mark H., *A Century of Jewish Life in Dixie,* revd., 278–79
Ely, James W., Jr., revs., 106–107
Emancipation, 299, 305, 306, 307; Lincoln and, 41 ff.
Emancipation of Angelina Grimkė, by Katharine Du Pre Lumpkin, revd., 259–60
Emergence of the Presidential Nominating Convention, by James S. Chase, revd., 103–104
Emory, William Helmsby, 33
Empire and Liberty, by Allan Rogers, revd., 401–402
Energy crisis, papers on, 74
Endris, Joseph P., 518–19
Endris, Mrs. Joseph P., 518

Engerman, Stanley L., coed., *Race and Slavery*, revd., 533–34
Episcopal church, Negro and antebellum sou., 317, 454, 458, 459, 464*n*
Equiano, Olaudah, 479
Era of Franklin D. Roosevelt, comp. by William J. Steward, noted, 285–86
Essays on Urban America, by Robert F. Oaks *et al.*, noted, 436
European Discovery of America: The Southern Voyages, by Samuel E. Morison, revd., 397–98
Evans, Henry, 464, 471
Evans, Henry Clay, 505, 508, 510*n*, 513
Evans, Sara M., paper by, 80–81
Evans, William McKee, 291; comment by, 81–82
Everett, Donald E., revs., 575–76
Evitts, William J., *A Matter of Allegiances*, revd., 118–19
Ewald, Ursula, comment by, 72
Ewart, Hamilton Glover, 507
Ezell, John S., 234, 291

Falconer, John Ironside, 155
Family, art. on effect of Civil War on Negro, 369–80; of slaves, 309–10
Farmers Improvement Society of Texas, 200
Farr, Richard R., 179
Fate of a Nation, by William P. Cumming and Hugh F. Rankin, noted, 583
Favrot, Charles Allen, 350, 351, 352
Fayette Co., Tenn., fear of slave insurrection in, 322, 323, 324
Federal Machine, by Matthew A. Crenson, revd., 553–54
Fehrenbacher, Don E., 46
Fences, and antebellum sou. agriculture, 157–60
Fenians, 382 ff.
Ferris, Norman B., revs., 561–62
Ferris, William R., Jr., 481–82, 483
Field, Alex., 457
Finance, art. on sou., 391–96
Financial history, book on, revd., 409–10
Finger, Stephen, 457
Finley, Hugh Franklin, 506
Finster, Jerome, ed., *The National Archives and Urban Research*, revd., 242–43
Fires of Jubilee, by Stephen B. Oates, revd., 554–55
Fischer, Roger A., *The Segregation Struggle in Louisiana*, revd., 265–66
Fisher, Perry G., *Materials for the Study of Washington*, noted, 286
Fisher, Walter, 291; comment by, 65
Fisk University, interviews of former slaves by, 489
Fite, Gilbert C., 59, 88, 135, 235–36; "The Historian as Teacher: Professional Challenge and Opportunity," 3–18
Fleener, Charles J., paper by, 72
Fleming, Julius J., book on, revd., 267–68
Florida, books on, noted, 289; books on, revd., 266–67, 400–401; and livestock, 154, 158, 159
Florida Place Names, by Allen Morris, noted, 289
Florida, University of, book on, revd., 571–72
Foley, David M., sess. chmn., 67
Folk history, book on, revd., 578–79
Folklore, in testimony of former slaves, 484 ff.
Folmsbee, Stanley J., death of, 235; obituary notice on, 293
Folsom, James E., book on, revd., 131–32
Foner, Eric, ed., "Andrew Johnson and Reconstruction: A British View," 381–90
Foner, Jack D., *Blacks and the Military*, revd., 133–34
Foote, Shelby, *The Civil War*, revd., 418–19
Ford, George Burdett, 354
Ford, Henry, 3
Forestry, book on, noted, 290
Forgie, George B., revs., 542–44
Fort Crawford, 517, 519, 520
Fort Gibson, 518
Fort McIntosh, book on, noted, 585–86
Fort Macomb, 21
Fort Saint Philip, 21
Fort Winnebago, 517–19
"Fortieth Annual Meeting," by Richard M. Brown, 59–88
Fortune, Timothy Thomas, 515
Foster, Lillian, 464
Foust, James D., paper by, 75
Fox, William Lloyd, coed., *Maryland*, revd., 398–99
France, 386; book on, noted, 290; book on, revd., 105–106
Franklin, Jimmie L., sess. chmn., 67; revs., 578–79
Frantz, Joe B., comment by, 61–62
Frassanito, William A., *Gettysburg*, revd., 560–61

Frazier, E. Franklin, 369
Fredrickson, George M., "A Man but Not a Brother: Abraham Lincoln and Racial Equality," 39–58; revs., 545–47
Free Men All, by Thomas D. Morris, revd., 99–100
Freedmen, autobiographies of, 479–80; British views of, 383; and contraband camps, 373–74; in Pike Co., Ohio, 524–25; Lincoln and colonization of, 55–57; Negro churchmen as leaders of, 471; U. S. Army and La., 32–38
Freedmen's Bureau, 164–65; and Negro family, 379
Freedmen's Bureau bill, 382, 386
Free-Soil party, 45
Frémont, John C., 335, 336
Fridley, Russell W., panelist, 85
Friend, Llerena, 61
From Colony to Country, by Ralph Ketcham, revd., 250–51
From Prescription to Persuasion, by John C. Rainbolt, revd., 93–94
Frontier, book on, noted, 584; book on, revd., 255–56
Fry, Gladys-Marie, *Night Riders in Black Folk History,* revd., 578–79
Fugutive Slave Law, 474
Fugitive slaves, and family ties, 371
Funders, Va. Negroes and, 170 ff.
Furlong, Patrick J., revs., 539–40

Gaines, William H., Jr., *Virginia History in Documents,* noted, 287
Gallagher, Thomas F., paper by, 70
Garfield, James Abram, 75, 177
Garrett, Franklin M., *Yesterday's Atlanta,* noted, 289
Garrison, William Lloyd, 299
Garson, Robert A., *The Democratic Party,* revd., 273–74
Gaspar, David Barry, comment by, 64
Gaston, Paul M., revs., 89–90
Gatewood, Willard B., Jr., 88, 136; revs., 574–75
Genovese, Eugene D., 480; *Roll, Jordan, Roll,* revd., 240–42; coed., *Race and Slavery,* revd., 533–34; and sou. agriculture, 154–55
Gentleman Boss, by Thomas C. Reeves, revd., 567–68
Gentry, Judith F., 135
Georgia, art. on slave religion in, 299–320; books on, noted, 287–88, 289, 587; books on, revd., 429–31, 570–71, 580–81; and Colored Farmers' Alliance, 190; interviews of former slaves in, 484–85, 488; and livestock, 147, 153, 154, 158, 160
Georgia, University of, books on, revd., 268–69, 580–81
Germany, papers on, 77
Gerrymander, 512
Gettysburg, by William A. Frassanito, revd., 560–61
Gettysburg, Battle of, book on, revd., 560–61
Gibbs, Georgianna, 485
Gibson, Arrell M., 88
Gibson, Scott L., coauth., *The Yeas and the Nays,* noted, 437
Gill, Harold B., Jr., *The Gunsmith in Colonial Virginia,* noted, 288
Gillespie, Neal C., comment by, 68
Gilmore, J. L., 190
Girardeau, John Lafayette, 453
Giraud, Marcel, *A History of French Louisiana,* Vol. I, revd., 94
Gist, Mordecai, book on, noted, 437
Glazer, Joe, paper by, 81
Godbold, E. Stanly, Jr., revs., 434–35
Goddard, Will, book on, noted, 284–85
Goff, Nathan B., 498, 499*n*, 505, 509
Gómez, Severo, paper by, 79
Goodrich, Ernest Payson, 354
Goodwyn, Lawrence C., paper by, 80
Gorham, George Congdon, 177
Graduate Student Award (1972–73), 136–37, 236
Graham, Hugh Davis, revs., 131–32
Grandy, Charles, 485
Granger movt., book on, revd., 423–24
Grangers, 167, 170; and Negroes, 191
Grant, John William, 345
Grant, Ulysses Simpson, 174, 525
Gray, Lewis Cecil, and sou. agriculture, 151, 155, 162
Great American Frontier, ed. by Thomas D. Clark, noted, 584
Great Awakening, 299
Great Britain, books on, revd., 90–91, 115–16, 401–402, 561–63, 566–67; papers on, 70, 83
Greece, papers on, 86–87
Greenbackers, 167, 170
Greenberg, Louis M., 138
Greene, Jack P., revs., 402–403

Grider, George, coauth., *Isaac Shelby*, noted, 284
Griffith, Lucille, revs., 279–80
Grimké, Angelina, book on, revd., 259–60
Gruber, Ira D., book note by, 283
Guide to the Microfilm Edition of the Mordecai Gist Papers, by Richard J. Cox, noted, 437
Guide to the Official Records in the Mississippi Department of Archives and History, comp. by Thomas W. Henderson and Ronald E. Tromlin, noted, 286
Gun in America, by Lee Kennett and James L. Anderson, revd., 577–78
Gunderson, Robert G., 291
Guns, book on, noted, 288; book on, revd., 577–78
Gunsmith in Colonial Virginia, by Harold B. Gill, Jr., noted, 288
Gurr, Charles Stephen, revs., 433
Gutman, Herbert G., *Slavery and the Numbers Game*, noted, 584–85

Haas, Arthur G., sess. chmn., 87
Haas, Edward F., *DeLesseps S. Morrison*, revd., 576–77
Haase, Charles J., 349
Hackney, Sheldon, sess. chmn., 68
Hale, Douglas D., Jr., comment by, 87
Hall, Jacquelyn Dowd, paper by, 80
Hall, L. Marshall, Jr., 292
Halleck, Henry Wager, 29, 31
Halliburton, Rudia, Jr., paper by, 76–77
Halsell, Willie D., death of, 235
Hamilton, Alexander, books on, revd., 412–13
Hamilton, Holman, 135, 234; revs., 107–109
Hamilton, Ross, 173, 174
Hampton Institute, interviews of former slaves by, 489
Haney, James E., 291
Hanks, George H., 34
Hansen, Klaus J., comment by, 68–69
Harding, Warren G., paper on, 69
Hargreaves, Mary W. M., coed., *The Papers of Henry Clay*, Vol. 5, revd., 550–52
Harlan, Louis R., 234; coed., *The Booker T. Washington Papers*, Vol. 3, revd., 125–26; paper by, 73
Harrell, David Edwin, Jr., sess. chmn., 76
Harris, Carl V., paper by, 85–86
Harris, D. Alan, revs., 424–25
Harris, Della, 485
Harris, Julian, paper on, 63
Harris, William C., 135; comment by, 82; revs., 123–24
Harrison, Benjamin, 505, 509
Harrison, Joseph H., Jr., revs., 103–104
Harrison, Lowell H., *The Civil War in Kentucky*, noted, 586
Hart, Joel Tanner, book on, noted, 284–85
Hartdagen, Gerald E., paper by, 78
Hartje, Robert G., revs., 417–18
Harvest and the Reapers, by Kenneth and Mary Clarke, noted, 284–85
Harvey, Cecil, cocomp., *A List of References for the History of Black Americans in Agriculture*, noted, 587
Haskell, Thomas L., revs., 531–33
Hattaway, Herman M., 291; comment by, 73
Hatzenbuehler, Ronald L., 291
Hawke, David Freeman, *Paine*, revd., 98–99
Hawkins, William George, 475
Hay, Thomas Robson, 236; death of, 235
Hayden, J. Carleton, comment by, 65
Hayes, John D., revs., 538–39
Hayes, Rutherford Birchard, 169, 170, 172, 499
Haynes, Robert V., revs., 128–29
Haywood, C. Robert, revs., 93–94
Helguera, J. León, sess. chmn., 66, 135
Hemings, Madison, art. on Jefferson and, 523–28
Hemings, Sally, art. on Jefferson and, 523–28
Hemphill, W. Edwin, ed., *The Papers of John C. Calhoun*, Vol. VIII, revd., 549–50
Henderson, H. James, *Party Politics*, revd., 407–408
Henderson, James D., paper by, 66
Henderson, Thomas W., cocomp., *Guide to the Official Records in the Mississippi Department of Archives and History*, noted, 286
Hendricks, J. Edwin, revs., 535–36
Hendrix, James P., Jr., revs., 431
Henri, Florette, coauth., *The Unknown Soldiers*, revd., 128–29
Henry, G. Seldon, 291
Henry, Patrick, book on, revd., 406–407
Henson, Josiah, 474, 479
Hepzibah Baptist Church, 378
Herbert, A. Otis, comment by, 71
Herdsman, art. on antebellum sou., 147–66
Heth, Henry, book on, revd., 263–64

Higginbotham, Sanford W., 234
Hill, Walter B., book on, revd., 268–69; paper on, 86
Hilliard, Sam Bowers, and sou. agriculture, 153 ff., 163
Hine, William C., 291
"Historian as Teacher: Professional Challenge and Opportunity," by Gilbert C. Fite, 3–18
Historians, paper on, 59
Historical administration, papers on, 87–88
Historical Atlas of Alabama, by Donald B. Dodd, noted, 437
Historical preservation, papers on, 71–72, 79
Historical societies, papers on, 84–85
Historiography, art. on use of testimony of former slaves in, 473–92; book on, noted, 584–85; books on, revd., 529–31
History, art. on teaching, 3–18
History of French Louisiana, Vol. I, by Marcel Giraud, revd., 94
History of Mary Washington College, by Edward Alvey, Jr., revd., 279–80
History of the Old South, 3d ed., by Clement Eaton, revd., 529–30
History of the Supreme Court, Vol. V, by Carl B. Swisher, revd., 260–61
Hoar, George Frisbie, 177
Hobgood, Ben C., paper by, 67
Hobson, Fred C., Jr., *Serpent in Eden*, revd., 129–30
Hochman, Steven H., coauth., "A Note on Evidence: The Personal History of Madison Hemings," 523–28
Hodges, Anne-Marie, paper by, 85
Hodges, James A., revs., 570–71
Hoetink, Harry, 47
Hoffman, Donald B., 291; sess. chmn., 67
Hofstadter, Richard, 52
Hoglund, A. William, 291
Hogs, art. on antebellum sou., 147–66
Holden, William Woods, 497
Holley, Donald, comment by, 82
Hollimon, Blaine S., death of, 235
Hollon, W. Eugene, comment by, 61–62
Holloway, Lou, comment by, 65
Holmes, Jack D. L., revs., 94
Holmes, Michael S., *The New Deal in Georgia*, revd., 570–71
Holmes, William F., "The Demise of the Colored Farmers' Alliance," 187–200; revs., 270–72
Hooke, Miss, 521
Hooper, Benjamin Stephen, 184
Hooper, Benjamin W., 516
Hoover, Herbert, book on, noted, 286
Hope, John, paper on, 73
Hopkins, James F., coed., *The Papers of Henry Clay*, Vol. 5, revd., 550–52
Hopkins, Samuel, 304
Hopkinsville, Ky., and slave insurrection, 321, 329, 331, 333
Hopper, Isaac Tatem, 476
Hopson, Mobile, 485
Hornsby, Alton, Jr., paper by, 73
Horsman, Reginald, revs., 413–14
Horton, Louise, *Samuel Bell Maxey*, revd., 116–18
Houk, Leonidas Campbell, 498 ff.
Housing, sou. city planning and, 361
Howard, John G., 455
Howell, F. A., 190*n*
Hubbell, John T., 291
Huber, Leonard V., *Louisiana*, noted, 587
Hudson, Gossie H., comment by, 86
Huff, Archie Vernon, Jr., 137; *Tried by Fire*, noted, 588
Hugins, Walter E., Jr., comment by, 84
Hume, Richard L., paper by, 82
Hummel, Ray O., Jr., *More Virginia Broadsides Before 1877*, noted, 587
Humphrey, Richard Manning, 189 ff.
Hunt, John Wesley, book on, noted, 284–85
Hurst, James Willard, *A Legal History of Money*, revd., 409–10
Hurt, Joel, 346–47
Huston, Cleburne, *Deaf Smith*, revd., 115
Huthmacher, J. Joseph, 235; sess. chmn., 82
Hynds, Ernest C., *Antebellum Athens and Clarke County*, revd., 431

Illinois Colonization Society, 49
Impeachment, book on, revd., 563–64
Impeachment of a President, by Hans L. Trefousse, revd., 563–64
In Pursuit of Profit, by Edward C. Papenfuse, revd., 536–38
In the Common Cause, by David Ammerman, revd., 252–53
Incidents & Experiences in the Life of Thomas W. Parsons, ed. by Frank F. Mathias, revd., 579–80
Index to Maps of the American Revolution, by David S. Clark, noted, 286–87
Indian Territory, book on, noted, 585
Indians, book on, noted, 584; books on,

revd., 91–92, 253–55, 400–401, 413–14, 427–28, 555–58; papers on, 76, 79
Indians of the Lower South, edited by John K. Mahon, noted, 584
Ingle, H. Larry, 292
Insurance, art. on regional investments in, 391–96
Insurrection, art. on 1856 fear of slave, 321–38
Intellectual history, books on, revd., 97–98, 249–51, 547–49
Investments, art. on regional insurance, 391–96
Ireland, paper on, 66
Irish-Americans, 382 ff.
Iron industry, art. on slavery in, 321–38
Irwin, Harvey Samuel, 513
Isaac Shelby, by Sylvia Wrobel and George Grider, noted, 284
Isle, Walter W., revs., 129–30
Italy, paper on, 66

Jackson, Andrew, 40, 41; books on, noted, 289–90; books on, revd., 553–57
Jackson, Sara D., 291
Jacobins, papers on, 66
Jaffa, Harry V., 51, 52
Jamieson, Duncan R., paper by, 69
Jarausch, Konrad H., sess. chmn., 77
Jastremski, Leon, book on, revd., 575–76
Jefferson, Isaac, 477
Jefferson, Israel, 526*n*
Jefferson, Thomas, art. on Madison Hemings and, 523–28; books on, revd., 107–10, 256–58, 542–45
Jefferson and His Time, by Dumas Malone, Vol. V, revd., 109–110
Jefferson Barracks, 517–18, 520
"Jefferson Davis Ponders His Future, 1829," ed. by Lynda J. Lasswell, 517–22
Jefferson the President: Second Term, by Dumas Malone, revd., 109–110
Jefferson's Louisiana, by George Dargo, revd., 544–45
Jenkins, Brian, *Britain & the War for the Union,* Vol. I, revd., 561–62
Jenkins, William T., obituary notice on, 442
Jesuits, papers on, 72
Jewell, Robert Berry, coauth., *Uncle Bill of Wildwood,* noted, 284–85
Jews, book on, revd., 278–79
Jim Crow laws, 194, 359
Johannsen, Robert W., 234, 291
John James Tigert, by George C. Osborn, revd., 571–72
John Marshall, by Leonard Baker, revd., 106–107
John Wesley Hunt, by James A. Ramage, noted, 284–85
Johnson, Andrew, art. on Recon. and, 381–90; book on, revd., 563–64; and Miss. Recon., 58
Johnson, Herbert A., coed., *The Papers of John Marshall,* Vol. I, revd., 410–12
Johnson, Jerah W., 135
Johnson, Ludwell H., 57
Johnson, Samuel, 159
Johnson, Thomas R., paper by, 64–65
Jones, Charles Colcock, 453, 463; art. on slave religion and, 299–320
Jones, J. Ralph, 484–85
Jones, James P., coed., *Civil War Marine,* noted, 585
Jones, John A., 526, 527–28
Jones, Mary, and slave religion, 301 ff.
Jones, Robert H., revs., 100–101, 266–67
Jones, Walk Claridge, 349
Jones, Wilbur Devereaux, *The American Problem in British Diplomacy,* revd., 115–16; comment by, 83
Jordan, Weymouth T., Jr., comp., *North Carolina Troops,* Vol. V, noted, 588
Jordan, Winthrop D., 47; paper by, 67–68
Journal of Southern History, 233
Juhl Letters to the Charleston Courier, ed. by John Hammond Moore, revd., 267–68
Justice Accused, by Robert M. Cover, revd., 545-57

Kansas-Nebraska Act, 45
Kelly, Kevin P., paper by, 78
Kennedy, W. Benjamin, paper by, 66
Kennett, Lee, coauth., *The Gun in America,* revd., 577–78
Kentucky, art. on 1856 slave insurrection in, 321–38; books on, noted, 284–85, 437, 586; books on, revd., 574–75, 579–80; and livestock, 147, 148, 159 ff.; and Negro, 493 ff.
Kentucky Colored Democratic Club, 513
Kentucky Moonshine, by David W. Maurer, noted, 284–85
Ketcham, Ralph, *From Colony to Country,* revd., 250–51
Keuchel, Edward F., coed., *Civil War Marine,* noted, 585

Key, James Lee, 345, 346
King, A. L., paper by, 65
King, Doris Elizabeth, 234
Kirkpatrick, J. L., 469
Kirwan, Albert D., book on, noted, 584
Kitchens, John W., paper by, 87
Klein, Philip S., revs., 398–99
Klement, Frank L., paper by, 67
Knepper, George W., revs., 94–96, 579–80
Know-Nothing party, 336
Knoxville, and city planning, 343, 344, 354, 355*n*; mountain Repubs. in, 500–501, 512; voter registration in, 512
Kousser, J. Morgan, *The Shaping of Southern Politics*, revd., 270–72
Kownslar, Allan, paper by, 85
Kraehe, Enno E., 137; comment by, 87
Krebs, John M., 469–70
Kynerd, Byrle, paper by, 63

Labor, paper on, 78
Labor contracts, army and, 32–34; Civil War Negro family and, 377
Lambert, Joseph C., trans., *History of French Louisiana,* Vol. I, revd., 94
Lander, Ernest M., Jr., 135, 234
Langley, Wright, coauth., *Yesterday's Florida Keys,* noted, 289
Laredo, Texas, book on, noted, 585–86
Lasswell, Lynda J., ed., "Jefferson Davis Ponders His Future, 1829," 517–22
Latin America, book on, noted, 436–37
Laurens, Henry, book on, revd., 402–403
Law, Jefferson Davis and the, 518, 520
Lear, Floyd Seyward, obituary notice on, 442
Lee, Robert E. (fl. 1974), *Blackbeard the Pirate*, revd., 399–400
Leflore Co., Miss., racial violence in, 195–96
Legal history, books on, revd., 106–107, 544–47
Legal History of Money, by James W. Hurst, revd., 409–10
LeMaster, Edward B., 349
Lemmon, Sarah McCulloh, revs., 540–41
Lester, Charles E., 475–76, 477
Lester, Malcolm, revs., 98–99
Lester, Ruth W., coed, *The Papers of Thomas Jefferson,* Vol. 19, revd., 256–58
Lewis, George, 469
Lewis, John Francis, 178
Lewis, Ronald L., revs., 581–82
Lewis, Roscoe E., 484, 485
Liberty Co., Ga., slave religion in, 300 ff.
Liberty party, 45
Library of Congress, book on, noted, 437
Lidtke, Vernon L., comment by, 77
Life of Andrew Jackson, by John Reid and John Henry Eaton, noted, 289–90
Lincoln, Abraham, 23, 34, 35, 527; art. on racial equality and, 39–58
Linden, Glenn M., paper by, 81; sess. chmn., 85
Link, Arthur S., coed., *The Papers of Woodrow Wilson,* Vols. 15–17, revd., 425–57; sess. chmn., 73
List of References for the History of Black Americans in Agriculture, comp. by Joel Schor and Cecil Harvey, noted, 587
Literacy test, 194
Livestock, art. on antebellum sou., 147–66
Lodge, Henry Cabot, 506
Lodge election bill, 189–90; sou. mountain Repubs. and, 505–508
Loewen, James W., coed., *Mississippi*, noted, 286
Logan, John Alexander, 177
Loguen, Jermain, 479
Lokken, Roy N., revs., 401–402
Long, Charles H., comment by, 67
Long, Everette B., 291
Longton, William H., paper by, 68
Longwood College, and Simkins Prize, 137, 236
Lorantas, Raymond M., comment by, 84
Loring, James S., 475, 477
Lotchin, Roger W., revs., 126–27
Lottinville, Savoie, ed., *Travels in North America,* revd., 113–14
Louis, William Roger, comment by, 72
Louisiana, art. on fear of Negro violence in, 19–38; art. on Negro family during Civil War in, 369–80; books on, noted, 290, 587; books on, revd., 94, 265–66, 274–75; 421–23, 540–41, 544–45, 575–77; papers on, 70–71; Lincoln and Recon. in, 57–58; livestock in, 147, 154, 158
Louisiana, by Leonard V. Huber, noted, 587
Louisiana in French Diplomacy, by E. Wilson Lyon, noted, 290
Louisiana lottery, 192
Louisiana Native Guards, 29–31, 36
Louisiana Reconstructed, by Joe G. Taylor, revd., 421–23
Lovejoy, Joseph C., 475, 477
Lovejoy, Owen, 47*n*

Loveland, Anne C., revs., 99–100
Lowitt, Richard, 135, 234
Lowry, Robert, 195
Lumpkin, Katharine Du Pre, *The Emancipation of Angelina Grimké*, revd., 259–60
Lumpkin, Mrs. Samuel, 345
Lutherans, Negroes and antebellum sou., 458, 459, 464*n*
Lux, Guillermo, paper by, 71
Lyell, Sir Charles, 469
Lynching, 482; and 1856 slave insurrection scare, 330, 333, 337; and sou. Repubs., 501–502; and sou. agrarian reform, 195, 198
Lyon, E. Wilson, *Louisiana in French Diplomacy*, noted, 290; *The Man Who Sold Louisiana, noted, 290*

Macaluso, Leonard A., paper by, 66
McBride, Robert M., coauth., *Biographical Directory of the Tennessee General Assembly*,noted, 583–84
McCall, Harry, 190*n*
McColley, Robert M., paper by, 67; revs., 256–58
McCorkle, James L., Jr., revs., 274–75
McCormack, Eleanor O'Donnell, 349–50
McDonald, Forrest, coauth., "The Antebellum Southern Herdsman; A Reinterpretation," 147–66; *The Presidency of George Washington*, revd., 104–105
McEachern, Leora H., coed., *Wilmington–New Hanover Safety Committee Minutes*, noted, 287
McGimsey, Charles R., III, paper by, 79
McGovern, James R., ed., *Andrew Jackson and Pensacola*,noted, 290; ed., *Colonial Pensacola*, noted, 290
Machado, Manuel A., Jr., comment by, 71
McIntosh, William H., 453
McKale, Donald M., paper by, 72
McKenney, Thomas L., book on, revd., 413–14
McKinney, Gordon B., "Southern Mountain Republicans and the Negro, 1865–1900," 493–516
McMaster, Fitz Hugh, 391–94
McMath, Robert C., 292
McMurtry, Larry, papers on, 79–80
McTyeire, Holland Nimmons, 453
McVey, Frances Jewell, coauth., *Uncle Bill of Wildwood*, noted, 284–85
McWhiney, Grady, coauth., "The Antebellum Southern Herdsman: A Reinterpretation," 147–66; *Southerners and Other Americans*, revd., 89–90; paper by, 73
Maddex, Jack P., Jr., paper by, 68
Madison, James; 527
Maehl, William H., paper by, 77
Mahon, John K., ed., *Indians of the Lower South*, noted 584; sess. chmn., 83
Mahone, William, 498, 503 ff.; and Negro in Readjuster movt., 167–86
Making of the TVA, by Arthur E. Morgan, revd., 428–29
Malone, Bill C., paper by, 81
Malone, Dumas, coauth., "A Note on Evidence; The Personal History of Madison Hemings," 523–28; *Jefferson The President: Second Term [Jefferson and His Time*, Vol. V], revd., 109–10
Malone, Henry T., revs., 523–55
Man but Not a Brother: Abraham Lincoln and Racial Equality, by George M. Fredrickson, 39–58
Man Who Sold Louisiana, by E. Wilson Lyon, noted, 290
Mandle, Jay R., paper by, 62
Manifest Destiny, 51
Manly, Basil, Jr., 456, 470
Manning, Richard Irvine, book on, revd., 127–28
Mantell, Martin E., revs., 567–68
Manufacturing, paper on, 75
Manuscripts on Microfilm, comp. by Richard B. Bickel, noted, 437
Maps, books on, noted, 283, 286–87, 437; book on, revd., 94–96
Marcella, Gabriel, comment by, 66
Marines, U. S., book on, noted, 585
Marius, Richard C., 138
Mark Twain & the South, by Arthur G. Pettit, revd., 434–35
Marquardt, Louis P., 345
Marriage, and slaves, 369–72
Marshall, Andrew, 466–71
Marshall, John, books on, revd., 106–107, 410–12
Martin, William Harrison, 189*n*
Martineau, Harriet, 454
Mary Washington College, book on, revd., 279–80
Maryland, book on, noted, 583; books on, revd., 96–97, 118–19, 398–99, 536–38; paper on, 78

Maryland, ed. by Richard Walsh and William L. Fox, revd., 398–99
Maryland and the Empire, ed. by Peter S. Onuf, revd. 96–97
Maslowski, Peter, revs., 122–23
Massey, Mary Elizabeth, death of 235; obituary notice on, 292–93
Materials for the Study of Washington, by Perry G. Fisher, noted, 286
Mathews, Donald G., "Charles Colcock Jones and the Southern Evangelical Crusade to Form a Biracial Community," 299–320
Mathews, Jane DeHart, 88
Mathias, Frank Furlong, ed., *Incidents & Experiences in the Life of Thomas W. Parsons*, revd., 579–80; *Albert D. Kirwan*, noted, 584
Mathis, G. Ray, ed., *College Life in the Reconstruction South*, revd., 268–69; ed., *"Uncle Tom" Reed's Memoir*, revd., 580–81; paper by, 86
Matter of Allegiances, by William J. Evitts, revd., 118–19
Mattes, Merrill J., sess. chmn., 79
Matusow, Allen J., book note by, 586–87
Maurer, David W., *Kentucky Moonshine*, noted, 284–85
Maxey, Samuel Bell, book on, revd., 116–18
May, Ernest R., paper by, 64
May, Robert E., revs., 120–21
Meade, William, 317
Medary, Milton Bennett, Jr., 350
Meerse, David E., 292; revs., 118–19
Meier, August, comment by, 68; revs., 569–70
Memoirs of Henry Heth, ed. by James L. Morrison, Jr., revd., 263–64
Memphis, 196, 324; art. on city planning in, 339–68; book on, revd., 581–82; papers on, 69–70
Memphis and Charleston R. R., 324
Mencken, Henry Louis, book on, revd., 129–30
Merchants, book on, revd., 536–38
Merry, Nelson, 464–65, 471
Merwin, Miles M., revs., 399–400
Messner, William F., "Black Violence and White Response: Louisiana, 1862," 19–38
Methodists, book on, noted, 588; and Negro family, 378; Negroes and antebellum sou., 453 ff.; and slaves, 317
Mexican-Americans, papers on, 71
Mexican War, book on, noted, 585; book on, revd., 262–63
Mexican War, by K. Jack Bauer, revd., 262–63
Mexicans, papers on, 79
Mexico, 382, 386; papers on, 72, 83–84
Microfilm, books on, noted, 437
Midway Church (Ga.), 300, 303
Miles, Edwin A., and program comm., 135, 136
Military history, books on, noted, 283, 583, 585–86, 588; books on, revd., 122–23; 133–34, 262–65, 418–19, 538–39; papers on, 73
Miller, Richard G., coauth., *Essays on Urban America*, noted, 436
Miller, Robert Moats, comment by, 76
Miller, Samuel, 302
Miller, Zane L., sess. chmn., 69
Mind of America, by Rush Welter, revd., 548–49
Mining, and sou. Negroes, 502–503
Minor, William J., 370
Mintz, Sidney W., *Slavery, Colonialism, and Racism*, noted, 290
Miscegenation, 43, 54; art. on Jefferson and, 523–28
Missions, Negroes and antebellum sou. Protestant, 465–66; to slaves, 299 ff.
Mississippi, book on, noted, 286; books on, revd., 120–21, 281–82, 433; paper on, 63; and livestock, 147, 153 ff.
Mississippi, ed. by James W. Loewen and Charles Sallis, noted, 286
Missouri, and livestock, 147
Mitchell, John, book on, revd., 94–96
Mitchell, Memory F., ed., *Addresses and Public Papers of Robert Walter Scott*, noted, 288
Money, book on, revd., 409–10
Mooney, Chase C., *William H. Crawford*, revd., 112–13
Moore, James T., "Black Militancy in Readjuster Virginia, 1879–1883," 167–86; *Two Paths to the New South*, revd., 269–70; revs., 127–28
Moore, Jamie W., comment by, 64
Moore, Jessie T., Jr., comment by, 70
Moore, John Hammond, ed., *The Juhl Letters to the* Charleston Courier, revd., 267–68
Moore, John Hebron, sess. chmn., 75; and nominating comm., 234, 291

Moore, John R., paper by, 84
Moore, Thomas Overton, 29
More Virginia Broadsides Before 1877, by Ray O. Hummel, Jr., noted, 587
Morgan, Arthur E., *The Making of the TVA*, revd., 428–29
Morgan, George T., book note by, 285–86
Morgan, Thomas S., obituary notice by, 292–93; paper by, 82
Morison, Samuel Eliot, *The European Discovery of America: The Southern Voyages*, revd., 397–98
Morris, Allen, *Florida Place Names*, noted, 289
Morris, Margaret Francine, coed., *Essays on Urban America*, noted, 436
Morris, Thomas D., *Free Men All*, revd., 99–100
Morrison, deLesseps Story, books on, revd., 274–75, 576–77
Morrison, James L., Jr., ed., *The Memoirs of Henry Heth*, revd., 263–64
Morrison Era, by Joseph B. Parker, revd., 274–75
Morton, Richard Lee, death of, 235
Moser, Harold D., coed., *The Papers of Daniel Webster: Correspondence*, Vol. 1, revd., 541–42
Mott, John J., 499*n*, 509
Mugleston, William F., paper by, 63
Mullin, Gerald W., paper by, 63; revs., 245–46
Mullins, Edgar Young, paper on, 76
Municipal government, city planning and sou., 339 ff.
Music, book on, noted, 587; papers on, 81
Music Books of Ruebush & Kieffer, by Grace I. Showalter, noted, 587
Myrdal, Gunnar, 53

Nance, Joseph Milton, revs., 115
Napoleon III, 386
Nash, Gary B., *Red, White, and Black*, revd., 91–92
Nash, Gerald D., comment by, 74–75
Nashville, and city planning, 343, 344
National Archives and Urban Research, ed. by Jerome Finster, revd., 242–43
National Association of Business Agents and State Exchanges, 192–93
National Colored Alliance, 188
National Urban League, by Nancy J. Weiss, revd., 126–27
Naval history, papers on, 83
Navy, U. S., and La. Slaves, 25
Nebenzahl, Kenneth A., *A Bibliography of Printed Battle Plans*, noted, 583
Negro, art, on fear of violence by La., 19–38; art. on Lincoln and equality of, 39–58; art on Va. politics and, 167–86; art on Colored Farmers' Alliance and, 187–200; art. on religion and antebellum, 299–320; art. on 1856 insurrection and, 321–38; art. on Civil War and family of, 369–80; art. on Andrew Johnson and, 381–90; art. on antebellum sou. Protestantism and, 451–72; art. on use of slave testimony on life of, 473–92; art. on sou. mountain Repubs. and, 493–516; art. on Jefferson and, 523–28; books on, noted, 283–84, 290, 587; books on, revd., 91–92, 110–12, 119–20, 123–29, 133–34, 240–42, 246–48, 265–66, 275–77, 403–406, 416–17, 533–34, 563–64, 569–70, 578–79, 581–82; papers on, 64–65, 69–70, 73–74, 81–82, 86; economic condition of Va., 168; population distribution in sou. mountains of, 502–503; statistics on church membership of, 458; and theft of livestock, 164–65
Neitzel, Sarah C., paper by, 77
Nelson, Bill, paper by, 85
Neuenschwander, John A., revs., 252–53
Neutrality, book on, revd., 105–106
New Country, by Richard A. Bartlett, revd., 255–56
New Deal in Georgia, by Michael S. Holmes, revd., 570–71
New Mexico, paper on, 83–84
New Negro on Campus, by Raymond Wolters, revd., 569–70
New Orleans, 187; art. on city planning in, 339–68; books on, revd., 274–75, 576–77; biracial worship in, 454; and blacks in Civil War, 19 ff.
New Urban History, edited by Leo F. Schnore, revd., 531–33
Newcomb, W. W., revs., 427–28
Newspapers, and 1856 insurrection scare, 335
Nicholas, William E., paper by, 86
Nichols, Irby C., Jr., paper by, 87; and Snell Memorial Prize comm., 138
Nicks, William, 327
Night Riders in Black Folk History, by Gladys-Marie Fry, revd., 578–79

Nitske, W. Robert, trans., *Travels in North America,* revd., 113–14
Nixon, Richard Milhous, book on, noted, 586–87
Nor Is It Over Yet, by Jerrell H. Shofner, revd., 266–67
Nordin, D. Sven, *Rich Harvest,* revd., 423–24
Norris, J. Frank, paper on, 76
North Carolina, books on, noted, 287, 288, 289, 588; books on, revd., 248–49, 558–59, 574–75; papers on, 82, 85; and city planning, 343; and livestock, 147, 158 ff.; mountain Repubs. and Negro in, 493 ff.
North Carolina Governors, by Beth G. Crabtree, noted, 289
North Carolina Higher-Court Records, Vol. IV, ed. by William S. Price, Jr., revd., 248–49
North Carolina Troops, Vol. V, comp. by Weymouth T. Jordan, Jr., noted, 588
Northern Alliance, and Negro, 192
"Northern Institutions in Southern Financial History: A Note on Insurance Investments," by B. Michael Pritchett, 391–96
Northup, Solomon, 474, 475, 479, 491–92
Norton, Charles Dyer, 341
"Note on Evidence: The Personal History of Madison Hemings," by Dumas Malone and Steven H. Hochman, 523–28
Nugent, Walter T. K., revs., 409–10

Oaks, Robert F., coauth., *Essays on Urban America,* noted, 436
Oates, Stephen B., *The Fires of Jubilee,* revd., 554–55
O'Connor, Rachel Swayze Bell, book on, revd., 540–41
O'Donnell, James H., *Southern Indians,* revd., 253–55
Office of Education, U. S., 5
Offley, G. W., 480
Oil industry, papers on, 74
Old Dominion in the Seventeenth Century, edited by Warren M. Billings, revd., 535–36
Olien, Roger M., paper by, 69
Oliphant, Louise, 488
Olmsted, Frederick Law, 159, 455, 464
Olson, Alison Gilbert, *Anglo-American Politics,* revd., 90–91; comment by, 78
O'Neill, William L., panelist, 82–83
Onuf, Peter S., ed., *Maryland and the Empire,* revd., 96–97
Open-range system, in South, 156–60
Oral history, slave testimony as, 476 ff.
Ordnance Dept., U. S., book on, revd., 121–22
Organization of American Historians, 7
Orlando, and city planning, 354
Osborn, George Coleman, *John James Tigert,* revd., 571–72
Osbourne flotilla, 385
Osthaus, Carl R., revs., 133–34
Otis, Robert R., 346, 347, 363
Owen, Allison, 351, 352
Owens, William A., paper by, 61
Owsley, Frank Lawrence, and sou. agriculture, 149–53, 158, 163
Owsley, Frank Lawrence, Jr., ed., *The Life of Andrew Jackson,* noted, 289–90

Paige, Richard G. L., 172*n*, 173
Paine, by David Freeman Hawke, revd., 98–99
Paine, Thomas, book on, revd., 98–99
Painter, Nell Irvin, paper by, 86
Palmer, Dave Richard, *The Way of the Fox,* revd., 538–39
Paludan, Phillip S., revs., 260–61, 410–12
Papenfuse, Edward C., *In Pursuit of Profit,* revd., 536–38
Papers of Alexander Hamilton, Vols. XX, XXI, ed. by Harold C. Syrett *et al.*, revd., 412–13
Papers of Daniel Webster: Correspondence, Vol. 1, ed. by Charles M. Wiltse and Harold D. Moser, revd., 541–42
Papers of Henry Clay, Vol. 5, ed. by James F. Hopkins, Mary W. M. Hargreaves, *et al.*, revd., 550–52
Papers of Henry Laurens, Vol. IV, ed. by George C. Rogers, Jr., David R. Chesnutt, *et al.*, revd., 402–403
Papers of John C. Calhoun, Vol. VIII, ed. by W. Edwin Hemphill, revd., 549–50
Papers of John Marshall, Vol. I, ed. by Herbert A. Johnson *et al.*, revd., 410–12
Papers of Thomas Jefferson, Vol. 19, ed. by Julian P. Boyd and Ruth W. Lester, revd., 256–58
Papers of Woodrow Wilson, Vols. 15–17, ed. by Arthur S. Link *et al.*, revd., 425–27
Parker, Harold T., paper by, 79

Parker, Joseph B., *The Morrison Era*, revd., 274–75
Parks, sou. city planning and, 361
Parsons, Thomas W., book on, revd., 579–80
Parton, James, 523, 524
Patronage, sou. Repub. Negro, 499, 510–11
Party and Faction, by Rudolph M. Bell, revd., 101–102
Party Politics, by H. James Henderson, revd., 407–408
Patent Office, U. S., 147
Patrick Henry, by Richard R. Beeman, revd., 406–407
Patterson, Ben, 198
Paul, John, 178
Pease, Jane H., coauth., *They Who Would Be Free*, revd., 416–17; revs., 259–60
Pease, William H., 292; coauth., *They Who Would Be Free*, revd., 416–17
Peckham, Howard H., ed., *The Toll of Independence*, noted, 283
Peirce, Neal R., *The Border South States*, revd., 574–75
Pells, Richard H., comment by, 80
Peninsula Campaign, by Joseph P. Cullen, revd., 122–23
Pennington, James W. C., 475, 476, 479
Pensacola, book on, noted, 290
Peonage, 482
People's party, and Colored Farmers' Alliance, 190
Perdue, Robert D., 471
Perkins, Dexter, 4
Perrie, Mr., 386
Persistent Tradition, by George B. Tindall, revd., 573
Personal liberty laws, book on, revd., 99–100
Pessen, Edward, revs., 553–54
Peterson, Merrill D., 524; revs., 97–98; and Simkins Prize comm., 236
Pettit, Arthur G., *Mark Twain & the South*, revd., 434–35
Pharmacy, book on, revd., 433
Phelps, John Wolcott, 26–27
Phillips, Edward H., death of, 235
Phillips, Ulrich Bonnell, and sou. agriculture, 149–50, 165, 166; and slave narratives, 473–74, 477
Phillips Academy (Andover), 300
Phillis (a slave), 457
Pickens, Donald K., revs., 432
Pierce, Edwin Lillie, 31
Pierce, Franklin, 335
Pike Co., Ohio, Negroes and, 524–25, 526
Pills, Pen & Politics, by Edward Pinkowski, revd., 575–76
Pindell, Richard, 42, 43, 47
Pinkowski, Edward, *Pills, Pen & Politics*, revd., 575–76
Pioneer-at-Law, by George Edwards, revd., 280–81
Piracy, book on, revd., 399–400
Pittman, Frank A., 347
Pitts, Floyd B., comment by, 85
Place names, book on, noted, 289
Plantations, paper on, 62; Civil War and La., 19, 22, 31 ff.; interviews with former slaves and, 490; and sou. agriculture, 149 ff.
Planter class, Andrew Johnson and sou., 384, 389
Poe, William A., revs., 277–78
Polish Pioneers in Virginia, by Sigmund H. Uminski, noted, 288
Political South, by Monroe L. Billington, revd., 568–69
Political theory, book on, revd., 97–98
Politics, art. on Negro and Va., 167–86; art. on mountain Repubs. and Negro in sou., 493–516; books on, revd., 90–91, 101–104, 118–21, 131–33, 269–75, 407–408, 428–30, 542–45, 558–59, 562–64, 568–69, 573–77; papers on, 67, 69–70, 81–82, 85–86; Jefferson Davis and, 518; and Lincoln's racial views, 40–41, 50
Poll tax, 194
Pollock, Norman H., paper by, 70
Polser, Charles W., comment by, 72
Popular sovereignty, 49 ff.
Population, and city planning, 342, 352–53
Populist party, 193; and sou. Repubs., 509
Portraits, book on, noted, 587
Powdermaker, Hortense, 481
Powell, William S., comment by, 72
Presbyterian church, 156*n*, 300, 302, 313, 315, 317; paper on, 68; Negroes and antebellum sou., 458 ff.
Presidency of George Washington, by Forrest McDonald, revd., 104–105
Price, Samuel Woodson, book on, noted, 284–85
Price, Thomas, 475, 477
Price, William S., Jr., ed., *North Carolina Higher-Court Records*, Vol. IV, revd., 248–49
Prince (a slave), 371

Princeton Theological Seminary, 300, 302, 305
Pritchard, Jeter Connelly, 509, 510*n*, 514
Pritchett, B. Michael, "Northern Institutions in Southern Financial History: A Note on Insurance Investments," 391-96
Problem of Slavery in the Age of Revolution, by David B. Davis, revd., 403–406
Procter, Ben H., sess. chmn., 61
Proctor, Samuel, 234; sess. chmn., 72
Progress, papers on, 68
Progressive party (1948), book on, revd., 132–33
Progressivism, books on, revd., 127–28, 424–25
Progressivism in America, by Arthur A. Ekirch, Jr., revd., 424–25
Prohibition, paper on, 63
Protestantism, art. on race relations and antebellum sou., 451–72
"Protestantism and Afro-Americans in the Old South: Another Look," by Kenneth K. Bailey, 451–72
Pryor, Alfred S., 181
Public Papers of the Presidents . . . Herbert Hoover . . . 1929, noted, 286
Public Papers of the Presidents . . . Richard Nixon . . . 1972, noted, 586–87
Pugh, David, 33
Pulley, Raymond H., comment by, 86
Purifoy, Lewis McCarroll, Jr., 453

Quantitative history, books on, revd., 531–33; paper on, 64
Quarles, Benjamin, *Allies for Freedom*, revd., 119–20

Rabinowitz, Howard N., revs., 275–77
Rabun, James Z., 234
Race, books on, revd., 265–66, 533–34; papers on, 80–81
Race and Slavery, ed. by Stanley L. Engerman and Eugene D. Genovese, revd., 533–34
Race relations, art. on antebellum sou., 451–72; book on, noted, 436–37; interviews with ex-slaves and, 481–84; religion and antebellum sou., 299 ff.; sou. mountain Repubs. and, 493 ff.
Rachel of Old Louisiana, by Avery O. Craven, revd., 540–41
Racial equality, art. on Lincoln and, 39–58
Racism, 45 ff.; book on, noted, 290; papers on, 65–66, 67–68; and Colored Farmers' Alliance, 191 ff.; and 1856 slave insurrection panic, 338; Va. politics and, 169 ff.
Radford, Ruby Lorraine, 488
Radical Republicans, 57–58; Andrew Johnson and, 386, 388, 389
Ragland, Samuel Evan, 349
Railroads, book on, revd., 552–53
Raimey, Solomon D., 327, 337
Rainbolt, John C., *From Prescription to Persuasion*, revd., 93–94
Ramage, James A., *John Wesley Hunt*, noted, 284–85
Rambaut, Thomas, 470
Rampp, Donald L., coauth., *The Civil War in the Indian Territory*, noted, 585
Rampp, Lary C., coauth., *The Civil War in the Indian Territory*, noted, 585
Randall, Henry S., 523
Randolph, Edmund, book on, revd., 539–40
Randolph, Wassell, 348–49, 358
Rankin, Hugh F., coauth., *The Fate of a Nation*, noted, 583; sess. chmn., 79
Rasor, Eugene L., paper by, 83
Rawick, George P., 480
Ray, Frederic E., *Alfred R. Waud*, noted, 289
Readjuster movt., 499, 502 ff.; art. on Negro and, 167–86; book on, revd., 269–70
Ready, Milton L., revs., 400–401
Reardon, John J., *Edmund Randolph*, revd., 539–40
Rebellion, art. on 1856 fear of slave, 321–38
Reconstruction, art. on Andrew Johnson and, 381-90; books on, revd., 123–24, 265–69, 419–23, 563–64; papers on, 62, 64–65; Lincoln and, 57–58; and Negro, 20, 35, 38; sou. mountain Repubs. and, 493–99
Red River expedition, book on, noted, 585
Red, White, and Black, by Gary B. Nash, revd., 91–92
Redeemers, papers on, 85–86
Reed, Daniel J., sess. chmn., 84
Reed, Merl E., 135
Reed, Thomas Walter, book on, revd., 580–81
Reeves, Thomas C., *Gentleman Boss*, revd., 567–68
Reform, books on, revd., 424–25, 576–77; papers on, 62–63; city planning and, 338 ff.; motivation of Amer., 317–18

Reid, John, coauth., *The Life of Andrew Jackson*, noted, 289–90
Reinerman, Alan J., paper by, 87
Relief, papers on, 82
Religion, art. on Charles C. Jones and slave, 299–320; art on race relations and antebellum sou., 451–72; book on, noted, 588; books on, revd., 258–59, 277–78, 434; papers on, 67, 75–76, 78; Negro family and, 378–79
Representative Government, ed. by Melvin Yazawa, noted, 583
Republican party, art. on Negro and sou., 493–516; book on, revd., 419–21; papers on, 67, 69, 81–82; and Andrew Johnson, 382; and 1856 slave insurrection panic, 334 ff.; and Colored Farmers' Alliance, 193; in Pike Co., Ohio, 524–25; and Lincoln's racial views, 41, 45 ff.; and Va. Readjuster movt., 167 ff.
Reservation system, book on, revd., 557–58
Revels, Hiram Rhodes, 466, 471
Revivalism, book on, revd., 258–59
Rice, Otis K., revs., 577–78
Rice University, 233
Rich Harvest, by D. Sven Nordin, revd., 423–24
Richard Irvine Manning, by Robert M. Burts, revd., 127–28
Rideout, William M., paper by, 67
Riley, Edward M., panelist, 85
Riley, James D., paper by, 72
Ripley, C. Peter, "The Black Family in Transition: Louisiana, 1860–1865," 369–80
Risjord, Norman K., 135
Riznik, Barnes, paper by, 87
Robert R. Churches, by Annette E. Church and Roberta Church, revd., 581–82
Robinson, Charles Mulford, 340
Robinson, W. Stitt, revs., 557–58
Robison, Dan M., coauth., *Biographical Directory of the Tennessee General Assembly*, noted, 583–84
Rodabaugh, James H., 523
Rodgers, H. P., 198
Rogers, Alan, *Empire and Liberty*, revd., 401–402
Rogers, George C., Jr., 136, 292; coed., *The Papers of Henry Laurens*, Vol. IV, revd., 402–403; revs., 246–48
Rogers, J. J., 190, 191
Roland, Charles P., 236; sess. chmn., 73; and Sydnor Award comm., 136, 236
Roll, Jordan, Roll, by Eugene D. Genovese, revd., 240–42
Roman Catholic church, papers on, 72; and antebellum Negroes, 452, 454
Roosevelt, Franklin D., book on, noted, 285
Rose, Willie Lee, 234, 291; comment by, 68
Rosemont Plantation, 517–18, 519*n*
Rosengarten, Theodore, *All God's Dangers*, revd., 275–77
Ross, Steven T., sess. chmn., 66
Rothblatt, Sheldon, comment by, 70
Rowan County [N. C.], by James S. Brawley, noted, 289
Royalty, Dale M., revs., 105–106
Ruchames, Louis, revs., 414–15
Rudwick, Elliott, sess. chmn., 80
Ruebush & Kieffer, book on, noted, 587
Ruffin, Edmund, 157, 164
Rule, William, 500–501
Rundell, Walter, Jr., 88; revs., 255–56
Russell, C. Allyn, paper by, 76
Russell, Daniel Lindsay, 510*n*, 513
Rutman, Darrett B., comment by, 78
Ryland, Robert, 453

Sabers on the Rio Grande, by Jerry Thompson, noted, 585–86
St. Thomas College, 517
Sallis, William Charles, 292; coed., *Mississippi*, noted, 286
Sambo, 19, 36
Samuel Bell Maxey, by Louise Horton, revd., 116–18
Sanchez, Joseph P., paper by, 71
Sanders, Newell, 513
Sanders, Charles Richard, *The Cameron Plantation*, noted, 288
Satz, Ronald N., *American Indian Policy*, revd., 555–57
Savannah, Negro Baptists in, 467–70
Sayward, William J., 345, 352, 353, 364
Scarborough, William K., revs., 529–30
Schenck, Carl Alwin, *Birth of Forestry in America*, noted, 290
Schlegel, Marvin W., and membership comm., 234; and Simkins Prize comm., 292
Schmitt, Hans A., 135, 234
Schnore, Leo F., ed., *The New Urban History*, revd., 531–33
Schools for All, by William P. Vaughn, revd., 123–24
Schor, Joel, cocomp., *A List of References*

for the History of Black Americans in Agriculture, noted, 587
Schuessler, Hermann E., obituary notice on, 593–94
Science, paper on, 68
Scotch-Irish, and antebellum sou. agriculture, 156–60, 166
Scots, in South, 156–57
Scott, Anne Firor, 291
Scott, Nathan Bay, 510*n*
Scott, Robert Walter, book on, noted, 288
Scroggs, Jack B., revs., 116–18
Secession, book on, revd., 120–21
Secessionist Impulse, by William L. Barney, revd., 120–21
Seckinger, Ron L., comment by, 87
Secondary schools, teaching of history in, 5
Sectionalism, book on, revd., 273–74
Segregation, books on, revd., 133–34, 265–66; and sou. city planning, 357 ff.; and sou. Repubs., 510, 511–12
Segregation Struggle in Louisiana, by Roger A. Fischer, revd., 265–66
Selby, John E., sess. chmn., 63
Self-Evident Truths, by Paul K. Conkin, revd., 97–98
Sellers, Charles G., revs., 550–52
Senate, U. S., book on, noted, 436
Senter, DeWitt Clinton, 495, 497
Sequestration Comm., 32
Serpent in Eden, by Fred C. Hobson, Jr., revd., 129–30
Servin, Manuel P., comment by, 84; sess. chmn., 71
Seward, William Henry, and Anglo-American relations, 382 ff.
Seward, William J., comp. and annotator, *The Era of Franklin D. Roosevelt*, noted, 285–86
Sex, papers on, 67, 80–81
Shade, William G., revs., 548–49
Shaffer, John Wilson, 34–35
Shalhope, Robert E., revs., 547–48
Shankman, Arnold, revs., 278–79
Shaping of Southern Politics, by J. Morgan Kousser, revd., 270–72
Shapiro, Henry D., paper by, 77
Sharecropping, book on, revd., 275–77
Shaw, Nate [Cobb, Nate], book on, revd., 275–77
Shelby, Isaac, book on, noted, 284
Sherer, Robert G., revs., 265–66
Sheridan, Richard B., *Sugar and Slavery*, revd., 245–46
Sherrill, Peter T., revs., 562–63
Shiloh, by Wiley Sword, revd., 264–65
Shipp, Nelson, *A Vagabond Newsman*, noted, 287–88
Shofner, Jerrell H., *Nor Is It Over Yet*, revd., 266–67
Showalter, Grace I., *The Music Books of Ruebush & Kieffer*, noted, 587
Shuffer, J. J., 189
Silberstein, Gerard E., 138
Silverman, Catherine, paper by, 85
Simkins, Francis Butler, 137
Simkins Prize, establishment of, 137
Simmons, Furnifold McLendel, 514
Simpson, Amos E., 88, 137
Singer, J. David, paper by, 64
Single tax, Colored Farmers' Alliance and, 193*n*
Sisson, Daniel, *The American Revolution of 1800*, revd., 542–44
Skaggs, David Curtis, paper by, 78
Skipper, Ottis Clark, revs., 281–82
Slaughter, Richard, 485
Slave management, and Evangelical Christianity, 308–14
Slave narratives, art. on, 473–92
Slave rebellion, book on, revd., 554–55
Slavery, art. on religion and reform of, 299–320; art. on 1856 insurrection panic and, 321–38; art. on Jefferson and, 523–28; books on, noted, 290, 436–37, 584–85; books on, revd., 110–12, 240–42, 245–48, 403–406, 416–17, 533–34; papers on, 63–64, 68; Lincoln's attitude toward, 39 ff.; sou. mountaineers and, 495; sou. Protestantism and, 451 ff.
Slavery and the Numbers Game, by Herbert G. Gutman, noted, 584–85
Slavery, Colonialism, and Racism, ed. by Sidney W. Mintz, noted, 290
Slavery and Race Relations, ed. by Robert B. Toplin, noted, 436–37
Slaves, art. on Civil War and La., 19–38; art. on Civil War family life of La., 369–80; art. on interviews with former, 473–92; confiscation of, 24–25, 28, 31
Slemp, Campbell, 516
Slemp, Campbell Bascom, 516
Small, Melvin, paper by, 64

Smiley, David L., 292; and Graduate Student Award comm., 292
Smith, Erastus (Deaf), book on, revd., 115
Smith, Hoke, 346
Smith, Howard W., revs., 268–69
Smith, James Morton, comment by, 72
Smith, John, book on, revd., 534–35
Smith, Lillian, paper on, 65
Smith, Richard, sess. chmn., 84
Smith, Sam B., coed., *Tennessee History*, noted, 275
Smith, W. Calvin, revs., 267–68, 580–81
Social control, and sou. city planning, 365–66, 368
Social history, book on, noted, 588
Socialism, papers on, 77
Society in North Carolina, by Alan D. Watson, noted, 588
Society of Enquiry Concerning Africans, 302
Sorin, Gerald, revs., 243–45
Sosna, Morton P., paper by, 65
South, art. on herdsman in antebellum, 147–66; art. on Negroes and agrarian reform in, 187–200; art. on city planning in, 339–68; art. on financial history of, 391–96; art. on race relations and Protestantism in antebellum, 451–72; art. on Negro and Repub. party in mountain, 493–516; book on, noted, 584; books on, revd., 89–90, 123–24, 129–30, 253–55, 270–72, 275–77, 434–35, 529–30, 552–53, 564–65, 568–69, 573–75; papers on, 62–63, 68, 69–70, 75, 76, 80–81, 85–86
South Carolina, books on, revd., 127–28, 246–48, 267–68, 402–403; cotton pickers' strike in, 197*n*; interviews with former slaves in, 488–89; and livestock, 157 ff.
Southern Alliance, and Negro, 188 ff.
Southern Baptist Convention, by Robert A. Baker, revd., 277–78
Southern Historical Assn., 40th annual meeting, 59–88, 135, 235; 41st annual meeting, 135, 438; 42d annual meeting, 135–36; bylaws, 236; committees of, 135–36, 291–92; European History Section officers, 137; European History Section Snell Memorial Prize, 137–38; Executive Council actions, 233–34, 236; financial statement, 237–39; Graduate Student Award (1972–73), 136–37, 236; membership of, 235; nominating comm., 234; nominees (1974), 234; (1975), 291; officers of, 234; presidential address, 3–18; report of sec.-treas., 233–39; Simkins Prize, 137, 236; and Sydnor Award (1972–73), 136, 236
"Southern History in Periodicals, 1974: A Selected Bibliography," 201–32
Southern Indians in the American Revolution, by James H. O'Donnell, revd., 253–55
Southern Methodist University, by Mary M. H. Thomas, revd., 432
"Southern Mountain Republicans and the Negro, 1865-1900," by Gordon B. McKinney, 493–516
Southern University, interviews of former slaves by, 489
Southerners and Other Americans, by Grady McWhiney, revd., 89–90
Southwest, papers on, 60, 61, 76, 79
Space, Time, and Freedom, by Major L. Wilson, revd., 547–48
Spalding, Phinizy, revs., 249–50
Spanish America, papers on, 72
Sparks, Eliza[beth], 485
Spencer, H. J., 189
Sprague, Stuart Seely, revs., 406–407
Sprague, William Buell, 471, 472*n*
Stampp, Kenneth M., 382–83
Stamps, Anna Aurelia, 521*n*
Stamps, Jane Davis, 521*n*
Stamps, Isaac Davis, 521*n*
Stamps, Lucinda Farrar Davis, art. on letter of Jefferson Davis to, 517–22
Stamps, William, 518, 519*n*, 521
Stanly, Edward, book on, revd., 558–59
Stanton, Edwin McMasters, 28, 29, 387
Starobin, Robert S., ed., *Blacks in Bondage*, revd., 110–12
Starr, J. Barton, 292
States' rights, Andrew Johnson and, 387
Stealey, John E., III, revs., 113–14
Steelman, Joseph F., comment by, 85
Sternsher, Bernard, *Consensus, Conflict, and American Historians*, revd., 530–31
Steward, Austin, 479
Stickle, Warren F., paper by, 69–70
Stockton, Carl R., paper by, 86
Stoesen, Alexander R., revs., 429–30
Stokes, William Brickly, 497
Stone, Ralph A., comment by, 69
Stout, Harry S., revs., 419–21
Stowe, Harriet Beecher, 527
Strausberg, Stephen F., paper by, 82
Streets, and city planning, 353 ff.
Strickland, Arvarh E., 88; revs., 416–17

Strike, by sou. cotton pickers, 188, 196–99
Struggle for Neutrality, by Albert H. Bowman, revd., 105–106
Stumpf, Vernon O., revs., 90–91
Suffrage, book on, revd., 270–72; Andrew Johnson and sou., 382, 386; Lincoln and black, 57–58; sou. mountain Repubs. and Negro, 495 ff.
Sugar and Slavery, by Richard B. Sheridan, revd., 245–46
Sunbury (Ga.) Baptist Assn., and antebellum sou. Negro, 461–62, 467–68, 471
Supreme Court, U. S., books on, revd., 106–107, 260–61
Susman, Warren I., paper by, 79–80
Swisher, Carl B., *History of the Supreme Court,* Vol. V, revd., 260–61
Sword, Wiley, *Shiloh,* revd., 264–65
Sydnor Award (1972–73), 136, 236
Syrett, Harold C., coed., *The Papers of Alexander Hamilton,* Vols. XX, XXI, revd., 412–13
Szasz, Margaret, *Education and the American Indian,* revd., 427–28

Tachau, Mary K., 292
Taiwan, papers on, 84
Talmadge, Eugene, book on, revd., 429–30
Taney, Roger Brooke, 51; book on, revd., 260–61
Taylor, A., 455
Taylor, A. Elizabeth, sess. chmn., 82
Taylor, Alfred Alexander, 506, 507–508
Taylor, George V., sess. chmn., 79
Taylor, Joe Gray, 292; *Louisiana Reconstructed,* revd., 421–23
Taylor, Lonn, 87
Taylor, William S., 510*n*
Taylor, Zachary, 518
Teach, Edward, book on, revd., 399–400
Teaching, art. on history, 3–18; papers on, 59, 85
Tennessee, art. on 1856 slave insurrection in, 321–38; books on, noted, 285, 289, 583–84; books on, revd., 574–75, 581–82; and law on slave insurrections, 338; and livestock, 161 ff.; mountain Repubs. and Negro in, 493 ff.
Tennessee, by Mary F. Caldwell, revd., 251–52
Tennessee During the Revolutionary War, by Samuel C. Williams, noted, 289
Tennessee History, comp. and ed. by Sam B. Smith and Luke H. Banker, noted, 285
Tennessee Supreme Court, and lynching, 337–38
Tennessee Valley Authority, book on, revd., 428–29
TePaske, John J., revs., 397–98
Territorial growth, and city planning, 342–43, 352–53
Territories, book on, revd., 100–101
Terry, Fred J., 347
Texas, books on, revd., 115–18; papers on, 61, 65, 71, 79–80, 84; cotton pickers' strike in, 197*n*; fear of slave insurrection in, 322, 334; livestock in, 147, 154, 158, 159
Texas Observer, papers on, 79–80
Theisen, Gerald, paper by, 83–84
They Who Would Be Free, by Jane H. Pease and William H. Pease, revd., 416–17
This Sheba, Self, by J. E. Crowley, revd., 249–50
Thomas, Mary Martha Hosford, *Southern Methodist University,* revd., 432
Thomas, Robert C., receives European History Section Snell Memorial Prize, 137–38
Thomas, Rosemary, paper by, 85
Thomas Jefferson, by Fawn M. Brodie, revd., 107–109
Thomas L. McKenney, by Herman J. Viola, revd., 413–14
Thompson, Jerry, *Sabers on the Rio Grande,* noted, 585–86
Thompson, John, 480
Thornbrough, Emma Lou, sess. chmn., 65; revs., 125–26
Three Kentucky Artists, by J. Winston Coleman, Jr., noted, 284–85
Tigert, John James, book on, revd., 571–72
Tilley, Nannie M., revs., 248–49
Tindall, George Brown, 59; *The Persistent Tradition,* revd., 573
Tinkle, Lon, sess. chmn., 79
Tobacco, book on, noted, 437; book on, revd., 566–67
Tobacco and Kentucky, by W. F. Axton, noted, 437
Toll of Independence, ed. by Howard H. Peckham, noted, 283
Tomlin, Ronald E., cocomp., *Guide to the Official Records in the Mississippi Department of Archieves and History,* noted, 286
Tompkins, E. Berkeley, revs., 132–33
Toplin, Robert Brent, *Slavery and Race Relations,* noted, 436–37

Toppin, Edgar A., paper by, 74
Torrey, Charles T., 477
Totalitarianism, papers on, 72
Tourgée, Albion Winegar, 199
Townsend, Charles R., comment by, 81
Transylvania University, 517, 520*n*
Trapier, Paul, 453
Travel, books on, revd., 113–14, 552–53
Travels in North America, by Paul Wilhelm, Duke of Württemberg, revd., 113–14
Travels on Southern Antebellum Railroads, by Eugene Alvarez, revd., 552–53
Treasury Dept., U. S., and plantations, 375, 380
Trefousse, Hans L., *Impeachment of a President,* revd., 563–64
Trelease, Allen W., 234; sess. chmn., 81
Trennert, Robert A., Jr., *Alternative to Extinction,* revd., 557–58; comment by, 77
Tried by Fire, by Archie V. Huff, Jr., noted, 588
Troye, Edward, book on, noted, 284–85
Trumbull, Henry, 475
Trust in Tobacco, by Maurice Corina, revd., 566–67
Tulane University, 233
Turner, Frederick Jackson, and sou. agriculture, 150–53, 166
Turner, Nat, 19, 306, 489; book on, revd., 554–55
Twelvetrees, Harper, 475
Two Hundred Years of Pharmacy in Mississippi, by Leslie C. Campbell, revd., 433
Two Paths to the New South, by James T. Moore, revd., 269–70

U. S. Military Academy, 517, 520
Ullman, Daniel, 37
Uminski, Sigmund H., *The Polish Pioneers in Virginia,* noted, 288
Uncle Bill of Wildwood, by Frances J. McVey and Robert B. Jewell, noted, 284–85
"*Uncle Tom" Reed's Memoir,* by Ray Mathis, revd., 580–81
Unknown Soldiers, by Arthur E. Barbeau and Florette Henri, revd., 128–29
Urban history, books on, revd., 242–43, 272–73, 531–33; papers on, 69–70
Urbanism, art. on 1920s sou., 339–68; book on, noted, 436
"Using the Testimony of Ex-Slaves: Approaches and Problems," by John W. Blassingame, 473–92
Uzee, Philip D., sess. chmn., 70

Vagabond Newsman, by Nelson Shipp, noted, 287–88
Vandiver, Frank E., 135, 234; paper by, 60–61
Vansina, Jan, 487
Vari, Diana G., paper by, 76
Vaughan, Alden T., *American Genesis,* revd., 534–35
Vaughn, William Preston, *Schools for All,* revd., 123–24
Vesey, Denmark, 458
Vigil, Ralph H., comment by, 84
Vigilantes, 1856 slave insurrection and, 323 ff.
Viola, Herman J., *Thomas L. McKenney,* revd., 413–14
Violence, art on fear of black, 19–38; books on, revd., 577–79; papers on, 66; and sou. agrarian reform, 194–200
Virginia, art. on Negro and politics in, 167–86; books on, noted, 288, 587; books on, revd., 93–94, 122–23, 269–70, 406–407, 410–12, 534–36, 574–75; papers on, 78, 85; and Colored Farmers' Alliance, 190, 191; interviews of former slaves in, 485; livestock in, 147, 157 ff.; mountain Repubs. and Negro in, 493 ff.
Virginia History in Documents, by William H. Gaines, Jr., noted, 287
Voegeli, V. Jacque, 87; and Sydnor Award comm., 292

Wacker, Charles Henry, 341
Wade, Richard C., coauth., *Essays on Urban America,* noted, 436
Walker, Gilbert Carlton, 497
Walker, Jacob, 465
Walker, James Alexander, 509, 512
Walker, Peter F., comment by, 73
Wall, Bennett H., 88, 234; "Annual Report of the Secretary-Treasurer," 233–39; paper by, 74
Wall, Neva, 88
Walsh, Richard, coed., *Maryland,* revd., 398–99
War casualties, book on, noted, 283
Wars, paper on, 79
Warwick, William H., 190
Washburn, Wilcomb E., panelist, 85

Washington, Booker T., 188; paper on, 73
Washington, D. C., book on, noted, 286; SHA meeting in, 135, 438
Washington, George, 527; books on, revd., 104–105, 251–52, 538–39
Washington Street United Methodist Church, book on, noted, 588
Watson, Alan D., *Society in North Carolina*, noted, 588
Watson, Meredith, 173
Watson, Richard L., Jr., 291; sess. chmn., 86
Waud, Alfred R., book on, noted, 289
Waverly, Ohio, and Jefferson's slaves, 523, 525
Waverly (Ohio) *Pike County Republican*, 523 ff.
Waverly (Ohio) *Watchman*, 526
Way of the Fox, by Dave R. Palmer, revd., 538–39
Wayles, John, 527
Wayne, John, 156
Weare, Walter B., sess. chmn., 86
Weaver, John C., paper by, 69
Webb, Walter Prescott, 156, 163; paper on, 61
Webb, Mrs. Walter Prescott, 61, 62
Weber, Michael, 79
Webster, Daniel, book on, revd., 541–42
Weed, Charles, 33
Weir, Robert M., 135
Weisiger, Kendall, 345
Weiss, Nancy J., *The National Urban League*, revd., 126–27
Weiss, Thomas J., paper by, 75
Weldon, Edward L., 135
Welsh, Peter C., paper by, 87
Welter, Rush, *The Mind of America*, revd., 548–49
West, book on, noted, 584; book on, revd., 113–14
West, Elliott, coed., *Essays on Urban America*, noted, 436
West Indies, book on, revd., 245–46
West Virginia, book on, revd., 574–75; mountain Repubs. and Negroes in, 493 ff.
Wetmore, S. F., 524, 525, 527
Wharton, Vernon Lane, 165
Wheeler, William Bruce, revs., 101–102
Whig party, book on, revd., 558–59; Lincoln and, 41, 44, 46
White, Albert Blakeslee, 510*n*
White, John Daugherty, 498, 508
Whitfield, Henry L., book on, revd., 281–82
Whitten, Robert Harvey, 347, 359
Wickersham, Charles A., 347
Wiener, Jonathan M., paper by, 62
Wiggins, Sarah Woolfolk, 292
Wild Man from Sugar Creek, by William Anderson, revd., 429–30
Wiley, Bell Irvin, 234–35; *Confederate Women*, revd., 559–60
Wilkinson, Mell R., 345
Willard, George-Anne, 68
William H. Crawford, by Chase C. Mooney, revd., 112–13
Williams, Frank B., Jr., obituary notice by, 593
Williams, Isabel M., coed., *Wilmington–New Hanover Safety Committee Minutes*, noted, 287
Williams, James (slave), 477
Williams, Lorraine A., 135
Williams, Sally, 478
Williams, Samuel Cole, *Tennessee During the Revolutionary War*, noted, 289
Williamson, Joel R., sess. chmn., 62
Williamson, Samuel R., Jr., sess. chmn., 64
Willis, Joseph, 461, 465, 471
Willson, Augustus Everett, 516
Wilmington–New Hanover Safety Committee Minutes, ed. by Leora H. McEachern and Isabel M. Williams, noted, 287
Wilson, David, 474, 475, 477
Wilson, Major L., *Space, Time, and Freedom*, revd., 547–48
Wilson, Spencer, paper by, 79
Wilson, William H., *Coming of Age*, revd., 272–73
Wilson, Woodrow, books on, revd., 425–27
Wiltse, Charles M., coed., *The Papers of Daniel Webster: Correspondence*, Vol. 1, revd., 541–42
Windhorn, Stan, coauth., *Yesterday's Florida Keys*, noted, 289
Wise, John J., 175
Wish, Harvey, 322
Wolf, Dan, 349
Wolters, Raymond, *The New Negro on Campus*, revd., 569–70
Women, book on, revd., 559–60; papers on, 65–66, 80–81, 82–83
Women's Christian Temperance Union, paper on, 63
Wood, Forrest G., revs., 533–34
Wood, Peter H., *Black Majority*, revd., 246–48; comment by, 63–64

Woodman, Harold D., 88
Woolfolk, George R., 234
Works Progress Administration, and interviews with ex-slaves, 480–91
Worcester, Donald E., comment by, 79
World War I, book on, revd., 128–29
Wright, Gavin, comment by, 75
Wrobel, Sylvia, coauth., *Isaac Shelby*, noted, 284
Württemberg, Wilhelm Paul, Duke of, *Travels in North America*, revd., 113–14
Wyatt-Brown, Bertram, revs., 240–42
Wyllie, Irvin G., death of, 235
Wynes, Charles E., sess. chmn., 85

Yardley, William, 500–501
Yarnell, Allen, *Democrats and Progressives*, revd., 132–33
Yates, Bowling C., revs., 121–22
Yazawa, Melvin, ed., *Representative Government*, noted, 583
Yeas and the Nays, by Albert Castel and Scott L. Gibson, noted, 437
Yesterday's Atlanta, by Franklin M. Garrett, noted, 289
Yesterday's Florida Keys, by Stan Windhorn and Wright Langley, noted, 289
Yetman, Norman R., 480, 484, 486
Yi-liang, Chow, 13
Young, Mary E., sess. chmn., 77
Younger, Richard D., 292

Zaire, papers on, 67
Zimmer, Anne Y., 292
Zoning, and city planning, 353 ff.

U. S. POSTAL SERVICE

STATEMENT OF OWNERSHIP, MANAGEMENT AND CIRCULATION

(Act of August 12, 1970: Section 3685. Title 39. United States Code)

SEE INSTRUCTIONS ON PAGE 2 (REVERSE)

1. TITLE OF PUBLICATION
Journal of Southern History

2. DATE OF FILING
12 Sept. 1975

3. FREQUENCY OF ISSUE
Quarterly

4. LOCATION OF KNOWN OFFICE OF PUBLICATION *(Street, city, county, state, ZIP code) (Not printers)*
Rice University, P. O. Box 1892, Houston, Harris County, Texas 77001

5. LOCATION OF THE HEADQUARTERS OR GENERAL BUSINESS OFFICES OF THE PUBLISHERS *(Not printers)*
Southern Historical Association, History Department, Tulane University, New Orleans, La. 70118

6. NAMES AND ADDRESSES OF PUBLISHER, EDITOR, AND MANAGING EDITOR

PUBLISHER *(Name and address)*
Southern Historical Association, History Department, Tulane University, New Orleans, La. 70118

EDITOR *(Name and address)* Managing
S. W. Higginbotham, Rice University, P. O. Box 1892, Houston, Texas 77001

MANAGER EDITOR *(Name and address)*
None

7. OWNER *(If owned by a corporation, its name and address must be stated and also immediately thereunder the names and addresses of stockholders owning or holding 1 percent or more of total amount of stock. If not owned by a corporation, the names and addresses of the individual owners must be given. If owned by a partnership or other unincorporated firm, its name and address, as well as that of each individual must be given.)*

NAME	ADDRESS
Southern Historical Association	Department of History
	Tulane University
	New Orleans, Louisiana 70118

8. KNOWN BONDHOLDERS, MORTGAGEES, AND OTHER SECURITY HOLDERS OWNING OR HOLDING 1 PERCENT OR MORE OF TOTAL AMOUNT OF BONDS, MORTGAGES OR OTHER SECURITIES *(If there are none, so state)*

NAME	ADDRESS
None	

9. FOR OPTIONAL COMPLETION BY PUBLISHERS MAILING AT THE REGULAR RATES (Section 132.121, Postal Service Manual)

39 U. S. C. 3626 provides in pertinent part: "No person who would have been entitled to mail matter under former section 4359 of this title shall mail such matter at the rates provided under this subsection unless he files annually with the Postal Service a written request for permission to mail matter at such rates."

In accordance with the provisions of this statute, I hereby request permission to mail the publication named in Item 1 at the reduced postage rates presently authorized by 39 U. S. C. 3626.

(Signature and title of editor, publisher, business manager, or owner)

10. FOR COMPLETION BY NONPROFIT ORGANIZATIONS AUTHORIZED TO MAIL AT SPECIAL RATES *(Section 132.122, Postal Manual)*

(Check one)

The purpose, function, and nonprofit status of this organization and the exempt status for Federal income tax purposes

[X] Have not changed during preceding 12 months

[ ] Have changed during preceding 12 months

(If changed, publisher must submit explanation of change with this statement.)

11. EXTENT AND NATURE OF CIRCULATION	AVERAGE NO. COPIES EACH ISSUE DURING PRECEDING 12 MONTHS	ACTUAL NUMBER OF COPIES OF SINGLE ISSUE PUBLISHED NEAREST TO FILING DATE
A. TOTAL NO. COPIES PRINTED *(Net Press Run)*	5,274	5,381
B. PAID CIRCULATION 1. SALES THROUGH DEALERS AND CARRIERS, STREET VENDORS AND COUNTER SALES	none	none
2. MAIL SUBSCRIPTIONS	4,563	4,608
C. TOTAL PAID CIRCULATION	4,563	4,608
D. FREE DISTRIBUTION BY MAIL, CARRIER OR OTHER MEANS 1. SAMPLES, COMPLIMENTARY, AND OTHER FREE COPIES	none	none
2. COPIES DISTRIBUTED TO NEWS AGENTS, BUT NOT SOLD	none	none
E. TOTAL DISTRIBUTION *(Sum of C and D)*	4,563	4,608
F. OFFICE USE, LEFT-OVER, UNACCOUNTED, SPOILED AFTER PRINTING	711	773
G. TOTAL *(Sum of E & F—should equal net press run shown in A)*	5,274	5,381

I certify that the statements made by me above are correct and complete.

(Signature of editor, publisher, business manager, or owner)
S. W. Higginbotham

PS Form 3526 July 1971

APPLICATION FOR MEMBERSHIP

(Detach and mail, with remittance, to Secretary-Treasurer)

The Southern Historical Association
BENNETT H. WALL, Secretary-Treasurer
c/o History Dept., Tulane University
New Orleans, Louisiana 70118

MEMBERSHIP CLASSES

☐ Annual	$ 10.00	
☐ Family	$ 12.00	
☐ Five-years	$ 45.00	
☐ Enrolled Student	$ 5.00	(Send Certification)
☐ Life Membership	$200.00	(Payable in quarterly installments)
☐ Retired	$ 3.00	
☐ Sustaining	$ 15.00	and above

NOTICE: By action of the Executive Council all memberships are on a calendar year basis. Back issues for the year you enroll will be sent you. For our records, please indicate when they are received.

I enclose $ ______________ to pay my dues in the Southern Historical Association.

Name ______________________________

Address ______________________________

____

Applications for student membership must be accompanied by this certificate signed by a faculty representative of the institution in which the applicant is currently enrolled.

I hereby certify that the person whose name appears on this application is currently enrolled as a student in ______________________________

Signed ______________________________

Position ______________________________

THE IMPROBABLE ERA
The South Since World War II
Charles P. Roland

Here the South since 1940 is viewed by a distinguished historian as an era wholly astonishing for its economic, political, and social developments which the traditions of the region have managed to endure.

– "A fresh, authoritative interpretation of those elusive intangibles that enter into the southern mystique."–Dewey W. Grantham

– ". . . remarkably objective. . . . especially interesting and revealing chapters dealing with race relations, religion, literature and the arts."–Bell I. Wiley

248 pages / photographs / $11.95

THE LADY & THE PRESIDENT
The Letters of Dorothea Dix & Millard Fillmore
Charles M. Snyder

Recently discovered and previously unpublished, these letters provide a wealth of raw material for a reinterpretation of these two national leaders. / *$9.50*

JOHN HUNT MORGAN & HIS RAIDERS
Edison H. Thomas / $3.95bb

FRONTIER KENTUCKY
Otis K. Rice / $3.95bb

BLACK CHURCH IN THE SIXTIES
Hart M. Nelsen
& Anne Kusener Nelsen / $11.50

The University Press of Kentucky Lexington 40506

STRAIN OF VIOLENCE
historical studies of American violence and vigilantism
Richard Maxwell Brown